D1044541

**Essential Papers on Short-Term
Dynamic Therapy**

ESSENTIAL PAPERS IN PSYCHOANALYSIS

Essential Papers on Short-Term Dynamic Therapy

Edited by

James E. Groves, M.D.

NEW YORK UNIVERSITY PRESS
New York and London

Library of Congress Cataloging-in Publication Data
Essential papers on short-term dynamic therapy / edited by James E.
Groves.
p. cm. — (Essential papers in psychoanalysis)
Includes bibliographical references and index.
ISBN 0-8147-3076-0 (cloth : alk. paper). — ISBN 0-8147-3083-3
(paper : alk. paper)
1. Brief psychotherapy.   2. Psychodynamic psychotherapy.
I. Groves, James E.   II. Series.
RC480.55.E886   1996
616.89′14—dc20   96-37145
                    CIP

Contents

Preface

The editor of a collection inherits not one but two Original Sins. The first sin is the inclusion of papers that "don't belong" because they are misaligned somehow theoretically, clinically, or stylistically. The second sin is omitting papers that "absolutely ought to be included" because of their historical importance, value to the field, or obvious excellence. A book calling itself "Essential Papers" is bound to displease someone, especially when a favorite paper is missing or, worse, when a disliked paper or an exemplar of a rival school has been chosen instead. "How could Erich Lindemann's seminal work on grief be missing!" someone will say, "Or Balint's work—he *invented* the focus." And "Why on earth put Beck's cognitive therapy with short-term dynamic psychotherapy?" Or Kelly, or Klerman. Or Eric Berne? "And *why* Winnicott?"

The following apology will have to concern several papers and assuage many individuals: Readings were chosen or discarded for reasons ranging from the whimsical (I happened to like it or wanted to juxtapose it with another for comparison) to the practical (it was difficult to secure permission and an equally suitable paper was available). I hope this book contains *most* of the papers that are *most* essential. In general I have included a paper if for some reason it spoke to me or seemed useful in narrating the history of the field. I omitted a paper if it did not or if it had recently been reprinted or was available to a wide readership (for example, the Lindemann paper just a few months prior to this writing appeared in a festschrift of the *American Journal of Psychiatry*). But mainly a paper is here because I want it available to the therapist who may need it for a particular patient in short-term therapy. The point of psychotherapy, after all, is the patient who needs help.

I regret that many excellent papers could not be included, but this is an anthology, not an encyclopedia. (Also, most important papers not included are cited in my chapter or the part introductions.) An omission does not mean that a theorist lacks historical priority. It is said, for instance, that Rank[1] pioneered in setting a termination date, and it would have been interesting to include a selection pertinent to the preset termination date; but this would involve sifting through a great deal of Rank's material about "birth trauma," something rather far afield from the needs of the average person who picks up this book. (And besides, Freud beat Rank to the punch if I recall, setting a termination date for the treatment of the Wolf Man.) Turning from historical to futuristic, the very interesting work of Lorna Smith Benjamin[2] will probably be of increasing importance as the field matures, but at this stage her model involves a lot of instrumentation that I somehow felt would not actually be used by most practitioners at this time. I would have liked to include something of Lester Luborsky,[3] who not only synthesized and codified many important principles of psychoanalytic therapy but did so in one of the earliest examples of the manual-driven approach to psychotherapy. I had to choose not to, again for reasons of space, and because I felt the manual form was well-exemplified by Klerman and colleagues. Concerning the one-session therapy of B. L. Bloom,[4] my sense is that papers by Sifneos, Horowitz, Malan, and Winnicott cover much of his material. (The Bloom book's *title*, however, is unrivaled for delicious irony.)

In the introductory chapter that begins this collection, I summarize the papers in the book and, in the bridges between parts, try to fill any holes. I have attempted to give a panoramic view of the field, at least as it appeared to me over the years, reading the literature and treating patients under the inspiration of the various ideas and techniques gleaned. (In this connection, I received help from two superb reviews,[5,6] those of Marmor and of Burke, White, and Havens.) I have also tried to provide an overview of the field in the commentary bridging sections and by means of the order of selections. I believe an afterword or final summarizing chapter to be redundant in this particular book, but I know many people like collections constructed that way; for them, the introductory chapter can serve equally well as a finale and can be saved to read later. (Besides, in this book I want Donald Winnicott to have the last word.)

But what actually constitutes an *essential* paper in short-term dynamic therapy? I confess that I did not begin with a notion of what characterized "essentialness" and then lixiviate papers through that notion. Rather, I assumed that since I do a great deal of therapy and since I do read, a paper would come to me if it somehow possessed some essence of short-term therapy. I know how this method opens me to criticism, but I can only plead that there is a case to be made for working from exemplars toward essences, not the reverse, when there is no solid consensus in a field. John Ruskin did something of the sort last century in characterizing the nature of the Gothic: he studied examples of Gothic art and architecture, chose the ones he felt were "most Gothic" (in my terms, not his), and came up with a canon of Gothic characteristics (such as inspiration by forms found in nature, fierceness of originality, rhythmicity in repeated elements, and so on). No one of these made something Gothic, but the more of such characteristics a particular example possessed, the more "Gothicness" it had (in his terms, not mine), so that the absence of one or two such characteristics did not exclude the example from the canon. (As I write this, it comes to me that the Gothic simile appears because, fundamentally, I consider therapy an art form, not a science. This being so, my method is even more open to criticism, especially from the scientific wing of our field.)

For me, the four characteristic elements of short-term dynamic therapy are brevity, focus, therapist activity, and patient selection. Whether these four are in an Aristotelian sense "essential" and exhaustive is open to debate. I am sure that someone is going to argue that at least one of them is not essential (merely "accidental" in this metaphor). And someone else is going to come up with another characteristic that person deems "essential" and I have not. I look forward to this happening and am quite prepared to add another characteristic to the list of "short-term-dynamic-therapy-ness" criteria if the argument seems persuasive.

An explanation is probably now in order for the plan of this book. Some readers will in all likelihood feel that its plan is in places too like other large collections on short-term dynamic therapy; others will feel it is quirky and perverse—especially that I have reversed the contents of the parts on focus and therapist activity. In the last analysis the shape of the book is a compromise between the papers finally chosen for inclusion in the body of it and—for lack of a better word—my *esthetic* sense of how they wanted to fit together. As a result, the plan of the book is as follows: Introduction (about the four aspects or "essences" of short-term dynamic therapy, *brevity, focus, therapist activity,* and *patient selection*) and editor's overview. Then five parts follow dealing with dynamic short-term therapies or other short-term therapies rooted somewhere in psychoanalytic theory: (1) papers illustrating why brevity is not only a formal part of these therapies but also that flexibility and rigidity have content implications as well; (2) explorations of the focus— in two senses—what the patient sees as focal and what the therapist does to harmonize with this (or not) and to hold the focus in the treatment; (3) the therapist's activity—what is done and why, especially with regard to the therapist's theory of cure in relation to psychoanalytic theory, most particularly the transference; (4) patient selection for a given form of treatment, principally moving along the health/sickness dimension; and (5) a reconsideration of all of the above by means of ultra-short therapies, including none at all.

Missing from this volume are several *categories* of papers, and perhaps this is the time to justify those lacunae. First, I have not devoted much space to discussions of *why* short-term therapy, as opposed to long-term treatment. That dead horse has been flogged enough; herein shall be no political statements about efficiency, no hand-wringing about economics, and no aspersions cast on long-term treatments; the reader knows these arguments perfectly well or this volume would not be in hand. (Also, frankly, I consider the fifty-year dogfight over long-versus-short to be ideology at the expense of the patient; whether you agree with Davanloo[7] that short-term work is *always* better with some patients or with Shafer[8] that long-term is *always* better, these issues are still not proved. A thorough initial evaluation of any given patient should determine the choice of therapy—not reference to dogma.) Secondly, I have not made a special place for discussions of efficacy or outcome research; these are mentioned in many of the papers included here, and, quite candidly, this subfield is outside my purview; I refer the reader to the excellent meta-analysis published by Crits-Christoph.[9] Finally, I consider several categories of brief therapy beyond the scope of this volume—group, marital, and family therapies—and they are available elsewhere. I particularly like Budman's collection[10] for its readability and Wells and Gianetti's[11] for their attempt at comprehensiveness.

In addition to the therapists and theorists who have inspired me, my teachers, my students, and (it cannot go without saying) my patients, many people have made this book possible. At New York University Press, I wish to thank my editor, Timothy Bartlett, and the series editor, Dr. Leo Goldberger. At Harvard, Professor Roger W. Brown and Jack Yeats as usual asked the right questions. My mentors at the Massachusetts General Hospital, Drs. Anne Alonso and Scott Rutan, provided continuous support. Dr. Robert Abernethy, head of the General Psychiatry Practice, gave the book financial help, put a roof over my head for years, and made a home for the many colleagues whose ideas continue to fertilize my work—Ms. Marilyn Schwartz, Drs. Mark Blais, and Theodore Powers, among others. Dr. Ned Cassem, my chief, not only brought me up in psychiatry, but more than any other single person over the years provided the interesting and inspirational patients who taught me more than all the books. And finally, my son John Daniel gave me hope and necessary daily reminders of the value of caregiving (and did so while mostly managing to keep the chocolate milk away from the white sofa).

REFERENCES

1. Rank, O. *The Trauma of Birth.* 1929. Reprint, New York: Harper & Row, 1973.

2. Benjamin, L. S. "Brief SASB-Directed Reconstructive Learning Therapy." In *Handbook of short-term dynamic psychotherapy,* P. Crits-Christoph and J. P. Barber. ed. New York: Basic Books, 1991, 248–86.

3. Luborsky, L. *Principles of Psychoanalytic Psychotherapy: A Manual for Supportive-Expressive Treatment.* New York: Basic Books, 1984.

4. Bloom, B. L. "Bloom's Focused Single-Session Therapy." In B. L. Bloom, *Planned short-term therapy.* Boston: Allyn and Bacon, 1992, 97–121.

5. Marmor, J. "Short-Term Dynamic Psychotherapy." *Am J Psychiatry* 136 (1979): 149–55.

6. Burke, J. D., Jr., H. S. White and L. L. Havens. "Which Short-Term Therapy? Matching Patient and Method." *Arch Gen Psychiatry* 35 (1979): 177–86.

7. Davanloo, H. *Short-Term Dynamic Psychotherapy.* New York: Jason Aronson, 1980.

8. Shafer, R. "Termination of Brief Psychoanalytic Psychotherapy." *Int J Psychoanal Psychother* 2 (1973): 135–48.

9. Crits-Christoph, P. "The Efficacy of Brief Dynamic Psychotherapy: A Meta-Analysis." *Am J Psychiatry* 149 (1992): 151–58.

10. Budman, S. H., ed. *Forms of Brief Therapy.* New York: Guilford Publications, 1981.

11. Wells, R. A., and V. J. Gianetti, eds. *Handbook of the Psychotherapies.* New York: Plenum Press, 1990.

1. Introduction: Four "Essences" of Short-Term Therapy: Brevity, Focus, Activity, Selectivity

James E. Groves

Toward the end of the nineteenth century, when Breuer and Freud were busy inventing psychoanalysis, hysterical symptoms defined the focus of the work. These early treatments were brief and symptom-focused, the therapist was active, and, basically, desperate patients selected themselves for the fledgling venture. In time, free association and dream analysis replaced hypnosis as the method of treatment, increasing the duration of treatment. As time went on, the trauma theory of the neuroses was replaced by the Oedipus complex, and a broader, more free-ranging exploration replaced the symptom as focus. Still later, as exploration of the transference replaced direct suggestion, the interaction of the therapist with the patient necessarily diminished. Soon, only the rare therapist, most notably Ferenczi,[1] practiced psychoanalysis still using the more directive techniques. Freud and his followers, refining their technique to foster transference, found analyses growing longer and longer. At the same time, the analyst's activity with the patient, confined mainly to interpretations of transference resistance, grew less and less. In this way, psychoanalysis became more and more unfocused.

The history of psychoanalysis mirrors differences between short-term and long-term psychotherapy. Analyses grew longer and longer and more and more unfocused as the therapist grew less and less interactive. Half a century later, as therapies became briefer and briefer, they became more focused and the therapist became more active. But *brevity, focus,* and *therapist activity* are parameters in which short-term therapies differ, not only from long-term therapy but also from one another. Patient *selection* makes up a fourth "essence" in the description of the short-term psychotherapies.

Table 1.1 shows brevity, focus, activity, and selection on one axis and a quasi-historical, quasi-ideological grouping on the other. From top to bottom, it shows five main divisions of short-term dynamic therapies currently in use. They are the interpretive short-term therapies,[2-4] the existential psychother-

Edited and reprinted by permission of Guilford Publications from *Psychotherapy for the 1990s,* J. S. Rutan, ed., New York, 1992, pp. 35–59.

Table 1.1. "Essences" of Short-Term Dynamic Therapy

School	Short-term dynamic therapies:	Brief # sessions	Focused	Active	Selective
Analytic	SIFNEOS Anxiety suppressive	4–10	Narrow: on crisis, coping, at conscious level	Therapist: Teacher — Clarifies, supports, decreases transference	Less healthy patients but able to work and recognize psychological nature of illness
	SIFNEOS Anxiety provoking	12–20	Very narrow; oedipal conflict, grief; unconscious level; transference	Teacher — Interprets transference, resistance. Idealizing becomes ambivalent transference	Very rigid standards: "top 2–10% of clinic population;* oedipal conflict or grief; motivation essential; psychological-mindedness tested by trial interpretation
	MALAN	20–30 Fixed date*	Narrow, implicit (therapist finds it), unconscious, similar to Sifneos A-P	Doctor — Similar to Sifneos—"insight" held to be curative	Similar to Sifneos; healthy but some character pathology; able to work analytically. Responds to trial interpretation with deepened affect and increased associations if focus is correct.
	DAVANLOO	1–40 25 ca.	Broader but similar to Malan and Sifneos, plus: resistance and retroflexed anger	Critic* — Confrontive of resistance, especially around anger, D/A/I (conflict) and C/T/P (persons) triangles	Less healthy than Sifneos group: "top 30–35%"—some long-standing phobic, obsessional, or masochistic personalities but must respond to "trial therapy" first session
Existential	MANN	12 Exactly*	Broader focus: (Time Itself*) & "Central Issue" Termination, affective state	Empathic Helper — Therapist, by being-with patient through separation, helps in mastering developmental stage parents failed patient	Broader patient selection but usually not borderline; some ego strengths, especially passive-dependent patients and delayed adolescents

		Sessions	Focus	Therapist Role	Technique	Patient Selection
Behavioral	COGNITIVE	1–14 acutely Additional 24 if chronic	Conscious: "Automatic Thoughts"*	Coach or Director*	Therapist helps define governing slogans, refutes them, assigns homework,* mandates practice of new cognitions and behaviors	Not psychotic. In crisis. Coped previously. Not cognitively impaired. Not borderline
	INTERPERSONAL	12–16	Interpersonal Field	Coach or Doctor	Defines interpersonal deficits, role problems and helps reshape interpersonal behaviors*	Depressed patients at any level of health, with losses or interpersonal deficits, causing maladaptation or depression
Analytic	ECLECTIC	Horowitz: 12 — Budman: 20–40 Variable spacing,* re-up option — Leibovich: 36–52	Interpersonal + Cognitive Precipitating event — Interpersonal + Developmental + Existential — One problematic borderline trait* e.g., low frustration tolerance	Counselor — Doctor — Real Person	Combines all of the above strategies, especially interventions aimed at shoring up defenses, repairing stress response damage	Any level of health (except organic and psychotic conditions), but progress relates to level of health
	WINNICOTT	1–14 On demand*	Broad; unconscious: transference, termination, separation, aggression	Empathic Helper/ Playmate	Maintains holding environment, actively interprets transference, unconscious conflicts; supplies missing developmental capabilities*	Broad, individualized; looks for response to trial interpretation

*Unique feature

apy of Mann,[5] the cognitive short-term therapies,[6] (usually lumped with the behavioral therapies), interpersonal psychotherapy,[7] a group of practitioners and theorists subsumed under "eclectic"—Horowitz and colleagues,[8] Budman and Gurman,[9] Leibovich.[10,11] The sixth "school" of short-term therapy belongs to Winnicott,[12] showing how arbitrary, in some sense, it is to group disparate methods at all. Winnicott could be classified with the interpretive group or with Mann but is placed at the end to suggest something beyond eclecticism.

THE INTERPRETIVE METHODS: SIFNEOS, MALAN, AND DAVANLOO

Foremost in modern short-term therapy is, of course, Franz Alexander's manipulation of the interval and spacing of sessions.[13] He formulated "flexibility" in such a way that even his critics had to take a fresh look at the nature of the therapeutic frame. Decreased frequency, irregular spacing, therapeutic holidays, and therapist-dictated scheduling (rather than patient- or symptom-dictated scheduling) all decreased irrational transference elements and enhanced the reality orientation of therapy, (and increased preconscious conflicts and affect, which Alexander also called *transference*.) Alexander's discoveries in manipulating the interval and scheduling of sessions suddenly caused the frame of dynamic therapy to become as interesting as the picture it surrounded. Freud, of course, had been willing to adapt the therapeutic frame to the temporal situation of the patient,[14] but his willingness waned over time.

With the Second World War came a glut of patients suffering from "shell shock" and "battle fatigue." New concepts emerged and new theories developed from treating so many patients so rapidly. In 1944, Grinker and Spiegel,[15] working with soldiers, and Lindemann,[16] working with survivors of the Coconut Grove fire, rediscovered the active short-term therapies Ferenczi and Rank[1] had advocated and even Freud practiced earlier. Alexander and French now popularized their method of modifying the length and spacing of sessions ("flexibility") and neutral role of the psychotherapist to achieve a "corrective emotional experience," in which the therapist becomes an actor consciously playing a role counter to the patient's past experience.

Working in Boston and in London, Sifneos[2,17] and Malan[3] can be credited with independently fashioning various psychoanalytic techniques and deviations into the first whole, coherent short-term methodologies still widely in use today. The increased activity of Ferenczi and Rank, Lindemann's crisis work, Grinker and Spiegel's push for brevity, Alexander and French's flexible framework, and Balint's[18] finding and holding of the focus were all technical innovations, but none constituted a whole new method. Yet Malan and Sifneos invented ways of working that were not just arrays of techniques but whole new therapies born in the outpatient clinic. Before, with modifications added to the analytic structure, it was as if the "house of therapy" was being renovated, a room here, a new roof there. Malan and Sifneos moved next door, as it were, and built a whole new house.

The "interpretive" short-term therapies feature brevity, narrow focus, and careful patient selectivity, but the common feature lies in the nature of the therapist activity. Psychoanalytic interpretation of defenses and appearance of unconscious oedipal conflicts in the transference appear in other short-term therapies (and are often downplayed), but only in these methods are interpretation and insight the leading edge, the apex of the method, and, as in psychoanalysis, the main "curative" agent.

Sifneos contrasts anxiety-suppressive with anxiety-provoking[17] psychotherapies. Anxiety-suppressive therapy serves less healthy patients who are able to hold a job and recognize the psychological nature of their illness but unable to tolerate the anxiety of deeper levels of psychotherapy. Anxiety-provoking psychotherapy is longer, less crisis-oriented, and aimed at the *production* of anxiety—which then is used as a lever to get to transference material. (In psychoanalysis, transference emerges, but often in short-term therapy it is forced out.)

Sifneos's anxiety-provoking therapy runs twelve to twenty sessions but may extend to forty or more. The focus is narrow: failure to grieve a death, inability to finish a project because of success fear, triangular, futile love relationships—the standard grist of the analytic mill—these high-level neurotic conflicts are the province of anxiety-provoking therapy. The therapist serves as a detached, didactic figure who iterates the focus, keeps it in view, and challenges the patient in a firm, dry fashion that discourages dependency and appeals to the intellect. One can think of this method as a classical oedipal-level defense analysis with all the lull periods removed and the anxious periods (castration anxiety, not separation anxiety) strung together. One important feature is that it serves only 2 to 10% of the population, the subgroup able to tolerate its unremitting anxiety.[19]

Malan's method is similar, but the therapist discerns and holds the focus without explicitly defining it for the patient. (In the initial trial, if the therapist has in mind the correct focus, there will be a deepening of affect and an increase in associations as the therapist tests it.) A unique feature is that Malan sets a date to stop, once the goal is in sight and the patient demonstrates capacity to work on his or her own; the *date,* rather than a set number of sessions, avoids the chore of keeping track if acting out causes missed sessions or scheduling errors.

Malan's early work is reminiscent of the British object-relations school. Like Sifneos, he sees interpretation as curative but aims less at defenses than at the objects they relate to. In other words, the therapist will call attention to behavior toward the therapist, but rather than asking what affect is being warded off, Malan wants to know more about the original object in the nuclear conflict who sets up the transference in the first place. Malan's later work converges toward that of Davanloo, so that at present, Malan's and Davanloo's approaches are pretty much identical.

Davanloo's method is similar to the others at its theoretical core, although it can appear dramatically different in the famous videotapes shown in Montreal. What occurs in Davanloo's method is that the therapist's relentless, graduated, calculated clarification, *pressure,* and challenge elicit *anger* that is used to dig out the transference from behind "superego resistance." (In Sifneos, anxiety is the lever; in early Malan, typically it is dependency and depression.)

Davanloo[4] starts therapy right in the first session (after a half hour of ruling out sicker patients). He begins by criticizing the patient's passivity, withdrawal, or vagueness while pointing out the body language and facial expressions demonstrating them. Patients who do not decompensate or withdraw are then offered a trial interpretation: The patient's need to fail and clumsiness in the interview disguise aggression toward the therapist; the patient's need to become "a cripple," to be "amputated" and "doomed," disguises rage. The therapist works with this "triangle of conflict" (which goes from defense to affect to impulse in relation to the "triangle of persons").

The "triangle of persons" begins with a problematic current object, one mentioned in the first half of the initial interview. Then investigation moves to the therapist the patient has just been protecting from anger, then to the parent who taught such patterns in the first place. One or two circuits around the "D/A/I" (conflict) triangle in relation to three points of the "C/T/P" (persons) triangle constitute the "trial therapy," *Figure 1.1.* The "trial therapy" is a more elaborate version of trial interpretations Malan and Sifneos use to test motivation and psychological-mindedness. Davanloo's patients

Figure 1.1: Davanloo's "Trial Therapy"

lack the ability to distinguish between points in the "conflict [defense/affect/impulse] triangle" or to experience negative affects directly. By trolling the D/A/I triangle around the "persons [current object/therapist/parent] triangle," Davanloo forces the frigid patient to *feel* and thus creates a mastery experience for the patient. (These are nonpsychotic, nonaddicted, nonorganic individuals who have a combination of retroflexed aggression and harsh superegos but, at the same time, enough observing ego to discount the apparent harshness. His patients somehow find the Davanloo method supportive; up to 35% of an average clinic's population are said to tolerate it, a range broader than either Sifneos or Malan claimed.[19] Failures of the Davanloo "trial therapy" typically are referred to cognitive therapy.) (Davanloo's ideas on patient selection have changed over the years, and he has repudiated some of the notions in this paragraph; for a survey of his current thinking, see the introduction to Part IV, below, on patient selection.)

Davanloo is currently the most controversial of all the theorists reviewed in this book. Especially therapists steeped in psychoanalytic culture see Davanloo as not merely too active but at times downright cruel. I myself do not agree, having watched many hours of tapes of Davanloo doing his therapy; my opinion is that the videocamera that is *always present* serves to "protect" the patient by bringing the community into the consulting room, helping the patient feel that Davanloo's confrontations are not "personal." On the other hand, I wonder whether the lack of privacy in this videotaped situation may prevent the patient from really "being in" treatment and rather may produce a kind of "as-if" therapy. Gustafson's criticism of Davanloo is somewhat similar. In a dry but carefully argued essay (and what is perhaps the longest footnote published in this field), Gustafson and Dichter[20] argue that Davanloo's patients appear to be argued into compliance or persuaded into a posture of cure, rather like someone being brainwashed into a religious conversion.

THE EXISTENTIAL METHOD OF JAMES MANN

Mann's insistence on a strict limit of exactly 12 sessions is unique in all the field. Twelve sessions, which Mann chose somewhat arbitrarily and then empirically tested to his satisfaction, is sufficient time to do important work but short enough to put the patient under pressure. This set number with no reprieve is both enough time and too little; it thrusts the patient and the therapist right up against existential reality they both tend to deny: Time is running out.

No other short-term therapy seems to require so much of the therapist. And Mann's treatment is open to patients further down the continuum of psychological health than patients acceptable to Sifneos and Malan. In theory, at least, even the occasional borderline patient with some well-developed strengths, some mastery of adolescent issues, and some capacity to make and break relationships with a modicum of skill is a candidate. And even if this method does not appeal to all short-term therapists, almost every subsequent theorist in the field seems to have been influenced by Mann to some degree (even Budman and Gurman, whose use of time appears so unlike Mann's).

Underlying the focus the patient brings, Mann posits a "Central Issue" (analogous to a core conflict) in relation to the all-important issue Time Itself. The therapist is a time-keeper who existentially *stays with* the patient through separations, helping master the developmental stages in which parents failed the patient. Mann's theoretical point of departure (which probably *followed* the empirical finding that 12 sessions was about right) is Winnicott's notion that time sense is intimately connected to reality testing, which underlies the depressive position; the attainment of the depressive position is a prerequisite for the development of the "capacity for concern" and, with it, the attainment of object relatedness.

The most succinct way to view Mann's treatment is that, in some sense, unconscious mental processes are timeless; neurotic and character-disordered structures are timeless as well; Mann's therapy starts out timeless and rapidly becomes time-constrained, unburying the issue of unconscious timelessness and, with it, childish wishfulness versus actual grown-up time. In other words, the steady ticking of the clock is used as a chisel to resculpt magical, timeless thinking.

After an initial evaluation determining that the patient is not psychotic, borderline, or organically impaired, the therapist begins to think about the "central issue" (such as problems with separation, unresolved grief, failure to move from one developmental stage to another—delayed adolescence especially). This central issue is couched not in terms of drive or defense but existentially, in terms of the patient's chronic suffering as a result. Then the therapist solicits the patient's agreement to work for a total of 12 sessions of standard psychotherapeutic length. The patient will at this point express some disbelief that 12 sessions will be enough, and Mann says that if the evaluation has been accurate and the method is suited to this patient, the therapist should look the patient in the eye and say that 12 sessions will be just enough. The therapist should not compromise the time limit by suggesting at any point that further sessions will be permitted.

The early sessions are marked by an outpouring of data and the formation of a positive or idealizing transference. During this phase the therapist's job is to hold the focus on the central issue and allow the development of a sense of perfection. At about the fourth session disillusionment often appears and the return of a focus on symptoms. At this point the therapist makes the first interpretation that the patient is trying to avoid seeing time as limited and avoiding feelings about separation. This sequence is repeated and deepens through the middle of therapy.

After the midpoint, overt resistance often occurs, perhaps as lateness or absence on the part of the patient, and the emergence of negative transference. The therapist examines this in an empathic and welcoming way, while inwardly examining countertransference issues which may impede the work. And finally, in the latter sessions comes a working through of the patient's pessimism and recollection of unconscious memories and previous bad separation events, along with an expectation of a repetition of the past. By the therapist's honest acceptance of the patient's anger and ambivalence over termination, the patient moves from a state of neurotic fear of separation and its attendant depression to a point where the patient is ambivalent, sad, autonomous, and realistically optimistic.

This method is probably one of the hardest of the short-term methods because it demands so much of the therapist. So much happens in such a short period of time, and the impact of emotions upon the therapist is so condensed. But, while it appears to be a method that many therapists shy away from, properly selected and skillfully applied, it can be powerful in its effect and quite beautiful in its theoretical simplicity.

THE COGNITIVE APPROACH

Because the cognitive approach is so often associated with behavioral therapy, it is hard to recall that it has its roots in psychoanalysis and therefore the dynamic therapies. The intellectual parent of cognitive therapy is Freud, not Pavlov or Thorndike or Skinner. To see why this is so, think of mental life as consisting of an abecedarian triangle of *a*ffect (or feeling), *b*ehavior (the outcome of affect and thought), and *c*ognition (or thinking). Figure 1.2 depicts the relation among these three elements of mental life, each affecting the other reciprocally (as well as showing the relation among limbic system, neocortex, and motor strip). The figure compares psychoanalysis to cognitive therapy: Freud's focus is mainly on the relation of unconscious processes to affect and behavior as mediated through cognition. Aaron Beck's[6] focus is the relation of *conscious* thought processes to mental life. Thus the focus of behavior therapy is *behavior,* treating affects and conscious cognitions only secondarily. The focus of psychoanalysis is affect and unconscious cognition (C_{ucs}). Cognitive therapy, however, focuses on affect and conscious cognition, C_{cs}, (or "automatic thoughts" as Beck calls them). It seeks to alter syllogisms that impinge on both affect and behavior.

The two cognitive therapies dealt with here are those of Aaron Beck, a method which one day may treat more psychiatric patients than any other method in the United States, and the all-but-forgotten Fixed Role Therapy of George A. Kelly.[21] The dry, practical aspect of Beck's therapy serves as a contrast to the drama and strangeness of Kelly's (but they are both cognitive therapies). Beck sees cognition as encompassing a broad spectrum ranging from discreet thoughts and self-verbalizations all the way to fantasy, imagery, and abstract beliefs and values. He posits that an individual's interpretation of events in the world is encapsulated in fleeting "automatic thoughts," which are often cognitions at the fringes of consciousness. These "automatic thoughts" mediate between an event and the affective and behavioral response. In other words, the patient labors under a set of slogans that, by their labeling function, influence his or her *weltanschauung* and hamper experimental forays into new behaviors that could change the representation of the world and of the individual in it.

The basic thrust of cognitive therapy according to Beck is to get the automatic thoughts completely into consciousness, to challenge them consciously, and to practice new behaviors that change the picture of the world and the self in it. The patient is actively exhorted to challenge these automatic

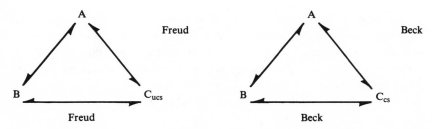

Figure 1.2: The Mind of Psychoanalysis and the Cognitive Mind

thoughts, and when any positive change occurs, this is used as a wedge against the monolithic power of the Negative Cognitive Assumption.

The therapist actively schedules the patient's day-to-day activity, and the patient is asked to list in some detail actual daily activities and rate the degree of "mastery" and "pleasure" that each affords. These allow the therapist to review the week with the patient and sculpt behaviors. Cognitive rehearsals are also used in forecasting the upcoming week to help the patient foresee obstacles.

The therapist explains to the patient the major premise of the cognitive model, that an intermediating slogan lies between an event and the emotional reaction. This slogan may take a verbal or pictorial form. The therapist then, using Socratic questioning, elicits from the patient statements of fact that lead to a more accurate conceptualization of the problem, while at the same time interfering with the patient's obsessive reiteration of the negative cognitive set. The patient's participation in the reasoning process gives a chance to experience the therapy in advance of actually putting it into practice. Most of the work, however, is not done in therapy sessions but in homework, in which the patient carries out the prescriptions of the therapist.

The "Fixed Role Therapy" of George A. Kelly[21] is based in personal construct theory. The personal construct is not just a representation of an event. It is not just a concept. Rather, it is the person's referent—a mental template, a deep structure—upon which events are projected in order to cope with them. Under personal construct theory every individual tries to achieve "maximal differentiation of events in the world with a minimum of constructs," or to have the greatest number of adaptive options with the smallest repertoire of interactional routines. Cognitive processes are channeled by individual expectations; one anticipates events by constructing referents based on past ones.

One way to look at the cluster of behavioral expectations placed on individuals in the world is through the notion of *role*. A simple-minded way to think of role is just the way it is used in drama: a part that one plays to which other characters throw cues for the purpose of advancing the play along the lines of the script. One of the problems with personal constructs and roles is that roles may be aberrant and constructs may be erroneous. For Kelly, however badly one chooses to act, it is in role relationships that people have their best chance of reframing constructs, introducing novelty into routines, and changing their patterns in the world.

The patient is asked to write a character sketch of himself or herself from a particular point of view. The therapist then studies this sketch and writes an "enactment sketch" that might have been written by a hypothetical other self or the character in another role. In the next session the therapist shows the patient this sketch. If the patient's response is satisfactory the therapist asks the patient to pretend that the old self has "gone to the mountains" and that the new self materializes. The patient is then to enact, as much as possible, 24 hours a day, 7 days a week, all that this new self might do, say, think or even dream in the new role—not unlike method acting. At least three sessions a week are scheduled in which patient and therapist rehearse the enactment, plan tests of its effectiveness, and examine outcomes. At the end the old self "comes back" to evaluate the experience.

It is not that the therapist designs a new, "better" self, it is that the patient sees a universe of selves that can fit into the roles of life. The experiment convinces the patient of the relativity of personal constructs and provides the motivation and skills for a change into new roles.

The self-characterization is elicited in such a way as to imply that neither diagnosis nor therapy is based on hidden facts. Rather, it can be based on superficial aspects of the individual. The patient may begin to see that there is a sense in which we are what we represent ourselves to be. The therapist tells the patient to write a character sketch just as if the patient were the character in a play, to write it as it might be written by a friend who knows the patient intimately and sympathetically, perhaps better than anyone could really know anyone, and write it in the third person, "John Doe is. . . ."

The therapist's role in writing the enactment sketch is quite difficult. The therapist needs to discern in the patient's sketch at least one testable hypothesis about roles and personal constructs, and it is explicitly stated in the therapist's sketch for the new self. The hypothesis may be one that the patient has already set up in the self-characterization. For example, if the self-characterization describes the patient as "meticulous," the therapist may want to cast the patient in the role of an individual who is "casual," or relaxed; this way the patient can see what would happen in this new role. By structuring the new self's behavior, the psychotherapist tries to make the whole of daily living take shape in a new world that the patient never suspected is actually there. Examples often involve spotting a character trait central to the personality structure of the individual and enacting its opposite. For instance, a selfish, rigid, intolerant patient may be asked to play a role that is otherwise similar but differs in that the new self is constructed as "tolerant." Pivotal in the enactment sketch is not only its construction but also its presentation to the patient. "Is this the kind of individual *you* would like to *know?*" If the answer is yes, the enactment can proceed.

Kelly describes a two-week course of an every-other-day regimen of seven sessions. In each session the therapist becomes a director mediating the living-through of the enactment sketch.

Therapy sessions rehearse five kinds of situations: (1) interaction with a teacher or supervisor on the job; (2) interaction with peers; (3) interaction with a spouse or intimate; (4) interaction with parents; and (5) interaction in a situation involving a religious experience. Only a day or two should elapse between the assignment and when the patient comes in to announce that it cannot be done. At this point the therapist must be prepared to support the endeavor vigorously, starting with the more superficial area of daily living, for instance, the job situation. Rehearsing such a situation is an early treatment goal and it is a strenuous experience for both therapist and patient. It is so constructed that the patient can withdraw before becoming overwhelmed. Job supervision or student-teacher relationships usually lend themselves to this goal. It is better to hold off a role enactment with a spouse or intimate because the patient is likely to be reproached for behaving strangely and needs time to get used to the idea.

The integrity of the original self of the patient is protected. Kelly's value-free mode of operating is receptive to the unfolding of the truth, whether it is something the therapist likes or not. The new self is not the kind of person that the patient is to become. "At this point neither of us knows what kind of person you *should* be. That is something that will have to be developed as we go along."

The essential point of this complex endeavor is mainly that the patient is to *be* the new self and observe others reacting to the new self at the same time the old self is forgotten. The object of being the new self for two weeks is not to "find" oneself but to see that the inner person is something that one *creates* as one goes along rather than something solely dictated from inside or imposed only from without.

THE INTERPERSONAL APPROACH

Interpersonal psychotherapy is brief and active. Like the cognitive therapies, it de-emphasizes the transference—not investigating unconscious distortions of the interpersonal field. Interpersonal psychotherapy focuses not on mental content but on the *process* of the patient's interaction with others. In interpersonal psychotherapy, behavior and communications are taken at face value. Consequently, it may be disliked by psychologically minded therapists who find it mechanical. The strength of the method is that it poses little risk of iatrogenic harm, even to the fragile patient, even in the hands of the inexperienced therapist.

Klerman and colleagues'[7] interpersonal therapy, or IPT (along with Beck's cognitive model) will be increasingly important as the United States searches for cheaper psychotherapy. (And to provide the historical perspective, transactional analysis, or TA, is compared with the others; it was influential in its day and popular to a degree now hard to remember two or three decades later.)

Klerman and colleagues' interpersonal therapy, IPT, acknowledges its debt to other therapies in stance and technique but claims distinction at the level of "strategies," meaning an orderly series of steps in evaluation and treatment (nowadays called "manual driven"). For patients with depression related to *grief,* they first review depressive symptoms, relate them to the death of the significant other, reconstruct the lost relationship, construct a narrative of the relationship, explore negative and positive feelings, and consider the patient's options for becoming involved with others.

For patients with *interpersonal disputes* causing depression, they conduct a symptom review, relate symptom onset to the dispute, take a history of the relationship, dissect out role expectations, and focus on correcting nonreciprocal expectations.

For patients with *role transitions,* they review the symptoms, relate symptoms to life change, review positive and negative aspects of new and old roles, review losses, ventilate feelings, and find new role options.

And finally, with patients with *interpersonal deficits* leading to depression, they review symptoms and relate them to social isolation or unfulfillment, review past relationships, exploring repetitive patterns, and (unlike the be-havioral therapies) discuss the patient's conscious positive and negative feel-ings about the therapist and use them to explore the maladaptive patterns elicited earlier.

IPT is strongly faithful to *method* (*à la* the St. Louis School of Psychiatry, the Research Diagnostic Criteria or RDC, and DSM IV); this fidelity provides a clear algorithm for decisions at every stage of evolution of the therapy. Thus, interpersonal therapy should "do no harm" and is so straightforward that it appears within the technical reach of the intelligent lay person, making it ideal for psychotherapy outcome research and low-cost managed health care.

As one example of method, here is the algorithm for communication analysis: Therapists should identify (1) ambiguous or nonverbal communica-tion, (2) incorrect assumptions that the other has indeed communicated, (3) incorrect assumptions that one has understood, (4) unnecessarily indirect verbal communication, and (5) inappropriate silence—closing off communi-cation. If the therapist identifies one or more of these, this list is run through another list of therapeutic investigations of the therapeutic relationship itself to give the patient concrete examples. Then decision-analysis, the major action-oriented technique of IPT, is utilized to help the patient diagnose and treat depressing interpersonal problems by finding other options.

Strupp and colleagues[22] also specifically claim the interpersonal model. In their method, the focus the patient brings helps the therapist to generate, recognize, and organize therapeutic data. The "focus" is commonly stated in terms of a cardinal symptom, a specific intrapsychic conflict or impasse, a maladaptive picture of the self, or a persistent interpersonal dilemma. This "focus" is not an end but a "heuristic guide to inquiry" that helps the therapist organize the therapeutic experience. It is supposed to exemplify a central pattern of interpersonal role behavior in which the patient unconsciously casts him or herself. (By "unconscious" they do not appear to mean Ucs in its strict sense, but more Freud's "preconscious," or Beck's concept of "automatic thoughts.") The arena for the investigation is interpersonal, the method for such investigations is narrative: "the telling of a story to oneself and others. Hence, the focus is organized in the form of a schematic story outline" providing a structure for "narrating the central interpersonal stories of a patient's life."[22]

This narrative or story contains four structural elements or subplots which are the keys to the therapy: (1) acts of self, (2) expectations of others' reactions, (3) acts of others toward the self, and (4) acts of self toward the self. While learning this narrative, the therapist is supposed at the same time to bear in mind it is a map, not the territory itself. Nonetheless, it is a map of human actions embedded in interpersonal transactions. These transactions, originating in cyclic psychodynamic patterns, cause recurrent maladaptation and pain—and narrating and editing these four subplots form the basis of the Strupp method.

Transactional analysis,[23] or TA, Eric Berne's brainchild, has the same skeleton used by IPT and Strupp and colleagues. There is a systematic analysis of communication and interpersonal interaction, working from presenting complaint back to previous patterns and forward to interaction with the therapist. But its characteristic construct is that interpersonal transactions come from three "ego states,"—"child," "parent," and "adult" (corresponding to id, ego, and superego). Alternation among ego states is a function of the permeability of the boundaries of each. Too much or too little permeability leads to pathology: Excluding the "child," prohibits play and creativity from other states; conversely, extreme permeability keeps the patient from staying in the "adult" mode long enough to complete an undistorted interpersonal transaction.

Two principal forms of interaction give rise to interpersonal distortions: the crossed transaction, in which one individual speaks, for instance, from the adult state but the other actor speaks from, say, his or her own parent to the other's child. And the communication in which both individuals are in complementary (not crossed) communication but where the problem is two parallel communications, one overt, one covert—one for one agenda, one for another, hidden agenda. This transaction is a "game," which has a "payoff" as its aim. This payoff is usually gratification of the "child's" goal.

Historically TA evolved as group treatment but can be adapted by imaginatively bringing the patient's social set into the therapy room and examining this "group." The therapist who recognizes, for instance, that a game is going on in therapy can expose the game, go along with the game, ignore some games and not others, or propose alternative games.

THE ECLECTICS

The "eclectic" brief therapies are characterized by combinations and integrations of other theories and techniques. Three important exemplars are considered in this chapter. Horowitz and colleagues combine theories of the stress response syndrome with information-processing theory and the psychology of coping in various personality types; this yields an interpersonal and cognitive mixture that takes into account the dynamic unconscious as well. Budman and Gurman explore three dimensions of mental life—the interpersonal, the developmental, and the existential—to assemble a methodology that leaves no other school of short-term therapy unexploited, with the stated exception of James Mann's. And Leibovich sails into uncharted waters, not in the reality-based, supportive techniques he uses but in the individuals who are his brief therapy constituency, healthier borderline patients.

Horowitz and colleagues[8] owe a debt to a broad literature on stress, coping, and adaptation that spans the cognitive, behavioral, phenomenological, and ego psychological realms. The point of departure is the normal stress response: The individual perceives the event, a loss or death. The mind then reacts with *outcry* ("No, no!") then denial ("It's not true!"). These two states, denial and outcry, alternate, so that the subjective experience is of unwanted intrusion of the image of the lost. Over time "grief work" proceeds so that "working through" goes to completion. The pathological side of this normal response to stress occurs in the stage of perception of the event when the individual is overwhelmed. In the outcry stage there is panic, confusion, or exhaustion. In the denial stage there is maladaptive avoidance or withdrawal by suicide, drug and alcohol abuse, dissociation or counterphobic frenzy. In the more complex stage of intrusion, the individual experiences alternation of flooded states of sadness and fear, rage and guilt, which alternate with numbness. If working through is blocked, there ensue hibernative or frozen states, constriction, or psychosomatic responses. If completion is not reached there is ultimately an inability to work or to love.

Horowitz's therapy basically proceeds like the older models of Lindemann or Grinker and Spiegel, with ego psychology and information-processing theory woven in. The therapist identifies the focus—in this therapy usually a traumatic event or a loss—and tries to determine whether the patient is in *denial* or the intrusion phase of maladaptation. In the denial phase, perception and attention are marred by a dazed state and selective inattention. There is partial amnesia or emotional isolation. Information-processing is crippled by disavowal of meanings. Loss of a realistic sense of connection with the world occurs. There is emotional numbness. In the type of maladaptation marked by the patient's being stuck in the *intrusion* phase of the trauma response, perception and attention are marked by hypervigilance, overactive consciousness, and inability to concentrate. Emotional attacks or pangs of anxiety, depression, rage, or guilt intrude. Psychosomatic symptoms are common here as the sequelae of the chronic flight-or-fight response ensues.

A dozen or so sessions are used to focus on the recent stress event and work it through. In the early sessions the initial positive feelings for the therapist develop as the patient tells the story of the event and the preliminary focus on the loss is discussed. There ensues a sense of decreased pressure as trust is established. The traumatic event is related to the life of the patient as a psychiatric history is taken. In the middle phase of therapy the patient tests the therapist and the therapist elicits associations to this stage of the relationship. A realignment of focus takes place, with interpretations of resistances. The patient is asked to understand why these resistances, based on past relationships, are currently unreasonable. The therapeutic alliance deepens as this phase continues and the patient works on what has been avoided. Further interpretation of defenses and warded off contents and linkage of these contents to the stress event occur. In the late middle phases, transference reactions are interpreted as they occur. There is continued working through of central conflicts which emerge as termination relates them to the life of the patient. In termination there is acknowledgment of problems as well as real gains and an adumbration of future work, for instance, anniversary mourning.

A major feature of Horowitz's work is on defensive styles. The "hysterical" personality style has an inability to focus on detail and a tendency to be overwhelmed by the global; the "compulsive" style is the converse, with the patient unable to experience affect because of details. The therapist acts in either event to supplement the missing component and to damp out the component flooding the patient.

In the borderline patient the well-known tendency to split is damped out by the therapist anticipating that, with shame and rage, there is going to be a distortion of the patient's world into its good and bad polarities. For the patient with a narcissistic personality style, the tendency to exaggerate or minimize personal actions is gently but firmly confronted. The schizoid patient is allowed interpersonal space.

One of the most attractive features of Horowitz's eclectic style is that it is not competing with other schools of short-term psychotherapy but can be integrated or added in parallel with other styles.

The work of Budman and Gurman[9] rests on the "IDE focus," interpersonal, developmental, and existential. None of these ideas is novel, but the way they are combined systematically is nicely realized with reference to eliciting the precipitating event, its relation to the focus, the relation to development, and working through with a balance of techniques. The major focus in the IDE perspective includes (1) losses, (2) developmental dysynchronies, (3) interpersonal conflicts, (4) symptomatic presentations, and (5) personality disorders.

In the IDE method, Budman and Gurman pursue a systematic approach beginning with the individual's reason for seeking therapy *at this time*. The patient's age, date of birth, and any appropriate developmental stage-related events or anniversaries are brought in. Major changes in the patient's social support are reviewed. Especially important in the Budman-Gurman system is substance abuse and its contribution to the presentation *at this time*.

A major feature here is the belief that maximal benefit from therapy occurs early, and the optimal time for change is early in treatment. The law of diminishing returns sets in as therapy becomes prolonged. Budman and Gurman are not snobbish about the capacity of any one course of treatment to cure the patient completely and they welcome the patient back again in successive developmental stages at developmental crises. A particular value of this treatment is its nonperfectionistic approach, both in pulling a particular phase of therapy to an end and the lack of any feeling of failure on resuming treatment. The picture one develops of this approach is of clusters of therapies ranging along important nodal points in the individual's development.

The short-term psychotherapy of Leibovich[11,12] for borderline personality disorders has much in common with several other short-term therapies. The main difference is that he accepts the diagnosed borderline patient. While he does seem to exclude the schizotypal, acting-out, and sickest types of "core" borderline patients, he does accept the borderlines who are on the border with the neuroses, the anaclitic type, (and by implication the as-if borderlines). What Leibovich is mainly aiming at is to find borderline patients who have a greater than average (for borderlines) capacity for growth.

In terms of brevity this is the longest of the short-term psychotherapies, usually running a year. In terms of focus it is unique; Leibovich asks the patient to consider a single recurrent borderline personality behavioral trait such as low frustration tolerance or tendency to explode in rages or tendency to throw oneself into overvaluing and devaluing relationships—the standard DSM IV list—and choose one and only one of these as a focus. The patient will complain that the problem is too large for short-term therapy, and Leibovich will say, Well, let's try to do what we can with the time available.

The patient should have evidence of sufficient reality testing, some evidence of good motivation, and a degree of intrapsychic and emotional separateness or personality distinctiveness (lack of tendency to fuse suddenly). Some connection with the therapist must be present (avoidance of schizoid traits that are too extreme). The patient should not be in a major depression. The patient must have a capacity to do some verbalization, and there should be some stable and intact ego functions which assisted the patient at one point at least during previous developmental stages. The patient must be able to recognize the existence of a focal troublesome issue or a central problematic pattern around which many difficulties revolve. The patient must be able to harbor at least some realistic expectations.

Exclusion criteria for Leibovich are individuals in crisis and dyscontrol, fixed psychotic projection and denial, schizoid defenses, absence of any current relationships, acute psychotic episodes, inability to accept the appropriate boundaries of the therapeutic setting, and lack of any observing ego.

The therapist's activity in the short-term therapy of the borderline is basically to focus and to remain as a real person without overly empathizing or fusing with the patient. The therapist's main job is to restrain the patient's tendency to become diffuse. The therapist here is more like a coach than in some other therapies, evoking ego mechanisms of defense and acting as a fiduciary at times as ego functions fail.

THE TIMELESS GENIUS OF DONALD WINNICOTT

The idea of being a short-term therapist probably would have made Winnicott laugh. He no doubt would have described himself as a therapist of whatever duration the *patient* needed. Even a cursory understanding of the "holding environment" or the "maturational process" shows Winnicott's commitment to an equitable framework for life and psychotherapy and an implicit hostility to unfair infringements on the right to time of the child—the child of any age. So given a presumed preference for open-ended therapy, how is his remarkable work capable of shedding light on short-term therapy?

The themes of brevity, focus, therapist activity, and patient selection discriminate among short-term therapies, and there is no reason to abandon them with Winnicott. In terms of brevity, he was apparently capable of removing important blocks to development in a single session. *Therapeutic Consultations in Child Psychiatry*[24] provides examples of one, two, or three sessions being sufficient to push the individual through a block and resume normal development. He was willing to analyze "the Piggle" in 14 sessions.[12] (He tended to call something "analysis" if it proceeded at deeper levels of the psyche and to consider the length and frequency of therapy less important.) But he agreed to intermittent therapy of the Piggle *only* *if* it were "on demand," only if the child could request the next session when needed. He explicitly states that if therapy can not be daily analysis, then it had better be "on demand," otherwise it becomes superficial.

In terms of focus, Winnicott had a broad-ranging interest in impediments to normal development, especially as pathological manifestations of aggression. His cases suggest he worked from the patient's first communication disclosing the nature of the developmental block (what he is supposed to have called the "sacred" moment),[25] and this tended to be the focus he came back to. When in doubt, he tended to tell the patient so and go back to the original communication about the developmental block.

In terms of therapist activity, Winnicott always keeps the holding environment firm. Not that he caters to the patient or is unnecessarily gratifying; he was ever aware of the demands of the real world in terms of time and money. On the other hand, he tries not to put the patient in a place where the original loss is again repeated, this time at the hands of the therapist. Winnicott proceeds by first framing the treatment and then interpreting. He leaves the Piggle in the waiting room, takes himself into the consulting room, and by the time she wanders over to him, he has "already made friends with" the toys—he has established the frame and entered the work, awaiting her there. (And he is not just being cute, he *means* he has made friends with the toys.) This rapid alternation between making a secure frame (or holding environment) and plunging into the therapeutic work is one of Winnicott's most characteristic features. Of the other therapists considered here, James Mann seems closest to this balance: First: frame, then—work.

In the realm of patient selection, Winnicott also resembles Mann. Winnicott has an openness to patients at almost any level of pathology and accepts their need to regress in service of removing developmental blocks. On the other hand, neither Winnicott nor Mann is a daredevil where the patient's welfare is concerned. Winnicott unsentimentally and without apology states some patients are too sick to grow, too damaged, and for these, he works toward containment and management.

It is in the area of brevity that Mann and Winnicott, otherwise often similar, appear most at odds. How to explain this paradox: Mann with his insistence on exactly 12 sessions, Winnicott with his insistence on either daily analysis or therapy-on-demand? Perhaps it is one of those instances where the extremes converge. Both Mann and Winnicott are realists—time is running out, reality in the end will prevail. On the other hand, they are optimistic about the power of human loving to defeat developmental stagnation. The twelve sessions of Mann and the on-demand therapy of Winnicott actually take place in the same world, the child's world, by the child's clock. Perhaps Mann's 12 sessions and Winnicott's 'on-demand' are the same therapeutic lifetime. The time-world of Mann's 12 sessions may be reality viewed in one dimension, say 'from above,' and Winnicott's on-demand is 'cross-sectional,' perhaps from the vantage point of those crucial moments in life or therapy when the clock stops, when we are dissociated from clock time—for good or ill—for survival and for growth. Perhaps the 'on-demand' schedule reproduces the stopped clock of mother love and the strict 12 sessions of Mann reproduce its sheltering but realistic framework. There are moments in *The Piggle* that support this notion, when the little girl and the dying old man discuss his death and her survival. For Winnicott, the evanescence of life lends love its ultimate force.

This leads to a final stylistic marker of Winnicott's therapy, one even more mysterious: his empathy for the nature and level of the communication and its timing. In so many of his cases, there is the special moment when he remarks, "And then I knew I must say . . ." or "At this point I knew I must call her [the Piggle] Gabrielle . . ."—an uncanny moment of pure intuition.

PATIENT SELECTION

It is fitting that issues of selectivity should bring the discussion full circle: Patient selection begins and ends with the initial evaluation, and without a good clinical evaluation, choice of a therapy for any given patient is a house built on sand.

Certain patients should be excluded from short-term dynamic treatment: patients with severe, chronic Axis I disorders that have not responded fully to biological treatment, chaotic acting-out personality disorders, patients specifically rejecting brief treatment, patients for whom it is impossible to find a focus or for whom there are multiple, diffuse foci. The list is long.[26,27]

And there are patients who will do well in almost any form of short-term treatment, for instance the highly functioning graduate student who cannot complete a dissertation. But between these ranges fall a majority of patients who present to the outpatient clinic or private practice. How does one decide which patient will do well in which therapy?

If the patient is relatively healthy, there are more options: Sifneos may be beyond the reach of the average patient, but there are Malan, Mann, and Davanloo. If the patient is moderately healthy, the methods of Budman and Gurman may work well, or of Horowitz, especially if there is a traumatic event to serve as a focus. If the patient is considerably less healthy, Sifneos anxiety-suppressive treatment is often useful, or cognitive therapy or IPT, depending on the extent to which the focal problems are cognitive or interpersonal. Even some patients with borderline personality disorder may find help, in the methods of Leibovich. But before a choice of treatment is finalized, the level of health must always be matched with the likely focus of treatment. There are patients who, by virtue of their level of health, might seem right for one form of treatment but who, because of the focus that emerges in the initial evaluation, are better suited to an altogether different treatment modality. Also, temperamental fit between patient and therapist may pertain: Crits-Christoph[28] notes that "patients who have more interest in examining the subtle, complex meanings of events and interpersonal transactions are a better match" for, say, expressive treatment, whereas those with a more concrete style may prefer, say, cognitive therapy or IPT.

Table 1.1 summarizes patient selection criteria in the last column, and it is possible to run down the list and narrow the range to three or four therapies likely to be best. This list can be narrowed by working leftward along the rows summarizing each therapy. Under therapist activity and focus are criteria that may help narrow the list of most-likely-to-succeed short-term therapies even further. And the duration of treatment of various therapies may be weighed against the patient's means or insurance coverage.

How does one really choose a short-term therapy for any given patient? The answer contains four aspects: (1) the therapist's therapeutic armamentarium of therapies to choose from (what this book hopes to enlarge); (2) the patient's goals, aims, wishes, and requests; (3) the patient's psychobiosocial situation as determined by a good initial evaluation; and (4) the *fit* among these factors set against the backdrop of real-world demands. It all boils down to a match between the resources of the patient—time and money—and the resources of the therapist—time and skills. What they have in common is time. But for patient and therapist, there is one undeniable fact about termination: Time always runs out.

REFERENCES

1. Ferenczi, S., and O. Rank. *The development of psychoanalysis.* Trans. C. Newton. New York: Nervous & Mental Disease Publishing, 1925.
2. Sifneos, P. E. *Short-term psychotherapy and emotional crisis.* Cambridge, Mass.: Harvard University Press, 1972.
3. Malan, D. H. *The frontier of brief psychotherapy.* New York: Plenum Medical Book, 1976.
4. Davanloo, H. Techniques of short-term dynamic psychotherapy. *Psychiat Clin No Amer* 2(1979):11–22.
5. Mann, J. *Time-limited psychotherapy.* Cambridge, Mass.: Harvard University Press, 1973.
6. Beck, A. T., and R. L. Greenberg. Brief cognitive therapies. *Psychiat Clin No Amer* 2(1979):23–37.
7. Klerman, G. L., M. M. Weissman, B. J. Rounsaville, and E. S. Chevron. *Interpersonal therapy of depression.* New York: Basic Books, 1984.
8. Horowitz, M., C. Marmar, J. Krupnick, N. Wilner, N. Kaltreider, and R. Wallerstein. *Personality styles and brief psychotherapy.* New York: Basic Books, 1984.
9. Budman, S. H., and A. S. Gurman. *Theory and practice of brief therapy.* New York: The Guilford Press, 1988.
10. Leibovich, M. A. Short-term psychotherapy for the borderline personality disorder. *Psychother Psychosom* 35(1981):257–64.
11. Leibovich, M. A. Why short-term psychotherapy for borderlines? *Psychother Psychosom* 39(1983):1–9.
12. Winnicott, D. W. *The Piggle: An account of the psychoanalytic treatment of a little girl.* Madison, Conn.: International Universities Press, 1977.
13. Alexander, F. The principle of flexibility. In *Brief therapies,* ed. H. H. Barton. New York: Behavioral Publications, 1971, pp. 28–41.
14. Freud, S. Studies on hysteria (1893–95). *Standard Edition,* vol. 2. London: Hogarth Press, 1955, pp. 125–34.
15. Grinker, R. R., and J. P. Spiegel. Brief psychotherapy in war neuroses. *Psychosom Med* (1944):123–31.
16. Lindemann, E. Symptomatology and management of acute grief. *Am J Psychiatry* 101(1944):141–48.
17. Sifneos, P. E. Two different kinds of psychotherapy of short duration. In *Brief therapies,* ed. H. H. Barton. New York: Behavioral Publications, 1971, pp. 82–90.
18. Balint, M., P. H. Ornstein, and E. Balint *Focal psychotherapy.* Philadelphia: J. B. Lippincott, 1972.
19. Flegenheimer, W. V. *Techniques of brief psychotherapy.* New York: Jason Aronson, 1982.
20. Gustafson, J. P., and H. Dichter. Winnicott and Sullivan in the brief psychotherapy clinic. *Contemp Psychoanal* 19(1983):624–37.
21. Kelly, G. A. Fixed role therapy. In *Direct psychotherapy,* ed. R.-R. M. Jurjevich. Coral Gables, Fl.: University of Miami Press, 1973, pp. 394–422.

22. Schacht, T. E., J. L. Binder, and H. H. Strupp. The dynamic focus. In *Psychotherapy in a new key,* ed. H. H. Strupp and J. L. Binder. New York: Basic Books, 1984, pp. 68.

23. Berne, E., C. M. Steiner, and J. M. Dusay. Transactional analysis. In *Direct psychotherapy,* ed. Jurjevich R.-R. M., Coral Gables, Fl.: University of Miami Press, 1973, pp. 370–93.

24. Winnicott, D. W. *Therapeutic consultations in child psychiatry.* New York: Basic Books, 1971.

25. Gustafson, J. P. An integration of brief dynamic psychotherapy. *Am J. Psychiatry* 141(1984):935–44.

26. Burke, J. D., Jr., H. S. White, and L. L. Havens. Which short-term therapy? Matching patient and method. *Arch Gen Psychiatry* 36(1979):177–86.

27. Marmor, J. Short-term dynamic psychotherapy. *Am J Psychiatry* 136(1979):149–55.

28. Crits-Christoph, P. The efficacy of brief dynamic psychotherapy: A meta-analysis. *Am J Psychiatry* 149(1992):157.

PART I

Brevity: Rigidity and Length of Time Frame

Three very different essays in this part illustrate the temporal essence of short-term dynamic psychotherapy.

Franz Alexander's manipulation of the interval and spacing of sessions was designed to solve several problems related to transference resistance — therapeutic impasse, stagnant treatment, therapy as a way of life, addiction to therapy, and inability of the patient to carry over lessons learned in treatment to real-world situations. He was particularly concerned with what he saw as the patient's "procrastination." Alexander felt that shaking up the regularity of time allotted to spend with the therapist might succeed where classical transference interpretation had failed. While one might argue that these maneuvers worked by giving the patient symbolic nonverbal interpretations, they did work — and sometimes the results were impressive. (Alexander's name was permanently linked with French[1] when they invented another manipulation that worked, the "corrective emotional experience," also criticized by some of their colleagues.) Notwithstanding the reaction of orthodox psychoanalysis, Alexander's experiments in lengthening the interval between sessions (or — rarely — decreasing the interval), mandating therapeutic holidays, and shortening the length of the therapy made even his critics take a fresh look at the nature of the therapeutic envelope. For the first time, the frame of dynamic therapy had started to become as interesting as its content.

Half a century later, Budman and Gurman display the same impatience with the open-ended time frame. In long-term psychotherapy, the sessions fall into a regular rhythm that becomes almost hypnotic after a while — with diminishing marginal return on the time investment. Budman and Gurman are similar to Alexander in their reluctance to let that happen, but their theories are dissimilar. Here, the time allotment is related to how fast the patient is working through issues related to the *focus* (the "IDE focus," for *i*nterpersonal, *d*evelopmental, *e*xistential). The interpersonal and existential aspects of their method are all well and good, but it is the impact of development that has the strongest voice. Budman and Gurman provide an integration of many previous theories and techniques—which entitles them to the label "eclectic"—but their method has a feeling of clinical wholeness to it. There is little of the patchwork quality that is sometimes termed "eclectic," and this selection is also included because it contains rich practical knowledge about how to treat actual patients. Although Budman and Gurman may seem diametrically opposite James Mann in regard to time structure, the acute time-sensitivity that runs all through their work is not dissimilar.

Who but a fool or a saint would choose to know in advance the exact moment of his own death? James Mann's insistence on a therapy of exactly twelve sessions—no more and no less—thrusts patient and therapist right up against the existential reality they both tend to deny: Time is running out. Compared with Mann's, no other method requires so much in the way of stamina and emotional maturity in the therapist (one might almost say "wisdom"). And Mann's treatment is open to patients further down on the spectrum of psychological health than patients acceptable to Sifneos, Malan, and Davanloo (early Davanloo, that is, not later Davanloo). Even the occasional borderline patient with well-developed strengths, some mastery of adolescent issues, and a capacity to make and break relationships somewhat skillfully is a candidate for Mann's method. And every subsequent short-term therapy is influenced by Mann to some degree (even Budman and Gurman, who spend more than a little energy reacting *to* Mann). In this selection Mann discusses Winnicott's idea of time sense as developmentally connected to reality testing, which, in turn, results from passage into Melanie Klein's "depressive position," or what Winnicott calls the stage of "capacity for concern." (Later, in the last part, Winnicott is seen working with these same issues—as his own time is running out.)

REFERENCE

1. Alexander, F., and T. M. French. *Psychoanalytic Therapy*. New York: Ronald Press, 1946.

2. The Principle of Flexibility

Franz Alexander

As long as the psychoanalytic method of treatment was considered a single procedure, the analyst—whether he was aware of it or not—selected his patient to fit his technique; only a few tried to adapt the procedure to the diversity of cases they encountered. Such a state of affairs is far from satisfactory. In all medicine there are very few instances in which the therapeutic tool is rigidly fixed and the patients made to conform. The logical solution to the problems of therapy is rather the converse. Not only do their ailments differ greatly, but the patients themselves present many physical and psychological differences. In psychotherapy, as in all therapy, the physician must adapt his technique to the needs of the patient.

Today the tendency among psychoanalysts is to be less rigid in matters of technique. In the research cases described in this volume, the psychoanalytic method has been used in a flexible manner. We have experimented with frequency of interview, the use of chair or couch as the situation required, interruptions of long or short duration in preparation for terminating the treatment, and the combination of psychotherapy with drug or other treatment. Above all, we have sought to learn how to control and manipulate the transference relationship so as to achieve the specific goal and fit the particular psychodynamics of each case.

When a patient consults us, we do not accept him for any specific method of psychotherapy; the procedure is based upon diagnostic opinion. Yet, not even after the initial diagnostic appraisal can we foretell what technique will be necessary for a later phase of the treatment. As we now practice psychoanalytic therapy, we seldom use one and the same method of approach from the first to the last day of treatment.

The number and variety of psychotherapeutic techniques will probably continue to multiply. Our aim, however, is always the same: to increase the patient's ability to find gratifications for his subjective needs in ways accept-

Reprinted by permission of Plenum Publishing Company from *Brief Therapies,* H. H. Barton, ed., New York, 1971, pp. 28–41.

able both to himself and to the world he lives in, and thus to free him to develop his capacities.

This therapeutic aim can be achieved by the use of various therapeutic techniques. Only the nature of the individual case can determine which technique is best suited to bring about the curative processes of emotional discharge, insight, and a thorough assimilation of the significance of the recovered unconcious material, and, above all, the corrective emotional experiences necessary to break up the old reaction pattern. Whether the abreaction and the corrective experience take place on the couch during free association or in direct conversation between patient and therapist sitting vis-à-vis, whether it is effected through narcosis, or whether it occurs outside the analytic interview in actual life situations while the patient is still under the influence of the psychoanalytic interview—all these are technical details determined by the nature of the individual case. In some cases the development of a full-fledged transference neurosis may be desirable; in others it should perhaps be avoided altogether. In some it is imperative that emotional discharge and insight take place very gradually; in others with patients whose ego strength is greater, interviews with great emotional tension may be not only harmless but highly desirable. All this depends upon the needs of the patient in a particular phase of the therapeutic procedure.

IS SUCH A PSYCHOTHERAPY PSYCHOANALYTIC?

Some psychoanalysts who have used the standard method exclusively may feel we are not justified in calling all these different techniques "psychoanalytic." They may argue that the expression should be reserved for the procedure developed by Freud and practiced by his followers for the last forty years.

Whether the designation "psychoanalytic therapy" is justified depends upon one's definition of psychoanalysis. That concept of psychoanalysis which is based on superficial conformity to the requirements of daily interviews, uninterrupted free association, and the use of a couch, and which regards the transference neurosis as inevitable, obviously does not include the flexibility we advocate. However, if one defines psychoanalysis by more essential criteria as any therapy *based on psychodynamic principles* which attempts to bring the patient into a *more satisfactory adjustment to his environment* and to assist *the harmonious development of his capacities,* then all forms of therapy, however flexible, having this basis and this goal, may be considered psychoanalytic.

Yet even the so-called standard psychoanalytic therapy does not consist merely in the patient's dreams, fantasies, free associations, and the analyst's interpretations thereof. Even this technique often entails direct questioning by the analyst, steering the material in the direction which seems most significant to the course of the analysis. It may require advice to the patient concerning the conduct of his affairs outside the treatment; it may even, in some instances, demand active interference by the analyst.

Then too, assimilation of newly acquired insight cannot be credited to the analyst's skillful interpretations alone, any more than the healing of an incision can be said to result solely from the surgeon's skillful suture. Just as the healing of a wound is a natural function of the human body, so the integration of new insight is a normal function of the ego. The surgeon endeavors to create the best possible conditions for the healing of the wound; the psychoanalyst tries to create the most favorable conditions for the integration, by the ego, of its recently liberated psychic energy. Integration is the ego's main function; the psychoanalyst merely supports it by proper management of the transference relationship.

And finally, the analytic process is not confined to the analytic interview. Abreaction and the development of new emotional reaction patterns take place not only in the presence of the therapist but throughout the rest of the day or week—at home, at the club, in the office. The importance of this fact has been gradually impressed upon us and we have become progressively aware that what transpires during this interval between the therapeutic sessions is of tremendous significance to the patient's progress toward health. Moreover, actual events within the family life or in business or other pursuits may help or hinder therapeutic progress. The careful analyst, therefore, is actively concerned not only with the analytic situation but also with the patient's other relationships, how they are affected by the analysis and how they in turn affect the analytic work.

FREQUENCY OF INTERVIEW

Procrastination: Regression

The standard procedure of daily interviews tends, in general, to gratify the patient's dependent needs more than is desirable. In a large number of cases the same results—emotional insight and relief of anxieties—could have been achieved with fewer interviews and less time if a technique of changing the frequency of interview according to need had been used from the very beginning of the treatment. Just as a person who is fed every half-hour never becomes conscious of the feeling of hunger, so the analytic patient whose needs for dependence are continually gratified never becomes emotionally aware of them. In such a situation, reducing the frequency of interview will suddenly bring into consciousness the dependent needs, together with all the reactive resentments for their frustration.

One should not forget that daily interviews exercise a seductive influence on a patient's regressive and procrastinating tendencies. The neurotic's proneness to evasion (after all, the most fundamental factor in his withdrawal from the actual life situation) is favored by the expectation of an almost infinite number of interviews. "If not today, tomorrow we will solve the problem—or next month, in the next half-year, the next two or three years."

This expectation of a protracted treatment has its therapeutic value, of course, in a patient who comes to the analyst in despair, sensing his utter incapacity to endure his given life situation. The initial improvement in severe neurotics is, to a large degree, due to the soothing effect of the procrastination sanctioned by the psychoanalytic technique. One relieves the patient by allowing him to evade the pressing issues of his life and to regress to a more comfortable infantile position, not only in fantasy but in reality, in the real relationship between patient and analyst.

By allowing such an actual regression, however, we later find ourselves involved in new difficulties. The initial soothing effect of the prolonged outlook gradually becomes corruptive and the therapist, faced with the task of driving the patient from his comfortable infantile position, realizes anew how difficult it is to force anyone to give up acquired rights.

When pregenital material (that which applies to sensations experienced in early infancy) appears in psychotherapy, it is frequently considered significant traumatic material when it may actually be merely an escape back to the early pretraumatic, highly dependent emotional state in which the patient felt safe and contented. Although it is true the deeper a patient sinks into a dependent transference neurosis the more regressive pregenital material he will produce, it is a fallacy to consider an analysis in which the patient brings up much regressive material as more thorough than one primarily centered around the actual life conflict. Regressive material is a sign not of the depth of the analysis but of the extent of the strategic withdrawal of the ego—a neurotic withdrawal from a difficult life situation back to childhood longings for dependence gratifiable only in fantasy.

In every neurosis we look for that time in the patient's life when he refused to yield to the ever-changing requirements of the process of maturation, to "grow up." This refusal may take place in almost any phase of life from early infancy through adulthood, and the severity of the neurosis is determined in part by how early in life the individual set himself against growing up. This point marks the beginning of the neurosis. When regressive material is brought which antedates this point, it should be evaluated, therefore, as a sign of resistance and not as deep penetration into the sources of the neurosis.

The more skillfully a treatment is conducted, the less time will be spent with such regressive material. It is the therapist's duty to lead the patient from his retreat back into the present, and to induce him to make new attempts to solve the problem from which he fled into the past. With the correct interpretation and handling of the transference relationship, the need for such deep regressions can be almost entirely avoided.

It should, therefore, be a general principle in all psychotherapy to attempt to check this regressive tendency from the very beginning of the treatment, allowing no more procrastination and regression than is absolutely necessary to calm panic, anxiety, and despair.

Intensity: Emotional Level

An extreme generosity with interviews is not only uneconomical but, in many cases, makes the analysis emotionally less penetrating. Daily interviews often tend to reduce the patient's emotional participation in the therapy; they become routine, and prevent the development of strong emotions by allowing the patient to verbalize his transference feelings as they emerge. This is particularly the case with aggressive impulses felt toward the analyst, for if the patient can give vent to them daily in small amounts he never becomes aware of them in a convincing manner. When the intensity of such hostile impulses is too low, it may be well to let it increase by lessening the frequency of interviews; when it is very great, more frequent interviews become imperative.

It is a common experience that an analysis in which the emotional level is low progresses extremely slowly. The whole procedure becomes intellectualized, without the real emotional participation of the patient. In general, stronger emotional participation brings the issues more clearly to the foreground and makes insight more vivid, thereby speeding up the progress of the treatment. Consequently, every analysis should be conducted on as high an emotional level as the patient's ego can stand without diminishing its capacity for insight.

This level, of course, varies from case to case. Roughly speaking, in patients with a so-called "weak ego" (poor integrative power), the emotional discharge and accompanying insight must take place very gradually. Such severely neurotic individuals cannot tolerate intense emotional participation and require small abreactions in almost daily interviews over a long period. Patients with good integrative faculty ("strong ego"), who can endure more intense sessions without developing too strong defenses, often need relatively infrequent interviews. With many such patients, as soon as a fairly good rapport has developed—which in some cases may require only a few interviews—the entire treatment may be carried out in infrequent interviews. These are apt to become more dramatic and of greater emotional intensity than the psychoanalytic interviews in the standard technique.

Manipulation of Frequency

Every psychoanalyst must at some time have unwittingly frustrated a patient—when circumstances forced him to cancel an appointment or when, for some reason, the patient had to leave without seeing the physician—and found that association material which had seemed meaningless or obscure because of the small amount of emotion involved, had suddenly become crystal clear. Vacations which were not intended to be technically indicated interruptions of treatment but were solely to refresh the analyst, have often had a similar vitalizing effect upon a treatment become stale in the routine of daily interviews. Many psychoanalytic treatments owe their progress to such an accident which precipitates more relevant material than can the most astute interpretations on material devoid of emotion.

The point to be considered, then, is how to use such incidents intentionally as an integral part of the therapeutic procedure, how to manipulate the frequency of interview so as to secure the patient's emotional participation and to maintain it at the desired level.

Frequency of interview must be regarded as a relative affair. Weekly interviews in some instances may be regarded as the normal frequency, in others constitute a drastic reduction, in still others take on the character of an interruption of treatment. For instance, a patient who has been seeing the physician five times a week might find three times a week a radical reduction, whereas an interval of an entire week might be tantamount to an interruption of treatment.

When the therapeutic relationship has become well established and the patient's ego defenses have been sufficiently analyzed, the patient reaches a fairly stable equilibrium. In this equilibrium—which, in standard psychoanalysis, may develop in some patients after three or four months—the patient feels much as if he were to say, "Yes, I am acting like a child—but what of it? This is not real life anyway." This partial insight into his dependence retains a kind of theoretical quality since it has been gained on the basis of relatively unimportant matters. It therefore becomes almost imperative to increase the emotional intensity in order to make the patient's insight more realistic and convincing. In this phase of the treatment, a radical curtailing of the frequency of interview (from five a week to two or even one) tends to make the emotional insight much deeper and speeds up the analytic process.

It must be borne in mind, however, that reducing the frequency of the interviews can cause stronger emotional participation only if the patient has already developed a fairly intense transference relationship. A patient who is not yet interested in the analysis will not react to the reduction of interviews by developing more intense transference feelings. In most cases, therefore, it is advisable to ensure interest by a series of interviews before reduction of frequency can serve as a method of intensifying the emotional participation.

The opposite procedure of shifting from infrequent interviews to more frequent ones may become necessary in other emotional situations. It is a common observation that in some patients accustomed to daily interviews, a few days' intermission may increase the resistance to such an extent that the patient becomes unable to continue the treatment, may never return to it. This is true of the resistance which develops from repressed hostile impulses, from intense feelings of dependent coloring incompatible with the patient's self-esteem and pride, or from erotic feelings toward the analyst which produce anxiety. In such situations, an intellectual check of the too-strong emotions is needed. More frequent interviews at this point allow a gradual discharge of the emotional tension which has accumulated during the intermission. (Occasionally the opposite technique can be used with success.)

The "acting-out" character also benefits from careful manipulation of the frequency of interview. Since these individuals (feeling no restraint within themselves) tend to act on their impulses without regard for social standards, they frequently clash not only with convention but with the law. The psychiatrist must represent prohibition in his own person and must anticipate his patient's impulses in order to help him by restraint. It is obvious that such patients will at times require almost constant contact with the therapist.

Another important reason for manipulating the frequency of interview lies in the tendency of psychoneurotic patients (with the exception of the "acting-out" character) to substitute experiences of the analysis for life experiences. The transference neurosis comes to serve the purpose of the original neurosis: withdrawal from real participation in life. The original neurosis was a withdrawal into fantasy; the transference neurosis is a withdrawal into the relatively harmless realm of the therapeutic relationship. When the frequency of interview is reduced, the patient is given less opportunity to substitute these safe analytic experiences for life experiences. The sooner a patient can translate what he learns during the treatment into actual life experiences, the faster the analysis will progress.

Economical Psychotherapy

From the beginning, the therapist must persist in trying to counteract the patient's tendency to sink himself into a safe, comfortable transference neurosis.[1] Without this continuous, alert pressure from the analyst, even relatively mild neurotic disturbances may lead to a disproportionately prolonged treatment. A correct evaluation of how fast an analysis can progress, how intense an emotional strain the patient can stand, will decide whether the procedure will assume the character of the standard psychoanalysis or that of so-called brief psychotherapy.

The nearer the analyst can keep the patient to his actual life problems, the more intensive and effective the therapeutic process is. From the point of view of genetic research, it might be advisable to encourage the patient to wander way back into the Garden of Eden of his early youth; therapeutically, however, such a retreat is valuable only insofar as it sheds light upon the present. Memory material must always be correlated with the present life situation, and the patient must never be allowed to forget that he came to the physician not for an academic understanding of the etiology of his condition, but for help in solving his actual life problems.

The therapeutic maxim of an economical psychotherapy, therefore, must be to allow as little regression as the patient can stand, only that procrastination which is unavoidable, and as little substitution as possible of transference gratifications for life experiences.

Preparation for Interruptions

In most cases of standard psychoanalysis, the neurotic gratifications of the transference relationship sooner or later outweigh the patient's therapeutic desire for recovery. Freud expressed this as follows: "This transference soon replaces in the patient's mind the desire to be cured." The reason for this is that after the resistance against the emotions in relation to the therapist has been analyzed, the transference neurosis loses much of its painful aspect and the patient's shame for his dependence upon the analyst, his guilt for his hostile impulses, diminishes. The original neurosis was a combination of gratification, conflicts, and suffering; the transference neurosis repeats all these features but, with progressive analysis of the ego's defenses, the conflictful elements diminish and its gratifications increase.

No wonder the patient is not inclined to give it up if he can afford to continue treatment. It is naive to think that most patients stick to their prolonged treatments so consistently, often year after year, only because of their desperate desire to be cured. This may be true in the first phase of the treatment, but later they cling to it because it gives them neurotic gratification without much suffering. It is, nevertheless, true that the patient can frequently be observed behaving more normally in his daily life during this phase because, in a sense, the transference situation serves as a crutch and at the same time lessens his neurotic needs.

As the patient has no emotional need for a change, it may be extremely difficult to break up this inertia—particularly if there are no external inconveniences connected with the analysis, such as an excessive financial burden or awkward time arrangements. Freud was aware of this impasse in standard psychoanalysis when he stated that in the early years of his practice he had difficulty in persuading his patients to continue their treatment; later he had difficulty in inducing them to give it up. Today an efficiently handled psychotherapy does not allow such a dilemma to occur but combats the growing inertia while still in an incipient stage.

The status quo can now be disturbed only by diminishing the gratifications of the transference neurosis through as radical a reduction of interviews as is at all tolerable for the patient, leading up to an interruption of the treatment which will serve as a test of his capacity to use in his daily life the new reaction patterns acquired in the therapy.

INTERRUPTIONS AND TERMINATIONS OF TREATMENT

Many patients in this phase, having instinctively learned their therapist's predilections, bring seemingly interesting material to allay the analyst's impatience and give an impression of steady progress and deepening of analytic insight. While the analyst may believe that they are engaged in a thorough "working-through," in reality the procedure has become a farce, a clever technique of procrastination on the part of the patient. Or a patient may reach that place in treatment where he merely repeats material he has brought many times before, in order to avoid opening up other conflicts. Or again, a patient may make a "flight into health" in order to avoid painful insight. The genuineness of these attitudes is not always easy to divine. The therapist may take them for indications that the patient is ready to leave treatment and to meet life entirely on his own, or he may realize that the patient is employing unconscious subterfuge. In either case, an interruption will show whether the patient is able to lead a normal life without his regular interviews.

During an interruption the patient learns which of his previous difficulties he still retains, and the following interviews usually center around those emotional problems in which he needs further help. The author of this section has used the method of one or more preparatory interruptions almost exclusively during the last twelve years (the interruptions varying in length from one to eighteen months) and has found that the analysis after interruption has, without exception, become much more intensive, accomplishing more in the following few weeks than had been achieved in months before.

At first, the interruption may have to be imposed by decree and the patient forced to rely on his own strength and judgment. Soon, however, he may recognize that he actually does not need the therapist as much as before. This diminishes the resentment brought on by the patient's feeling of helplessness and increases his confidence in his own powers.

It is advisable to make the interruption not too short. The patient should have an opportunity to struggle with his problems alone and should not be encouraged to turn to the analyst at the first hint of relapse. On the other hand, he should have the assurance that if he really needs his therapist, he can always return to him. We thus avoid recrudescence of the patient's resistance to giving up his neurotic escape reactions and the panic reactions which have been observed in experiments with the termination technique developed by Ferenczi and Rank.

Termination of treatment, if the method of preparatory interruptions is used, will not be artificial but will become a natural ending to the therapy. Experience—how the patient actually reacted to previous interruptions—will determine when the therapy should be brought to a close, not such theoretical criteria as the filling in of memory gaps and complete understanding of the etiological factors, nor even the depth of intellectual insight. In some cases, the patient will be capable of completely changing the life situation in which he failed before and which precipitated his neurosis, adapting it to his needs and to his capacity for gratifying them. In all cases, the patient will have given actual, tested proof of his ability to find ego-syntonic gratification for his needs.

At the present state of our knowledge, it is difficult to make precise predictions concerning the length of a treatment or the number of interviews required in any given case. Our task is to make the patient self-reliant by exerting a constant but not excessive pressure, blocking the patient's neurotic retreat into fantasy and into the past, and urging him toward the actual difficulties of his current life situation. The intensity of this pressure—upon which the rate of progress, and thus the length of treatment, depends—can be determined only through repeated testing during the treatment, observing the patient's reactions as they manifest themselves either in recrudescence of resistance, or in progressive efforts in his everyday life.

How much preparatory experience in the transference relationship a patient needs before he becomes capable of handling the corresponding interpersonal situations in real life, depends upon the nature of the case. With patients whose ego's functional capacity is only temporarily impaired under trying life conditions, a few interviews to relieve acute anxiety may suffice. The intensity of the neurotic regressive trends in the different patients, however, is of such extreme variety that the length of treatment may be anything from a few isolated interviews to the standard technique of daily interviews extending over several years.

EXTRA-THERAPEUTIC EXPERIENCES

The so-called normal individual, when he fails in a life situation and has suffered a serious setback, will make new attempts to solve his actual problem instead of having recourse to the substitutive solutions of neurotic regression. An essential feature of neurosis is the giving up of systematic efforts of trial and error to overcome those difficulties which precipitated the neurotic breakdown. This neurotic reaction to traumatic experiences appears in all degrees of intensity. In some cases, no more help is needed than temporary support to enable the patient's ego to make new attempts at finding gratifications for its needs, even in the new baffling situation. At the other extreme are patients who react to almost every change in their life situation with neurotic escapes into fantasy and regressive behavior. Between these two extremes, there is a continuous gradation from the more acute to chronic types of neurosis.

The degree to which one should rely upon the therapeutic effect of the patient's experiences in life depends upon the nature of the case and the phase of the treatment. In general, a greater part of the therapy may take place outside the sessions with the less severe cases, in which an interview a week or every other week may have enough influence on the patient's daily life to insure progress. At the other extreme is the patient who must be hospitalized and under constant supervision. Another generalization of approximate validity is that, with the progress of treatment, one can rely more and more on the beneficent effect of actual experiences in life; these experiences, of course, have been made possible by the preparatory interviews in which the patient has learned to handle certain emotional situations in his relationship to the analyst.

It is important to keep in mind that the patient will finally have to solve his problems in actual life, in his relationships to his wife and his children, his superiors and his competitors, his friends and his enemies. The experiences in the transference relationship are only preparations, a training for the real battle. The sooner the patient can be led against those real obstacles in life from which he retreated and can be induced to engage in new experimentation, the more quickly can satisfactory therapeutic results be achieved.

In every psychotherapy, therefore, whether it takes the form of the standard technique or that of some briefer method, an integral part of the treatment consists in observing and systematically influencing the patient's experiences in life.

The attitude has been overstressed that a "real psychoanalyst"—in contrast to the "practical psychotherapist" who might give advice and directives to the patient—should not try to guide the patient in his daily life and should encourage or discourage his activities as little as possible. It was formerly felt (and sometimes still is) that during treatment the patient really need not do much concerning his practical problems, and that in any case to influence his daily activities was not the concern of the therapist. This assumption that the interviews will solve everything as if by magic has prolonged many treatments unduly. Freud himself came to the conclusion that in the treatment of some cases, phobias for example, a time arrives when the analyst must encourage the patient to engage in those activities he avoided in the past. (A patient who retreats into isolation, for instance, should in the different phases of the treatment try again and again to have human contacts.) This is a fundamental principle of every treatment, an intrinsic part of the therapy.

Even more generally accepted than the motto "As little interference in the patient's daily life as possible" is another rule all students of psychoanalysis were formerly taught: "No important changes in the life situation until after the completion of treatment." Back of this rule was the sound observation that some patients were inclined to act out in life their ever-changing trends as they became liberated during the treatment. For example, a formerly very cautious, intimidated patient, when he becomes aware of the dependent attitude responsible for his former habit of never standing up for his rights, may impulsively give up a good job just to prove his independence and courage. Or a patient whose sexual repressions have been relieved, may impulsively rush into promiscuous activities.

And yet, in a certain phase of the treatment the patient may be ready to marry, for instance, even though he still needs further treatment. Serious delay of therapeutic progress may result from adherence to the rule of "no important, irreversible changes during treatment." Marriage, change of occupation, even change of profession, may be indispensable to the therapeutic success of a case, and waiting for the end of treatment before such a change may destroy all possibility of success. The advice not to make important decisions during treatment, therefore, should be given the patient in a modified, more flexible form: "No important, irreversible changes in the life situation, *unless both therapist and patient agree.*"

First Attempts

The therapeutic process must at no time be thought of as restricted to the emotional experiences within the transference relationship. Too often it is forgotten that transference experiences and life experiences take place simultaneously and parallel to each other. Having learned to handle hitherto-conflictful emotional constellations in the transference relationship, the patient must then be helped to experiment with the same type of constellation in real life.

Like the adage "Nothing succeeds like success," there is no more powerful therapeutic factor than the performance of activities which were formerly neurotically impaired or inhibited. No insight, no emotional discharge, no recollection can be as reassuring as accomplishment in the actual life situation in which the individual failed. Thus the ego regains that confidence which is the fundamental condition, the prerequisite, of mental health. Every success encourages new trials and decreases inferiority feelings, resentments, and their sequelae—fear, guilt, and resulting inhibitions. Successful attempts at productive work, love, self-assertion, or competition will change the vicious circle to a benign one; as they are repeated, they become habitual and thus eventually bring about a complete change in the personality.

The chief therapeutic value of the transference situation lies in the fact that it allows the patient to experience this feeling of success in rehearsal, a rehearsal which must then be followed by actual performance. And curbing the patient's tendency to procrastinate and to substitute analytic experience for reality (by careful manipulation of the transference relationship, by timely directives and encouragement) is one of the most effective means of shortening treatment. Fostering favorable experiences in the actual life situation at the right moment in the treatment tends to make for economical psychotherapy, bringing it to an earlier conclusion than otherwise. The therapist need not wait until the end of treatment but, at the right moment, should encourage the patient (or even require him) to do those things which he avoided in the past, to experiment in that activity in which he had failed before.

While it is important not to urge the patient prematurely, the therapist's fear that his patient will fail is usually stronger than it should be. The therapist must prepare the patient for failures, explaining that they are unavoidable and that the most important thing for him is to be always ready to try new experiments. Moreover, failures can be turned to advantage when they are carefully analyzed and their cause thoroughly understood by the patient.

REFERENCE

1. Rado, S. The relationship of patient to therapist. *American Journal of Orthopsychiatry,* 1942, 12, No. (3).

3. Theory and Practice of Brief Therapy

Simon H. Budman and Alan S. Gurman

All forms of brief therapy emphasize the importance of having a clear area of focus for the treatment. The theoretical inclinations of the developer of the treatment determine the major focus or foci.

What is meant by "treatment focus"? How does one stick with the focus? And what are common foci in brief therapy from an I-D-E (interpersonal, developmental, existential) perspective? These are some of the questions we attempt to address in the following pages.

Human behavior is so complex, and can be organized according to such a wide variety of principles, that the therapist has literally an infinite number of choices regarding the potential core focal issue or issues. Kinston and Bentovim (1981), in describing the value of a therapeutic focus for brief treatment, have written:

A focal hypothesis refers to an "ad hoc clinical theory" developed to clarify or bring into focus a large number of disparate and apparently unrelated phenomena. It integrates and provides continuity to the manifestations of the person or family. It also serves as a beacon to guide the therapist as he or she becomes involved in the detailed specifics of work with the individual or family. For this reason, it must be brief and highly pertinent. . . . (p. 367)

We believe that a focus relating to interpersonal, developmental, and existential factors has the greatest potential for being quickly relevant to the patient, closely related to his or her reason for seeking therapy, and useful to the therapist as a theme around which to organize his or her interventions. The foci we describe in this chapter are frequently seen in the general outpatient practice of psychotherapy with adults. Except for our final category, severe personality disorders, they generally relate to events or states of being that may be relatively independent of diagnostic category. As such, they represent what we view as the most prominent and immediate feature in the patient's life, which is directly related to the patient's decision to seek therapy at this particular point in time.

Reprinted by permission of Guilford Publications from *Theory and Practice of Brief Psychotherapy*. New York, 1988, pp., 62–73; 283–90, 373–94.

In considering any of the possible central foci proposed below, the therapist should always taken into consideration the patient's life stage as a factor affecting the significance of the given focus for that person. For example, the death of a spouse has very different meanings for a 30-year-old widow and for a 75-year-old widow. There is intense pain and mourning in both circumstances. However, the 75-year-old woman may have friends who have also lost their husbands; there may have been more of an expectation that her husband might die before her; the couple's children are probably grown adults; and so on. For the 30-year-old woman, there would have been no expectation nor anticipation that she would be widowed at this point in her life; there are likely to be young children to raise alone; the support systems for young widows or widowers are likely to be minimal; and so forth.

In addition, the therapist should remain attuned to the interpersonal context of the patient. What supports exist? What are his or her familial and friendship networks like? What and who are the most powerful interpersonal influences in the patient's life?

THE FIVE MOST COMMON FOCI

We describe here the five most commonly occurring foci.

Losses

Past, present, or impending losses often constitute a major reason for seeking psychotherapy. Examples include the loss of an attachment figure through moves, separation, divorce, or death; the loss of one's own health and well-being through illness, accident, or victimization; the loss of a home or a job; and so on. Not infrequently multiple areas are affected at once, as when an illness or disability leads to the loss of a job. It should be borne in mind that losses are not always dealt with directly by the patient at the time of their occurrence. That is, for a variety of reasons at the time of a particular loss, the patient may be unable to acknowledge the full meaning or power of that loss. It may take months or years before the impact manifests itself overtly. By that time, the patient has detached the original experience from its now manifest symptomatology. The symptoms are therefore viewed as mysterious, as unrelated to events in the present, and often as indicative of characterological deficits. In a similar manner, the patient who realizes that a loss will soon occur may deny its importance, thereby excluding from consciousness the cause of his or her discomfort.

Developmental Dysynchronies

Development throughout life is a dynamic process, with a variety of changing hopes, expectations, and role demands at various points. When our expectations at transition points are not fulfilled, and in particular when our age-mates are moving to achieve things that we ourselves have been unable to achieve, a disequilibrium occurs that may lead to help seeking.

For example, the single, unattached 28-year-old man or woman who finds that more and more of his or her friends are becoming involved in long-term, committed relationships, are living with lovers, or are getting married may feel an increasing sense of loneliness and heightened desire for such a relationship himself or herself. Similarly, the 64-year-old man who is quickly moving toward retirement without any real savings, sense of security, or plan for how he will spend the remainder of his life may be filled with fear, anxiety, and depression. This may be especially true if he has friends who have saved money and/or who are better organized to deal with retirement. When the therapist fails to take a dynamic (not psychodynamic) view of adult development, it may be easy to forget that the same symptomatology in those of different ages may have very different meanings and causes. We believe that for the patient to realize that the therapist can truly understand and empathize with his or her plight is of enormous value. Therefore, for many patients it is not as effective simply to comprehend that the patients are depressed as it is to convey an understanding of their developmental and existential pain.

Interpersonal Conflicts

A third major area of difficulty that frequently brings people to psychotherapists is the exacerbation of interpersonal conflicts. Frequently such interpersonal conflicts occur within the context of an intimate relationship. At times, conflict relates to different developmental sequencing between partners in that relationship, as when, for example, a woman feels ready to have children while her spouse does not. However, severe interpersonal conflicts certainly may occur with friends, employees, coworkers, and so on. Although conflicts may relate to potential losses or to developmental factors, they also may occur independently of either.

Symptomatic Presentation

Another major reason for presentation to a therapist is in regard to a particular clear and discrete symptom or set of symptoms. Not infrequently the patient has suffered with the symptom for an extended period of time, but chooses to seek therapy after a major loss or when he or she has just passed or is about to pass a particular developmental milestone. Unlike those circumstances in which understanding a particular loss, grieving for it, and so on is helpful, it is our impression that if the patient presents exclusively or almost exclusively with a symptomatic concern (e.g., "I have been an insomniac for 10 years and it has nothing to do with the circumstances of my life"), the patient *must* be treated first and foremost around that symptom. Even if other issues are clearly (to the therapist) the pivotal factor(s) driving the patient to seek help at this point—and they almost invariably are—the patient must be accepted on his or her own terms. This means an immediate focus upon the presenting discrete symptomatology. The range of symptomatic presentations is enormous, but usually includes habit disorders, sexual dysfunctions, fears, and phobias.

Severe Personality Disorders

There are some patients who simply never make progress when therapy deals with the major foci described previously. In addition, their presentation to a therapist often ceases to be clearly tied in to the losses, transitions, and conflicts described above. Rather, such patients present repeatedly for mental health therapy, with little indication that any change has occurred after any brief intervention. They present with constant reports of loneliness, isolation, depression, anger, and so on. Their pain is rarely alleviated by a problem-focused intervention. Moreover, such patients' characterological impediments often interfere with their abilities to relate productively with a therapist. The portrait that usually emerges is one of a patient with severe (at times borderline) character problems. It should not be assumed, however, that such a patient cannot be treated in brief therapy. We have seen such patients briefly using one or more of the major foci described for numerous courses of brief therapy, and this has appeared to be the treatment of choice. There are, however, other patients for whom the usual format does not appear to have sufficient useful effect and for whom other approaches seem to be more beneficial. For such patients, it may be necessary to focus on characterological issues per se if any change is to occur. This does not preclude brief therapy, according to our definition, for these patients; rather, it may indicate a longer but still cost-effective and time-effective intervention.

A Note on Substance Abuse

In choosing any of these five frequent foci, the therapist must always be aware of the problems of drug addiction and alcoholism. If, as the therapist is beginning treatment, it becomes clear that a major issue for the patient is that of a severe (alcohol or drug) addiction problem, this problem must take precedence over all others. A patient who is drinking heavily or using illicit drugs is unlikely to be able to profit from treatment, regardless of the therapist's best efforts. It is essential that the issue of addiction be addressed just as soon as the therapist is sure that this is a significant disruption in the patient's life. Enormous amounts of time in therapy can be wasted if the therapist neglects, ignores, or misses a substance abuse problem.

THE PROCESS OF FINDING A FOCUS

Figure 3.1 illustrates the process of finding a focus for the therapy. It is conceivable that more than one of the areas mentioned above may constitute the therapeutic focus. Once, however, the major focal area is clarified and agreed upon, it is most important that it be made the central theme of the therapy that follows. Whereas other issues may, of course, come up and be discussed, it is the responsibility of the therapist to keep the major theme of the treatment always at the forefront of the interaction. This has a number of important implications:

1. As early in the interviews as possible, the therapist presents the focus as he or she sees it and seeks clarification from the patient regarding whether or not the proposed focus appears consonant with his or her experience of the problem and goals for change. For example, one might say to a 48-year-old widower, "I believe that your wife's death from cancer 2 years ago left you feeling in enormous pain. I know that you originally said that you were depressed about your current relationships and did not know why these were

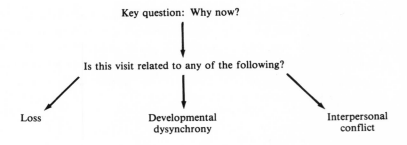

Key question: Why now?

Is this visit related to any of the following?

Loss   Developmental   Interpersonal
              dysynchrony   conflict

If the patient does not view the above focal areas as relevant, *or* if the patient defines the symptom itself as the major issue,

Symptomatic focus

If the patient has had repeated presentations around any or all of the foci above, without clear benefit, *or* if character issues preclude these foci because of constant interference with the therapeutic process,

Character focus

Warning: Under circumstances of active alcohol or drug abuse, this problem *must* be addressed before or simultaneously with the development of any other focal area.

Figure 3.1: Major Foci in Brief Therapy

going so poorly. But I think that the issue of your wife is central here. Perhaps we can, at least initially, focus on that and see if it is helpful to do so. What do you think?"

2. Once a relevant focus is established and accepted, the therapist deals with digressions by always maintaining clarity for himself or herself about what the central theme for this patient is. Some patients may have to be urged or guided to stick with the theme even after accepting it, whereas for others this comes easily. Certainly there are occasions when a particular crisis or real-life event may preclude dealing with the focal theme. For example, a young woman whose therapy was focused around a particular habit disorder (picking and scratching the inside of one of her nostrils)

developed a very critical situation at work. The therapist under such circumstances should not behave as an automaton and must maintain empathy with the patient. However, even during a crisis or a temporary change of focus, the central theme can be brought up briefly and its importance remembered.

3. Sessions should end with some summary statement from the therapist regarding what has gone on during that session and how he or she views the situation in regard to the central theme. For example, "You've spoken a good deal today about the death of your brother. I know it's hard for you to do, but it looks to me as though you are really becoming more able to recognize just how much he meant to you and how much his loss hurt you."

Thus, the individual session and a given course of sessions are both like a fine fabric, woven together by the thread of the central theme. The theme opens the session, maintains a unity within the session, and closes the session. It is also part of what keeps a coherence between different sessions. Although people's lives tend to be multifaceted and complex, and we believe that it is quite important to give credence to this complexity, we also feel that without a focus brief therapy cannot exist. Were we to treat whatever came up for patients without tenaciously maintaining a focus, there would be no target, no direction, and no clarity about the utility of the treatment.

BRIEF INTERVENTION: SOME ASSUMPTIONS

In describing an I-D-E model of brief therapy, it is most helpful to begin with some theoretical assumptions about how psychopathology and other psychological difficulties develop and are maintained, since such views should directly influence what the brief therapist does in the face of such problems.

1. *It is our first assumption that the patient-to-be has been subjected to faulty learning at some point during his or her early growth and development.* This faulty learning may take a variety of forms and/or relate to various aspects of the child's life. It may be direct and cognitive (as when a parent states; "Sex is dirty and you should stay away from it"), and/or subliminal, symbolic, and emotional (the parent grimaces whenever sexual issues are portrayed on TV or in movies, etc.). Furthermore, it may be and remain conscious, or may be unconscious and not readily available to the individual. In any event, a cognitive-emotional map of the world is internalized and to a greater or lesser degree becomes a template for future behaviors and relationships. It is supposed that the greater the intensity of the faulty messages, the

greater the psychopathology subsequently displayed. It is also assumed by psychoanalytically oriented clinicians that the earlier the occurrence of the faulty learning, the greater the psychological disturbance that results.

Many major systems of personality and psychotherapy make similar assumptions regarding the issues of faulty learning. Writing from a social learning perspective about internalized belief systems, Bandura (1982) states:

People seek and hold firmly to beliefs because they serve valuable functions. Indeed, life would be most taxing and chaotic if people had no conceptions of themselves and the world around them. Their experiences would lack coherence; they would cede the substantial benefits of foresight, which requires a system for predicting conditional happenings in daily affairs; they would lack guides for action with situational influences pulling in all directions; and finally, they would be without basic goals for organizing their efforts over long time spans. Belief systems thus help to provide structure, direction, and purpose to life. Because personal identity and security become heavily invested in belief systems, they are not readily discardable once acquired. (p. 753)

Strupp and Binder (1984), from the perspective of object relations theory, likewise conclude: "Every current relationship is more or less influenced by past relationships which have become organizing themes in the personality structure and, as such, are reenacted in the present" (p. 34). From the Ericksonian viewpoint, Lankton and Lankton (1983) also present a very similar set of concepts:

[Milton] Erickson believed that "maps" or rules for recombining experience, are so automatized that they become unconscious and the experiences and perceptions attached to them become automatized. Since the map is rarely in a person's conscious awareness, it is not scrutinized and updated with the passage of time. It is, instead, reinforced by the outcomes of the person's selective behavior and perceptions. Symptoms are generally the result of the client's making the best choice among options determined unconsciously by those associations available in his or her map. (pp. 34–35)

2. *The person and his or her environment are in constant interaction and are reciprocally influential.* Many theories of personality, until more recent years, were based upon what Bandura (1977) has called "unidirectional determinism." This model maintains that either the environment acts upon the person to structure and shape behavior and experience, or, as the alternative, that the individual's mind creates reality. This point of view fails to consider the fact that the person, behavior, and the environment are in constant interaction and determine one another in a process of "reciprocal

determinism" (Bandura, 1977). This can also be described as a nonlinear systems perspective. The individual operates within a particular, or at least relatively consistent, belief system; however, he or she is also changing and being modified over time as are his or her environment and behavior. Each aspect of the human ecology interlocks with all others, making it nearly impossible to effectively separate the elemental parts from one another.

A simple illustrative example might be the training of a young gymnast. Due to a variety of factors, such as the child's physical attributes, parental interest and support, recollections of champion gymnasts on TV, and so on, a child might begin gymnastics training. Skill level achieved might lead to further training and improved environmental supports and to the child's modification of her belief system regarding what she is capable of. However, it may also be that modified environment (e.g., going to a better gym) precedes improved skill level and modified belief system ("I am a very good gymnast"), or that beliefs, environment, and skills change simultaneously and are synergistic to one another.

Because even the most basic reciprocal systems are in fact highly complex, most psychotherapy theoreticians have chosen to deal with only one aspect of interpersonal systems (i.e., either behavior, environment, or beliefs). It is our contention that the effective brief therapist will have in his or her repertoire interventions that may modify the system at any of these three levels, and will choose from among intervention possibilities by trying to consider where the greatest leverage can be exerted with the least expenditure of time or effort.

3. *The patient's existing, current interpersonal environment (and his or her view of that environment) either may provide a buffering effect in the management of major or minor stress and distress, or may be a factor leading to the exacerbation of these factors. The interpersonal environment is never neutral.* Everyone, other than hermits or those who are living alone on isolated deserted islands (who, for obvious reasons, are rarely seen by psychotherapists or anyone else), exists as part of some social interpersonal systems. These systems are often central factors in mitigating the effects of adverse life experiences, or may be exacerbating factors, or may themselves be the adverse life experiences that contribute to symptomatology. In our view, the patient's real interpersonal system is obviously of great importance in a number of ways. However, of at least equal importance is the patient's *perceived* interpersonal system. Until recently, it was simply assumed that those with the fewest social contacts and the most impoverished social

systems would be the most highly susceptible to psychiatric symptoms. Contemporary epidemiological research has indicated that *perceptions* of the environment are as important in the development of neurosis as, if not more so than, actual number of contacts or relationships. Henderson, Byrne, and Duncan-Jones (1982), reporting the results of a major study of the relationship between neuroses and the social environment, conclude:

[T]he actual availability of social relationships probably has little to do with the causes of neurosis. The perceived adequacy with which others meet the individual's requirements, especially under adversity, seems much more important. . . . Under adversity, it is those who construe their social relationships as inadequate who are more likely to develop symptoms. (p. 197)

This means that patients can be helped in a variety of ways (which we describe later) to re-evaluate their social environments. Furthermore, a social system that the individual patient has initially described as impoverished often includes many more supports than are readily apparent to the patient.

4. *Although personality, character, social supports, and so on play an important part in contributing to an individual's life pattern, chance encounters are also prominent factors in shaping the life course.* Both psychoanalytic and humanistic theorists assume that the individual is the major determiner of his or her life course, either because of early development or through free choice. The role of chance encounters is either minimized or ignored. Bandura (1982), in presenting a psychology of chance encounters, defines such events as "an unintended meeting of persons unfamiliar to each other" (p. 748). As an example, he presents the story of Paul Watkins, who was

. . . a talented teenager headed on a promising course of personal development—He enjoyed a close family life, was well liked by his peers, excelled in academic activities, and served as student-body president of his high school, hardly the omens of a disordered destiny (Watkins & Soledad, 1979). One day he decided to visit a friend who lived in a cabin in Topanga Canyon in Los Angeles. Unbeknown to Watkins, the friend had since moved elsewhere and the Manson "family" now lived there. This fortuitous visit led to a deep entanglement in the Manson gang in the period before they embarked on their "helter skelter" killings. To an impressionable youth the free flow of communal love, group sex, drugs, spellbinding revelations of divine matters, and isolation from the outside world provided a heady counterforce that launched him on a divergent life path requiring years to turn his life around. (p. 748)

Bandura continues:

In the preceding case the initial meeting was entirely due to happenstance. Human encounters involve degrees of fortuitiveness. People often intentionally seek certain types of experiences, but the persons who thereby enter their lives are determined by a large element of chance. (p. 748)

In a similar vein, a recently popular foreign film, *The Return of Martin Guerre,* is based upon the true story of two 16th-century French peasants who meet, fortuitously, as comrades in arms. The two look very similar and are often mistaken for each other. One of the peasants, Martin Guerre, has run off and abandoned his wife, child, and village many years before as a youth, and tells his comrade that he will never return to them. Thus, the other, upon leaving the army, surreptitiously goes to Guerre's village, masquerading as the true Martin. He is accepted as genuine, moves into his old comrade's house, lives with his wife and has children by her, works his fields, and totally assumes Guerre's identity, until another series of chance encounters lead to the imposter's unfortunate discovery and ultimate execution.

The assumption of chance encounters is not meant to imply that one has no control over one's own life. Rather, we believe the following:

a. All of our lives are determined, at least in part, by good and bad fortune, which cannot be fully under the individual's influence and are not predetermined by experiences up to the age of 4.
b. Chance encounters may be significant events (for better or for worse) in shaping the individual's life.
c. There are probably ways in which individuals can be helped both to put themselves in circumstances where positive and useful chance encounters are more likely to occur, and to maximize the benefits of such environmental events.

A final example in this regard comes from Bergin and Lambert (1978), who call positive chance encounters "naturalistic therapy":

One example of a naturalistic therapy process comes from our experiences in conducting extensive personality assessments of normal persons for a governmental agency. During these evaluations we have occasionally noted an exceptionally effective person who has come from a chaotic and ordinarily pathology-inducing family life. A young college graduate illustrated this well. He came from an extremely disturbed home setting in which every member of his family except himself had been hospitalized for severe mental illness; and yet he had graduated from a renowned university with honors, had starred on the football team, and was unusually popular. During his government training he was held in the highest esteem by staff members and was rated as best liked and most likely to succeed by his peers.

In examining this young man's history we discovered that during his elementary school years he had essentially adopted a neighborhood family as his own and spent endless hours with them. Certain characteristics of this family appear most significant. They were a helping family in the sense that love emanated from them and was freely available to all. Of special significance for the fellow under consideration was his relationship with a boy in the family, a year older than he, who formed for him a positive role model with whom he closely identified and whom he followed to his considerable satisfaction.

An even more crucial factor was his relationship with the mother in this family, who became his guide, counselor, and chief source of emotional nurturance. His reports indicate that while this relationship was intense, it was not symbiotic, and seemed to foster his independence and self-development. This particular woman was apparently the prototypical mother and influenced more than one stray youth toward security, resilience, and accomplishment. It is difficult to deny the potent therapeutic impact of this woman, at least as it was portrayed by her protégé's report. Although there are probably few like her, she represents a dimension of socially indigenous therapy that may be more significant than is usually recognized. Her home became a neighborhood gathering place. It might be characterized as an informal therapy agency, a kitchen clinic! Certainly, it makes the possibility of "spontaneous" remission more believable. (pp. 149–150).*

5. *Experience is always understood by the individual (at least in part) on the basis of his or her stage of life development.* It is clear to us that one's stage of life development is an important lens through which experience in the world is viewed. A 24-year-old with obsessive concerns about death may be viewed as having a serious psychiatric problem, whereas a 75-year-old with major concerns in this area may be normative. Symptoms such as depression, loneliness, problems with intimacy, and so on all have different meanings, depending upon the patient's stage of life development. Although each of us follows an individual and unique life course, there are similarities regarding what most people in a given age cohort value in regard to issues such as intimacy, financial stability, and so on.

6. *Our final assumption is that little or no therapy will actually occur unless or until the patient is ready for change.* Ability to profit from treat-

* This quotation is taken from "The Evaluation of Therapeutic Outcomes," by A. E. Bergin and M. J. Lambert, 1978, in *Handbook of Psychotherapy and Behavior Change* ed. S. L. Garfield and A. E. Bergin, 2nd ed. New York: Wiley, pp. 139–90. Copyright 1978 by John Wiley and Sons. Reprinted by permission.

ment is far more closely related to this concept of readiness than it is to diagnosis or psychopathology. We emphasize the notion of "Why now?" because it is the question most central in clarifying patients' readiness to work on change. Patients with very severe diagnoses, levels of pathology, and long-sustained problems may be confronted by developmental milestones or find themselves dealing with other events that make them "ready" and available for treatment.

In finding a focus for treatment the clinician helps to clarify where the push for change is from, so that this healthy thrust can be capitalized upon and enhanced. As we have indicated, alcohol and drug abuse *must* be addressed early in therapy, and it may be necessary to delay or refuse therapy to a patient who is actively drinking or abusing drugs.

The common foci and the six assumptions that we have described provide the clinician with a conceptual frame of reference in the practice of brief therapy. Clearly, patients come to us with their own unique personalities, areas of conflict, and ways of being in the world; however, we believe that the overall perspective we are providing offers the brief therapist a method for determining the area or areas that may be most readily and beneficially addressed in treatment. The assumptions provide a general orientation to our theoretical position, which in turn lead to our intervention strategies.

THE USE OF TIME IN BRIEF PSYCHOTHERAPY

> Look upon that last day always. Count no mortal happy till he has passed the final limit of his life secure from pain.
> —Sophocles, *Oedipus the King* (ca. 429 B.C/1949)

Most brief and long-term psychotherapists have applied a notably low degree of creativity to the use of time in treatment. Perhaps because of convenience, insurance restraints, and habit, there is nearly universal application of the 50-minute, weekly psychotherapy session. Groups and families tend to be seen for about 90 minutes, also on a weekly basis. The major "mainstream innovation" in the last 80 years regarding the application of time in psychotherapy has been the use of clear time limits set early in the treatment. However, the most truly novel uses of therapy time about which we have heard or read are Milton Erickson's (1980) approaches to this issue, and Alexander and French's (1946/1974) time utilization.

Erickson, in some cases, would see people for very brief sessions (sometimes just several minutes), and at other times he would see a patient for many hours without a break. On occasion some patients would be seen for daily visits; on other occasions an individual might be seen very intensively and then not again for many months. As with so many other aspects of Erickson's approaches, it is not usually easily discernible from his writings how and why he made his differential decisions regarding whom he would treat in one way as opposed to another.

Alexander and French (1946/1974), in many of their case studies, described strikingly flexible and innovative uses of time. For example, in their "Case P" (pp. 293–297), a young man of 19 came for treatment because of severe and debilitating depression. He was to leave for the Army in less than 3 months, and because of scheduling difficulties he could come in for only very brief (15- to 20-minute) interviews once or twice a week. The therapist saw him for a total of 35 visits, which appeared to have been extremely helpful. He had two more brief contacts with the therapist several years after entering the Army. In addition, Alexander and French (1946/1974) provided many examples in their book of increasingly "spread-out" sessions as a method of weaning the patient away from therapy, (e.g., "Case K," pp. 234–244). The authors also presented a number of other cases in which the therapists seemed to use time in a variety of flexible ways.

We believe that even if a therapist does not often choose to modify his or her uses of time, it is important for him or her to be aware that there *are* infinite possibilities for its use. We also believe that some clinical and empirical principles may be applied when the therapist wishes to maintain a time-effective perspective and does have the inclination and opportunity to modify his or her time utilization more radically.

Our empirical data regarding this issue come in part from D. H. Johnson and Gelso's (1980) excellent review of the effectiveness of time limits in psychotherapy, and in part from Howard et al.'s (1986) analysis of the dose–effect relationship in psychotherapy. One of Johnson and Gelso's conclusions is as follows:

Apparently a minimal amount of counseling may be needed to get improvement started; after this point, the actual duration of the counseling is not predictive of long-term improvement. Thus, with at least weekly treatment contact to begin the improvement process, time alone (with or without counseling) seems to be the actual variable in producing optimal improvement in our clients. In other words, it may be that it is not "the more counseling time the better" but "the more time after beginning counseling the better." (pp. 73–74)

Howard et al. (1986), on the other hand, conclude that up to a certain point (about 52 weekly sessions) there is a clear, positive dose–effect relationship in psychotherapy; that is, for the first year, the more once-a-week therapy the better. How can these seemingly different findings be reconciled? It appears to us that neither the studies reviewed in the Johnson and Gelso (1980) paper nor those cited in Howard et al. (1986) compared, in a careful, randomized experimental design, therapy that was provided intermittently over an extended period of time with therapy that was provided weekly (or more frequently) over this same extended period of time. In the absence of such research, what is apparent from a careful examination of both sets of data is that the early stages of an episode of treatment (the first six to eight visits) are extremely important in initiating the change process. (Howard and his colleagues believe that 50% of patients treated in psychotherapy will show some response to therapy with six to eight sessions.)

Thus, if the therapist wishes to use time in an innovative, time-effective manner, he or she might consider seeing a patient initially for longer visits (more than 50 minutes) and/or for a number of sessions close together. Once the treatment has been initiated (after perhaps four to eight visits), the therapist who is continuing to see a patient might move to briefer visits and/ or visits that are "spread out" over longer periods. Most importantly, the therapist should remember that there is nothing sacred about seeing patients in a particular way as regards the timing of visits. We have found that even the most disturbed patients can respond to the flexible use of time in a favorable manner. Indeed, setting up twice-a-month visits with such patients may at times be viewed as a vote of confidence in their abilities to survive without the therapist. Even less disturbed patients may profit considerably from such unusual scheduling of appointments. In addition to suggesting the patients' capacity to "survive" without the commonplace weekly meeting, such scheduling—particularly when used in the context of the active, focused style of intervention described in this book—also implies the need for patients to work on their problems outside the therapist's office. That is, dependency is minimized, and self-responsibility is enhanced. The therapist should consider the fact that time and timing are just as much types of interventions as are interpretations, tasks, and so on, and need not be applied in an unquestioned, unchangeable manner. In any case, the flexible brief therapist should place particular emphasis upon making maximal use of early sessions in a given episode of care, and may consider a move to less frequent or less "time-intensive" visits later in a given episode.

THE ISSUE OF TERMINATION

Psychoanalytically oriented thinkers, in particular, have been interested in the issue of termination in psychotherapy. Since "good" treatment is viewed as having a prophylactic effect, the need for additional treatment once the therapy is "completed" is often perceived as indicating a therapeutic failure. The following excerpt from Firestein's (1978) review of psychoanalytic termination criteria will give the reader some idea of what many analytically oriented thinkers see as the ideal state for the terminating patient:

A typical characterization would indicate approximately the following: Symptoms have been traced to their genetic conflicts, in the course of which the infantile neurosis has been identified, as the infantile amnesia was undone ("insight"). It is hoped all symptoms have been eliminated, mitigated, or made tolerable. Object relations, freed of transference distortions, have improved, along with the level of psychosexual functioning, the latter attaining "full genitality." Penis envy and castration anxiety have been mastered. The ego is strengthened by virtue of diminishing anachronistic countercathectic formations. The ability to distinguish between fantasy and reality has been sharpened. Acting out has been eliminated. The capacity to tolerate some measure of anxiety and to reduce other unpleasant affects to signal quantities has been improved. The ability to tolerate delay of gratification is increased, and along with it there is a shift from autoplastic to alloplastic conflict solutions. Sublimations have been strengthened, and the capacity to experience pleasure without guilt or other notable inhibiting factors has improved. Working ability, under which so many aspects of ego function, libidinal and aggressive drive gratification are subsumed, has improved. (pp. 226–227)

Furthermore, not only must the patient be in this extraordinary (and unlikely) state of mental health, but there should be no looking back. That is, "when you are done, you are done."

Ticho (1972) strongly advises against reassuring the patient that he or she can recontact the analyst if the need arises. Indeed, such reassurances are viewed as suspect. The therapist's need to make such a statement and the patient's need to hear this reassurance probably mean that the treatment is not really complete and perhaps should not be terminated.

This rigid and unrealistic view of termination in psychotherapy and psychoanalysis has pervaded long-term dynamically oriented thinking (Panel, 1969, 1975). In a modified form, this view has also influenced brief dynamic therapies (Davanloo, 1978; Mann, 1973; Sifneos, 1972, 1979). That is, little attention is paid to the possibility of the patient's returning, because successful treatment will have been curative, and additional therapeutic input should not be required. Indeed, as Davanloo (1980) writes regarding his approach, "[A]t the time of termination there is definite evidence of the *total resolution* of the patient's core neurosis" (p. 70, italics added). Moreover, this minimizing of the possibility, need, or appropriateness of the patient's returning contradicts the theoretical and research evidence we have considered in previous chapters in favor of an I-D-E framework for brief psychotherapy. The Davanloo position would seem to deny the likelihood of developmental changes across the life span.

Mann and Goldman (1982) warn against telling the patient, in their form of time-limited therapy, that there will be a follow-up interview about 1 year after termination. They write:

At no time during the treatment does the therapist make any mention of a follow-up interview. It is incumbent on the therapist to make certain that the separation phase of treatment is *unequivocal;* anything less will suggest to the patient that the separation is not genuine, that more time will be available. (p. 13, italics added)

Thus, in their model, the termination is presented to the patient as absolute because to do otherwise would intrude upon the fantasies, anxieties, and "working-through" process evoked by the separation. In brief behavioral treatments, termination appears to be seen as an issue of no major importance and is generally addressed only minimally (e.g., Beck, Emery, and Greenberg, 1985), if at all. When the issue is addressed by cognitive-behavioral therapists, return for treatment is viewed (pejoratively) as indicating a "relapse" (see Beck et al., 1979, p. 327; Lazarus, 1981, p. 30). (Should those who return to physicians or dentists for more care be viewed as "relapsers" or "treatment failures"? We hope not. However, this terminology and the underlying mythology pervade mental health care.)

In contrast to the views expressed in such illustrations from the psychoanalytic and behavioral literature on the matter of returning patients, our experience has been that a patient's returning often indicates not only that a positive working alliance has been established, but also that the patient has derived some benefit from his or her initial therapy experience.

"Working Through" Termination in Brief Dynamic Therapy

Strupp and Binder (1984) write:

A central purpose of psychodynamic psychotherapy is to help the patient come to terms with previous separation and object losses, whether these be emotional or actual. Accordingly, one may say that many patients enter psychotherapy because they failed to resolve reactions to earlier traumas or losses. Symptoms and complaints often embody a return to earlier lost objects with whom the patient has unfinished business. (p. 260)

In working out a "better" ending for the treatment, the therapist tries to help the patient change his or her previously unsatisfactory pattern of handling separations.

Mann's (1973) emphasis in time-limited therapy upon termination issues has as its goal the working through of separation-individuation issues:

It is absolutely incumbent upon the therapist to deal directly with the reaction to termination in all its painful aspects and affects if he expects to help the patient come to some vividly affective understanding of the now inappropriate nature of his early unconscious conflict. More than that, active and appropriate management of the termination will allow the patient to internalize the therapist as a replacement or substitute for the earlier ambivalent object. *This time the internalization will be more positive (never totally so), less anger laden and less guilt laden, thereby making separation a genuine maturational event.* Since anger, rage, guilt, and their accompaniments of frustration and fear are the potent factors that prevent positive internalization and mature separation, it is these that must not be overlooked in this phase of the time-limited therapy. (p. 36, italics in original)

Although dealing with and "working through" terminations in psychotherapy have taken on almost mythical proportions, there are no empirical data of which we are aware that indicate any relationship between outcome and focus upon termination. Indeed, Clara Hill (personal communication, June 20, 1986) and her colleagues, in their interesting study of process and outcome in time-limited therapy, found that the highly experienced therapists in that study tended to spend extremely short periods of time discussing termination with their patients.

Furthermore, although the termination of psychotherapy is often described as a very painful event for the patient, engendering strong emotions of grief, loss, anger, and abandonment (Edelson, 1963; Firestein, 1978; Mann, 1973), the single careful study on the topic of which we are aware seems not to support this contention. Marx and Gelso (1987), in a field study of former counseling center clients, reported: "Perhaps the most surprising finding of the study was participants' pervasive positive reactions to ending counseling in sharp contrast to the literature's emphasis on termination as a painful loss. . . . It is clear that clients in the study expressed largely positive feelings about ending" (p. 8).

We do not mean to imply by what we have said that termination is an inconsequential issue which should be ignored by the brief therapist. Certainly, in our description of time-limited group psychotherapy, the ending of the group is viewed as one of the important foci in the treatment. Similarly, we believe that for those individual patients and/or couples for whom a "break" in the therapy engenders major insecurities or issues regarding previous losses, the separation should be examined and clarified. There may, however, be numerous circumstances in which excessive focus upon the so-called "termination" is unwarranted. This may be because such issues have little relevance to the particular patient in question and his or her circumstances, or because the "intermittent" and "as-needed" nature of the treatment relationship has been emphasized by the therapist and accepted by the patient. It may be unnecessary to analyze the "termination" if one is simply "interrupting" treatment for some period of time.

We also believe that the view that therapy is *totally* terminated at a given point has led to some serious ethical issues. In a national study of psychiatrists (Gartrell, Herman, Olarte, Feldstein, and Localio, 1986), it was found that 10% at one point developed a sexual relationship with a patient. The vast majority of such liaisons developed after the formal termination of therapy. This study has moved the American Psychiatric Association to consider revising its ethical standards so that a "dual relationship" with a patient is eschewed *at any time*. Once a person is a patient, he or she is always a patient.

The Reality of "Finality"

As we have mentioned, the data on how patients actually make use of psychotherapy appear to tell a different story from that told in the theoretical literature. Many patients return for multiple courses of mental health treatment over the span of their lives.

In a research project by V. Patterson, Levene, and Breger (1977), about 60% of the patients in brief psychodynamic or brief behavioral therapy who were studied returned within 1 year for more treatment. Furthermore, it was learned that almost 60% of the patients interviewed had had psychotherapy prior to entrance into that study. Kovacs, Rush, Beck, and Hollon (1981), in a randomized clinical trial comparing cognitive-behavioral therapy and imipramine for depression, found that about 50% of the patients studied in either condition had had additional treatment after the formal termination of the study therapy. Weissman et al. (1981), comparing pharmacotherapy and interpersonal therapy for depression, reported at the 12-month follow-up that "most patients received some treatment. . . . Only about one-third of the patients received no psychotherapeutic drugs and did not see a mental health professional during the year [following therapy]" (p. 52).

The phenomenon of patients' returning to treatment after the formal "termination" of a course of therapy is not limited to brief approaches. Goldensohn (1977), in a survey of graduates of the William Alanson White Psychoanalytic Institute, found that 55% had additional therapy after their analyses. Hartlaub, Martin, and Rhine (1986) surveyed analysts at the Denver Psychoanalytic Society, who reported that within 3 years of termination two-thirds of their "successfully analyzed" patients had recontacted them. Grunebaum (1983) and Henry et al. (1971) also found that psychotherapists themselves had received many courses of long-term treatment over their life spans, and that return for more therapy was unrelated to the perceived quality and/or outcomes of previous therapies. In fact, Grunebaum reported that in his sample the most striking determinant of returning for treatment was the patient/therapist's age: The older a patient/therapist, the more likely it was that he or she had received more episodes of therapy.

Several years ago, one of us had an interesting experience that highlighted the (frequent) interminability of brief psychotherapy.*

I was asked to do a consultation at a local mental health center on a somewhat problematic outpatient. As the patient was described to me by the psychiatrist who was treating him, I had a *déjà vu* experience. I wondered whether I had supervised some of the patient's previous therapy. Suddenly, I recalled that this was a man I had seen presented (on videotape) at a large national mental health conference, by one of the nation's foremost practitioners of brief dynamic therapy and described as a stunningly successful case of short-term therapy—a "cure." When I later met the patient face to face for a consultation interview, I asked him if he had, in fact, seen Dr. X in therapy.

"Oh, yeah," he said. "Dr. X was a great guy. I saw him for some sessions before I left computer school. Then when I moved here I got into a therapy group to work on some of the issues that had come up later. After that, me and my wife went into about 6 months of couple therapy with Dr. Y.

---

* For the sake of clarity, this description is written in first-person singular.

Following that, I felt like I needed to work more on my own issues, so I saw an individual therapist for awhile. After a year we began to have trouble with our kid, so we came here and started being seen."

It was my impression that Dr. X had done an excellent job. He was remembered fondly by the patient, and had helped the patient view "talking with someone about my problems" as a very beneficial endeavor. However, in contrast to the impressions conveyed in Dr. X's writings and lectures, the therapy was far from definitive.

In our view, although a therapist may "terminate" a patient's treatment by arbitrarily setting a date after which the therapist will no longer see that patient, patients can and do (with great frequency) seek out more treatment elsewhere when they want and need it. While there do exist circumstances in which it may be useful for the therapist to emphasize what it is like "to separate" from another person, we believe that this can be accomplished by the use of "treatment-free" periods. That is, we often suggest to the patient that after a course of brief therapy, he or she might wait 3–6 months before seeking more treatment. This period without therapy may be most helpful in allowing the patient to clarify and consolidate gains. Of course, if the patient needs to be seen before the end of this period, we are flexible and accommodating.

From our perspective, it is usually best to maintain a primary care perspective with patients—that is, to keep in mind a model of care like the model maintained by the family general practitioner. He or she may first see a patient for the flu, later for a back problem, and still later for family or emotional issues.

Both of us have seen patients for as many as 15 years in successive courses of brief therapy, and have treated children (now grown) of some of our early cases. As we say to psychology and psychiatry trainees, "There is nothing easier than getting a patient *not* to come back." Indeed, many therapists seem to have exceptional innate skills in getting patients never to return to them. We believe that patients can and should return as needed. This perspective does not preclude doing therapy efficiently and effectively, and it encourages a more flexible perspective of "not needing to do it all at once." Moreover, even relatively few visits may be viewed as sufficient if seen in the larger context of an overall primary care relationship. On the other hand, a rather large number of visits may be experienced as depriving if this is understood as *the* definitive course of therapy.

REFERENCES

Alexander, F., and T. M. French. 1974. *Psychoanalytic Therapy: Principles and Application.* Lincoln: University of Nebraska Press. (Original work published 1946).

Bandura, A. 1977. "Self-Efficacy: Toward a Unifying Theory of Behavioral Change." *Psychological Review,* 84. 191–215.

Bandura, A. 1982. "The Psychology of Chance Encounters and Life Paths." *American Psychologist,* 37:747–755.

Beck, A. T., G. Emery, and R. L. Greenberg. 1985. *Anxiety Disorders and Phobias.* New York: Basic Books.

Beck, A. T., J. A. Rush, B. F. Shaw, and G. Emery. 1979. *Cognitive Therapy of Depression.* New York: Guilford Press.

Bergin, A. E., and M. J. Lambert. 1978. "The Evaluation of Therapeutic Outcomes." In *Handbook of Psychotherapy and Behavior Change,* ed. S. L. Garfield and A. E. Bergin 2nd ed. New York: Wiley, 139–190.

Davanloo, H. ed. 1978. *Basic Principles and Techniques in Short-Term Dynamic Psychotherapy.* New York: Spectrum.

———. 1980. "A Method of Short-Term Dynamic Psychotherapy." In *Short-Term Dynamic Psychotherapy,* ed. H. Davanloo New York: Jason Aronson, pp. 43–71.

Edelson, M. 1963. *The Termination of Intensive Psychotherapy.* Springfield, Ill.: Charles C. Thomas.

Erickson, M. H. 1980. "An Introduction to the Study and Application of Hypnosis for Pain Control." In *Innovative Hypnotherapy: Collected Papers of Milton H. Erickson on Hypnosis,* ed. E. L. Rossi, New York: Irvington, vol. 4, pp. 237–245 (Original work published 1967).

———. 1980. *Innovative Hypnotherapy: Collected Papers of Milton H. Erickson and Hypnosis.* E. L. Rossi, ed. New York: Irvington, vol. 4.

Firestein, S. K. 1978. *Termination in Psychoanalysis.* New York: International Universities Press.

Garfield, S. L., and A. E. Bergin, Eds. 1978. *Handbook of Psychotherapy and Behavior Change,* 2nd ed. New York: Wiley.

Gartrell, N., J. Herman, S. Olarte, M. Feldstein, and R. Localio. 1986. "Sexual Contact: Results of a National Survey, Psychiatrist-Patient Contact. Part I: Prevalence." *American Journal of Psychiatry* 43:1126–31.

Goldensohn, S. S. 1977. "Graduate Evaluation of Psychoanalytic Training." *Journal of the American Academy of Psychoanalysis* 5:51–64.

Grunebaum, H. (1983). "A Study of Therapists' Choice of a Therapist." *American Journal of Psychiatry,* 140:1336–39.

Hartlaub, G. H., G. L. Martin, and M. W. Rhine. 1986. "Recontact with the Analyst Following Termination: A Survey of Seventy-One Cases." *Journal of the American Psychoanalytic Association* 34:895–910.

Henderson, S., D. G. Byrne, and P. Duncan-Jones. 1982. *Neurosis and the Social Environment.* Sydney: Academic Press.

Henry, W. E., J. H. Sims, and S. L. Spray. 1971. *The Fifth Profession*. San Francisco: Jossey-Bass.

Howard, K. I., S. M. Kopta, M. S. Krause, and D. E. Orlinsky. 1986. "The Dose-Effect Relationship in Psychotherapy." *American Psychologist* 41:159–64.

Johnson, D. H., and C. J. Gelso. 1980. "The Effectiveness of Time Limits in Counseling and psychotherapy: A Critical Review." *The Counseling Psychologist* 9:70–83.

Kinston, W., and A. Bentovim. 1981. "Creating a Focus for Brief Marital or Family Therapy." In *Forms of Brief Therapy* ed. S. H. Budman. New York: Guilford Press, pp. 361–86.

Kovacs, M., A. J. Rush, A. J. Beck, and S. Hollon. 1981. "Depressed Outpatients Treated with Cognitive Therapy or Pharmacotherapy." *Archives of General Psychiatry* 38:33–39.

Lankton, S. R., and C. H. Lankton. 1983. *The Answer Within: A Clinical Framework of Ericksonian Hypnotherapy*. New York: Brunner/Mazel.

Lazarus, A. A. 1981. *The Practice of Multimodal Therapy*. New York: McGraw-Hill.

Mann, J. 1973. *Time-Limited Psychotherapy*. Cambridge, Mass.: Harvard University Press.

Mann, J. and R. Goldman. 1982. *A Casebook in Time-Limited Psychotherapy*. New York: McGraw-Hill.

Marx, J. A., and C. J. Gelso. 1987. "Termination of Individual Counseling in a University Counseling Center." *Journal of Counseling Psychology* 34:3–9.

Panel. 1969. "Problems of Termination in the Analysis of Adults,, S. K. Firestein, reporter." *Journal of the American Psychanalytic Association* 17:222–37.

———. 1975. "Termination: Problems and Techniques, W. S. Robbins, reporter." *Journal of the American Psychoanalytic Association* 23:166–76.

Patterson, V., H. Levene, and L. Breger. 1977. "A One Year Follow-up Study of Two Forms of Brief Psychotherapy." *American Journal of Psychotherapy* 31:76–82.

Sifneos, P. 1972. *Short-Term Psychotherapy and Emotional Crisis*. Cambridge, Mass.: Harvard University Press.

Sifneos, P. E. 1979. *Short-Term Dynamic Psychotherapy: Evaluation and Technique*. New York: Plenum Press.

Sophocles. 1949. Oedipus the King, trans. D. Grene. In *An Anthology of Greek Drama, First Series* ed. C. A. Robinson. New York: Holt, Rinehart & Winston, pp. 51–100. (Original work produced ca. 429 B.C.)

Strupp, H. H., and J. L. Binder. 1984. *Psychotherapy in a New Key: A Guide to Time-Limited Dynamic Psychotherapy*. New York: Basic Books.

Ticho, E. 1972. "Termination of Psychoanalysis: Treatment Goals, Life Goals." *Psychoanalytic Quarterly* 41:315–33.

Watkins, P., and G. Soledad. 1979. *My Life with Charles Manson*. New York: Bantam Books.

Weissman, M. M., G. L. Klerman, B. A. Prusoff, D. Sholomskas, and N. Padian. 1981. "Depressed Outpatients: Results One Year after Treatment with Drugs and/or Interpersonal Psychotherapy." *Archives of General Psychiatry* 36:51–55.

4. Time-Limited Psychotherapy

James Mann

TIME: CONSCIOUS AND UNCONSCIOUS

The link between time and reality is insoluble. We can divorce ourselves from time only by undoing reality, or from reality only by undoing the sense of time. Categorical time is measured by clocks and calendars; existential time is that which is experienced, lived in, rather than observed. "Each moment is the fruit of forty thousand years. The minute-winning days, like flies, buzz home to death, and every moment is a window on all time."[1] Thomas Wolfe is only one, and a latecomer at that, among the great writers in history whose awareness of the vicissitudes of living embraced sensitivity to the meaning of time. St. Augustine called a person's present the memory of things past and the expectations of things to come. This definition of the existential now needs no adumbration. In psychoanalysis, the genetic and adaptive viewpoints reflect these dimensions of time. A. D. Weisman points out, "The genetic version [of emotional development] is to the past what the adaptive viewpoint is to the future—the genetic viewpoint is only a way to recognize and to compare recurrent themes throughout emotional development."[2] Time and the subjective meaning of time are inseparable elements, therefore, in every life history, and all significant human behavior is forever linked with time.

Schecter, studying the development of the concept of time in a normal group of children ranging from age three to six, found that when they learned how to tell clock time, external factors became increasingly important in establishing time sense. Prior to this age, with many individual variations, to be sure, diurnal rhythm (the concept of the day as a unit of twenty-four hours) was described in terms of immediate *personal* experiences. These first included physiological functions, such as bowel movements, sleeping, and eating, and later such factors as interpersonal and play activities. Seasonal time, with its enormous and often unpredictable variations, was poorly understood in all the children studied. The conclusion of the observers was that

Reprinted by permission of Harvard University Press from *Time-Limited Psychotherapy*. Cambridge, 1973, pp. 3–23, 30–38.

the emergence of the concept of time in children is the result of the interaction between the child with his private experiences and his own rhythmic needs and an external world with external physical forces (light, dark, cold, and so forth) and significant adults, both of which have rhythmic patterns of their own. They postulate that a sense of past, present, and future follows a hunger-feeding-satisfaction sequence that necessitates an adequate mother-child relationship as well as physical need satisfaction.[3]

Fisher and Fisher made a study of the influence of parental figures on the perception of time. They found consistent evidence that the more their subjects unconsciously conceived the parent of the same sex or both parents as highly dominant, the more was their time sense an overevaluating one. In addition, a very suggestive finding was that the individual's unconscious concept of the parent of the same sex most determines the extent to which that relationship will influence his perception of time.[4] Thus, the emotional determinants of time sense prove to be inescapably related to the early nurturing objects. The development of a sense of reality is, of course, entirely incorporated within the same sequence of events. That the children studied related early time sense to oral and anal functions along with a nirvanalike state of bliss (sleep) is not unexpected.

We should not be surprised, then, that the later acquisition of real time sense remains loaded with the experiences and symbols and fantasies of the past. In the way that folklore so often exposes unconscious conflict and meaning, time as a limited commodity is portrayed as Father Time, with a beard and a scythe; limitless time, immortality, is invariably presented in the figure of a woman. Time always represents the reality principle, and the time to wake up is connected with father. By contrast, the attributes of the pleasure principle, the primary process and timelessness, are related to the mother. Ambivalence in respect to time is exemplified in our images of finite time as Father Time and immortality as a woman.[5]

The past continues its active existence in the unconscious at every point in the now of a person's life. Time and the unconscious meanings of time are the constant accompaniments of the now, and every now is an indivisible conglomerate of past, present, and future. The timeless quality of the unconscious was elaborated by Freud and the generations of analysts who have followed. Scott questioned whether the timelessness of the unconscious might be more a function of omnipotent fantasies than of the unconscious itself.[6] It may be difficult and is perhaps unnecessary to separate the two. In his "New Introductory Lectures on Psychoanalysis," Freud remarks: "There is nothing in the id that could be compared with negation; and we perceive with surprise an exception to the philosophical theorem that space and time are necessary forms of our mental acts. There is nothing in the id that corresponds to the idea of time; and there is no recognition of the passage of time, and—a thing that is most remarkable and awaits consideration in philosophical thought—no alteration in its mental processes is produced by the passage of time."[7]

The psychological meaning of time is elaborated in some detail in the beautiful paper of Marie Bonaparte on "Time and the Unconscious," published over thirty years ago.[8] She focuses on the notion of the "paradise" of childhood, which is popular, even poetical, although with small effort most people can recall the torment of smallness and the burning impatience to grow up. She describes a quality of memory which gives that childhood world a vision and a feeling of golden sunlight that is overbrilliant and unreal. She attributes this not only to the amnesia of many childhood events, but more to the actual experience of infinite time, or timelessness, in the world of childhood. It is not at all unusual to hear from patients in psychoanalysis a description of this same intense recollection, and it is always found to be related to close body contact with the mother. Two of my own analytic patients drew the sunny state of California into such a fantasy, although neither one had been born there, and another used the image of bright white wool, pressing close. The yearning for what once was remains vigorously alive.

Bonaparte observes that in adolescence, life seems to be spread out in a limitless expanse and death does not seem to exist. This concept of time opposes the remarkable intellectual and reality development characteristic of adolescence. Thus, adolescents become sorely conflicted because they know that there is limited time available for making certain life decisions, so that the characteristic ambivalence at this developmental period is heightened by preoccupations with time. "We destroy time from the moment we begin to use it . . . for in living our time we die of it."[9]

Although there are no effective means for struggling against time, we do try. Bonaparte describes five situations in which the pleasure principle prevails and time can cease to exist. (1) Dreams in which we guard the illusions of childhood and defeat time by immersing ourselves in the infinite time of childhood. (2) Daydreams in which fairytale fantasies of omnipotence dominate, and reality and time are conquered. (3) The intoxication of love, which, with its remarkable idealization of the loved object, allows the lover to transcend time, to vow eternal love, and to ignore reality. (4) Intoxication from drink or drugs, which is used to minimize or erase reality and allow full reign to the pleasure principle. Bonaparte was able to point out even then that the psychotoxic drugs such as heroin and marijuana diminish or eliminate the sense of time and that the euphoria produced by these drugs arises from the escape from the constriction and passage of time. Carefully controlled experiments today on the effects of marijuana highlight the alterations in time sense as a major effect. (5) States of mystic ecstasy, which are not unlike the ecstatic states experienced by drug users and lovers. In all three, but particularly in the mystic states, subjective feelings of eternity are projected and given an objective existence, which effectively conquers time.

If one can eliminate time sense, one can also avoid the ultimate separation that time brings—death. In a period of history of heightened alienation and separation of one from the other such as exists today, drugs that slow or stop the sense of time relieve the pain of loneliness now and the future threat of total aloneness. For example, while in analysis, an unmarried man with powerful ambivalent attachments to his mother who was living in another city was invited to have Thanksgiving dinner with a couple who were his friends. All became "stoned" on marijuana before dinner. He noted that he continued to feel very warm about the total set and had a good feeling about it all. Time, however, seemed to be extremely prolonged. "It all seemed like forever. Time stretched out incredibly." He described the woman of the couple as very caring, very womanly, a good cook, and added that she "seemed like a generation out of phase." By this he meant that the dinner that she made was what his mother would make. Thus, the effect of the drug was to promote a sense of foreverness, of eternity, which is linked to the taking in of good things from the mother.

Baba Ram Dass, who as Alpert was once a colleague of Leary in the use of hallucinogens as the new religion, now achieves the same goal without the use of drugs. He quotes the Third Noble Truth of Buddha, saying that one must give up attachment and desire and make an end of births, deaths, suffering.

> You end the whole thing that keeps you stuck.
> If I'm not attached to this particular
> Time-Space locus then I can free my
> Awareness from my body and I can become
> One with it all
> I can merge with
> The Divine Mother.[10]

The sense of time may serve as a major reassurance to the ego of its own existence, while the existence of past time, of memories, can also be used by the ego to create the illusion of timelessness.[11] Since the perception of time is always a confrontation with reality and its limitations, memory may be employed as a means of making every past event an occurrence of now, thereby reducing time to zero and giving new life to the sense of magical omnipotence.[12] The passage of time symbolizes the period of separation. Observation of the phases of the moon and other phenomena are based on this anxiety. "Timelessness is the fantasy in which mother and child are endlessly united. The calendar is the ultimate materialization of separation anxiety."[13] The remarkable ambivalence about time is seen in the common attributes of time as a teacher, as a healer, and as a friend.

All these situations constitute clearcut evidence for the presence of a sense of timelessness residing in the unconscious of all humans. An even more remarkable expression of it is the fact that no person *feels* himself to be growing old. In the presence of good health, we do not experience the advance of old age. We do perceive the effects of the aging process and we are aware *inwardly* of having grown older. The pursuit of timelessness, of eternity, is dramatically accented by the usual portrayals of Time as an old man with a scythe, and Death as a grinning skeleton with a scythe. We seek to avoid destruction by avoiding time.

Winnicott considers the depressive position as a normal stage in healthy infant development occurring in the weaning age, that period when the infant can begin to give things up, throw things away. Significantly, he adds that this normal depressive position depends on the development of a sense of time which is a prerequisite for the appreciation of the difference between fact and fantasy. In an individual who has achieved this normal developmental stage, future reactions to loss are grief and sadness. If there is some degree of failure at the depressive position, loss leads to depression. Furthermore, a well-established depressive position is accompanied by introjects of personal enrichment and stabilization as well as memories of good experiences and of loved objects. These allow for sustaining loss without undue environmental support.[14]

In recent years, attention has been directed more than ever before to the dying patient; what goes on in his mind and his feelings; what goes on in the minds and feelings of family and caretakers; and how the interaction of the two sides confronted by the ultimate limitation of time allows for dying with greater or lesser degrees of dignity and serenity. Eissler was among the first to give extended study to the state of dying, and since death and time are indelibly connected in our subjective experience, his consideration of time is pertinent. While physical time is reduced to a pinpoint, the moment observed on the clock, psychological time, by contrast, expands or constricts in accordance with age, mood, and other factors such as Weisman mentions (qualitative fluctuations in reality sense, cycles of interpersonal activity, discontinuities of perception, and alternating expansion and contraction of libidinal fields).[15] For the child, the next day may be felt to be somewhere in the remote future, while in an adult, next week may be experienced as the immediate present. For the aged, there is no experience of future time except for that which can be contrived by such ego defenses as denial of an end to time.

Both Eissler and Winnicott attribute crucial impact on personality development to the development of a sense of time. There is no contradiction here, since Winnicott sees the development of time sense as a necessary ingredient in mastering the repetitive losses that must be endured in the course of living. Eissler also correctly points out that the indivisible union between reality and time sense undoes forever in the life of the person his timeless paradise, so that the appreciation of time as an explicit content brings with it the knowledge of death as an explicit content.[16]

Eissler believes "that society by its impact upon the emotional sphere, upon a person's attitude toward his body, upon the concept of death, and in many more ways, leaves a characteristic imprint upon time experience."[17] Surely the evidence for this is even more certain fifteen years after Eissler's statement. We live in a historical period when time has been shattered, or at least seems to be shattered, as it is experienced. We no longer measure profound social change in generations, but rather by the decade or less. The conquest of space and time by satellite communication and the immediate availability of visual events all over earth and even beyond this planet further fashion time experience and meaning into a steadily shrinking mold. Time seems to rush by more rapidly than we can comprehend what is happening.

All means of communication are now breathlessly rapid; all vehicles move rapidly; change occurs swiftly. The resultant sense of impermanence, instability, and unharnessed speed is reflected in a charged-up sense of time, such that the limitation of time appears to be omnipresent and equally oppressive. Time-limited psychotherapy has a particular suitability now that time is an ever-present urgency for everybody all the time. We cannot help but feel that there is *less* time available for any of us to get whatever it is that we want or think that we want. As the rushing experience of time forces the end of personal time—death—even more urgently upon us, death becomes increasingly unacceptable. We ask medicine to eliminate death itself. We demand instant change as well as instant cure. We try to refuse to accept the visible effects of the passage of time. Thus, the enormous market among older people for young fashions, a vast array of cosmetics, the widespread use of plastic surgery, and the popularity of hair dyes and wigs—for men as well as for women. The social expression of futile attempts to slow up time is seen, for example, in the reissue of a Sears, Roebuck catalogue of over fifty years ago which has become a bestseller. This kind of nostalgia reflects on the deepest level the wish to return to past time, to make past time now and thereby to restore infantile omnipotence and, with it, timelessness. "In all human hearts there is a horror of time." [18]

All short forms of psychotherapy, whether their practitioners know it or not, revive the horror of time. Whatever differences there may exist among the various kinds of short forms of psychotherapy, or among their proponents, the factor common to all is the obvious and distinct limitation of *time*. However, despite the profound awareness of the influence of unconscious mental processes on both the development and present daily life of the individual patient, no attention, or at best the most casual attention, is paid to the subjective and objective meanings of time both to the patient and to the therapist.

Of all the pioneers of psychoanalysis and of psychotherapy, only Otto Rank called attention to a specific aspect of time and used it in his treatment of patients. He felt that the patient is always aware that the treatment must one day be finished, and, moreover, that in every single treatment hour the patient repeats in miniature his original "mother-fixation" and the severance of that fixation until he is finally able to master it and finish it. When Rank succeeded in overcoming the patient's mother-fixation through analysis of the transference, "then a definite term is fixed for the analysis within which period the patient repeats automatically the new severance from the mother (substitute) figure, in the form of the reproduction of his own birth." [19] He adds in a footnote that patients choose a gestational and hence a termination period of from seven to ten months, and that the choice refers in fact to the patient's own birth. Insofar as Rank believed that the trauma of birth stood at the center of all later human development and experience, his approach was highly idiosyncratic, and only a very small group of therapists continue to use and promote his ideas. Moreover, his concept of time was a limited one, albeit extremely important in respect to the difficulties and complexities of the termination process in psychoanalysis as well as in any psychotherapy.

The specific limitation of time as an unvarying constant from the beginning of treatment and the train of unconscious dynamic events that follows as a result not only serve as guidelines in treating the patient, but also can provide a means of studying and coordinating the meaning and effects of time, so that at least some aspect of the horror of time is reduced or eliminated. None of the short forms of psychotherapy has approached treatment of emotional disorders from this stance. One of the critical problems in the humane management of the dying patient is the denial of death by all the caretakers, professional, family, relatives, and friends. One way of understanding the failure to give time central significance in short forms of psychotherapy lies in the will to deny the horror of time by the therapists themselves.

Since there is only a now in existential time, whatever the patient's presenting distress, it is linked firmly to enduring events in his inner life which extend to the remotest past and into a foreseeable future. They are felt as *now*. All events that occurred in the past are not necessarily important; only those that have endured over time and are again inseparable from time. Any psychotherapy which is limited in time brings fresh flame to the enduring presence in all persons of the conflict between timelessness, infinite time, immortality and the omnipotent fantasies of childhood on the one hand, and time, finite time, reality, and death on the other hand.[20] The wishes of the unconscious are timeless and promptly run counter to an offer of help in which time is limited. Thus, any time-limited psychotherapy addresses itself both to child time and to adult time. At the least, this gives rise to powerful conflicting reactions, responses, and most of all, conflicting expectations. The greater the ambiguity as to the duration of treatment, the greater the influence of child time on unconscious wishes and expectations. The greater the specificity of duration of treatment, the more rapidly and appropriately is child time confronted with reality and the work to be done.

In any dynamic psychotherapy, the restless guardians of time are aroused. It is unavoidable. We have tended to pay little attention to it until the issue of termination of treatment arises. At that point, all sorts of ambiguities and resistances in respect to termination are allowed to intrude by both patient and therapist. If we undertake psychotherapy of limited duration, it would be wise to begin where the patient is; namely, that as soon as he learns that the amount of time for help is limited, he is actively subject to the magical, timeless, omnipotent fantasies of childhood, and his expectations in respect to the treatment arise from them as he lives them now. It is on the basis of this meaning of a real-unreal, conscious-unconscious *now* that we move into active consideration of the treatment itself.

THE TREATMENT AGREEMENT
AND TREATMENT GUIDELINES

The treatment agreement in this method of time-limited psychotherapy reflects a studied, structured approach based on psychoanalytic concepts of mental functioning. It is designed to take advantage of, to utilize constructively in the service of the patient, the element of time that is in itself implicit in every kind of short-form psychotherapy and that is so steadfastly avoided in the mental lives of both patients and therapists, as well as in the psychiatric literature.

The failure to give time, that horror in all human hearts, full recognition has effectively obstructed efforts to establish a sound methodology of any short-form psychotherapy. The natural result has been a growing reliance upon eclecticism—seizing upon anything that seems to be humane as also being helpful. The next step in the progression can only be to assert that short-form psychotherapy requires only common sense, whereupon blindness and ignorance of mental functioning shall, in fact, prevail.[21]

The lack of any kind of adequate methodology in short-term therapy has been decried by Wolberg: "We apply the same tactics that we find useful in prolonged treatment, namely, relaxed listening, permitting the relationship to build up and move into zones of transference, waiting expectantly for the patient to acquire motivations for self-direction, and peeling off layers of resistance to reach the treasures of the unconscious."[22] Despite his sharp criticism, Wolberg goes no further in outlining any kind of methodology; rather he calls upon therapists to make a series of compromises from the traditional, psychoanalytic-like position that will enable them to accept limited treatment goals, greater activity, and greater flexibility, including a readiness to be genuinely eclectic in method. Only in respect to the actual termination of treatment does he give any attention specifically to time, and even then he disposes of it so casually as to encourage the reader to pay no more attention than that. "Termination will be accepted without protest if the patient has been apprised of and has accepted the fact that he will be in therapy just as long as is deemed necessary."[23] It is not made clear who will so deem it, patient, or therapist, or both. Semrad and his colleagues show understanding of the need for methodology when they suggest that a sensitive and organized approach to a patient will make for a shorter treatment period. However, no mention is made of time or of the duration of treatment.[24]

Many clinicians have recognized and appreciated specific aspects of the problem of time but all have stopped short of seeing it as a nodal point for the construction of a methodology. Alexander, the only contributor in Wolberg's standard reference on short-term psychotherapy who makes any reference to the meaning of time, makes the point that since no patient wishes to face up to the source and nature of his conflicts (to face himself as he is), the prolongation of treatment always serves the neurosis. Therefore, he impresses his patients with the fact that they will press toward the completion of treatment as quickly as possible. Alexander remarks, "Of course, we are not magicians, but our intention is to make therapy as brief as we can." His use of the word *magician* implies that he knows what the patient's expectations and fantasies are, especially in short-term treatment, but even so he does not press for any specific use of them.[25]

In a vast experience with short-term dynamic psychotherapy, Sifneos has established a variable time limit based on symptomatic improvement. He speaks of termination as soon as the patient is symptom-free and is relating and working better.[26]

Another standard reference is *Emergency Psychotherapy and Brief Psychotherapy* by Bellak and Small. Their definition is that brief psychotherapy "is to be accomplished in the short range of one to six therapeutic sessions of customary duration (45 to 60 minutes)."[27] In practice, there appears to be some confusion, or lack of precise definition, among the terms emergency psychotherapy, crisis intervention, and brief psychotherapy. The limitation of one to six sessions appears to be more directive to the therapist than any reasoned aspect of the dynamic process of treatment. In a clinic designed to provide immediate psychiatric service, such a directive may be a realistic accommodation to pressure. Time, an immediate association to both *emergency* and *brief,* is understood and utilized only in its categorical, not in its existential, sense.

In his study of the psychotherapeutic relationship, Frank emphasizes that it is the ambiguity of the situation that assures the patient's participation as well as his willingness to be influenced. The paradigm here is "I know what is wrong with you, but you have to find out for yourself in order to be helped." He is critical in his description of the end point as indeterminate, the constant striving of the patient until he is cured without any criteria of cure to pursue, and he notes that the therapist's permissiveness increases the ambiguity and thus helps to deprive the patient of a target. Frank also maintains that there is "some evidence that the speed of the patient's improvement may be influenced by his understanding of how long treatment will last," and that "there is some experimental evidence that patients respond more promptly when they know in advance that therapy is time-limited."[28]

One will immediately note that there is the least possible amount of ambiguity in the treatment setting described herein, and that time, the most significant element, will be quite deliberately employed to achieve certain ends that will be of use to the patient. What Frank omits, as do so many others, are two critical reasons that contribute to ambiguity in psychotherapy. One is that the problem of time with its meaning of separation, loss, and death is as vital in the emotional life of the therapist as it is in that of the patient; the other, which follows from the first, is manifest in the remarkable uncertainty of therapists that they can be of help in a short period of time.

The study by Meyer and his coworkers comes very close to the target but then veers sharply away. Their patients were informed verbally and in writing prior to the first therapeutic interview that treatment would be limited to ten weekly visits. The aim of the study, however, was only to compare the characteristics of patients who finished the ten sessions with those who dropped out. The therapists involved were free to manage their patients as they might in any psychotherapeutic situation "except for whatever constraints or pressures they felt as a result of the time-limited situation."[29] Fleck, discussing the study, remarks on the possibility of the ten-session dictum carrying the impact of a prescription, akin to dosage and number of pills, in contrast to the usual open-ended treatment, and that this might account for the surprisingly high percent of lowest socioeconomic groups finishing the ten sessions.

The specific limitation of time is constant in each case and includes a total of twelve treatment sessions. The choice of twelve treatment sessions was made somewhat arbitrarily. Perhaps ten or fourteen would have sufficed equally well. Long experience in psychotherapy suggested that twelve sessions might be adequate for the therapist to accomplish some amount of work with the patient. More important, to study the meaning of time in short-form psychotherapy, some arbitrary choice had to be made so that one could begin. By placing all patients within the same procedural framework, it is possible to assess the process and outcome with some degree of consistency and reliability. One can examine the work of a single therapist as well as compare several therapists. The relative uniformity of the scheme makes more evident the sequence of dynamic events present and facilitates comparison with those occurring in other patients.

There is also much to support a treatment plan which allows all participating therapists to direct their attention to the same thing—that is, to the relationship between individual problems and circumstances on the one hand, and to a rather constant operational medium on the other. The interaction can be more readily studied. The elaboration of goals and the selection of patients for such treatment may also be better clarified. Experience has demonstrated that twelve treatment sessions is probably the minimal time required for a series of dynamic events to develop, flourish, and be available for discussion, examination, and resolution. Other psychotherapists and investigators of the psychotherapeutic process can repeat and test, as far as testing and replication are possible in this field, by adopting this method.

Certain procedures and decisions naturally precede the formal treatment negotiations. First, there is the usual intake or consultative interview. This may be extended to two or more meetings in order to clarify what it is that the patient is seeking. From the data obtained, a formulation of the central conflict productive of the present manifestations of distress can be made. The formulation of the central conflict may or may not coincide with the patient's conscious motive for seeking help. The patient is generally very much aware of the pain that he is suffering, and he usually finds some reason or reasons to account for it. But we need not necessarily accept his reasons for the distress as the most significant. In fact, his reasons may have very little to do with the actual state of mind. For example, the patient may be anxious, depressed, and in a state of exacerbated conflict with a spouse. The patient may present some fairly succinct ideas about the relationship with the spouse and suggest that it is in that relationship that the present symptoms found their origin. We may agree that his temporal connection is correct; we may agree that the troubled relationship between patient and spouse is a precipitating cause. However, we may also conclude that the present disturbance is more directly related to an unresolved grief reaction in respect to a significant earlier figure.

From the historical data obtained, we seek to relate the present central issue to significant past sources, which enables us to sort out further unconscious determinants of the present focal conflict in the course of treatment without becoming lost in an unmanageable mass of material. Further, we assess the patient's general psychological state and make a tentative diagnosis. The next step is to determine how to distribute the twelve treatment interviews according to our best estimate of the patient's needs. A chronic schizophrenic patient who is functioning at a marginal level, but functioning, may be helped over some current difficulty by weekly half-hour visits over a period of twenty-four weeks, in one instance, for example, by weekly fifteen minute visits for forty-eight weeks. As one might expect, the majority of patients in time-limited psychotherapy are seen for forty-five to sixty minutes once each week for twelve weeks. The twelve may be referred to as twelve treatment hours if it is intended that the patient will be seen for sixty minutes in each interview; but if the therapist can allow only forty-five or fifty minutes for each meeting, the term sessions, interviews, or meetings is preferable. This may appear to be an obsessional adherence to literalness. However, when the meaning of time is to be the lever that motivates and moves the patient, there is a sufficient mix of fantasy and reality without making for an unnecessary additional complication by calling a less than sixty minute meeting an hour.

The data described here are derived primarily from my own work with patients and supported by material obtained in supervising a number of psychiatric residents in their treatment of a large number of patients. Most of these patients were seen for forty-five or fifty minutes once each week. In some instances, the twelve meetings were completed in seven or eight weeks by seeing the patient more than once each week, a procedure required when patients or therapists themselves had only a limited amount of time in the geographic area.

With these decisions made, the patient is told by the therapist that after due consideration of the available data, it would appear that the patient's central difficulty is of a particular nature, and he tells the patient what, in his opinion, it is. In so doing, the therapist has informed the patient not only of his diagnosis, but also of the goal of the mutual work to be undertaken.

Implicit in the selection of a patient for time-limited psychotherapy is the assumption, based on the evaluation interview(s), that the patient is neither in a state of acute decompensation (acute psychotic reaction) nor so profoundly depressed as to be unable to engage in the work of psychotherapy. The substance of the work here is derived from the treatment of patients who, although they have had severe and disabling complaints in many instances, were nevertheless possessed of sufficient ego strength to be able to negotiate a treatment agreement and to tolerate a treatment schedule.

How does one go about choosing what seems to be the central genetically and adaptively important issue? A clear understanding of psychoanalytic concepts of unconscious determinants of thoughts, feelings, and actions and their relation to maturational phases of personality development as well as to the elaboration of structural elements (id, superego, and ego) is requisite for an appreciation of the modes of expression of intra-psychic conflict. In general, the central issue is apt to be of immediate use to the patient if it is couched in terms of feelings or in terms of maladaptive function. Such a selection tends often to make for a broad statement of the patient's central difficulty. While this may seem ambiguous and nonspecific at the start, there will ensue a rapidly growing clarification and specification of the central issue for both patient and therapist.

The most effective means for involving the patient in the treatment process lies in selecting a central issue that is both genetically and adaptively relevant, hence one that has been recurrent over time. A close study of the patient's history will disclose some thin red line that began in the past and remains active in the present, one that denotes both genesis and adaptive effort dictated by the genesis. But adaptation always implies defense. That is to say that the patient has devised methods for mastering early difficulties. An important part of such mastery is the erection of psychological defenses which will keep out of awareness the origins of the problem as well as the pain suffered at that time.

In practice, therefore, it may seem important to decide whether to pose the central issue in terms of its genetic sources or its adaptive expression. In either instance, we may fully expect that the patient will summon his characteristic defenses when he is confronted with a central issue. Understanding the nature of conflict and of defense and the significance of the latter for the maintenance of the integrity of the individual allows for a third kind of approach which will not reinforce defenses but will rather increase the patient's motivation for help. In turn, this leads to more immediate involvement in the treatment process.

The third approach lies in formulating a general statement that speaks to the therapist's understanding of the patient's present and chronically endured pain. This is the kind of pain that is recognized by the patient as a consciously acceptable part of his human condition that need not warrant denial. It is one, moreover, that carries with it some degree of feeling unjustly put upon by an insensitive world. The patient's history has highlighted this affective state. Statement of the central issue in terms of his own chronic pain immediately brings the patient closer to the therapist out of his feeling that he is in the presence of an empathic helper. The closeness that he feels effectively promotes a rapid therapeutic alliance.

The statement of the central issue in these affective terms makes unnecessary any attempt by patient, or by therapist for that matter, to intellectualize the situation or to defend himself from awareness and from closeness to the therapist. The patient cannot but help to wish to move further into this kind of promising relationship, so he responds readily to the remainder of the treatment structure and sets the predictable series of dynamic events in motion. Further, the patient will feel free to move from the general, central issue to the specific genetic and adaptive issues over the course of the next four or five meetings. The genetic and adaptive issues will continue to be elaborated in the continuing affective milieu, and the therapeutic experience will remain throughout the twelve meetings at a high, alive, emotional level.

For example, a woman of thirty-three is single, rather alone in the city, and finds herself in something of a state of limbo despite considerable talent and substantial education in a particular field. She would like to marry, to have a family, and to engage in the meaningful career for which she had prepared herself. She has none of these. A study of her history reveals that life changed drastically for her when she was thirteen years old and her father died suddenly. One could clearly outline the effect of this loss and the adaptive efforts made to overcome its effects in the course of the next twenty years. The central issue might have been stated to her in terms of her never having gotten over the loss of her father and of her various attempts to master it leading to her present state. Although the patient presented herself in her diagnostic interviews as a smiling, rather charming, undepressed woman, the central issue was posed to her in this way: "I gather from all that you have told me that the greatest problem facing you at this time is your very deep disappointment with yourself to find yourself as you are at this time in your life." Her immediate acceptance was indicated first by a depressed silence and then by her expressed willingness to go further into it.

In the patient whose case will be presented in detail, the central issue was posed as one in which the patient was told that she "was suffering from a constant sense of nagging discontent, irritation, and irritability." She moved quickly from this acceptable generalization of pain to the adaptive efforts over time that did everything for her except to spare her from a variety of displaced painful symptoms.

The detection of the most telling feeling state and the diagnosis of some kind of maladaptive behavior are readily made in very few cases. Even as each patient comes for help, he brings with him an array of defenses which are designed precisely to keep from his awareness what he is feeling, how he is feeling, what he would wish, and what behavior is maladaptive and what he is achieving or trying to achieve with the particular behavior. There are many variations within all of the above. Some patients will know how they are feeling, but will have no conscious knowledge of the source of the feeling; others may be aware of maladaptive behavior but not recognize that they are even deeply depressed, and the like. The task of selecting the central issue must depend, therefore, on the skill of the therapist as an interviewer. This is primarily a demonstration of his familiarity with the role and manifestation of the patient's unconscious thoughts and feelings and fantasies. While free association is the method of choice for obtaining information that lies outside conscious awareness, it is hardly applicable in any kind of short-form psychotherapy. The pioneer in exploring and adapting psychoanalytic principles and techniques to a short-form psychotherapy was Felix Deutsch. In his two major works, Deutsch outlined and illustrated in extensive clinical examples his "associative anamnesis" and his sector, or goal-directed, therapy.[30] The associative anamnesis was based upon the concept of free association, but was limited in that the interviewer directed his attention to particular words, the behavior accompanying the words and the particular moment in the interview when the word and/or the behavior appeared. The words most often expressed some kind of feeling—hurt, fear, rage, disappointment, and so on. His aim was to make conscious to the patient the kinds of feelings and fantasies that existed in his mind in respect to a particular symptom and that symptom alone (hence, goal-directed). Deutsch's special interest lay in the study of psychosomatic conditions, so that the relief of the particular psychosomatic symptom could be defined as the directed goal. The patient knows, of course, that he is suffering physically and is looking for relief of the same symptom that his therapist is interested in.

The principles enunciated by Deutsch in his associative anamnesis are equally applicable to arriving at a central issue in the course of an interview, although in general clinical practice we are less likely to be dealing with a clearly defined psychosomatic symptom. However, his work remains an excellent guide for obtaining information about any patient's secret (even to him) feeling state or behavior, which the clinician can then relate to the patient's conscious reasons for seeking help. The relationship between the two establishes a genetic-adaptive continuity, an inclusive now that can then be stated to the patient as the central issue, the diagnosis, the mutual work of treatment.

Thus, "Your major difficulty is that you feel inadequate and chronically depressed as a result of your need to challenge and to pacify men who are important to you," is the statement of the central issue in a young woman who had lost her father in early adolescence. She had been an only child and had lived with her widowed mother. The relationship between the significant adolescent loss and her present dysfunction was established in the statement of the central issue.

A thirty-one-year-old married man was taking several university courses in an extended effort to get a college degree. His reason for seeking help was his consuming fear of failing and accompanying difficulty in studying. In his background was an alcoholic father, who one day was found hanging, a mother chronically disabled with arthritis, a one-month-old son who had been found dead in his crib five years before, a boss with whom he was very close who died very quickly of acute leukemia one year before, and an always present fear that his job will suddenly end by his being fired. The central issue for the twelve treatment sessions was expressed to him as, "Because there have been a number of sudden and very painful events in your life, things always seem uncertain, and you are excessively nervous because you do not expect anything to go along well. Things are always uncertain for you." Again, a clear relationship is established between the drastic loss of sustaining objects and the expectation that the present and future will be the same.

A twenty-two-year-old female student depressively stated that her chief problem was that she was "all fucked up." Sufficient anamnestic data was obtained to support the statement of the central issue as being that she wished "not to be hurt by so many people." Early in the course of treatment this was refined to "How did you come to think so little of yourself?"

Always, since the central issue is determined by the therapist, the patient should be told that if, in the course of their work, the therapist's original diagnosis is found to be incorrect, both patient and therapist will know it and will change direction appropriately.

In the course of these negotiations, the therapist informs the patient that twelve treatment interviews will be made available to him to work on the central problem and that, according to the therapist's best judgment, the time would best be used, for example, in weekly forty-five minute visits. He should add that unforeseen interruptions may occur as the result of illness, bad weather, or the like, but that these will not reduce the total treatment time offered the patient. Finally, the time for each appointment is given as well as the *exact* date of the last or twelfth meeting. I consult my calendar overtly, so that the patient is witness to its role in setting the exact date of the final interview. This practice was initiated on the assumption that patients would defend themselves even more vigorously from continuing awareness of the reality of time coming to an end unless confronted with real time, the calendar. This is in accord with the observation of Bergler and Roheim that "The calendar is an ultimate materialization of separation anxiety."[31] The use of the calendar in establishing the treatment agreement serves as a stimulus and as a reinforcement to unconscious fantasies and defenses in respect to the meaning of time. Generally, the session with the patient at which these negotiations are transacted is considered the first of the twelve, unless treatment negotiations have consumed all of the appointment time.

Lastly, the patient is asked for his agreement to all of the items in the treatment proposal. It is unusual for a patient to refuse this carefully ordered plan, and why this is so will be clarified later. Patients often ask whether anything can really be done for them in so short a time, which is certainly a reasonable query. The response of the therapist is determined by his understanding that the question emerges from at least three sources—unconscious yearning for child time, which is linked to eternity; adult, realistic perception of limited calendar time; and the enormously accelerated time of the present historical period, which contributes substantially to the patient's concern about the swift passage of time, that so little of it is for him. The appropriate response to the patient's question, therefore, is a quiet and genuinely confident "yes."

It is an appropriate response because, more than anything else, it pays tribute to that quantum of adult self-esteem, however diminished it may be, which demands some degree of self-satisfying performance or work of oneself. It is appropriate also because it responds affirmatively to the unconscious demand for the satisfaction of infantile fantasies. The patient sitting before us always speaks in a "multitude of tongues," and we are well advised to know as much as we can of these multi-level messages as we formulate our responses.

The following dialogue ensued when a patient was offered a typical treatment agreement:

Pt.: Suppose I talk myself into feeling better?

Dr.: Should that happen, it would be useful to you if you would let me know that. *(The response suggests to the patient that it is his responsibility to be of help to himself by telling the doctor about it.)*

Pt.: Suppose I feel better at the end—will it last?

Dr.: This is typical of your fear of failure in advance and your preparation for it. You would like a gilt-edge guarantee, and I can't give that to you. *(This response was determined by material gained in the anamnesis, including his reasons for seeking help. Having been given responsibility for himself in the answer to his first question, he promptly poses another demand which is not granted. Again I direct my answer to the adult in the patient.)*

Pt.: Why the short amount of time you are giving me?

Dr.: Because that's all you need. *(This response incorporates the earlier questions that center around his self-esteem as well as the patient's conscious and unconscious expectations of the treatment. The unconscious fantasy is that he will have an eternity to fulfill his infantile demands for gratification by virtue of the doctor's omnipotence which he hears in the doctor's confident remark that the work can be done in the short time prescribed. The resistance and the demand implied in the question as well as other lurking doubts will be effectively managed by a positive response. These are the details of the treatment guidelines.)*

The therapist has asked the patient for his agreement to the treatment plan. The patient has his reasons for not objecting. That these reasons are chiefly unconscious does not alter his verbal acceptance of responsibility in the process. We know that in any case in which a therapist offers his help, unconscious fantasies about the outcome may have little or nothing to do with the realities of the treatment agreement. The patient is consciously free to say no and refuse to continue under such terms. Unconsciously he is far from free, but, as noted, this condition obtains regardless of the therapist's stance. It is the therapist's obligation to give the patient the clear opportunity to question and to accept or refuse.

A treatment agreement of some kind is consummated in every instance in which patient and therapist arrange to provide help for the patient. Appointment hours, appointment dates, fees, and some statement as to the nature of the patient's problems are usually settled. With rare exceptions is any time limit established, but for those cases in which the therapist or patient have a limited stay on the service, in the clinic, or in the geographic area. Since so much of psychiatry clinic service is provided by psychiatric residents, medical students, student social workers, and so forth, the duration of treatment is most often determined simply by the duration of the professionals' commitment to the particular service. Even in those cases where the treatment agreement includes a time limit, the duration of treatment remains more or less ambiguous, since a degree of uncertainty is invariably communicated directly or indirectly by the therapist. The most usual situation is one in which a certain number of meetings is offered with a "we shall see then" proviso.

The treatment agreement described here aims at making use of the patient's conscious and unconscious anticipations in coming to a psychotherapist, anticipations that become even more florid if the therapist is a physician. Out of the welter of ideas, feelings, symptoms, and incidents presented by the patient, the therapist extracts what he judges to be the central issue and asserts the time-honored role of the physician in telling the patient what it is that ails him.[32] Further, the patient knows that the stated central issue is, in effect, both the diagnosis and the mutual work of the treatment. The therapist then *prescribes* an *exact* amount of time, the model presented here being one hour each week for twelve weeks, and with calendar in hand he announces the date of the final interview. The patient is encouraged to review and discuss the proposed agreement and to accept or reject it. The therapist deliberately tones down (but not out) the patient's expectations of omnipotence by adding that if it becomes evident to both that the chosen central issue is erroneous, they will be free to leave it and to move on to the more appropriate issue.

Ambiguity in this kind of treatment agreement is minimal. If these guidelines are followed, the failure of a patient to consent will be a rare occasion indeed. As a by-product, of course, the breakage rate, which is usually inordinately high in most clinics, will be drastically reduced. Therapists often tend to underestimate how great are the resources of most people for doing for themselves when given a modest amount of help.

THE SEQUENCE OF DYNAMIC EVENTS

The most significant dynamic element in the treatment agreement lies in the exact proscription of time. Philips and Johnston remark that "what is important is that the interview series has a beginning, an end and other discernible features." Their emphasis in treating children is making certain that "the treatment experience itself has a structure."[33]

A time limit is one of the elements in the structure. Malan in his admirable study of brief psychotherapy comments on this aspect of the therapy which, after all, is announced in the adjective *brief*. "The technique that we eventually developed for conveying the limitations of therapy to the patient was to put to him, at the beginning, in some such statement as the following: 'My idea is to go ahead with treatment, once a week, for a few months and see where we can get. At the end of that time we will review the situation, but if it looks as if you need more you will be transferred to a longer form of treatment. If we feel that we have got far enough, then I will stop seeing you *regularly*. This does not mean that you will necessarily stop seeing me altogether—you can ask to come back at any time for further occasional sessions if you feel you need further help.' "[34]

Philips and Johnston limited their patients to a block of ten sessions, although in some instances one or more sessions were added, as were, in other instances, a whole new series or indefinitely extended treatment. They view the time limit as only one of a number of restrictive, structuring agents and do not direct attention to the meaning of time. This is unfortunate, since time is probably even more an intrusive specific when one is treating a child-parent pair. In this connection, Proskauer, considerably later, picks up on the impact of time itself in the child patient by stressing the termination-separation problem.[35] Malan's treatment plan expresses a large measure of easy flexibility but promotes at the same time greater ambiguity in respect to time and misses out on the use of time as a powerful motivating force in treatment. Oberman takes very much the same position as Malan with patients diagnosed as borderline. This is more in the nature of a special instance that will be considered along with the selection of patients.[36]

It has been my practice not to compromise the time limit by making any suggestions during the course of treatment about further treatment after the twelve treatment visits have elapsed. In so doing, it has been possible to reinforce and to clarify the meaning of a beginning, a middle, and an end. A major problem in many long-term psychotherapy cases, and one which unfortunately all too often dictates that psychotherapy shall be long-term or indefinite, is the very problem of arriving at an end. Too frequently, long-term psychotherapy dribbles to an unspoken end mediated by a move to another city by the patient or therapist, rotation to another service, inconvenient appointment hours, or a chronic impasse situation between patient and therapist that relates to a transference-countertransference situation which is neither understood nor resolved. This problem prevails in many short forms of psychotherapy also.[37]

Patients coming to see a psychiatrist expect the worst. The clear definition of the central problem or focus is experienced with a sense of relief. The proscription of time touches neatly on the unconscious wish to have treatment fulfill infantile fantasies and creates paradoxically both a sense of optimistic urgency and a sense of pessimism and predetermined disappointment. The time limit is not only a proscription, it is also a prescription. The specific time limit has a message for the eternity of the infantile in the unconscious and for the reality sense and real time sense of the conscious in the adult. Hence, the impatient optimism of the child in the unconscious is tempered by its opposite, the pessimism of the adult. The contradiction between the two poses no problem for the human mind, in which contradictions exist readily side by side without influence upon each other.

At the same time, the degree and intensity of the relationship to the therapist, also limited by time, harmonizes with the patient's conflicting unconscious desire for closeness and for distance. This may be understood in terms of the opposing wishes found in every person who seeks help from another, and particularly so when it is the emotional and/or physical well-being that is at stake. The situation promptly arouses the never-ending struggle between the wish to be dependent, taken care of, relieved of responsibility, and gratified, and the wish to maintain one's sense of self, autonomy, independence, and self-esteem. The established time limit becomes and is experienced as a suitable compromise in that the patient is invited to be dependent, but not for very long.

The total effect is to reproduce very keenly the original ambivalence experienced with early important objects. If the therapist is correct in his choice of the focus of treatment, he also effects a response in the patient that is related not only to the present stress, but also to stress that is important genetically. For most patients, a crisis is generally an exacerbation of a lifelong conflict situation that may find what seems to be different avenues of discharge at different times. The treatment agreement suggests without hesitation that something can be done for the patient in the time allotted. The notion of *what* can be done undoubtedly reaches beyond the desire for relief in the present conflict state and again arouses unconscious expectations of infantile fulfillment.

Knowing the termination date at the start increases anxiety in respect to loss as well as defenses against loss. The termination date is quickly repressed, and the intensification of defenses against separation and/or loss serves to highlight much of the nature of the present central issue, its past history, and the means employed to master it. The distinct limitation of time, the selection of a focus that may be conscious (among many others that are conscious) but which is particularly cogent in the unconscious life of the patient, the confidence of the therapist that something will be done in a short period of time, and the *known* termination date all serve to fuse past objects, past fantasies, and past conflicts in a telescopic manner to the extent that the therapist becomes an intensely positive transference object very quickly. The details of the treatment agreement consolidate the various dynamic forces that are streaming in the emotional life of the patient so that a treatment set has been created which is entirely in tune with the meaning of now to the patient.

If, in this circumstance, the therapist resists every effort of the patient to divert him from the agreed area of investigation, the area of regression in the transference will remain limited. The single focus, that is, the present state around which the patient finds it impossible to act without conflict or painful anxiety in his present encounter with the world, and the constriction of time together promote a well-organized, defined, and limited regression downward through existential time, which at the same time is moderated by enormous forward pressure to the real end of time. Regression now increases in respect to the amorphous "golden sunshine" of the patient's beginnings and diminishes in respect to confrontation with a known end. Union and separation become the major poles of treatment, thereby diminishing in intensity all other phase-specific conflicts and the anxieties attached to them.

It is as a result of these dynamic events that one will regularly see rapid symptomatic improvement in the patient within the first three or four meetings. The beginning can now be understood as consisting mostly in a surge of unconscious magical expectations that long ago disappointments will now be undone and that all will be made forever well, as they should have been so long ago. The warm sustaining golden sunshine of eternal union will be restored—and in the unconscious it is restored. For the patient it is truly a literal beginning when he makes known to the therapist that his distress is greatly diminished or even entirely gone. Within the context of time-limited psychotherapy, this is one explanation of the process of the so-called transference cure.[38]

So it is that in this rapid mobilization of a positive transference, one can observe the dynamics of the transference cure within the first three or four of the twelve meetings. In essence, the ambivalence experienced and endured in relation to early significant persons is temporarily resolved in the expectation of enormous fulfillment and relief. During this positive phase, important aspects of the current problem, adaptive maneuvers, and the genetic roots of the central issue will become known to the therapist. In the midst of this positive state, the patient will be inclined to pour out much important anamnestic data and secret feelings and fantasies. The therapist will be tempted to explore one or another fascinating avenue of data, and it is in this setting that any variety of psychotherapy may become excessively diffused and the goals of treatment increasingly blurred. The therapist must remain insistent in confining attention to the central issue and use only those data that relate to it. His persistence not only serves to bring to light associations directly relevant to the central issue, but also increasingly constricts the boundaries of the flowing positive transference. In this way, the tendency to regress also becomes limited, since the patient is being persuaded to direct his attention and his affect to a limited area of living.

As the therapist continues to attend only to the central issue, the patient's initial enthusiasm begins to wane. He has many things to talk about, many problems to solve, and he feels willing to do so as he continues under the influence of the beginning fantasies. The failure of the therapist to go along with him has the effect of moving the patient more and more in the direction of the original ambivalent relationship as it had been an affective fact of the patient's life, rather than as it was temporarily undone in the beginning, positive, "golden glow" phase of the treatment. Now the first glimmers of disappointment begin to appear, and these are generally heralded by a return of symptoms, or of problems, or of a sense of pessimism as to what will be achieved in treatment.

Symptoms, character traits, and life styles that have served to defend against awareness of the conflict contained in the central issue reappear or take on new strength "in vivo." At this point, six or seven of the twelve meetings are apt to have been held, and clearly the "honeymoon" is over. In fact, the middle of treatment has been reached. The characteristic feature of any middle point is that one more step, however small, signifies the point of no return. In the instance of time-limited psychotherapy, the patient must go on to a conclusion that he does not wish to confront. The confrontation that he needs to avoid and that he will actively seek to avoid is the same one he suffered earlier in his life; namely, *separation without resolution from the meaningful, ambivalently experienced person.* Time sense and reality are co-conspirators in repeating an existential trauma in the patient.

So it is that by the seventh or eighth meeting, in addition to protective symptoms, character traits, and life styles, resistance will take form in lateness or absence or in generally subtle, but readily apparent manifestations of negative transference. The end phase is in progress and will encompass the final third of the twelve meetings.[39] The predetermined sense of pessimism and disappointment described as aroused in the phase of treatment negotiations lies in the unconscious recollection of the patient of a similar ending earlier in his life. The need to ward off and to deny the separation and end is regularly manifested in the patient's rapid repression of the termination date and/or of the number of meetings that are left to him. In most instances, the midpoint of treatment is reached and passed without any verbal expression of awareness of it. Instead, defensive reactions are set in motion. To test this hypothesis, I have made it a point in my own cases to inquire, rather blandly and almost parenthetically at about the seventh or eighth meeting, how many more meetings were left to us. The repeated response has been a hasty, "I don't know." If pressed for a further reply, each patient has given two answers—"four or five more," for example—of which one is precisely correct. If the twelve meetings have been interrupted by the therapist's absence, the patient is likely to be even more confirmed in his ignorance of the amount of time left to him.

The last three or four of the twelve meetings must deal insistently with the patient's reaction to termination. It is in this end phase that the definitive work of resolution will be done, and it will incorporate, of necessity, understanding of all the highly concentrated and intensely experienced dynamic events that have preceded it. Sadness, grief, anger, and guilt with their accompanying manifestations in fantasy and in behavior must be dealt with. The genetic source of these affects is relived in the disappointing termination and separation from the therapist in whom he has become heavily invested, and the therapist must not hesitate to examine with the patient all these feelings and fantasies and the behavior derived from them in the light of the central issue as it brought the patient for help in his present life circumstance.

The process of termination in this time-limited procedure is intensely affect-laden. More often than not it is as difficult for the therapist as it is for the patient. The dynamics of a beginning, a middle, and an end reverberate in the therapist, too. The intensity of the time-restricted relationship not only arouses doubt in the therapist's mind as to the extent to which he can be effective in helping the patient, but also exposes him to his own unconscious conflicts of exactly the same nature. That is, the therapist, too, faces the *possibility* of separation without resolution—a circumstance which one can confidently predict occurred in the past history of every therapist, in fact, in the life history of every human being. In this circumstance, resistance to termination by the therapist will not be unexpected. It is the inability to confront squarely and boldly the separation and termination process that most often accounts for the interminability of much of long-term psychotherapy. It is so often apparent, too, that even in those cases of long-term psychotherapy or of psychoanalysis where the treatment is brought to an agreed-upon conclusion, the painful termination-separation phase is worked through somewhat raggedly and far from completely. It is likely that therapists of all persuasions founder to some extent at this point. The issue is emphasized here not to point an accusing finger, but rather to underline the presence of a universal problem to which therapists must pay unrelenting attention. Further, it is in the nature of this time-limited psychotherapy to aggravate and accentuate the therapist's own troubled responses to termination-separation. The number of hiding places and opportunities for procrastination and denial are simply fewer in number. It cannot be accepted as accidental that specific references to time and the meaning of time are so prominently noted by their absence in the literature on all short forms of psychotherapy.

Resistance by the therapist becomes visible not only in his avoidance of the patient's reactions to approaching termination, but also by the nature of his responses to the patient's resistance. A common experience, for example, is for the patient to inquire anxiously as to what will happen when treatment is over and he feels as upset as ever, possibly even worse. The therapist may respond in a number of ways in which the message is communicated to the patient that the twelfth hour termination will not be for real. The reply "we will see" is a frequent one and clearly informs the patient that the patient's uncertainty is shared and therefore subject to a decision that will prolong therapy.

It is absolutely incumbent upon the therapist to deal directly with the reaction to termination in all its painful aspects and affects if he expects to help the patient come to some vividly affective understanding of the now inappropriate nature of his early unconscious conflict. More than that, active and appropriate management of the termination will allow the patient to internalize the therapist as a replacement or substitute for the earlier ambivalent object. *This time the internalization will be more positive (never totally so), less anger-laden, and less guilt-laden, thereby making separation a genuine maturational event.* Since anger, rage, guilt, and their accompaniments of frustration and fear are the potent factors that prevent positive internalization and mature separation, it is these that must not be overlooked in this phase of the time-limited therapy.

Experience indicates that one cannot expect in time-limited psychotherapy the kind of full-blown expression of these that is found, or is at least possible, in long-term psychotherapy or in psychoanalysis. This can be understood as a logical consequence of treating the patient in such a way as to limit the area of regression in the transference. Because defenses are not generally weakened, and because ego defenses characteristically employed to maintain unawareness of the presenting unconscious conflict are reinstated, open expressions of anger or rage tend to be limited. However, they are present. Lateness or absence has already been noted. Irritation, annoyance, sullenness, and depression are observable. Slips of the tongue are revealing, as are details of bits of behavior outside the treatment situation. The patient's dreams may be particularly revealing of the warded-off powerful feelings of anger. Changes in the patient's attire and face may be blatant clues. Direct expression of disappointment with the course of events may take place.

The following excerpt is from the first few minutes of the tenth session with a young male patient:

Pt.:   Well, it is rather a nice day out today.
Dr.:   Yes. Were you at home?
Pt.:   Yes, I slept a lot and ate a lot.
Dr.:   It's nice to be at home.
Pt.:   Especially physically. My bed at home is so much better than what I have in my apartment, and I just slept like a log.
Dr.:   It smells better, too, doesn't it?
Pt.:   Mmmm. I had an experience on the way over here. I was driving by school—I had to take care of a few things in my office—and getting out of my car I see this man coming down the street. Oh, oh, I've got to avoid him if I possibly can. He is an important doctor, and he is a John Birch man. He said, "I haven't seen you lately," and I said, "That's right." So he said, "What's been happening to you?" So I thought, "What's been happening to you, you jerk."— I only thought that, and I made my excuses and left. That was one guy I didn't want to see.
Dr.:   The two of you go to the same church?
Pt.:   Ya. He's one of those guys. Boy oh boy, get him away from me. I was afraid I might say something that was in real bad taste. He is a guy with a fine education, graduate education and all those kinds of things, but he is just completely off the deep end, just so off—

Dr.: In what way? What is your objection?
Pt.: Well, he is one of my brother's supporters, and he goes around speaking for
the Birchers, and I stand for the opposite. The sort of thing the John Birch
society stands for—no place for democracy. He takes the extremes to such an
extreme. Anyway, he was on his way to the—clinic, so perhaps he'll get
some help.
Dr.: What kind of help?
Pt.: Psychiatric help.
Dr.: Are you an advocate of psychiatric help?
Pt.: Let me ask you a question in a round about fashion.
Dr.: You want to duck it slowly?

While one might say that it is understandable that a patient might well
report early in an interview some event occurring immediately before coming
to see the therapist, the fact is that the patient—every patient—sorts out a
limitless number of impressions, thoughts, and feelings and is impelled out
of need and the pressure of the emotional situation to choose and to speak of
what is of urgent concern to him. He will protect himself in characteristic
modes from overt direct expression of what he is feeling. In this instance, the
end of treatment nears and the patient lets it be known that he has been
visiting his home where certain basic gratifications, food and shelter, are
open to him. He then has to tell of his encounter with the well-educated,
physician John Birch jerk who has no respect for democracy. The meaning
of this in respect to the treatment situation requires no further elaboration. It
is by no means an unusual or exceptional example of the kind of concealed,
angry feelings present as termination approaches.

In every case, one can find ample evidence for the angry feelings precipitated anew by the termination. Termination without as much consideration of
the anger as possible (and more rather than less is invariably possible) will
lead to a termination that may be repetitive almost to the last detail of the
separation experienced early in the life of the patient with the significant
person. In this connection it may be helpful to note that in some cases the
patient has been told at the conclusion of the last interview that he might at
some time experience angry thoughts about me, or that he might experience
a general sense of anger, unattached to any person or idea, and that this
anger, too, might well belong to feelings about me. I remind him that he
need not be surprised or guilty should this happen, and that he will be able
to elaborate further for himself what it was about in the light of our discussions.

NOTES

1. Thomas Wolfe, *Look Homeward Angel* (New York: Charles Scribner's Sons, 1952), p. 3.

2. A. D. Weisman, *The Existential Core of Psychoanalysis* (Boston: Little, Brown, 1965).

3. D. E. Schecter, M. Symonds, and I. Bernstein, "The Development of the Concept of Time in Children," *Journal of Nervous and Mental Diseases,* 121 (1955), 301.

4. S. Fisher and R. L. Fisher, "Unconscious Conceptions of Parental Figures as a Factor Influencing Perception of Time," *Journal of Personality,* 21 (1953), 496.

5. Bertram D. Lewin, "Phobic Symptoms and Dream Interpretation," *Psychoanalytic Quarterly,* 21 (1952), 295.

6. W. Clifford M. Scott, "Some Psycho-dynamic Aspects of Disturbed Perception of Time," *British Journal of Medical Psychology,* 21 (1948), 111.

7. Sigmund Freud, "The Dissection of the Psychical Personality," *Complete Psychological Works* (London: Hogarth Press, 1964), XXII, 57.

8. Marie Bonaparte, "Time and the Unconscious," *International Journal of Psychoanalysis,* 21 (1940), 427.

9. Bonaparte, "Time and the Unconscious."

10. Baba Ram Dass, *Remember Be Now Here* (New York: Crown Publishers, 1971), p. 38.

11. Franz S. Cohn, "Time and the Ego," *Psychoanalytic Quarterly,* 26 (1957), 168.

12. J. Meerloo, "Father Time," *Psychiatric Quarterly,* 24 (1950), 657.

13. E. Bergler and G. Roheim, "Psychology of Time Perception," *Psychoanalytic Quarterly,* 26 (1946), 190.

14. D. W. Winnicott, "The Depressive Position in Normal Emotional Development," *British Journal of Medical Psychology,* 28 (1955), 89.

15. K. Eissler, *The Psychiatrist and the Dying Patient* (New York: International Universities Press, 1955); Weisman, *Existential Core of Psychoanalysis,* p. 90.

16. Eissler, *The Psychiatrist and the Dying Patient,* p. 266.

17. Eissler, *The Psychiatrist and the Dying Patient,* p. 282.

18. Bonaparte, "Time and the Unconscious."

19. Otto Rank, *The Trauma of Birth* (New York: Harcourt Brace Co., 1929).

20. In children and in young adolescents, the slow passage of time becomes agonizing in its apparent purpose of delaying biological and psychological gratifications. "When will I be big enough to do as I please, to have a woman, to control others"—all the adult pleasures which illuminate an illusory but glowing future of freedom. As adults grow older, the gratifications of life are recognized for their temporary nature, and the swift passage of time is all too real. Wishing for the passage of time then becomes asking for old age, infirmity, and death.

21. C. K. Aldrich, "Brief Psychotherapy: A Reappraisal of Some Theoretical Assumptions," *American Journal of Psychiatry,* 125 (1968), 5–37.

22. L. R. Wolberg, "The Technique of Short-Term Psychotherapy," in *Short-Term Psychotherapy*, ed. L. R. Wolberg (New York: Grune and Stratton, 1965), p. 128.

23. Wolberg, "Technique of Short-Term Psychotherapy," p. 189.

24. E. V. Semrad, W. A. Binstock, and B. White, "Brief Psychotherapy," *American Journal of Psychotherapy*, 20 (1966), 576–596.

25. F. Alexander, in Wolberg, *Short-Term Psychotherapy*.

26. P. E. Sifneos, "Short-Term, Anxiety-Provoking Psychotherapy: An Emotional Problem-Solving Technique," *Seminars in Psychiatry*, I, no. 4 (November 1969).

27. L. Bellak and L. Small, *Emergency Psychotherapy and Brief Psychotherapy* (New York: Grune and Stratton, 1965).

28. J. Frank, "The Dynamics of the Psychotherapeutic Relationship," *Psychiatry*, 22 (1959), 17.

29. E. Meyer, et al., "Contractually Time-Limited Psychotherapy in an Out-Patient Psychosomatic Clinic," *American Journal of Psychiatry*, 124 (1967, suppl.), 4.

30. F. Deutsch, *Applied Psychoanalysis* (New York: Grune and Stratton, 1949), p. 5. F. Deutsch and W. E. Murphy, *The Clinical Interview* (New York: International Universities Press, 1955), II.

31. E. Bergler and G. Roheim, "Psychology of Time Perception," *Psychoanalytic Quarterly*, 15 (1949), 190–206.

32. The same role is assumed by social workers, psychologists, and others as therapists. However, they have a little less going for them in terms of the patient's expectations because of the centuries-long designated role of physicians as preservers of life as well as life savers.

33. E. L. Philips and M. S. H. Johnston, "Theoretical and Clinical Aspects of Short-Term Parent-Child Psychotherapy," *Psychiatry*, 17 (1954), 267.

34. D. H. Malan, *A Study of Brief Psychotherapy*, Tavistock Publications (Springfield, Ill.: Charles C. Thomas, 1963).

35. S. Proskauer, "Some Technical Issues in Time-Limited Psychotherapy with Children," *Journal of the American Academy of Child Psychiatry*, 8, no. 1 (January 1969).

36. Edna Oberman, "The Use of Time-Limited Relationship Therapy with Borderline Patients," *Smith College Studies in Social Work* (February 1967).

37. I do not intend to suggest that only treatment with a time limit can help a patient. Obviously this is not so. I do suggest, however, that if we understand the meaning and effect of observing a real time limit, we may not only be able to give help to a greater number of patients, but also we may be able to give more lasting and more meaningful help. Further, a real time limit promotes structure and process so effectively as to allow therapists everywhere to test the method.

38. Transference cures are not to be demeaned, since we know that they may sustain some patients over impressive periods of time. Psychiatrists should guard their zeal in setting as their goal the "cure" or "to cure" each patient, however. Not only is the definition of cure quite impossible, but, more important, since all adult neurotic

and psychotic states are manifestations of a chronic state of dysfunction, is it not asking too much of ourselves to seek always for widespread and thoroughgoing personality change as the sole criterion for being effective? As in other branches of medicine, there is reason to be pleased with the number of five-year "cures" and even with the number of one-, two-, or three-year remissions we can effect as we employ the best means available to us. This is one aspect of the therapist's work where a self-administered reduction in therapeutic omnipotence can be of inestimable value to both patient and therapist.

39. A beginning phase cannot be strictly limited or delineated within meetings one to four, nor the middle phase meetings five to eight, nor the end phase nine to twelve. There are variations, shading, and overlapping of one with another. However, because the total amount of time available to the patient for delaying tactics is so stringently limited, the three phases are often remarkably equal.

PART II

Treatment Focus: The Patient in the Outside World

The six essays in this part chosen to illustrate *focus* may seem rather to illustrate the idea of therapist *activity* discussed in the next section. All six readings feature methods in which the therapist is quite active in comparison to those of Mann, Sifneos, or Malan. Horowitz's activity is aimed at information-processing; the work of Klerman, Berne, and Strupp centers on the interpersonal field, and the methods of Kelly and of Beck are cognitive therapies—often lumped with the behavior therapies. So how, as a group, do these essays enlarge our knowledge of focus?

The focus is an essential part of short-term therapy. In practical terms, without focusing, the therapy goes on and on, ranging over many topics, eventually turning into long-term therapy. Focus is a *sine qua non* of brief treatment in quite another sense as well, a sense theoretical as much as practical: Without a focus, a "treatment" consisting of a small number of sessions cannot justly be called short-term *therapy* because it will in all likelihood be spread too thin to justify the name "therapy." *Focus* for dynamic therapists means a developmental stage (such as separation), a state (such as grief), a conflict (such as writer's block), a symptom (such as anxiety), an activity (such as how to parent), a drive (such as sex), a life pursuit (such as a job), a role (such as being a father), an identity (such as being gay), a—the list is endless. There are almost as many possible foci as there are patients. But what they all have in common is *coherence* as an issue for the individual. A handle. A subject heading. An index entry. James Mann's therapy, for instance, has a two-layered focus—the issue the patient understands is a problem and wants to work on, and the central issue the therapist feels underlies the patient's focus causing other neurotic issues as well—but Mann's focus is still a single, coherent entity.

There is a tendency in the recent short-term literature to pull techniques and ideas from many schools together—yet to maintain coherence in the focus by always departing from the patient's presenting *symptom*. And returning to it when things get diffuse. One can picture the therapy as a wheel with various spokes of technique and theory but an axis that is the symptom that the patient presented with. (This is not a bad idea at all, and in fact it was where psychoanalysis started out.) Friedman and Fanger,[1] for instance, put it well when they advise starting with the "metaphoric function of the symptom . . ." and then planning a treatment with goals that can be stated in positive language, assessed as observable behavior, that are dear to the patient, that are congruent with the patient's culture, and that are—*possible*. After the departure from the symptom-as-metaphor, the therapist's cognitive task is to keep focused on the *central strategy* of the therapy, which is *reframing* the patient's experience into ideas congruent with the patient's goals.

So how do the six therapies in this section—featuring information-processing, cognitive therapy, and interpersonal treatment—illustrate *focus* as well as treatment methods or therapist activities? The answer is, focus is a noun, yes, but it is also a verb. What the long-term dynamic therapist does is listen, empathize, understand, contain, frame, support, clarify, interpret, and so on. What the short-term therapist does is—all of these—*plus* focusing the treatment. How the therapist finds and holds the focus grows out of the therapist's theoretical basis. The therapist can focus by saying something like, "This business about your job is important I know, and a hot issue today, but I'm wondering how it relates to the marriage problems that brought you here that we wanted to work on." Or, more crudely, "I want to get back to that fight you had with John last night." The act of focusing in this instance is useful, even essential if it is to be short-term *therapy*. But this is only a mechanical operation, like a sheepdog herding the flock and preventing strays breaking away. The *intellectual* act of focusing never gets far away from the therapist's *theory* of how emotional growth occurs.

If the reader is puzzled by the inclusion of interpersonal and cognitive therapies in a collection of papers on "dynamic" brief treatments, it should be remembered how much in our field theory influences technique. Interpersonal and cognitive treatments have an impact even on therapies that consider themselves purely psychodynamic, especially short-term ones. Theories in one area influence clinical practice in another, a striking example being the impact of self psychology on practitioners who do not at all think of themselves as Kohutians. I know of only one widely cited self psychology paper[2] in the whole brief therapy literature, yet short-term therapists of the 1990s tend to pay as much attention to the impact of an empathic rupture upon the transference as in the 1970s they would have attended to defenses related to the transference. (And lest a reader be puzzled by the inclusion of two antiques, TA and Fixed Role therapy, it is worth remembering how little is truly new under the sun.)

In the treatments described in this part, the focus is pretty much predetermined. In Horowitz it is trauma and its impact; in Klerman, the patient's interpersonal behaviors; in Beck, an influential false cognition. But while the focus is fairly obvious given the theoretical stripe of the practioner, it is the *focusing* that varies—from treatment to treatment and from patient to patient. In the method of Schacht, Binder, and Strupp, it is the patient's narrative— the story he or she tells about the self—that generates the focus, and it is particularly instructive how the therapist leads the work again and again back to that narrative.

Ironically enough, in part III after this, on therapist *activity,* practitioners are outwardly more *passive* and focus more on inner life and its relation to the past. Here in this section, practitioners focus more on the patient's interface with the outer world at present. In both sections the focus grows out of the patient's presenting problem intersecting the therapist's philosophy of cure and treatment skills. In a certain sense—once the two people sit down together and begin their relationship—the *focus chooses itself,* growing naturally out of the intersubjective space between the two. This is true of the methods in both sections, but these six papers are presented first, because here, the therapist's focus*ing* is more concrete and easier to grasp.

REFERENCES

1. Friedman, S. and M. T. Fanger. *Expanding Therapeutic Possibilities: Getting Results in Brief Psychotherapy.* Lexington, Mass.: Lexington Books, 1991, 58.

2. Goldberg, A. "Psychotherapy of Narcissistic Injuries." *Arch Gen Psychiatry* 28(1973):722–26.

5. Stress Response Syndromes: Character Style and Dynamic Psychotherapy

Mardi J. Horowitz

Stress response syndromes are the topic, but the larger aim of this report is to test a model for organizing clinical knowledge. The model integrates variables that characterize current state, personal style, and treatment technique. To reduce information to a coherent level, particular categories along each dimension are designated. The interactions are then examined. Here, a particular domain is circumscribed by state in terms of stress response syndromes, disposition in terms of obsessional and hysterical personality, and by treatment in terms of focal psychodynamic psychotherapy. If this model works for circumscribing a domain and assembling assertions within it, then it can be used with other states, styles, and treatments. The resulting organization of clinical knowledge would allow a clear focus for resolution of disputes about observation and therapy.

RATIONALE FOR CHOICES

State: Stress Response Syndromes

Stress response syndromes have been chosen because the general symptomatic tendencies are well documented, observed across various populations, and usually change rapidly during psychotherapy. External stress events are usually clear and provide the therapist with a point of reference for consideration of other material.

Disposition: Hysterical and Obsessional Neurotic Styles

"Obsessional" and "hysterical" styles are classical typologies in dynamic psychology. Theorization about these styles is at the same level of abstraction as theories of stress, in that both stress response syndromes and obsessional

Reprinted by permission of the American Medical Association from *Archives of General Psychiatry* 31(1974):768–81.

and hysterical styles have been described in terms of potentially conscious cognitive and emotional processes. Information processing theory will thus provide a useful language.[1-3]

Technique: Crisis-Oriented Psychodynamic Therapy

The goals of psychotherapy are infinite. Here they will be limited to conceptual and emotional working through of the stress response syndrome to a point of relative mastery, a state in which both denial and compulsive repetition are reduced or absent.

Nuances of techniques such as repetition, clarification, and interpretation will be focused on, since these maneuvers are on an information processing level of abstraction. The nature of the relationship between patient and therapist will also be examined, but the complexities of transference and resistance will not be discussed in detail.

The basic knowledge relevant to each choice will now be summarized and followed by development of their interactions.

The Natural Course of Stress Response Syndromes

Multiple meanings confound the use of the word "stress." In psychiatry, the central application is concerned with the stress event that triggers internal responses and evokes potentially disruptive quantities or qualities of information and energy. A prototype of a stress event is a highway accident and an elaboration of this prototype will be used to provide a concrete reference for what follows.

Before developing this example, some reminders set the stage. Freud and Breuer[4] found that traumatic events were repressed and yet involuntarily repeated in the form of hysterical symptoms. While some "reminiscences" of their hysterical patients stemmed more from fantasy than from reality, the central observation of compulsive repetition of trauma was validated in many later clinical, field, and experimental studies.[5-8] A second common set of stress responses includes ideational denial and emotional numbing. These signs seem antithetical to intrusive repetitions and are regarded as a defensive response.[9-11] Tendencies to both intrusive repetition and denial-numbing occur in populations that vary in predisposition, after stressful events that vary in intensity and quality, and may occur simultaneously in a given person or in patterns of phasic alteration.

There is a common pattern to the progression of phases of stress response. With the onset of the stress event, especially if it is sudden and unanticipated, there may be emotional reactions such as crying out or a stunned uncomprehending daze. After these first emotional reactions and physical responses, there may be a period of comparative denial and numbing. Then an oscillatory period commonly emerges in which there are episodes of intrusive ideas or images, attacks of emotion, or compulsive behaviors alternating with continued denial, numbing, and other indications of efforts to ward off the implications of the new information. Finally, a phase of "working through" may occur in which there are less intrusive thoughts and less uncontrolled attacks of emotion with greater recognition, conceptualization, stability of mood, and acceptance of the meanings of the event.[11-15]

THEORY OF PSYCHIC TRAUMA

Freud's theories about trauma have two important aspects: the neurotic and energic definitions of traumatization. In early theory, a traumatic event was defined as such because it was followed by neurotic symptoms. To avoid circularity, a theoretical explanation of traumatization was necessary. The energic explanation defined as traumatic those events that led to excessive incursions of stimuli. In a series of energy metaphors, stimuli from the outer world were postulated to exceed a "stimulus barrier" or "protective shield." The ego tried to restore homeostasis by "discharging," "binding," or "abreacting" the energy. Energy, instinctual drives, and emotions were often conceptually blended together in this model.

While Freud repeated energy metaphors throughout his writings, he also conceptualized trauma in cognitive terms more compatible with contemporary psychodynamic models. As early as 1893 in his lecture "On the Psychical Mechanism of Hysterical Phenomena," he spoke of how one could deal with the affect of a psychic trauma by working it over associatively and producing contrasting ideas.[16] Also, implicit in his formulations of signal anxiety is the concept of ideational appraisal of events and their implications.[17]

The concept of information overload can be substituted for excitation or energy overload.[3,18] Information applies to ideas of inner and outer origin as well as to affects. The persons remain in a state of stress or are vulnerable to recurrent states of stress until this information is processed. It is the information that is both repressed and compulsively repeated until processing is relatively complete. Emotions, which play such an important part in stress response syndromes, are not seen as drive or excitation derivatives, but as responses to ideational incongruities and as motives for defense, control, and coping behavior. This view of the centrality of ideational processing is consistent with French's conceptualization of integrative fields[19] and the concept of emotion with ideational incongruities is concordant with cognitive formulations of emotion,[20] and cognitive-neurophysiological formulations.[21]

Prototypic Example

These generalizations will be given concrete reference in the form of a story. The story is intended as a prototype and will be elaborated in various ways as an exercise. That is, the story will allow a hypothetical constancy of events and problems but a variation in personality style. We shall imagine this story as if it happened to two persons, one with an hysterical neurotic style, the other with an obsessional style. Thus, similar response tendencies to the same stress event can be contrasted in terms of stylistic variations and the nuances of treatment applicable to these variations.

Harry is a 40-year-old truck dispatcher. He had worked his way up in a small trucking firm. One night he himself took a run because he was short-handed. The load was steel pipes carried in an old truck. This improper vehicle had armor between the load bed and the driver's side of the forward compartment but did not fully protect the passenger's side.

Late at night Harry passed an attractive and solitary girl hitchhiking on a lonely stretch of highway. Making an impulsive decision to violate the company rule against passengers of any sort, he picked her up on the grounds that she was a hippy who did not know any better and might be raped.

A short time later, a car veered across the divider line and entered his lane, threatening a head-on collision. He pulled over the shoulder of the road into an initially clear area, but crashed abruptly into a pile of gravel. The pipes shifted, penetrated the cab of the truck on the passenger's side, and impaled the girl. Harry crashed into the steering wheel and windshield and was briefly unconscious. He regained consciousness and was met with the grisly sight of his dead companion.

The highway patrol found no identification on the girl, the other car had driven on, and Harry was taken by ambulance to a hospital emergency room. No fractures were found, his lacerations were sutured, and he remained overnight for observation. His wife, who sat with him, found him anxious and dazed that night, talking episodically of the events in a fragmentary and incoherent way so that the story was not clear.

The next day he was released. Against his doctor's recommendations for rest and his wife's wishes, he returned to work. From then on, for several days, he continued his regular work as if nothing had happened. There was an immediate session with his superiors and with legal advisors. The result was that he was reprimanded for breaking the rule about passengers but also reassured that, otherwise, the accident was not his fault and he would not be held responsible. As it happened, the no passenger rule was frequently breached by other drivers, and this was well known throughout the group.

During this phase of relative denial and numbing, Harry thought about the accident from time to time but was surprised to find how little emotional effect it seemed to have. He was responsible and well-ordered in his work, but his wife reported that he thrashed around in his sleep, ground his teeth, and seemed more tense and irritable than usual.

Four weeks after the accident he had a nightmare in which mangled bodies appeared. He awoke in an anxiety attack. Throughout the following days, he had recurrent, intense, and intrusive images of the girl's body. These images together with ruminations about the girl were accompanied by anxiety attacks of growing severity. He developed a phobia about driving to and from work. His regular habits of weekend drinking increased to nightly use of growing quantities of alcohol. He had temper outbursts over minor frustrations, experienced difficulty concentrating at work and even while watching television.

Harry tried unsuccessfully to dispel his ruminations about feeling guilty for the accident. Worried over Harry's complaints of insomnia, irritability, and increased alcohol consumption, his doctor referred him for psychiatric treatment. This phase illustrates the period of compulsive repetition in waking and dreaming thought and emotion.

Harry was initially resistant, in psychiatric evaluation, to reporting the details of the accident. This resistance subsided relatively quickly and he reported recurrent intrusive images of the girl's body. During the subsequent course of psychotherapy, Harry worked through several complexes of ideas and feelings linked associatively to the accident and his intrusive images. The emergent conflictual themes included guilt over causing the girl's death, guilt over the sexual ideas he fantasied about her before the accident, guilt that he felt glad to be alive when she had died, and fear and anger that he had been involved in an accident and her death. To a mild extent, there was also a magical or primary process belief that the girl "caused" the accident by her hitchhiking, and associated anger with her, which then fed back into his various guilt feelings.

COMMENTS

Before continuing with those conflicts triggered by the accident, it is helpful to consider, at a theoretical level, the ideal route of conceptualization that Harry should follow. To reach a point of adaptation to this disaster, Harry should perceive the event correctly; translate these perceptions into clear meanings; relate these meanings to his enduring attitudes; decide on appropriate actions; and revise his memory, attitude, and belief systems to fit this new development in his life. During this information processing, Harry should not ward off implications of the event or relevant associations to the event. To do so would impair his capacity to understand and adapt to new realities.

Human thought does not follow this ideal course. The accident has many meanings sharply incongruent with Harry's previous world picture. The threat to himself, the possibility that he has done harm, the horrors of death and injury, and the fear of accusation by others seriously differ from his wishes for personal integrity, his current self-images, and his view of his life role. This dichotomy between new and old concepts arouses strong painful emotions that threaten to flood his awareness. To avoid such unbearable feelings, Harry limited the processes of elaborating both "real" and "fantasy" meanings of the stressful event.

Because of complex meanings and defensive motives that impede conceptualization, the traumatic perceptions are not rapidly processed and integrated. They are stored because they are too important to forget. The storage is in an active form of memory that, hypothetically, has a tendency toward repeated representation. This tendency triggers involuntary recollections until processing is completed. On completion, the stored images are erased from active memory.[2,8] (This memory is called "active" rather than "short-term" because of the extended duration of intrusive repetitions of stress-related perceptions.) The repetitions, however intrusive, can be adaptive when they provoke resumption of processing. They can be maladaptive when they distract from other tasks, elicit painful emotions, evoke fear of loss of mental control, and motivate pathological defenses.

Defensive operations that oppose repetition can also be adaptive because they allow gradual assimilation rather than overwhelming recognition. Defense maneuvers can be maladaptive if they prevent assimilation, lead to unrealistic appraisals, perpetuate the stress response symptoms, or lead to other problems, such as Harry's alcoholism.

The six problematic themes of Harry's psychotherapy can now be reconsidered as ideational-emotional structures in schematic form. These themes will provide a concrete referent during the ensuing discussion of character style variations. In Table 5.1, each theme is represented as a match between a current concept and enduring concepts. Since there is an incongruity between the new and the old, the elicited emotion is also listed.

Three themes cluster under the general idea that Harry sees himself as an

Table 5.1. Themes Activated by the Accident

Current concept—	incongruent with—	"enduring" concept—	emotion
A. Self as "aggressor"			
1. Relief that she and not he was the victim		Social morality	Guilt
2. Aggressive ideas about girl		Social morality	Guilt
3. Sexual ideas about girl		Social morality	Guilt
B. Self as "victim"			
1. Damage to her body could have happened to him		Invulnerable self	Fear
2. He broke rules		Responsibility to company	Fear (of accusations)
3. She instigated the situation by hitch-hiking		He is innocent of any badness: the fault is outside	Anger

aggressor and the girl as a victim. For example, he felt relief that he was alive when someone "had to die." The recollection of this idea elicited guilt because it is discrepant with social morality. He also felt as if he were the aggressor who caused a victim to die because of his wish to live, a primitive concept that someone has to die, and a belief in the magical power of his thought. Similarly, his sexual ideas about the girl before the crash were recalled and were incongruent with his sense of sexual morality and marital fidelity. All three themes are associated with guilty feelings.

Three other themes center around an opposite conceptualization of himself, this time as a victim. Harry is appalled by the damage to the girl's body. It means his body could also be damaged. This forceful idea interferes with his usual denial of personal vulnerability, and is inconsistent with wishes for invulnerability. The result is fear. Harry also conceives of himself as a victim when he recalls that he broke company rules by picking up a passenger. Since the breach resulted in a disaster, and is discrepant with his sense of what the company wants, he believes accusations would be justified and is frightened. "Harrys" with varying character styles would experience this same theme in different ways. A Harry with a paranoid style might project the accusation theme and suspect that others are now accusing him. He might use such externalizations to make himself feel enraged rather than guilty. If Harry had a hysterical style, he might have uncontrolled experiences of dread or anxiety without clear representation of the instigating ideas. Were he obsessional, Harry might ruminate about the rules; about whether they were right or wrong, whether he had or had not done his duty, about what he ought to do next, and on and on.

The last theme cited in Table 5.1 places Harry as a victim of the girl's aggression. His current ideas are that she made the disaster happen by appearing on the highway. This matches with his enduring concept of personal innocence in a way that evokes anger. These angry feelings are then represented as a current concept and responses occur to these concepts that again transform Harry's state. His felt experience of anger and his concept of the girl as aggressor do not mesh with his sense of reality. The accident was not her fault and so, as the state of ideas change, his emotional experience (or potential emotional experience) changes. He feels guilty for having irrational and hostile thoughts about her. With this switch from the feelings of victim to the feelings of aggressor, there has been a change in emotions from anger to guilt and, as diagrammed in Table 5.1, in state from B3 to A2.

All six themes might be activated by the accident. In "Harrys" of different neurotic character styles, some themes might be more important or conflictual than others. In a hysterical Harry, sexual guilt themes (A3) might predominate. In an obsessional Harry, aggression-guilt (A2), concern for duty (B2), and "self as an innocent victim" themes (B3) might predominate. Other themes, such as fear of body vulnerability (B1) and guilt over being a survivor (A1) seem to occur universally.[7,10]

Harry had a period in which there was relative denial and numbness for all the themes. Later, at various times after the accident, some themes were repressed and others emerged; eventually some were worked through so that they no longer aroused intense emotion or motivated defensive efforts. The first emergent themes were triggered by the nightmare of mangled bodies and the daytime recurrent unbidden images of the girl's body. The themes of bodily injury and survivor guilt (A1 and B1) were no longer completely warded off but rather occurred in an oscillatory fashion with periods of both intrusion and relatively successful inhibition. In psychotherapy, these intrusive themes required first attention. The other themes such as sexual guilt emerged later.

General Stratagems of Treatment for Stress Response Syndromes

At least two vectors effect stress response syndromes: the tendencies to repeated representation and the tendencies to inhibited representation to prevent disruptive emotions. The general rationale of treatment is to prevent either extreme denial, which might impede conceptual and emotional processing, or extreme intrusive-repetitiousness, which might cause panic states or secondary avoidance maneuvers. Various "schools" of therapy have evolved techniques for counteracting extremes of denials or repetitious states, and these are tabulated in Table 5.2.

Once extreme symptoms are reduced, the task is to bring stress-related information to a point of completion. This "completion" can be defined, at the theoretical level, as a reduction of the discrepancy between current concepts and enduring schemata. The crucial feature is not discharge of pent-up excitation, as suggested by the terms "abreaction" and "catharsis," but processing of ideas. To complete the response cycle, either new information must be reappraised or previous concepts must be modified to fit an altered life. Emotional responses will occur during this process when conflicts of meanings are fully considered.

Investigation, in focal psychodynamic treatment, includes examination of conflicts present before and heightened by the immediate situation, as well as the loaded meanings given to stressful events because of prior development experiences and fantasies. Conscious representation is encouraged because it promotes the solving of problems not resolved by automatic, out-of-awareness thought or dreaming. The communicative situation encourages representation and reexamination, and techniques of repetition, clarification, and interpretation enhance the on-going process.[22]

The state of stress imposed by a particular life event may impose a general regression in which developmentally primitive adaptive patterns will be noted, latent conflicts will be activated and more apparent, and increased demand for parental objects will affect all interpersonal relationships. These general regressive signs will subside without specific therapeutic attention, if the state of stress is reduced by working through the personal meanings of the particular life event.

The problem in therapy is to provide tolerable doses of awareness because knowledge of the discrepancies between desire and reality leads to painful emotional responses. On his own, the patient has warded off such knowledge to avoid pain and uncertainty. In therapy, while the affective responses are painful, they are held within bearable limits because the therapeutic relationship increases the patient's sense of safety.[23] In addition, the therapist actively and selectively counters defensive operations by various kinds of intervention. These interventions are, most commonly, clarification and interpretation of specific memories, fantasies, and impulse-defense configurations.

Table 5.2. Classification of Treatments for Stress Response Syndromes

	States	
Systems	Denial-Numbing Phase	Intrusive-Repetitive Phase
Change Controlling processes	Reduce controls Interpretation of defenses Hypnosis & narcohypnosis Suggestion Social pressure & evocative situations: e.g., psycho-drama Change attitudes that make controls necessary Uncovering interpretations	Supply controls externally Structure time & events for patient Take over ego functions, e.g., organize information Reduce external demands & stimulus levels Rest Provide identification models, group membership, good leadership, orienting values Behavior modification with reward & punishment
Change Information processing	Encourage abreaction Encourage: Association Speech Use of images rather than just words in recollection & fantasy Enactments, e.g., role playing, psychodramas, art therapy Reconstructions (to prime memory & associations) Maintenance of environmental reminders	Work through & reorganize by clarifying & educative type interpretive work Reinforce contrasting ideas, e.g., simple occupational therapy, moral persuasion Remove environmental reminders & triggers Suppress or dissociate thinking, e.g., sedation, tranquilizers, meditation
Change Emotional processing	Encourage catharsis Supply objects & encourage emotional relationships (to counteract numbness)	Support Evoke other emotions, e.g., benevolent environment Suppress emotion, e.g., sedation or tranquilizers Desensitization procedures Relaxation & biofeedback

The aim of these techniques is completion of ideational and emotional processing and hence, resolution of stress state rather than extensive modification of character. However, persons of different character structure will manifest different types of resistance and transference during this process. The general techniques will be used with various nuances depending on these dispositional qualities of the patient. As illustration, hysterical and obsessional variations on these general themes will now be considered.

HYSTERICAL STYLE IN RESPONSE TO STRESS

Background

The concept of hysterical character was developed in the context of psycho-analytic studies of hysterical neuroses, even though these neuroses may occur in persons without hysterical character and persons with hysterical styles do not necessarily develop hysterical neurotic symptoms, even under stress. The discussion will briefly develop the "ideal" typology of hysterical style with the assumption that most persons will have only some of the traits and no person will fit the stereotype perfectly.

The main symptoms of hysterical neuroses are either conversion reactions or dissociative episodes.[24] Both symptom sets have been related to dynamically powerful but repressed ideas and emotions that would be intolerable if they gained conscious expression.[4,16] In classical analytic theory, the intolerable ideas are a wish for a symbolically incestuous love object. The desire is discrepant with moral standards and so elicits guilt and fear. To avoid these emotions, the ideational and emotional cluster is warded off from awareness by repression and denial. Because the forbidden ideas and feelings press for expression, there are continuous threats, occasional symbolic or direct breakthroughs, and a propensity for traumatization by relevant external situations. While later theorists have added the importance of strivings for dependency and attention ("oral" needs), rage over the frustration of these desires, and the fusion of these strivings with erotic meanings, the correlation of hysterical symptoms with efforts at repression has been unquestioned.[25-27]

Psychoanalysts view hysterical character as a configuration that either *predisposes* toward the development of conversion reactions, anxiety-attacks, and dissociative episodes, or exists as a *separate entity* with similar impulse-defense configurations but different behavioral manifestations. The hysterical character is viewed as typically histrionic, exhibitionistic, labile in mood, and prone to act out.

Because of a proclivity for acting out oedipal fantasies, clinical studies suggest that hysterical persons are more than usually susceptible to stress response syndromes after seductions, especially those that are sadomasochistic; after a loss of persons or of positions that provided direct or symbolic attention or love; after a loss or disfigurement of body parts or attributes used to attract others; and after events associated with guilt about personal activity. In addition, any event that activates strong emotions, such as erotic excitement, anger, anxiety, guilt, or shame, would be more than usually stressful, even though an hysteric might precipitate such experiences by his behavior patterns.

Clinical studies also indicate what kinds of responses may be more frequent in the hysteric during and after the external stress event. Under stress, the prototypical hysteric becomes emotional, impulsive, unstable, histrionic, and possibly disturbed in motor, perceptual, and interpretive functions.

Styles of thought, felt emotion, and subjective experience are of central relevance to the present theses and have been described by Shapiro.[28] He emphasized the importance of impressionism and repression as part of the hysterical style of cognition. That is, the prototypical hysteric lacks a sharp focus of attention and arrives quickly at a global but superficial assumption of the meaning of perceptions, memories, fantasies, and felt emotions. There is a corresponding lack of factual detail and definition in perception plus distractability and incapacity for persistent or intense concentration. The historical continuity of such perceptual and ideational styles leads to a relatively nonfactual world in which guiding schemata of self, objects, and environment have a flat, depthless quality.

Dwelling conceptually in this nonfactual world promotes the behavioral traits of hysterical romance, emphasis on fantasy meanings, and *la belle indifférence*. For example, the prototypic hysteric may react swiftly with an emotional outburst and yet remain unable to conceptualize what is happening and why such feelings occur. After the episode he may remember his own emotional experiences unclearly and will regard them as if visited on him rather than self-instigated.

This general style of representation of perception, thought, and emotion leads to patterns observable in interpersonal relations, traits, and communicative styles. A tabular summary of what is meant by these components of hysterical style is presented below.

Information Processing Style

Short-order patterns—observe in flow of thought and emotion on a topic
  Global deployment of attention
  Unclear or incomplete representations of ideas and feelings, possibly with lack of
    details or clear labels in communication; nonverbal communications not trans-
    lated into words or conscious meanings
  Only partial or unidirectional associational lines
  Short-circuit to apparent completion or problematic thoughts

Traits

Medium-order patterns—observe in interviews
> Attention-seeking behaviors, possibly including demands for attention, and/or the use of charm, vivacity, sex appeal, childlikeness
> Fluid change in mood and emotion, possibly including break-throughs of feeling
> Inconsistency of apparent attitudes

Interpersonal Relations

Long-order patterns—observe in a patient's history
> Repetitive, impulsive, stereotyped interpersonal relationships often characterized by victim-aggressor, child-parent, and rescue or rape themes
> "Cardboard" fantasies and self-object attitudes
> Drifting but possibly dramatic lives with an existential sense that reality is not really real

Shapiro's formulations differ from clinical psychoanalytic opinion in terms of the stability of such patterns. Shapiro regards the patterns as relatively fixed, perhaps the result of constitutional predisposition and childhood experiences. Other analysts regard these patterns as more likely to occur during conflict. The following discussion will not contradict either position, since both allow us to assume a fixed base line of cognitive-emotional style and an intensification of such patterns during stress.

Controlling Thought and Emotion: Harry as "Hysteric"

Harry will now be considered as if he responded to stress and treatment in a typically hysterical manner. One of his six conflictual themes, as described earlier, will be used to clarify the hysterical mode of controlling thought and emotion. This theme concerns Harry's relief that he is alive when someone had to die (see A1, Table 5.1).

Considered in microgenetic form, Harry's perceptions of the dead girl's body and his own bodily sensations of being alive are matched with his fear of finding himself dead. The discrepancy between his perceptions and his fears leads to feelings of relief. The sense of relief is then represented as a conscious experience.

In the context of the girl's death, relief is incongruent with moral strictures. Harry believes that he should share the fate of others rather than have others absorb bad fate. This discrepancy between current and enduring concepts leads to guilt. Harry has low toleration for strong emotions and the danger of experiencing guilt motivates efforts to repress the representations that generate the emotions.

While repression helps Harry escape unpleasant ideas and emotions, it impedes information processing. Were it not for controlling efforts, Harry might think again of the girl's death, his relief, and his attitudes toward survival at her expense. He might realize that he was following unrealistic principles of thought, forgive himself for feeling relief, undertake some act of penance and remorse if he could not change his attitude, or reach some other resolution of the incongruity between the current concept with his enduring schemata.

If repression is *what* Harry accomplishes, one can go further in microanalysis to indicate *how* it is accomplished in terms of cognitive operations. These operations can be abstracted as if they were in a hierarchy. The maneuver to try first in the hierarchy is inhibition of conscious representation. The initial perceptual images of the girl's body are too powerful to ward off and, immediately after the accident, Harry might have behaved in an "uncontrolled" hysterical style. Later, when defensive capacity was relatively stronger, the active memory images can be inhibited, counteracting the tendency toward repeated representation. Similarly, the initial ideas and feelings of relief might be too powerful to avoid, but later, as components of active memory, their reproductive tendency can be inhibited.

Suppose this inhibition fails or is only partly successful. Warded off ideas are expressed in some modality of representation. In a secondary maneuver, the extended meanings of the ideas can still be avoided by inhibition of translation from initial modes to other forms of representation. Harry could have only his visual images and avoid verbal concepts concerning death, relief, and causation.

A third maneuver is to prevent association to meanings that have been represented. This is again, hypothetically, an interruption of an automatic response tendency. Harry might conceptualize events in image and word forms but not continue in development of obvious associational connections. The purpose would be avoidance of full conscious awareness of threatening meanings.

These controlling efforts are three typically hysterical forms of inhibition: avoidance of representation, avoidance of translation of threatening information from one mode of representation to another, and avoidance of automatic associational connections. If these efforts fail to ward off threatening concepts, there are additional methods. A fourth maneuver is the reversal of role from active to passive. Harry could avoid thinking about his own active thoughts by deploying attention to how other factors (fate, the girl, or the listener to his story) are involved. He could then change the attitude that he was alive because he *actively* wished to be alive, even if another person died, by thinking of one's *passivity* with regard to fate, of the girl's activity in hitch-hiking, and of how she got herself into the accident.

The fifth and last "hysterical" maneuver is alteration of state of consciousness. Metaphorically, if the hysteric cannot prevent an idea from gaining consciousness, he removes consciousness from the idea by changing the organization of thought and the sense of self. Harry used alcohol for this purpose, but no outside agents are necessary to enter a hypnoid state, with loss of reflective self-awareness. These five cognitive maneuvers can be listed as if they were a hierarchy of "rules" for the avoidance of unwanted ideas:

1. Avoid representation
2. Avoid intermodal translation
3. Avoid automatic associational connections (and avoid conscious problem-solving thought)
4. Change self-attitude from active to passive (and vice versa)
5. Alter state of consciousness in order to: (1) alter hierarchies of wishes and fears; (2) blur realities and fantasies; (3) dissociate conflicting attitudes; and (4) alter the sense of self as instigator of thought and action.

The hysteric has further maneuvers, but these extend longer in time. Harry could manipulate situations so that some external person could be held responsible for his survival. This reduces the danger of a sense of guilty personal activity. In terms of very long-range maneuvers, Harry could characterologically avoid experiencing himself as ever fully real, aware, and responsible. He could identify himself with others, real or fantasied, which would make any act, or thought crime, their responsibility and not his.

Clarity in Therapeutic Interventions: An Important Nuance with Persons Who Have Hysterical Style

If the person of hysterical style enters psychotherapy because of stress response symptoms, the therapist will try to terminate the state of stress by helping him to complete the processing of the stress-related ideas and feel-

ings. The activity will include thinking through ideas, including latent conflicts activated by the event, experiencing emotions, and revising concepts to
reduce discrepancies. The interpretation of defense may be useful to remove
impediments to processing, but the main goal in the present model is to end
or reduce a state of stress rather than to alter the character style. Even with
such limited goals, character style must be understood and the usual therapy
techniques (as in Table 5.2) used with appropriate nuances.

These nuances are versions, variations, or accentuations of major techniques such as clarification. One example is simple repetition of what the
patient has said. The therapist may, by repeating a phrase, exert a noticeable
effect on the hysteric who may respond with a startle reaction, surprise,
laughter, or other emotional expressions. The same words uttered by the
therapist mean something different from when they are thought or spoken by
the hysteric himself: they are to be taken more seriously.

Additional meanings accrue and some meanings are also stripped away.
For example, a guilty statement by Harry, repeated by the therapist in a
neutral or kind voice, may seem less heinous. More explicitly, to call this
"repetition" is to be correct only in a phonemic sense. Actually, the patient
hears meanings more clearly, hears new meanings as well, and the previously
warded off contents and meanings may seem less dangerous when repeated
by the therapist.

Simple repetition is, of course, not so "simple." The therapist selects
particular phrases and may recombine phrases to clarify by connection of
causal sequences. At first, when Harry was vague about survivorship, but
said "I guess I am lucky to still be around," the therapist might just say "yes"
to accentuate the thought. A fuller repetition, in other words such as "you
feel fortunate to have survived," may also have progressive effects; it
"forces" Harry closer to the potential next thought . . . "and she did not, so I
feel badly about feeling relief."

Left to his own processes, Harry might have verbalized the various "ingredients" in the theme, might even have painfully experienced pangs of guilt
and anxiety, and yet might still not have really "listened" to his ideas. In
response to this vague style, the therapist may pull together scattered phrases:
"You had the thought, 'Gee I'm glad to still be around, but isn't it awful to
be glad when she's dead?'" Harry might listen to his own ideas through the
vehicle of the therapist and work out his own reassurance or acceptance. This
seems preferable to giving him permission by saying "You feel guilty over a
thought that anyone would have in such a situation"; although this is, of

course, sometimes necessary. As will be seen, *these simple everyday maneuvers are not as effective with persons of obsessional style.*

Other therapeutic maneuvers oriented toward helping the hysteric complete the processing of stressful events are equally commonplace. To avoid dwelling further on well-known aspects of psychotherapy, some maneuvers are listed in tabular form as applicable to specific facets of hysterical style (Table 5.3). Each maneuver listed has additional nuances. For example, with some hysterics, interpretations or clarifications should be very short and simple, delivered in a matter-of-fact tone that would serve to counter their vagueness, emotionality, and tendency to elaborate any therapist activity into a fantasy relationship.

Nuances of Relationship with the Hysterical Patient in a State of Stress

Hysterical persons have a low toleration for emotion, although they are touted for emotionality. Because motivations are experienced as inexorable and potentially intolerable, the ideas that evoke emotion are inhibited. If toleration for the unpleasant emotions associated with a stressful event can be increased, then cognitive processing of that event can be resumed. The therapeutic relationship protects the patient from the dangers of internal conflict and potential loss of controls, and so operates to increase tolerance for warded off ideas and feelings. The therapist effects the patient's sense of this relationship by his or her activities or restraint. How this is typically done is also a nuance of technique.

After a stress event, the hysterical patient often manifests swings from rigid overcontrol to uncontrolled intrusions and emotional repetition. *During these swings, especially at the beginning and with a desperate patient, the therapist may oscillate between closeness and distance within the boundaries that characterize a therapeutic relationship.*

The hysteric may consider it imperative to have care and attention. This imperative need has been called, at times, the "oral," "sick," or "bad" component of some hysterical styles.[25,26,29] During the period of imperative need, especially after a devastating stress event, the hysteric may need to experience warmth and human support from the therapist. Without it, the therapeutic relationship will fall apart, the patient may regress or develop further psychopathology. During this phase the therapist moves, in effect, closer to the patient: just close enough to provide necessary support and not

Table 5.3. Some "Defects" of the Hysterical Style and Their Counteractants in Therapy

Function	Style as "defect"	Therapeutic counter
Perception	Global or selective inattention	Ask for details
Representation	Impressionistic rather than accurate	"Abreaction" & reconstruction
Translation of images & enactions to words	Limited	Encourage talk Provide verbal labels
Associations	Limited by inhibitions Misinterpretations based on schematic stereotypes, deflected from reality to wishes & fears	Encourage production Repetition Clarification
Problem solving	Short circuit to rapid but often erroneous conclusions Avoidance of topic when emotions are unbearable	Keep subject open Interpretations Support

so "close" as the patient *appears* to wish.

As the patient becomes more comfortable, he may begin to feel anxiety at the degree of intimacy in the therapeutic relationship because there may be a fear of being seduced or enthralled by the therapist. The therapist then moves back to a "cooler" or more "distant" stance.

The therapist thus oscillates to keep the patient within a zone of safety by sensitive modification of his manner of relating to the patient. Safety allows the patient to move in the direction of greater conceptual clarity.[30,31] Naturally, the therapist's manner includes his nonverbal and verbal cues. This is what the therapist *allows* himself to do in the context of his own real responses and qualities of being. This is *not* role playing. The therapist allows or inhibits his own response tendencies as elicited by the patient.

If the therapist does not oscillate in from a relatively *distant* position, and if the patient has urgent needs for stabilizing his self-concept through relational support, then the discrepancy between need and supply will be so painful that the patient will find it unendurable to expose problematic lines of thought. Inhibition would continue. If the therapist does not oscillate from a relatively *close* position, then conceptual processing will begin but transference issues will cloud working through the stress response syndrome. Neither clarity nor oscillation by the therapist may be a suitable nuance of technique with the obsessional.

OBSESSIVE STYLE IN RESPONSE TO STRESS

Background

Contemporary theory of obsessional style evolved from analysis of neurotic obsessions, compulsions, doubts, and irrational fears. Abraham[32] and Freud[33] believed the obsessional neuroses to be secondary to regressions to or fixations at the anal-sadistic phase of psychosexual development. The manifestations of the neuroses were seen as compromises between aggressive and sexual impulsive aims and defenses such as isolation, intellectualization, reaction formation, and undoing. Underneath a rational consciousness, ambivalent and magical thinking were noted to be prominent. Common conflicts were formed in the interaction of aggressive impulses and predispositions to rage, fears of assault, and harsh attitudes of morality and duty. These conflicts lead to coexistence and fluctuation of dominance and submission themes in interpersonal situations and fantasies.

Salzman[34] emphasized the obsessional's sense of being driven, his strivings for omniscience and control, and his concerns for the magical effects of unfriendly thoughts of both the self and others. Homosexual thoughts may also intrude, although often without homosexual behavior.

Vagueness seems less possible for the obsessional than the hysteric. Since they tend more toward acute awareness of ideas, staying with one position threatens to lead to unpleasant emotions. Seeing the self as dominant is associated with sadism to others and leads to guilt. Seeing the self as submissive is associated with weakness and fears of assaults; hence, this position evokes anxiety. Alternation between opposing poles, as in alternation between sadistic-dominance themes and homosexual-submissive themes, serves to undo the danger of remaining at either pole.[35,36]

To avoid stabilization at a single position and to accomplish the defense of undoing, obsessionals often use the cognitive operation of shifting from one aspect of a theme to an oppositional aspect and back again. The result is continuous change. At the expense of decision and decisiveness, the obsessional maintains a sense of control and avoids emotional threats.[37-39]

While the obsessional moves so rapidly that emotions do not gain full awareness, he or she cannot totally eliminate feelings. Some obsessionals have intrusions of feelings either in minor quasi-ideational form, as expressed in attacks of rage. Even when this occurs, however, the event can be undone by what Salzman calls "verbal juggling." This process includes alterations of meaning, the use of formulas to arrive at attitudes or plans, shifts in valuation from over- to under-estimation, and, sometimes, the attribution of magical properties to word labels.

Shapiro[28] has described the narrowed focus of the mode of attention of the obsessional person, how it misses certain aspects of the world while it engages others in detail. Ideal flexibility of attention involves smooth shifts between sharply directed attention and more impressionistic forms of cognition. The obsessional lacks such fluidity.

He also describes how the obsessional is driven in the course of his thought, emotion, and behavior by "shoulds" and "oughts" dictated by a sense of duty, by his fears of loss of control, and by his need to inhibit recognition of his "wants." In spite of his usual capacity for hard work, productivity, and "will power," the obsessional person may experience difficulty and discomfort when a decision is to be made. Instead of deciding on the basis of wishes and fears, the obsessional must maintain a sense of omnipotence and, therefore, must avoid the dangerous mistakes inherent in a trial-and-error world. The decision among possible choices is likely to rest on a rule evoked to guarantee a "right" decision or else is made on impulse, to end the anxiety. The result of these cognitive styles is an experiential distance from felt emotion. The exception is a feeling of anxious self-doubt, a mood instigated by the absence of cognitive closure.

This discussion has focused on aspects of cognitive style. These are summarized below with common traits and patterns of behavior.

Information Processing Style

Short-order patterns—observe in flow of thought and emotion on a topic
  Detailed, sharp focus of attention on details
  Clear representation of ideas, meager representation of emotions
  May shift organization and implications of ideas rather than follow an associational line to conclusion, as directed by original intent or intrinsic meanings
  Avoid completion or decision of a given problem, instead switch back and forth between attitudes

Traits

Medium-order patterns—observe in interviews
  Doubt, worry, productivity and/or procrastination
  Single-minded, imperturbable, intellectualizer
  Tense, deliberate, unenthusiastic
  Rigid, ritualistic

Interpersonal Relations

Long-order patterns—observe in a patient's history

Develop regimented, routine and continuous interpersonal relationships low in "life," vividness, or pleasure: often frustrating to "be" with

Prone to dominance-submission themes

Duty-filler, hard worker, seeks or makes strain and pressure, does what he "should" do rather than what he decides to do

Experiences himself as remote from emotional connection with others, although feels committed to operating with others because of role or principles

Controlling Thought and Emotion: Harry as an "Obsessive"

Stressful events may so compel interest that there may be little difference in the initial registration and experience of persons with hysterical or obsessional style. But, short of extreme disasters, the obsessional person may remain behaviorally calm and emotionless in contrast to the emotional explosions of the hysteric. (This report demands such generalizations, but it should be noted that during some events, obsessionals may become quite emotional and hysterics may remain calm. The difference remains in the quality of the person's conscious experience. The hysterical person can have a "hysterical calm" because it is based on an inhibition of some aspects of potential knowledge, no emotion occurs because implications are not known. If and when the obsessional behaves emotionally, it may be experienced by him as a loss of control, one to be "undone" by retrospective shifts of meaning, rituals, apologies, or self-recriminations.)

After a stressful event, the obsessional and the hysteric may both exhibit similar general stress response tendencies, including phases of denial and intrusion. But they may differ in their stability in any given phase. The obsessional may be able to maintain the period of emotional numbing with greater stability, the hysteric may be able to tolerate phases of episodic intrusions with more apparent stability and less narcissistic injury.

During the oscillatory phase, when the uncompleted images and ideas of the current stressful concepts tend to repeated and intrusive representation, the hysteric is likely to inhibit representation to ward off these unwelcome mental contents. The obsessional may be precise and clear in describing the intrusive images, but may focus on details related to "duty," for example, and away from the simple emotion-evoking meanings of the gestalt of the image.

It is during the oscillatory phase of both intrusions and warding off maneuvers that styles stand out in starkest form. Instead of, or in addition to, repressive maneuvers as listed earlier, the obsessional responds to threatened repetitions with cognitive maneuvers such as shifting. By a shift to "something else," the obsessional is able to jam cognitive channels and prevent emergence of endurance of warded-off contents, or to so shift meanings as to stifle emotional arousal. That is, by shifting from topic to topic, or from one meaning to another meaning of the same topic, the emotion-arousing properties of one set of implications are averted.

Treating Harry: Modeled Here As an Obsessional Personality

In discussion of a hysterical Harry, the theme of survival guilt was used as an example. An obsessional Harry might share a tendency toward emergence of the same theme but react to this threat with a style characterized by shifting rather than vagueness and inhibition.

In psychotherapy, Harry begins to talk of the unbidden images of the girl's body. He associates now to his memory of feeling relieved to be alive. The next conceptualization, following the idealized line of working through, outlined earlier, *would be* association of his relieved feelings with ideas of survival at her expense. This cluster *would be* matched against moral strictures counter to such personal gain through damage to others, and Harry *would* go on to conceptualize his emotional experience of guilt or shame (theme A1 in Table 5.1). Once clear, he could revise his schematic belief that someone had to die, accept his relief, feel remorse, even plan a penance, and reduce incongruity through one or more of these changes.

Harry does not follow this idealized route because the potential of these emotional experiences is appraised as intolerable at a not fully conscious level of information processing. A switch is made to another ideational cycle in order to avoid the first one. The second cycle is also associatively related to the images of the girl's body. A common element in both ideational cycles allows a pivotal change and reduces awareness that the subtopic has changed.[40]

The pivot for the switch is the idea of bodily damage. In the second ideational cluster, the concept is that bodily damage could happen to him, perhaps at any future time, since it has now happened to her. Through the comparison with his wishes for invulnerability and his dread of vulnerability, fear is aroused (B1 in Table 5.1).

While fear is unpleasant and threatening as a potential experience, the switch allows movement away from the potential feelings of guilt (theme A1). When the second theme (B1) becomes too clear, fear might be consciously experienced. The procedure can be reversed with return to A1. Harry can oscillate in terms of conscious and communicative meanings between A1 and B1 without either set of dangerous ideas and emotions being fully experienced.

Harry need not limit switching operations to the two contexts for ideas about bodily damage. He can switch between any permutations of any themes. He can transform, reverse, or undo guilt with fear or anger.[41] He can see himself as victim, then aggressor, then victim, and so forth. These shifts dampen emotional responsivity but reduce cognitive processing of themes.

This does not imply that inhibition of representation will not be found in obsessional Harry or shifts of theme will be absent in hysterical Harry. Obsessional Harry will attempt inhibitions and use his shifts when inhibitory efforts fail. Hysterical Harry might shift from active to passive, as noted earlier, but timing and quality of the shifts would differ. Obsessional Harry would tend to shift more rapidly, with less vagueness at either pole. The shift could occur in midphrase, between an utterance of his and a response from the therapist, or even as virtually simultaneous trains of thought.

It is because of rapid shifts that therapists who attempt clarity with obsessionals may be thwarted in their task. Suppose the therapist makes a clarifying intervention about A1, the survivor guilt theme. Obsessional Harry may have already shifted to B1, his fear of body injury, and thus hear the remarks in a noncongruent state. The clarification procedure may not work well because Harry was not unclear or vague in the first place, is not listening from the earlier position, and will undo the therapist's intervention by further shifts. An interpretation to the effect that Harry fears bodily damage as a retribution for his survivor relief and guilt would be premature since, at this point, he has not fully experienced either the fear or the guilt.

Holding to Context: Important Nuances with Persons Who Have Obsessive Character Style

Holding the obsessional to a topic or to a given context within a topic is equivalent to clarifying for the hysteric. *Metaphorically, the obsessional avoids conceptual time where the hysteric avoids conceptual space. The goal of holding is reduction of shifting, so that the patient can progress further along a given conceptual process.* The patient must also be helped to tolerate the emotions that will be experienced when he cannot quickly divert ideas into and out of conscious awareness.

Holding to context is more complicated than clarification. One begins with at least two current problems, such as the dual themes of A1 and B1 in Harry. When the patient is not shifting with extreme rapidity, the therapist may simply hold the patient to either one or the other theme.

The patient will not comply with this maneuver and the therapist must not confuse "holding" with "forcing." Ferenczi,[42] in an effort to speed up analysis, experimented with various ways to make the obsessional stay on topic until intensely felt emotions occurred. For example, he insisted that his patient develop and maintain visual fantasies relevant to a specific theme. During this technical maneuver his obsessional patients did experience emotions, they even had affective explosions, but the transference complications impeded rather than enhanced the therapy.

The therapist has to shift, even though he attempts to hold the patient to a topic. That is, the therapist shifts at a slower rate than the patient, like a dragging anchor that slows the process. This operation increases the progress of the patient in both directions. That is, with each shift, he is able to go a bit further along the conceptual route of either theme, even though he soon becomes frightened and crowds the theme out of mind with an alternative.

The therapist may use repetitions, as with the hysteric, in order to hold or slow the shift of an obsessional patient. But this use of the same maneuver is done with a different nuance. With the hysteric, the repetition heightens the meaning of what the patient is *now* saying. With the obsessional, the repetition goes back to what the patient was saying *before* the shift away from the context occurred. With the hysteric, the repetition may be short phases. With the obsessional, greater length may be necessary, in order to state the specific context that is being warded off. For example, if Harry is talking about bodily damage and shifts from a survivor guilt context to his fears of injury, then a repetition by the therapist has to link bodily damage specifically to the survivor guilt theme. With the hysteric, such wordy interventions might only diminish clarity.

At times, this more extensive repetition in the obsessional may include the technique of going back to the very beginning of an exchange, retracing the flow carefully, and indicating where extraneous or only vaguely relevant details were introduced by the patient. Reconstructions may add warded off details. This technique has been suggested for long-term character analysis,[31,34] during which defensive operations are interpreted so that the patient increases conscious control and diminishes unconscious restrictions on ideas and feelings. In shorter therapy, aimed at working through a stress, this extensive repetition is still useful, because, during the review by the therapist, the patient attends to the uncomfortable aspects of the topic.

Increased time on the topic allows more opportunity for processing and hence moves the patient toward completion. Emotions aroused by the flow of ideas are more tolerable within the therapeutic relationship than for the patient alone. Also, time on the topic and with the therapist allows continued processing in a communicative state, emphasizing reality and problem solving rather than fantasy and magical belief systems. Identification with and externalization onto the relatively neutral therapist also allows temporary reduction in rigid and harsh introjects that might otherwise deflect thought.

Focusing on details is sometimes a partial deterrent to shifting in the obsessional, just as it may aid clarity with the hysteric. The nuances of focusing on details differ because the purposes differ. In general, the aim with the hysteric is to move from concrete, experiential information, such as images, toward more abstract or more extended meanings, such as word labels for activities and things. The aim with the obsessional is to move from abstract levels, where shifts are facile, to a concrete context. Details act as pegs of meaning in concrete contexts, and make shifts of attitude more difficult. This maneuver utilizes the obsessional's predisposition to details but allows the therapist to specifically select them. Again, the nuance of asking for concrete details is part of the general aim of increasing conceptualization time.

In states where shifts are so rapid as to preclude simple repetition or questioning, the therapist may use a more complex form of repetition. The therapist repeats the event, for example, Harry's intrusive image of the girl's body, and then repeats in a single package the disparate attitudes that the patient oscillates between. For example, the therapist might tell Harry that the image of the girl's body led to two themes. One was the idea of relief at being spared from death that made him feel frightened and guilty. The other was the idea of bodily harm to himself. Were the rate of oscillation less rapid, this form of "packaged" intervention would not be as necessary, since simpler holding operations may be sufficient and the therapist can focus on a single theme.

These efforts by the therapist encroach on the habitual style of the patient. The patient may respond by minimizing or exaggerating the meaning of the intervention. The obsessional is especially vulnerable to threats to his sense of omniscience, especially after traumatic events. If the therapist holds him on a topic, the obsessional senses warded off ideas and feelings and develops uncertainties that cause his self-esteem to fall.

To protect the patient's self-esteem, the therapist uses another technical nuance. He uses questioning to accomplish clarification and topic deepening, even when he has an interpretation in mind. The questions aim the patient toward answers that contain the important, warded off, but now emerging ideas. The obsessional patient can then credit himself with expressing these ideas and experiencing these feelings. The therapist with the hysterical person might, in contrast, interpret at such a moment, using a firm, short delivery, since a question might be followed by vagueness.

To the obsessional, incisive interpretations often mean that the therapist knows something he does not know. A transference bind over dominance and submission arises as the patient either rebels against the interpretation with stubborn denial, accepts it meekly without thinking about it, or both.

Timing is also important with obsessionals working through stress-activated themes. After experience with a given patient, the therapist intuitively knows when a shift is about to take place. At just that moment, or a trifle before, the therapist asks his question. This interrupts the shift and increases conceptual "time and space" on the topic about to be warded off. These technical nuances are put in a crude, broad context in Table 5.4.

Nuances of Relationship with Obsessional Patients in a State of Stress

The oscillation described as sometimes necessary with the hysterical style is not as advisable with the obsessional style. Instead, the therapist creates a safe situation for the patient by remaining stable within his own clear boundaries (e.g., objectivity, compassion, understanding, concern for the truth, or whatever his own personal and professional traits are).

The patient learns the limits of the therapist within this frame. It gives him faith that the therapist will react neither harshly nor seductively. This trust increases *the patient's* breadth of oscillation. He can express more aggressive ideas, if he knows the therapist will neither submit, be injured, compete for dominance, or accuse him of evil. Harry could express more of his bodily

Table 5.4. Some "Defects" of Obsessional Style and Their Counteractants in Therapy

Function	Style as "defect"	Therapeutic counter
Perception	Detailed & factual	Ask for overall impressions and statements about emotional experiences
Representation	Isolation of ideas from emotions	Link emotional meanings to ideational meanings
Translation of images to words	Misses emotional meaning in a rapid transition to partial word meanings	Focus attention on images & felt reactions to them
Associations	Shifts sets of meanings back & forth	Holding operations Interpretations of defense & of warded off meanings
Problem solving	Endless rumination without reaching decisions	Interpretation of reasons for warding off clear decisions

worries when he knew the therapist would not himself feel guilty or overresponsible.

If the therapist changes with the obsessional's tests or needs, then the obsessional worries that he may be too powerful, too weak, or too "sick" for the therapist to handle. Also, the obsessional may use the situation to externalize warded off ideas or even defensive maneuvers. The therapist shifts, not he. This is not to say the obsessional does not, at times, need kindly support after disastrous external events. But his propensity for shifting makes changes in the degree of support more hazardous than a consistent attitude, whether kindly-supportive, neutral-tough, or otherwise.

Suppose the therapist becomes more kindly as Harry goes through a turbulent period of emotional expression of guilt over survival. Harry may experience this as an increase in the therapist's concern or worry for him. He might shift from the "little" suffering position that elicited the therapist's reaction, to a "big" position from which he looks down with contempt at the "worried" therapist.

Similarly, if the therapist is not consistently toughminded, in the ordinary sense of insisting on information and truth-telling, but shifts to this stance only in response to the patient's stubborn evasiveness, then the patient can shift from strong stubbornness to weak, vulnerable self-concepts. Within the context of this shift, the therapist comes to be experienced as hostile, demeaning, and demanding.

Unlike the hysteric, then, *the obsessional's shifts in role and attitude within the therapeutic situation are likely to be out of phase with changes in demeanor of the therapist.* The obsessional can chance further and more lucid swings in state when he senses the stability of the therapist.

Transference resistances will occur in spite of the therapist's effort to maintain a therapeutic relationship. The stability of the therapist will be exaggerated by the patient into an omniscience that he will continually test. When negative transference reactions occur, the therapist will act to resolve those that interfere with the goals of therapy. But some transference reactions will not be negative even though they act as resistances. The hysteric may demand attention and halt progress to get it. The obsessional may take an oppositional stance not so much out of hostility or stubbornness, although such factors will be present, as out of a need to avoid the dangerous intimacy of agreement and cooperation. Since the therapist is not aiming at analysis of transference to effect character change, he need not interpret this process. Instead, with an obsessional patient in an oppositional stance, he may word his interventions to take advantage of the situation.

That is, interventions can be worded, when necessary, in an oppositional manner. Suppose Harry was talking about picking up the girl and the therapist knew he was predisposed to feeling guilty but was warding it off. With a hysterical Harry the therapist might say, "You feel badly about picking up the girl." With an obsessional and cooperative Harry he might say, "Could you be blaming yourself for picking up the girl?" With an oppositional obsessional stance, the therapist might say, "So you don't feel at all badly about picking up the girl." This kind of Harry may disagree and talk of his guilt feelings.

Provided the context is a basically stable therapeutic relationship, one in which the patient has an image of the therapist as objective, kindly, and firmly competent, the inflection need not be the sincere, neutral, firm tone helpful with hysterics. *Slight* sarcasm or *mild* humor may help the obsessional Harry assume a tough position while trying out his own tender ideas.[34]

By sternness, as implied in the above comments, the therapist may have the effect of "ordering" the obsessional to contemplate warded off ideas. This seeming unkindness is kind in that it removes responsibility from the patient and permits him to think the unthinkable. But this sternness, mild sarcasm, or slight humor has to remain a relatively consistent characteristic of the therapist.

This is not as difficult as it may sound, for *these nuances involve what the therapist allows himself to do or not do in natural response to the situation. They are not assumed or artificial roles or traits.* For some therapists, kindliness, openness, gentleness, and a nonjudgmental air are preferable nuances to any toughness, sternness, sarcasm, or humor and may accomplish the same purpose. These latter remarks are meant more as illustrations than assertions because it is here that we encounter that blurred border between the "science" and "art" of psychotherapy.

CONCLUSIONS

This report has taken a state of stress, considered the variations between two dispositional types within that state, and discussed the nuances of psychodynamic psychotherapy aimed at symptom relief. These dimensions, state, typology, and mode of treatment, define a frame of reference. Assertions have been made that are clearly positioned within this frame of reference. For example, stress response syndromes have been characterized by phases of denial and intrusion, hysterical persons have been described as using inhibition of representation to ward off intrusive and repetitive ideas and feelings, and clarity has been posited as an important nuance of their therapy. Obsessional persons were characterized by switching operations for the same purpose and holding operations were asserted to be important nuances of technique in their therapy.

Such assertions involve standard psychiatric knowledge. What is gained through this model is an organization for the systematic assemblage of such knowledge. With clear conceptual positionings of assertions, many of the arguments and divergencies that characterize psychiatry and psychology would fall away in favor of renewed empirical observation and formulation. The key is comparable rather than incongruous levels of abstraction.

To the extent that the model is worthwhile, the assertions here can be specifically challenged. General stress response tendencies may not follow the pathways defined, there may be better ways to typologize what was called "hysterical" and "obsessional," the nuances of focused psychodynamic psychotherapy described may be incomplete or inappropriate. A specific site of disagreement can be localized by following the same dimensions. For example, *an argument about a nuance of treatment would have to be connected with a specific kind of person, in an intrusive-repetitive phase after a stressful external event, involved in psychodynamic treatment aimed at relief of intrusions and resolution of the state of stress.*

While this type of model localizes conceptualization, it may be argued that it defines restrictively small areas. Within the general field of psychopathology and psychotherapy there would be multitudes of such areas. I believe that the field is so large that many specific subdivisions are indicated, and that knowledge will be accumulated and clarified by this method. The complexity is not overwhelming. The present model can be extended by keeping any two dimensions constant while extending the boundaries of the third. For example, extensions may involve other variations of personality, other versions of pathological states, and other views of therapy.

Variations in typology would include narcissistic, schizoid, impulsive, and paranoid personalities. Each would be contrasted with hysterical and obsessional styles of response to stressful life events. Each would be considered in the context of brief dynamic therapy aimed at working through the life event and so central conceptual anchoring would be maintained.

Variations in state would include other formulations of the meaning of a crisis episode. For example, a contrasting view within the framework of brief psychodynamic therapy regards the life events as secondary in importance to enduring conflicts. The predominant state is seen as character patterns rather than phases of stress response. Separation from a lover would be seen as an occasion to work further on dependency-independency conflicts present for a long time.[43,44] Would the same nuances of treatment for varying styles apply in therapy oriented toward character conflicts?

Variations in treatment would maintain the set of stress response syndromes in certain common character types. Other technical approaches would provide contrasting points of view. For example, a behavior therapist would discuss treatment of such intrusive images as noted in Harry. He might advocate such approaches as systematic desensitization and implosion.[45] Learning theory hypotheses would be advanced equivalent to the repetition-until-completion tendency described in this paper. A rationale of treatment would be based on these hypotheses. Assertions would be advanced about how systematic desensitization and implosion work. The behavior therapist might assert that desensitization would be more suitable for hysterical styles because there is a progressive clarification of anxiety-provoking representations and a supportive patient-therapist relationship. He might prefer implosive techniques for obsessional styles, as this method can hold attention to a specific aspect of an ideational complex, provoke emotional response, and engage the patient in a "tough" appearing role-relationship.

These nuances of techniques within a behavior therapy point of view could then be contrasted with the assertions of the dynamic point of view, as well as with other technical possibilities. Nuances across schools might be developed. Hysterical vagueness might be seen as altered by any clarification technique such as role playing, psychodrama, transactional analysis, or gestalt therapy. Obsessional shifting of topics might be seen as altered by any holding technique such as systematic desensitization, implosion, or guided imagery techniques. Contrary assertions would, at least, be assembled at similar levels of abstraction. Disagreements could be resolved by further observation of given types of persons in a given state. In this way we might hope to pass beyond brand names as our professional disagreements become productive rather than schismatic.

REFERENCES

1. Miller GA, Galanter E, Pribram K: *Plans and the Structure of Behavior.* New York, Henry Holt & Co Inc, 1960.

2. Horowitz MJ: *Image Formation and Cognition.* New York, Appleton-Century-Crofts Inc. 1970.

3. Peterfreund E: Information systems and psychoanalysis: An evolutionary, biological approach to psychoanalytic theory. *Psychol Issues* 7:1–397, 1971.

4. Freud S, Breuer J: Studies on hysteria, in Strachey J (ed): *Standard Edition.* London, Hogarth Press, 1957, vol 2, pp 185–305.

5. Grinker K, Spiegal S: *Men Under Stress.* Philadelphia, Blakiston, 1945.

6. Freud S: Beyond the pleasure principle (1920), in Strachey J (ed): *Standard Edition.* London, Hogarth Press, 1953, vol 18, pp 7–64.

7. Furst SS: Psychic Trauma: A survey, in Furst SS (ed): *Psychic Trauma.* New York, Basic Books Inc, 1967.

8. Horowitz MJ, Becker SS: Cognitive response to stress: Experimental studies of a compulsion to repeat trauma, in Holt R, Peterfreund E (eds): *Psychoanalysis and Contemporary Science.* New York, Macmillan Co, vol 1, 1972, pp 258–305.

9. Hamburg DA, Adams JE: A perspective on coping behavior: Seeking and utilizing information in major transitions. *Arch Gen Psychiatry* 17:277–284, 1967.

10. Lifton RJ: *History and Human Survival.* New York, Vantage Books, 1967.

11. Horowitz MJ: Phase oriented treatment of stress response syndromes. *Am J Psychother* 27:506–515, 1973.

12. Davis DR: *An Introduction to Psychopathology.* London, Oxford University Press, 1966.

13. Lazarus RS: *Psychological Stress and the Coping Process.* New York, McGraw-Hill Book Co Inc, 1966.

14. Janis IL: *Stress and Frustration.* New York, Harcourt-Brace-Javanovich, 1969.

15. Bowlby J, Parkes CM: Separation and loss within the family, in Anthony EJ, Kopernik C (eds): *The International Yearbook for Child Psychiatry and Allied Disciplines*. New York, John Wiley & Sons Inc, 1970, pp 197–215.

16. Freud S: On the psychical mechanism of hysterical phenomena, in Strachey J (ed): *Standard Edition*. London, Hogarth Press, 1962, vol 3, pp 25–39.

17. Freud S: Inhibitions, symptoms and anxiety, in Strachey J (ed): *Standard Edition*. London, Hogarth Press, 1959, vol 20, pp 87–172.

18. Appelgarth A: Comments on aspects of the theory of psychic energy. *J Am Psychoanal Assoc* 19:379–416, 1971.

19. French T: *The Integration of Behavior, Volume 1: Basic Postulates*. Chicago, University of Chicago Press, 1952.

20. Lazarus RS, Averill JR, Opton EM: Towards a cognitive theory of emotion, in *Feelings and Emotions*. New York, Academic Press Inc, 1970.

21. Pribram KH: Emotion: Steps toward a neuropsychological theory, in Glass D (ed): *Neurophysiology and Emotion*. New York, Rockefeller University Press and Russell Sage Foundation, 1967.

22. Bibring E: Psychoanalysis and the dynamic psychotherapies. *J Am Psychoanal Assoc* 2:745–770, 1954.

23. Greenson R: The working alliance and the transference neurosis. *Psychoanal Q* 34:155–181, 1965.

24. Janet P: *The Major Symptoms of Hysteria*. New York, Hafner Publishing Co, 1965.

25. Easser BR, Lesser SR: Hysterical personality: A re-evaluation. *Psychoanal Q* 34:390–405, 1965.

26. Marmor J: Orality in the hysterical personality. *J Am Psychoanal Assoc* 1:656–675, 1953.

27. Ludwig AM: Hysteria: A neurobiological theory. *Arch Gen Psychiatry* 27:771–777, 1972.

28. Shapiro D: *Neurotic Styles*. New York, Basic Books Inc, 1965.

29. Lazare A: The hysterical character in psychoanalytic theory: Evolution and Confusion. *Arch Gen Psychiatry* 25:131–137, 1971.

30. Sandler J: The background of safety. *Int J Psychoanal* 41:352–356, 1960.

31. Weiss J: The emergence of new themes: A contribution to the psychoanalytic theory of therapy. *Int J Psychoanal* 52:459–467, 1971.

32. Abraham K: A short study of the development of the libido, viewed in the light of mental disorders, in *Selected Papers*. London, Hogarth Press, 1942.

33. Freud S: Notes upon a case of obsessional neurosis, in *Collected Papers*. London, Hogarth Press, 1949, vol 3.

34. Salzman L: *The Obsessive Personality*. New York, Science House, 1968.

35. Sampson H, Weiss J, Mlodnosky L, et al: Defense analysis and the emergence of warded-off mental contents: An empirical study. *Arch Gen Psychiatry* 26:524–532, 1972.

36. Weiss J: The integration of defenses. *Int J Psychoanal* 48:520–524, 1967.

37. Barnett J: Therapeutic intervention in the dysfunctional thought processes of the obsessional. *Am J Psychotherapy* 26:338–351, 1972.

38. Schwartz E K: The treatment of the obsessive patient in the group therapy setting. *Am J Psychotherapy* 26:352–361, 1972.

39. Silverman JS: Obsessional disorders in childhood and adolescence. *Am J Psychotherapy* 26:362–377, 1972.

40. Klein GS: Peremptory ideation: Structure and force in motivated ideas. *Psychol Issues* 5:80–128, 1967.

41. Jones E: Fear, guilt and hate. *Int J Psychoanal* 10:383–397, 1929.

42. Ferenczi S: *Further Contributions to the Theory and Technique of Psychoanalysis.* London, Hogarth Press and the Institute of Psychoanalysis, 1950.

43. Sifneos PE: *Short-Term Psychotherapy and Emotional Crisis.* Cambridge, Mass, Harvard University Press, 1972.

44. Mann J: *Time Limited Psychotherapy.* Cambridge, Mass, Harvard University Press, 1973.

45. Yates AO: *Behavior Therapy.* New York, John Wiley & Sons Inc, 1970.

6. Interpersonal Psychotherapy for Depression

Gerald L. Klerman, Myrna M. Weissman, Bruce Rounsaville, and Eve S. Chevron

THEORETICAL AND EMPIRICAL BASES

Interpersonal psychotherapy (IPT) is a psychological treatment especially designed and evaluated for depressed patients. It is a short-term, time-limited psychotherapy which focuses on the patient's current interpersonal relations. While genetic, biochemical, developmental, and personality factors have a role in the vulnerability to depression, clinical depression occurs in an interpersonal context. The authors are convinced, based on clinical experience and research evidence, that psychotherapeutic intervention directed at this interpersonal context will facilitate the patient's recovery from the acute episode and may possibly have preventive effects against relapse and recurrence.

Theoretical Basis

The theoretical basis for IPT derives from the interpersonal school of psychiatry, a distinctly American contribution to psychiatry and mental health. The earliest theoretical source was Adolf Meyer, whose psychobiological approach to understanding psychiatric disorders placed great emphasis on the patient's experiences (Meyer, 1957). In contrast to Kraepelin's concept of disease entities, derived from continental European psychiatry, Meyer applied Darwin's concept of adaptation to understanding psychiatric illness. Meyer saw psychiatric illnesses as part of the patient's attempt to adapt to the environment, usually the psychosocial environment, and considered that a patient's particular response to environmental changes reflected early developmental experiences, especially experiences in the family and social groups.

Among Meyer's associates, Harry Stack Sullivan stands out for his articulation of the theory of interpersonal relations. His writings linked clinical

Reprinted by permission of American Psychiatric Association Press, Washington, D.C., from *Psychiatry Update* 3(1984):56–67.

psychiatry to anthropology, sociology, and social psychology (Sullivan, 1953a; 1953b). Sullivan asserted that psychiatry is the scientific study of people and interpersonal processes, as distinct from the exclusive study of mind, society, or brain. In its emphasis on interpersonal and social factors in the understanding and treatment of the depressive disorders, IPT has drawn from the work of many other clinicians, especially the work of Fromm-Reichmann (1960) and Cohen et al. (1954) and more recently that of Arieti and Bemporad (1978). Becker (1974) and Chodoff (1970) are also among those who have emphasized the social roots of depression and the need to attend to the interpersonal aspects of the disorder, and Frank (1973) has stressed the general importance in psychotherapy of focusing on current interpersonal situations.

Empirical Basis

The empirical basis for the interpersonal approach to depression derives from several areas of research, including ethological and experimental work with animals, developmental research with children, and clinical and epidemiologic studies of adults.

Attachment theory has emphasized that the most intense human emotions are associated with the formation, disruption, and renewal of affectional attachment bonds. Based on findings of the animal ethologists, Bowlby studied mother-child relationships, and he demonstrated that attachment bonds were important in human functioning and that their disruption made individuals vulnerable to depression or despair (Bowlby, 1969). The individual learns to form these bonds largely through experience within the family, especially, but not exclusively, during early childhood. Bowlby's work has since been extended by Rutter (1972), who showed that relationships other than those between the mother and child have an impact on the formation of attachment bonds. The related work of Henderson and his colleagues (1978a; 1978b; 1978c) has shown that a deficiency of social bonds in an individual's current environment is associated with neurotic distress. Based on these observations, Bowlby (1977) has more recently proposed a rationale for interpersonal psychotherapy. Psychotherapy should assist the patient in examining current interpersonal relationships and how these relationships are based on experiences with attachment figures in childhood, adolescence, and adulthood.

Focusing on one aspect of attachment bonds, Brown et al. (1977) examined confiding relationships in connection with the development of depression. In a community survey of women living in the Camberwell section of London, they found that the presence of an intimate, confiding relationship with a man, usually the spouse, was an important protection against developing a depression in the face of life stress.

A considerable body of research has demonstrated a relationship between "stress," usually studied as recent life events, and the onset of psychiatric illness, particularly depression. The studies of the Yale group are most relevant to understanding stressful life events and depression (Klerman, 1979; Paykel et al., 1969). Exits of persons from the social field occurred more frequently with depressed patients than with normal subjects in the six months prior to the onset of depression. This group also found that marital friction was the most common stress reported by depressed patients prior to the onset of depression. Several studies relate to the emotional consequences of marital disputes, separation, and divorce, linking marital disruption with a wide variety of emotional disorders, including depression (Bloom et al., 1978). Ilfeld (1977) made similar observations in a survey of about 3,000 adults in Chicago. Depressive symptoms were closely related to stress, particularly to stress in marriage and, less frequently, to the stresses of parenting. In another study, chronic problems within intact marriages were as likely to produce distress and depressive symptoms as was the total disruption of the marriage by divorce or separation (Pearlin and Lieberman, 1977).

Impaired interpersonal relations can thus predispose to or precipitate mental disorders; at the same time, mental disorders have been found to produce interpersonal deficits. The impairment in close interpersonal relations of depressed women has been studied in considerable detail (Weissman and Paykel, 1974). Depressed women are considerably impaired in most aspects of their role functioning, as workers, wives, mothers, family members, and friends. This role impairment is greatest with close family members, particularly spouses and children, with whom considerable hostility, disaffection, and poor communication were evident. With recovery from symptoms, most, but not all, of the social impairments are diminished. Marital relationships often remain chronically unhappy and easily disrupted.

There has been debate about whether the marked difficulties associated with depression are antecedents or consequences of the disorder (Briscoe and Smith, 1973). Studying the interactions of depressed patients and normal subjects, Coyne (1976) has demonstrated that depressed patients characteristically elicit unhelpful responses from others.

Empirical findings add to the theoretical rationale for an interpersonal approach to understanding depression and for a psychotherapeutic approach based on interpersonal concepts. The research has documented both the importance of close and satisfactory attachments in the prevention of depression and the role of disrupted attachments in the development of depression.

PSYCHOTHERAPEUTIC GOALS

IPT assumes that the episode of clinical depression has three component processes. (1) *Symptom formation,* the development of depressive affect and other symptoms, stems from psychobiological and/or psychological mechanisms. (2) *Social and interpersonal relations,* which are based on learning from childhood experiences, concurrent social reinforcement, and/or personal mastery and competence, are disrupted, usually by an event. (3) *Personality problems* form part of the person's predisposition to depressive symptom episodes, particularly enduring traits such as inhibited expression of anger, guilt, poor psychological communication with significant others, and/or difficulty with self-esteem. IPT intervenes in the first two of these three processes, symptom formation and social and interpersonal relations. Because of IPT's relatively brief duration and low level of psychotherapeutic intensity, IPT is not expected to have a marked impact upon enduring aspects of personality structure, although personality functioning is assessed. While some longer-term psychotherapies have been designed to achieve personality change using the interpersonal approach (Arieti and Bemporad, 1978), these treatments have not been assessed in controlled trials.

IPT facilitates recovery from acute depression by relieving depressive symptoms and by helping the patient become more effective in dealing with those current interpersonal problems that are associated with the onset of symptoms. Symptom relief begins with helping the patient understand that the vague and uncomfortable symptoms are part of a known syndrome, which is well described, understood, and relatively common, and which responds to a variety of treatments and has a good prognosis. Psychopharmacologic approaches may be used in conjunction with IPT to alleviate symptoms more rapidly. Improvement in interpersonal relations begins with exploring which of four problem areas commonly associated with the onset of depression—grief, role disputes, role transition, or interpersonal deficits— is related to this particular patient's depression. IPT then focuses on the particular interpersonal problem as it relates to the onset of depression.

In the authors' experience, the psychotherapy of depressed patients has paid insufficient attention to techniques for reducing symptoms, for facilitating the patient's current social adjustment, and for improving interpersonal relations. With IPT, personality reconstruction is not attempted in the symptomatic state; instead, the technique emphasizes reassurance, clarification of emotional states, improvement of interpersonal communication, testing of perceptions, and performance in interpersonal settings. These techniques are conventionally grouped under the rubric of "supportive psychotherapy." In the authors' view, however, the term supportive psychotherapy is a misnomer. Most of what is called supportive psychotherapy attempts to assist the patient to modify interpersonal relations, to change perceptions and cognitions, and to reward behavioral contingencies.

PHASES IN IPT

As shown in Table 6.1, the conduct of IPT is best discussed in terms of three phases. The three phases include (1) an early phase devoted to assessment and the negotiation of the therapeutic contract, (2) a middle phase, which has the longest duration and which entails psychotherapeutic work on one or another of the four problem areas, and (3) the termination phase.

The Early Phase

The tasks of the early phase are to deal with the depression, to assess the interpersonal problems, and to negotiate a mutually agreeable therapeutic contract.

The first task, *dealing with the depression,* has a high priority during the early phase. To accomplish this, six more specific tasks are recommended.

First, the symptoms should be reviewed systematically, going through the DSM-III inclusion and exclusion criteria. A structured interview such as the SADS, DIS, or SKID is often helpful. The time course of a current episode should be reconstructed, with attention to the current sequence of symptoms, their intensity, and their characteristics. Assessment should also inquire into any current life event that may relate to the onset of the episode. A family history should be taken, with a systematic inquiry into the medical and

Table 6.1. Phases and Tasks in the Conduct of IPT

Phases	Tasks

EARLY	Treatment of depressive symptoms
	    Review of symptoms
	    Confirmation of diagnosis
	    Communication of diagnosis to patient
	    Evaluation of medication need
	    Education of patient about depression (epidemiology, symptoms,
	        clinical causes, treatments, prognosis)
	    Legitimation of patient's "sick role"
	Assessment of interpersonal relations
	    Inventory of current relationships
	    Choice of interpersonal problem area
	Therapeutic contract
	    Statement of goals, diagnosis, problem area
	    Medication plan
	    Agreement

MIDDLE	Treatment focusing on problem area
	    Grief reaction
	    Interpersonal disputes
	    Role transition
	    Interpersonal deficits

TERMINATION	

psychiatric status of all first-degree relatives, particularly parents, siblings, and offspring.

Second, the diagnostic possibilities should be assessed using standard operational criteria, particularly DSM-III. Differential diagnosis from anxiety conditions and alcoholism should receive particular attention. Within the DSM-III category of Affective Disorders, an attempt should be made to assign the patient to one of the subcategories such as Bipolar Disorder, Major Depression, or Dysthymic Disorder. Within Major Depression, attention should be given to the presence or absence of delusions and melancholic symptoms.

Third, if the patient does meet the criteria for a DSM-III diagnosis, the patient should hear the diagnosis confirmed with a statement such as, "We have reviewed your symptoms, and it appears that you meet the criteria for [diagnosis] and that you should receive treatment for this."

Fourth, as the symptoms and diagnosis are considered, the possible value of medication should be assessed. With IPT, in contrast to many other forms of psychotherapy, the authors do not believe that medication is theoretically or clinically contraindicated. Medication is indicated when the patient's symptoms are of sufficient intensity and when the syndrome shows features of the melancholic pattern or delusional symptoms. The authors have found that melancholic and delusional patients do not respond to psychotherapy alone, but will respond to the combination of medication and IPT.

Fifth, during one of the early interviews, the patient should receive explicit information about the nature of depression as a clinical condition and should learn something about its symptom pattern, frequency, and clinical course and about the alternative treatments and essentially good prognosis for depression. Many patients will have read about depression in the lay literature or in such books as *Moodswing* (Fieve, 1975) or *Unfinished Business* (Scarf, 1980).

Sixth, and finally, this whole process legitimizes the patient in the sick role. The authors place IPT, unlike other psychotherapies, in the general medical model and believe that an important part of the therapeutic improvement comes from the patient being legitimized in the sick role. Efforts should be made, nonetheless, to minimize dependency. If the patient is in the labor force, treatment should encourage the patient to keep working. The patient should also maintain a reasonable schedule of social and family activities. The tendency to withdraw socially and to avoid activity should be countered by explicit suggestion.

The second major task of the early phase is *assessment of the interpersonal problem area,* with a systematic inventory of the significant persons in the patient's current and past life. This assessment especially emphasizes the current relationships, their stability, and their possible disruption. On the basis of this, one can often make a judgment about which of the four problem areas is associated with the patient's depression and which requires further therapeutic work.

The formation of *the therapeutic contract* with the statement of goals constitutes the third and final main task of the first phase. When the other two tasks are completed, the patient should receive an explicit statement reiterating the diagnosis of the depressive symptoms and identifying the interpersonal problem area. If the patient agrees on both of these matters, a treatment plan should be proposed, including a medication plan where appropriate, and focusing on the interpersonal problem. The proposal to the patient might say, "There is good evidence that episodes of depression like yours are often related to interpersonal problems, and your problem seems to be [statement of interpersonal problem]. If you agree, we will work on these issues over the next few months."

The Middle Phase: Problem Areas and Treatment Tasks

Previous research indicates general and specific techniques for dealing with each of the four interpersonal problem areas in IPT—abnormal grief reaction, interpersonal role disputes, role transition, and interpersonal deficits.

Many depressions involve an *abnormal grief reaction*. This is not identical with normal bereavement, which is usually self-limiting and has approximately six to nine months' duration of symptoms, with a shorter period of social disability. Most people experiencing grief adapt without professional assistance. However, about 15 percent of patients have symptoms that persist beyond six to nine months, and others have anniversary reactions.

The tasks in treating abnormal grief reactions are to facilitate the mourning process which has been suppressed, delayed, or prolonged, to assist the patient with establishing new relationships, and to offer an attachment which may serve as a partial and temporary substitute for the lost relationship with the significant other. Along with these tasks, IPT with grief reactions entails reconstruction of the relationship with the dead person, with special attention to the patient's expression of positive and negative affects, unfulfilled expectations, and any guilt or self-remorse.

In clinical practice, *interpersonal role disputes* are among the interpersonal difficulties most commonly associated with depression, particularly for women. Role disputes develop when the patient and at least one significant other have nonreciprocal expectations about their role interactions and relationships. Specifically, they take the form of marital disputes, disputes between parent and child, disputes between work colleagues, or disputes within the extended family or friendship network.

The first treatment task with interpersonal role disputes is to help the patient identify the existence of a dispute and the issues involved. Since such disputes are very often masked, simply identifying the existence of a dispute and relating it to the onset and perpetuation of the depression can be of considerable assistance to a depressed patient (Spiegel, 1957). The task then is to guide and encourage the patient in examining and choosing alternative courses of action, which will include renegotiating the relationship and modifying any maladaptive communication patterns and expectations. The most important task is to facilitate the renegotiation of role expectations between the patient and the significant other. Often, as with a marital dispute, this can be accomplished best by bringing the other person into the session. When disputes require negotiations that cannot take place in the therapeutic session, as with disputes involving occupations and friends, IPT will entail the ongoing monitoring of the interactions.

Role transitions occur normally with the life changes that require a person to move from one social role to another. The developmental life cycle often includes such changes as graduating from high school or college, leaving home for college, entering the military, entering the labor force, being promoted or demoted, losing a job, having a child, changing residency, and retiring. Most people adapt to these role transitions with minimal difficulty. Some develop depressive symptoms, however, which under DSM-III may be considered an Adjustment Disorder with Depressed Mood or a Major Depressive Episode. Those who fail to cope adequately with transitions and develop symptoms often experience the role transition as a loss, and accordingly some psychodynamic theorists have interpreted these transitions as being akin to grief and bereavement. For work with IPT, however, the authors believe that grief reactions and role transitions should be distinguished.

IPT with the patient whose depression is related to a role transition includes the task of enabling the patient to regard the new role in a positive, less restricted manner and to view it as opportunity for growth. Other tasks are to restore self-esteem by encouraging the patient's sense of mastery and to explore the positive and negative aspects of the previous role. Disruptions of previous interpersonal relations with work colleagues, friends, and family are also explored, and the patient is helped to initiate new relationships and to examine the repertoire of social skills that may be involved in the new role.

Interpersonal deficits constitute the fourth and final area of IPT's focus. People often lack the skills for initiating or sustaining interpersonal relations. Some have the skills to initiate relationships, but cannot sustain them, particularly the close attachments that require commitment, intimacy, and expectations of fidelity and loyalty. Others have trouble initiating relationships because they lack the repertoire of skills and are shy, isolated, and lonely. In the authors' experience, depressed patients whose symptoms are associated with social isolation tend to have more severe disturbances, and IPT has been less successful with these patients. Long-term treatment is often necessary, to work on their underlying personality problems and to help them develop new social skills.

In IPT with patients who have interpersonal deficits, one can expect to accomplish the preliminary task of helping the patient identify past positive relationships and experiences which may serve as a model. Patients may also be guided to consider opportunities for forming new relationships. Beyond this, the techniques and therapeutic maneuvers for helping such patients cannot be detailed in this brief discussion. A manual has been available in unpublished form for some time (Klerman et al., 1979) and has recently been elaborated in a published volume (Klerman et al., 1984).

IPT COMPARED WITH OTHER PSYCHOTHERAPIES

The authors agree with Jerome Frank (1973) that the procedures and techniques in many of the different psychotherapies have much in common. Many of the therapies emphasize helping the patient to develop a sense of mastery, combating social isolation, restoring the patient's feeling of group belonging, and helping the patient to rediscover meaning in life. The psychotherapies differ, however, on whether the patient's problems lie in the far past, the immediate past, or the present.

IPT focuses primarily on the patient's present, and it differs from other psychotherapies in its limited duration and its attention to current depressive symptoms and the current depression-related interpersonal context. Given this frame of reference, IPT includes a systematic review of the patient's current relations with significant others. IPT also differs in that it was developed for the treatment of a single group of disorders—the depressive disorders. Table 6.2 summarizes the similarities and differences in the approaches of IPT and other psychotherapies.

IPT is *time-limited and not long-term*. Considerable research has demonstrated the value for most patients' current problems and for most symptom states of short-term, time-limited psychotherapies (usually once a week for less than 9 to 12 months). While long-term treatment may still be required for changing personality dysfunctions, particularly maladaptive interpersonal and cognitive patterns, and for ameliorating or replacing dysfunctional social skills, evidence for the efficacy of long-term psychotherapy is limited. Long-term treatment also has the inherent potential disadvantages of promoting dependency and reinforcing avoidance behavior. Psychotherapies that are short-term or time-limited aim to minimize these adverse effects.

IPT is *focused and not open-ended*. In common with other brief psychotherapies, IPT focuses on one or two problem areas in the patient's current interpersonal functioning, and these are agreed upon by the patient and the psychotherapist after several evaluation sessions. The content of sessions is therefore focused and not open-ended.

IPT deals with *current and not past interpersonal relationships.* The IPT therapist focuses the sessions on the patient's immediate social context, as it was just before and as it has been since the onset of the current depressive episode. Past depressive episodes, early family relationships, and previous significant relationships and friendship patterns are, however, assessed in order to understand overall patterns in the patient's interpersonal relationships.

IPT is concerned with *interpersonal, not intrapsychic* phenomena. In exploring current interpersonal problems with the patient, the psychotherapist may observe the operation of intrapsychic defense mechanisms such as projection, denial, isolation, undoing, or repression. In IPT, however, the psychotherapist does not work on helping the patient see the current situation as a manifestation of internal conflict. Rather, the therapist explores the patient's behavior in terms of interpersonal relations. The example of how dreams are handled is analogous. Although the therapist does not usually ask the patient to recall dreams, patients may spontaneously report them. When this occurs, the psychotherapist may work on the dream by relating its manifest content and associated affects to relevant current interpersonal problems.

IPT is concerned with *interpersonal relationships, not cognitive-behavioral phenomena* per se. IPT attempts to change how the patient thinks, feels, and acts in problematic interpersonal relationships. Specific negative cognitions or behaviors such as lack of assertiveness and lack of social skills are not in themselves a treatment focus in IPT. They are considered only in relationship to significant persons in the patient's life and for the ways that they impinge upon these interpersonal relationships.

In common with cognitive-behavioral therapy, IPT is concerned with the patient's distorted thinking about him or herself and others and with the relevant options for change. The IPT therapist may work with the patient about his or her distorted thinking by calling attention to discrepancies between what the patient is saying and doing or between the patient's standards and those of society in general. Unlike cognitive-behavioral therapies, however, IPT does not attempt systematically to uncover such distorted thoughts, give homework, or prescribe methods of developing alternative thought patterns. Rather, the IPT psychotherapist calls the patient's attention to distorted thinking in relation to significant others as the evidence arises during the psychotherapy. The IPT psychotherapist will often visit with the patient to explore the effect of his or her maladaptive thinking on interpersonal relationships.

In IPT, *personality is recognized but is not the focus*. The patient's personality is very frequently the major focus in psychotherapy. IPT does not expect to make an impact on personality. It recognizes, but does not focus on, the patient's personality characteristics. Moreover, IPT does not make the assumption that persons who become depressed have unique personality traits. This assumption is still questionable and requires further testing; so far, research on this question has not yielded any conclusive answers.

IPT AND PSYCHODYNAMIC THEORY

The authors' goal in developing IPT was not to create a new psychotherapy, but to make explicit and operational a systematic approach to depression and to base that approach on accepted theory and empirical evidence. Much of IPT resembles what many, perhaps most, psychoanalytic and dynamic psychotherapists do. This reflects the extent to which the interpersonal approach has permeated American psychotherapeutic practice, a trend whose historical roots are probably twofold. In the first place, most of the founding psychotherapists and practitioners of the interpersonal approach, including Sullivan, Fromm-Reichmann, Cohen, and Stanton, were initially trained in Freudian psychoanalysis. While they disagreed with some aspects of psychoanalytic theory and practice, the role of early childhood experience and the existence of unconscious mental processes were not the sources of this disagreement. Their disagreement arose over the existence of libido, the dual instinct theory (eros and death instincts), and the relative importance of biological, instinctive forces, compared with social and cultural influences, on personal development and current functioning. A second historical force was the expansion of psychotherapy following World War II, which coincided with widespread national concerns about social change, racial and sexual equality, personal well-being, and the enhancement of personal potential and individual happiness. Such cultural values are highly compatible with scientific and professional pursuits that focus on interpersonal relations and personal development throughout the life cycle.

For purposes of theoretical clarity and research design, the authors have nonetheless often found it useful to highlight the differences between the

Table 6.2. Comparison of IPT with other psychotherapies

	IPT	Other psychotherapies
ASSESSMENT QUESTIONS	What has contributed to this patient's depression right now?	Why did the patient become what he or she is, and/or where is the patient going?
	What are the current stresses?	What was the patient's childhood like?
	Who are the key persons involved in the current stress?	What is the patient's character?
	What are the patient's current disputes and disappointments?	
	What are the patient's assets?	What are the patient's defenses?
TREATMENT QUESTIONS	How can I help the patient clarify his or her wishes and have more satisfying relationships with others?	How can I understand the patient's fantasy life and help the patient get insight into the origins of his or her behavior?
	How can I help the patient ventilate and unburden himself or herself of painful emotions (i.e., guilt, shame, resentment)?	How can I find out why this patient feels guilty, shameful, or resentful?
	How can I correct misinformation and suggest alternatives?	How can I help the patient discover false or incorrect ideas on his or her own?
OUTCOME QUESTION	Is the patient learning how to cope with the problem?	Is the patient cured?

interpersonal and the psychodynamic approaches to human behavior and mental illness. The essential focus of a pure psychodynamic approach is on unconscious mental processes and the role of intrapsychic memories, wishes, fantasies, and conflicts in determining behavior and psychopathology. The essential focus of a pure interpersonal approach is on social roles and interpersonal interactions in the individual's past and current life experiences. Both the interpersonal and the psychodynamic approaches are concerned with the person's life span and the important role of early experiences and persistent personality patterns at all developmental stages and in all areas of personal functioning. However, in understanding personal functioning, the psychodynamic psychotherapist is concerned with object relations, while the interpersonal psychotherapist is concerned with interpersonal relations. Put another way, the psychodynamic psychotherapist listens for the patient's intrapsychic wishes and conflicts, while the interpersonal psychotherapist listens for the patient's role expectations and disputes.

A comprehensive theory would ideally incorporate both these approaches, along with biological, behavioral, and other views. Given the current state of knowledge, however, the authors believe it timely and valuable to focus clearly on one approach, to explore its validity, and to examine its utility through systematic research, especially through controlled trials of efficacy and other outcomes.

REFERENCES

Arieti S, Bemporad J: Severe and Mild Depression. The Psychotherapeutic Approach. New York, Basic Books, 1978.

Becker J: Depression: Theory and Research. New York, John Wiley & Sons, 1974.

Bloom BL, Asher SJ, White S W: Marital disruption as a stressor: A review and analysis. Psychol Bull 85:867–894, 1978.

Bowlby J: Attachment and Loss, vol 1: Attachment. New York, Basic Books, 1969.

Bowlby J: The making and breaking of affectional bonds: II. Some principles of psychotherapy. Br J Psychiatry 130:421–431, 1977.

Briscoe CW, Smith JB: Depression and marital turmoil. Arch Gen Psychiatry 28:811–817, 1973.

Brown GW, Harris T, Copeland JR: Depression and loss. Br J Psychiatry 130:1–18, 1977.

Chodoff P: The core problem in depression, in Science and Psychoanalysis. Edited by Masserman J. New York, Grune & Stratton, 1970.

Cohen MB, Blake G, Cohen R, Fromm-Reichmann F, Weigert E: An intensive study of twelve cases of manic-depressive psychosis. Psychiatry 17:103–137, 1954.

Coyne JC: Depression and the response of others. J Abnorm Psychol 85:186–193, 1976.

Fieve RR: Moodswing. New York, Bantam Books, 1975.

Frank J: Persuasion and Healing: A Comparative Study of Psychotherapy. Baltimore, Johns Hopkins University Press, 1973.

Fromm-Reichmann F: Principles of Intensive Psychotherapy. Chicago, Phoenix Books, 1960.

Henderson S, Duncan-Jones P, McAuley H, Ritchie K: The patient's primary group. Br J Psychiatry 132:74–86, 1978a.

Henderson S, Duncan-Jones P, Byrne DG, Scott R, Adcock S: Social bonds, adversity, and neurosis. Presented at World Psychiatric Association, Comm on Epidemiology and Community Psychiatry, St. Louis, Oct 18–20, 1978b.

Henderson S, Byrne DG., Duncan-Jones P, Adcock S, Scott R, Steele GP: Social bonds in the epidemiology of neurosis. Br J Psychiatry 132:463–466, 1978c.

Ilfeld FW: Current social stressors and symptoms of depression. Am J Psychiatry 134:161–166, 1977.

Klerman GL: Stress, adaptation and affective disorders, in Stress and Mental Disorder. Edited by Barrett JE, Rose RM, Klerman GL. New York, Raven Press, 1979.

Klerman GL, Rounsaville BJ, Chevron ES, Neu C, Weissman MM: Manual for Short-Term Interpersonal Psychotherapy (IPT) of Depression. Unpublished manuscript, fourth draft, June 1979.

Klerman GL, Weissman MM, Rounsaville BJ, Chevron ES: Interpersonal Psychotherapy of Depression. New York, Basic Books, 1984.

Meyer A: Psychobiology: A Science of Man. Springfield Il, Charles C Thomas, 1957.

Paykel ES, Myers JK, Dienelt MN, Klerman GL, Lindenthal JJ, Pepper MP: Life events and depression: A controlled study. Arch Gen Psychiatry 21:753–760, 1969.

Pearlin LI, Lieberman MA: Social sources of emotional distress, in Research in Community and Mental Health. Edited by Simmons R. Greenwich CT, JAI Press, 1977.

Rutter M: Maternal Deprivation Reassessed. London, Penguin Books, 1972.

Scarf M: Unfinished Business: Pressure Points in the Lives of Women. New York, Doubleday & Co, 1980.

Spiegel JP: The resolution of role conflict within families. Psychiatry 20:1–16, 1957.

Sullivan HS: Conceptions of Modern Psychiatry. New York, WW Norton & Co, 1953a.

Sullivan HS: The Interpersonal Theory of Psychiatry. New York, WW. Norton & Co, 1953b.

Weissman MM, Paykel ES: The Depressed Woman: A Study of Social Relationships. Chicago, University of Chicago Press, 1974.

7. Transactional Analysis

Eric Berne, Claude M. Steiner, and John M. Dusay

This chapter is in three sections: a historical introduction (Berne), a theoretical outline (Steiner), and a discussion of clinical application (Dusay).

THE DEVELOPMENT OF TRANSACTIONAL ANALYSIS

Psychoanalysis owes its birth to Mrs. Emmy von N., who "gave permission" to Freud to listen to her by frequent admonitions of "Keep quiet—don't talk." This was a license to Freud to disregard his teachers and their injunctions to impose his will on his patients. If he had been unable to avail himself of this license, psychoanalysis would not have come into being at that time, and perhaps never. Similarly, I had been trained for almost twenty years to listen to my teachers and not to my patients. The clinical question was always, "What would my teachers say about that the patient is saying?" rather than "What is the patient telling me?" The theory and practice of transactional analysis began to develop after I received permission (to use a transactional expression) to reverse this trend and listen to patients rather than to teachers. Thus, when a patient remarked: "I feel as though I had a little boy inside of me," I was supposed to interpret the "little boy" to mean an introjected penis, as in the similar case cited by Otto Fenichel. But instead of saying to myself, "What would Otto Fenichel think about this?" I asked the patient: "What do you think about it?" It was thus established that at times the patient really did feel like a little boy (for whatever reason), and this feeling was the most convincing and significant clinical fact in determining the course of his life. The next step was to ask him at appropriate times: "Which part of you said that, the little boy or the grown-up man?" This question marked the birth of transactional analysis.

Of the many influences that gave me permission to be grateful to my teachers but to listen to my patients, only the external ones will be mentioned. For someone who was accustomed to the exigencies of medical

Reprinted by permission of Miami Press from *Direct Psychotherapy: 28 American Originals*. Coral Gables, 1973, pp. 370–93.

practice from early childhood, an analogy existed between the treatment of coughs and the treatment of neurotics. Psychoanalysis was like listening to the patient cough, year after year, learning more and more about various kinds of coughs and becoming very skillful in discussing them and diagnosing them. Formal psychoanalysis was like treating all kinds of coughs, even the common cold, by prolonged sanitarium care; psychoanalytic therapy was like treating tuberculosis by a weekly auscultation and an occasional mustard plaster, without looking for more specific remedies. Although with these approaches one might learn an enormous amount about the natural history of coughs, and become very expert at auscultation, neither of them seem profitable therapeutic measures in the rough and tumble of ordinary practice if there is to be any expectation of cure within a reasonable time. An added difficulty was that the most thorough treatment, psychoanalysis, the prolonged equivalent of "sanitarium cure," was by Freud's own statement, supported by the experience of others, not applicable to the most serious cases and could only be used for the milder ones. These paradoxes indicated a need for something better, not merely better "sanitariums" or better auscultation but better therapeutic methods.

The progress from the first question, "Which of the two is talking now," arose from further observations communicated by the patients and made by the therapist. It soon appeared that not all feeling and behavior patterns fitted into the two entities little boy and grownup, now called "ego states" in honor of Dr. Paul Federn. There must be a third. What was it, and where did it come from? It soon became apparent that this was a Parental ego state. This conclusion gave rise to a tripartite framework which could now contain every manifestation of every patient studied. This new framework was quite independent of Freud's tripartite system and stood on its own merits; on the other hand, it did not contradict anything in Freud, and in fact, the two systems reinforced each other while each maintained its own inner consistency. One was based on free association, the other, dealing with the same kind of patient population, was based on introspection and observation, both of which had gone out of style when psychoanalysis became predominant. This aspect of the theory, the diagnosis of ego states, constitutes structural analysis.

The next question that came into focus was: "If each of these two people talking is three different people, who is talking to whom?" This question emerged very cogently one day in a therapy group, which is its natural matrix, and led to the evolution of the analysis of individual transactions:

e.g., "His grownup (or Adult, as it was now called) is talking to her grownup, but it is her little girl (or Child) who is answering. Aha! Where does this lead us?"

The next step was the observation one day that a conversation in the group (or what was now called a series of transactions) seemed familiar. This *déja vu* quality was not due to the content, which was new, but to the way the conversation went, to the operations which the speakers were performing on one another, the way they were "manipulating" each other, to use the vulgar term. It thus appeared that there was a class of conversations which was independent of the overt content and depended on the transactions: a kind of algebraic classification, in which the specific x's and y's under discussion were irrelevant, but the functional relationships between the parties were the same. Further study of such phenomena resulted in the concept of games.

The question after that was, "Why did people want to go through such stereotyped sets of transactions, and what did they add up to in the long run?" To answer this question required a longitudinal view of the patient's whole life, with the gratifying result that it became possible to extrapolate and predict what the patient was going to do with his life in the future. This gave rise to the study of scripts. All this process took about four years from 1954 to 1958.

By 1958, so many other people had become interested in learning the new approach that more formal meetings became necessary. Hence the formation of the San Francisco Social Psychiatry Seminars, which met weekly. As people from other cities, states, and countries soon began to use the method, further organization was necessary, and the International Transactional Analysis Association was established about ten years from the time the crucial question was asked of the first patient.

There was also another kind of interest. Because all clinicians deal with the same kinds of psychopathology, many of the things that transactional analysts say have been said in somewhat similar fashion in other contexts. Thus a volume of mail and personal communications appeared which stated that transactional analysis was not new; it was only revised Adler, Jung, Freud, Krishnamurti, Rudolph Steiner, Horney, Grinker, Rank, Heidegger, Fairbairn, and so on. Thus, a criterion was necessary to distinguish transactional analysis from other approaches. This criterion may be succinctly stated as follows: transactional analysis is based on the personality theory of ego states; everything follows from that premise and cannot be clearly understood without that. Therefore whatever explains human behavior on the basis of

Child, Parent, and Adult ego states is transactional analysis. Whatever does not explain human behavior in terms of these ego states is not transactional analysis, even though many statements from other fields may sound similar to true transactional statements. Thus, similar conclusions may be arrived at starting from a different theoretical standpoint and traveling a different route. But only those conclusions which are derived from the existence of three ego states constitute transactional analysis, and it is this starting point which is new. Even a "flirtation" with ego states, such as has been carried on by R. Ekstein and R. Fairbairn, is not enough. As Freud remarked, it is one thing to flirt with an idea and another to be married to it.

The International Transactional Analysis Association now has about 600 members scattered across 30 states and four countries, which is evidence of an awakening interest in the therapeutic use of the theory of ego states, transactions, games, and scripts, particularly in group treatment.

THE TRANSACTIONAL THEORY OF PERSONALITY

As a theory of personality, Eric Berne's transactional analysis can be seen to be a branch, rather close to the roots, on the tree of psychoanalytic personality theory. Thus, transactional analysis is essentially sympathetic to psychoanalytic concepts of personality. As a theory and method of treatment, however, it differs from psychoanalytic theory in a number of significant ways which will be elaborated in the section on treatment.[1]

The building blocks of the theory of transactional analysis (TA) are three observable modalities of ego function, the Parent, the Adult, and the Child. Because of the apparent similarity between these and the three basic psychoanalytic concepts, the ego, the superego, and the id, the difference and relationship between them will be outlined forthwith.

Transactional analysis can be called an ego psychology, but it must be remembered that ego psychology is a name reserved, perhaps rightfully, for that body of theory developed by Hartmann, Kris, Loewenstein, and Rapaport, all of whom are dedicated to psychoanalytic concepts but desire to modify what they consider to be an excessively narrow view of the ego. According to these writers, Freud's description of the ego does not do justice to the much broader spectrum of functions which they see the ego performing. Ego psychology, an extension of Freud's theories, deals largely with considerations of psychic energy available to the ego and has not produced, as Ford and Urban (9), point out, any notable innovations in treatment. Thus, if TA is to be called an ego psychology, it must be remembered that TA departs from orthodox psychoanalytic theory not so much on the issue of psychic energies but on the issue of the scientific and practical value of observable ego variables rather than dynamic hypothetical constructs. In addition, it might be pointed out that while the ego psychologists divide the ego in terms of functions (synthetic, adaptive, defensive, perceptual, etc.), TA divides the ego into three modalities, every one of which incorporates the several ego functions.

Structural Analysis

A person operates in one of three distinct ego states at any one time. These ego states are distinguishable by the observer on the basis of skeletal-muscular variables and the content of verbal utterances. Thus, certain gestures, postures, mannerisms, facial expressions, and intonations, as well as certain words, are typically associated with one of the three ego states. When the observer is examining his own behavior, he has, in addition, kinesthetic, perceptual, cognitive, and affective information that is part of the ego state being observed.

The Child. *The Child ego state is essentially preserved in its entirety from childhood.* Thus, for example, in this ego state the person behaves as he did when he was three years old. Current thinking holds that the Child is never more than about eight years old and can be as young as one hour old. Not only does the person sit, stand, walk, and speak as he did as a three-year-old, but he perceives, thinks, and feels as the three-year old did. Perception is syncretic (14), and thinking is at a prelogical or preoperational level of development (11). In psychoanalytic terms mental activity is dominated by the primary process, in which tension is discharged through wish fulfillment.

Response to stimulation is direct rather than mediated, and the person is stimulus-bound rather than able to delay response. Internal (proprioceptive and kinesthetic) stimulation is not distinguished from external, sensory stimulation, and the person responds to the primary aspects of stimuli—color (amplitude), intensity, and movement—rather than the "meaningful" aspects of them. In short, it can be said that all which is known about the psychology of children (motivation, perception, and thinking) applies to the person when he is in the Child ego state (12).

The Child is visible in a fixated form in schizophrenics and in certain kinds of superfeminine women or supermasculine men; it appears consistently and for varying periods of time in normal, well-functioning persons, and of course is the habitual ego state in three-year-old children. Colloquially, lest the value of the Child be misunderstood, it is said that "it is the best part of the person" and "the only part that can really enjoy itself."

The Adult. *The Adult ego state is essentially a computer,* an impassionate organ of the personality, the function of which is to gather and process data for the purpose of making predictions. Thus, the Adult gathers data about the world through the senses, processing them according to a logical program and making predictions when necessary. In its perceptual function it is diagrammatic; while the Child perceives in color, in space, and from one point of view at a time, the Adult perceives in black and white, usually on two dimensions, and from several points of view at the same time. The most detailed description of the operation of the Adult is the one by Piaget in *Logic and Psychology* (11) under the rubric of "formal operations." When in the Adult ego state, the person is isolated from his own affective and other internal processes, a condition that is indispensable for the proper observation and prediction of reality. Thus, in the Adult ego state the person "has no feelings," even though he may be capable of appraising his Child or Parent feelings. Often a rational Parent ego state is confused with the Adult ego state, the latter being not only rational but also without emotion.

In this context it should be noted that the Adult grows, according to Piaget, through a series of developmental steps stretching out through childhood. This development proceeds over time as a consequence of the interaction between the person and the external world. The Parent, on the other hand, is not a result of actual development but of a nondevelopmental process of direct acquisition rather than gradual change.

The Parent. *The Parent is essentially made up of behavior that is copied from parents or authority figures.* It has, therefore, the quality of being taken whole, as perceived, without modification. A person in the Parent ego state will behave as his parent or whoever was or is *"in loco parentis."*

Thus, the Parent ego state is essentially nonperceptive or cognitive, being simply a parameter or arbitrary but constant basis for decisions and feelings. It is the repository of traditions and values and therefore vital to the survival of civilization. It operates validly when adequate information for Adult decision is not available, but in the case of certain pathologies it operates in spite of adequate Adult information.

Structural analysis, then, is organized around these fundamental concepts, the ego states. Some further concepts in structural analysis will be advanced.

Ego states are seen to operate one at a time, that is, the person will always be in one and only one of the three ego states. This ego state is called the executive, or will be said to have executive power. It is possible, however, that while one ego state has the executive power, the person is aware of literally standing beside himself, observing his own behavior. This feeling, that the self is not the ego state in the executive, is usually associated with a situation in which the Child or Parent has the executive power, while the "real self," perhaps the Adult, observes without essentially being able to behave. Thus, while only one ego state is cathected—that is imbued with the psychic energy necessary to activate muscular complexes involved in behavior—it is possible for another ego state to be cathected sufficiently to become conscious to the person even though it is not able to activate the musculature.

A clinical observation that might be seen to militate against the postulate that ego states occur one at a time is the situation where two sets of muscles seem to be powered by two separate ego states. For instance, a lecturer's voice and facial muscles might seem to indicate an Adult ego state whereas an impatient toss of the hand might reveal a Parent ego state. In cases such as this it is likely that the behavior is Parent in Adult disguise and therefore Parent or that Parent and Adult are alternating rapidly.

The possibility for alternation between ego states is a function of the permeability of the ego state boundaries. This permeability is an important variable in psychopathology. Low permeability leads to exclusion of appropriate ego states. Exclusions of the Parent, Adult, and Child ego states are all pathological since they preclude the use of ego states that, in a given situation, may be more adaptive than the excluding ego state. For example, at a party the excluding Adult is less adaptive than the Child, whereas a father who has an excluding Adult is preventing the more adaptive Parent from properly raising his children.

On the other hand, extreme permeability represents another form of pathology often manifested in an incapacity to remain in the Adult ego state for a sufficiently enduring period of time.

The above discussion is based on the assumption that every ego state, being a substructure of the ego, is, in its own way, an adaptive organ. The manner in which the ego as a whole functions adaptively has been elucidated by Hartmann (10); all three ego states share in this adaptive function, each ego state being especially suited for certain specific situations. It might be said that the Parent is ideally suited where control is necessary: control of children, of unknown situations, of fears, of unwanted expression, and of the Child. The Adult is suited to situations in which accurate prediction is necessary. The Child is ideally suited where creation is desired: creation of new ideas, procreation, creation of experiences, and so on.

One more concept is of first-hand importance: contamination. This phenomenon is characterized by an Adult ego state holding as fact certain ideas stemming from the Parent or the Child. An idea, such as "excessive masturbation leads to insanity," could presumably be part of a person's Adult ego state. Decontamination of the Adult is an early therapeutic requirement in treatment and is accomplished through an accurately timed confrontation by the therapist's Adult with the inaccuracy of the ideas that are causing the contamination.

To recapitulate, every person has three ego states which manifest themselves in sequence and which adapt to three different kinds of situations. These ego states have boundaries which can, in the case of pathological states, prevent the shift of ego states or the enduring application of them. The Adult is capable of developing contaminations from the Parent or Child.

Thus, TA is a theory committed to verifiable and observable variables. This commitment implies that variables are seen as observable and verifiable by patients as well as therapists or theorists. The wish to include the patient in the understanding, observation, and verification of behavior theories generates the extensive use of colloquialisms, the preference for group treatment over individual treatment, and the insistence that most relevant variables in treatment are conscious and therefore available to the patient himself by the simple application of attention to certain areas of his behavior. Because of these preferences, TA falls clearly within the area of direct therapy which constitutes the scope of these volumes.

Transactional Analysis

Just as the ego state is the unit of structural analysis, so the transaction is the unit of transactional analysis. The theory holds that the behavior of one person is best understood if it is examined in terms of ego states and that the behavior between two or more persons is best understood if examined in terms of transactions. A transaction consists of a transactional stimulus and a transactional response, and stimulus and response occur always between specific ego states. In a simple transaction, there are only two ego states.

One example might be between two Adult ego states, "How much is 5 times 7?" "Thirty-five"; all other combinations of ego states may occur in a transaction. Transactions will follow one another smoothly as long as the stimulus and response are parallel or complementary.

In any given series of transactions, communication will proceed if the response to a previous stimulus is addressed to the ego state that was the source of the stimulus and is emitted from the ego state to which that source addressed itself. Any other form of response will create a crossed transaction and will interrupt communication. In Figure 7.1, transaction A is complementary and will lead to further communication whereas transaction B is crossed and will break off communication. Crossed transactions are of interest not only because they account for the interruption of communication but also because they are usually part of the transactions in games.

In addition to simple transactions, a very important form of transaction is the complex, ulterior transaction. This form of transaction has two levels: social and psychological. Each level involves two ego states. In Figure 7.1, transaction C is between A and A, "Come to my apartment and look at my blueprints," and between C and C, "Ever since I was a little girl I have loved blueprints." Usually, in the case of an ulterior transaction, the social level is a cover for the real (psychological) meaning of the transaction; thus, interpersonal behavior is not understandable until the ulterior level and ego states involved are understood.

Games

A game is a carefully defined event. To satisfy the definition of a game, a behavioral sequence has to: (1) consist of an orderly series of transactions with a beginning and an end; (2) contain an ulterior motive, that is, contain a psychological level different from the social level; and (3) result in a payoff for both players.

The payoff of games constitutes an important part of TA theory and can be seen as the motivational aspect of it. To use an analogy, structural analysis describes the relevant parts of the personality just as a parts list describes the parts of an engine. Transactional analysis describes the way in which the parts interact in the same manner in which a cutaway display engine operates and exemplifies the manner in which the engine parts relate to each other. But to understand *why* people transact with each other, some sort of motor power has to be postulated, and this explanation is found in the motivational

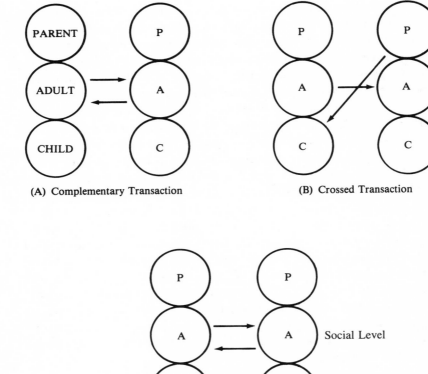

(A) Complementary Transaction   (B) Crossed Transaction

(C) Complex Ulterior Transaction

Figure 7.1: Three Types of Transactions

concepts of stimulus hunger, structure hunger, and position hunger. Games derive satisfaction for all three of these hungers, and this satisfaction is referred to as the advantage or payoff of the game.

1. The satisfaction of stimulus hunger is the biological advantage of the game. There is considerable research in the literature indicating that stimulation is one of the primary needs of higher organisms. On the basis of these findings and clinical evidence, Berne (1) has evolved the concepts of stimulus hunger and stroking. Stimulus hunger is satisfied by stroking or recognition. Stroking is a more basic need than recognition, and it is said that a person

needs stroking "lest his spinal cord shrivel up." Actual physical stroking can be replaced with symbolic stroking or recognition. Thus, the average adult is able to satisfy his hunger for stroking through, among other things, a ritual that is essentially an exchange of recognition strokes. For example, the following is a six stroke ritual:

A: Hi.
B: Hi.
A: How are you?
B: Fine, and you?
A: Fine. Well, see you.
B: Yeah, see you around.

A game is transactionally more complex than the previous ritual but is basically still an exchange of strokes. It might be noted in passing that "Go to hell!" is as much a stroke as "Hi," and people will settle for the former form of stroking when they cannot obtain the latter.

2. The satisfaction of structure hunger is the social advantage of the game. Structure hunger is satisfied by the establishment of a social matrix within which the person can transact with others. Thus, to satisfy structure hunger, the individual seeks social situations within which time is structured and organized for the purpose of obtaining strokes. This need for structure can be seen as an elaboration of stimulus hunger and therefore as a more complex form of the basic need for stimulation. By virtue of being played, a game provides a series of ways in which time can be structured. For instance, a game of "If it Weren't for You" (IWFY), provides for considerable time structure with its endless face-to-face recriminations. It provides for additional time structure in that it makes possible the pastime of "If it Weren't for Him (Her)" played with neighbors and relatives and possibly "If it Weren't for Them" played at bars and bridge clubs.

3. The satisfaction of position hunger is the existential advantage of the game. Position hunger is satisfied by an internal transaction, within the player, in which a basic, lifelong, existential position is vindicated. This existential position, colloquially known as the patient's "racket," can be illustrated with a sentence, such as "I am no good," "They are no good," or "Nobody is any good." The internal transaction takes place between the player and another person, usually a parent, and it is a form of stroking or recognition in which the stroke is given internally.

Thus, after a game of RAPO,[2] the players go home and White may say to will answer, "That's my good little girl." This transaction has stroking value, and at the same time it reinforces the existential position of the player. As will be elaborated later, every game has the added effect of advancing the script, or life plan of the person.

At the same time that a game provides strokes for the player, it also provides protection from intimacy. Intimacy, which is a social situation free of rituals, pastimes, and games, can also be seen as a situation in which strokes are given directly and therefore most powerfully. Intimacy, therefore, can be a threat to the person, essentially a threat of excessively intense stroking. Thus, a game is a carefully balanced procedure, the purpose of which is to obtain an optimal amount of stroking.

It should be noted, in addition, that strokes can be obtained without resorting to games which are basically subterfuges and that games are learned in childhood from parents as a preferred method of obtaining stimulation. Thus, a person giving up a game has to develop an alternate way of obtaining strokes and structuring time, and, until he does, he will be subject to despair, a condition parallel to marasmus in deprived children.

Two games will be described in detail. The first, a "soft" game called "Why Don't You Yes But" and the second, a "hard" version (second degree)[3] of RAPO.

Why Don't You Yes But. This is a common "soft" game played wherever people gather in groups, and it might proceed as follows. Black and White are mothers of grade-school children.

White:　I sure would like to come to the PTA meeting, but I can't get a baby sitter. What should I do?
Black:　Why don't you call Mary? She'd be glad to sit for you.
White:　She is a darling girl, but she is too young.
Black:　Why don't you call the baby-sitting service? They have experienced ladies.
White:　Yes, but some of those old ladies look like they might be too strict.
Black:　Why don't you bring the kids along to the meeting?
White:　Yes, but I would be embarrassed to be the only one to come with her children.

Finally, after several such transactions, there is silence followed possibly by a statement by Green, such as, "It's sure hard to get around when you have kids."

The above game (YDYB), which incidentally was the first game to be analyzed by Berne, fulfills the three parts of the definition as follows. First, it is a series of transactions beginning with a question and ending with a silence. Second, at the social level it is a series of Adult questions and Adult answers; at the psychological level it involves a series of questions by a demanding, reluctant Child unable to solve a problem and a series of answers by increasingly irritated Parents anxious to help in a quandary.

The payoff of the game is as follows: It is a rich source of strokes; it provides a readily usable form of time structure wherever people congregate; and finally, it reinforces an existential position. The position, in this case, is exemplified by Green's statement, "It's sure hard to get around when you have kids." In the case of White, the game successfully proves that parents are no good and always want to dominate you, while at the same time it proves that children are no good and prevent you from doing things. In the case of Black, the game successfully proves that children are ungrateful and unwilling to cooperate. In the case of both Black and White, the existential advantage fits into their script. Both White and Black can come away from the game feeling angry or depressed according to what their favorite "feeling racket" is. After a long enough succession of such similar games, both White and Black may feel justified in getting a divorce, attempting suicide, or quitting.

RAPO. This game is played by a more specialized type of personality; that is to say, while YDYB can be played by almost anyone, RAPO's psychological content is such that it only attracts certain persons. It is a sexual game so it requires a man and a woman, although it may be played between homosexuals as well. It might proceed as follows.

At a party, after considerable flirtation White finds herself alone with Black reading aloud from the Decameron. Aroused by the inviting situation, Black makes an advance and attempts to kiss White. Indignant, White slaps Black's face and leaves in a huff.

Again we have a series of transactions, beginning with a sexual invitation and ending with a sexual rebuff. On the social level the game looks like a straightforward flirtation ended due to a breach in etiquette by Black, rightfully rebuffed by White. On the psychological level, between Child and Child, White has first enticed and then humiliated Black.

The payoff, again, consists of strokes, a way to structure time, and existentially, a ratification of the position holding that "Men (women) are no good" followed by feelings of anger or depression as the case may be, according to preference. Again the script is advanced since enough episodes of this game may justify a murder, rape, suicide, or depression for the players.

Script Analysis

When games are seen as parts of an on-going life course rather than isolated events, their existential meaning comes into relief. As previously mentioned, every game has an existential advantage. This advantage is the promotion of the script.

The script is a manifestation of the Child. The Child is the motor of the personality, not only in the biological sense, but also in a mental sense because ideas lodged in the Child have a pervasive influence upon the life course of the individual. Ideas in the Child will find expression and are not subject to correction by observation of their results.

The script is essentially a life course, decided upon by the person early in life, and therefore lodged in the Child. The decision is seen by the youngster who is making it as a valid solution or adaptation to the pressures under which he exists. The script is a product of the synthetic function of the ego, the Adult in the youngster (the professor),[4] who with all of the information at his disposal at the time decides that a certain position and life course are a reasonable resolution of his problems.

These pressures can be diagrammed in a script matrix. (See Figure 7.2.) It will be noted that the influences on the youngster are seen to be limited to influences by the parents. This essentially implies that culture has no effect on an individual other than as transmitted specifically by one of the parents or parent surrogates.

The most important influence or pressure impinging on the youngster originates from the parental Child. That is, the Child ego states in the parents of the person are seen as the determining factor in the formation of scripts. Present theory holds that in post-Oedipal scripts the contrasexual parent's Child is crucial or "calls the shots," whereas in the pre-Oedipal scripts the crucial parent is the mother, no matter what the sex of the offspring (13).

As previously pointed out, games produce as part of their gains the existential payoff. With every repetition of a game, the script is advanced, because every game's last dramatic move is an acquiescence to the person's parental Child (C_M or C_F), colloquially called the "witch mother" or "ogre." Acquiescence to C_M or C_F, as discussed previously, results in stroking and recognition.

In the example of an alcoholic, the game begins with a sober individual whose predominant ego state is Parent and who ruthlessly restricts and castigates his Child. The end of the game or payoff takes place when the person is

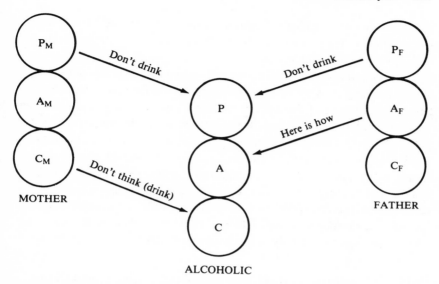

Figure 7.2: Script matrix. P, Parent; A, Adult; C, Child; M, Mother; F, Father

in a self-damaged Child ego state, essentially having done his parent's Child's (C_M or C_F) bidding. Figure 2 illustrates the alcoholic script. For this particular male alcoholic, the parent calling the shots is mother, and it is mother's Child (the witch mother) who says, "Don't think," "I will protect you when you are damaging yourself" (5). This statement, usually made nonverbally, may seem improbable at first blush. But it becomes more plausible when one considers that it originates from a three-year-old girl who enjoys caring for and forgiving people and who resents self-sufficiency (seen as rejection). This patient happens to have an alcoholic father who throughout him shows how being an alcoholic is a good adaptation to mother's Child's injunction. The patient decides that to obtain mother's protection and to avoid her Child's harassment, he must become self-destructive. As he does this, he observes that mother protects him; when he does not, he is subjected to subtle pressures to return to the self-destructive behavior. He might start playing such minor self-destructive games as delinquency, etc., but eventually he hits on alcohol and finds that it does exactly what his mother's Child wants him to do, namely not thinking, and damaging himself.[5] At this point he decides that he will become an alcoholic. This decision, made by the Adult in the young person, will seem reasonable and cogent and will continue to be seen as reasonable unless the script is changed. It should be noted that while, essentially, C_M is saying, "Drink," P_M

and P_F, as well as the patient's Parent are saying, "Don't drink." The influence of the Parent is felt periodically during sober periods, but the witch mother (C_M) always wins out in the end.

The implications of this theory for the understanding of psychopathology are far-reaching. Diagnosis of psychopathology is far more meaningful in terms of TA, in which behavior is observed and pathology is described in terms of what the patient does, than in terms of psychoanalytic dynamics. "He is drinking himself to death" is a script diagnosis, in contrast to its psychoanalytic counterpart, "He is a passive, aggressive character with strong oral features." The script diagnosis implies (1) that the patient is carrying out an early life decision that is an adaptation to the pressures of the parental environment, specifically of the wishes of a parental child; (2) that the pathology is lodged in the Child ego state; and (3) that the elements of a cure are contained essentially in the psychology of persuasion of children.

CLINICAL APPLICATIONS OF TRANSACTIONAL ANALYSIS

The goal of transactional analysis is to cure as many patients during the first treatment session as is possible. This means that the aim is 100% success and any failure to achieve this percentage is viewed as a challenge. "Cure" is not an ambiguous and vague term around which the patient and the therapist play mutually attractive games but is clearly defined early in the course of treatment. The means of establishing criteria of "Cure" is by defining a clear, concise contract between the patient and therapist. The patient is asked a question, worded differently by different therapists, determining "How will you know and how will I know when you have achieved what you are consulting me for?" This is a variation of "What do you want?" which is avoided in some forms of psychotherapy. At times a clear Adult–Adult contract between the therapist and patient can be readily established. For example, "I will be able to make $100 a week in take-home pay" or "I will no longer be impotent with my wife," etc. When such a contract is established, treatment can proceed rapidly. Frequently other ego states will get involved in the formation of the contract; particularly noticeable is the Child of the patient and the Parent of the therapist. For example, "Doctor, I'm suffering, do something for me." "Of course, my dear, just relax and everything will be all right." Under some circumstances, the therapist may choose to enter into a Parent–Child type of contract. For example, when a very confused, disoriented, frightened, and contaminated Child ego state of a patient causes this individual to be hospitalized against his will, the therapist may, for some period of time, provide a protective and judicial position with which he will treat the patient. However, when the therapist is doing this in full awareness, he will soon be able to establish a more suitable contract with the patient, if it is indicated.

One distinct advantage of forming a clear, concise contract is that both the patient and the therapist, as well as other group members, will know when the patient is getting what he came to treatment for (6). The contract is not determined just by the patient but also by the therapist. If the goal in treatment is not acceptable to the therapist, he will not enter into a contract with the patient. The therapist himself, in forming a contract, will need to know what his Adult will be doing in the group, what his Parent will be doing, and what his Child will be doing. The training of therapists for transactional analysis has been discussed extensively in the book, *Principles of Group Treatment* (4). As frequently happens, group treatment is carried out in institutional settings. Therefore, another consideration is the goal of the institution. The therapist entering into some type of contract with the patient will clearly have in mind his contract with the institution in which he finds himself practicing. To facilitate this, the therapist outlines prior to the onset of group treatment a clear authority diagram including all of his supervisors and administrators, himself, and the patients. Without this diagram a conflict may arise; i.e., when a supervisor who holds some theoretical position that patients can be cured only after months and months of depth unconscious exploration is reluctant to allow a patient who has not "worked through his inner conflicts" to pass from the institution. A patient who has had considerable experience with the game "Let's you and him fight" may delightfully exploit the confused situation that results when the therapist does not have a clear-cut authority diagram in mind. Those persons familiar with institutional and hospital practices probably recall many instances in which the patient sat gleefully on the sidelines as the doctor and nurse had a nonproductive argument about his management. Games played between administrative supervisors, co-therapists, and other persons involved in a patient's treatment may affect the outcome of the patient's treatment. In the preceding illustration, the patient may decide, "Why should I do anything around the hospital, I can go home and watch my mother and father fight."

Historically, transactional analysis evolved as a group treatment, and there are many advantages in this respect. There is a much larger variety of response to any individual patient in the group. When a patient and therapist are sitting together in a room, there is the Parent, the Adult, and the Child of the patient, and the Parent, the Adult, and the Child of the therapist. In this setting, actually six different people are in the room, and transactions will proceed from one ego state in one person to another ego state in the other person. A group of eight, then, has twenty-four primary ego states available to any one particular person in the group, and an increasingly large number of transactions are possible. (Refer to Figure 7.2.) A patient entering a group will stimulate other members in the group by one of his characteristic ego states and will in turn respond and be stimulated by others, whether he says anything or not. He can perhaps find a feeding mother, a punitive father, a gleeful child, and a logical adult, and because of the individual's characteristic background, he will be able to enter into transactions with the particular ego state of another individual in the group which appeals to him at that particular time. The therapist, by observing this carefully or by entering into the transactions, will soon be able to evaluate one person's characteristic ways of transacting with another person.

It has been found advantageous to select patients for group treatment at random without respect to age, sex, diagnosis, etc. This method is used because certain people with similarities in their background tend to pass the time with familiar topics that prevent more useful interaction. For example, a geriatric group may characteristically pass the time by saying "Ain't it awful that juvenile delinquency is on the rise, etc., etc." A group of juvenile delinquents, on the other hand, may pass time in saying things like "Ain't it awful, our parents are, etc., etc." There are also mutually compatible games that certain select groups tend to play. For example, a group of prisoners may play "How do you get out of here" and "Let's pull a fast one on Joey." A random selection saves a great deal of time and energy on the therapist's part in breaking up mutually compatible pastimes and games, and, where it is impossible to avoid this occurrence, such as in a penal institution, it becomes a subject for special consideration (8). Group attendance at a voluntary group can be used by the therapist as a gauge of the effectiveness of group treatment. When his attendance falls below approximately 70%, probably something is wrong with the treatment, and this is called an "ailing" group. On the other hand, with attendance at 100%, the therapist must realize that this percentage is beyond the bounds of normal group attendance at voluntary functions. Perhaps the therapist at this point needs to check his Parent aspects. When it is noted that there is an "ailing" group, the therapist needs to review the contract with the patient, the contract with the institution if he is practicing in an institutional setting, the authority diagram, and then question what his own Parent, his own Adult, and his own Child is doing in the group. Usually an "ailing" group means that an undiagnosed game is being played. Contract review with special attention to "Why aren't you getting what you want" promotes Adult–Adult assessment of expectations and limitations of the patient, therapist, and the institution. The authority diagram review will pinpoint the individuals between or among whom the game is being played, and ego-state review will further clarify what attitudes, beliefs, and feelings are involved. The transactional analyst does not spare examination of his own ego-state involvement and most prefer to use chalk and blackboard to insure direct examination. The therapist draws his own Parent, Adult, and Child ego state, including the actual transactions as diagrammed in Figure 7.1. In this position, the therapist is not passive or anonymous and the "ailing" group knows why it is ailing.

Procedures in transactional analysis are direct and active on the part of the therapist. As has been outlined previously, the very structure of the group implies that the therapist take an active role in determining how he is going to be in the group, in contradistinction to just getting a group of people together and seeing what happens. Different therapists have reported different sequences in undertaking group treatment. However, the usual course is to begin with a structural analysis. In this respect, each individual patient in the group, by confrontation or interpretation by the therapist or other group members, becomes aware of when he is thinking, feeling, and behaving as a Parent; when he is thinking, feeling, and behaving as Adult; and when he is thinking, feeling, and behaving as a Child. The diagnosis of different ego states can be made from the behavior of the individual, his attitudes, and his gestures, etc. For example, when the therapist is confronted with the upright finger of the lecturing Parent in the group, he points it out immediately and does not let it be lost to posterity, unless he has decided there is some contraindication to confrontation at that point. The voice of the patient is also important. It is well known that an individual has two or three different voices that he uses in different circumstances, and awareness of this fact is readily made available to the patient. Vocabulary content, likewise, is indicative of the ego state that is predominant. For example, such words as "should, ought, must," etc., would be indicative of the Parent state. Adult ego-state content is characterized by such things as "probability, indications are, etc.", and Child ego-state words are usually spontaneous, terse, and well known to most readers. Frequently seen is the use of "Wow." An historical verification of an ego state is also important and strived for by the therapist. For example, the question, "When was the first time you placed your finger in the air like that?" might be met with the response, "I was six and my father did that when I said something naughtily to my mother." Another important verification of the ego state involved is the social response of others in the group. A Child attitude, gesture, and vocabulary will often elicit a Parent response from another individual, and the opposite, of course, is frequently seen. A prejudicial Parent statement will be met by rebellious comment from the Child of another patient. In a typical countertransference situation, the Adult of the patient may attempt to transact with the Adult of the therapist by asking the question, "Do you think I need further treatment?" and the therapist may respond from his Parent and say, "Don't ask that, be patient," and at that point the rebellious Child may appear. Final verification, sometimes attained only with difficulty, is the subjective phenomenological reexperiencing of the ego state. The sooner the patient is aware which particular ego state is functioning and operating in the group, the sooner he will be able to fulfill his contract successfully. This condition implies that the therapist observe and confront in an active manner.

A successful realigning of ego state and awareness on the part of the patient sometimes allows the patient to meet his contract. In two forms of psychopathology which are well known, a simple structural analysis may allow the patient to gain a social control. For example, in a manic depressive-type illness during the depressed stage, a strong, rigid, punitive Parent is the only ego state at that point which is in operation, and no laughter, spontaneity, or creativity characteristic of the Child is in evidence at that point. This rigidity, as discussed previously, is known as exclusion. The therapist at this point, in addition to diagnosing the ego state, talks to the Child. In delusional states, it is seen that the boundary between the Adult ego state and the Child ego state has become fused. Ordinarily the Adult can clearly distinguish what is real and what is fantasy, but with contamination present, the child's fantasies and nightmares merge with the Adult to the extent that what appears like Adult functioning is actually programmed by the Child. Therefore, Child fantasies are experienced as Adult reality. The therapist gains access to the fantasies by entering the Child's world. It would be the Child of the therapist intuitively reacting in an active way with the Child of the patient who has a contaminated ego state. Once in the Child state with the patient, the therapist can suggest that there are other alternatives and discuss these with the Adult. This contamination must be clarified before going on to other therapy sequences, and in many cases a simple structural analysis will suffice to allow the patient to attain his treatment contract.

Therapy may proceed to analyzing transactions and the diagnosis of crossed transactions. Some therapists prefer to begin with these because they are so dramatically presented in groups, sometimes at the onset of group treatment. Occasionally games have little to do with treatment contracts which have been arrived at. However, it is usually found that the predominant game that an individual displays in the group is incompatible with what he wishes to attain as his goal in group treatment. When this is so, a detailed analysis of the game is undertaken. Having clearly in mind the structure of the Parent, Adult, and the Child ego states, the patient is in a good position to analyze what particular ego state is involved in any set of transactions with another individual. An awareness of the particular game an individual is playing then allows him to choose whether or not he wishes to continue this game. Knowing that there are advantages that a person gains by playing certain games, the therapist chooses the interventions to make. When the therapist recognizes that a game invitation has been extended to him, he has four types of choices open to him (6). He may respond by exposing the game. This action is taken when he feels that the patient has some alternative method available to him to make up for the loss that he will experience when giving up a certain game. The therapist at the point of exposure of the game stands ready to intervene actively if necessary. On some occasions the therapist may respond by going along with the game. This action would be taken only after carefully considering if continuing the game is beneficial to the patient's condition. Infrequently, but occasionally, the therapist will choose to ignore a particular game, usually for diagnostic purposes. It could also be utilized to acquaint the patient with the idea that perhaps he does not need to utilize his old patterns to achieve recognition with people. Alternative games are sometimes proposed by the therapist.

Games as an on-going part of the life course of an individual are not readily abandoned by the patient, and when given up the Child may experience a loss. Clinically there is usually a depression at this point in treatment. As seen in the script matrix, the life course, including the essential games, has been decided upon early in life and is determined by transactions from the biological parent to the Child. The therapist has intervened in the life of the patient and is distinguished from the biological parent. The Adult of the therapist clearly assesses the on-going treatment, the Parent of the therapist is available to the Child of the patient when a loss is present, and the Child of the therapist intuitively reacts with the Child of the patient. The laughter and humor common in transactional analysis groups is reminiscent of children playing together.

With the loss of the script position, the Child is free to create new pleasures, find more acceptable games, and perhaps attain intimacy.

NOTES

1. The material presented in this section is based on Berne's books (1–4), writings in the *Transactional Analysis Bulletin,* and discussions at scientific meetings of the San Francisco Transactional Analysis Seminars.

2. See RAPO, below.

3. The softness or hardness of a game refers to the intensity with which it is played and the morbidity of its effects. First degree is the soft version, and third degree is the hard version of a game.

4. The professor is the colloquialism for the precocious Adult ego state in young children.

5. It is because of this that the hangover is seen to be the payoff of the alcoholic game.

REFERENCES

1. Berne, E. *Transactional analysis in psychotherapy.* New York: Grove Press, 1961.

2. Berne, E. *Games people play.* New York: Grove Press, 1963.

3. Berne, E. *The structure and dynamics of organizations and groups.* Philadelphia: J. B. Lippincott, 1963.

4. Berne, E. *Principles of group treatment.* New York: Oxford University Press, 1966.

5. Crossman, P. Permission and protection. *Transact. Anal. Bull.,* 1966, 5, 9.

6. Dusay, J. M. Scientific proceedings (abstract). *Transact. Anal. Bull.,* 1965, 4, 16.

7. Dusay, J. M. Response in therapy. *Transact. Anal. Bull.,* 1966, 5, 18.

8. Ernst, F. H., & Keating, W. C. Psychiatric treatment of the California felon. *Amer. J. Psychiat.,* 1964, 120, 10.

9. Ford, D. H., & Urban, H. B. *Systems of psychotherapy.* New York: John Wiley and Sons, 1963.

10. Hartmann, H. *Ego psychology and the problem of adaptation.* New York: International Universities Press, 1958.

11. Piaget, J. *Logic and psychology.* New York: Basic Books, 1957.

12. Steiner, C. Psychological functions of the child. *Transact. Anal. Bull.,* 1965, 4, 16.

13. Steiner, C. Script and counterscript. *Transact. Anal. Bull.,* 1966, 5, 18.

14. Werner, H. *Comparative psychology of mental development.* New York: Science Editions, 1961.

8. The Dynamic Focus

Thomas E. Schacht, Jeffrey L. Binder, and Hans H. Strupp

The Dynamic Focus addresses the problem of gathering and organizing therapeutically relevant information, and of incorporating this information systematically into the therapy. The dynamic focus as construed in TLDP (Time-Limited Dynamic Psychotherapy) is a heuristic. The focus helps therapists to generate, recognize, and organize psychotherapeutically relevant information. This active and explicit approach to discovery contrasts with the passive, broadly exploratory, and open-ended model advocated in some time-unlimited approaches. In such long-term psychotherapies, for example, it may be expected that spontaneous organizing tendencies will suffice if therapists conduct themselves properly and if patients are suited to the tasks of treatment. Thus Gill and Hoffman (1982) assert: "Presumably the analysis of transference becomes, during the course of the work, the analysis of a *more organized* set of perceptions and reactions *without any special effort* on the analyst's part to bring this about" (p. 143, emphasis added). While a few patients may do well in the absence of special effort on the therapist's part, many others do not easily accommodate to such an approach.

HISTORICAL OVERVIEW

The term *dynamic focus,* or just *focus,* has been widely associated with the central problem of maximizing therapeutic efficiency in time-limited treatments (Armstrong 1980; Bellak and Small 1978; Binder 1977; Binder and Smokler 1980; Budman 1981; Davanloo 1980; Flegenheimer 1982; Malan 1976; Mann 1973; Ryle 1979; Sifneos 1972). Indeed, several of the aforementioned authors claim that inability to find or maintain a focus is a fundamental contraindication for brief psychotherapy. At least one research group has honored this seminal concept by labeling its brief dynamic treatment approach "focal" psychotherapy (Balint, Ornstein, and Balint 1972).

Reprinted by permission of HarperCollins, Publishers, Basic Books from *Psychotherapy in a New Key.* New York, 1984, pp. 65–82, 98–109, 314–23.

Related concepts include "nuclear conflict" (Alexander and French 1946); "core neurotic conflict" (Wallerstein and Robbins 1956); central "transference predisposition" (Racker 1968); "residual trauma" (Blos 1941; Ekstein 1956); "central issue" (Mann and Goldman 1982); and "core conflictual relationship theme" (Luborsky 1977).

A dynamic focus is commonly stated in terms of a cardinal symptom, a specific intrapsychic conflict or developmental impasse, a maladaptive conviction about the self, an essential interpretive theme, or a persistent interpersonal dilemma or pattern of maladaptive activity. The content and form of the dynamic focus may vary across theoretical orientations and from therapist to therapist. For example, a therapist may attempt to focus on dependency wishes connected with a patient's struggles during the developmental crisis of autonomy versus shame; or, a treatment might focus on unresolved aggressive feelings connected with the process of grieving for a lost object, on pervasive sexual guilt, or on unconscious castration anxiety stimulated by the oedipal implications of impending graduation from college. Although specific authors have clearly defined favorites, such as Sifneos's (1972) preference for oedipal conflicts, the psychotherapy literature offers no consensual limits to the list of potential focal topics.

Unfortunately, current clinical literature offers few explicit procedures and only a handful of general principles for identifying a dynamic focus. It is more usual to encounter the view that identifying a dynamic focus is a high-level intuitive art. Malan (1976) for example, holds that a focus "crystallizes" in the sensitive therapist's mind. While there is agreement among students of brief psychotherapies that a dynamic focus should function as an orienting beacon or frame of reference for the therapist's interventions, there is no consensus on the specific form such a focal beacon should take (intrapsychic conflict, interpersonal dilemma, developmental impasse, persistent affective theme), nor is there agreement on how the therapist should pursue, develop, and elaborate a focal formulation (Kinston and Bentovim 1981), or even regarding how the quality of a particular focus may be evaluated. Progress toward greater conceptual specificity of the dynamic focus has occurred largely in a research context (Gill and Hoffman 1982; Luborsky 1977; Ryle 1979; Schacht, in press). However, since research procedures are often too specialized or cumbersome for routine clinical application, therapists have little in the way of concrete guidance and must usually rely on their own inventiveness, theoretically informed intuition, and clinical experience.

Despite its theoretical centrality, practical application of the dynamic focus concept has remained vague and unfocused. The purpose of this chapter is to outline an explicit model.

CONCEPTUAL FOUNDATIONS OF THE TLDP* FOCUS

In TLDP a focus is not used simply to limit, constrict, circumscribe, or shorten a therapy. A focus should not hinder the patient's awareness or expression; nor should it reduce a patient's complaints to stereotyped forms. A TLDP focus is also different from a target problem (an unfortunate metaphor which implies that a therapist is some sort of marksman and that clinical techniques are weapons in a therapeutic armamentarium).

The TLDP focus should be understood as an ad hoc individualized theory which clarifies and connects behavioral and experiential phenomena that otherwise appear unrelated and discontinuous. The focus is not an absolute or final formulation (which may, in any case, be a naive and impossible goal). Rather, it is a heuristic guide to inquiry. Both the process of generating a focus, and the focus itself, help patients expand their sense of themselves, integrate bewildering experiences, and master complex problems in living. The major value of a TLDP focus rests in the way in which it may help to organize a therapeutic experience. If therapy is thereby shortened, the reduction in the time required for effective treatment is generally a byproduct of this enhanced organization. When therapy must be brief it is best shortened straightforwardly by setting time limits. A focus then becomes a tool for making efficient use of the allotted time.

Clinicians should be careful lest their focal work transform a good therapeutic environment into one in which the patient acquiesces to a domineering professional. Thus, the focus ought not be imposed by the therapist; this would contravene the basic principles of TLDP by augmenting the patient's dependency on a powerful authority figure, proving more hindrance than help in the long run. Although therapeutic confrontation may be valuable in certain circumstances, such confrontation should not be confused with subtly or overtly pushing, manipulating, seducing, coercing, badgering, controlling, exhorting, or indoctrinating the patient. TLDP requires a collaboration between patient and therapist, for which the patient freely takes active responsibility. The focus, in this spirit, should be arrived at jointly in a manner that brings more of the patient's world into relief and interrelation.

* Time-Limited Dynamic Psychotherapy

TLDP Focus as a Structure for Interpersonal Narratives

The TLDP focus is a working model (Peterfreund 1983) of a central or salient pattern of interpersonal roles in which patients unconsciously cast themselves, the complementary roles in which they cast others, and the maladaptive interaction sequences, self-defeating expectations, and negative self-appraisals that result. The focus helps therapists to make their description and understanding of these problematic patterns more systematic and coherent. The focus provides labels and an organizing structure that makes therapeutically relevant information more accessible and that ideally helps both patient and therapist to reach meaningful discriminations and integrations.

The TLDP focus is grounded in two principles:

1. *For the kinds of psychological problems treated by TLDP, the primary arena for construing life experience is interpersonal.*
2. *The primary psychological mode of construing life experience, for the therapeutic operations central to TLDP, is narration: the telling of a story to oneself and others.* Hence, the TLDP focus is organized in the form of a schematic story outline. The TLDP focus combines the two principles, providing a generic structure for narrating the central interpersonal stories of a patient's life.

Why an Interpersonal Emphasis? Interpersonal transactions are emphasized because they provide a common psychological stage on which problematic life dramas originate and are repeatedly played out. Yalom (1980), for example, illustrates this point with the case of unresolved death anxiety. He points out that such anxiety is associated with (and perhaps maintained by) characteristic patterns of interpersonal transactions. In one common pattern, persons comfort themselves with fantasies of rescue, which lead to desperate dependency on powerful figures. Alternately, death anxiety may elicit defensive belief in one's specialness and secret invulnerability; these beliefs, in turn, are associated with arrogantly narcissistic devaluation of other persons who become, in this view, less special.

People develop cognitive, affective, and motivational structures, struggle with existential and philosophical issues, and form visions of self and reality in a deeply interpersonal context that itself unfolds one transaction at a time. Each transaction contains something of the larger whole. Correspondingly, issues become evident in therapy primarily through the role they play in patients' transactions with significant others and, more immediately, with the therapist. The TLDP focus attempts to capture the most therapeutically central aspects of these transaction patterns.

What Is Narration and Why Is It Important? The central model of psychological activity, structure, and organization, for psychotherapeutic purposes, is the story—also referred to by cognitive psychologists in a more restricted sense as the script (Schank and Abelson 1977). In a story, experiences and actions become sequentially organized into more or less predictable patterns of situational feeling, perceiving, wishing, anticipating, construing, and acting. These patterns, when they lead to problems in living, become the subject matter of psychotherapy.

Many aspects of life stories are frequently, even typically, unconscious. Because we are unaware, we live out these organizing life scripts as if they represented absolute truths, rather than being simply versions of reality. Conscious knowledge of these life stories is promoted by TLDP so that patient and therapist may come to see the currently problematic reality as relative, and together may make appropriate revisions. Knowledge of a life story is acquired in the course of attempting to tell it; narration is the name given to this process of coming to know one's organizing life stories through the effort of telling them. Narration is thus a process of discovery, a kind of investigation. Retelling or renarrating refer to the concomitant process of change through creating alternative (therapeutic) understandings of a life story. Although the terms *narration* and *renarration* have a certain cognitive quality, the processes themselves should not be intellectualized and to be therapeutically useful must be sustained by vividly experienced emotions.

In TLDP the patient and therapist are engaged in a joint narration and renarration of the central interpersonal dilemmas of the patient's life (Schafer 1983; Sherwood 1969; Spence 1982). Through this activity patient and therapist collaboratively author a framework for understanding, a new story, within which the patient's awkward, confusing, and self-defeating experiences appear intelligible and purposeful, as occurring for reasons that are understandable within the world as the patient has construed it and within the dramas being enacted in that world. Through the process of reiterative story making the patient and therapist come to appreciate different possibilities for understanding, feeling, and acting with more flexible and perhaps controllable outcomes. This recognition of alternate possibilities signals the beginning of therapeutic change.

Defining Characteristics of a TLDP Focus

The focus takes the form of a prototype or schematic interpersonal narrative. This narrative is built upon an abstract format or conceptual template (to be described) which aids in its construction.

Just as the rules of English grammar do not specify the content of any particular sentence (but do specify that an intelligible sentence should contain a subject, verb, object, and so on), the abstract form of the TLDP focus likewise provides a structural standard, a way of organizing specific and individual meanings into a narrative that makes interpersonal sense. To achieve this goal, a focus must tell something about: (1) the kinds of distinctions the patient makes about himself or herself and others; (2) based on those distinctions, the kinds of actions (including making further distinctions) in which the patient characteristically engages; and (3) the way in which these distinctions and actions are organized by the patient into a rigid and problematic interpersonal drama. More specifically, a focal narrative describes:

1. human actions,
2. embedded in a context of interpersonal transactions,
3. organized in a cyclical psychodynamic pattern, that have been
4. a recurrent source of problems in living and are also currently a source of difficulty.

Each element of this definition will be taken up in turn.

Human Actions. This phrase means that a TLDP focus is constructed of actions and is not simply a collection of traits or other static hypothetical constructs. A life story is a narrative account of a responsible person doing (and experiencing) certain things, in particular situations, for potentially identifiable (albeit often unconscious) reasons. The characters in a life story act: they perceive, think, sense, emote, move, anticipate, and remember. Furthermore, they may do these and other things in various ways, such as reluctantly, enthusiastically, desperately, angrily, sexually, unconsciously, conflictedly, and so on. Conflict may be expressed by attempting to perform incompatible actions, such as submissively ingratiating oneself with an authority while voicing an assertive concern for one's rights, or by striving simultaneously to feel incompatible emotions, such as affection and anger.

As Schafer (1976, 1983) argues in depth, the language of actions is a kind of "native tongue" for constructing narratives about human behavior and experience. In contrast, a focus phrased in abstract jargon or technical language poses significant heuristic and communication problems. It is very difficult, for example, to achieve consensus on the precise referents of constructs like repressed orality, unconscious castration anxiety, or primitive rage. To communicate such constructs intelligibly requires translation from the jargon into terms more resonant with ordinary experience. Castration anxiety, for example, may be redescribed in terms of specific action patterns, such as "feels physically small and incapable of expressing himself in the presence of older males who occupy positions of authority." This translation process can be largely bypassed, however, if therapy proceeds from the beginning with language that is simple, direct, and action oriented. Such language better retains the ability to evoke in both patient and therapist the full experiential complexity that originally gave birth to the focal formulation.

As Schafer (1976) has described, both private actions (thoughts, feelings, images) and public actions (speaking, moving) are best designated by verbs and adverbs, not by nouns and adjectives. For example, it is better to think in terms of feeling angry or acting angrily for some reason than to speak of "my anger making me do it." Correspondingly, the statements which comprise a focal narrative should emphasize verbs and adverbs (actions) rather than nouns and adjectives (entities, traits, reifications). Actions are characteristically concrete; they lend themselves to empathy because their description may evoke in the therapist some experience, remembered or imagined, of acting (feeling, sensing, thinking, choosing, and so on) in a similar manner. For therapists accustomed to thinking in terms of reifications or trait names (dependent, introverted, grandiose, paranoid, narcissistic, obsessive, hysteric, and so on), some mental effort may be required at first to recast these familiar labels in terms of the specific patterns of action to which they inevitably refer. This effort is worthwhile since, as Schafer has persuasively argued, action formulations are "good to think with."

The TLDP focus organizes actions into a structured pattern. This pattern clusters actions into meaningful groups on the basis of their role or function in the narration of interpersonal scenarios. For example, in telling an interpersonal story the actions of the storyteller and the actions of other characters should be grouped separately, lest it becomes unclear who did what. A story which failed to distinguish between acts of the narrator and acts of others may be incomprehensible (although the fact that a patient chose to tell such an incomprehensible story would be of great interest, perhaps suggesting a severe defect in self-boundaries or excessive reliance on projection). In a similar manner, it is useful to identify the role of other groups of actions, such as the narrator's anticipating or reacting to the activities of other persons.

Interpersonal Transactions. Focal action patterns should be embedded in a context of interpersonal transactions, the basic unit of interpersonal scripts. In contrast to simple actions, which may be executed by one person, transactions are executed by two people acting in relation to each other. In telling the story of a transaction, one person's actions are portrayed as explicitly evoking another person's actions. For example: "After you told him the secret, he got angry and slammed the door, and you imagined that you would never see him again." In this case the action of telling a secret is understood as evoking the actions of becoming angry and slamming the door, which in turn evoke the action of imagining a final separation.

Nontransactional narratives may fail to refer to action ("That's a pretty painting"); they may fail to involve interpersonal action ("I mowed the lawn today"); or they may involve interpersonal actions that nevertheless do not describe the actions of one person as evoking the actions of another ("She yelled at me and then she cried and hugged me"). Narration of a transaction, in contrast to narration of an action which occurs merely in the presence of other persons (real or imagined), thus reflects not only one person's contribution to a relationship, but also takes into account the expressed or imagined actions (thoughts, wishes, fears, motives, and so on) of others in response. The concept of transaction will be elaborated further in the discussion of how to actually construct and work with a TLDP focus.

Cyclical Psychodynamic Pattern. The TLDP focus must be organized in a way that makes sense of the self-defeating persistence and inflexibility of a patient's maladaptive and stereotypic interpersonal transactions. The concept of a "cyclical psychodynamic pattern" (Anchin and Kiesler 1982; Wachtel 1982; Wender 1968) best reflects this characteristic rigidity, chronic repetitiveness, and self-perpetuating nature of neurotic problems in living. Traditional explanations invoke linear models of cause and effect to account for this self-defeating persistence and rigidity. These linear accounts view early trauma and unfortunate developmental circumstances as continuing to exert an influence on later behavior, much as a series of billiard balls are set into motion by a first strike with the cue. Unfortunately, such linear models of cause and effect (typified, perhaps, in hydraulic interpretations of Freudian metapsychology) have often led to postulation of highly complicated systems of hypothetical psychic forces and mental structures, and to a misplaced emphasis on distantly past "original" causes.

In a cyclical account the psychodynamic process is not located in the anachronistically preserved past. Instead, this process is understood in terms of presently enacted self-propagating vicious circles. In these vicious circles, self-confirming patterns of repetitive social interchange serve to verify patients' maladaptive views and to validate and reinforce their problematic actions. While some past events set these vicious circles into motion, present continuation of these self-defeating patterns does not depend on the perpetual causal influence of those past events (as a "repressed" psychic force). For this reason, a detailed veridical knowledge of the past (which may be an impossible goal in any case) is not crucial to a cyclical psychodynamic account. The following schematic scenarios exemplify the cyclical psychodynamic concept:

George's mother was abusive and neglectful; his father abandoned the family when George was four years old. As an adult, George now imagines himself to be ugly and unlovable. This perception leads to painful self-rejecting thoughts and to occasional bouts of moderate depression. Rather than endure additional rejection from others, which he is certain is forthcoming because of his ugliness and unlovable nature, George withdraws from others and involves himself in self-destructive overeating, while preoccupying himself with angry ruminations about the "hypocrisy" of other people with regard to standards for physical attractiveness. Although he imagines his behavior to be self-protective, in fact others experience George's withdrawal and anger as unrewarding or even noxious, and they are led to subsequently reject and avoid him. George interprets their behavior not as a reasonable response to his own actions, but rather as proof that he is hopelessly ugly and unlovable. Awareness of this "proof" supports George's self-rejection and also prompts his continued self-defeating withdrawal from and preemptive rejection of others.

Mary was alternately and unpredictably pampered and punished by her father. With him, Mary learned that her own wishes and feelings were inconsequential, and she spent a great deal of time obsessively and anxiously analyzing his behavior, searching for clues that might portend his next change of mood. Mary developed an obsequious and ingratiating style of relating to her father, in the hope that such behavior on her part might induce him to continue pampering her and might minimize the seemingly inevitable episodes of harsh punishment. This ingratiating interpersonal style was also particularly attractive to men whose own role preferences involved the complementary stance of dominance and control. Consequently, Mary had the greatest social success with dominant men who showered her with gifts and who enjoyed their ability to extract unquestioning submission and obedience from her. She married such a man after a brief courtship and discovered only later that he was also inclined to episodes of heavy drinking and physical violence. While Mary recognizes her husband's faults and fears for her safety, she also imagines that if she only tries harder she can "bring out the good" in him. Consequently, she spends a great deal of time obsessively and anxiously analyzing his behavior, looking for clues that might help her know better how to please him. He, in turn, regards her as contemptibly weak and deserving of whatever punishments he elects to inflict. Mary does not interpret these intermittent punishments as evidence of her husband's sadistic nature, but continues to view the problem in terms of her own failure to please him. Consequently she feels guilty and berates herself for imagined inadequacies, and resolves to try harder.

These examples illustrate the self-confirming selection and shaping of experience that is central to a cyclical psychodynamic process. This self-confirming shaping of experience results from both private actions (selective thinking, feeling, perception) and also interpersonal (public) actions that elicit responses from others which validate one's preconceived characterizations of them. Through these largely unconscious patterns of action, patients repeatedly reaffirm the implicit premises with which they construe themselves, others, and situations; accordingly, contradictory evidence and experience are unlikely to be encountered or appreciated. Neurotic problems in living thus acquire a persistent and self-defeating quality, and this persistence becomes an understandable function of the patient's repetitive transactions with others, including, eventually, the therapist.

Historic and Current Significance. A TLDP focus should ideally encompass a pattern of interpersonal transaction that is both historically significant and also a source of current difficulty. However, while currently enacted patterns are of primary importance, the specific nature of these patterns may be ambiguous, even when they are enacted within the treatment relationship. Historical knowledge aids therapeutic understanding by providing a disambiguating context in which confusing meanings of present events may be more easily interpreted. Because the primary value of historical material in a cyclical psychodynamic account is limited to clarifying current actions, the search for historical antecedents should always be subordinate to a reconnaissance of the present. This emphasis is diametrically opposite to a linear-causal approach, in which evidence from the present is used to deduce and confirm some supposedly crucial events which presumably occurred in the past.

Therapists must understand that veridical historical knowledge may be impossible to obtain, and that a psychotherapeutic history is always a history as narrated—a story told to a particular clinician under the constraints of a particular conversational situation. Because memory processes are reconstructive, and because these reconstructive processes are influenced by experiences apart from the events being recalled, what transpires between patient and therapist in the here-and-now exerts a significant influence on what is remembered. As Spence (1982:95) succinctly puts it: "Recall of the past is a hostage to the transference." A dynamic focus furthers the TLDP process by participating in this here-and-now reconstructive narration of the past, and more importantly, the present. Most often, as the therapeutic narration progresses, patients develop a greater tolerance for anxiety, an increased trust in the therapist, and a richer sense of their own past. Consequently, while it is not uncommon to begin a therapy with little sense of the patient's past, in a successful case at least a partial life history (that most relevant to the patient's main problems) will have been collaboratively authored by the end of the treatment. The TLDP focus thus facilitates the collaborative making of a meaningful history, in contrast to the traditionally unilateral taking of a history.

Because history is always as narrated, and because the narrative process cannot be separated from the present patient-therapist relationship, TLDP therapists rely on that relationship as the primary arena for psychological exploration and change. In order to use the patient-therapist relationship in this manner, the patient's problematic interpersonal patterns must become manifest in that relationship. Of course, to allow or encourage patients' interpersonal difficulties to become evident in their present relationship with a therapist poses some risk, since it is typically these same difficulties that underlie the problems for which the patient seeks help. However, along with this risk comes an enormous potential benefit. When a patient's interpersonal difficulties become evident in the therapeutic relationship, the subsequent therapeutic work may acquire a persuasive sense of immediacy and affective conviction that cannot be duplicated by even the most penetrating and astute analysis of material about other relationships.

GENERAL FORMAT OF A TLDP FOCUS

This format of a TLDP focus was empirically derived from analysis of the categories of information to which expert therapists addressed their comments when constructing focal interventions (Schacht, in press). It specifies four categories of information which constitute minimal requirements for a well-formed narrative about an interpersonal transaction pattern. To make minimal narrative sense of an interpersonal transaction we should know something about (1) what the interpersonal actors do (perceive, think, feel, expect, and so on); (2) what each actor expects his or her behavior will or should lead the other to experience; (3) how each actor believes the other will or should behave in response; and (4) how the aforementioned activities influence the actors' opinions and treatment of themselves.

The TLDP focus contains four structural elements which express, in schematized fashion, these narratively fundamental categories of action. Collectively, these four categories of action, and their interrelations, compose a framework for the narrative description of interpersonal action patterns. The four action categories are as follows:

1. *Acts of self.* These may include all domains of human action, such as affects and motives ("I feel affectionate toward my mother" or "I wish my wife would pay more attention to me"); perceiving situations ("I sensed we were in a competition together"); cognitions ("I can't stop thinking about how ugly and inferior I am when I meet someone attractive."); or overt behaviors ("I can't refrain from avoiding eye contact with my boss when I'm angry with him"). Acts of self include both private and public actions (feeling affectionate as well as displaying affection), and may vary in the degree to which they are accessible to awareness.

2. *Expectations about others' reactions.* These are imagined reactions of others to one's own actions and may be conscious, preconscious, or unconscious. To achieve a transactional understanding, these should be articulated in specific relation to some acts of self. Statements in this category should emphasize imagined anticipation of others' actions rather than overtly voiced demands regarding others' behavior (these latter events are classed under acts of self). Expectations about other's reactions often take a form such as: "If I speak up, I imagine that she will disapprove of me" or "If I ask her out she will just laugh at me."

3. *Acts of others toward self.* These are observed acts of others that are viewed as occurring in specific relation to the acts of self. That is, these actions of others appear (or are assumed) to be evoked by the patient's own actions. As previously, acts may include all domains of human action, including both public and private actions. Acts of others are typically expressed in a form such as this: "When I asked for the money he ignored me."

4. *Acts of self toward self (introject).* This category of actions refers to how one treats oneself (self-controlling, self-punishing, self-congratulating, self-destroying). These actions should be articulated in specific relation to the acts of self, expectations of others' reactions, and acts of others which compose the remainder of the format. An introject prototypically takes a form such as: "When my husband praises me I feel guilty and remind myself of my shortcomings" or "When I get angry I just try to slow myself down and think things through. I give myself all the time I need."

In a complete TLDP focus, information about the foregoing categories of action is organized into an outline of a prototypic, maladaptive, cyclical interpersonal transaction pattern. If therapists systematically compare the structure of their formulations to this standard, then the format may also aid in recognizing when a tentative focus is incomplete and it may organize the pursuit of missing information. Like many other conceptual tools available to a psychotherapist, the TLDP focus format is primarily a heuristic aid for the clinician and should not be mistaken for what is ordinarily communicated directly to the patient. Everything the therapist understands about a focus is not necessarily transformed into an interpretation.

EXAMPLE OF A TLDP FOCAL NARRATIVE

This example outlines a problematic interpersonal transaction pattern that was observed first in the patient's current relationship with her therapist, and later was narratively integrated with her childhood history and her current marriage.

Presenting problems. The patient complains of depression and marital difficulties.

Acts of self. Frances assumes a passive interpersonal position in which she refrains from disclosing her inner self, avoids social contact by withdrawal or procrastination, defers and submits to others' wishes, and spends much time in private thinking and wondering rather than in active communication.

Expectation of others' reactions. Frances expects that other people will ignore or reject her. She validates this expectation with recollections of being ignored or rejected by her mother and by various significant others.

Observed reactions of others. Others find Frances's passivity unappealing and do not spontaneously recognize her distress and come to her aid. However, Frances does not see this as an understandable reaction to her passivity, but instead interprets this as evidence that others are actively rejecting and ignoring her.

Introject (how patient treats herself). Frances views herself as helpless in a hopeless situation. Rather than endure the imagined negative reactions of others, she inhibits and controls herself and refrains from asserting her desires or complaints (hoping that this interpersonal passivity will make her mere presence more palatable to others).

HOW TO CONSTRUCT A TLDP FOCUS

Formulation of a TLDP focus does not require that therapists adhere to any particular theory of personality. Most personality theories identify certain interpersonal or action patterns as prototypic. For example, in the Freudian psychosexual scheme, interpersonal behaviors are understood in terms of prototypic oral, anal, phallic, and genital patterns. The TLDP focus, in contrast, does not identify any particular interpersonal perspective, theory, or pattern as primary. Rather, the focus mainly addresses how a complete and intelligible interpersonal story may be told, and speaks less to what specific content the story should convey. Accordingly, the content of a TLDP focus may be drawn from any number of broad story metaphors, cultural myths, and psychological theories of personality.

For clinical purposes the ability of a personality theory to sustain a process of intelligible and collaborative therapeutic narration is more important than its so-called objective or scientific validity. In practice this means that a focal formulation must respect the phenomenology of the patient's and therapist's experience. Although there are many possible variants in telling any life story, neither stereotyped theoretical assumptions nor sheer imaginative fiction can substitute for a narrative that is reasonably faithful to the specific details of the patient's life and the particular therapeutic relationship. Sheer charismatic persuasion *cum* coercion may lead some individuals to uncritically adopt a ready-made life story; however, there is no place in TLDP for this kind of Procrustean "one-size-fits-all" formulation.

Malan (1976:55) points out that ability to formulate a focus is separate from a patient's motivation and ability to work within the focus. In TLDP this distinction between formulating and working with a focus has less meaning since the two processes are joined. That is, formulating a focus in TLDP is understood as a central part of the therapeutic work, rather than being simply a precursor to it. Both the process and the outcome of this activity are useful to the patient. The process of constructing a focus, for example, may require activities which improve patients' ability to introspect; to differentiate feelings, images, and thoughts; to regulate and organize their attention; and to observe themselves and others interacting.

The first step in constructing a TLDP focus is to refrain for a while from doing so, and rather to observe patients telling their stories in their own language, their own time, and with their own structure. This permits assessment of patients' spontaneous capacity for gaining access to their inner lives and for organizing their life stories in a continuous, coherent, and relevant way. By initially allowing the patient free rein, the therapist may observe the ordinary complexity of the patient's narrative themes and the influence of emotion and interpersonal relatedness (especially with the therapist) on the patient's narrative capacity. When certain affectively charged material is discussed or when the therapeutic relationship moves into certain domains, some patients may respond with loosened or disorganized thinking, with seemingly inappropriate affects, with heightened anxious struggles to control impulses, or with defensive maneuvers designed to restore psychic and interpersonal equilibrium. Therapists who too vigorously take the lead may handicap themselves by short-circuiting the patient's expression of these important tendencies.

However, by the second or third session therapists often have sufficient information to begin more systematic work toward and/or with a focus. This systematic work involves two general steps. The first step is to gather information about recurrent patterns of interpersonal transaction from the ongoing flow of the therapeutic dialogue. The second step is to sort, interpret, organize, and assemble these raw data about interpersonal transactions into a coherent outline of a repetitive problematic interpersonal transaction pattern, using the four-element structure of the TLDP focus as a guide.

In actual practice, these two steps occur at virtually the same time. That is, the therapist simultaneously gathers and interpretively organizes information. For convenience and clarity each step will be discussed separately. Also, as presented here these activities are laid out in a very deliberate step-by-step manner. Ordinarily, with sufficient practice therapists can work more fluently and less deliberately than this presentation might suggest. However, the value of having an explicit step-by-step model of the therapist's task becomes evident even for experienced clinicians when something unexpected or disorienting happens in therapy. At such times it may be extremely helpful to have a consciously available guide to fall back on.

GATHERING INTERPERSONAL INFORMATION

As various microanalytic studies have shown, even brief conversational interchanges contain overwhelming amounts of interpersonal information (Labov and Fanshel, 1977). When extracting information about interpersonal transaction patterns from the ongoing flow of communicative activity in therapy, clinicians must reconcile their desire to be thorough with the numerous limits to information gathering posed by constraints of time, motivation, financial resources, and human intellectual capacity. It is important to recognize that a therapeutic reconnaissance can never approach exhaustive completeness, and that, fortunately, effective psychotherapeutic work does not ordinarily depend on having an encyclopedic familiarity with the patient. Two basic principles aid in the task of gathering interpersonal information. These include: (1) seeking transaction, and (2) evaluating the functional salience of identified transactions.

Seeking Transaction

Because the TLDP focus expresses a prototypic transaction pattern, therapists naturally cannot generate a focus until they have understood the patient's problems in transactional terms. However, while much that transpires in therapy may relate to interpersonal transaction patterns, patients' spontaneous narratives about interpersonal events are often fragmented or superficial. Consequently, their accounts lack information necessary for a fully transactional understanding of what is being discussed. Consider the following verbatim example from an early therapy hour with a college student:

They could, like you could use it when your friends, when it was like something you had had always, or feelings you had acquired, you know, when you were a child or something like that. Something that comes to mind was when, when my mother was, when we were living in (name of town) when I was in the second and third grade, my (pause) we were living with my grandparents too (pause) it was my grandparents and my mother and my sister and my brother and my mother was going to school (pause) and I often got, you know, scolded and things like that for (pause) one thing that sticks in my mind is one night my mother came in late and we were watching TV and she was tired and, uh, or something (pause) or maybe she wasn't even there (pause) she wasn't even there (pause) and it was just with my grandmother and I (pause) somehow an argument started and she started screaming, you know, at me (pause) I was sort of a (pause) I could, I could, I guess I could provoke fights easily when I was young 'cause I got into a lot of them with my mother and grandparents and people, and I can't remember (pause) well anyway, somehow I was told that you don't love your mother, you don't love your mother, this sort of thing (pause) and then I don't know if that happened before (pause) something happened, and then when my mother came home I told her about it, and then something else started. I can't remember, I can remember.

Clearly, this narrative represents a major challenge to even the most insightful interpreter of interpersonal transactions. Although the context for the patient's remarks is clearly interpersonal, his account is vague, loosely organized, self-contradictory, and does not clearly present one person's actions as eliciting or evoking another person's actions. Consequently, the therapist's task of seeking out the transactional implications of whatever the patient is saying and doing becomes very difficult.

In the foregoing example, what appeared at first to be disorganized thinking was, in fact, part of an organized interpersonal scenario being enacted between patient and therapist that did not become apparent until some time later in the session. This patient had heard in a psychology class about the concept of free association and was attempting to say everything that came to mind without consideration of interpretability. He construed his efforts to free associate as a gift to the therapist, whom he consciously wanted very much to please (the patient made similar efforts to please in his relationships with significant others). The fact that the patient at first neglected to tell the therapist about this experiment in free association revealed other meanings of this behavior, including an opposite wish to challenge or test the therapist's authority and competence ("You're so smart, see if you can figure *this* out!") and a fear of being interpersonally inaccessible ("Can you, or anybody, understand me?").

Vagueness, disorganization, and defensive avoidance are not the only factors which may obscure the transactional significance of patients' symptoms and problems. Psychological difficulties often appear in a symbolized, metaphorically transformed, or poorly differentiated manner that disguises their functional roots in maladaptive patterns of interpersonal transaction. . . .

USING INTERPERSONAL INFORMATION TO FORMULATE A TLDP FOCUS

It is quite unlikely that any two clinicians will gather information in precisely the same way. This variation occurs because each therapist possesses idiosyncratic perceptual and narrative-constructing capabilities, and because each therapist-patient dyad will find unique portions of the possible common experiential range on which to base their communication. In the course of their initial assessments, therapists will accumulate a variety of clinical observations, empathic intuitions, preconscious impressions, personal fantasies, emotional reactions, and so forth. Although these intuitive processes underlying much clinical information gathering will lead to differences among therapists, the inescapable role of intuition should not be used to rationalize a casual abandonment of disciplined and critical thinking. Indeed, effortful reflective thought is an important means of training one's clinical intuition (what is at first effortful later becomes fluent and intuitive with practice).

Sometimes collected observations and impressions may not seem to hang together in a coherent manner, and therapists may ignore, discard, or devalue certain observations simply because they can't understand their significance. This temptation to close one's eyes to confusing information must be resisted. It is necessary to persevere in the faith that one may ultimately make sense of what seems, at first, like an impossibly ambiguous and complex aggregation of information. To persist in this way demands that therapists be willing and able to sustain the tension which results from confronting such ambiguity and that they be diligent enough to accept responsibility for the hard work of doing so.

The TLDP focus format provides a heuristic structural standard for the evaluation, organization, interpretation, and analysis of *both* systematic observations and intuitively derived impressions. The format helps the therapist to organize his or her impressions into a prototypical schematic narrative which: (1) includes central problematic aspects of a patient's habitual modes of relating to others, and (2) organizes these interpersonal transactions into a self-defeating cyclical psychodynamic pattern. Using the four-element TLDP focus model as a template for structuring inquiry, a therapist begins to assemble a focus by considering pertinent questions such as: Which actions and transactions appear redundantly? What cyclical-causal relationships appear among the observed actions and transactions? Which expectations of others appear related to which of the patient's actions; and which of these actions, in turn, lead others to behave in ways that confirm the patient's initial expectations? How have behaviors of others toward the patient (past or present) led him or her to introject? How does a particular way of treating himself or herself affect the patient's expectations of others and transactions with them?

The result of this systematic reflection is a set of statements, organized into the four categories of the TLDP focus format, that express a patient's central interpersonal difficulties in a schematic narrative. While this preliminary focus may be well developed, and the therapist may feel convinced of its validity, a useful rule of thumb is to regard the focus as always partial and preliminary (and therefore subject to continued scrutiny and revision as necessary). Maintaining a tentative attitude toward a focus is a reminder that people's lives are complex and multifaceted, and that therapists cannot hope to achieve an exhaustive or final understanding of a patient, no matter how long or intensely therapy continues.

Difficulty in Formulating a Focus

It is possible that a therapist may be unable to construct a complete focus, either because information relative to one or more of the four action categories is deficient, or because the available information cannot be organized into a coherent cyclical-psychodynamic account. The first hypothesis should generally be that the therapist lacks sufficient information to formulate a focus. However, persistent difficulty in formulating a focus may point to other handicapping factors, including problems with the information-gathering process or even becoming overwhelmed by too much information. More specifically, these difficulties may include the following issues:

1. The patient's character organization may be too rigidly armored, preventing the therapist (and the patient) from obtaining necessary information. Such patients often have very constricted and poorly differentiated inner lives. Alternately, the information may be available but presented in such disguised, transformed, chaotic, or unusual (psychotic) forms that it goes unrecognized or is uninterpretable even by experienced and sensitive observers.

2. Maladaptive modes of relating may be so pervasively woven into the patient's character structure (ego-syntonic) that the boundaries between

problematic and reality-oriented interpersonal patterns may be virtually nonexistent. Patients whose characterological difficulties are this rigidly entrenched often maintain that any problems in their lives are due to the unreasonableness of other people, and it may be impossible to establish an effective therapeutic collaboration.

3. The patient's capacity for experiencing and relating to other persons may be severely constricted. Rather than experiencing others as whole objects with thoughts, wishes, fears, and inner lives of their own, these patients may experience others predominantly in terms of fragmented attributes (what they wear, own, or do for a living) or in terms of functions which gratify basic needs. Such patients are unable fully to perceive themselves in transaction with another person, and hence cannot easily provide the information necessary for a complete TLDP focus.

4. The patient may have a problem that is not maintained in a cyclical psychodynamic fashion. Typical examples of such problems include various adaptive failures caused by ego defects which result from central nervous system or metabolic disorders (attention deficits, impulsivity, problems with affect modulation), or stress reactions due to extreme but discrete trauma. Ordinarily such patients will not meet the basic criteria for selecting TLDP as an appropriate treatment. However, because the selection criteria cannot be perfect, therapists may (erroneously) attempt TLDP with some patients whose problems don't fundamentally arise in a transactional matrix (although they may have interpersonal sequelae). Persistent difficulty in formulating a complete focus may be a clue to this possibility.

5. Therapists' own experiences may interfere with their perceptions, producing a confusingly fragmented and overly selective picture of their patients, or yielding a premature and misplaced sense of conviction. Negative enactments by the therapist may alter the openness and content of the patient's self-disclosure. Patients who persistently keep the therapist in the dark often believe something like this: "If I let you really know me, then you will humiliate me." Although this behavior and its underlying reasons may properly become part of the work toward a focus, therapists should not fail to consider the possibility that their own behavior contributes to this enactment.

6. The therapist may be attempting to integrate too much information. As discussed previously under "Seeking Transaction," people may enact

interpersonal transaction patterns in numerous forms and contexts. The picture may be further complicated by various ways in which a manifest or currently operative interpersonal pattern may serve as a functional component in a concealed or warded-off pattern (the patient uses one mode of maladaptive relating as a means of avoiding a more feared alternative). If the therapist fails to recognize that a variety of superficially different behaviors and experiences all express a common underlying transaction pattern, then it can be very difficult to formulate a focus because the apparent amount of relevant information becomes overwhelming. When struggling to understand a patient whose transaction patterns seem overwhelmingly numerous, a useful rule of thumb is to cluster actions or transactions that all make the patient feel the same way about himself or herself (transactions that converge on a common introject). This common introject—usually experienced as a redundant affective theme—may provide the clearest clues to what the patient is reenacting.

In TLDP, difficulty in formulating a focus does not necessarily portend therapeutic failure. Since the explicit focal format represents both a description of a recurrent problem and also a plan for inquiry and action, it offers a basis for identifying what remains to be accomplished if a focus is to be generated. Suppose, for example, that a patient recounts a pattern of problematic transactions with his wife but in his telling fails to include any mention of her expectations or of how he felt about himself while with her. The therapist should then inquire about the missing information, using the structure of the TLDP focus as a general guide to formulating questions. What does the patient imagine his wife might have expected? How would he have acted had he been aware of that expectation? How did the way he felt about himself influence his choice of what to do and his construal of his wife's beliefs and motives or how she felt about herself?

Using the TLDP focus format as an observational guide makes it very difficult for patients to be uninteresting and makes failure to generate a focus almost as informative to the therapist as a successful fabrication of a focus. The TLDP therapist who has been unable to chart a focal direction for treatment may always refer to the structure of the focus for clues about where to go next. Each time difficulty is encountered in formulating a focus, the problem may be related to the basic definition of a focus and to the fundamental tasks of: (1) gathering interpersonal information relevant to the four elements of the focal narrative; and (2) organizing that information into a narratively coherent cyclical psychodynamic account. The four elements of the TLDP focus model, as a standard for structural comparison, allow therapists to judge when and how completely a focus has been formulated. Or, if a focus has not been formulated, the model points to what is absent and the therapist may then set about obtaining the missing information.

When assessed against the focus format, partial data tell the therapist which aspects of the therapeutic reconnaissance should be emphasized if a complete or well-formed focus is to be generated. For example, it may be that the patient has failed to provide information that is interpersonally or transactionally interpretable. This can occur when patients talk about objects or abstractions rather than human activities. In this instance, the therapist knows that he or she should work toward understanding the action implications of what the patient is reporting, because a focus requires understanding in action terms. In other cases, patients may have discussed only the activities of others, or only those of themselves, or may have avoided discussion of their expectations or of how they treat themselves. Here, the therapist's task in generating a focus is to pursue information pertinent to the unarticulated categories. With the guidance of the explicit four-element focal model, this work toward a focus may be just as systematic (and therapeutically important) as subsequent work with a focus. A brief clinical example will illustrate:

The patient was a professional man in his mid-thirties who complained of depression and inability to accomplish goals. Predictably this problem with accomplishing goals was also enacted in therapy, which quickly became a rather stagnant and boring affair. When the content of the therapeutic dialogue was reviewed with reference to the interpersonal information required to formulate a focus, it became apparent that neither the patient nor the therapist had discussed anything which fell into the category of expectations of others. Accordingly, the patient's self-report had the quality of a travelogue, in which he simply recounted a series of "I went there . . . I did this . . . then she did that." Other people, including intimates such as two former wives, were presented as uncomplicated characters without inner lives or expectations of their own. This patient's inattention to or denial of others' expectations was further acted out in the therapy when he neglected to pay his bill, thereby communicating that, among other things, the therapist's expectations were also insignificant. When the therapist became aware of this pattern and brought her own expectations into the therapeutic relationship by confronting the patient over the unpaid bill, this marked a turning point in the heretofore becalmed treatment process. Subsequent therapeutic work productively continued to give attention to the neglected subject of other people's expectations and inner states.

WORKING WITH A COMPLETED FOCUS

The TLDP focus is not a substitute for an overall clinical assessment, and it should be considered in its overall clinical context. Just as treating a cut finger becomes a very different therapeutic task depending on whether or not the patient is a hemophiliac, so dealing with a particular maladaptive transaction pattern must proceed according to each patient's characteristic strengths and weaknesses for participating effectively in the therapeutic work. Collaboration in generating a focus does not mean that patients can effectively participate in the extended psychotherapeutic tasks. They must also meet other criteria of suitability for TLDP.

Ideally there is no single event that is isolated and labeled as the "presentation" of a focus to the patient. Rather than speaking of presenting a focus to the patient, it is better to understand the process as one of collaboratively arriving at a shared view of what is important to work on in therapy. This work involves more than simply creating intellectual generalizations about experience. Thus, while the focal work should be broad enough to serve as a prototype for dealing with other important situations in the patient's life, it must also involve specifically detailed and vivid reliving of pertinent emotional and transactional experiences. Throughout this process the therapist should maintain an atmosphere of collaboratively finding out rather than one of authoritatively having the answer.

A focus should be articulated as a specific problematic interpersonal scenario that the patient consistently anticipates as his or her fate. This perceived interpersonal destiny ideally unites the technical and experiential components of the therapeutic process by capturing a pattern of interpersonal transaction that is significant both outside of therapy and also in the patient's relationship with the therapist. In an ideal (and therefore impossible) therapy, material emerges during each session that is clearly related to the focus (expresses some part of the focal pattern or defends against such expression). This material typically updates and elaborates the core understanding captured in the focus. "Deep" interpretations should not be required for these relationships to be evident.

Focal comments should rarely (if ever) address the entire cyclical psychodynamic pattern, as this would ordinarily be too much for a patient to digest at once and would probably lead to overly intellectualized understanding. Rather, therapists should work toward clarifying, elaborating, and interpreting the individual manifestations of the focus before attempting to interpret patterns or links between the elements. Like storytellers, therapists should organize their comments and questions so that the proper affective and associative background is in place for focal narratives to make convincing sense. However, the therapist cannot force this background into being and validation of this process must come from the patient. Often it is necessary to work slowly, bit by bit, or even simply to wait for the patient to take an expectable next step. This is an essential feature of that aspect of psychological interventions traditionally called "timing."

Focal comments should also strive for specificity (in action terms) and should avoid overly broad generalizations such as "conflicts over anger," "competitiveness with older men," or "attacks of feeling inadequate." Because it is important for patients to feel affectively as well as intellectually understood, and because excess verbiage may interfere with access to mental imagery and affective experiences (Appelbaum 1981; Spence 1982), therapists should value brevity and should phrase their remarks in concrete and emotionally evocative language. Highly abstract words and long compound sentences rarely belong in psychotherapy. Indeed, it is often a sign of important relationship difficulties (a patient who makes the therapist feel insecure) when it seems necessary to speak in a pompous or jargon-laden manner.

While a focus may be extremely useful as a structure for listening and for interpreting and organizing ongoing observations and impressions, therapists should beware of overextending a focal narrative. It is dangerously easy to force therapeutic events to fit a focal formulation and, subsequently, to find "corroborating" evidence. The fact that something can be plausibly related to the focus doesn't mean that the connection is affectively convincing or, most important, that it is consonant with the patient's experience at the time. The risk is that once sensitized to the presence of a particular characteristic in a patient, and especially once that characteristic has been named and incorporated into an organized formulation, a therapist becomes more likely to perceive that same characteristic again, and becomes less likely to perceive opposite, contradictory, or alternate characteristics. For example, a comment by the patient about the therapist's clothing or appearance will be understood one way if the prior interpersonal process was perceived as expressing aggressive competitiveness, whereas the same comment will be heard quite differently if the process was perceived to be one of nurturance or seduction. Likewise, if a patient casts himself in the role of a bad boy, the therapist may become especially alert to evidence that the patient is seeking signs of displeasure or forgiveness in the therapeutic relationship. Correspondingly, the therapist may become less sensitive to alternate possibilities which do not fit the bad boy formulation. Therapists do well to be skeptical of themselves and to alert themselves to the possibility that their observations are contaminated by the effects of self-fulfilling prophecy and selective perception.

Having created a plausible focus, therapists may subsequently feel a certain narrative pressure to apply their hard-won understanding. This pressure is increased by the therapists' need for mastery, order, and understanding (which a focus appears to fulfill) and by patients' demands for a quick fix. If therapists yield to this narrative pressure indiscriminately, the result may be a rigid or even frenzied interpretive pursuit of focal connections. Therapists may succumb to an unwarranted sense of conviction in the correctness of their formulations (hardening of the categories) and become blind and deaf to evidence from the patient and the therapeutic relationship. It is crucial to repeatedly reconfirm the validity of the focus by establishing an elaborated experiential and associational context for what the patient brings to each session. In this process patients must be working partners who experience what is being verbalized and who are able to support, revise, or disconfirm the therapists' comments as well as make contributions of their own. *A focus does not explain everything: it is a map, not the territory itself.* There will inevitably be significant residual ambiguity in any narrative formulation. Therapists should not forget the essentially tentative and incomplete nature of any focus.

Patients, too, may embrace a focus with excessive zeal, learning what their therapist "wants" to hear and shaping their comments and reactions accordingly. To some extent this is unavoidable and can even be positive: a patient may develop an enhanced capacity for empathy. However, patients who persistently say what the therapist wants to hear may seem to confirm the focal formulation, when in fact the focal work is being distorted by the interpersonal enactment between patient and therapist.

In this circumstance, the patient-therapist collaboration may itself reenact the focal problem, with the content of the focus being unconsciously shaped by both participants' needs for certain things to be true in order to maintain their relationship. For example, patients' needs to please may impel them to make things hang together for therapists who, for their part, feel duty bound to make sense of their patients' problems. Such patients may be willing to accept plausible constructions uncritically, but such acceptance may in fact represent an enactment of an excessively deferent and dependent interpersonal pattern. In this case, a therapeutic misalliance risks yielding only a maladaptive illusion of understanding. Therapists should beware of being seduced by the seeming coherence of a patient's narrative (what Spence 1982, refers to as "fool's gold"). What patients say, no matter how plausible or coherent, should not be interpreted outside the context of when, how, and why they say it. In particular, a patient's responses to focal work should always be evaluated with the status of the treatment relationship in mind.

Efforts to articulate a focus should simultaneously foster patients' beliefs that their difficulties and suffering are being understood and that their situation is not hopeless. However, helping patients to feel understood (or even understandable) is a delicate task that cannot be accomplished merely by saying "I understand" or by nodding empathically at regular intervals. To this end it is important to respect patients' affective distress and to recognize how their symptoms and maladaptive actions also represent healthy motives and genuine (if failed) efforts to deal with their problems. Therapists also will inevitably make some inappropriate assessments and interpretations. Indeed, sometimes it is only through such errors that the therapist gets to observe, in the patient's reactions, details that elaborate further understanding. To participate effectively in TLDP, patients must occasionally tolerate such failures of empathy and then be able to return to collaborative work. Therapists, for their part, must openly allow themselves to be corrected by feedback from the patient.

Another problem occurs when patients' implicit requests for understanding are also woven into the maladaptive interpersonal patterns that are the subject of therapy. Patients frequently entertain curative fantasies as corollaries to their focal patterns. In such fantasies, patients imagine that if they are to feel or act "better," they must have a certain kind of person who will interact with them in a particular way. Thus, as part of their maladaptive transaction patterns, patients may need to cast the therapist in a certain role in order to feel that he or she is capable of listening, understanding, or accepting. For example, a patient who relates to others deferentially and dependently may feel most comfortable with a therapist who enacts a complementary authoritative and directive role. However, by assuming such a role, which the patient implicitly demands as a precondition for being understood, the therapist may also foreclose important opportunities for the patient to develop a more autonomous mode of relating. Of course, to meet their own needs, patients may perceive a therapist as authoritative and directive even when objective observers would make a different assessment. The therapist's task is to understand the patient's experience without necessarily validating any distorted perceptions or maladaptive interpersonal preconditions for being understood.

Patients' responses to development of a focal narrative are often a mixture of both positive and negative reactions. On the positive side a patient may respond with appreciative recognition, acknowledging that despite previous awareness of this area of discomfort, it was never so clearly articulated as a problem. Or, patients may realize for the first time that various disturbing elements in their experience are not disconnected, but can be organized and understood as part of a pattern of conflictual interpersonal relationships. This recognition sets the stage for investigations into how patients play an active role in creating and maintaining their difficulties. Alternately, since the focal subject matter is painful, patients may become anxious and back away from the therapist, or they may back away from themselves by responding with habitual defensive techniques that ward off awareness of experiences associated with the focus.

All reactions to the focus, whether positive or negative, may provide further material for the elaboration of the focus. Both avoidance or zealous embracing of the focal content in the therapeutic dialogue may paradoxically be accompanied by an enactment of the focal pattern in the therapeutic relationship. To examine these enactments without thereby suppressing them, therapists must give the patient adequate latitude to respond. Specifically, therapists should maintain a collaborative approach and should ordinarily abstain from forcing the direction of the dialogue.

While refraining from overtly managing or directing their patients, TLDP therapists must also deal effectively with diversionary resistances, such as persistent vagueness or avoidant changing of topics. Throughout, however, emphasis should be placed on understanding when, how, and why defensiveness occurs, rather than on confrontively getting patients to admit to their defensive actions. Avoiding a controlling or adversarial stance also does not imply that therapists do not exert persuasive influence. It is impossible for a therapist to be truly nondirective, and it is undesirable to pretend or even aspire to the myth of neutrality. It is most important that therapists exert influence in a manner that fosters autonomy, allowing patients to discover and own their personal capacity for change. While exerting influence to increase patients' autonomy may seem self-contradictory, properly accomplished the task is no more paradoxical than the influence a mother uses to ease a young child into opportunities for independent activity.

Staying with a Focus. If a patient's communications repeatedly seem irrelevant to the focus, then the therapist should attempt to bring the patient back to pertinent material. This work should follow two guidelines: (1) the principle of "selective attention and selective neglect" (Balint, Ornstein, and Balint 1972), and (2) the principle of "least possible confrontation."

Selective attention and selective neglect are not the same as arbitrarily ignoring whatever appears unrelated to a focus. Ignoring anything that a patient says or does is an unfriendly and generally counterproductive action in TLDP, since everything that a patient says or does communicates something, however disguised, and thus cannot be safely disregarded. Selective attention and selective neglect properly involve a subtle process of influencing what is figure and what is ground in the therapeutic discourse. The therapist's patterning of questions, the timing and shaping of the context for questions, the choices of what to name and what to leave nameless, should all create an associative atmosphere in which focally relevant material predominates because it seems most narratively natural.

The principle of least possible confrontation instructs therapists to use the gentlest means available to promote awareness. It is almost never useful to sacrifice a collaborative therapeutic relationship in order to confront a patient. To paraphrase Peterfreund (1983:198), the adversary is not the patient but the patient's problem. While some patients may forgive a therapist's abruptness and tactlessness, this forgiveness may well be part of their difficulties; in any case, the fact of a forgiving patient does not justify a coercive approach to the therapeutic relationship. It can be necessary at times to provoke anxiety, especially with obsessional patients (Sifneos 1972; Davanloo 1980), and this may even be desirable, so long as patients do not become so anxious that they lose the capacity to observe themselves and to collaborate effectively. However, even anxiety-provoking confrontation can be gentle, and ideally, therapists should prefer to help patients learn how to confront themselves. The inevitable impediments to speaking freely should arise from within the patient, and not from reactions to a confrontive relationship offered by the therapist. The principle of least possible confrontation recognizes that a TLDP focus is a means, not an end. It should never be understood as some sort of critical interpretation which produces change all by itself and therefore must be gotten across to the patient at almost any expense.

Although the principles of selective attention/neglect and least possible confrontation may sound simple, a therapist's task in this regard can be quite delicate and difficult. The therapist must function somewhat as a narrative artist, creating a background of associations and interpretive elements that makes focally relevant themes easy to see. If carried out in a crude, mechanical, or unempathic manner the patient may reject the therapist's efforts as tedious carping and the therapy may reach an impasse. An empathic collaborative relationship is an essential prerequisite for selective attention/neglect and for therapeutic confrontation, and maintaining this relationship generally takes precedence over other therapeutic work.

If therapists persistently fail in their efforts to engage the patient in focally relevant dialogue, they should: (1) review the patient's overall clinical status to ensure that the patient possesses the basic resources for effective participation in TLDP, and/or (2) consider the possibility that the content of the chosen focus is currently unworkable. A focus is, after all, just a hypothesis. If correct it may not be uniquely so, or it may be excessively inaccurate or incomplete. In some cases, exploration of the focal topics evokes unmanageable anxiety. This is especially likely if the therapist fails to take an affirmative approach and places excess emphasis on the defective, pathological, and maladaptive aspects of the patient's life. In such cases patients may self-protectively divert themselves from the focal material by becoming preoccupied with unconnected events, current or historical. Although such events may be relatable to the focus, the connections may be too obscure to be plausibly interpreted. Furthermore, in such a case the therapist's primary task would be to establish (or restore) the patient's sense of safety in the therapeutic relationship.

If excessive anxiety and defensiveness persist, a therapist may have to abandon or revise a focus in order to restore an effective collaborative process. In general, however, a focus should not be abandoned unless there is reasonable evidence suggesting the potentially greater viability of another focal pattern. It is important to persevere, and to tolerate the ambiguity, uncertainty, and tension which inevitably accompany efforts to make sense of the heretofore incomprehensible. Such perseverance, if not carried to fruitless extremes, is frequently rewarded by new understandings based on generation of unexpected connections between seemingly unrelated events.

If through their therapist's example patients also elect to persist in trying to understand, rather than choosing to run away from themselves and others, the result may be increased hope, a strengthened sense of mastery, and a heightened awareness of themselves as active agents in their lives.

REFERENCES

Alexander, F., and T. M. French. 1946. *Psychoanalytic Therapy: Principles and Applications*. New York: Ronald Press.

Anchin, J. C., and D. J. Kiesler, eds. 1982. *Handbook of Interpersonal Psychotherapy*. New York: Pergamon Press.

Appelbaum, S. A. 1972. "How Long Is Long-term Psychotherapy?" *Bulletin of the Menninger Clinic 36*:651–55.

———. 1981. *Effecting Change in Psychotherapy*. New York: Jason Aronson.

Armstrong, S. 1980. "Dual Focus in Brief Psychodynamic Psychotherapy." *Psychotherapy and Psychosomatics 33*:147–54.

Balint, M., P. Ornstein, and E. Balint. 1972. *Focal Psychotherapy: An Example of Applied Psychoanalysis*. London: Tavistock Publications.

Bellak, L., and L. Small. 1978. *Emergency Psychotherapy and Brief Psychotherapy*. 2d ed. New York: Grune & Stratton.

Binder, J. L. 1977. "Modes of Focusing in Psychoanalytic Short-term Therapy." *Psychotherapy: Theory, Research, and Practice 14*(3):232–41.

Binder, J. L., and I. Smokler. 1980. "Early Memories: A Technical Aid to Focusing in Brief Psychotherapy." *Psychotherapy: Theory, Research, and Practice 17*:52–62.

Blos, P. 1941. *The Adolescent Personality*. New York: Appleton-Century-Crofts.

Budman, S. H., ed. 1981. *Forms of Brief Therapy*. New York: Guilford Press.

Davanloo, H., ed. 1980. *Short-term Dynamic Psychotherapy*. New York: Jason Aronson.

Ekstein, R. 1956. Psychoanalytic Techniques. In *Progress in Clinical Psychology*, vol. 2, edited by D. Bower and L. E. Abt. New York: Grune & Stratton.

Flegenheimer, W. V. 1982. *Techniques of Brief Psychotherapy*. New York: Jason Aronson.

Gill, M. M. 1982. *Analysis of Transference I: Theory and Technique*. New York: International Universities Press.

Gill, M. M. and I. Hoffman. 1982. "A Method for Studying the Analysis of Aspects of the Patient's Experience of the Relationship in Psychoanalysis and Psychotherapy." *Journal of the American Psychoanalytic Association 30*:137–67.

Kinston, W., and A. Bentovim. 1981. "Creating a Focus for Brief Marital Therapy." In *Forms of Brief Therapy*, edited by S. H. Budman. New York: Guilford Press, pp. 361–86.

Labov, W., and D. Fanshel. 1977. *Therapeutic Discourse: Psychotherapy as Conversation*. New York: Academic Press.

Luborsky, L. 1977. "Measuring a Pervasive Psychic Structure in Psychotherapy: The Core Conflictual Relationship Theme." In *Communicative Structures and Psychic Structures,* edited by N. Freedman and S. Grand. New York: Plenum Press.

Malan, D. H. 1976. *The Frontier of Brief Psychotherapy: An Example of the Convergence of Research and Clinical Practice.* New York: Plenum Press.

Mann, J. 1973. *Time-limited Psychotherapy.* Cambridge: Harvard University Press.

Mann, J., and R. Goldman. 1982. *A Casebook in Time-limited Psychotherapy.* New York: McGraw-Hill.

Mortimer, R. L., and W. H. Smith. 1983. "The Use of the Psychological Test Report in Setting the Focus of Psychotherapy." *Journal of Personality Assessment 47:*134–38.

Peterfreund, E. 1983. *The Process of Psychoanalytic Therapy: Models and Strategies.* New Jersey: Analytic Press.

Racker, H. 1968. *Transference and Countertransference.* New York: International Universities Press.

Ryle, A. 1979. "The Focus in Brief Interpretive Psychotherapy: Dilemmas, Traps, and Snags." *British Journal of Psychiatry 134:*46–54.

Schacht, T. E. In press. "Toward Operationalizing the Transference: A Research Method for Identifying a Focus in Time-limited Dynamic Psychotherapy." In *Empirical Studies of Psychoanalytic Theory,* vol. 3, edited by J. Masling. Hillsdale, N.J.: Erlbaum/Analytic Press.

Schafer, R., 1976. *A New Language for Psychoanalysis.* New Haven, Conn.: Yale University Press.

———. 1983. *The Analytic Attitude.* New York: Basic Books.

Schank, R. C., and R. Abelson. 1977. *Scripts, Plans, Goals, and Understanding.* Hillsdale, N.J.: Erlbaum.

Sherwood, M. 1969. *The Logic of Explanation in Psychoanalysis.* New York: Academic Press.

Sifneos, P. 1972. *Short-term Psychotherapy and Emotional Crisis.* Cambridge, Mass.: Harvard University Press.

Spence, D. P. 1982. *Historical Truth and Narrative Truth.* New York: W. W. Norton & Co.

Wachtel, P. 1982. "Vicious Circles: The Self and the Rhetoric of Emerging and Unfolding." *Contemporary Psychoanalysis 18*(2):259–72.

Wallerstein, R. S. and L. L. Robbins. 1956. "The Psychotherapy Research Project of the Menninger Foundation: Rationale, Method, and Sample Use IV: Concepts." *Bulletin of the Menninger Clinic 20:*239–62.

Wender, P. H. 1968. "Vicious and Virtuous Circles: The Role of Deviation-amplifying Feedback in the Origin and Perpetuation of Behavior." *Psychiatry 31*(4):309–24.

Yalom, I. 1980. *Existential Psychotherapy.* New York: Basic Books.

9. Fixed Role Therapy

George A. Kelly

Fixed role therapy is an experimental procedure that may be followed in cases where one wishes to activate psychotherapeutic processes without resorting to applied psychology. This is to say that it represents a form of inquiry designed to shed light on an urgent problem rather than a treatment warranted only by previous research. It is essentially experimental, not simply because it is novel, but because it involves the client in a calculated venture the extended outcome of which he must assess. In a strict sense it is not even a form of treatment but an investigative project in which the client is himself the principal investigator—and knows it!

CONSTRUCTIVE ALTERNATIVISM

The form of the procedure is embedded in personal construct theory, which, in turn, is anchored in an epistemological position called constructive alternativism. Constructive alternativism holds that man understands himself, his surroundings, and his potentialities by devising constructions to place upon them and then testing the tentative utility of these constructions against such *ad interim* criteria as the successful prediction and control of events. It assumes that man's construction of events may ultimately converge upon reality, in the manner of non-Euclidian parallel lines, but that it is presumptuous to claim the convergence has already taken place. Any present construction is then open to an undetermined amount of reconsideration, no matter how obvious it may appear to be or how objective the evidence which supports it at the moment. Constructive alternativism stands in contrast to a view we may call accumulative fragmentalism, the notion that knowledge is a growing collection of substantiated facts—when we get all the facts we shall find ourselves arrived at the truth.

Reprinted by permission of Miami Press from *Direct Psychotherapy: 28 American Originals.* Coral Gables, 1973, pp. 394–422.

PERSONAL CONSTRUCT THEORY

Personal construct theory starts with the postulate that a person's processes are psychologically channeled by the ways in which he anticipates events. It goes on to propose that one anticipates events by construing the manner in which future occurrences can be thought to replicate past ones. The unit of construction is the personal construct, which is defined as a way in which two or more events can be regarded as similar and in contrast to one or more other events. The personal construct is not a representation of an event or a group of events, as is sometimes said of a concept. It is, instead, a referent devised by the person upon which he may project events in order to cope with them. It need not be verbalized and it may be regarded as structuring smooth muscle and glandular processes, as well as skeletal muscle or verbal enactments.

The development of a personal construct system for the anticipation of events poses a "minimax" problem for the person—how to achieve maximum differentiation of events with a minimum of dichotomous discrimination units, or constructs. It also involves problems of ordinal relations between constructs, the employment of constructs in experience, commitment to behavioral inquiry, and the revision of constructs in the light of particular outcomes and the integrity of the system as a whole.

THE SCIENCE PARADIGM

For purposes of understanding fixed role therapy there are two features of personal construct theory that must be kept clearly in mind. Both represent wide departures from the views of other personality theories. The first is the notion of the scientist as the paradigm of man. The second is the notion that one enacts a role, in the personal construct theoretical sense, only to the extent that he is guided by a construction of another person's outlook. Both notions require a little explaining.

A description of scientific method as it is practiced by scientists can quite properly be regarded as a personality theory—applied, of course, to persons who happen to be scientists. But the basic features of scientific method can be considered as basically human too. One can scarcely say the scientist does anything a human being cannot do, though he may do some things that not all his fellow humans do as well. But the behavior of the scientists is altogether human behavior, and a construction of his actions can provide guidelines for understanding all human behavior. Moreover, the tactics that scientists follow in pursuing their investigations are no less available to other men who have inquiries to pursue.

The thoughtful exploration of this line of theorizing suggests, then, that what a scientist does, man can do, and what a scientifically minded psychologist does, his client can do. It suggests, furthermore, that it may be as inept to try to get a client up on his feet by treating him or conditioning him as it would be to try to get a psychologist to make a monumental contribution by ordering him to do precisely what he is told. But if a client can begin to use the better methods of inquiry himself, if he can experiment appropriately, and if he can reformulate his hypotheses in the light of the relationships between his predictions and his observation of occurrences, he may be on his way to living his life in a manner that leads somewhere rather than going round and round in "healthy" orbits prescribed by his psychiatrist. Fixed role therapy casts the client in the role of a scientist intent on inquiring into his most perplexing problems. It casts his psychotherapist in the role of a colleague who has as much to learn as he does.

ROLE

The other feature of personal construct theory that must be particularly well understood is its definition of role. The two conventional notions of role—a course of action articulated with the actions of others, and a set of behavioral expectations imposed upon a man—are both externalized definitions. That is to say their determinants are outside the person. Personal construct theory, however, makes every effort to employ terms which refer to the outlook of the person himself. The theory's definition of role represents such an effort.

If I attempt to understand another man mechanistically or behavioristically, it probably means that I am not concerned with the construction he is placing on me or the other events in his life, but only with those actions which I can observe and how I myself choose to construe them. For all I care, he could just as well be a combination of levers and wires. I may even refer to him as "an organism," rather than as "a person," in the manner of psychologists who think there is something unscientific about being a person. To be sure, I may be able to anticipate some of his behavior better by construing him in this way than if I listen to him too intently. This may turn out to be particularly true if I make the mistake of assuming that the words he uses have only the meanings attributed to them by the dictionary.

But however efficient may be this manner of construing my friend, personal construct theory would not call any of my ensuing behavior a role. On the other hand, if I make an attempt to see the world through his spectacles (through his constructs, I mean) and I structure my own actions in the light of what I think I see, what I do then is, for me, a role. This is not to say that my interpretation of his viewpoint is accurate, or even that I shall then choose to act in a manner compliant with his wishes. Indeed, my perception may be grossly inaccurate, which could result in considerable confusion, and I may even choose to use my version of his outlook to undo him, which also could have chaotic consequences. But in any case, my actions would constitute a role.

IMPLICATIONS OF ROLE ENACTMENT

However badly I may choose to act, or some other individuals may choose to act, it should not be necessary to go into great argumentative detail to suggest that, notwithstanding, it is in role relationships that men may hope to combine their ingenuities as well as their labors. Thus they may advance mankind's cultural achievements beyond what can be accomplished simply by assembly line divisions of labor or by the imposition of regularized behavioral expectations upon the masses. On the other hand, a socialization of human institutions which is based on the two conventional notions of role is all too likely to lead to the suppression of human ingenuity, as, in the case of one of the notions, it did in the early stages of the industrial revolution, or as, in the case of the other, it has done in the headlong rush of ideological socialism.

The notion of role as a man's course of action articulated with the actions of others leads one to envision a society populated with a species of economic man. The notion of role as a set of expectations conjures up an image of a society of ideological man. I suppose we could add that, if the current notions of psychotherapy continue to catch on, we may look forward to a society of the self-conscious man. But personal construct theory envisions a different kind of society, a society of the inquiring man. Fixed role therapy depends greatly upon both client and therapist understanding the meaning of role in this personal construct sense, rather than in the sense of either of the conventional definitions, or in the implied sense that emerges out of present-day psychotherapeutics.

Having said only this much, we could easily break off the discussion and leave the reader with the impression that fixed role therapy is going to turn out to be no more than an epistemological pastime of gentle people. But this might be misleading. Fixed role therapy is as much an ontological venture as it is a perceptive psychoanalysis of one's neighbors. Personal construct theory is not a cognitive theory but a theory about how the human process flows, how it strives in new directions as well as in old, and how it may dare for the first time to reach into the depths of newly perceived dimensions of human life.

Personal construct theory's epistemology is an epistemology of creative action: Man understands his world by finding out what he can do with it. And he understands himself in the same way, by finding out what he can make of himself. Man is what he becomes. What he becomes is a product of what he undertakes—expected or by surprise. The peculiar genius of psychology, if it has one, is to see man in this perspective, as what the continuing effort of living can make of him. Here, beyond epistemology, lies the ontological rationale of fixed role therapy.

OTHER FORMS OF PSYCHOTHERAPY WITHIN PERSONAL CONSTRUCT THEORY

Although fixed role therapy embodies the principles of personal construct theory, the reader should not be left with the impression that it is the only form of psychotherapy that may do so. It stands out as an example of the theory in action primarily because, on the face of it, it appears to disregard so much of what other systems hold to be essential. Psychoanalysis probes and strives for insight, yet fixed role therapy offers no necessary interpretations of the client's present problem. Behavior therapy prescribes a cure, yet fixed role therapy may propose an enactment no client or therapist would want to see continued. The client-centered therapist must offer his client "an unconditional positive regard" for the feelings he has so long experienced in dread, but fixed role therapy recognizes no such autonomy of feelings. Yet fixed role therapy is articulate about what it undertakes, it ventures to undertake unfamiliar modes of behavior, and it relies upon acute sensitivity to feelings arising out of one's own experimentation.

But however much at odds with better known approaches fixed role therapy appears to be, its rationale does not rest on any necessary conviction that they are wrong. The philosophical position, constructive alternativism, which underlies the theory and the method, does not require one to discredit one set of assumptions before daring to examine the implications of others. Indeed, this is, in effect, just what is proposed to the client: He need not invalidate his "neurotic" outlook before actively exploring what other outlooks have to offer. He has only to undertake psychotherapy as an ontological venture rather than as an epistemological exercise designed to convince himself of what he does not feel is so. All of this is a way of saying that one's personality is not altogether shaped by what he knows and what he accepts, but emerges continuously through his modes of pursuing what he hopes to be and what he would like to find out.

Personal construct theory, more than any other system of psychotherapy I know, envisions an orchestration of techniques—perhaps as wide a variety of techniques as the human armamentarium stocks. Unlike psychoanalysis, in which Freud precisely combined the techniques of his mentor Charcot and his colleague Breuer, personal construct theory does not prescribe for the therapist a single orthodox procedure. Nor does it see the salivating dog as the prototype of the client, or an abiding faith in man as the climate in which all good things grow. Yet what the psychoanalyst does to help his client articulate what has remained estranged from language, the personal construct theorist may do also. He may, as well, see conditioning as an experiment the client performs rather than an operation performed on him, and he may offer his client the acceptance of feelings as a hypothesis worth experimenting with.

APPROPRIATENESS OF FIXED ROLE THERAPY

One thing more: for my own part I do not employ fixed role therapy in the majority of cases I see, perhaps in no more than one out of fifteen. There are too many other orchestral possibilities for one to sit and hum the same therapeutic tune to his clients morning, noon, and night. Sometimes I employ the procedure when I can see the client for less than a month but can have him come in several times a week. I may resort to fixed role therapy when a client has become surfeited with other therapeutic efforts, including my own. It can be used to break through overintellectualization, and it can serve to direct the client to resources outside the therapy room which are not for hire. Now and then I use it to prepare the client for a protracted psychotherapeutic sequence and sometimes to finish off such a sequence. Occasionally it proves useful when a psychotherapist whom I am supervising becomes preoccupied with the "interesting material" that accumulates in session after session and starts "peeling his onion."

As for the appropriateness of fixed role therapy in various diagnostic categories, our experience so far does not permit us to put our finger precisely on the outer boundaries. My early apprehension about using it with "schizophrenics" has been allayed; it does not foster the delusions I was afraid it might. I am also less reluctant to employ it with mild "paranoid schizophrenics," now that I have had some experience with it. Handled properly, it seems to offer some stabilization for the aura of urgency that "manics" display. "Depressives," of course, experience difficulty mobilizing themselves for the continued enactment, but, since continued mobilization of their efforts is generally judged to be a good thing, this difficulty need not be taken as a contraindication for the method. I have even seen it work rather well in "conversion" cases and in cases of "immature personality." It has been tried with some success in cases of mental retardation, though not to "cure" the symptoms of mental deficiency itself, of course. Thus far I have not approached a "phobic case" through fixed role therapy; I must try that the next time a client comes in complaining of his inability to get along with snakes.

THE SEQUENCE OF STEPS IN FIXED ROLE THERAPY

It would perhaps be helpful at this point to turn from rationale to technique, starting with a sketch of the process as a whole, and then following with a step-by-step account of the sequence of procedures. The client, call him Q. M., is asked to write a character sketch of himself from a particular point of view. The therapist then studies this sketch in consultation with colleagues and, with their help, prepares an enactment sketch, one that might have been written by a hypothetical "E. S." in response to a similar request.

In the next therapy session Q. M. is shown the "E. S." sketch and his superficial reaction to it is tested. If the test is passed satisfactorily, he is asked to pretend that he, Q., "has gone to the mountains to enjoy himself," and that, in his stead, "E. S." materializes. The client is to enact as best he can, twenty-four hours a day, all that "E. S." might do, say, think, or even dream. At least three therapy sessions a week are scheduled, and in them client and therapist rehearse the enactment, plan critical tests of its effectiveness, and examine outcomes. At the end of the period Q. M. "comes back," whether he wants to or not, and is invited to appraise the experience in whatever ways make sense to him.

The undertaking is not as simple as it probably sounds. Our experience —

the experience of my colleagues and myself—suggests many points at which variation in the procedure can lead to trouble, especially in the hands of a therapist who thinks of fixed role therapy as a form of "treatment." Although the method does not require one to make the usual psychoanalytic "interpretations," it is scarcely any the less vulnerable to the blunders of clinically insensitive therapists. It is neither easy nor routine. Clinical skill and perceptiveness are as crucial as they are known to be in a psychoanalytic relationship where volatile transference involvements are present. But, of course, the terms of reference are different.

THE SELF-CHARACTERIZATION

At first glance it may appear that the self-characterization the client is asked to write is not essential to the experiment. I am convinced, however, that it is an important step in the process. The particular way in which the self-characterization is elicited is intended to imply that neither psychodiagnosis nor the ensuing psychotherapy is based on "confession." Moreover, having written the self-characterization, the client should be better prepared to see the "E. S." sketch as having both subjective and objective authenticity. "E. S." is a man, such as Q. himself is, who can see himself as a man, just as Q. has been asked to see himself, who faces human problems too and makes no pretense of psychological perfection. Furthermore, Q. may begin to see that there is a sense in which one may credit a man with being what he represents himself to be, this being an application of the principle of the credulous approach, about which personal construct theory has a great deal to say.

As I write these sentences I recall that last night—by an actual count of candy bars—exactly seventy goblins, witches, and sundry suspicious characters of assorted sizes came to our door, some of them piping in small voices, "Trick or treat, trick or treat!" To be sure, you and I might be constrained to say that "they were not goblins, or witches, or even very suspicious," both of us being quite willing to assume that we know what real spooks look like. But if we agree to make such a denial, do we approach the psychological truth about these visitors, or do we retreat from it? Which, psychologically, is the real child: The child behind the mask, or the child "unmasked," standing barefaced in the bright light of the living room, surrounded by adults, and saying proper "pleases" and "thank yous?" Do I understand the child half as well if I refuse to see the part he is enacting? I think not!

A man becomes the President of the United States. But come now, between us psychologists, is he really the President? Or must we not diagnose him as the small-time politician who has been playing "trick or treat" most of his life? No, I think that if he now undertakes to enact the part, he is, indeed, *The President.* If we are to understand psychologically a man who enacts such a commitment, we can do so only by empathizing the commitment, by being credulous to it. Of course, this does not mean that he will play the part the way we think we might or the way we think Abraham Lincoln or George Washington played it.

Psychological perceptiveness does not depend upon the precision with which we can fit our client into one of our own preconceived categories but upon our grasp of his construction of events and of the part his construction leads him to take in coping with them. The therapist, too, has a role to enact, a role in the personal construct theoretical sense, one that comes to life only after he puts the client's glasses on over his own and sees as best he can what the client sees.

ELICITING THE SELF-CHARACTERIZATION

"I want you to write a character sketch of Q. M., just as if he were the principal character in a play. Write it as it might be written by a friend who knew him very intimately and very sympathetically, perhaps better than anyone ever really could know him. Be sure to write it in the third person. For example, start out by saying, 'Q. M. is. . . .' " This is the way Q. M. is asked to write a character sketch of himself.

The phrasing of this request has been carefully chosen and has gone through a good many revisions in the light of experience with it. The term, "character sketch," seems to work best in suggesting to the client that he is to present himself as a coherent whole rather than to catalogue his faults and virtues. The object is to see how he structures himself, and within what kind of framework, not to force him to diagnose himself within a psychologist's framework. He may find it difficult to present himself as an integral person. If so, it is worth knowing, and, furthermore, an appreciation of this fact should help the clinician structure his own role. A responsible therapist will seek to know something of how both Q.'s self and his outside world are seen through those glasses he wears.

It is easy to see that the therapist cannot suggest an outline for the sketch, though he may be asked to prescribe one. It is Q.'s outline, his own structural framework, however inadequate that may be, that is sought, not a burlesque of a man vainly juggling words to present himself in the alien language of a presumed expert. Nor is Q. expected to encapsulate himself in the terms of any particular friend, as the phrase, "perhaps better than anyone ever really could know him," is intended to suggest.

To be sure, Q. may find himself at a loss for words. If so, then that may be how it is with him—a self held together without the structure of language. Or he may say only, "I live at 35½ Commercial Street. I am five feet two inches tall. I am 32 years old, and I weigh 190 pounds." Can we then say he has offered us nothing of psychological importance? I think no sensitive clinician would say that! He may thus indeed have put his identity in the most poignant perspective.

Or suppose he says only, "I am of medium height and build, I live in an average community, and I have never been in trouble." Can we allow ourselves to think for one moment that this tells us nothing of his inner experience or of the illusive issues that plague his daily life?

There are occasions when a client will protest he is quite incapable of writing down anything about himself. Ordinarily one suggests then that he give it a try and come in next time with whatever he has managed to write. But the therapist can add, if he wishes, "Just suppose I have never seen Q. M. or talked to him. How would this friend, who knows him so much more intimately and sympathetically than anyone really does know him, write the character sketch? You and I need his help." It does not seem advisable to go further than this, if indeed to go even this far. After all, the success of therapy rarely hinges on the client's avoiding all confrontation with his own unproductiveness.

PREPARING THE ENACTMENT SKETCH: AN EXPERIMENT

There is much more to be said about systematic methods of analyzing the self-characterization. But that is a whole chapter in itself, and the reader, if he plans to have a go at fixed role therapy, is urged to read what is written elsewhere about it (3). The analysis should be carried to the point where the therapist has some notions of the principal construct dimensions the client uses in identifying himself, of how he utilizes experience, and of the directions in which his sense of movement appears to carry him. One can begin to infer also what his words mean, although finding out precisely what a client's language means is an undertaking not likely to get very far in the brief course of a fixed role therapy sequence.

It may seem trite to say that "E. S." must, first of all, present himself as human. The image of mental health that most psychotherapists manage to project is not of a person that most of us would warm up to, much as we might admire his stark realism, his overpowering release of libidinal energy, and his unfailing competence in manipulating his associates. Such realism robs the world of mystery, the energy makes all obstacles trivial, and the competence eliminates any exciting risk of failure. Certainly personal construct theory does not for one moment paint such a picture of mental health.

There is no implicit guarantee of success in the character of "E. S." Like Q., he is a man of dreams, striving, and uncertainty. His answers turn out to be questions in another form, and his questions, if they are to lead him anywhere in his life, must be posed in judicious behavior, not merely in words. Any attempt to portray "E." as a walking solution to Q.'s problems makes him into a Madison Avenue advertiser's layout rather than an honest experiment. This portrayal would be as fraudulent as most applied psychology turns out to be, whether on Madison Avenue or in a practitioner's office.

HYPOTHESES IMBEDDED IN "E. S."

The task one faces in writing the enactment sketch is, then, to design a genuine experiment in which both client and therapist are active participants and both are prepared to be surprised by the outcomes. That means there should be at least one hypothesis to be tested, and it should be stated explicitly in the "E. S." sketch. The hypothesis may be one Q. has already set up in his characterization of himself. Since, in human affairs, there is nothing that corresponds to the statistician's null hypothesis, we can examine Q.'s hypothesis only by testing its substantial alternatives. For example, if he has described himself as "meticulous," the alternative (from his point of view) might be to play the part of an "E." who was "casual," and then to see what would happen.

But more often than not the psychotherapist will want to cast the enactment in a new dimension, one that has never occurred to Q., and, indeed, one he may not initially be able to visualize. "E.," for example, may be characterized as "generous," and the implications of being so versus being "grasping," may be explored by actually playing the part. By structuring Q.'s behavior with respect to a new axis, the psychotherapist begins to make the whole of living take shape in a world Q. never suspected was there.

Contrast this kind of undertaking with one in which the client would simply play the part of a person who is "casual," as against Q.'s "meticulousness." He may even have tried it before; most clients have rattled back and forth in their slots. But to launch out in an altogether new dimension, through successive rehearsals and field trials, is to find a new kind of life space and to break out of the ruts that have too long channeled his life. The novel products of such a venture can, if properly recognized as outcomes of his initiative, be woven into the fabric of Q.'s life experience.

But without such sallies in new directions, life is no more than a series of accidental collisions with events, and the outcomes can be judged only as fortunes or misfortunes. The impact of an event, when no venture has been risked, leaves one's personality intact or bruised but, in either case, essentially unchanged. But a true commitment, the outcome of which is reflected back upon its design, recreates personality by carrying through the full cycle of human experience.

"E. S." IS A ROLE

The reader may recall my early insistence that one must keep two features of personal construct theory in mind when he employs fixed role therapy—the science paradigm and the notion of role. Let us hope I have now said enough about the science paradigm to make it clear that fixed role therapy is a genuine experiment in which client and therapist are co-investigators and the major hypotheses are stated in the "E. S." sketch.

Now it will come as no surprise for me to say also that the enactment sketch must embody a role, a role in the personal construct sense. This is to say that "E. S." is to be depicted as a man who acts in the light of his continuing attempt to catch a glimpse of the way things seem to others. Not only, then, is he an anthropomorphized hypothesis for Q. to test, but he is such a man as would attempt to try on other men's glasses and to discover through experimentation if what he observed by looking through them was indeed what other men observe. Perhaps I had better say that "E." actively concerns himself with the outlooks of others, not merely with their behaviors, and he is prepared to verify his perception of how the world looks to them.

Whether his friends perceive accurately or not is another matter, and this he realizes too.

Sometimes I am asked if the client himself should not write, or at least take part in writing, the enactment sketch. This would seem to follow from the view of the client as a participating scientist. But when I have tried this approach I have noted that he does not often introduce a novel construct dimension. Probably it is not easy for him to express on the spur of the moment what has never before occurred to him. What he does then, if he tries anything new at all, is propose a reversal of his position on one of his prevailing construct axes. Although this reversal may eventually lead him to a new vantage point in construing his circumstances, it does not offer the dramatic possibilities that an experiment initially designed by an imaginative therapist might disclose. Nor is it likely to open up a world proportioned in new dimensions.

Nevertheless, there are stages and forms of therapy in which the client's design of his own experiments is not only valuable but essential. Indeed, we may hope that the design and calculated execution of experiments is something he will be doing for the rest of his life.

What I have mentioned here does not by any means exhaust the considerations that should be taken into account when one attempts fixed role therapy in a particular case. A therapist should be prepared to consider not only the wealth of his own clinical experience but also the skills, the perceptions, the weaknesses, the perplexities, and the preoccupations of his client with "causes" and "circumstances." Moreover, he must respect the integrity of the Q. personality, lest, by invalidating particular neurotic approaches to life, he destroys the man himself.

ILLUSTRATIVE ENACTMENT SKETCHES

A few years ago the following enactment sketch was used in a fixed role therapy sequence:

K. M. is a man whose basic integrity governs all his daily acts. Never are his actions incompatible with his convictions. He has found from experience that this kind of integrity enables him to rise above life's vexing obstacles and personal handicaps. This quality in his personal make-up may not always be noted by others, yet it subtly flavors all his interpersonal relations.

One of the conspicuous features of Mr. M.'s character is his obvious respect for the personalities of other people, even those who do not meet the standards he applies to himself. It is his basic integrity that makes him unique in this respect. While he is always free to express his own point of view, it would never occur to him that, by doing so, he would be trying to compel others to conform to his views. When he expresses himself, it is meant as a sincere invitation to others to express their own particular viewpoints also. Thus he interacts with people without feeling he must either teach or concede.

When Mr. M. was an adolescent, his relations with his parents were sometimes strained because of their rigid insistence that he look at certain situations from their viewpoint. Out of this experience has developed the point of view which now has become the characteristic feature of his personality.

Sometimes his friends find him a stimulating companion—willing both to give and to take. At other times he falls silent to the company of others, perhaps because he is hesitant to stifle another's self-expression. Although on these latter occasions he gives the impression of being withdrawn and reticent, actually he always remains an alert, though sometimes quiet, participant in any social situation.

The above sketch was prepared for enactment by a client who was easily threatened by persons who did not subscribe to his "upright" virtues and often became disputatious. The initial "integrity" theme in the sketch was designed to maintain this feature of his perception of himself, or his pose if you prefer, but to derive from it a mode of action which lent itself to the development of rudimentary role constructs. His experiences, as he remembered them, with his parents made the development of role constructs a tricky matter. It seemed best to incorporate somewhat similar "experiences" when writing the enactment sketch. It will be noted that the sketch also tried to provide grounds for his keeping his mouth shut while still "participating" in a group.

Following is a self-characterization written by a client for whom an enactment sketch was later prepared. The misspellings in her type-written manuscript are reproduced.

In my opinion C. N. is not a shy girl by no means. She mixes well with both sexes but is frequently moody and therefore is irritible to those surrounding her. Carrie lies quite often; knowing she is doing wrong, but continues to do so. She exaggerates about things concerning herself which she feels would like to be true but are not. I find she's becomes dissatisfied with herself and the things she is doing quite often. For example, she gets disgusted with school and wants to quit and has no desire to study. Also she feel as if she wants to go to a new environment to meet new people. I also feel she possess a selfish character at time and other times quite generous depending upon her so-called mood. She has a strong desire to be happy and satisfied with the things she has and therefore have peace of mind. She sometimes has the feeling that she wants everything to come her way without working for it and she would like to possess of feeling of wanting to give as much as receive. She would like very much to fall in love and not only look for what he could give her, now but first look for how ambitious he is and what he will have in the future. She is dead set against marry a doctor because of that life a doctor's wife leads. She feels she requires constant attention and love in order not to have that sence of insecurity she so frequently feels.

The following enactment sketch was prepared for this client and used in fixed role therapy.

Julie Dornay is a good person to have for a friend. She is spontaneously and sympathetically interested in people. She is a good listener. She is sensitive to the ways other people feel. People value her friendship, not only because of the things she can give them or the favors she can do, but more because of the encouragement and strength her friendship gives them. Having had problems of her own, she is well equipped to play a sympathetically supporting role to the people who confide in her. While she does not feel that all her own problems are solved, when others come to her, she lays her own problems aside in order to be of help. Basically she believes that all people are worthwhile in their own right, regardless of their accomplishments or worldly successes. Because of this fundamental belief in people her own worthwhileness is simply and naturally taken for granted.

There is an undercurrent of impatience in Julie's way of life. She is quick to express her liking for her friends. She is always ready to speak up in their behalf. When she sees someone being pushed around she really stands up and lets her voice be heard. But this impatience never seems to come into conflict with her underlying feeling of kindliness and sensitivity for others. Indeed, one might almost say that her impatience is a result of this feeling.

Julie's capacity to be a good friend leads her into many new and interesting adventures. While some people pick and choose the friends who conform to their own narrow specifications, Julie selects a tremendous variety of friends, no two of whom fit precisely the same set of specifications. Thus her own life is enriched and widened and new horizons are continually opening up before her.

When you talk to Julie you soon become aware of the fact that she is interested in you because, first of all, she fundamentally accepts you as you are and wholeheartedly believes that you are genuinely a worthwhile person. She responds to you spontaneously and takes your acceptance of her for granted. But most of all you discover that she is ready and eager to know you as a unique and different personality among her many and varied friends.

In this enactment sketch the role construction is frankly stated, though in a concrete behavioral form. As can be seen, the enactment is designed to involve her in commitments, perhaps even premature ones. Her search for a Lochinvar is not invalidated, but she is to be kept busy attending to lesser characters along the way.

PRESENTING THE ENACTMENT SKETCH TO THE CLIENT

The usual procedure is to present a copy of the enactment sketch to the client and ask him to follow as the therapist reads a copy of it. Then the therapist asks two questions: (1) "Has E. S. described himself in a manner that makes him seem genuine?" and (2) "Does he sound like a person you would like to know?" If the answer to both questions is "yes," the enactment can proceed.

If the answer to the first question is "no," the therapist should ask what there is about the sketch that makes "E. S." seem artificial. Sometimes this calls for rewriting a part of the sketch, but more often "an interpretation" will suffice. Sometimes the interpretation can be composed on the spot as an addendum to the sketch.

If the answer to the second question is negative, the therapist can seek to find out what feature of the sketch is threatening. Sometimes this difficulty, too, can be handled by "an interpretation" of "E." In any case, unless the sketch can be made acceptable in terms of both questions, it is better to start over by writing another characterization before attempting the enactment.

The enactment can be proposed somewhat in the following manner: "During the next two weeks, instead of dealing directly with your problems, I would like to suggest that we do something altogether different. Let us suppose that Q. M. is going to have a two week vacation in the mountains, and, in his place, you are going to be 'E. S.' You will act like 'E. S.,' talk like him, think like him, do the things you think he might do, eat the way you think he would eat, and, if you can, even have the dreams you think he might have.

"Here is another copy of 'E.'s' character sketch. Keep one copy with you all the time and read it at least four times a day—particularly at night when you go to bed, and again in the morning. Read it also whenever you have difficulty playing the part.

"During these two weeks I'll be seeing you every other day, so we can rehearse. We'll try to anticipate some of the situations that will arise so that you can be ready to be as much like 'E.' as possible.

"Don't worry about Q. We don't even need to think about him. Besides, he is going to be away enjoying himself, and we can assume he doesn't want to be bothered. In any case, he will be coming back two weeks from today and that will be time enough to see what he has on his mind.

"Now, let's see, your supervisor is who? Angus McGillicuddy? OK, let us suppose it will be 'E. S.' who shows up for work this afternoon. How would 'Mr. S.' greet Mr. McGillicuddy? I'll be Mr. McGillicuddy. Good afternoon, 'Mr. S!' "

It is important to get the enactment under way immediately. Rather than attempting to persuade Q. that he should be "E.," the client is treated as if he actually was "E.," with the therapist expressing surprise or disbelief at any expression that is out of character. Even though Q. is speechless, or fails to play the part convincingly, his confrontation with a therapist who sees him as "E.," and as "E." only, cannot be ignored. Somehow he must cope with the novel situation in which he now finds himself. Though he may run the gamut of familiar manipulative devices to get out of it altogether, the most obvious pathways for movement are those staked out by the constructs "E." envisions.

During this stage of the enactment, the therapist may feel quite as strange as the client does. In fact, I find it generally more difficult to persuade therapists to commit themselves to the undertaking than to get clients to give it an honest experimental trial. I suppose that is because most clients expect to invest something in therapy, whereas all too many therapists, being applied psychologists rather than scientists, want little more than to be successful in the easiest possible manner. Perhaps we should remember that there is a great deal of difference between coming to a session to wager one's way of life and coming only to put in an hour of professional time.

Perhaps the most difficult thing for the therapist to realize is that, even when his client says nothing, a few moments of being perceived as "E." rather than Q. will stick in the troubled mind long after the session is ended. A man can scarcely fail to wonder, amidst all the tortured doubts about ever being anything other than his miserable self, what it would be like, what it really would be like, to walk out into the world and be recognized, not as Q., but as "E." Certainly, unless our observations have been quite misleading, the effectiveness of the therapeutic effort does not depend upon the glibness with which the part is played. Indeed, it seems to me that the reverse may be true; the client who finds the experience disruptively novel and his first words in the part labored and inept may be the one most deeply affected by the experience. He is the one who invests himself, who performs an experiment, not the skilled actor who makes a burlesque of the part and risks nothing.

PROTECTING THE INTEGRITY OF Q.

Important as it is not to become embroiled in a debate with the client about whether he can or cannot enact the part of "E.," some questions should be answered. The one most likely to be asked first is what the purpose of the enactment is or how it "will help." It is a fair question and must be answered honestly, as I believe all questions must be in a psychotherapeutic relationship. Although I have not settled on any particular phraseology, as I have for some of the other steps in the sequence, something like the following is appropriate.

"We both need to know right off just how much you are prepared to invest in developing a new way of life for yourself. Sometimes people think they can simply close their eyes and have the therapist do something to them that will take all their troubles away without their having to take any risks themselves. But psychotherapy is not simply a matter of going to the doctor to be treated and then going back home to continue acting and thinking in the same old way. That won't work. Besides, life is an adventure from beginning to end, and right here is where we start. *I'm* ready; are *you?*"

Sometimes the client will persist: "But I don't see how this can help." The answer can be brief: "Of course not; you haven't tried it. Neither of us knows for sure what will happen. The only thing we know for sure is that nothing much is likely to happen until we start to experiment as thoughtfully as we can and keep our eyes open to what happens as a result. The first thing to find out is what happens this afternoon."

Now and then at this point the client may say, "But I'm afraid." The therapist may respond, "You mean, Q. is afraid. But 'E. S.' isn't. So let's send Q. to some place where he will have nothing to fear, and you simply be 'E.' I'll do everything I can to help. Now, 'E.,' at what time did you say you expect to arrive at work this afternoon?"

The second most common question is, "You mean 'E.' is the kind of person I should be?" Again, the answer must be candid. "No! At this point neither of us knows what kind of person you should be. That is something that will have to be developed as we go along, and let us hope it will continue to develop long after you stop seeing me. As far as you and I are concerned, 'E.' is simply an experiment, and the important thing for both of us to observe is exactly what happens when a man lives his life this way—what happens both inside his skin and what happens outside."

What is so important for the therapist to keep in mind, and so difficult for most of us brought up in the traditions of realism, determinism, and stimulus-response psychology, is that the object of therapy is not to eradicate Q. in order to replace him with some kind of "E." Q.'s integrity is neither criticized nor questioned. It is treated with respect and even reaffirmed. Certainly the client is never told that he is at odds with himself and thereby led to wonder what gremlins infest his psyche. The fact that "E.," by his contrast with Q., is so clearly make-believe rather than "real" is a key to the success of the venture, not a handicap.

And let us make no mistake about the basic methodology of science. For the genius of science is not its realism, but its calculated ventures into the world of make-believe—which scientists like to call "testing hypotheses." I doubt that an out-and-out realist could ever bring himself to test a hypothesis, any more than he could ever work himself out of a neurosis or a psychosis.

The "Q." the client has come to know is a hypothesis too. But how can a simple-minded realist know that? So he comes to the therapist for help. Since he can visualize no alternatives to the "Q." he knows, he cannot see that personality as hypothetical. All he can see are some of the outcomes of being "Q.," its "reinforcements," and he rarely needs a therapist to point out to him how unhappy those particular events are or that he is exhibiting a "neurotic paradox." Without constructive alternatives, without hypotheses, "reinforcements" can serve only as palliatives and irritants.

But "E." is so clearly a make-believe character, assuming the therapist is not too much of a realist himself to present him so or too much of an applied psychologist to risk an honest experiment, that he can be treated as a hypothesis indeed. From the moment the client experiences "E." as a hypothesis, science can have its day in the therapy room. And if "E." is a hypothesis the client finds he can test, the thought can scarcely escape him that there must be others too.

INITIATING THE REHEARSALS

Let us turn back to where we left off—the beginning of the first rehearsal. The therapist can hardly expect that his own initial attempt to play the part of "E's" supervisor will portray that person accurately enough to provide strong support for the enactment of "E." After a few sentences the client is likely to say, "But old Gillie wouldn't say that." "All right," says the therapist, "let me play the part of 'E.' and you play the part of his supervisor. Good afternoon, Mr. McGillicuddy."

The exchange of parts which follows is important to the experiment. If the client does not say something that suggests it, the therapist should take the initiative and propose it himself. In any rehearsal the client is likely to see one part as dominant over the other, and, if he finds himself in an awkward position, he will wonder if the therapist is not taking unfair advantage of the inequity by casting himself in the dominant part. Exchanging parts is therefore a good practice in all psychotherapeutic enactments and especially so with children. Besides, being engaged in what must be both a true experiment and a true role enactment, the client reaching for the outlooks of others is almost as essential as is getting the knack of being "E." The exchange facilitates this attempt.

The effectiveness of the rehearsals probably depends as much upon the therapist's ingenuity as it does upon the client's cooperation. If the therapist is inept it will be painfully obvious to both of them. He cannot hide behind esoteric terminology or owlish expressions of hidden wisdom. He, no less than the client, is caught up in an experiment, the outcomes of which cannot be accurately forecast. Both must take the risk that goes with being scientists. Fixed role therapy is a strenuous and demanding undertaking, as anyone who attempts it seriously will find out soon enough. It is not a job for dropouts who have taken up "psychotherapy" rather than continue to face the perplexities and frustrations of scientific inquiry.

THE SEQUENCE OF SESSIONS

Generally we have planned the therapy sessions to emphasize, in succession, rehearsals for five kinds of interpersonal situations: (1) "E.'s" interaction with a supervisor on the job or with a teacher, (2) his interaction with his peers, (3) interaction with his spouse or with someone with whom he has an affectionate attachment, (4) interaction with parents or their surrogates, and (5) interaction in a situation involving religious experience. While the therapist must continually call attention to the need for playing the part at all times, and not merely in the situations which have been previously rehearsed, the ventures can be somewhat scaled to the depth and difficulty of the anticipated enactment.

Sessions should be frequent. It is particularly urgent to schedule the second session within one or two days of the first. A minimum of three sessions a week seems to be essential if the project is not to be abandoned by the client in the face of his first obstacles. He is usually discouraged during all the first

week, and he will ordinarily come to the second session with a flat announce-
ment that he cannot play the part. The therapist who thinks behavior is
simply the pursuit of pleasant rewards will be easily "taken in." But he will
have to remind himself that the client and he are scientists and that the object
of the enterprise is to see precisely what happens under the conditions they
have set up, not to scratch an itchy ego.

What is undertaken in fixed role therapy is a vigorous experiment, not a
hit-and-miss search for the elixir of painless existence. Nothing short of
persistent and ingenious effort is effective. This means frequent and arduous
sessions that will tax the resources both of client and therapist.

Although many clients will maintain that their relations with their supervisors are more uncomfortable than with others, it seems best to point the
first rehearsals specifically at this kind of enactment situation. Supervisory
relations, even when strained, tend to be simple. This is to say they involve
relatively few personal construct dimensions, and those that are necessarily
involved tend to be ones which can be more easily put into words, or, as
some might say, are more "cognitive." Personal construct theory is not, of
course, a cognitive theory, as anyone who senses the depth of its personal
involvements must surely realize. But as "cognition" goes, the relatively
articulate and structured relationship between a work supervisor and an
employee, or between a teacher and a pupil, can be considered to fit the
category better than do most other important relationships.

There is another advantage in starting with this relationship. Playing out
the first specific situation for which a rehearsal has been held usually proves
to be a strenuous experience. It is just as well to make it one from which the
client can withdraw before he becomes overwhelmed. Supervisory or student-teacher relationships usually lend themselves to this kind of touch-and-
go dialogue.

The relations with one's peers, which usually mean with a group of
persons of the same age and often of the same sex, are not so highly and
articulately structured. To be sure, one may not feel himself under as much
restraint in dealing with friends, but the complexities of interaction and the
subtle invitations to impulse are greater, making one's unfamiliar enactment
of a new role considerably harder to keep under precisely structured control.
Moreover, it is in this particular enactment that the client is most likely to be
told for the first time that he is "behaving strangely." For this reason the
specific rehearsal for a peer enactment is scheduled after the one pointing
toward a supervisory enactment rather than before.

INITIATING ENACTMENTS

The client is often at a loss to think of some way he can precipitate a situation in which he can play the part of "E." In rehearsing the supervisory situation, the therapist may suggest that the enactment could start with some form of "shop talk." Usually that will be a question or a comment dealing with a matter of common concern between them. If the interaction is to be with a teacher, a brief after-class conversation on a topic recently discussed by the teacher is appropriate. Moreover, in this kind of situation it is quite reasonable for the client to play a role—in the personal construct sense. That is to say the interaction can be directed toward grasping the other person's point of view. Moreover, the feedback is immediate, thus lending itself to the purposes of a truly experimental venture.

As the first rehearsal gets under way, the therapist can begin to show the client how hypotheses can be used as a basis of interaction. What does the client think the supervisor will say? How will he say it? Can the client play the part, during the exchange, in the way he suspects the supervisor will play it? What variations might occur, and what clues should be particularly observed? What will his own feelings be at each stage of the enactment? Having raised such questions, the client may be urged to look for all deviations from the hypothesized responses of the supervisor and to make note of them, perhaps in writing as soon after the interaction as possible. He can, at the same time, make notes describing his own feelings.

When the second session is held, the client and therapist will want to go over the results of this particular enactment as well as what may have happened in others. The results may be reflected upon the hypotheses formulated in the previous session, though usually the therapist will not be as rigorous in comparing hypotheses with outcomes at this stage of therapy as later. When it comes to reporting feelings, it will be necessary to have the client make clear whether those feelings were ones that might be attributed to "E." or whether Q. is sneaking back from his vacation. Therapists who are used to exploring the "true feelings" of their clients are likely to get into trouble at this point, and I have seen some of them let the session deteriorate into an exploration of Q. rather than of "E."

Usually a replay of the supervisor enactment is in order during the second session. It can be played as it happened and again as it might have happened if the part of "E." were played to the hilt. Exchanges of parts between the client and the therapist are again in order. Subtle variations in feeling tone and in the trend of the dialogue can now be noted during the replays. The therapy session itself is part of the experiment, and its outcomes can be noted on the spot. What happens in the therapy room is a test tube experiment; what happens outside is a field trial. Both are component parts of the experimental undertaking.

But the second session must not bog down in postmortems. The next two days of enactment must be planned, and the peer interaction rehearsed. Here the problem is not likely to be so much a matter of initiating a conversation as contributing to it in the role of "E." The client will have to be alert to how the conversation is going and say what he has to say before it has gone off and left him. The rehearsal should prepare him for the quickened pace of the exchanges he may expect among a group of friends.

As I have already suggested, the enactment that follows the second session may confront the client with the reaction that he is acting strangely. It is just as well to prepare him for it. Rather than being disconcerted by his friends' surprise, he should take it as evidence that he has portrayed "E." as a person unlike Q. It is "E." with whom his friends must cope, and it will be important to him to note the various ways in which they attempt to do it. He may even ask them what they regard as "strange." Certainly it is an important part of any experiment to observe closely relevant changes in the dependent variables.

SUPPORT FOR THE ENACTMENT

Often a client will ask if he should not tell some of his friends that he is enacting a role. He may particularly want to tell his wife. What this request usually means is that he is anxious—in personal construct terms, confused—and he is willing to sacrifice some of the realistic feedback that he might obtain from the enactment in order to acquire support. If others know that he is "only playing a part," what he does may appear to have more structure. He wants to say, "Look, I am not really this incoherent. Disregard what I am doing, and continue to see me as Q. Q. may not be the most effectual person in the world, but at least he makes a kind of sense."

But there is little to be gained by the enactment if one's friends are invited to ignore the experiment's independent variable—"E." The enactment becomes an exercise rather than an experiment. As an exercise it does little more than put the client through the motions prescribed by the enactment sketch. And only the most insensitive of "learning" theories would attribute much of psychological importance to that!

In personal construct theory, support has a specific meaning, and it is distinguished from reassurance. Support is a broad response pattern on the part of the therapist which permits the client to experiment widely and successfully. Successful experimentation, in terms of the theory's basic assumptions, is that which leads to clear-cut answers to the questions he poses behaviorally, thus tending to dispel anxiety. Success is thus not defined in any of the usual ways of reward, drive reduction, satiation, feeling tone, need fulfillment, etc.

In fixed role therapy the therapist does supply support, and it is important that he do so. He offers candid comments on the client's enactment. He joins the client in predicting what may happen and shares the client's surprise when unexpected results arise. He lends himself to the enactment by playing, as best he can, the wide variety of parts required by the rehearsals. He joins the client in seeking ways to put enactment experiences into words or in clarifying them through reenactment in the therapy room. If the therapist performs his part of the task well, he will minimize the client's urge to divulge the "E. S." role prematurely, as the poor fellow may in an effort to find elsewhere the support he craves.

After all, the client should soon discover that he can experiment much more successfully, that is to say, elicit more definitive answers to his behaviorally posed questions, if he lets the enactment of "E." speak for itself rather than asking his friends what they think of the enactment sketch. The object of "being E." for two weeks is not to amuse his friends or to see if he has at last "found himself" but to realize here and now that his innermost personality is something he creates as he goes along rather than something he discovers lurking in his insides or has imposed upon him from without. What others may say about the "E." sketch is of much less therapeutic concern than what they think and do when confronted with "E." in the flesh. Besides, the client is committed to "being E" for no more than the brief period of the enactment, and he needs to get the most out of the experience.

THE DEEPER ENACTMENTS

When it comes to confronting his wife with "E.," the client has a more difficult task on his hands. Marriages can fall into rigid patterns, and often the partners, having struck a balance after years of painful interaction, are reluctant to risk breaking the uneasy truce. Yet each of them may wish he could refresh the relationship, and each may doubt the other's willingness to take chances.

It has been my experience that a client is often eager enough to have a different role relation to his wife but dreads what she may say when he attempts it. She may ridicule his fumbling efforts or tell him that he is doing only what he should have started a long time ago. But it has also been my experience that wives (or husbands) find the enactments of their spouses as exciting as they may be disconcerting. Susie M. may be a little nervous about living with "E. S." for two weeks while her husband is "away on a holiday," but that is not the same as saying she would not like to give it a whirl. Making love as "E. S." can make one feel like a different man, but being made love to by "E. S." can make one feel like a different woman. It is a dull client indeed who, having plunged into this phase of the enactment, does not sense that his life could be very, very different.

For his enactments with a supervisor or with peers, the client can prepare himself thoroughly for a limited series of relatively brief encounters. But keeping up the enactment with his experienced spouse requires sustained attention. Moreover, theirs is a relationship that may long since have settled into a routine. Now he must innovate continually, often violating the unwritten rules by which he and his wife have been unwittingly playing the marriage game. The third rehearsal is designed to meet this condition of sustained role enactment.

There is another matter to be confronted in this rehearsal and in the two which follow it. Many of the constructs in terms of which a client has structured his marriage may be preverbal. He cannot represent them as precisely by symbols as he can the more intellectualized dimensions of his life. He therefore cannot point to them and say, "There, that is a dimension in which I shall discontinue making distinctions;" or, "This is a notion I shall now apply to my daily circumstances in a different way." It is expecting too much of fixed role therapy to hope that the use of preverbal constructions can be so deliberately altered.

But it is not expecting too much to hope that the events produced by the enactment will be different. And when events are different, there is occasion to reflect them upon the reference axes of one's construct system in positions where previous events have not been plotted. Gradually the construct system, verbal and preverbal, adapts itself in some manner to that with which it must cope, and the intentionality of a personal construct slowly aligns itself to the shifts in its extensionality. Changes in operational definitions erode and enrich essential definitions, and one's definition of his marriage or of his spouse is no exception.

Extending the enactment to a situation involving one's parents often runs into a practical difficulty. The parents may be deceased or may live too far away for a day's visit. Sometimes a letter embodying the enactment can be sent to the parents. And, indeed, if it is written, it must be sent, else we shall have indulged in an intellectual exercise without venturing the commitment which makes it into an enactment.

It is all too easy, both for client and therapist, to let fixed role therapy degenerate into intellectualism on the one hand or dissolve into expressionism on the other. The method does not strive for "insight," nor does it invite "self-expression." Personal construct theory, by the way, generally takes a dim view of "insight," observing that this term is more appropriate to naive realism than to a constructive outreach to the world. The theory is a little more tolerant of "self-expression," though that, too, seems often to be predicated on the notion of an inescapable "real self" rather than a self one creates through the process of experimenting with his life.

As with one's spouse, relations with parents involve preverbal constructions and often stalemated interactions. The fourth rehearsal, which is directed particularly at this arena of enactment, must make maximum use of the temporary disengagement of the Q. personality from the situation and the commitment, instead, to an enactment of "E." My experience suggests that a great deal of the value of the parental enactment accrues from the rehearsal in which the client exchanges parts and undertakes to feel and act as one or both of his parents would experience their relationship with him. The therapist can make a great deal of this opportunity by speeding up the tempo of this rehearsal and by playing it out in a number of presumed settings. Since role in the personal construct theoretical sense is based on a construction of another person's outlook, here in this particular rehearsal is an opportunity to take a long delayed second look through the parental spectacles. The client is likely to be surprised by what he sees even before he has confronted his parents in the experimental role of "E."

The final situation, for which a specific enactment is rehearsed, is the one involving religion. Now and then someone who has had little or no experience with fixed role therapy protests that this is much too intimate a matter to be approached as an enactment of any part other than that of the vacationing

Q. himself. But the therapist need not prescribe any particular religious doctrine. He and his client can work out together the inferred religious outlook that would characterize such a man as "E. S." is. And why not? Must religion be a reluctant concession to the inevitable, or might it not be a commitment to an undertaking reaching far beyond the present self?

Just how the role is enacted through its religious implications will depend somewhat upon the situation available for its trial. At a minimum this will amount to holding a discussion of religious and ethical matters with others who have similar areas of concern. But I think the therapy works out best if the client takes the pains to search deeply for the implications of the part he has been playing. If he has had an incipient tendency to burlesque the part of "E. S." the man, the religious enactment should bring the client to the point of realizing that any man's commitment to behavior carries with it the profoundest of implications for the meaning his life will have and the deepest of obligations to take account of what happens as a result of his acts.

TERMINATING THE ENACTMENT

In the end, of course, Q. must come home. The therapist should see that he does and that he takes responsibility for appraising what has happened and for what he himself will choose to undertake. We hope Q. will see his life open to fresh undertakings, and that he will not be unwilling to take candid account of what happens when he embarks upon them. It will be just as well if he decides to discontinue acting the part of "E.," valuable as he may feel the experience turned out to be. His next urgent task is to create the new Q., and that will take a little time, say, a lifetime. But if there was once an "E." who, in the course of a mere two weeks, took on the flesh and vision of a man, there can be a "Q.," and after him a " 'Q.,' " and a " 'Q.!' "

Perhaps it is not necessary to remark at the end of this discussion that there is much more to be said. The reader who is impatient to get on to other matters may think I have tried to say too much. The therapist who undertakes fixed role therapy will certainly wish I had said more.

Let us hope that I have not focused so sharply upon fixed role therapy as to leave the impression that it is the only therapeutic method to be derived from personal construct theory. There are so many other implications of the theory it would be a pity if this particular method I happen to have used in no more than ten percent of my therapeutic efforts over the years were to be regarded as the definitive explication of personal construct psychotherapeutics.

It would also be a misfortune if I were to leave the impression that the steps I have outlined are the only ones that can profitably be followed. I have reported simply a part of what my experience seems to show, omitting, I fear, some of the interesting variants, such as fixed role therapy with groups of three to a hundred persons. But what experience I have reported I hope has been described in such a way as to make clear underlying assumptions about the nature of man and how he goes about making himself into what he is.

REFERENCES

1. Bannister, D. A. new theory of personality. In B. M. Foss (Ed.), *New horizons in psychology*. Baltimore: Penguin, 1966.

2. Bonarius, J. C. J. Research in the personal construct theory of George A. Kelly. In B. A. Maher (Ed.), *Progress in experimental personality research*. Vol. 2. New York: Academic Press, 1965.

3. Kelly, G. A. *The psychology of personal constructs*. Vols. 1 and 2. New York: Norton, 1955.

4. Kelly, G. A. Theory and therapy in suicide: the personal construct point of view. In E. Shneidman and N. Farberow (Eds.), *The cry for help*. New York: McGraw-Hill, 1961.

5. Kelly, G. A. The language of hypothesis: man's psychological instrument. *J. Indiv. Psychol.*, 1964, **20**, 137–152.

6. Kelly, G. A. The strategy of psychological research. *Bull. Brit. Psychol. Soc.*, 1965, **18**, 1–15.

7. Kelly, G. A. A psychology of the optimal man. In A. Mahrer (Ed.), *Goals of psychotherapy*. New York: Appleton-Century-Crofts, 1966.

8. Kelly, G. A. Sin and psychotherapy. In O. H. Mowrer (Ed.), *Morality and mental health*. Chicago: Rand-McNally, 1966.

9. Patterson, C. H. *Theories of counseling and psychotherapy*. New York: Harper and Row, 1966.

10. Sechrest, L. The psychology of personal constructs: George Kelly. In J. M. Wepman and R. W. Heine (Eds.), *Concepts of personality*. Chicago: Aldine, 1963.

10. Brief Cognitive Therapies

Aaron T. Beck and Ruth L. Greenberg

Although most forms of psychotherapy since Freud have addressed themselves in some way to the cognitive aspects of emotional disorders, only relatively recently have researchers advanced the suggestion that the "active ingredient" in psychotherapy may lie in the cognitive realm. This suggestion has gained credibility as the result of a growing body of experimental work, and has led to the formulation of methods of psychotherapeutic intervention that focus directly on cognition. A number of the "cognitive therapies" are designed to be brief therapies. It has been contended that they deliver efficiently and effectively those essential elements of change which may be produced indirectly, and at a more leisurely pace, by psychoanalysis, supportive psychotherapy, or other insight therapies.

Current cognitive therapies may vary in placement of emphasis and may use diverse techniques, but they share a number of basic principles. To paraphrase Mahoney and Arnkoff,[20] they hold in common these fundamental assumptions: that behavior and affect are mediated by cognitive processes; that maladaptive behavior and affect correlate with maladaptive cognitions; and that the task of the therapist is to identify these cognitions and to provide learning experiences which will modify them. Proponents of the cognitive therapies contend that correction of maladaptive cognitions will lead to improvement in psychiatric disorders. Since the term *cognition* generally encompasses a broad spectrum—from discrete thoughts and self-verbalizations to fantasy, imagery, and abstract beliefs and values—the cognitive therapies similarly include a wide range and diversity of concepts and techniques.

HISTORICAL BACKGROUND

The cognitive therapies draw on ample historical precedent. Contributions to a cognitive approach to treatment have been made by writers as diverse as Sigmund Freud, Eric Berne, Fritz Perls, John Rosen, and Albert Bandura;

Reprinted by permission of W. B. Saunders Co. from *Psychiat. Clin. N. Am.*2(1979):23–37.

explicitly cognitive therapies have been developed by Paul DuBois, Alfred Adler, Arthur W. Combs and Donald Snygg, and Albert Ellis (see Raimy).[26] Mahoney[19] traces to Immanuel Kant the philosophical assumptions underlying the cognitivist position. Mahoney also documents the complex history of interest in cognitive variables among academic psychologists and within the ranks of the behavior therapy movement.[20]

Of the earlier writers, Alfred Adler was perhaps the most kindred spirit with respect to the current cognitive movement. Adler explained psychopathology as a result of "a mistake made in the whole style of life, in the way the mind has interpreted its experiences, in the meaning it has given to life, and in the actions with which it has answered the impressions received from the body and from the environment."[1] These "mistaken opinions" were acquired in early childhood.[2] Adler saw abnormal behavior as the individual's attempt to protect mistaken ideas about himself in situations which he cannot meet adequately; he identified several misconceptions which he found to be common in disturbed individuals. The key to these misconceptions, Adler argued, was a lack of "social interest," the individual's failure to recognize his need to contribute to the welfare of others. Striving after unattainable goals, pursuit of personal superiority, and belief in the power and superiority of roles and traits identified as "masculine," are other "mistakes" which Adler held responsible for maladjustment and neurosis.

For Adler, psychotherapy was a process of getting the patient to recognize and understand his faulty beliefs, which might lie only at the periphery of consciousness; the process was facilitated by the "courage" the patient derived from his relationship with the therapist. Adlerian treatment consisted chiefly of discussions in which the therapist explained to the patient the nature of his misconceptions and their role in his maladaptive life style. While depending largely on empathy and intuition as a means of assessing the misconceptions, Adler also recommended "guessing"—suggesting tentative hypotheses which could be verified or disconfirmed as data accumulated. He encouraged the patient to recount dreams and childhood recollections, largely in order to obtain information regarding the patient's misconceived goals and beliefs. Adler also advised attending to symptoms, setbacks, physical traits, gait, voice and posture as possible clues to the beliefs and the mechanisms producing maladjustive behavior.[1,2] For a review of Adler's contribution, see Raimy.[26]

George Kelly's personal construct theory viewed the individual as defined psychologically by the way he construes and anticipates events.[17] Kelly advocated a form of psychotherapy which emphasized personal exploration and experiment: it was predicated on the assumption that man is self-creating—that it is the nature of the human enterprise to reach toward new constructions of experience. The personal construct psychotherapist, he wrote, employs a variety of procedures "as part of a plan for helping himself and his client get on with the job of human exploration and checking out the appropriateness of the constructions they have devised for placing upon the world around them."[18]

The work of Adler and Kelly, of course, was not shaped by the demand for demonstrable therapeutic results that has been evoked in the wake of the behavioral movement. Current cognitive therapies, more responsive to that demand, tend to be more structured, operationalized, and time-limited, and may have a significant behavioral component. The following discussion will concern forms of cognitive therapy developed chiefly by Albert Ellis, Donald Meichenbaum, and Aaron T. Beck.

ELLIS: RATIONAL-EMOTIVE THERAPY

The principles of rational-emotive therapy—probably the type of cognitive therapy best known to the general public—have been expounded in the voluminous writings of Albert Ellis.[10-12] Adopting the Stoic philosophy vis à vis human emotion, Ellis holds that there are virtually no causes for severe emotional distress except the misperceptions, incorrect evaluations, magical and absolutistic thinking, illogical beliefs, and misplaced values of the distressed person. Ellis is emphatic in attributing to certain commonly held ideas a large proportion of the maladjustment and emotional turmoil observed by clinicians. The "shoulds, oughts, and musts" that individuals impose on themselves and on others point to one set of pathogenic ideas. Other "core irrational ideas" include the notions that an adult needs to be loved by everyone around him, that certain acts are "awful or wicked" and should be severely punished, and that it is terrible when things are not as one would like them to be.

At the heart of rational-emotive therapy is the "ABC" method. The patient is taught that every upsetting event consists essentially of three parts. Beginning with "C," a recent Emotional Consequence, the therapist demonstrates that the client wrongly attributes the emotion to "A," the Activating Experience. The client is shown that "A" is powerless to produce "C" without the intervention of "B," the individual's Belief System: although the patient generally has rational beliefs about the activating experience, the therapist explains, these are often superseded by irrational beliefs which produce feelings of anxiety, worthlessness, depression, or anger.

The process continues as the therapist brings the client to point "D," where he energetically Disputes the irrational beliefs, and uses logical and empirical criteria as his guides. Here a form of semantic analysis may also come into play: what does it mean to be a "worthless person" . . . to "accept" oneself? A new point, "E," is reached when the client adopts the rational philosophies advocated by the therapist, and a behavioral Effect is established. However, the patient is warned that change necessitates constant work, observation, and practice in disputing irrational beliefs; homework assignments are used to accelerate the process of reeducation and behavioral change.

Rational-emotive therapy is not necessarily a brief form of treatment. According to Ellis,[11] it usually takes "from 1 to 20 sessions of individual and/or 20 to 80 sessions of group therapy. Consequently, many clients are seen for relatively brief periods of time. Ideally, however, clients are to be seen for a total period of about two years, during which time they will have about 20 individual and about 75 group sessions."

MEICHENBAUM: SELF-INSTRUCTIONAL TRAINING

A pioneering venture into cognitively oriented treatment methods must be credited to Donald Meichenbaum, whose research with hyperactive children led to the development of "self-instructional training" for these children and eventually for other client groups. Through laboratory and naturalistic studies, Meichenbaum determined that the "private speech" of impulsive, hyperactive children was more immature and more self-stimulatory (i.e., contained more animal noises, singing, word play, etc.) than that of "reflective" children. The private speech of reflective children showed more outer-directed "remarks" and was more self-regulatory and self-instructional in content. In contrast, the hyperactive children manifested a significant deficit in the ability to use verbal self-instruction to regulate their own behavior.

In an attempt to correct these deficits, Meichenbaum and Goodman[22] devised a procedure consisting of several stages. First, an adult performed a task while "talking to himself" aloud ("cognitive modeling"). Next, the child performed the same task under the adult's instructions ("external guidance"). A third stage consisted of "overt self-guidance"—the child performed the task while instructing himself out loud; during the fourth step, "faded, overt self-guidance," the child performed the task while whispering the instructions to himself. Finally, the child performed the task silently, guided by "private speech" ("covert self-instruction"). Training tasks were made increasingly difficult and grew in number to include games, puzzles, situations at home, and academic work. In the course of training, the adult deliberately made errors in completing tasks, and then modeled the recognition and correction of those errors. Parents and teachers were involved as additional modelers and reinforcers. The self-instructional program proved effective in improving performance with respect to a variety of tasks.

Meichenbaum has integrated aspects of self-instruction into a program of stress inoculation training. The underlying principle of stress inoculation was that the client might be trained to cope with small doses of stress, e.g., by confronting stressful situations other than those of primary concern, in preparation for dealing with the more distressing stimuli. Inoculation begins with an educational phase, which presents the patient with a way of conceptualizing his reactions to stress, provides a rationale for treatment, and suggests that he view the stress reactions as a succession of stages: preparation, confrontation, possible succumbing to stress, and self-reinforcement for coping. In the second or "rehearsal" phase of training, the client is trained in a broad variety of coping skills, including relaxation, breath control, and cognitive appraisal. Self-instructional training is included here and involves rehearsal of coping self-statements for each of the four stages of response to stress: "What is it you have to do? . . . Stay relevant . . . Relax . . . you did it!" In the third phase ("application"), the client applies his skills to a variety of laboratory stressors.

The stress-inoculation approach has been applied effectively to a wide range of psychological stresses, such as interpersonal anxieties, test anxieties,[23] phobias, and chronic anger.[25] It has also been used successfully in the control of pain. Turk[32] adopted Melzack's division of the pain experience into three components, and applied it to the stress-inoculation procedure. Thus, the client is introduced to a conceptualization of pain consisting of a sensory discriminative component, which can be controlled by relaxation and breathing techniques; motivational-affective components, such as feelings of helplessness, which are minimized by shifting attention, focusing on the pain itself, or manipulating imagery; and a cognitive-evaluative component. This last component is handled by mobilizing adaptive self-statements rehearsed earlier in conjunction with the four anticipated stages of response to stress.

Meichenbaum's work exemplifies the integration of cognitive interventions into a primarily behavioral treatment program. Although it focuses more exclusively on verbal "self-statements" than does the work of Ellis or Beck, its highly operationalized format lends itself readily to research, and there is increasing evidence of its usefulness in treating a variety of clinical problems.[22]

BECK: COGNITIVE THERAPY OF DEPRESSION AND ANXIETY

In writings derived in part from his long-term studies of clinical aspects of depression, Beck[3,4,6] suggested that emotions follow from meanings attributed to events, and that emotional disturbances result when events are given distorted meanings. Beck posited that an individual's interpretation of an event is encapsulated in fleeting "automatic thoughts," which are often at the fringes of consciousness, and mediate between an event and the affective response. A patient, he argued, can be trained to observe his maladaptive thoughts and formulate alternative interpretations. The "automatic thoughts" also provide clues by which to identify an individual's underlying belief system, which is ultimately responsible for the way he assigns meaning to events. Beck hypothesized that many forms of psychopathology—depression, anxiety, phobias, and obsessions—may be associated with characteristic cognitive distortions, and that these disorders would respond to therapy aimed at the correction of the distortions.

Beck's cognitive therapy was originally developed as a treatment for depression and suicidal behavior, but it has recently been applied successfully to the treatment of anxiety and other clinical problems. The therapy is brief, problem-oriented, and highly structured, and makes extensive use of written and behavioral homework, bibliotherapy, role-playing, and other teaching devices. It is technically eclectic, but uses its broad range of techniques in ways that are consistent with the goal of cognitive modification. It is concerned with the therapeutic relationship as a means of setting the stage for cognitive retraining, but puts little emphasis on the supportive and emotional aspects of the relationship as factors in clinical outcome. Similarly, Beck's therapy does not dwell on dreams and childhood memories, although when these are produced spontaneously, they may serve as valuable clues to particular cognitive patterns. The aim is to provide the patient with a set of practical self-help tools that he will continue to employ and to sharpen after termination of therapy.

Depression: Behavioral Techniques

The goal of cognitive therapy of the depressed patient is to train the patient to correct the idiosyncratic, negative thoughts and the underlying dysfunctional assumptions that perpetuate his depressed mood and lead to his lack of motivation, low activity level, and other symptoms.[5] In the initial stages, the therapist concentrates on behavioral methods: in order to "mobilize" the patient, he schedules activities with the patient. Also, the patient is asked to list in some detail his actual daily activities between sessions, and to rate the degree of "mastery" and "pleasure" he has obtained from each activity.

These behavioral records provide the therapist with factual information about the patient's actual activities, which may differ radically from the patient's oral report ("I did nothing," "I just sat around"). More important, they constitute evidence to counter the patient's idea that he has done nothing. If he has given ratings of mastery or pleasure to any activity, this information counters his idea that he *always* feels terrible and that *nothing* he does will give him pleasure or satisfaction. These operations are the first steps in the process of changing the patient's tendency to think in broad extremes ("all-or-nothing" thinking), and to correcting other typical cognitive distortions.

If the level of activities is low or the patient reports obtaining little gratification from them, the therapist may assign specific activities, such as preparing a dinner or attending a movie. Often, the patient will be reluctant to undertake the assignment because he is sure he will fail at it, or thinks he is too weak or incompetent to take even the first step (or he will believe there is no point in doing things he used to enjoy because they no longer give him satisfaction). The therapist may suggest that the patient carry out the assignment as an experiment, the purpose of which is to determine whether or not he is capable of accomplishing the task or gaining pleasure from it. Since the goal of the experiment is just to gather information, there is no way the patient can fail—any outcome will provide information to patient and therapist. Generally, the patient discovers that he can do more and enjoy more than he expected. The success generally leads to an improvement in affect; more important, it provides the therapist with an opportunity to point out that the patient's beliefs and expectations differed from reality.

When the patient is reluctant to attempt any activity, the therapist may introduce a graded task assignment. This method breaks an activity into a hierarchy of small steps, ranging from simple to more complex. The task is structured in such a way as to heighten the probability that the patient will accomplish each step; but here again it is understood that "failure" is acceptable because it too provides needed information. A severely depressed man, for example, believed he should take his life because he could no longer function; in fact, he had stopped making even routine efforts to care for himself. Therapist and patient agreed that the patient would begin to increase his activities by cooking an egg for breakfast the next morning; this goal too was broken down into specific segments, such as buying the eggs, finding the pan, boiling the water, etc. Eventually, he proceeded to the more formidable activity—preparing dinner for several friends.

Although the patient is likely to feel better after these small successes, he may disparage the accomplishment. A teenager who found that smoking marijuana made her feel "down" made sure she had none available one weekend. Although she achieved her goal of not smoking "grass" for a few days, she took no credit because, after all, "there was no marijuana around to smoke." The patient is encouraged to evaluate his achievement realistically; that is, to compare it to his previous level of activity when depressed and to his inaccurately low estimate of what he could accomplish, rather than to the levels of achievement he was accustomed to before he became depressed. This focus on small satisfactions and achievements is aimed at altering the tendency to think that if an achievement is not perfect, it is entirely worthless. Since in the graded task assignment the criteria for success and failure have been clearly defined, the procedure also provides an opportunity for the patient to observe his tendency to evaluate himself negatively even when he has met objective criteria for success.

Cognitive rehearsal methods may be used to help the patient foresee obstacles that may prevent him from reaching a given goal and to develop plans for overcoming such obstacles. The patient is asked to imagine going through all the steps necessary to attain a goal. One woman, for example, intended to take an exercise class the following day, but by using this technique, she realized that she lacked the proper shorts, might not have access to the car, etc. Solutions to these problems were devised, and she was able to take the class rather than being overwhelmed with a sense of futility and frustration as she often was in trying to achieve simple goals.

This procedure, like others described above, redirects the patient's attention from the abstract to the concrete. While the patient's abstract conceptualizations are pervaded by negativity, his concrete problems are often solvable. He is helped to secure *some* relief from the depressed mood, and becomes increasingly aware that his negative expectations are not completely borne out by the facts. After "experimental" demonstrations of the patient's negative evaluations and predictions, he becomes receptive to the suggestion that there may be systematic distortions in his perceptions of reality, and direct cognitive methods may be introduced.

Depression: Cognitive Strategies

The essential first step in the use of cognitive methods is to explain to the patient the major premises of the cognitive model. The patient is told quite explicitly that this approach presumes that his psychiatric disorder is related to the way he interprets reality, and that he can learn to think more logically in the specific areas that cause problems. He is introduced to the concept of the "automatic thought"—the almost instantaneous interpretation of a situation which appears to intervene between an event and the emotional reaction, and which may take a verbal or pictorial form. The concept of the negative cognitive set, which directs the depressive's attention to highly selected features of his experience, is also explained.

The therapist often uses a Socratic method of questioning to elicit from the patient himself the statements of fact that lead to a more accurate conceptualization of his problem. For example, a middle-aged housewife complained that she was depressed because her teenaged children no longer wanted to spend time with her. When the therapist began to inquire into the facts behind her statement, it became apparent to both therapist and patient that her children, indeed, enjoyed being with her. The therapist, however, does not assume from the outset that the patient's conceptualization is wrong, nor does he use his own perceptions as a basis for trying to convince the patient he is wrong.

The patient's participation in the reasoning process tends to make the more realistic conclusion more credible to him, and, in addition, provides experience in reality-testing. At times, patients receive active instruction in how to validate a conclusion. A student who was convinced that a mediocre grade on a paper indicated he was a poor student was induced to telephone his professor from the therapist's office and inquire about the meaning of the grade. The student was relieved by the information he received (viz., that his paper showed considerable creativity), and had also learned a way of gathering information directly that was helpful on subsequent occasions. Further, the experience served to disconfirm his negative cognitive set.

At a later stage, the patient's basic assumptions, rules, or formulas may also be questioned. For example, let us assume that the housewife above really did find that her children no longer desired her company on frequent occasions. In that case, the therapist looks into the meaning she assigns to the fact: possibly, "I'm no longer needed as a mother," or "My only pleasure in life is unavailable." She will be encouraged to look for alternative interpretations ("I should be proud of my success as a mother, because I've helped my children achieve independence"), to examine the underlying beliefs that give rise to her spontaneous interpretations ("My main purpose in life is to care for my children"), and to modify the underlying beliefs ("My purpose in life is to find personal satisfaction, for which my family is only one of many possible sources").

A basic method of cognitive therapy is to train the patient to identify and evaluate his automatic thoughts. He is asked to observe and record them, or sometimes simply to count them; he is immediately helped by "distancing" himself from his thoughts. The patient may be asked to use changes in affect as cues prompting him to look for the cognitions that precede them, or he may be asked to attend to automatic thoughts in specific situations or at particular times of day that are known to be problematic. The therapist may assign the patient as "homework" an activity that is somewhat distressing to the patient, so that the patient can "catch" the cognitions that are generated. Upsetting events that occur naturally are fully exploited—even welcomed— as opportunities to observe the thinking-feeling sequence and to articulate more clearly the underlying conceptual system. When it is apparent that a particular theme is common to many of the patient's thoughts, he may be asked to collect thoughts relating to that theme for a given period of time.

In the therapy session, the patient may be asked to recollect an event that has upset him—to replay it step by step in his imagination—and to look for the thoughts that actually gave rise to his distress. Or a cognitive rehearsal method may be used, in which a *potentially* upsetting event is imagined and related thoughts identified.

Homework

The therapist depends to a large degree on "homework" assignments in which the patient carries his observational and evaluative skills into daily life circumstances. In fact, the basic "data" which therapist and patient use to construct and refine their strategy are the written records which the patient compiles as "homework." "Homework" also provides the setting in which the patient learns and overlearns a new set of responses.

Testing Hypotheses

When enough data have been collected, the therapist may construct a hypothesis. If, for example, many of a patient's thoughts involve the theme of rejection, the therapist might propose that the patient sees himself as a person who is often rejected by others and consequently resorts to avoidance of social situations in which he runs the risk of being rejected or disapproved of—which in turn intensifies his sense of isolation and loneliness. The patient is asked to consider whether this conceptualization of his problem seems to fit his past experience, and on the basis of his feedback the original hypothesis may be discarded or modified to permit the introduction of new evidence. He is also asked to consider whether future experiences seem to confirm the hypothesis.

Alternative Explanations

At the same time, he is trained to provide alternative responses to the distressing automatic thoughts. He is asked to systematically consider alternative ways of conceptualizing an event or solving a problem. When, in severe cases, the patient is unable to conceive of any solution to his problem except suicide, the therapist cautiously reopens closed-off possibilities for consideration.

These principles of therapy lend themselves to a type of written homework assignment which uses the "triple column technique." This involves recording a distressing event and subsequent reactions in a predetermined format. Generally, in the first column, the patient records the event itself—a critical comment by a boyfriend, rejection from a graduate school, a daydream or fantasy. He then makes note of the resulting emotion, and writes down the intervening thought or image. In a final column, he reports his "rational response" to the original, dysfunctional thought. More complex homework forms require the patient to rate numerically the strength of his original emotional response, then to identify and rate his subsequent emotional response; they also ask for ratings of the strength of his belief in the dysfunctional thought and in the rebuttal. Since ratings of disturbed affect generally drop after the "rational response," they can later be used to demonstrate to the patient that he can assert control over his emotions.

Analysis of Dysfunctional Thoughts

The analysis of dysfunctional thoughts can follow at least three general courses. *Logical* analysis involves examining the types of inference leading to a conclusion. Although the automatic thought is instantaneous, it may compress a complex reasoning process, which can then be recapitulated. The patient asks whether it has involved such logical errors as (1) overgeneralization, (2) arbitrary inference, or (3) selective abstraction, which would cast doubt on the validity of the conclusion. (See Beck[6] for examples of these logical errors.) Patients may conclude that something is wrong simply on the basis of their own feeling states; they are trained to recognize and terminate the "cognition-affect spiral." A second approach is *empirical* analysis: the patient considers whether the thought corresponds to factual reality. If the facts are unknown to him, he determines how the relevant information might be obtained. *Pragmatic* analysis answers the question, "What are the practical consequences of holding this belief?" If the effects are likely to be self-defeating (or a self-fulfilling prophesy), this in itself constitutes sufficient reason to search for alternative ways of conceptualizing an event.

With practice, the patient begins to observe patterns in the kinds of events that distress him, and to note that he has stereotyped cognitive responses to these events—an interpretational bias. He may also recognize that his beliefs lead to behavior which may in turn reinforce the belief: the effect of an instructor's belief that he could not give a lecture was that he did not attempt to prepare it, and thereby confirmed his low self-image by failure to achieve. When automatic thoughts derive from basic belief systems which are firmly entrenched, these systems too may be subjected to critical review.

In addition to the general principles outlined above, a host of more specialized techniques have been developed. These are described in detail in a monograph, *Cognitive Therapy of Depression,* by Beck, Rush, Shaw and Emery.[8]

Beck's Cognitive Therapy: Anxiety

Like the treatment for depression, the cognitive approach to the treatment of anxiety derives directly from Beck's cognitive theory as well as from clinical research. Structured interviews with anxious and phobic patients confirmed the hypothesis that each patient could identify visual fantasies or verbal thoughts of danger preceding his attacks of anxiety. A typical "spiral" occurs when the patient reacts with symptoms of anxiety to a perceived danger to his physical person or to some element of his "personal domain." He then misinterprets these symptoms—increased heart rate, shortness of breath, etc.—as confirmation of the legitimacy of his fears or as evidence of some additional impending disaster, such as having a heart attack or becoming insane. The problem continues its spiral when the patient envisions negative social consequences of his anxiety problem, develops a disabling fear of the anxiety reaction itself, or increasingly underestimates his ability to cope with the feared situations and with his own anxiety symptoms. The anxiety may become associated with a greater and greater number of stimuli, and the patient may find himself continually avoiding threatening situations, and severely restricting his activities as a result.

The cognitive treatment, then, comprises a variety of techniques that focus on identifying the specific ideation or imagery that initiates and perpetuates the spiral. The therapist trains the patient to recognize that these thoughts and images do not necessarily correspond to reality, and educates him in ways of assessing how realistic the cognitions may be. Extensive use is made of behavioral assignments exposing the patient in graduated "doses" to the situations he fears. Generally, these are used in conjunction with written assignments: the patient is asked to record and rebut the cautionary thoughts he experiences. In the session, the therapist uses a rich mixture of imagery-based techniques and Socratic questioning designed to clarify the patient's thinking.

This method of treating anxiety has recently been elaborated in a book-length treatment manual.[7] The manual describes a variety of techniques for discerning and altering the "private meanings" which certain types of events hold for the anxiety patient. For example, the sound of a siren will stimulate anxiety if the private meaning of the sound is, "Someone has been hurt. I too could be hurt or die." The meaning can be detected by having the patient recollect the thoughts that preceded a recent attack, or vividly imagine himself in situations which have provoked anxiety in the past, and report the thoughts to the therapist as they occur: therapist and patient may be able to reconstruct the personal meaning on the basis of repeated themes.

At times, the patient may be asked to imagine the worst possible consequences of the feared event—death, illness, injury, impoverishment, humiliation—and to state what would disturb him about these unfortunate outcomes. Specific misinformation may then be corrected. ("If I get cancer, there will be no way to treat it." "Death would be painful." "He would reject me if he knew I have homosexual thoughts." "Other people will know what a fool I am." "If I lose my job, my children will go hungry.") Philosophical considerations may be raised: for example, the goals of meeting rigid standards for professional success, or of being perfectly moral, "normal," responsible, altruistic, etc., can be questioned. Alternative, noncatastrophic views of dying can be suggested.

Another major goal of therapy with the anxious patient is to train the patient to manage his anxiety in the stressful situation. One target is the patient's inaccurate predictions: typically, when confronting the feared situation, he grossly overestimates the probability that a particular negative outcome will ensue, although when away from the situation, he assigns a more reasonable probability. A second aim is to correct the patient's misconception of the effects of anxiety itself: that he "can't stand it," that it will cause him to go insane or have a heart attack, that it will necessarily have a negative effect on his performance, that it will continue indefinitely. A third set of techniques involves practical instruction in ways to reduce anxiety: distracting oneself by concentrating on trivial details, avoiding others who are anxious (such as anxious fellow-students before an important examination), modeling the behavior of nonanxious persons. The "triple column technique," cognitive rehearsal, review of basic beliefs and values, and other methods associated with Beck's treatment of depression, have also been adapted to the treatment of anxiety.

RELATIONSHIP BETWEEN COGNITIVE THERAPY AND RATIONAL-EMOTIVE THERAPY

Although these two forms of therapy are based on similar rationales and have many treatment procedures in common, there are major differences between them. First, Ellis attributes all emotional disorders to certain commonly held "irrational" beliefs. His methods are, in his own words,[11] "very much inner-directed, theory-based, and authoritative, and hence . . . *not* directly inspired by the client's productions." In contrast, cognitive therapy assumes that the problem-causing ideas are idiosyncratic, and must be detected on an individual basis. Further, Beck delineates specific cognitive patterns for each of the neurotic disorders.[5,6] Indeed, Beck and his colleagues have produced specialized manuals for the treatment of various syndromes—depression, anxiety, chemical dependency. Beck's formulation of these distinct therapeutic strategies is analogous to the prescribing of specific drugs for specific diagnostic groups. Secondly, Ellis assumes an extremely aggressive stance from the outset of therapy: "I do not hesitate, even during the first session, directly to confront the client with evidence of his irrational thinking and behaving." In general, cognitive therapy attempts to lead the patient himself, through skillful questioning, to question the validity of his own thinking. The initial sessions in particular are devoted to obtaining empirical data regarding the patient's behavior patterns, the occurrence of disturbed affect, and the content of related cognitions—basic beliefs and assumptions are not questioned at this stage.

STUDIES OF OUTCOME

The effectiveness of the cognitively oriented therapies described above has recently been subjected to a good deal of research. Studies of Rational-Emotive Therapy have been reviewed by DiGiuseppe, Miller, and Trexler[9] and Goldfried;[13] for studies of self-instructional training, see Meichenbaum.[22] In general, results are quite favorable to the cognitive therapies. Citing only a fraction of the relevant literature, we can state that promising results have been obtained using cognitive therapies in the treatment of test anxiety,[21,24] speech anxiety,[31] interpersonal anxiety,[15] and general anxiety;[16] in relief of tension headache;[14] and in the modification of unassertive behavior.[30]

Our own studies[27] found cognitive psychotherapy to be even more effective than antidepressant medication in the treatment of a group of 41 depressed, suicidal outpatients. These patients were moderately to severely depressed when admitted to the study, and 75 per cent were suicidal. Their depressions were longstanding—they had been chronically or intermittently depressed for a mean period of 8.8 years—and most had been treated previously with antidepressant drugs and/or psychotherapy; a large percentage (22 per cent) had a history of psychiatric hospitalization.

Patients undergoing cognitive therapy in this study were treated with a maximum of 20 interviews over a 12 week period, while the patients under pharmacotherapy received up to 250 mg of imipramine per day for the same period of time. On all measures, cognitive therapy produced significantly greater improvement than the antidepressant medication, and more patients treated with cognitive therapy showed marked improvement or complete remission (78.9 per cent compared to 22.7 per cent). There was also a substantially lower dropout rate among patients in cognitive therapy. At one-year follow-up, cognitive therapy patients manifested significantly less self-rated depressive symptomatology than the drug-related patients, and only half the cumulative relapse rate of the latter group.

Additional studies obtaining favorable results for cognitive therapy in the treatment of depression have been conducted by Shaw[28] and by Taylor and Marshall,[29] among others.

We suggest that the current tally of results underscores the potential significance of additional clinical research in this area.

REFERENCES

1. Adler, A.: What Life Should Mean to You. New York, Capricorn, 1958.
2. Ansbacher, H. L., and Ansbacher, R. R., eds.: The Individual Psychology of Alfred Adler. New York, Harper & Row, 1956.
3. Beck, A. T.: Thinking and depression: 1. Idiosyncratic content and cognitive distortions. Arch. Gen. Psychiatry, 9:324–333, 1963.
4. Beck, A. T.: Thinking and depression: 2. Theory and therapy. Arch. Gen. Psychiatry, 10:561–571, 1964.
5. Beck, A. T.: Depression: Clinical, Experimental, and Theoretical Aspects. New York, Hoeber, 1967. Republished as Depression: Causes and treatment. Philadelphia, University of Pennsylvania Press, 1972.
6. Beck, A. T.: Cognitive Therapy and the Emotional Disorders. New York, International Universities Press, 1976.
7. Beck, A. T., and Emery, G.: Cognitive therapy of anxiety and phobic disorders. Unpublished manuscript, University of Pennsylvania, 1978. Available from the Center for Cognitive Therapy, Philadelphia.
8. Beck, A. T., Rush, A. J., Shaw, B. F., et al.: Cognitive Therapy of Depression. New York, Guilford Press, in press.
9. DiGiuseppe, R. A., Miller, N. J., and Trexler, L. D.: A review of rational-emotive psychotherapy outcome studies. The Counseling Psychologist, 7:64–72, 1977.
10. Ellis, A.: Reason and Emotion in Psychotherapy. New York, Lyle Stuart, 1962.
11. Ellis, A.: Humanistic Psychotherapy: The Rational-Emotive Approach. New York, McGraw-Hill, 1973.
12. Ellis, A., and Harper, R. A.: A New Guide to Rational Living. Hollywood, Wilshire, 1975.
13. Goldfried, M. R.: Anxiety reduction through cognitive-behavioral interven-

tion. *In* Kendall, P. C., and Hollon, S. D., eds.: Cognitive-Behavioral Interventions: Theory, Research, and Procedures. New York, Academic Press, in press.

14. Holroyd, K. A., Andrasik, F., and Westbrook, T.: Cognitive control of tension headache. Cognitive Therapy and Research, 1:121–133, 1977.

15. Kanter, N. J.: A comparison of self-control desensitization and systematic rational restructuring for the reduction of inter-personal anxiety. Unpublished doctoral dissertation, State University of New York at Stony Brook, 1975.

16. Keller, J. F., Croake, J. W., and Brooking, J. Y.: Effects of a program in rational thinking on anxieties in older persons. J. Couns. Psychol. 22:54–57, 1975.

17. Kelly, G.: The Psychology of Personal Constructs. New York, Norton & Co., 1955.

18. Kelly, G.: The psychotherapeutic relationship. *In* Maher, B., ed.: Clinical Psychology and Personality: The Selected Papers of George Kelly. New York, Wiley, 1969.

19. Mahoney, M. J.: Cognition and Behavior Modification. Cambridge, Ballinger, 1974.

20. Mahoney, M., and Arnkoff, D.: Cognitive and self-control therapies. *In* Garfield, S. L., and Bergin, A. E., eds.: Handbook of Psychotherapy and Behavior Change: An Empirical Analysis. New York, Wiley, 1978.

21. Meichenbaum, D.: Cognitive modification of test anxious college students. J. Consult. Clin. Psychol., 39:370–380, 1972.

22. Meichenbaum, M.: Cognitive Behavior Modification: An Integrative Approach. New York, Plenum, 1977.

23. Meichenbaum, M., and Butler, L.: Toward a conceptual model for the treatment of test anxiety: Implications for research and treatment. *In* Sarason, I. G., ed.: Test Anxiety, Theory, Research, and Applications. Hillsdale, New Jersey, Lawrence Erlbaum, in press.

24. Meichenbaum, D. H., Gilmore, J. B., and Fedoravicius, A.: Group insight vs. group desensitization in treating speech anxiety. J. Consult. Clin. Psychol., 36:410–421, 1971.

25. Novaco, R.: Anger Control: The Development and Evaluation of an Experimental Treatment. Lexington, Massachusetts, Heath & Co., 1975.

26. Raimy, V.: Misunderstandings of the Self. San Francisco, California, Jossey-Bass, 1975.

27. Rush, A. J., Beck, A. T., Kovacs, M., et al.: Comparative efficacy of cognitive therapy and imipramine in the treatment of depressed outpatients. Cognitive Therapy and Research, 1:17–37, 1977.

28. Shaw, B. F.: Comparison of cognitive therapy and behavior therapy in the treatment of depression. J. Consult. Clin. Psychol., 45:543–551, 1977.

29. Taylor, F. G., and Marshall, W. L.: Experimental analysis of a cognitive-behavioral therapy for depression. Cognitive Therapy and Research, 1:59–72, 1977.

30. Thorpe, G. L.: Desensitization, behavior rehearsal, self-instructional training and placebo effects on assertive-refusal behavior. Europ. J. Behav. Anal. Mod., 1:30–44, 1975.

31. Trexler, L. D., and Karst, T. O.: Rational-emotive therapy, placebo, and no-treatment effects on public-speaking anxiety. J. Abnorm. Psychol., 79:60–67, 1972.

32. Turk, D.: An expanded skills training approach for the treatment of experimentally induced pain. Unpublished doctoral dissertation, University of Waterloo, 1976.

Therapist Activity: Focusing on (or Away from) the Unconscious

In part II, therapists focused on the patient's interface with the world of the present. Here in part III the focus is on inner life and its relation to the past, hidden areas revealed by the transference. In both instances the focus emerges from the patient's pain interacting with the therapist's philosophy of cure. The short-term dynamic therapies possess no unique intellectual content distinct from long-term dynamic therapy; rather, brief treatments differ from long-term and among themselves in brevity, focus, activity, and selectivity.

The selections in this part as a whole reflect the impact of theory on activity and illustrate Gustafson's [1] dictum to the effect that any single maneuver is useful only when utilized with a larger set of theory-based principles. In Gustafson's blueprint they are threefold: (1) find the missing developmental piece, (2) pay careful attention to managing resistance, and (3) use brief therapy to understand, resolve, and repair the missing developmental capabilities discerned in (1). And while this section concerns the therapist's activity, patient selection is obviously intimately linked, especially with regard to resistance and transference—generally, healthier patients get selected for interpretive work and sicker ones do not, as part IV will show. (An exception that proves the rule is Winnicott's, the last paper in this present part.)

Almost nobody disputes that transference occurs in short-term treatments. Almost nobody doing short-term therapy feels that transference can only be interpreted when there is a "full-blown transference neurosis" (as it is peculiarly called). What is at issue is the *utility* of interpretations, transference interpretations for two purposes: (1) to advance the treatment itself or prevent transference from sabotaging the therapeutic task, and (2) to help the patient see that the same distortions going on in treatment interfere with relationships outside. Although they are writing only about psychoanalysis, Gill and

Muslin[2] convincingly argue that transference distortions strong enough to compromise an analysis occur in the beginning *hours* of treatment and need to be interpreted, a position certainly applicable to short-term treatments, even very brief ones.

Practitioners in this section tend to have in common a keen interest in the transference. And even if one doubts the curative effect of transference interpretations (as Strupp does), the harmful effect of unempathic ones is obvious even to the skeptic. This section begins with a discussion of when and why to interpret transference in short-term therapy. Following that, Hans Strupp debates Michael Balint on the role of interpretation versus *in vivo* learning in the patient's improvement—a window into both Strupp's ideas and Balint's clinical genius. (For another view of Balint's famous case, see Gustafson's[3] summary and discussion.) The next chapter is not directly about brief treatments, it is about a specific component of *activity*—the language the therapist uses. Transference *is* projection, and Havens discusses the vicissitudes of the patient's projection as affected by two types of statements—counterprojective and empathic—and their different effects on "transference management." Next comes one of Davanloo's more recent accounts of his method of mobilizing affect and interpreting his version of "transference."

The next chapter is not about short-term therapy at all, it is about countertransference. Countertransference is little written about in the short-term literature, and where it is, the quality of discourse (except by Mann) tends to be mediocre. Langs's chapter is eccentric, brilliant, and difficult. The reward for persisting, however, is a new grasp of how countertransference must be considered if transference is to be interpreted—especially if the interpretations are vigorous and penetrating, as are Davanloo's, for instance. Disowned sadism, rage, and hate are central to Davanloo's focus on the transference and to Langs's analysis of countertransference. If one is to dive into transference, as Davanloo does, management of the countertransference is essential. Langs's complex theories are powerfully catalytic (if not always immediately accessible).

Speaking of self-analysis and the use of countertransference, this section ends with a brief tour de force of Donald Winnicott. His economy and skill hinge on his brilliant use of symbols in this case, illustrating Langs's ideal therapist in this regard.

REFERENCES

1. Gustafson, J. P. "An Integration of Brief Dynamic Psychotherapy." *Am J Psychiatry* 141 (1984):935–44.

2. Gill, M. M., and H. L. Muslin. "Early Interpretation of Transference." *J Am Psychoanal Assoc* 24 (1976):779–94.

3. Gustafson, J. P. "The Complex Secret of Brief Psychotherapy in the Works of Malan and Balint." In *Forms of Brief Therapy,* ed. S. H. Budman. New York: Guilford Press, 1981, 83–128.

11. Transference Interpretations in Focal Therapy

Allen Frances and Samuel Perry

Within the confines of focal therapy, when are transference interpretations indicated? The psychiatric literature contains three contradictory answers. Some authors (1–3), the "conservatives," believe that transference interpretation is indispensable in traditional psychoanalysis but out of place in briefer therapies. Others (4–9) present the so-called "radical" view that transference interpretation is the most powerful technique for promoting change, even in brief treatments. A third group (10–14)—we might call them "skeptics"— doubt that specific techniques like transference interpretation have much independent impact one way or the other when compared with the nonspecific interpersonal features common to all psychotherapies.

After brief comments on the rationale and research supporting each position, we will attempt to reconcile them by suggesting clinical guidelines to indicate when transference interpretations are and are not possible and appropriate in focal therapy. We use two cases for illustration. In one, transference interpretations seemed necessary and effective; in the other, treatment proceeded best with the intentional avoidance of transference material.

THE CONSERVATIVE VIEW

Not long after Freud encountered transference as a complication of the "talking cure," he realized that he had accidentally discovered a phenomenon of great therapeutic potential. As a psychoanalysis unfolded, the sources of a patient's neurosis were not just remembered but actually repeated. The patient transferred onto the analyst attitudes toward significant developmental figures and thereby brought past conflicts alive in the immediate analytic situation, where interpretations could then be made (15).

Strachey consolidated the conservative view in his influential paper "The

Reprinted by permission of the American Psychiatric Association from *American Journal of Psychiatry* 140 (1983):405–9.

Nature of the Therapeutic Action of Psychoanalysis" (16). He argued that "the ultimate instrument" is "the mutative interpretation" of the fully developed transference neurosis, because 1) the point of emotional urgency available for intervention is most likely to be the transference neurosis; 2) the distortions in the patient's perception of the analyst are the only ones that can be demonstrated with certainty; and 3) the patient's unrealistic superego can be modified only by the gradual introjection of the realistic images of the analyst that result from repeated transference interpretations. Implicit in this argument is the notion that characterological changes are not expected to occur without a prolonged working through of neurotic conflicts. A true transference neurosis is fostered by the patient's regression in the analytic situation and by the understanding, patience, and passivity of the analyst. Until this intense transference neurosis develops (and it does not in brief therapy), transference interpretations are "premature."

This conservative view is not supported by a body of scientific research. In fact, Schafer (17) argued that questions about analytic technique are inherently not answerable by the investigative methods of behavioral science. Therefore, relying on theory and accumulated clinical wisdom, the conservatives conclude that treatments other than analysis may be necessary for patients who are in crisis or lack resources or are otherwise unsuitable, but that such treatments should be viewed as a compromise unlikely to produce character change.

THE RADICAL VIEW

The radical view is represented by the current leading contributors to the brief therapy literature, such as Davanloo (8), Malan (4), Mann (9), and Sifneos (6). They argue that transference interpretations in brief therapy not only can provide symptomatic relief but also can promote lasting characterological change. Accordingly, they believe that focal therapy is often the treatment of choice and that conservatives are unnecessarily cautious about applying transference interpretations to treatment settings other than analysis. Malan supported the radical position with interesting clinical research (18). He and his colleagues at the Tavistock Clinic studied 60 focal treatments, with follow-ups extending in some cases to more than 10 years. Successful psychodynamic change was correlated with early and thorough interpretation of the transference, particularly statements that linked feelings about the therapist to feelings about parents (therapist-parent [T/P] link).

Serious methodological problems restrict the authority of Malan's conclusion. His studies had no control groups, did not precisely define the treatments, and did not sufficiently measure possibly relevant patient variables. Malan scored the process of treatment (such as T/P links) by reviewing therapists' notes, which had been dictated from memory after sessions and were subject to the systematic bias of analytically oriented therapists well aware of the hypotheses being tested. In addition, the scoring of process and outcome was often not blind, and the measures of psychodynamic change may be criticized for being subjective and superficial. Furthermore, as Malan acknowledges, correlations do not imply causality: perhaps good-prognosis patients simply enable or encourage their dynamically oriented therapists to make T/P linking interpretations while the cause of their improvement lies elsewhere. Despite these reservations, the radical view does have some scientific support, and some is surely better than none.

THE SKEPTICAL VIEW

The skeptics question whether the benefits of the various psychotherapies can be attributed to any of the specific technical interventions that distinguish them. They believe that psychotherapy works, but suspect that nonspecific factors—such as a good relationship between therapist and patient—are more crucial than either theoretical orientation or technical innovation. This view was originally stated by Rosenzweig long ago (10) and has been championed by Jerome Frank (11): in all therapies (ancient or modern) a client experiencing tension visits a wise authority who has been delegated special powers; the client's problem is explained within the context of an ideology accepted by both; and a healing ceremony leads to relief.

Several research studies support this position of skepticism about the specific value of transference interpretations. Strupp and Hadley (19) compared the results achieved with depressed male college students treated either by college professors or by dynamically oriented therapists. Although the experienced psychotherapists made more specific interventions, the outcomes of the two groups were not significantly different. The kind of patient and not the kind of treatment was the best predictor of outcome (20). Strupp and Hadley's study would be more convincing were it not for serious sampling problems. Many of the "patients" were actually recruited by advertising. Although they did score high on MMPI depression, psychasthenia, and social introversion scales, the recruited subjects may nonetheless have differed in important ways from real patients. Kindly professors might not have fared so well if they had been confronted with patients other than depressed and lonely undergraduates.

Sloane and associates (14) compared behavioral with psychodynamic brief therapy. Experienced therapists representing each orientation treated randomly assigned, nonpsychotic outpatients stratified for severity of illness. Although the psychodynamic therapists made more transference interpretations than the behavioral therapists did, the two groups were indistinguishable in outcome and in the patients' perception of what had occurred during treatment. Both groups did better than a waiting list control group, but the specific reasons for improvement could not be isolated.

The skeptical position has received additional support from a number of sophisticated reviews of outcome research. Aggregated results from hundreds of controlled studies have not thus far been able to document the advantages of one modality over another (21, 22). Since all sorts of very different treatments—behavioral, supportive, dynamic, experiential, directive, rational-emotive, gestalt, etc.—have produced equivalent measured results, possibly a fine point like transference interpretations may have little specific importance. The burden of proof now rests upon those who believe that specific interventions are differentially effective. Most of the research we reviewed, however, was insufficiently specific in design; the failure to demonstrate differences among treatments may simply reflect limitations in the research.

GUIDELINES FOR TRANSFERENCE INTERPRETATION IN FOCAL THERAPY

In summary, some advise against transference interpretation outside of traditional psychoanalysis, some believe transference interpretation is essential in focal therapy, and some say it does not matter so long as the therapist and patient are engaged in a meaningful therapeutic relationship. Because research has not been sophisticated enough to resolve this issue, none of the three positions is supported by very compelling data. The three views can be reconciled, however, if one accepts that all are sometimes true and none is always true. In some focal treatments, transference interpretation appears to be indispensable, in others it may be unnecessary or potentially harmful, and there may be times when fine points of technique do not make a difference. In the spirit of this reconciliation and on the basis of clinical judgment, we make the following tentative suggestions.

Transference interpretations in brief therapy are appropriate when 1) transference feelings have become the point of urgency and/or a major resistance; 2) transference distortions have disrupted the therapeutic alliance and interpretations are necessary to strengthen the alliance; 3) conflicts revealed in the transference directly reflect conflicts responsible for the presenting problem or maladaptive character traits; 4) the patient has the psychological-mindedness to observe, understand, tolerate, and apply transference interpretations; and/or 5) the length of remaining treatment will allow sufficient exploration of whatever transference interpretations are made.

Transference interpretations may be unnecessary or inadvisable if 1) the patient does not develop strong and apparent transference distortions; 2) the point of emotional urgency and the related intrapsychic conflicts are fixed on current events and relationships outside the treatment situation; 3) a fragile therapeutic alliance will be jeopardized further by a distressing and unacceptable transference interpretation; 4) the patient does not have the psychological-mindedness to observe, understand, tolerate, and use transference interpretations; 5) transference distortions are not related clearly enough to the presenting problem or to significant maladaptive character traits; and/or 6) remaining treatment time is too limited for even a partial analysis of transference material.

CASE ILLUSTRATIONS

Case 1. This case illustrates a brief treatment in which transference interpretations seemed crucially important.

Ms. A, a 24-year-old nurse, came to therapy with slashed arms and fears that she was going crazy. After weeks of bitter arguments, her boyfriend had abruptly ended their relationship. Ms. A was left with unbearable restlessness, hatred for both her boyfriend and herself, and an inability to sleep, ultimately leading to mild self-mutilation and psychiatric consultation.

During the first three sessions, Ms. A openly described how her recent relationship, like two previous ones, had turned sour for reasons she did not understand. She was aware that she had contributed to these failed affairs and at first appeared eager to explore how; but during the fourth session she sat like a pouting child, sullen and withdrawn, and only with encouragement mumbled that she "never believed much in psychiatry." The therapist, finding no recent event outside of treatment to explain this shift, considered her behavior likely to be a specific manifestation of transference resistance and asked what feelings she had about him. The patient replied that she was convinced the therapist did not like her and was finding her unworthy of his efforts. She had kept quiet about her doubts for fear of hurting his feelings.

An analysis of these transference distortions became the focus of Ms. A's brief therapy, which lasted for a total of 22 sessions over a 6-month period. The first resistance explored was her need to protect the therapist by remaining silent. She recalled a longstanding fear of accidentally hurting those she cared for, making a medication error with her hospital patients, making an inadvertent "nasty" remark to her boyfriends, or flippantly putting down her younger brother, who was addicted to drugs. She soon linked this need to "hold her tongue" to the experience of nursing her mother when the latter was dying of cancer. Ms. A had been afraid that she would make some "Freudian slip" and her mother would die feeling eternally hurt.

Although Ms. A spontaneously recalled lifelong concerns about hurting others, she could not provide examples of precisely what she was afraid she might say. When asked to be more specific, she was at first evasive and then irritated at the therapist for dwelling on trivial details and said she doubted that the therapist wasted his time in mundane gossip with his male patients. This notion about the therapist could then be traced to an intense though well-concealed resentment toward her parents for favoring her brothers over herself, as well as resentment of her brothers and men in general. She was struggling to contain an embittered hatred and feared that it would slip out undisguised. With further work Ms. A was able to understand that her conviction that the therapist did not like her and found her unworthy was based in part on her disparaging view of herself as a woman and in part on her unexpressed resentment, which made her feel unlovable. By exaggerating minor problems and by sulking, she had unconsciously sabotaged relationships with boyfriends before the extent of her rage could be realized and before her lovers would find out that she was "just another cow."

The highly charged concentration on material related to the transference precluded much discussion of Ms. A's current life outside of treatment, and yet, concomitant with her increased understanding, she began to dress more attractively and appear more relaxed. She could accept and even joke about whatever anger she felt toward the therapist for being late, toward her new boyfriend for being "a size Large jock," and toward her father, whom she now recalled more fondly. But 6 weeks before the date of termination, Ms. A once again became withdrawn during sessions. This time, however, Ms. A did not appear to be sulking; instead she was shy and reserved. By now she was able to work with transference material effectively, and she associated her feelings when she was with the therapist to her pubescent years when she would sit with her father in the living room, feeling very distant from him and fearing that he would ask "embarrassing questions." Before termination, Ms. A was able to realize that in her fantasy the price of womanliness was either acting illicitly or being abandoned.

On follow-up 3 months after treatment, Ms. A described how she was less inhibited with her new boyfriend and able to experience and express both angry and tender feelings. Other aspects of her life, such as her work and her relationship with her brother, had also improved.

Case 2. In contrast to the case of Ms. A, that of Mr. B illustrates a brief treatment in which transference interpretations involving the therapist seemed neither necessary nor advisable.

Mr. B, a 40-year-old successful executive, was forced into treatment by his wife, who threatened divorce unless he immediately changed his behavior toward her. A no-nonsense sort of fellow, Mr. B frankly admitted during the first visit that he was quite skeptical about psychiatry but loved his wife and wanted to preserve the marriage; if the psychiatrist would tell him what he was doing wrong, he would try to change. He himself was bewildered by his wife's dissatisfactions—he was not a drunk, he did not fool around, he gave her the very best that money could buy; what was wrong with him? Maybe she was just "high-strung."

Throughout the 12 sessions over a 3-month period, Mr. B related to the therapist in a friendly man-to-man fashion as if he were seeking advice about how to tune his high-performance sports car. While describing the ways he and his wife spent time together—such as their punctual and meticulous evening meal—Mr. B seemed unaware that he was such a perfectionist that little room was left for spontaneity in his marriage. When this observation was made to him, Mr. B noted with surprise that his wife had complained about the very same thing, although he had never before taken her complaints very seriously. The therapist then commented on the ease with which Mr. B had, over the years, been able to dismiss his wife's remarks and asked about similar experiences with other women. The modulated tone of the session suddenly changed. With intense feeling Mr. B described his mother as a domineering, demanding, critical woman who was impossible to manage and who could get under his skin in a way Mr. B could not easily dismiss.

Without ever commenting on Mr. B's need to control and at times dictate the sessions, the therapist concentrated on transferential distortions *outside* of the treatment setting. The patient was repeatedly shown how he was relating to his wife as if she were a new version of his mother. His effort to avoid being dominated and scrutinized was costing him a potentially loving relationship in which he could be cared for in the way he wanted yet feared. Mr. B responded by being more open and tender with his wife and more realistic in his dealings with his mother. On follow-up 6 months later, Mr. B was thankful for the way his marriage had continued to improve, but he still related to the therapist in his characteristic controlling and somewhat perfunctory manner.

DISCUSSION

Ms. A's initial transference distortions were so intense that the treatment was in jeopardy unless she realized that her feelings of being unworthy were unrealistic and based on relationships with significant others in her past. Her transference resistance was closely related to her presenting problem and her nuclear conflicts. Through the analysis of her misperceptions of the therapist, she could simultaneously correct the way she perceived and related to her boyfriends and family. In the therapist's judgment, interpretations of the transference were not only indicated but unavoidable.

In the case of Mr. B, the opposite appeared to be true. Transference interpretations involving the therapist would have disrupted rather than enhanced the flow of treatment. Although Mr. B's need to control the therapist was dynamically related to his fear of being controlled by his mother and wife, the manifestations of this fear within the therapeutic situation were probably too subtle for this no-nonsense kind of patient to observe and use. His need to control had, after all, worked adaptively both professionally and socially and was not a character trait he wanted "fixed." In addition, if the therapist had (perhaps defensively) commented on how the patient was "treating" him, Mr. B might have devalued the treatment altogether by viewing the therapist as one additional demanding and whining person in his life. On the other hand, it remains quite possible that Mr. B's transference reactions toward the therapist might have been usefully explored and related to the similar behaviors that he had manifested toward his wife. This was not done because the therapist's intuition was that such a confrontation would strain a fragile and inflexible therapeutic alliance and that the point of greatest and most available emotional urgency remained the patient's feelings about his wife, not the therapist.

The case of Mr. B also illustrates the distinction between transference interpretations focused on behavior toward the therapist as opposed to interpretations with respect to transference behavior toward other figures in the patient's current life—in this instance, Mr. B's wife. Because the technique of transference interpretation was developed within the context of psychoanalysis and has been specifically related to the distorted reactions of the patient to the therapist, some authors (16) believe that the term "transference interpretation" should refer only to remarks regarding misconceptions of the therapist. Others believe that the term should not be so tightly defined and may refer to interventions by the therapist designed to clarify and correct how the patient is "transferentially" relating to important current figures outside the therapeutic situation. In making suggestions about the indications and contraindications for transference interpretations, we have used the more restricted definition for fear that the broader sense of transference interpretation would blur the points we are trying to make.

Another definitional issue involves the way in which to best apply the term "focal therapy." Proponents of certain forms of brief psychodynamic therapy (particularly Sifneos) insist upon very restrictive, and rarely met, patient selection criteria, which among other things include a high level of psychological-mindedness and the capacity for making use of transference interpretations. One can certainly reserve the term "focal therapy" exclusively for treatments that rely primarily on interpretation of the transference, but this results in an unnecessarily restrictive definition which obscures the important fact that many patients who benefit from brief, focused, psychodynamic therapies do not meet the most stringent selection criteria and do not require transference interpretation.

We have considered the attributes of the patient that determine whether transference interpretations are indicated. We must acknowledge, however, that attributes of the therapist may trigger some transference reactions and may suppress others. Ms. A's presenting problem of difficulties with heterosexual relationships might not have been reflected in her initial transference reaction if the therapist had not been male; Mr. B might not have responded So "reasonably" to a female therapist, and, in fact, might well have experienced disruptive transference distortions requiring prompt interpretation. Features of the therapist other than sex—age, appearance, character style, and mode of interacting—also may catalyze or inhibit transference reactions in the limited course of brief therapy.

CONCLUSIONS

Accumulated research evidence and clinical experience should discourage therapeutic dogmatism concerning which interventions should be used and when. One cannot argue convincingly that brief therapy requires transference interpretations, that it precludes them, or that specific interventions are unimportant. Flexibility is required to meet the particular needs of any given patient. In the absence of more substantial scientific data, decisions about what is optimal must still be based on informed judgment and intuition. Accordingly, we have suggested certain tentative and unsupported guidelines for and against the use of transference interpretations in focal therapy.

REFERENCES

1. Deutsch F: Applied Psychoanalysis. New York, Grune & Stratton, 1949.

2. Pumpian-Mindlin: Considerations in the selection of patients for short-term therapy. Am J Psychother 7:641, 1953.

3. Berliner B: Short psychoanalytic psychotherapy: its possibilities and its limitations. Bull Menninger Clin 5:204–211, 1941.

4. Malan DH: The Frontier of Brief Psychotherapy. New York. Plenum, 1976.

5. Malan DH: A Study of Brief Psychotherapy. London, Tavistock, 1963.

6. Sifneos, PE: Short-Term Psychotherapy and Emotional Crisis. Cambridge, Mass, Harvard University Press, 1972.

7. Sifneos PE, Apfel RJ, Bassuk E, et al.: Ongoing outcome research on short-term dynamic psychotherapy. Psychother Psychosom 33:233–241, 1980.

8. Davanloo H: Basic Principles and Techniques in Short-Term Dynamic Psychotherapy. New York, Spectrum, 1978.

9. Mann J: Time Limited Psychotherapy. Cambridge, Mass, Harvard University Press, 1973.

10. Rosenzweig S: Some implicit common factors in diverse methods of psychotherapy. Am J Orthopsychiatry 6:422–425, 1936.

11. Frank JD: Therapeutic factors in psychotherapy. Am J Psychother 25:350–361, 1971.

12. Strupp HH: Psychoanalysis, "focal psychotherapy," and the nature of the therapeutic influence. Arch Gen Psychiatry 32:127–135, 1975.

13. Shapiro AK: Placebo effects in medicine, psychotherapy, and psychoanalysis, in Handbook of Psychotherapy and Behavior Change. Edited by Bergin AE, Garfield SL. New York, John Wiley & Sons, 1971.

14. Sloane RB, Staples FR, Cristol AH, et al.: Psychotherapy Versus Behavior Therapy. Cambridge, Mass, Harvard University Press, 1975.

15. Freud S: Remembering, repeating and working-through (1914), in Complete Psychological Works, standard ed, vol. 12. London, Hogarth, 1958.

16. Strachey J: The nature of the therapeutic action of psychoanalysis. Int J Psychoanal 15:127–159, 1934.

17. Schafer R: The termination of brief psychoanalytic psychotherapy. Int J Psychoanal Psychother 2:135–148, 1973.

18. Malan DH: Toward the Validation of Dynamic Psychotherapy: A Replication. New York, Plenum, 1976.

19. Strupp HH, Hadley SW: Specific vs. nonspecific factors in psychotherapy: a controlled study of outcome. Arch Gen Psychiatry 36:1125–1136, 1979.

20. Strupp HH: Success and failure in time-limited psychotherapy. Arch Gen Psychiatry 37:947–954, 1980.

21. Luborsky L, Singer B, Luborsky L: Comparative studies of psychotherapies: is it true that "everybody has won and all must have prizes"? Arch Gen Psychiatry 32:995–1008, 1975.

22. Smith ML, Glass G, Miller TI: Benefits of Psychotherapy, Baltimore, Johns Hopkins University Press, 1980.

12. Psychoanalysis, "Focal Psychotherapy," and the Nature of the Therapeutic Influence

Hans H. Strupp

The nature of the psychotherapeutic influence, by which I mean factors responsible for "mutative" changes, has traditionally been allocated to "transference interpretations." Such interpretations, when properly timed, are said to produce dynamic, economic, and structural changes in the patient's mental apparatus. These changes in mental structure and functioning are viewed as the unique contribution of psychoanalysis and are said to set psychoanalysis apart from psychotherapy in a fundamental sense. They are seen as radical rather than symptom-oriented; they are supposedly free from "suggestion"; and they are what Freud called the "pure" gold of "nontendentious" psychoanalysis. Elsewhere, to be sure, Freud spoke of psychoanalysis as a form of "after-education" (see also Stone,[1] p. 31) and he admitted that, at times, the analyst has to serve the patient as "mentor and guide." This influence, however, was regarded as secondary and subsidiary to transference interpretations, certainly as less desirable, and in any case a product of operations unworthy of the appellation "psychoanalytic."

While the foregoing distinction has historically served the important purpose of setting "psychoanalysis" apart from other forms of "psychotherapy," thereby elevating the former to a position of preeminence while denigrating the latter, I am taking the position that it is largely spurious. The distinction, in my view, is a resultant of political and propagandistic rather than scientific considerations; indeed, it is indefensible on scientific grounds. In other words, it will not suffice merely to state and to repeat that the psychoanalytic influence is categorically different from a psychotherapeutic influence, unless evidence can be produced to substantiate the claim. In fact, the burden of demonstrating the viability of the distinction rests on the proponents, not on the critics who can take a more parsimonious stance in asserting, as I have done in several places,[2,3] that there are only a limited number of techniques for influencing the feelings, attitudes, and behavior of another person, and

Reprinted by permission of the American Medical Association from *Archives of General Psychiatry* (1974) 32:127–35.

that psychoanalysis partakes of these techniques insofar as it is geared to the goal of effecting change. The latter goal, of course, is frequently disputed by psychoanalytic authors; however, it is difficult to see how any psychotherapist can dissociate himself from the *raison d'être* of his trade, i.e., producing change, however that change may be specified. Change, as everyone recognizes, can and does occur as a function of diverse interventions, and it is notoriously difficult to attribute change to particular operations.

I shall mention only in passing the kind of evidence called for above. For the distinction between "psychoanalytic" and other changes to hold, it would be necessary to show that treatment outcomes are *quantitatively* or *qualitatively* different. Unless it can be demonstrated that a patient whose treatment has been conducted along strictly orthodox lines is more mature, autonomous, independent, healthy, integrated, or what not than someone whose therapy has included subtle and perhaps not so subtle suggestions and whose therapist has steered, guided, and persuaded him in ways that are proscribed by psychoanalysis (at least to the extent that their purpose is clearly recognized), the difference would appear to be untenable. In other words, we shall need *empirical indicators* of some kind. These may be exceedingly subtle, but they have to be real and somehow they must make a difference in the person's functioning. A question may be raised why after decades of therapeutic work so little progress has been made in adducing such evidence. Part of the problem, of course, rests with the prevailing reliance on intrapsychic mechanisms as well as the difficulty of documenting behavioral change. But even qualitative differences are difficult to document. Could it be that they do not exist? (Stone[1] notes: "I think there is legitimate question as to whether analysis can be defined and differentiated from other methods *entirely* on the basis of techniques or other elements of outer phenomenology.")

The purpose of this chapter is to advance my argument by reference to a recent case history that illustrates my assertion that therapeutic changes can be conceptualized along lines different from those traditionally advanced by psychoanalytic therapists. Such "translations" into another theoretical framework are, of course, always possible and perhaps not particularly remarkable. It makes little difference whether a meat patty is called "hamburger" or "Salisbury steak," but, as I will try to document, it may be quite another matter whether therapeutic changes are attributed to insight into aspects of an infantile psychosexual conflict or whether they are seen as a function of interpersonal learning experiences occurring within the psychotherapeutic framework. As a third possibility, there may be shared elements.

The latter is precisely what I consider to be the case in all forms of psychotherapy, including psychoanalysis, operant conditioning, and a host of others.

FOCAL PSYCHOTHERAPY

The case history that will form the basis of this report exemplifies an approach called focal psychotherapy, advanced by the late Michael Balint and co-workers at the Tavistock Clinic in London. Balint's[4] interest in the possibility of shortening psychoanalytic psychotherapy grew out of earlier efforts by pioneers like Ferenczi,[5] Ferenczi and Rank,[6] and Alexander and French,[7] and it is cognate with contemporary work by Malan[8] (a co-worker of Balint's), Sifneos,[9] and Mann.[10] (Other case histories might have been chosen, and it could be argued that Balint is not truly representative. The reason I selected this material is the relatively comprehensive presentation and the insights it permits into the author's thinking and theorizing.) While Freud[11] recognized the need for alternatives to long-term psychoanalysis— which in his day tended to last no longer than approximately nine months (!)—and made some pragmatic statements along these lines, his attitude toward the "innovations" proposed by Ferenczi and Rank was strongly antagonistic. The opposition centered around the "activities" proposed by the innovators that were seen as "manipulative," hence nonanalytic or antianalytic. Presently, protracted arguments ensued concerning purportedly irreconcilable differences between "psychoanalysis" and "psychotherapy." The *bête noire* hovering in the background always appeared to be the model of the 19th century mesmerian hypnotist who made powerful direct suggestions and asserted an authoritarian attitude vis-à-vis his patients, all of which was obviously—and justifiably—anathema to the psychoanalysts. It is important to note that the battle was fought largely on ideological rather than empirical grounds, the credo of the orthodox analytic position being that classical analysis was essentially nonmanipulative, that the therapist did not influence his patients other than through transference interpretations, and that any other "activities" constituted "parameters" that needed to be carefully avoided or at least dealt with in special ways. While it was recognized that the therapist affected the patient in various ways, such influences tended to be downgraded, eschewed, and seen as radically different from that of the "true" psychoanalytic influence. There can be no question that, in terms of developing the patient's independence and autonomy, it is far more desirable to let him struggle and arrive at his own solutions rather than to "modify" his behavior in keeping with the therapist's (or society's) preconceived notions, and the analysts' emphasis on encouraging the patient to find his own answers to life's problems, including the management of impulses and needs, is altogether appropriate. Indeed, this emphasis constitutes one of the most important contributions analysis has made to the resolution of man's emotional problems in living. It is crucial, however, to examine what in fact occurs in the course of the therapeutic interaction. When this process is carefully dissected, I believe it will emerge with compelling clarity that the therapeutic influence is broad-gauged, that every patient is being influenced by the therapist in a wide variety of ways, of which interpretations are only one subset, and that it is arbitrary to elevate the latter to a position of preeminence. On the contrary, I believe that the weight of the therapeutic influence is brought to bear in numerous modalities and that interpretations of all kinds are a relatively minor factor in the total change that is wrought over the short as well as the long term. This proposition, I contend, is amply borne out by Balint's case. The most that can be said is that the effect of any class of therapeutic interventions is *relative;* conversely, I assert that to the extent that therapeutic operations are effective in producing change, they partake of *all* aspects that are characteristic of psychological influencing techniques known to produce modifications in feelings, attitudes, and behavior. In other words, insight—even deeply felt emotional insight—into one's dynamics enables the patient to change his feelings and behavior only to the extent that he has become willing to *listen* to the therapist and to accept his teachings concerning the "good life," as he sees it.

Returning to Balint's focal therapy, initial experimentation with a shortened technique proved abortive, in part because of the timidity of his collaborators who apparently were preoccupied with whether or not the new thinking and the new techniques might "endanger" basic psychoanalytic theory and practice[4] (p. 13). A renewed effort was undertaken and a "focal workshop" was constituted. As part of this enterprise, Balint began to treat a patient (whose case history will presently be described), composed notes following each therapeutic session, made some reasonably systematic observations, discussed the progress with his collaborators (Paul Ornstein and Enid Balint), and followed the patient's progress over a period of seven years. Balint's focal therapy was based on the major premise that, in order to carry out short-term treatment, it is essential to define the therapeutic aims clearly, to focus attention on their achievement, and to avoid being sidetracked by traditional interests in the *totality* of the patient's psychodynamics and his psychosexual development (p. 46).

REPORT OF A CASE

The patient was a 43-year-old business executive who was referred by his general practitioner because of "increasing preoccupation with his wife's feelings towards a young man who seriously courted her before their marriage about twenty years ago and with whom she had had no further contact whatsoever" (p. 20). The patient had one serious "breakdown" six years prior to the present referral that lasted for a few months and gradually improved. A similar, though less severe, disturbance occurred a few weeks prior to the referral.

The patient came from a wealthy family, was well educated, and was working in the parental firm. Recently the father had retired, and the patient with his two brothers, had acquired controlling interest in the business.

During World War II, the patient met his wife, a Turkish woman, when he was stationed in Cyprus. He was subsequently transferred to India, and it was during this period that his wife-to-be developed a fairly platonic love interest in another man. Eventually, she decided to marry the patient. The marriage was described as "very happy right from the start." The couple had three children, reportedly all well adjusted. The patient was described by the therapist as a "reliable, sensible and very loving man, a man with imagination and drive" (p. 22). The therapist responded positively to him. "Of course," he noted, "I was aware of [the] latent homosexual, paranoid nature [of the patient's appeal]; still, the appeal was there and was very strong." (p. 23).

By the second interview, Balint had arrived at a diagnosis: "a jealous paranoia with all the classical features of obsessional character, latent homosexuality, and so on" (p. 27). Good prognostic signs were seen as the patient's "very good ego structure" and the fact that his paranoid ideas were "strictly limited"; negative indicators were the long duration of the symptoms and the danger of antagonizing the patient if the therapist penetrated his "paranoid circle."

TREATMENT GOALS

The focal aims of the treatment were formulated as the amelioration of the guilt feelings caused by the patient's triumph over his homosexual rivals (the fellow officer in Cyprus, his father-in-law, and his own father). Since Balint thought this might be "too ambitious," he entertained a secondary aim: "to enable [the patient] in the transference to find a man with whom he can share his wife (symbolically)" (p. 27).

As noted, the patient's prominent symptomatology centered around a long-standing preoccupation with his wife's feelings toward his erstwhile rival, and his incessant questioning of her relation to the man with whom there had been no further contact since the marriage. The wife apparently submitted to her husband's persistent interrogations without violent protest, although one gathers that she felt her patience was being sorely tried, and at one time or another she resorted to untruths, presumably to gain some peace.

Events precipitating the earlier breakdown to which the therapist assigned considerable importance were the couple's move to a new and larger house, the death of the patient's father-in-law of whom he had been very fond, and the acquisition of control in the father's business. No data are presented concerning current conflicts or issues in the marital relationship or details of the wife's response to the patient's incessant interrogations. In fact, the reasons for the upsurge of the patient's ruminations remained obscure, although predictably there must have been important sources of marital friction. In other words, the picture of an idyllic marriage, except for the patient's obsession, strains one's credulity. I shall return to this problem shortly.

It was of some importance that the patient sought "a kind of symptomatic treatment," wanted to use the therapist "only as a sounding board," and envisaged the length of therapy between five and six sessions (p. 27). Balint considered 10 to 20 sessions more realistic. As it turned out, the patient was seen for 27 sessions, extending over a period of about 1½ years. The follow-up consisted of some correspondence and two interviews, the last of which occurred six years after the initial consultation. The last contact was a report from the patient's general practitioner to the therapist.

It is clear that the treatment plan and the principal theme running through the therapist's interventions derive from Balint's dynamic formulation of the patient's difficulties. He states (p. 29):

The choice [of foci] reflects the therapist's ideas about the possible dynamic etiology of the illness. He considered it a fairly classical instance of a jealousy paranoia, with the three classical sources, anal erotism, homosexuality, and rigid obsessional tendencies. The therapist thought that in this case the most important factor was the patient's homosexuality, which could not tolerate that there were men who would not love him. Expressed as distorted by the patient's projection this would run: Men would compete with him for his woman's love and become his rivals, i.e., his enemies instead of loving him. The fact that he could not accept was that in the case of his wife he defeated his rival, which was the final proof that his rival will forever remain his enemy and could never love him. It was in this sense that the first focal aim was described as the more ambitious one, to enable him to accept his ultimate victory, that is, the fact that he will never be able to enjoy the love of his rival.

The second focal aim is described as "symptomatic" because, by sharing his wife symbolically, he dispenses with the victory, nobody is the conqueror, so perhaps the men need not hate each other. There always remains a possibility of harmonious coexistence. This is, of course, based on by-passing the need for reality-testing. Expressed in homosexual terms, the ambitious focal aim would mean that he would be able to free himself from the homosexual attachment to the extent that he could beat his rival. The second aim would mean a compromise: The importance of the rival is reduced, but the patient must give him a symbolic share of his wife in order to retain his rival's affection (p. 29).

In the foregoing, Balint refers to the "possible dynamic etiology" of the patient's disturbance, and readers who have been trained in the psychoanalytic tradition will undoubtedly agree that the formulation is indeed *possible*. However, other formulations may be considered equally plausible, and a different formulation might have led to technical differences. For example, one might have begun by scrutinizing the marital relationship for conflicts, and one might have wondered why the husband, in a seemingly idyllic relationship, found it necessary to attack his wife in thoroughly sadistic fashion and why these attacks occurred at certain periods but not at others. Balint was correct in noting that his dynamic formulation was a *possible* one, but once he had convinced himself of its explanatory power, he proceeded to act as if it were *the only* possible one. On the basis of the clinical data provided in the book, it is fair to say that a sample of therapists—even therapists with a theoretical approach similar to Balint's—would have formulated the cause and the treatment plan along different lines (c.f., Strupp[12] for empirical data on this topic).

CRITIQUE

At this point, it may be questioned why this is an issue in the first place. In response, it is to be noted that whereas psychoanalytic theory provides certain guidelines in formulating clinical problems, acceptance of basic psychoanalytic tenets does not necessarily result in identical dynamic formulations, for the simple reason that the theory is not sufficiently precise or stringent. However, if a dynamic formulation is relevant to the ensuing therapeutic operations, the conceptualization of the patient's problem and the therapeutic task is hardly trivial. If this is denied, it cannot be asserted that the therapeutic operations are guided by specific theoretical assumptions concerning the nature of the symptoms and their cause. In the case under discussion, it is an open question, therefore, whether the results of the therapy (which were impressive) were due to the interpretations advanced by Balint throughout the treatment or to other factors, concerning which more needs to be said. In other words, it may be quite true that the patient was struggling with a homosexual problem, but there is no convincing demonstration that Balint's interpretations, which were undergirded by his particular assumptions concerning the cause of the patient's problems, were a primary source of the improvement. For example, having located the source of the current disturbance in the patient's psychosexual development, the therapist heavily focused on *past* events in the patient's life, which of course coincided with the patient's preoccupations. It is at least conceivable that the patient was far less threatened by discussions centering around a rival in the remote past than by contemporary issues.

It may be countered that a single case cannot be used to prove or disprove the foregoing point. However, as previously pointed out, the onus rests on the proponents of a particular formulation, not on the critics who can rest content with therapeutic factors *common* in all forms of psychotherapy. From this standpoint, it is relatively inconsequential whether the treatment in this case was "psychoanalysis" or "focal psychotherapy"; the same strictures apply in both instances.

Balint's basic unwillingness or inability to entertain alternative hypotheses emerges in other respects as well. For example, he views "psychoanalysis" as the only viable alternative to focal therapy (pp. 28, 58), ignoring the fact that many forms of relationship psychotherapy might at least be possible contenders. If the patient were suffering from a psychosis—a likely diagnosis hinted at in various places—orthodox analysts (including Balint p. 59) would in any case be highly cautious about the prognosis, if they considered the patient suitable at all. In short, Balint exemplifies an inordinately doctrinaire perspective on clinical data, clinical formulations, and treatment modalities, as well as a faith in the therapeutic utility of a procedure hardly warranted either by research or accumulated clinical experience. The same phenomenon is shown elsewhere in the volume, when Rorschach findings are treated as if the interpretations were immutable facts. The truth of the matter is that very often in clinical work we simply do not know, cannot be certain, and are greatly hampered by our theoretical perspectives that cause us to view the phenomena through the lenses of our particular biases. With due respect to the memory of a highly gifted and innovative analyst, my purpose is not to take issue with Dr. Balint's handling of the case or his concepts of focal therapy; rather, it is to raise questions concerning the prevailing practice of elevating tentative and fallible clinical observations to an exalted status that they cannot possibly deserve. It should be clear that any formulation—regarding cause, dynamics, and treatment modalities—can never be more than highly provisional. I shall note only in passing that progress in psychoanalysis has grievously suffered from a widespread reluctance to take seriously this self-evident truth.

Balint, Ornstein, and Balint have struggled hard to report a difficult case in considerable detail, an effort that is not nearly made with sufficient frequency by others. Even so, their account lacks verbatim transcripts of any patient-therapist transactions, and the reader must rely on the summaries of therapeutic sessions and other commentaries. The closest approach to primary data is the reproduction of an occasional letter by the patient to his therapist.

A careful reading of the material discloses the enormous complexity of the patient-therapist interactions, as well as the virtual impossibility of assigning proper weights to the factors that produced therapeutic change. There can be no doubt that the patient improved as a result of his therapeutic experience and that the therapeutic gains were maintained over a period of years. I am fully prepared to accept that something valuable transpired, but it cannot escape notice that previous flare-ups in the patient's life also had subsided after a period of time, for reasons that cannot readily be reconstructed. Leaving aside the problem of "spontaneous remission" (Bergin),[13] the basic question that concerns me in this article relates to the nature of the therapeutic action in this—and of course in other—cases. What accounted for the patient's clinical improvement? What factors in the patient-therapist interaction were responsible?

To anticipate my conclusion, the case history amply demonstrates that the therapeutic influence was exceedingly *broad-gauged and multifaceted.* Accordingly, I consider it largely futile to attempt isolation of single events, interpretations, and interventions as being responsible for "mutative" changes that occurred. This conclusion, I submit, is generally true—even when, as in the case of orthodox psychoanalysis, the therapist sharply restricts his "activities." Nevertheless, it appears worthwhile to isolate certain broad strands, which to this author appear at least as plausible as the foci chosen by Dr. Balint. Furthermore, it is my judgment that they make considerably fewer theoretical assumptions, which I consider a virtue.

REFORMULATION OF THERAPEUTIC FACTORS

First and foremost, it appears that the patient was able to form a *solid, reliable, and trusting relationship* with his therapist. There can be no doubt that Dr. Balint took a positive and enduring interest in this patient, far beyond and different from "another patient." He obviously liked the man; had a good deal of positive regard for him; accepted his "illness" without criticism or moral judgment; was willing to see the patient's wife and a male friend when such meetings seemed indicated; responded to emergencies; persisted in his therapeutic efforts, particularly at times when the going got rough and the patient's condition seemingly deteriorated; and in many other ways demonstrated that he was on the patient's side, willing and eager to help, never losing his patience, and always being a strong supportive figure. As the patient put it in a letter to Dr. Balint (p. 118):

"I will not forget your patience (what a stubborn patient I must have been at times), but you knew I did feel that all this difficulty would eventually resolve itself"[4] (p. 118).

While the therapist recognized the importance of this factor, I wonder whether he sufficiently credited the therapeutic outcome to the support he provided the patient by enabling him to develop an unusual sense of trust. The traditional concept of "identification" partly captures this ingredient, but, in my judgment, it fails to assign sufficient weight to the *human* quality of the process.

The second factor carrying major weight in the therapeutic success is encompassed by what I shall call the *learning experiences in constructive living,* which were mediated by the patient's positive relationship (alliance) with the therapist. Having created a situation in which the patient was willing to *listen* to the therapist, that is, having overcome mistrust and resistance to accepting the advice and guidance of persons in authority, Balint was able to "drive home" a number of important "lessons" that the patient was eventually able to accept as "insights" into his behavior, particularly in relation to his wife. A few examples will illustrate the point:

1. Balint notes: "I interpreted that whenever he is hurt, he must respond by reproaching [his wife] for her past deeds, that is, hurting her back, and thus quite a large part of his obsessional nagging and pestering [her] with questions is nothing but using the past to beat her with. He

did not like it but had to accept it, and this was the first time he was able to tell me the name of his rival . . ." (p. 56).

2. In a joint session with the wife, resulting from her distress at her husband's recent escapades with several prostitutes, which for unclear reasons he reported to his wife, Balint commented that "apparently [the patient's] liberation [he had previously been very inhibited with attractive women] has to be paid for by [the wife's] pains and that there is a real problem to be solved: How much liberation is to be achieved at the price of how much suffering?" (p. 63).

3. In another session, Balint summed up things by saying that "apparently he has the compulsion to mangle his wife until she says something that hurts him very badly; then he gets a very painful depression, but after that he can emerge as loving as ever. He became rather thoughtful and proposed that we should examine this process at the next session. He then asked me to come down to his wife to reassure her" (p. 72).

4. In the context of a discussion about being in love, romantic attachment, and sexual stimulation, Balint observed:

Although I expressed my sympathy with and worry about him, I remained adamant that what he asks from his wife is impossible. He must accept the fact that he will not be able to get more out of her than—that she flirted with this other man . . . but after a while decided that [the patient] was the right man for her. This seemed to settle him a bit and we were able to go on with some constructive work. This centered around the fact that he cannot accept that it is possible that anybody could be in love— though with different intensity—with two people at the same time (pp. 81–82).

And again:

. . . he can now see that it is possible to love two people at the same time, although not with the same intensity. Until now he could only imagine love on the either/or basis: Either exclusively one person or else no love for him at all. He sees now that this is a kind of childish theory, possibly coming from somewhere in his childhood, but he has no idea about its exact origins (p. 113).

It can readily be seen that in all of these situations (and numerous others), Balint identified a neurotic pattern in living, brought it to the patient's attention, and pointed out its self-defeating, complicating, and painful consequences. To be sure, these patterns referred to events of which the patient was "unconscious," in the sense that his behavior was "automatic" and predicated on certain assumptions (e.g., the "childish theory" referred to in the fourth example, as well as its fantasied consequences). They also exemplify what is perhaps the most crucial aspect of all analytic therapeutic work (traditionally called "working through"), that of demonstrating to the patient, in the context of a positive patient-therapist relationship, affectively charged patterns of behavior as they emerge in the here-and-now. What is "mutative" in such encounters, however, is not the history of these patterns (e.g., reference to rivalries with the father in childhood or the latter's sadistic behavior vis-à-vis the patient) but rather the emotional experience occurring in the present, correctly identified by Balint as *Erlebnis* (a meaningful experience) (p. 80). Here it may aid the patient to perceive a link between childhood experiences and the present, since it is often easier for a patient to accept a painful truth if he can recognize its infantile roots. It seems quite appropriate to call the process and the product of such experiences *insight*, i.e., a fusion of emotional experiences in the here-and-now with a cognitive appreciation of the antecedents and consequences of a maladaptive pattern in living.

Influence of the Therapist

Thus far, my account does not deviate substantially from the traditional psychoanalytic position except perhaps in the relative emphasis given to here-and-now (transference) factors. The description, however, remains incomplete unless we scrutinize more closely the nature of the therapist's influence in such situations, which in my view constitutes the bedrock of all forms of psychotherapy. I am referring to the *moral suasion* implicit in the therapist's seemingly neutral, task-oriented, and "clinical" stance. I would like to summarize this point in the form of a message that the therapist (Balint, too) continually sends and the patient continually receives. He says, in effect:

Look, we have established a pretty good working relationship, and you know by now that I have your best interest at heart. I don't criticize your behavior and I do not pass judgment concerning its propriety or impropriety. [p. 82] As far as I am concerned, you are entitled to lead your life as you see fit, and I won't try to dominate you, coerce you, intimidate you, or coax you. You are an adult, and I am not going to infantilize you. However, I am also not going to coddle you. I am not saying you are right, and the other important person in your life (in this case, your wife) is wrong. Nor am I saying that she is right and you are wrong. That's not my business. My business is to point out certain facts that complicate your life and lead to suffering. Since you are interested in bringing about a change (as demonstrated by your motivation for collaborative work), it behooves you to listen to my statements. As a fair, impartial, and relatively uninvolved observer, I have a better perspective on your life and your interpersonal operations than you do. I have no axes to grind; I am fully committed to helping you; but you have to listen if you want to get better.

In this statement, the therapist establishes the basic terms of the therapeutic contract and disarms the patient's habitual maneuvers of contradicting, dominating, and controlling the other person, thereby rendering well-meant advice and interpretations useless. The major task of all psychotherapy is to create a condition in which the therapist's interventions will not be sidetracked or neutralized by the patient's neurotic maneuvers, and the gist of all work on "resistances" is to neutralize or undercut the patient's perennial efforts at involving the therapist emotionally in his neurotic maneuvers for the purpose of ultimately defeating him and escaping his influence. It is only at relatively rare times when these resistances are at a low ebb that the therapist can proceed to the next step, as follows:

(With reference to paragraph 1, in "Reformulation of Therapeutic Factors"): We have seen that whenever you are hurt, you apparently respond by reproaching [your wife], that is, you have a great need to hurt her back. What do you suppose this will accomplish? Is it not reasonable to assume that this will alienate her and get her mad at you? What do you get out of that? It is predictable that this will result in further suffering and unhappiness for you, and you will surely not get your way if you proceed in this manner. In my judgment, this is a rather maladaptive, stupid, and self-defeating way of dealing with people. Don't you agree?

   (With reference to paragraph 2, in "Reformulation of Therapeutic Factors"): OK, so you have proved to yourself that you can pick up prostitutes and make it with attractive women. This is fine as far as I am concerned, but we may want to inquire whether it really raises your self-esteem. I don't think it does. And why do you have to tell your wife about it? Furthermore, is your 'liberation' to be paid for by [your wife's] suffering? The whole thing, it seems to me, is a pretty infantile way of behaving, and it surely does not impress me. I don't disapprove of your behavior, but I also do not approve of it. Draw your own conclusions, but you can see that I am subscribing to the tenet of reasonableness, rationality, and the Golden Rule in social relations.

   (Bypassing paragraph 3, I shall proceed to paragraph 4, in "Reformulation of Therapeutic Factors"): We have heard ample evidence that you are engaging in rather senseless behavior when you keep interrogating your wife concerning events that lie 20 years in the past. Surely, you can see that you are not going to get anything further out of her concerning the episode with [the other man]. Why can't you let bygones? Obviously, your pestering of [your wife] must serve other purposes that have much more to do with your *current* relationship. What are you trying to accomplish? What does it get you? Isn't it pretty silly to persist in this infantile behavior? There is another angle to consider: You seem to be operating on the theory that there is only a fixed quantum of love a person can bestow, and either you get it all or you get nothing. The idea of *sharing* affection with someone is quite alien to you. The only time in life when an individual believes that the world is structured in this manner is early childhood when a younger sibling is experienced as an intruder who will displace the older from a position he mistakenly construes as the center of the universe—that of mother's full and undivided devotion. Aren't your expectations from others rather excessive and grandiose? [p. 82] Can anyone deliver as much as you demand? Isn't it rather remarkable that [your wife] is putting up with your inquisitions? Isn't your view of the world based on rather infantile assumptions? You will have to scale these down if you want to lead a happier life.

Finally, it is important for you to recognize that instead of things "happening" to you (e.g., your suspicions of [your wife's] behavior prior to your marriage and your persistent ruminations), you play a *very active* part in bringing about the consequences, which then make you feel unhappy and about which you complain. Your assumptions about the world and your expectations of others play a very significant part in all of this. *You* are the only one who can put a stop to what is bothering you, and the responsibility for doing so clearly rests with you.

Therapeutic Learning

The foregoing examples suffice to document my point relative to the learning experiences in constructive living which all forms of psychotherapy explicitly or implicitly mediate: the therapist manages to establish himself as a "good" parent or authority figure; he creates conditions that maximize the chance of his being listened to and he seeks to neutralize or undercut roadblocks the patient places in the way of his teachings; he points out maladaptive patterns of behavior and their underlying infantile assumptions; he sets an example by remaining calm, unruffled, reasonable, and rational; he refuses to get entangled in the patient's neurotic machinations; he conveys the message that the patient must learn to accept *personal responsibility* for his own actions instead of blaming others and life circumstances for his predicament; he teaches basic lessons on how people in Western civilized society interact productively and nonneurotically; he teaches the patient to be less demanding and grandiose, to scale down his expectations of others, and to accept a more *active* role in managing his life; he conveys a philosophy of reasonableness, rationality, moderation, mutuality, and fairness as the guideposts of the "good life"; and, in broad terms, he combines love with discipline in helping the patient become a more autonomous, self-directing, and responsible adult.

Balint's case history demonstrates these basic ingredients exceedingly well, and the patient recognized them too when he stated at the end: "I had to mature, it was high time," and "You, Dr. Balint, started something very important and I was able to finish it. Now everything is peaceful" (p. 121). The question, however, must be raised: What, precisely, is "psychoanalytic" in this endeavor? How does it differ from what transpires in other forms of psychotherapy, or for that matter in any good human relationship, particularly the parent-child relationship?

My answer is that the differences are *relative* rather than *absolute*. Therapeutic learning, as I have stated elsewhere (Strupp),[14] always proceeds on a broad front, and in this sense it is the kind of "after-education" Freud spoke about. What psychoanalysis has specifically contributed to this enterprise is enormously important.

1. It has created a vehicle—the patient-therapist relationship—for bringing about personality and behavior change we call therapeutic (Stone[1] and Greenson).[15]
2. It has called forceful attention to the obstacles that every patient places in the path of his own progress because of the vagaries of his past interpersonal experiences, which in part have had the effect of closing him off from his ability to profit from parent-type interpersonal experiences.
3. It is shown the importance of steering clear of the patient's neurotic maneuvers that are characterized by a repetitive quality that continually threatens the very essence of the patient-therapist relationship and its potential therapeutic use.
4. It has shown a way of utilizing the deeply engrained human tendency of forming affectionate ties to a caring person, and by appeal to reason and rationality (the patient's adult or observing "ego"), to pit it against the neurotic patterns whose modification or abandonment is the ultimate goal of all psychotherapeutic interventions.
5. It has clearly pointed out a series of common maladaptive neurotic patterns and maneuvers by means of which the patient seeks to avoid reexperiencing painful affect relating to traumatic experiences, particularly in early life. These techniques are exemplified by rigid control, domination, negativism, stubbornness, and a wide variety of "symptoms" and "character trends," all of which serve to ward off inroads into the patient's profound sense of helplessness and vulnerability carried forward from childhood.
6. Closely related to the foregoing, it has made a lasting contribution by

identifying the relationship between so-called "symptoms" and their roots in irrational, unrealistic, and often mutually contradictory primitive strivings, as well as elaborate fantasies surrounding them. These powerfully influence the person's present-day behavior, partly because their nature has never been scrutinized by the patient and partly because he actively "denies" their existence. However, in all instances, he *acts* on the basis of these strivings while simultaneously disclaiming collusion or responsibility for the consequences. As Haley[16] has pointed out, he behaves like a hypnotized person who raises his arm while denying that he is doing so.

7. It has shown the importance of the therapist's steadfastness, reliability, trustworthiness, imperturbability, understanding, and respect—in short his *maturity,* which is quintessential in mediating a meaningful, incisive, and constructive human experience *(Erlebnis).* It is this emotional experience that carries by far the most important weight in therapeutic change and it constitutes the matrix within which the therapist brings his influence to bear: (1) by opening the patient up to the influence of a significant person; and (2) mediating the crucial lessons in constructive living that are the essence of psychotherapy.

In sum, given strong motivation to seek change (chiefly through suffering) and adequate personality resources, the patient has to be won over to a point of view different from the one that has in essential respects guided his life in the past, and he has to make these new teachings his own. That is, he must find them *meaningful* and a more desirable alternative to his former belief system. In this sense, the patient becomes persuaded and indoctrinated by a new philosophy of life, a philosophy of individualism and independence, reliability and responsibility, pride in his own strength and achievements, and acceptance of his own and the world's limitations that do not allow the unbridled expression or fulfillment of one's wishes, urges, and strivings. The resulting inner freedom is purchased at the cost of giving up one's selfishness, willfulness, and unbridled expression of infantile impulses and needs. It is won through self-discipline. In turn, the patient's relationships to others are based on mutuality rather than exploitation, cooperation rather than domination or subservience, and respect for the other person's needs, wishes, and rights. He becomes freer because he has learned to accept a leaner diet of gratifications than those vouchsafed the dependent child, and because he has learned to accept inner constraints and restraints.

Unless the patient accepts these messages on an *emotional* level (in the context of his personal experience), together with the painful relinquishment of neurotic aims, therapeutic change will not occur or it will remain sharply limited. It is for these reasons that many protracted analyses fail: either the therapist fails to deal with the inner core of the patient's problems (traditionally called his narcissism or deep childhood traumas), or he fails to mediate the crucial lessons in constructive living, or a combination of both.

Psychoanalytic Psychotherapy: Further Critique

While psychoanalytic teachings have recognized many of these truths, they have often remained implicit, and the undue emphasis on intrapsychic mechanisms, reconstructions of the past, and the giving of "correct" interpretations has all but obscured what is centrally important in therapeutic change. In Balint's case, such foci as "latent homosexuality" and "sharing the wife symbolically with the therapist" illustrate precisely what I mean. Fortunately for the patient and the outcome of the therapy, Balint taught the "lessons" set forth above, and it is the *cumulative character* of these experiences that must be credited with the mutative changes in the patient's feelings, attitudes, and behavior, rather than particular "interpretations." To reiterate my initial point: "interpretations" in the classical sense are but one class of interventions whose importance as "mutative" factors has been vastly exaggerated. At best, they can be seen as occasional markers of the broad therapeutic effort.

The egregious error of the psychoanalytic theory of psychotherapy has been a wholesale disregard of the *constructive aspects* of the therapeutic experience that are lessons in constructive living; instead, the latter have been smuggled in through the back door, as it were, because their frank recognition apparently meant to the older generation of analysts that the purity of the analytic influence was somehow being compromised. For these reasons as well as his preoccupation with psychic mechanisms, instincts, and libidinal energies, Freud transformed his profound insights into the problems of therapeutic change and the nature of the therapeutic experience into abstract discussions of warring impulses, psychic agencies, and libidinal cathexes—all of which gave the emerging system a pseudo-scientific respectability but effectively detracted attention from the therapist's influence in bringing about therapeutic change, as well as the patient's part in accepting the therapist's teachings and taking constructive action.

Fundamentally, psychoanalytic psychotherapy is a sophisticated technology for persuading a person to change his feelings, attitudes, and behavior; to assume responsibility (control) for his impulses, feelings, and actions; and to conduct his life in accordance with a philosophy extolling such values as personal strength, rationality, reasonableness, moderation, and the "golden rule" in interpersonal relations. It accomplishes its aim by subtly but consistently "letting down" the patient, strengthening his ability to accept disappointments and disillusionments with greater equanimity, but rewarding him for his achievement with a stronger sense of self and less guilt. The successfully treated patient is sadder but wiser, and he is more capable of (adult) enjoyment that does not produce guilt. At the same time, the interaction with the therapist who has taken the stance of a reasonable, loving but firm authority has—through his implied disapproval—closed many avenues of infantile gratifications that the patient had unwittingly sought but that resulted in conflicts, "symptoms," and a profound sense of guilt.

This approach to therapeutic change, however, presupposes a person who potentially finds the foregoing philosophy congenial or who can potentially be persuaded to accept and live by it. Many people, as Freud already recognized and as has been elaborated by a large literature since, are either not properly "motivated" or for many other reasons "unsuitable." The personality of the successfully treated patient shows a strange mixture of docility and submission to higher authority (the analyst as a representative of society), as well as a rugged sense of independence and selfhood, coupled with a keen sense of limitations both within himself, others, and life's circumstances.

It is difficult to say whether the "good life" proposed by psychoanalysis is one of freedom or conformity. In any case, it has become apparent that Western man, especially in America, has become greatly disenchanted with this model, which in many respects clearly embodies a Puritan ethic. The growth of the encounter movement and "humanistic psychology," not to mention the writings of Reich and Marcuse, certainly attest to the fact that many contemporaries believe that more "fun" can be derived from sensory experience than allowed by the Freudian doctrine. But even on its own terms, the goals potentially achievable within psychoanalysis are so beset with technical difficulties, partly encompassed by the problem of getting patients to accept the teachings mentioned above, and partly by the general difficulties of inducing anyone to change deeply engrained habits and beliefs that radical change is a relatively rare occurrence. Thus, what psychoanalysis has also contributed is a profound understanding of the obstacles impeding any effort at therapeutic change—the difficulties of changing human feelings and behavior that have their roots in childhood when the person was dependent and noticeably malleable and influenceable by the adults with whom he was involved in a powerful emotional relationship: who served as his models, inculcated in him their attitudes and values, and in numerous ways used his dependency to perform their educational function. In short, Freud made it abundantly clear that, in order to change a person in fundamental ways, it is necessary to involve him in an emotionally charged relationship and to utilize his dependency (strongly feared by all neurotic people) to influence him in desired directions. These directions are importantly determined by the culture and its values and are in no sense absolute.

The crux of all forms of psychotherapy is the achievement of self-direction, autonomy—what in psychoanalysis is called "ego control." If it is true that "where id was, there shall ego be," we are faced with the fundamental problem of how a person becomes socialized, how he develops techniques for subordinating his impulsive strivings to control from the outside, and subsequently to self-control. It might well be said that the paradigm is that of the domestic animal who becomes housebroken as a function of a congenital predisposition and human manipulations in which rewards and punishment prove decisive. The psychoanalytic credo states: if the growing organism can be brought to subordinate and adapt its asocial strivings to the social conditions, it can subsequently enjoy a sense of freedom, a freedom of the type that Robert Frost described as "moving easy in harness." As has long been recognized, the so-called neurotic person is in conflict and suffers because he has not learned to *modulate* his impulses such that they can find *partial* expression and gratification. Instead, he has learned to oppose ("resist") the influence of the parental authority figures, and he plays a duplicitous game of seeking to give expression to his impulsive strivings, while at the same time denying to himself and others his secret goals. This inner rebelliousness powerfully fuels his guilt, perpetuates his inner warfare as well as his relationships with others, and contributes paradoxically to a sense of weakness and helplessness. What therapy provides is an opportunity to let these impulses appear in clear awareness in relation to an essentially nonthreatening adult (therapist)—the "transference." Depending on the therapist's attitudes towards these emerging strivings (approval, disapproval, and neutrality), the patient is then placed in a position of giving them a new, less "automatic" direction. In this process, too, the patient comes face to face with the residues of the early interpersonal conflicts, partly intensified by misunderstandings, actual trauma, but also by his own fantasies, which inaugurated his struggle against accepting the teachings of those in authority. The following alternatives are open to the patient in this quest: (1) he can reject the parental authority once and for all; (2) he can accept it and abandon his inner strivings that bring him into conflict with others and established authority; or (3) he can modify the internalized parental authority, as well as his strivings, and bring about a better modus vivendi both within himself and in relation to others. In successful therapy, the latter is generally embraced. It is this struggle that Freud conceptualized in ego-id-superego terms.

In sum, the battle fought in analytic therapy is between the individual's impulsiveness (self-will, narcissism) and the discipline-imposing outside world that demands a measure of conformity from all adult members of society. Freud showed conclusively that no one can have it both ways, unless he succeeds in molding his social milieu and the behavior of significant others to adapt to his inner needs. Most of us succeed more or less in this dual task, and the extent to which this solution presents a viable balance between inner needs and outer demands is a measure of our "mental health." The therapist's task is to help the patient work out such a viable solution—a solution that is maximally noncoercive, maximally responsive to the patient's own needs, and relatively tolerant of—but by no means oblivious to—the demands of reality and society. Thus, analytic therapy is an education for optimal personal freedom in the context of social living. At its best, it preaches neither conformity nor libertinism but it clearly recognizes that controls and restraints are essential. However, its preference is for *rational* rather than authority-imposed control. Freud, especially toward the end of his life, harbored strong ambivalence as to whether the foregoing solution is ever viable, lasting, or productive of a sense of productivity and happiness.

One of the major problems not adequately dealt with in the psychoanalytic theory of psychotherapy is the precise manner in which *accretions to the person's intentionality* come about; how it happens that an individual who has previously been "lived by" forces over which he has inadequate control gradually acquires strength, so that henceforth he can exert greater control over his life. It is clear that in every psychotherapy (including Balint's patient), the patient eventually must be brought to take a stand, to assume cognizance and responsibility for his impulses and his actions. Instead of construing himself as a passive object that is buffeted by forces over which he has not control, he must reach a point where he says "*I* feel a particular way," "*I* deal with my feelings in a given manner," "*I take action.*" Paradoxically, he achieves this control to the extent that he can surrender some of his willfulness and go-it-alone attitude to a stronger benevolent person, the therapist; he gains strength as he learns to trust his helper and, for crucial moments, can feel sufficiently secure to place his fate in the other person's hands. It appears that in order to develop a strong sense of self it is necessary first to be able to trust others and gradually to grow out of this dependency-trust instead of being jolted out of it. Therapy seeks to bring about a correction, and where it succeeds—through long-term "analysis," "focal therapy," or whatever—it produces the kind of growth and maturation that is the ideal outcome of psychotherapy. Unhappily, the magical combination of the "right" patient, the "right" therapist, and the "right" circumstances are as rare as is perfection anywhere else in this imperfect world; yet this is not to say that approximations are to be scorned.

REFERENCES

1. Stone L: *The Psychoanalytic Situation*. New York, International Universities Press, 1961, 31, 32.
2. Strupp HH: On the basic ingredients of psychotherapy. *J Consult Clin Psychol* 41:1–8, 1973.
3. Strupp HH: Toward a reformulation of the psychotherapeutic influence. *Int J Psychiatry* 11:263–327, 1973.
4. Balint M, Ornstein PH, Balint E: *Focal Psychotherapy: An Example of Applied Psychoanalysis*. London, Tavistock Publications, 1972.
5. Ferenczi S: The future development of an active therapy in psychoanalysis (1920), in Suttie J (trans): *Further Contributions to the Theory and Technique of Psycho-analysis*. London, Hogarth Press, 1950, pp 198–216.
6. Ferenczi S, Rank O: The development of psycho-analysis. *Nervous and Mental Diseases Monograph*, No. 40, 1925.
7. Alexander F, French TM: *Psychoanalytic Therapy: Principles and Application*. New York, Ronald Press, 1946.
8. Malan DH: *A Study of Brief Psychotherapy*. London, Tavistock Publications, 1963.
9. Sifneos PE: *Short-Term Psychotherapy and Emotional Crisis*. Cambridge, Mass, Harvard University Press, 1972.
10. Mann J: *Time-Limited Psychotherapy*. Cambridge, Mass, Harvard University Press, 1973.
11. Freud S: Lines of advance in psycho-analytic therapy (1919), in *Standard Edition*. London, Hogarth Press, 1955, vol 17.
12. Strupp HH: *Psychotherapists in Action: Explorations of the Therapist's Contribution to the Treatment Process*. New York, Grune & Stratton Inc, 1960.
13. Bergin AE: The evaluation of therapeutic outcomes, in Bergin AE, Garfield

SL (eds): *Handbook of Psychotherapy and Behavior Change*. New York, John Wiley & Sons Inc, 1971.

14. Strupp HH: On the technology of psychotherapy. *Arch Gen Psychiatry* 26:270–278, 1972.

15. Greenson RR: *The Technique and Practice of Psychoanalysis*. New York, International Universities Press, 1967, vol 1, 358–411.

16. Haley J: *Strategies of Psychotherapy*. New York, Grune & Stratton Inc, 1963.

13. Explorations in the Uses of Language in Psychotherapy

Leston L. Havens

> . . . it was she who first gave me the idea that a person does not (as I had imagined) stand motionless and clear before our eyes with his merits, his detects, his plans, his intentions with regard to ourself exposed on his surface, like a garden at which, with all its borders spread out before us, we gaze through a railing, but is a shadow which we can never succeed in penetrating, of which there is no such thing as direct knowledge, with respect to which we form countless beliefs, based upon his words and sometimes upon his actions, though neither words nor actions can give us anything but inadequate and as it proves contradictory information—a shadow behind which we can alternately imagine, with equal justification, that there burns the flame of hatred and of love.
>
> —*Proust*

The purpose of these explorations is to find language effective in particular psychotherapeutic situations. One would like to have on hand a large number of verbal tools that are sharp-edged enough to shape even resistant situations.

I have suggested (Havens 1978) that the principal verbal tools can be characterized as interrogative, imperative, rhetorical, and declarative. The interrogative label is obvious; questions remain the principal device for even psychotherapeutic investigations. It is not so obvious that free associative work operates under a subtle imperative. The "fundamental rule" of psychoanalysis is an imperative, "say whatever comes to mind," and the silences, repetitions, and urgings that make up much of the analyst's work all sound at least a supplicatory note.

Empathic work is necessarily rhetorical. This is because "the imaginative projection of one's own consciousness into another being" (Webster's 1963), which is empathy, requires an imaginative expression of that new consciousness if it is to be shared; and rhetoric is the art of expressive speech (Havens 1978, 1979).

Further, it occurred to me that declarative statements could also have a

Reprinted by permission of the W. A. White Institute from *Contemporary Psychoanalysis 16 (1980):53–67.*

systematic place in psychotherapy. Of course, clarifications and interpretations usually take a declarative form and already have a systematic place in psychoanalysis and psychoanalytic psychotherapy, but in the course of studying Sullivan's intuitive remarks (Havens 1976) and listening to everyday speech I noted some functions of declarative statements that did not fit comfortably within either the clarifying or interpreting function. I have characterized these as "making marks and remarks" and "counterprojective statements." I could also speak of casting shadows or the mind revealing itself by the way it sees other things.

Listen on the bus or subway. Note that everyday speech consists heavily of exchanges of statements, each statement declaring and then ratifying, correcting or erasing the previous declarations. The declarers do not so much talk to one another, for example quiz one another, as they talk about something. This is dramatically evident when strangers meet at a disaster or parade. A "situational alliance" (Gutheil and Havens 1979) is formed that often permits revelations in other circumstances forbidden. I will suggest that one source of this freedom is the relative inattention to each other; personal projections are not being thrown on one another, but out there on the situation shared.

It is no accident that polite conversation frequently starts with comments about the weather. I suspect that is an example of what Tinbergen has called looking past one another, which many birds do on meeting, and which Tinbergen found useful in approaching autistic children (Tinbergen 1974). The weather is a relatively neutral subject, observed and shared out there. Prematurely directing attention to one another is avoided.

In contrast, medical examining and history-taking characteristically concentrate attention on the patient, moreover, as a source of pathology. Everyone who has been medically examined knows the sharp rises in anxiety as this attention falls on delicate matters. To continue Proust's metaphor, the medical person looks into the flame; he does not stand aside to watch the shadows.

The weather may prompt comments that are highly revealing. Like an inkblot it can attract and expose personal projections. This is what is meant by the mind's capacity to reveal itself in the way it sees other things. In essence, I am proposing the extension of this principle of projective testing into investigative and psychotherapeutic speech. We will see, too, that the same principle is already active in the play therapy of children and many other seemingly different psychotherapeutic devices.

Sullivan's intuitive understanding of the approach to shy, suspicious, or angry people foreshadowed the same idea. He suggested sitting beside or at an angle to the patient, not only to avoid staring at self-conscious people but, in addition, to direct attention somewhere else. This somewhere else was society, which in his social psychiatry constituted the source of pathology, and was experienced out there. Redirecting clinical attention moved the "screen" away from the therapist or patient, where it is put in psychoanalysis, "out there," as in projective testing or the miniature world of children's play therapy.

COUNTERPROJECTIVE STATEMENTS

The everyday management of people responding to acute pain or insult provides a useful illustration. For example, stubbing one's toe typically results in anger towards the object, blaming of it, even the desire to kick the offending object again. An observer standing close to the offending object may also be resented, suggesting a stimulus generalization or transference process. Moreover, the acutely hurt person often resents questioning, sometimes implying he thinks the observer must know what the matter is, suggesting a temporary loss of ego boundaries.

The treatment of such small, paranoid psychoses is, first, empathy with the pain and then alliance against the object. The latter is gained by kicking the offending object for the hurt person or speaking against the offending object. Just as certain exclamations form a prototypic form of empathic speech ("how painful," "that must hurt"), so another exclamation, "that damn chair!" is a prototypic form of counterprojective speech.

A counterprojective statement has three components. First, it must point "out there," because in part projection follows attention. Second, it must speak about the figures being projected: counterprojective statements place the chair, boss, girlfriend, or parent on the projective screen before the therapist and patient. Perhaps "speak about" is not right. No interpretation or explanation concerning these figures is offered; that would invite discussion centered back again on therapist and patient: the figures are simply put "out there."

Finally, in order to move projections, some part of the patient's feelings about those figures must be expressed by the therapist. This is similar to what Sullivan called "setting an example of desperation and rage" (Kvarnes and Parloff 1976). The therapist joins the patient for a moment in the patient's attitude toward the figures because his standing aloof would reinvite the projections.

In short, counterprojective statements move attention, place the critical figures and to some measure share feelings.

They have two purposes. Not only is the mind enabled to reveal itself in the way it sees other things—as in projective testing—the clinical relationship is partly relieved of the projections that have fallen on it: therapist and patient can examine the projections in an emotional field relatively free of them.

The importance of the second purpose is dramatically evident with very paranoid patients. Such patients attack our objectivity to comment because they have made us part of their paranoid fields. Moving the projections is then an essential part of continuing therapeutic work.[1]

I have discussed elsewhere (Havens 1976) the specific role of these counterprojective statements in managing other overwhelming or volatile transferences, what are best called psychotic transferences. Indeed, whenever transferences are outside the neurotic or interpretable range, counterprojective statements should be considered.[2] It is perhaps chiefly for this reason that the psychoanalytic therapy of children makes use of play objects; these provide a focus not only for the child's remembering but for the child's projections as well, reducing the projections on the therapist to a manageable level.

COUNTERPROJECTING: THE COMMON DENOMINATOR OF MANY THERAPEUTIC DEVICES

I will briefly review a number of therapeutic devices that appear to have counterprojection as one element in common.

With Beck's cognitive therapy, an image is elicited that accompanies a symptom, perhaps an image of large dangerous people accompanying anxiety (Beck 1970). This is then put out before therapist and patient to establish its pervasiveness, its difference from reality and later its experiential roots. The emphasis is first on fantasy, as with projective testing, and then on experience and differences from contemporary reality. Something similar occurs with Shorr's psychoimagination therapy (Shorr 1972).[3]

With both these devices the goal is narrative development and the surfacing and gaining perspective on significant fantasies. Transference management is not to my knowledge emphasized by either author, but it may be playing an unnoticed part.

Winnicott developed a technique for children that invites a still closer comparison with what I am describing. In the squiggle game (Winnicott 1971), one person makes lines or marks on a piece of paper, the other is invited to add additional lines or marks, perhaps to complete a specific representation. Indeed, Winnicott's technique might better have been named making marks than what I have termed "making marks and remarks." Call, in turn, has used the resulting drawings as the basis for a projective test of the more familiar sort. In his addition the child is invited to tell a story about the squiggle objects (Call 1975).

Many students of group therapy and psychodrama, too, have used distancing devices. Perls (1973) has emphasised them heavily. This element of his therapeutic work seems to overshadow even the empathic and cathartic ones so prominent in his suggestions. As in Beck's method, transference management takes a lesser, even inadvertent role.

Bowen's family therapy is also prominently counterprojective. Here are some revealing quotations.

The new effort was to work out problems in the already existing intense relationships within the family and to specifically avoid actions and techniques that facilitate and encourage the therapeutic relationship with the therapist. (Bowen 1978, p. 308)

The therapist is to be neutral and prevent the development of transference entanglements; the latter were to be worked out between family members themselves. Almost as in play therapy, transference is to be resolved "out there."

My best operating emotional distance from the family, even when sitting physically close, is the point I can "see" the emotional process flowing back and forth between them. The human phenomenon is usually as humorous and comical as it is serious and tragic. The right distance is the point it is possible to see either the serious or the humorous side. (p. 313)

It is necessary for the therapist to keep his focus on the process between the two. If he finds himself focusing on the content of what is being said, it is evident that he has lost sight of the process and he is emotionally entangled on a content issue. (p. 313)

What Bowen calls the "magic of family therapy" is the process of "externalizing the thinking of each spouse" (p. 314); in part each is to examine the other's transference; feelings are avoided; emphasis is on facts and ideas. I suspect that Bowen's capacity to elicit this material is heavily dependent on his having moved projections off himself.

Much of the therapeutic action of "paradoxical intention" also seems counterprojective. In this technique the patient is encouraged to do what he fears to do. In Frankl's words, "The specifically human capacity for self-detachment is mobilized and utilized for therapeutic purposes" (Frankl 1967, p. 3). From my own experience with this device, not only does self-detachment seem a significant part of the process (or what I will discuss as gaining distance or perspective), but also the change in the therapist's usual position. In paradoxical intention the therapist typically places himself on the side of the forbidden wish! Any prohibiting forces that are projected on the therapist are thereby counterprojected. The patient's internal conflict is not supported, and if the strength of this conflict is directly related to the intensity of the symptoms, the latter must abate.

As a final example, Kernberg includes among his recommendations for the treatment of borderline patients what he calls deflection.

The main characteristics of this proposed modification in the psychoanalytic procedure are (i) systematic elaboration of the manifest and latent negative transference without attempting to achieve full genetic reconstructions on the basis of it, followed by "deflection" of the manifest negative transference away from the therapeutic interaction through systematic examination of it in the patient's relations with others. . . . (Kernberg 1968, p. 601)

Deflection overlaps with counterprojection. They are not identical because implied in this passage is an assignment of the patient's responsibility for the negative transferences characteristic of Kernberg's way of working. In some patients, of course, such an assignment will exacerbate negative transferences.

We could also speak of supporting certain defenses, for example displacement and externalization. From the viewpoint of social psychiatry, however, the issue of what is defensive, on the one hand, or accurately attributive, on the other, depends upon the separation of fact from fantasy.

In a simple form these ideas are as old as the hills. Wise clinicians have always known there were other people in the room. And the wisest have formed some way of saying to the obstreperous patients "Your mother (or your father or your brother or sister) must be in the room!" And wise parents have themselves done the same thing: for example, setting their own difficult days before the children so the latter do not expect too much on tired evenings.

UNITING MEDIUM AND MESSAGE

We can work away from the patient (in contrast to working close to the patient in both the interrogative and empathic modes). Note in the following exchange how attention is directed away from the clinical relationship. At the same time some distance or perspective is gained on a fact about that relationship.

Pt: My father asked if I was through the treatment. (This begins away from the relationship but ends squarely on it.)

Th: Something troubled him. (I take it back "out there," to father.)

Pt: Maybe you didn't give him enough hope. (Stays between Th and father.)

Th: Maybe not.

Pt: I blew it last night. It was a wonderful evening. I really enjoyed that couple, you know the Br's. I was feeling so hopeful. Then at the end I got all excited and grandiose.

Th: Well so much for hope. (Pt has been living off grandiose hopes: he is constantly tempting Th to provide more of them. In fact, such hopes are serious distractions from accomplishing Pt's actual life tasks. Th's final comment is meant to convey: "hopes disorganize you": "I know you'd like them from me"; "sorry, no," all without getting into an argument about Pt's entitlements in the relationship.)

Note that hope, too, is treated as if it were something "out there," that is, as if it were something the patient could take or leave, not necessarily part of himself. (One might equally well speak of the therapist treating hopefulness as a *symptom* in this patient for whom it was ego-syntonic.) I wanted Pt to gain distance or perspective on a personal attribute, hopefulness, that in exaggerated form had helped to cripple him.

The message of my last remark could have been given in other ways: as a question, "Is hope good for you?" or as an interpretation directed at his rational understanding, "Again we see how great hopes, which you also have towards me and your parents, serve to overstimulate you." The therapist chose to use a medium that itself embodied the very distance or perspective he wanted the message to carry too.

These explorations in the uses of language in psychotherapy have the same purpose: to find and develop a language or medium of therapeutic discourse that supports the message conveyed. Because the selection of the language in which therapists work has been so largely neglected, the medium in which therapeutic messages are carried too often contradicts the messages themselves. This is laughably evident in the so-called "therapeutic double-binds" (Haley 1968) in which, for example, the imperative or authoritarian language of "Be spontaneous" contradicts the freedom prescribed.[4] Such examples are only tips of the iceberg, however.

Here is another, more common example: The provision of clear explanations and incisive comments about a patient's excessive dependence and hopefulness can inadvertently reinforce the very hopefulness and dependence they are intended to reduce. What we do speaks louder than what we say: With such a helpful and knowing therapist why not hope and depend? (Contradictions of medium and message can be thought of as inducing inner oppositions of insight-oriented and behavioristic models of learning.)

I will illustrate how working away from the patient can reduce some contradictions of medium and message. The material will demonstrate, in addition, how the declarative mode can move attention away from the clinical relationship and with it, specific projections. Later we will see that the elimination of some contradictions and the counterprojective function are at root one.

Patients often wonder: "why doesn't the therapist, who is trained, being paid, and knows my suffering, do more: why is so much left to me?" In the case of the particular patient to be considered, the contradiction has been unexpressed out of his expectation that the therapist would someday "do" something; the patient had only to wait. In the meantime, the expectation allowed the patient to do very little. Implicit in these attitudes were two projections: that the therapist had a secret knowledge or power he could impart and that he had some undetermined reason for withholding it.

Note that the two projections could not be dealt with directly. They were largely unconscious to the patient and if interpreted would probably have been denied. If, by chance, the interpretations did reach the patient, they must surely confirm his magical expectations ("What a clever therapist"); or if taken on faith, his dependency.

(In making the following interventions Th had decided not to let the transference develop freely, to the discovery of the paternal magic and its withholding for mother which were later reached. He believed that Pt's projections would be disruptive if left unchecked, producing a paranoid transference psychosis. He had also decided against an empathic elaboration of Pt's helpfulness and hopefulness, although this too was partly achieved later in the course of developing his superego and ego ideal structures.)

Pt: Why don't you clarify this? You know me very well. I'm confused. (Th's intuitive association was "Pt wants to see my penis": One of Pt's principal symptoms was his preoccupation with the "other men" in his triangular relationships, and their penises. Th did not utter it, however, because he thought that if it "took," it would again seem to Pt like magic and reinforce the little boy expectations: if it did not, it would only add to the complained-of confusion.)

Th: That's right. (Th is attempting to put Pt's confusion "out there." "Let's get this clear: it's confusing." The remark is both distancing and empathic: it acknowledges both the confusion and the irritation.)

Pt: I can't do this alone. (Pt might have been returned to the past of his alternately indulged and besieged childhood with the empathic "Often you were alone." Th, however, wanted to deal first with the gradually surfacing indignation at Th's withholding: this was too real to be handled as only transference. Nor would it have been wise to invite a therapeutic collaboration of examining it: "Let's look at why you feel indignation now." Pt might have cooperated in this on the basis of Th's authority-doctor knows best—but again his submissiveness and dependence would have been exploited.)

Th: Neither your boss nor the girlfriend have clarified things either.

Pt: They haven't.

Th: Everywhere you look: No one helps. (Said empathically.)

Pt: But you're supposed to.

Th: I suppose your parents were, too.

Pt: They didn't.

Th: No wonder you want someone to take their place. (Both empathic and externalizing: Th shares Pt's understandable yearning and locates its source outside the treatment.) They left such a hole!

Th has, first, attempted to preserve Pt's independence and self-respect; he has not wanted to reward the regressive entitlement to be, this time, properly taken care of. Understandable as that demand was, its satisfaction would imply, Pt cannot now perform these functions himself, and, more dangerously, Th was under an obligation to compensate for what the parents neglected. This could lead to an escalating series of demands.

Second, Th attempted to move the angry feelings generated by boss, girlfriend, and parents away from Th and "out there" to be examined, a counterprojection. If successful, Th will have allowed Pt to be more realistic about the treatment. Pt should also be able to see his expectations towards others more clearly. In fact, just after this exchange Pt inquired of himself whether he did not ask too much of the treatment and was therefore disappointed; he also said that he remembered fantasying that both boss and girlfriend would be far better than father and mother.

Th did not support Pt's suspicion that he had expected too much of boss and girlfriend. Th did not know whether indeed this was the case or, as possible, that Pt had picked as boss and girlfriend individuals who would, like mother and father, disappoint him. In other words, the therapist did not know if Pt's difficulty was one of repetitive, perhaps neurotic expectations or a neurotic recreation of a original family scene.[5]

Th could therefore not explain to Pt what the difficulty was. Indeed Pt may have picked and stayed with a therapist also bent on withholding from him! Above all, Th wanted to escape the vexing decision of whether he should give Pt more or less, which any attempt to work by means of a "corrective emotional experience" would have demanded. Nor could he work by providing interpretations, that is explanations to Pt's rational ego: beyond the issue of their correctness, they might be seen as gratifying gifts and therefore justifying Pt's demands. Moreover, they would have concentrated attention on Th with the danger of bringing more of Pt's projections back.

Now it is clear why avoiding double messages and moving projections are sometimes identical. This is because the medium of the message may reinforce a projection that itself undercuts the message. In this case, by supporting the patient's expectation of the therapist's helpfulness, the therapist would have undercut the patient's need to help himself. By moving this projection away from the therapist, a contradictory communication was avoided.

PSYCHOLOGICAL GOALS

I have already suggested (Havens 1979) that working empathically provides an opportunity gradually to build in or increase the empathic function in patients lacking it, both empathy towards oneself and towards others. I suggest that counterprojective statements offer another and equally important opportunity: to gain distance or perspective on historical experience and emotional investments that have been carried over into contemporary experience as projections—in short, to lift the shadows.[6]

These two opportunities are in one respect the opposite of each other. The lack of empathy toward some aspect of oneself suggests distance between the judged and judging psychic parts; at its most extreme in psychosis, the critical part may even be experienced at a considerable distance from the patient, as in paranoid hallucinations. Gaining empathy on oneself can be represented as loss of psychological distance, a coming together that in psychosis is literally felt as a reduction of distance between psychic parts (Havens 1962).

In contrast, gaining distance or perspective suggests a movement away from identification with some psychic part; the psychic element goes from being ego-syntonic to being ego-alien. Some hitherto unconscious part of the ego is then "seen" by the ego itself.

These two and contrasting alterations in internal dynamics offer themselves as goals in equally contrasting clinical situations. Narcissistic and many psychotic patients lack empathy for others; their incapacity to enter into relationships, to see another's point of view, to form a transference neurosis and accept interpretations block out therapeutic efforts. Not until their empathic resources have been extended—as by the cultivation and maturation of what Kohut has termed the narcissistic or self-object transferences (Kohut 1971)—is a collaborative effort of analytic interpretation possible. It is to this process that the development of empathic language makes a contribution.

On the other hand, the difficulties that many other patients (and sometimes the narcissistic ones as well) bring into treatment spring not from a lack of transferences, not from their flat, indifferent or affectless relationships, but from their overwhelming, premature, even volcanic transferences. Here the need is not transference cultivation but transference management.

The volatile transferences spring in turn from two phenomena: the rapid projection of historically developed expectations on the therapist and their equally rapid changes of sign; these patients love and hate intensely and they alternate love and hate abruptly. But however passionate and changeable, these patients do not experience the present as something new, distinct, and unique. However surprised, angry, excited by the apparent present they may be, it is really a surprise, anger, or excitement rooted in the past. The observer experiences surprise in turn that they themselves can still be surprised. The historical pervades the borderline present.

Similarly, however much pain, even torment they experience, it is seldom experienced symptomatically. We can say that, just as they have little distance from their pasts, so do they have little distance from their internal torments, little perspective on their characters. It is the world, particularly the present world, that is likely to be seen as symptomatic.[7]

I do not mean that such patients have no lack of empathic resources. But what they seem to lack most is inner distance, perspective on their past and themselves. Empathy may even be clinically dangerous, leading to heightened excitements and hopes. It is here that making marks and remarks and counterprojection seem most useful.

Sometimes by confronting these patients with interpretations, especially of the transferences, perspective can be achieved. Kernberg has been the foremost advocate of this approach. Too often, however, the patients are enraged, become more paranoid, and indeed, as Kernberg himself has emphasized, require some hospital or other controlling structure close at hand. The first advantage of counterprojective work is the reduction of transferences to manageable proportions at relatively little risk; the way to interpretations is smoothed. At the same time, I suspect something enduring may be begun. We can speak of "learning perspective" or of a differentiation of inner agencies or of gaining distance on introjected parts of the ego.

I do not mean that this learning perspective is an automatic result of working away from the patient, that distance from the screen "out there" automatically becomes part of the patient's inner distance. Rather than being an automatic result, learning perspective follows from opportunities that the outer screen provides.

Working on the screen means quite concretely addressing, facing, looking at hitherto undifferentiated parts of the ego. These are not talked about, as in interpretative work, or shared as in empathic work, but perceived. Distance, we can say, is inherent in the mode of work. Just as artistic perspective depends upon such pictorial details as the size of objects, their distance apart, shades and shadows or the color modulations that Cezanne exploited, so psychological perspective depends upon historical details; perspective springs from seeing things at once and in relationship to one another. Something similar was suggested by Novey (1968) who found gaining distance on the past facilitated by actual visits to scenes of the past. This is not always possible, and much more often patient and therapist must paint the picture instead. Sullivan spoke of reconstructing the past: "What I would have seen if I had been there" (Kvarnes and Parloff 1976). Writers, as well, speak of putting their pasts behind them in the course of composing their autobiographies.

In addition, I wonder if this gaining of perspective is not assisted by its being shared with someone from whom projections have been for at least a little while lifted. At such moments there is a unique present; the past is not falling on the other person. Perhaps that provides the sharpest perspective of all.

In summary, I suggest that we can see by way of the shadows and that seeing in this way has some notable advantages. Narrative flow can be stimulated, in part because projections do not fall so heavily on one another. And some difficult clinical situations are relieved. Perhaps, too, a basic attribute can be cultivated in this way, perspective on the past, differentiation of the structures internalized in the past, above all freedom from the past.

NOTES

1. In a subsequent paper I will discuss expressions useful in dealing with those, generally depressed, patients who do not project their internal objects but instead hold them close and identify with them. The need is for counter*introjective* comments because counterprojective ones, attacking the projections, are resented by these patients who identify with the introjects.

2. And conversely, may be contraindicated when transference development is sought or when externalization is for other reasons disadvantageous.

3. Shorr suggests a number of devices for stimulating patient's imaginative expressions, for example asking patients to imagine themselves in various situations. The goal is to explore the world through the patient's eyes. Again the emphasis is more on fantasy than on reality.

4. Bandler and Grinder (1975) give examples of the occasional therapeutic *usefulness* of double-binding statements, to highlight already existent inner conflicts. It seems to me however, that in their almost exclusive dependence on questions these workers introduce many other, unintended contradictions of medium and message.

5. To my knowledge, there is no accepted term for the second type of repetitive act, which depends on selection rather than misperception, in fact on accurate perception of the selected objects. Enactment seems a good term, but this is already in the literature with a broader meaning, of any acting out of any unconscious process (Sandler et al. 1973).

6. Psychotherapeutic work is often conceptualized as moving between a distant or objective position and one of closeness or trial identifications; and of having the twin goals of producing perception and intimacy. See, for example, the summary statement on the last page of Wyss's review of the psychoanalytic schools (Wyss 1966). The present work is essentially a methodological development of this same view.

7. Therefore, it is sometimes argued, the patients need to take responsibility, not be encouraged to externalize further, as by counterprojection. The present writer responds, people cannot be forced to take responsibility: they will be responsible for what they perceive to be their responsibility and what they are strong enough to take responsibility for: the situational alliance often increases both perceptiveness and the sense of strength.

REFERENCES

Bandler, R., and Grinder, J. 1975. *The Structure of Magic*. Palo Alto: Science and Behavior Books.

Beck, A. T. 1970. Cognitive Therapy: Nature and Relation to Behavior Therapy. *Behavior Therapy*, 1:184–200.

Bowen, M. 1978. *Family Therapy in Clinical Practice*. New York: Jason Aronson.

Call, J. D. 1975. Psychologically Based Conjoint Therapy for Children and Their Parents. In *American Handbook of Psychiatry*, vol. V. New York: Basic Books.

Frankl, V. E. 1967. *Psychotherapy and Existentialism*. New York: Washington Square Press.

Gutheil, T. G., and Havens, L. L. 1979. The Therapeutic Alliance: Contemporary Meanings and Confusions. *International Review of Psycho-Analysis*, in press.

Haley, J. 1968. *Uncommon Therapy*. New York: Grune and Stratton.

Havens, L. L. 1962. The Placement and Movement of Hallucinations in Space: Phenomenology and Theory. *International Journal of Psychoanalysis* 43:426–35.

———— 1976. *Participant Observation*. New York: Jason Aronson.

———— 1978. Explorations in the Uses of Language in Psychotherapy: Simple Empathic Statements. *Psychiatry* 41:336–45.

———— 1979. Explorations in the Uses of Language in Psychotherapy: Complex Empathic Statements. *Psychiatry* 42:40–48.

Kernberg, O. 1968. The Treatment of Patients with Borderline Personality Organization. *International Journal of Psychoanalysis* 49:600–19.

Kohut, H 1971. *The Analysis of the Self*. New York: International Universities Press.

Kvarnes. R., and Parloff. G., eds. 1976. *A Harry Stack Sullivan Case Seminar*. New York: W. W. Norton.

Novey, S. 1968. *The Second Look: The Reconstruction of Personal History in Psychiatry and Psychoanalysis*. Baltimore: Johns Hopkins University Press.

Perls, F. 1973. *The Gestalt Approach: Eyewitness to Therapy*. Palo Alto: Science and Behavior Books.

Sandler, J., Dare, C., and Holder A. 1973. *The Patient and the Analysis*. New York: International Universities Press.

Shorr, J. E. 1972. *Psychoimagination Therapy*. New York: Intercontinental Medical Book Corporation.

Tinbergen, N. 1974. Ethology and Stress Diseases. *Science* 185:20–27.

Webster's Third New International Dictionary. 1963. Phillip Babcock Gove, ed., Springfield, Mass.: G. & C. Merriam Co.

Winnicott, D. W. 1971. *Therapeutic Consultations in Child Psychiatry*. New York: Basic Books.

Wyss, D. 1966. *The Psychoanalytic Schools from Beginning to Present*. New York: Jason Aronson.

14. Unlocking the Unconscious

Habib D. Davanloo

The discovery of the technique of unlocking the unconscious by the author provides a unique opportunity for both the therapist and the patient to have a direct view of the patient's multifoci core neurotic structure.

As I outlined in previous publications, this technique of a rapid uncovering of the unconscious offers the clinical researcher in the field of psychoanalytic psychotherapy an unrivaled opportunity to check aspects of psychoanalytic theory of neurosis against empirical evidence.

HANDLING THE RESISTANCE

I have already discussed the nature of resistance, resistance of repression, and superego resistance. I outlined that patients who are at the extreme left of the neurotic spectrum, who are highly motivated and responsive, show major fluidity in their character structure, and suffer from neither character pathology nor resistance arising from the superego. But as we move to the right-hand side of the spectrum of structural neurosis we see cases suffering from severe character and superego pathology. Here we can generalize based on our extensive clinical data and state that in all patients on the right side of the spectrum the ego and its major functions are paralyzed by powerful forces generated by: (1) repression, and (2) the superego, both of which manifest themselves as impenetrable resistance in the clinical situation. While in previous publications I described various types of intervention that can be used in handling resistance and making direct access to the patient's unconscious possible, in this present article I primarily will focus on the central dynamic sequence essential in the process of the unlocking of the unconscious. The process will be illustrated by an analysis of the trial therapy of a patient.

Reprinted by permission of John Wiley & Sons, Ltd. from *Selected Papers*. New York, 1990, pp. 217–49.

THE CENTRAL DYNAMIC SEQUENCE

The whole process which is used in trial therapy is divided into a series of phases, each consisting of a specific type of intervention with its corresponding response. But the phases tend to overlap, and most interviews contain a good deal of repetition and the process proceeds in a spiral rather than a straight line. The central dynamic sequence can be summarized as follows:

Phase (1) Inquiry. Exploring the patient's difficulties, initial ability to respond; is the phase of descriptive, dynamic phenomenological approach to patient's psychopathology.

Phase (2) Pressure. Leading to resistance in the form of a series of defenses.

Phase (3) Clarification and Challenge to Defenses. This phase can be summarized as:

   (a) Rapid identification and clarification of the defenses.
   (b) Challenge to the defenses, leading to rising transference and intensification of the resistance.
   (c) Further clarification of the defenses; casting doubt on the defenses.
   (d) Systematic attempt to make the patient acquainted with the defenses that have paralyzed his functioning.
   (e) To turn the patient against his resistance; the patient must clearly see that his resistance that has paralyzed his functioning is being challenged.
   (f) Challenge that is directed against the resistance; challenge to the resistance against experience of impulse/feeling outside of the transference; challenge to the resistance against experience of the impulse/feeling in the transference: challenge to the resistance against emotional closeness in transference.
   (g) Head-on collision with character resistance with special reference to the resistance against emotional closeness in the transference and resistance maintained by the superego.

Phase (4) Transference Resistance.

   (a) Clarification and challenge to the transference resistance. The emphasis is on the resistance in the transference.
   (b) Head-on collision with the transference resistance with special reference to that maintained by the superego.

(c) Exhaustion of the resistance and communication from the unconscious therapeutic alliance.

(d) To maximize the inner tension between unconscious therapeutic alliance and resistance.

Phase (5) Intrapsychic Crisis.

(a) High rise in the complex transference feeling; direct experience of the C.T.F.; the triggering mechanism for the unlocking of the unconscious.

(b) Mobilization of the unconscious therapeutic alliance; creation of internal conflict and tension between therapeutic alliance and resistance; finally to turn the therapeutic alliance against the resistance.

(c) The first unlocking of the unconscious.

Phase (6) Systematic Analysis of the Transference. Leading to the resolution of the residual resistance with partial or major de-repression of the current or recent past (C) and distant past (P) conflicts.

Phase (7) Further Inquiry Exploring the Developmental History.

Phase (8) The Phase of Direct Access to the Unconscious. Direct view of the multifoci core neurotic structure and its relation to the patient's symptoms and character disturbance; and psychotherapeutic planning.

As I have already stated, not all therapies proceed in exactly this simple sequence. The phases tend to overlap and proceed in a spiral rather than a straight line. However, for those interested in learning the technique of Intensive Short-Term Dynamic Psychotherapy, the central dynamic sequence can be seen as a framework which the therapist can use as a guide, constantly working from one phase to another. With the exception of patients who suffer from severe fragile ego structure, the whole spectrum of structural neurosis are good candidates for Intensive Short-Term Dynamic Psychotherapy. But the evaluator should take into consideration that the ease with which the breakthrough can be achieved and the relative emphasis on different types of intervention depends on a number of variables. For example, the phase of inquiry which is a dynamic phenomenological approach to the patient's psychopathology outlining the patient's symptom disturbances and character disturbances varies from the left-hand side of the spectrum to the right-hand side of the spectrum. Patients on the extreme left are highly responsive with major fluidity in their unconscious and with great lucidity they describe their problems. But patients on the right-hand side of the spectrum, particularly those with ego-syntonic character pathology, are not able to respond. They have heavily identified with their resistance and they enter the interview with major character resistance, and the process immediately moves to the phase of identification and clarification of the patient's defenses.

PARTIAL AND MAJOR UNLOCKING OF THE UNCONSCIOUS

The degree of unlocking of the unconscious is exactly in proportion to the degree that the patient has experienced the complex transference feeling. In major unlocking of the unconscious under systematic challenge and pressure to the patient's resistance there is a breakthrough of the impulse in the transference which is accompanied by the breakthrough of the guilt and grief-laden unconscious feelings (the case of the machine gun woman, the case of the woman who frequently bruised her leg). But if the therapist aims at the partial unlocking of the unconscious the therapist must monitor the central dynamic sequence in such a way that the breakthrough of the impulse in the transference is partial. In this procedure the breakthrough of the aggressive impulse in the transference is partial but the breakthrough of the guilt and grief-laden unconscious feelings is at a much higher degree. The partial breakthrough into the unconscious is extremely important in controlled clinical research where a waiting list is essential.

I have repeatedly emphasized the care and vigilance with which this technique must be used and the therapist must undergo extensive training in utilizing such a powerful technique. In this article I give an example and analyze the case in depth and again emphasize the technical skill and vigilance in the process of the unlocking of the unconscious.

THE CASE OF THE FRAGILE WOMAN

The patient is a 32-year-old divorced woman. She had been interviewed one week previously by a relatively experienced trainee who had suspected the presence of a severely fragile ego structure. The present author, the second independent evaluator, undertook to interview her not knowing anything about the patient except a question mark of the possibility of a severely fragile ego structure. The interview needs to be considered in advance in terms of the phases listed above. As described, the therapist usually opens with a question about the patient's presenting complaints and continues with a certain amount of psychiatric inquiry. However, many patients—including the present one—arrive at the interview betraying obvious feelings which usually have an important transference component. The therapist then opens with a question, "How do you feel right now?" and begins to clarify and then challenge the patient's resistance against acknowledging transference feeling, at first cautiously and then with increasing power. When this happens not only does the central dynamic sequence begin at once, but the phases of pressure (2) and challenge to the resistance outside the transference (3) are bypassed. The therapist proceeds immediately to phase (4), namely, *Challenge to the resistance in the transference,* while as always vigilantly monitoring the patient's responses for danger signals. However, because the present patient had already been described as potentially fragile and entered the interview with a great deal of anxiety, the therapist had to modify his technique and proceed with much greater caution. In the opening phase, therefore, he employed the following devices:

(1) exerting gentle pressure toward transference feelings;
(2) concentrating on physical manifestations rather than actual feelings;
(3) frequently taking pressure off the transference by inquiring about situations outside the interview;
(4) avoiding challenge;
(5) allowing the patient escape routes by which she would describe something less anxiety provoking than feelings; and
(6) proceeding less fast.

As will be seen, these interventions to a great extent decrease the level of anxiety and the patient is able to describe the disturbing transference feelings stirred up in her by her previous interview, and doing so in such a way as to make it absolutely clear that she was not suffering from a fragile ego structure at all and was a good candidate for Intensive Short-Term Dynamic Psychotherapy. (See Davanloo, Trial Therapy as a Psychodiagnostic Tool.)

Therefore, the therapist quickly passed over into systematic use of the central dynamic sequence, putting pressure on the patient to experience her transference feelings, steadily escalating his challenge, and finally bringing about a head-on collision with the transference resistance (Phases 3 and 4 of the Central Dynamic Sequence). This resulted in a major breakthrough (Phase 5). There followed a phase of inquiry alternating with both challenge and interpretation directed against the defenses in general and the residual resistance, culminating in a second head-on collision. From then on it was possible to move to the phase of direct access to the unconscious, which consisted of exploring first the patient's sexual fantasies, and then past events and relationships. The therapist was now able to bring to the surface some of the patient's deepest pain.

It is worth mentioning also that this interview, similar to those I have already published, demonstrates signs indicating the operation of an unconscious therapeutic alliance, which in the author's opinion is the most reliable criterion for Short-Term Dynamic Psychotherapy.

The "Fragile" Woman: Interview

For the sake of brevity the dialogue has been shortened and paraphrased in places, but nothing important has been omitted.

The Phase of Gentle Pressure toward the Transference Alternating with Inquiry

The patient enters the interview visibly anxious, and the focus is immediately on her anxiety here and now, exploring the physiological concomitants of the anxiety and reducing the level of her anxiety.

TH: How do you feel right now?
PT: A little bit nervous.

The patient has mentioned a feeling, and the natural step is to direct her toward her actual experience. Here, however, the therapist carefully allows the escape route of describing only the physical manifestations of her nervousness:

TH: What is it like right now physically?
PT: My hands are cold. I feel my heart is racing a bit. It feels somewhat uncomfortable.

The therapist knows that this nervousness is likely to be concerned with the patient's feelings about the present interview. He seeks confirmation of this, and having received it, he directs the patient's attention toward these feelings. Thus he is already approaching the transference.

TH: How long have you been like that?
PT: Since about five minutes after arriving here.

TH: So you didn't have it before, you mean?
PT: Uh hmm.
TH: So it has to do with here?
PT: Yeah, I'm fearful, I'm not really sure what's going to happen.
TH: What do you have in mind about what's going to happen?
PT: I don't know.

Thus the patient has avoided the question, but the therapist makes no attempt to challenge this. Instead, he continues with a question which is purely factual and leads away from the transference—thus serving to reduce the pressure—but at the same time is designed to throw light on the transference indirectly:

TH: Usually you are like that? You get nervous in situations like this?
PT: Not all situations, but there is a certain reaction that I have in going for interviews or meeting people for the first time professionally. Not so much in personal interactions like meeting friends.

The therapist asks a question which gives the patient the choice of speaking about feelings or continuing with physical manifestations. She chooses the latter:

TH: What else do you experience besides pounding of the heart?
PT: And cold hands.

The therapist receives the message that she would rather not talk about feelings. He does not challenge this for the moment.

TH: Your hands get cold. Any other experiences physically?
PT: Uh, I have to urinate more often.

The therapist has noted that her present anxiety is a general phenomenon, and he now asks a question which is part of the psychiatric inquiry (Phase 1), but can also be used to lead naturally into the psychodynamics.

TH: How long would you say you have been like this, that when you meet a new situation or person professionally you develop this?
PT: Probably . . . the first time I was aware of this was when I was about ten. I was aware of being nervous and having to urinate. I wasn't so aware of my heart racing or cold hands but I remember cold.
TH: You are talking about elementary school, am I right?
PT: Yes, when I had to put on a performance I was very nervous.
TH: Were there incidents when you were called to the front of the class and you would become anxious and nervous?
PT: I went first to a parochial school which was very strict, and we weren't allowed

to speak out of turn—so that was a very nerve-racking situation, and I really was never asked to . . . Oh no, wait a minute, when I was in first grade, first year, the teacher humiliated me in front of the class.

The therapist's exploration of the physiological concomitants of anxiety and his cautious approach are paying dividends. She is feeling more at ease with an indication that the conscious therapeutic alliance is being cemented. Moreover, as will emerge much later, this memory is actually a "cover memory" for one of the most significant situations in her early life. The therapist continues his line of inquiry.

TH: What age would you say?
PT: Six, seven, eight.
TH: What was the humiliating situation?
PT: I was given a series of photographs, and I had to draw lines to indicate the way they related to each other, and I went up to the front of the class and gave it to her, and she smacked me across the face because I had done it incorrectly.

In the following question the therapist uses the word "reaction," which allows the patient the escape route of saying what she did without describing how she felt:

TH: And what was your immediate reaction?
PT: I cried and I know . . .
TH: So it is a situation that in front of the class she humiliated you, but then your reaction was weepiness, hmm?

The use of the word "weepiness" needs to be discussed. At first sight it may seem rather unfair on the therapist's part—after all a child of eight is humiliated by a person in authority has little option but to cry and (as we see later) to appeal to her parents for help. At the same time, however, the therapist knows that crying can be used as a way of avoiding massive underlying anger; and moreover that this defense can become ingrained and be used in later life at times when the expression of anger would be much more appropriate. Also, the patient has made the link between this incident and her current anxiety in interview situations, and she has arrived at the present interview in a state of considerable anxiety which is giving rise to somatic symptoms. The therapist knows that anger is likely to be one of the underlying feelings that the patient is avoiding. Thus the use of the word "weepiness" constitutes a subtle indirect message to the patient's unconscious that he knows all about defenses against anger, including anger in the here and now, and this can be considered as his first and only challenge in this early phase. He repeats the word, for emphasis:

TH: Any other reaction besides weepiness?
PT: Well, I don't remember reactions in the classroom. I remember crying to my father. I refused to go to school.
TH: Oh I see, you did actually refuse?

So, another of the patient's character defenses may be avoidance.

PT: Yes, so I was changed into another class and had a new teacher. It seems my parents took great offense to me being slapped, my father more so.
TH: You say the teacher humiliated you in front of the class, and it was so bad that you didn't want to go back to the class anymore. And you got your parents to help, and finally you went to another class. But if you go to that situation, you are weepy and crying, but what other physical reaction did you have?
PT: It's a blank in my mind. All I remember is being smacked and the feeling of shame and humiliation, and crying.
TH: So the only manifest things are weepiness and crying. You don't know what was your physical reaction, hmm?
PT: I don't remember.

The therapist begins to exert a little more pressure (Phase 2).

TH: Any other incidents of a similar kind that mobilized anxiety in you? This is very important to look at, because you say it goes back to the very early part of your life.
PT: Before that, no, I don't remember anything. Uh, after that . . .

The therapist draws attention to the here and now. He notices nonverbal clues which presumably betray the patient's reaction to the pressure. He decides to bring this into the open at once, but mentions only "tension" without making any attempt to ask about the cause of the tension:

TH: How do you feel right now? Still you are tense?
PT: A little tense.
TH: And usually you clench your . . . ?
PT: Yeah, my hands are very cold right now, I want to put them under my arms.
TH: The nervousness is still as bad as a few minutes ago, or a little better or what?
PT: It feels a little bit less.
TH: Uh hmm. Okay.

The content should be avoided in this phase, should only be acknowledged. This intervention of bringing into the open the patient's immediate reaction in the here and now even though it is only her anxiety has helped a great deal. Anxiety has been reduced and we have a manifestation of her conscious therapeutic alliance. Then she mentions recurrent dreams which might have a bearing on her psychopathology; but the therapist should keep in mind that resistance is in operation and moving to content while the patient is in a state of resistance would be totally counter-productive. In addition he has to clear up the transference. Moving into content would lead to pure intellectualization, but at the same time the therapist should not convey an atmosphere of rejection. He therefore carefully acknowledges her communication and then goes back to trying to understand the reason for her anxiety. In the early stages of this exploration his whole approach is still very cautious and he confines himself to asking about outside situations, but his ultimate aim—provided there are no contraindications—is that this will eventually lead him to the transference.

PT: What comes to my mind is that there are many things I'd like to understand about myself. Since I was a child I have been plagued by a certain type of dream which I feel is "somewhat representative of some of my behavioral patterns."

TH: You mean you have recurrent dreams?

PT: Uh hmm, and I think it's indicative of a certain split sometimes in the way I feel.

TH: And what you say is that those dreams reflect on some of your problems in life?

PT: Yes.

This apparently rich content is in the service of resistance, would only lead to intellectualization of the dream, an attempt to move away from the transference. The therapist gently moves to the anxiety.

TH: Okay, let's stay with this anxiety for a moment. Do you have any other incidents in recent years? When you are in front of a crowd, for example, do you experience it?

PT: Uh, in general no, I've always felt fairly comfortable speaking in front of crowds. It's when I feel that I'm being tested in some way that I feel this.

TH: Like an examination, or going to an interview to see if they're accepting you for a job?

This is a message to the patient's unconscious about the parallel situation of being accepted for therapy. The phase of inquiry continues.

PT: Yes.

TH: Could we look to the examination, because that is a situation in which you have to perform? Let me ask you, what is your occupation?

PT: Right now I'm a graduate student in economics.

TH: What is it like in examinations?

PT: Uh . . . I feel anxious. My hands are cold, my heart is racing when I go into the classroom and sit down.

TH: How about before? Do you have anticipation anxiety?
PT: Some anticipation. I'm not too bad where I know it's something I have to write down. The anxiety is more when I'm being tested verbally.
TH: In written you have less? What is the extent of the anxiety then? Is it to the level that your hands shake?
PT: No, I just notice that what I have to do is urinate, or I sweat.
TH: Does it interfere with your sleep the night before?
PT: Yeah, yeah, sometimes it does. Usually after an exam I feel worse than before. I usually dream more profoundly.
TH: After the exam you are worse in the form of a dream. Now in oral you say it is much worse? So you have gone through many oral exams?
PT: No, I haven't.
TH: You said you are a graduate, maybe I . . .

The patient makes a disguised reference to her previous interview, which takes the form of a mis-statement about what happens in the class. This is a clear indication that she is ready to deal with transference issues. The therapist notes this and decides to keep it at bay. He continues to check further on the degree to which she experiences somatization of her anxiety.

PT: No . . . I'm just saying that when I'm being asked a question in class—"Elena, what do you think?" or "Elena, what's the answer, how do you feel?" . . . not "How do you feel?" . . . they don't ask how do you feel, they ask you what do you think—I feel intimidated.
TH: What are the physical symptoms that you get?
PT: Tightness, choking uh . . .
TH: And then what else? Heart pounding?
PT: Yes, not very heavily, but I feel all of a sudden a sensation of stopping.
TH: Do you get severe tremors, shaking?
PT: No.
TH: Any other physical experiences such as faintness?
PT: No.
TH: Finally what happens? Do you overcome this?

The therapist continues in the line of psychiatric inquiry, Phase (1), to determine the extent the cognitive function of the ego becomes disrupted under the impact of anxiety.

PT: I'm able to sometimes muster up some words, but I feel that my mind goes blank and I can't think of an answer, so I feel frightened.

The therapist is immediately on the alert, since this is one of the important signals.

TH: You mean you lose track of your thoughts?

PT: Yeah.

TH: How do you master that situation, because if you lose track of your thoughts then it obviously must be very difficult for you?

PT: I don't think I do it very successfully. I might sometimes keep very quiet, or just say any answer, or talk about the question, or try to divert the question in some way.

TH: So this is quite a disturbing symptom for someone in academic life?

PT: Yes.

TH: How was it in high school, was it better or worse than now?

PT: I don't remember all that well. I did well and I was generally well liked by my teachers. I don't remember being nervous. I think my anxiety in front of people started when I came to Canada because all of a sudden I was in a new uh . . . a new . . .

TH: When did you come to Canada?

PT: Eleven years ago.

TH: From where?

PT: Philadelphia.

TH: Okay. Now you said that when you have to perform, like a test or an examination, then this anxiety mobilizes?

PT: Uh hmm.

Transference

At last the therapist is ready to open up the issue of transference directly. However, it is not the present transference that the patient wants to talk about, but her transference in the previous interview. This is a crucial issue and the therapist concentrates upon it. By this time the level of anxiety is greatly reduced. Here it is worth summarizing the sequence of events in advance. The patient described the disturbing effects of the previous interview and mentions that very soon after the end of the interview she felt great anger. She is able at the cognitive level without anxiety to declare anger in relation to the first evaluator. So far for the therapist there is no sign of fragility and he concentrates her attention on the actual experience of anger and the impulses it involved. The patient becomes resistant. Now the process enters the phase of clarification and challenge to the patient's resistance. She finally is able to acknowledge the way she would have wanted to verbally lash out at the first evaluator with no sign of anxiety. This is further reassurance about her supposed fragility. The therapist then undertakes a very important step which will be discussed more fully later, namely to acquaint her with the inner mechanism responsible for one of her major symptoms. He points out to her repeatedly and with great emphasis the fact that she doesn't feel anger but feels anxiety in its place, so that at least part of the mechanism responsible for her anxiety has to do with her inability to face her anger. It must be mentioned, too, that she began to suffer from anxiety soon after she entered the hospital for the present interview, so that opening up this will lead to dealing with the present transference as well. From now on the therapist can proceed relentlessly with the whole of the central dynamic sequence though by concentrating at first on the physical manifestation of her anger.

TH: And then how does that apply here with me, because here also you say you are very anxious? What is the nature of the performance here?

As mentioned above, it is not the present but the previous interview that the patient wants to speak about:

TH: What was it about that shook you?
PT: Well uh . . . (she laughs).
TH: You smile when I say . . .

The focus of the session is further on transference, countertransference evaluation, and her feeling toward the first independent evaluator; she indicates that she felt under attack.

Parenthetically it is important to emphasize, based on the clinical data that emerges, that the first evaluator had not done work on Phase (3) of the central dynamic sequence, and also the patient left the interview with unresolved transference feelings which have to be worked through in this interview. Now we return to the interview. The therapist is still troubled by the patient's previous mention of thought block:

TH: When you say you didn't know what was going on, did you lose track of your thoughts?
PT: I don't know exactly what you mean.
TH: I mean that you are talking about a subject but then suddenly you don't know what you were talking about.
PT: That happened, yeah. Because he kept on asking me, how do you feel, or what do you think, what do you feel, what do you feel? And when I said I didn't remember, "what do you mean you don't remember?" I said I can't remember.
TH: So actually during the interview you lost the train of your thoughts?

The patient's answer is very reassuring—she does not run away from disturbing feelings:

PT: Well immediately after I walked out I felt, uh, anger, immense anger toward him.

TH: You mean you felt anger toward him after you left, but not while you were there?

PT: I . . . I . . . for some reason I couldn't feel anger while I was here. I was so frightened that I couldn't feel my anger.

The therapist now prepares to make the link between the underlying feeling and the anxiety:

TH: So then let's look at it. While you were with him you had a lot of anxiety. Am I right?

PT: Yeah.

TH: There was no anger.

PT: I didn't feel anger.

TH: I know, that is what I mean. You did not experience the anger while you were with him. What you experienced was anxiety, hmm?

PT: Uh hmm.

TH: But how long after you left did you start to experience the anger?

PT: About five minutes.

TH: So you were still in the hospital when you had this anger toward him?

PT: Yeah.

Throughout the following passage he takes her through her impulses in detail, challenging her resistance as necessary, but at the same time supporting her by constantly reassuring her that what she is describing consists only of thoughts and ideas:

TH: How then did you experience that anger? You know, physically? When you are anxious we know how you experience anxiety—you have palpitations, tension, tightness. How do you physically experience the anger?

PT: (She sighs.) The same way almost.

TH: You mean anxiety?

PT: Except that there's a switch, that I want to lash out verbally or physically in some way.

TH: Both physically as well as verbally.

PT: Or I feel that my physical movements become, uh, more pronounced.

TH: Uh hmm. These were the thoughts and ideas in your head, that you wished you could have verbally and physically lashed out at him?

PT: Yes.

She has frequent sighs in talking about her anger toward the first evaluator which indicates that the impulse of anger gives rise to the anxiety which discharges itself in the form of tension in the intercostal muscles as well as the subdiaphragmatic muscles. The therapist moves to challenge.

TH: Now this is only thoughts and ideas, hmm?
PT: Uh hmm.
TH: Now in terms of thoughts and ideas, if you had lashed out—I mean you
         didn't—but if you had, what would that have been like? What are you like
         when you lash out verbally?
PT: Uh . . . my voice is raised, I yell.
TH: You yell, your voice goes up, uh hmm.
PT: I . . . I have not too much control on exactly what I'm saying.
TH: What would you have told him? . . . You smile.
PT: (Laughing) What would I have told him?
TH: I know it is difficult to tell me what you wanted to tell him. We are talking
         about thoughts and ideas.
PT: I . . . I don't remember what I would have told him.

The therapist begins his systematic challenge to the resistance against
experience of the impulse in relation to the (C), the first evaluator.

TH: We are not talking about remembering. Let's portrait a situation like that. It's
         not too far, it's a week ago, hmm? You smile again, hmm?
PT: (Laughing) I'm feeling embarrassed.
TH: Why? Because you want to tell me you wanted to tell him off verbally?
PT: Yes.
TH: So let's see in terms of thoughts and ideas how you would have told him off?

Finally she indicates that she would have verbally lashed out at him. Then
the therapist turns his attention to the physical impulse, which is likely to be
even more disturbing than purely verbal.

TH: If you physically had lashed out what would that have been like? You didn't do
         it but if you had done it? In terms of thoughts again?
PT: I . . . uh . . . I wanted to smack him across the face with the back of my arm.
TH: How?
PT: I'd like to go . . . wham! Across his face.
TH: And then? Only once?
PT: Yeah, that would have been sufficient.

The therapist sees a parallel with the distant past which seems to still live
on her.

TH: But you had the impulse to verbally tell him off, and there was also the impulse,
         like the teacher in school did to you . . . *(The patient laughs.)* You smile when I
         say that. Then you had the impulse to smack him in the face, hmm?
PT: Uh hmm.

The next passage needs discussion. One of the principle manifestations
that has been brought to light is that in the previous interview instead of

anger the patient experienced anxiety. This must mean that she has a powerful unconscious anxiety of the expression of anger, which needs to be brought into the open.

Analysis of Two Triangles—An Important Principle of Technique

During the course of this work I have become quite certain that it is extremely important for the patient not merely to respond to interpretation about some of her inner mechanisms, but to achieve lasting insight into them—particularly the way in which some fleeting feeling or impulse is immediately replaced by something else. If the patient is not given this insight there will be a failure of prophylaxis, and it will be only too easy for the same mechanism to re-establish itself as an automatic reaction on future occasions. Since there is a considerable amount of unconscious resistance against this insight, it is often necessary to repeat the interpretation over and over again in order to consolidate it.

It is very important to give a full impression of this process, so that I shall include almost all the therapist's interventions; but for brevity, I shall omit many of the patient's responses, almost all of which consisted simply of showing that she was following what the therapist said.

Link between the Impulse of Anger and Anxiety (Phase 3)

TH: But do you think the anxiety is a mechanism of dealing with the anger? Do you see what I mean? . . . The anger is not experienced in the moment, what is experienced is more the anxiety . . . There was a situation that mobilized anger in you but you did not immediately experience the anger . . . And what you experienced immediately was anxiety. You see? . . . It is very important that we see this: that the immediate reaction is anger but the mechanism that comes to the fore is anxiety . . . And anger is pushed underneath but later on it comes out . . . And what did you do with the anger? You wanted to lash out, but what happened to that anger? Where did it go?

Making the patient well acquainted with the impulse, anxiety, and defense (Phase 3).

PT: I don't know where it went.
TH: It's very important we look at it, because you cannot say the anger evaporates.
PT: In other situations the anger does not evaporate, it stays with me for a long time; but with him for some reason there was a part of me that was very accepting of the whole process.

TH: That is intellectually true; but still, where does the anger go?

PT: Well, immediately after I felt angry, which didn't last very long, I felt very shaken.

TH: Oh I see. First anger, and then again the anxiety.

PT: No, this was more trembling, total body trembling. I felt as if, uh, I had just been through a cyclone, or that something very traumatic just happened and the after-effects finally hit me.

It becomes more and more clear that she has a very powerful unconscious anxiety in relation to the expression of the anger, and the therapist continues to make her well acquainted with the three parts of the triangle of the conflict: the impulse-feelings, anxiety, and defense.

TH: The reason I say it is very important is because first there is the anger, but it immediately mobilizes a great deal of anxiety in you. In the session, obviously the anger was there but then you had anxiety. Then away from here the anger comes out, but then the massive anxiety takes over again, hmm? . . . As if the anger is something that disturbs you a great deal.

PT: Well, I was taught not to express anger.

The therapist dismisses this attempt to avoid the central issue:

TH: We can get to that, but first is to see that you are really terrified of a situation that mobilizes anger.

We saw the repeated emphasis on the link between anxiety and anger. Then she talked about the way she felt after the first interview.

PT: That is exactly what I realized after I left. After I got angry and then I felt trembling, all of a sudden I had a feeling of calmness; and, I don't know if it was a sadness, but I felt as if something had been exposed inside of me and chiselled out, or a hole poked in; and the release of emotions associated with that, psychologically, physically, made me feel very centered and very solid within myself, almost withdrawn but very much myself; and my actions the rest of that day were very quiet and more observant of people, but I felt better about myself for some reason, because I realized that I have to deal with my anger. I have to learn how to express it, I have to say it when it comes out.

The therapist does not want her to form the impression that she has to go around expressing her anger on all occasions:

TH: But obviously expressing it is not necessarily going to be constructive. I mean if you slap another person . . . The most important thing for us to see is what it is that happens when something mobilizes anger in you and this tremendous anxiety takes over. Do you see what I mean?

PT: Yes.

The therapist searches for confirmation that talking about her anger has led to relief in the here and now.

TH: How do you feel right now?
PT: Better.
TH: Because I have a feeling that you have a tremendous difficulty to even talk about anger. Am I right to say you prefer I don't talk about anger?
PT: I think I prefer you talk about anger. I need to talk about my anger.
TH: But talking about anger disturbs you? Is painful?
PT: Yes.

The therapist now approaches the issue of her transference in the present interview:

TH: Then do you think that something like that would happen here with me? Namely it might mobilize the impulse in you to lash out at me? You see, if I focus on something painful you don't want to focus on, then . . .
PT: I won't feel that I'll want to lash out with you right here. If anything I'll start feeling my hands getting cold.
TH: I know, the anxiety takes over.
PT: I'll just keep on being anxious, I feel that.

At this point the therapist delivers a message to both the patient's conscious and her unconscious therapeutic alliance, speaking of the devastating effect that this mechanism of replacing anger with anxiety has on her life. His aim is to prepare the way for much later work about her self-destructive tendencies which arise out of the repressed impulses, with guilt and grief-laden unconscious feelings.

Challenge to the Patient's Defenses, Leading to Rising Transference (Phase 3)

TH: Okay, so one thing so far we can understand is that it is very crippling, this anxiety—I don't know, you can say it is or it isn't—and it is very diffuse in many areas of your life. And then when a situation mobilizes anger, you don't experience anger but anxiety; and later anger comes, and then you become anxious again . . . But my question was, where does the anger go?
PT: It goes (*smiling*) somewhere here inside. That's where it goes.

The therapist takes the smile as an indication of transference feelings:

TH: Do you feel like smiling or is this a cover-up of something else?
PT: I feel embarrassed.

TH: Is it embarrassed or something else?
PT: (Smiling again) I don't know.
TH: I don't know, you know yourself better. I only met you for a short period I have a feeling that you have a tendency to cover up, to put up a facade.
PT: That's right.
TH: And do you think there is something of a facade with me?
PT: No, I feel that you see through the facade, and it makes me embarrassed. I feel a little bit naked. It's almost as if I'm sitting here with no clothes on and you're just looking at me.

The Issue of Emotional Closeness

Extensive clinical data indicate the importance of realizing that many patients defend themselves as strongly against the positive feelings as against their negative, and therefore they put up a barrier against any form of emotional closeness. In some patients resistance against emotional closeness is much more extensive than others. Here the therapist senses that the word "naked" refers to such a problem in the transference, and immediately sets about trying to bring this into the open.

(It is worth noting that at this moment many therapists might feel inclined to take up the sexual implications of the patient's remark. I am quite convinced that this would completely miss the point and would divert the whole interview and put the process of unlocking into impasse. There are indeed sexual implications present, but their relevance is quite secondary—in this context sexuality is merely an aspect of closeness, and closeness is the issue that needs to be dealt with, so that sexuality does not need to be mentioned at all.)

TH: "Naked" has to do with closeness, if you carefully look at it, hmm?
PT: Closeness?
TH: Yeah, that I am getting close to your intimate thoughts and feelings. Do you have a problem with closeness, intimacy?
PT: Uhh . . .
TH: I have a feeling that here with me you are trying to cover up your feelings.
PT: Yes.

The therapist's conclusion by this time is that there is resistance against emotional closeness in the transference which at the appropriate time needs to be systematically challenged. Then he decided to undertake the psychiatric inquiry.

PSYCHIATRIC INQUIRY (PHASE 1)

The patient has given conclusive evidence of her capacity to respond well to a rapid uncovering approach, but the therapist now needs to make doubly sure. He carefully inquires about depression, quality and severity, assessment of suicide.

This part of the interview will be summarized because it consisted entirely of question and answer. On the other hand, the fact that it is summarized must not be taken as an indication of its lack of importance, since psychiatric inquiry, a comprehensive dynamic phenomenological approach, forms an essential part of every trial therapy.

Her answers made it clear that while she suffers from a fairly severe depressive illness, she has so far always possessed the strength to survive without breakdown.

The answers that indicated the fine balance between severity on the one hand, and absence of danger signals on the other, were as follows.

In her depressive states she feels indifferent and that life is a failure, but she does not suffer from more serious or delusional depressive ideation, examples of which might be the feeling that she is an "empty shell," or that she has "destroyed the world." She says she does get into a state of withdrawal and may cancel her activities for a day at a time; but on inquiry it emerges that she usually counteracts this state by going to school or by energetic physical activity. There was no evidence that such activities were hypomanic. Her longest attack of depression lasted two months, but this was clearly reactive—to a major life event, the separation from her husband.

She can trace some kind of depressive state back to her teens, her description of this is not of true clinical depression, and there is no evidence for an "endogenous" depressive cycle, i.e., attacks without obvious external cause. Finally, although she does entertain thoughts of suicide she has never attempted it nor made serious plans to do so.

When she was asked about other psychiatric disturbances she mentioned a "dream state," which could be manifestation of schizophrenia, and "confusion," which could indicate an organic condition; but on inquiry both of these seemed to be no more than states of indecision.

This part of the inquiry ended with the following statement by the patient:

PT: . . . I think all my anxiety comes from the fact that my personal—my intimate relationships have not been stable.

This immediately led the therapist back to investigating the psychodynamics.

Pressure, Challenge to the Resistance Outside the Transference (Phases 2 and 3)

Since the only other disturbances that the patient has mentioned are concerned with personal relations, the therapist is satisfied that he has covered the psychiatric inquiry. He therefore asks about the nature of these disturbances, preparing to make the transition to more dynamic inquiry. In fact a brief passage of challenge to the resistance leads back into the transference in a way that could not have been foreseen.

The therapist asked first whether her problems in personal relationships were more pronounced with men than with women. The answer was that they are more pronounced with men, but that she does have problems with certain women in her professional life. This led to the relation with a fellow student named Priscilla, by whom the patient felt rebuffed, which had caused the patient to feel anxious. In answer to the question of what else she had felt, she said that she felt angry, but that she had only become aware of the anger later. The therapist immediately made the link with the previous evaluation interview:

TH: It's always later on, like last week here, hmm?
PT: Yeah.

Pressure and challenge to the resistance against experience of anger in relation to (C) (Phases 2 and 3).

TH: How did you experience the anger in relation to her?

This question produces some kind of inner turmoil, to which the therapist immediately draws attention:

PT: Uh . . . wheww . . .
TH: As soon as I asked how do you experience anger, you said "whewww."

The patient laughs in such a way as to indicate that some further reaction has been touched off in her. Once more the therapist immediately draws attention to this:

TH: Again the smile comes.
PT: Because I hide it so well I don't even feel it.

The therapist returns to challenging the defense:

TH: I know, you have a mastery of covering it up.
PT: That's right.

The therapist now introduces the word "crippling," repeating it for empha-sis—an intervention that he could not have known would eventually lead into the depths of her pathology:

TH: You are the master of covering up, to put the facade. This is a "crippling" force in your life.
PT: That's right, yes.

Making the Patient Acquainted with the Defenses That Have Paralyzed Her Functioning (Phase 3)

TH: And as this is a crippling force in your life, it is very important for you and I to examine it—unless you prefer not to examine it?
PT: No, I want to examine it.
TH: Because obviously this is a very crippling force for a young woman of your age, hmm?
PT: Yes.
TH: So then it is very important for us to examine it, for if we can see what it is like, then later on hopefully we can get to the core of it.

Rising Transference, Resistance, Challenge to Transference Resistance (Phases 3 and 4)

The following passage is extremely important because it illustrates almost all the aspects of transference that were described in my other publications. The therapist concentrates exclusively on the transference, employing challenge. He deals with all three corners of the triangle of conflict in connection first with negative and then with positive transference feelings, and ends up with a head-on collision with the transference resistance. The result is a major breakthrough. When this patient is compared with the left side of the spec-trum the far greater complexity of the transference in a severe character neurosis, as opposed to a symptom neurosis, will be evident.

An overall view of this passage is as follows.

(1) The patient herself suddenly re-introduces the transference, say- ing that she is angry about the therapist's use of the work "crip- pling."

(2) The therapist focuses on the actual experience of anger. The patient responds with a mixture of defenses such as somatization and laugh- ter on the one hand, and nonverbal cues betraying her inner feelings on the other, to both of which the therapist draws attention (two corners of the triangle of conflict in the transference).

(3) The patient's anger is now very close beneath the surface, and with the help of repeated challenge the therapist succeeds in bringing out the actual impulses involved.

(4) He then sees that in order to free her further it is important to deal with the third corner of the triangle of conflict, and he there- fore focuses on the anxieties that make it difficult to express her anger.

(5) He makes a move toward positive transference feelings by men- tioning her need to protect him from her anger, where by implication the anxiety is of causing him harm, but in fact this does not seem to be the important issue.

(6) She eventually names her anxiety as fear of his retaliating by re- jecting her, either if she expresses her anger or, indeed, if she fails to do so.

(7) As she speaks of this she begins to betray an underlying sadness which she tries to control, and he draws her attention to this.

(8) He now focuses on her fear of emotional closeness in the transference and her defenses against it (two corners of the triangle of conflict involving positive feelings).

(9) He senses that this needs a major effort on his part, and therefore it is here that he introduces the head-on collision with the transference re- sistance.

(10) This brings out intense feelings about her disappointment and disillu- sion with close relationships, and her fear that she can never love anyone again. Her ability to share these feelings with the therapist represents the emergence of the underlying positive feelings, the third corner of the triangle of conflict in the transference.

(11) Now that this major breakthrough has been achieved, he suggests taking a five-minute break.

We may now take up the interview where we left off.

Negative Transference

PT: Well, I'll tell you, I'm experiencing anger right now because you keep on saying crippling force, crippling force. It sounds like . . . well what the hell are you trying to say?

TH: So you say right now you are angry with me?

PT: Yes! Yes.

TH: Then how do you experience this anger with me?

PT: Well I feel I want to tell you to stop saying crippling force, crippling . . .

The Link between Negative Transference and Various Defenses against It

TH: But how do you experience this physically? You didn't like me to use the word crippling?

PT: No, I didn't.

TH: And then this mobilizes anger in you? Let's see how you experience this anger physically?

Challenge and pressure to the resistance against experience of anger in the transference.

PT: I don't remember . . . I didn't feel anything. I felt maybe a little tension in my stomach.

TH: But that is anxiety, you see. What is the way you experience anger? It is very important you look at it because last time you walked out from here with your anger. Now are you going to repeat that this time as well?

PT: No.

TH: Or do you want to experience it?

PT: I want to experience it.

The therapist emphasizes that this is a golden opportunity to acquaint her with her mechanisms for avoiding anger while they are actually happening:

TH: So let's see, because it's a very split-second process that needs to be examined. I use the word crippling, and for whatever reason—it doesn't make a difference—you didn't like it.

PT: No.

TH: That mobilized certain irritation and anger in you.

PT: Yeah.

Nonverbal Cues

He now draws attention to a number of nonverbal cues betraying her inner feelings:

TH: And I don't know if you noticed, but immediately your fist also became clenched, like that. You see?

PT: Yeah.

TH: And is still like that. *(The patient starts giggling)* And I'm sure you don't like it when I tell you your fist goes like that.

PT: No, it's okay.

TH: The smile comes to the forefront.

PT: I laugh, yeah.

TH: Which is a cover-up for your underlying feeling.

PT: That's right.

TH: Then let's see what is the underlying feeling. Is the anger, hmm?

PT: Yeah, that's right.

TH: Were you aware that when you got angry your fist went like that?

PT: No.

TH: But it is very important. And when you get angry, physically you take a very defensive, on-guard position, hmm?

PT: Yes, I'm feeling very anxious right now. Because you're probing me. I feel a tension here in my stomach.

TH: And you take a deep . . . *(Patient has frequent deep sighs.)*

PT: Yeah, I'm having trouble breathing.

TH: And then also you are holding onto the anger.

PT: Yes.

TH: So let's see how you experience the anger. You experience anxiety.

PT: That's right, yes.

TH: But let's see how physically you experience the anger. You see, a smile comes again. Let's face it, you can laugh . . .

PT: I know, I know, I know. But this defense mechanism is so good.

TH: But this defense mechanism is your worst enemy. Of course I am not the one to decide that. You have to decide, because that is your life.

PT: Well I don't know if laughing is my worse enemy.

TH: No, I'm not talking about laughing. It is the cover-up.

The patient is now using the defense of somatization against her anger. The therapist explores the extent of her somatic symptoms:

PT: I feel such pain right now. I think I have indigestion.

TH: Usually when you become very anxious you get indigestion?

PT: Yes.

TH: By indigestion you mean what? Vomiting or . . . ?

PT: No, just a tightness, inability to eat.

TH: What else do you get when you say indigestion?

PT: Diarrhea, gas.

TH: Do you feel that way right now?

PT: Not that profound, but yeah, I feel a little bit of it. And I'm having trouble breathing.

TH: Now let's see how you experience this anger, because there is always a delayed reaction. With Priscilla you were angry, hmm? But then the anger came later on, hmm?

PT: That's right.

TH: And now you are angry with me because you don't like the word crippling.

Negative Transference, Impulse

There is a drop in the level of anxiety, and the process indicates that the physiological concomitant of impulse is surfacing, the therapist maintains the focus on the actual experience of impulse.

TH: Or, you don't like me to focus on your facade, hmm? Okay, let's see how you experience the anger. We know there is a link between anxiety and anger, but that doesn't tell us how you experience the anger. Did you feel you wanted to verbally lash out at me? Or physically? You mean I am the exception?

The patient avoids the impulse by rationalizing, which the therapist challenges:

PT: Why should I be that angry at you because you said crippling? I mean there are degrees of anger.

TH: Yeah, but you are rationalizing it . . .

The patient admits the impulse but then starts to weaken it by further rationalization, which the therapist interrupts, bringing her back to the impulse:

PT: I experience the anger by wanting to raise my voice, and I don't understand . . .

TH: You feel you want to raise your voice?

Absence of anxiety and tension in vocal cords.

PT: Yes.

TH: So if you raise your voice what will you be like here?

PT: Uhh . . .

Negative Transference, Anxiety

Having exposed part of the impulse, the therapist senses that further freeing can only take place if he exposes the anxiety:

TH: Because obviously you are protecting me against your anger.

PT: Yes.

TH: Why? Why do you want to protect me against your anger? Let's look to your thoughts and ideas of what my reaction would be.

The patient is evasive:

PT: I don't know what your reaction is going to be.
TH: No, I'm saying in terms of thoughts and ideas.
PT: Well, my reactions of your reactions?
TH: You said yourself that I would have a reaction to it. That it might hurt me or it might . . . hmm?
PT: I don't know. I imagine you will be hurt.
TH: What else besides me getting hurt?
PT: That you would get angry at me.
TH: Okay, could we look to this? Because it is very important. I am sure it is a pattern outside of here. I cannot be an exception, hmm?

The therapist now embarks upon an extremely important procedure with any patient who has such difficulty over anger, namely driving home cognitive insight about the inner mechanisms involved and the reasons for them.

TH: Let's look to the pattern step by step. First is me focusing on crippling.
PT: That's right.
TH: This immediately mobilizes anxiety, but under the anxiety you experience anger.
PT: That's right.
TH: Then verbally you want to tell me off, but the idea is that I would get angry at you, and then what would happen? In terms of thoughts again.
PT: I'm afraid that you might put me in my place or say something hurtful to me, which either means I'd have to cover up or be more angry.
TH: So then could we look to that? The idea is that I would become revengeful toward you.

The therapist introduces this word, because he knows that almost certainly it would be an appropriate description of someone in the past.

PT: That's right.
TH: That I would retaliate with you? Could we look to this?

The therapist now emphasizes the irrational nature of the anxiety, thus informing her unconscious that he knows it comes from the past:

TH: Now could we look to see what evidence there has been that I would retaliate, or react with anger if you get angry with me?
PT: I have no evidence.
TH: So where does that come from? It is very important you look at it. So you say it comes from your head.

PT: That's right.

TH: Was there the thought also that I might terminate, or tell you, look, if you don't want it . . . did that thought pass through your head?

PT: It didn't pass through my head but it's maybe . . . I don't know.

TH: It is very important you examine that.

PT: Well yeah, maybe to some degree. It's something that passed through my head.

One of the fundamental principles of the technique is that the patient's whole psychic system is loosened by the direct experience of feelings about the therapist, of which a negative impulse is often the first component. These feelings are complex and they have their genetic roots in all the unresolved feelings and impulses in relation to the past. The patient's major unconscious anxiety has its links with repressed sadistic impulses as well as guilt-laden, grief-laden unconscious feelings in relation to the people in her past life orbit.

It is important to highlight that the challenging language such as crippling, in which many of the therapist's interventions are phrased, has come from patients themselves during the course of a large series of interviews over a span of 30 years.

Here it is worth anticipating; later in the interview it emerges that self-punishment in the form of crippling herself is a central part of her pathology. Not only this, but there is a link with the most important person in the patient's life, toward whom she felt the deepest guilt and remorse, who in the end had herself become crippled. This is why she reacts with anger every time the word is mentioned. We may now resume the interview.

Direct Experience of Anger in the Transference (Phase 5)

TH: What evidence is there that I intentionally want you to get angry? Because you are saying that I am dishonest, in a sense. If I do something intentionally to create a reaction in you then that becomes more dishonesty. So then you perceive me as a dishonest person, hmm?

PT: That's right.

TH: But what evidence have I given that I am intentionally doing something like that? Let's face it, you describe your life as paralyzed in many ways, I feel that your life is in some way crippled, okay? But now the issue is this: you are the master of your life.

PT: Right.

TH: Maybe you want to live in a crippled, paralyzed fashion. *(Addressing superego resistance.)*

PT: No.

TH: If you want to do it, so that is your life. But what I am saying is this: why does a young women of your age—and obviously you have potentiality, you have got yourself to college and so forth—want to carry on a life like this? *(Putting further pressure toward unconscious therapeutic alliance.)*

PT: Yeah.

TH: So where does the idea come from that I want intentionally to get you angry with me?

PT: That was the experience that I had last time I was here.

TH: You see, that is your perception of the situation, not that the situation is like that.

PT: That's right.

TH: Because you give me a single evidence.

PT: Wait, wait, wait, you're talking so much, though.

TH: How do you feel when I talk too much?

PT: *(Laughing)* You're getting on my nerves.

TH: My talking too much also gets on your nerves?

PT: Yeah.

TH: What else do you experience besides . . . ?

PT: I want to shrug you away. I want to say, stop it. Stop pushing me. Stop talking so much.

TH: How do you feel right now?

PT: Movemented.

There is a major change in her posture, her voice is loud, absence of tension in her vocal cords.

TH: So your position is no longer like that. Now it is like this, hmm? Which is more positive.

PT: That's right.

TH: Because this is a crippled position. The other one . . .

PT: That's right (laughing).

TH: You smile when I said that this is crippled.

PT: Right, it is.

TH: But you see it is very important that you look at it . . . One perception of me is that I would retaliate, okay? The other is that I would be dishonest in a sense. Of course later on we can look at it to see where this distorted perception of me comes from. Because I am sure if you examine it—you can laugh again—this is in operation in other relationships, because I cannot be an exception.

PT: Yeah.

TH: And if it is, then it is a fundamental job for us to examine it—unless you don't want to.

PT: Ohhh God, why do you . . . ? Yes! I want it. Yes, see I'm open. Okay that's what you want. Yes I want it. I want to examine my anger, my inability to express and feel it.

Sadness

Suddenly there is a major change in atmosphere:

TH: But I am sure it is not only anger, there are other things as well.
PT: I am sure there are too.
TH: How do you feel right now? Because one of the other things I feel—I might be wrong, I don't know—is that there are moments when there are waves of sadness coming. I see it in your eyes, but then you go dry. If you examine yourself, was there a moment that you had waves of sadness?
PT: I felt it more in my face, like a tightening here.
TH: How about your eyes?
PT: Throughout this, since I've arrived, yes.
TH: You try to control it, why?
PT: Because I feel that's another way of escaping.

Challenge to Resistance against Emotional Closeness in the Transference (Phase 3)

TH: Maybe it has to do with the issue of closeness with me. I have a feeling that you are terrified of closeness with me and you are putting a wall between you and me.
PT: Terrified?
TH: That I want to get to know you, I want to get to your intimate thoughts and feelings, but a part of you is very strongly fighting that.
PT: Yeah, because my feeling is, what gives you the right to be close to me?
TH: And that is very important that we look at it. What you say is what right has this stranger to pass the barrier and get to your intimate thoughts and feelings?
PT: That's right.
TH: So then we have a major obstacle between us, hmm?
PT: That's right.

Head-on Collision (Phase 4)

The therapist now embarks on a head-on collision with the resistance, speaking directly to the therapeutic alliance about the self-destructive consequences of maintaining her defense of distancing.

TH: But then as long as this barrier is there, this process is doomed to fail.
PT: Yes.
TH: Let's look at it.

One of the ways of dealing with major resistance is to look ahead in imagination to the end of the interview, and to face the patient with the disappointment that she will feel if she goes away having made the whole undertaking useless:

TH: It's very important you look at it, because as long as that wall, that barrier, is there and you don't want me to get to your intimate thoughts and feelings, then in a while when this session finishes, at the end of it, then when we say good-bye to each other, we will not have been able to understand the central core of your problem. You say good-bye to me and I say good-bye to you, you go on your own and I go. But you go on and carry on your crippled life—you carry your problems with you and carry on the miserable life that you have. I don't know, you have to decide, is it or isn't it? And then I will be useless to you.

PT: You're talking too much.

This is a defense of diversification, the therapist challenges it.

TH: Again that is another way of distancing.
PT: Is it really?
TH: Because I will be useless to you.

The resistance is swept aside in favor of the therapeutic alliance. The patient opens up an important issue contributing to her resistance in the transference.

The Issue of Control

PT: How can I feel that you want to get to know me if you're trying to overpower me? This is what I feel. You're trying to overpower me. You're trying to take control.
TH: So passing the wall becomes the issue of control, hmm?
PT: That's right.
TH: If I pass the wall and get to your intimate thoughts and feelings . . .
PT: Maybe I'll feel that you have more control and I don't like having less control.
TH: So that is another problem.
PT: That's right.
TH: So then let's see what you are going to do about it. Because, let's face it, if the distance remains there, if you don't want me to get to your intimate thoughts and feelings, I will be useless to you. It's as simple as that. But why does a young intelligent woman of your age want to do that?
PT: I don't want you to be useless to me.
TH: But it will happen if the wall is there, if you don't want me to get to your intimate thoughts and feelings, then I will be useless. Look, right now you have a lot of feeling. Tears are there but you are very strongly fighting them. Why?
PT: I'm not *(she smiles).*
TH: You are, with a smile. If you be honest with your feeling right now, if you really let your feelings come out what would you feel right now?

PT: Sad.

TH: And you don't want to share it with me.

PT: It's very painful. I don't understand you.

TH: I'm not sure it's that. You see, right now you are very sad and you don't want to let it go.

PT: I'm trying to let go.

TH: You want to control.

PT: But I'm afraid you're going to talk so much that you're not going to let me let it go.

In the following passage the therapist carefully avoids getting involved in what the patient is saying, and repeatedly confronts her with the central issue.

TH: Right now I am saying you are fighting the feeling. Let's look to your feelings.

PT: I feel very tight in my throat and I feel my eyes . . .

TH: You see, right now you talk, not to let the feeling come out. And I don't know why.

PT: Because I don't want you to come too close to me. I'm afraid of you in some way. I don't trust you.

Patient's tactical defense is swept aside.

TH: I'm not sure it is trust. It is tremendous conflict and fear, I don't know from where it comes. There is a tremendous fear of intimacy and closeness. Obviously it is sad.

PT: Somehow I'm afraid you'll make fun of me or something.

The patient's tactical defense is again swept aside.

TH: You see, these are all mechanisms you use to avoid your painful feelings. You know it well.

PT: *(Pause)* Maybe I don't believe that you can . . .

TH: Yeah, but right now you know that these are all mechanisms for fighting your very painful feelings.

PT: I can't go around crying in front of people every time they hurt me.

Direct Experience of Sadness, Breakthrough of Grief-Laden Unconscious Feelings (Phase 5)

TH: The issue really is this: I don't know what has happened in your life that you are so terrified of closeness. You want to keep all these painful feelings to yourself. You don't want me to get there.

There is a long pause. The patient is charged with feeling.

TH: You see, a while ago I was saying that you have a tremendous problem with the issue of intimacy and closeness.

PT: *(Whispering, hardly audible)* I keep people very far away.

TH: Far away, uh hmm. *(Pause)* Is it much more with men or women?

PT: *(She sighs deeply.)* I don't know. *(Hardly audible)* I don't know. I really don't know. Men have hurt me more, but I don't know if it's . . .

TH: So it has been more with men?

PT: Only because I've had a series of relationships with men that didn't work out.

TH: You mean a series of relationships with men that ended up in disappointment?

PT: Uh hmm. *(She is very sad, crying.)* The disappointment is so deep. *(She is very emotionally charged.)* Disillusionment is so deep that I wonder if I can ever love anyone.

TH: I don't know what has happened, but maybe a part of you has decided that you will never let any person get close to you again.

PT: *(Whispering)* I think so.

TH: What in a sense you have decided that you are going to live the rest of your life in a cave, so to say.

PT: Yeah. Do you have any kleenex?

TH: Conflict over control, conflict over closeness and intimacy. And hopefully you and I today will get to the core of your problem and get that into the open, so that you can see what it is. And we both can see where it originates and then a new avenue opens for you in life, hmm? And then there is a hope that, for the balance of your life—because you are very young now, you have a long way ahead—you can live the way you want to live rather than be affected by all these problems that you have. Then if we achieve that today, we can say good-bye to each other in a positive atmosphere. How do you feel toward me now?

PT: I feel better, but I can tell you honestly I think I'd feel differently if you were a woman . . .

This also is being used as a defense and must be challenged:

TH: But that doesn't solve the problem.

PT: No, but I have difficulty being close to you.

TH: I know, but we are here to solve the problem. You have been trying to avoid the problem. "If I was a woman"—still, avoidance. But avoidance doesn't solve the problem. You don't need me to expound on that. Running away, closing your eyes, facade, avoiding, doesn't solve it. We have to examine it. I am sure it is painful, but that is the only way we have, hmm?

PT: That's right.

At this point the therapist suggests having a five-minute break.

Now that the first breakthrough has been achieved the therapist embarks on fact-gathering. As always the aim is first to explore the patient's adult life and relationships. This will give him a picture of the disturbances that need to be explained, which will help to direct him in his later exploration of the past.

SUMMARY

In this chapter I have outlined the central dynamic sequence in the process of direct access to the unconscious and pointed out that the whole process can be divided into a series of phases, each consisting of a particular intervention with its corresponding response, and emphasized that these phases tend to overlap and proceed in a spiral rather than a straight line. The central dynamic sequence can be seen as a framework which the therapist can use as guide. The two major protocols, partial and major unlocking of the unconscious, were presented; and the trial therapy of a case, the "Fragile" Woman, was presented to demonstrate the technique of the major unlocking of the unconscious.

She entered the interview with a great deal of anxiety and in a state of transference resistance. The therapist for a moment bypassed the transference resistance and employed a set of interventions and came to the conclusion that there was no sign of a severely fragile ego and there is a major anxiety in relation to aggressive impulses. Then he quickly moved to pressure and challenge to the transference resistance and there was a head-on collision with the transference resistance. This finally led to a breakthrough of the aggressive impulse in the transference and the emergence of a deep sadness with a major communication from the unconscious therapeutic alliance.

REFERENCES

Davanloo, H. (1978). *Basic principles and techniques in short-term dynamic psychotherapy.* New York: Spectrum.

Davanloo, H. (1980). *Short-term dynamic psychotherapy.* New York: Jason Aronson.

Davanloo, H. (1984). Short-term dynamic psychotherapy. In *Comprehensive textbook of psychiatry* (4th ed., Chap. 29.11), H. Kaplan and B. Sadock (Eds.). Baltimore, MD: Williams & Wilkins.

Davanloo, H. (1986a). Intensive short-term dynamic psychotherapy with highly resistant patients I. Handling resistance. *Int. J. Short-Term Psycho., 1,* 107–133.

Davanloo, H. (1986b). Intensive short-term dynamic psychotherapy with highly resistant patients. II. The course of an interview after the initial breakthrough, *Int. J. Short-Term Psycho., 1,* 239–255.

Davanloo, H. (1987a). Intensive short-term dynamic psychotherapy with highly resistant depressed patients: Part I. Restructuring ego's regressive defenses. *Int. J. Short-Term Psycho.*, *2*, 99–132.

Davanloo, H. (1987b). Intensive short-term dynamic psychotherapy with highly resistant depressed patients: Part II. Royal road to the unconscious. *Int. J. Short-Term Psycho.*, *2*, 167–185.

Davanloo, H. (1987c). Clinical manifestations of superego pathology. Part I. *Int. J. Short-Term Psycho.*, *2*, 225–254.

Davanloo, H. (1987d). Clinical manifestations of superego pathology. Part II. *Int. J. Short-Term Psycho.*, *2*, 225–254.

Davanloo, H. (1988a). The technique of unlocking of the unconscious. Part I. *Int. J. Short-Term Psycho.*, *3*(2), 99–121.

Davanloo, H. (1988b). The technique of unlocking of the unconscious. Part II. *Int. J. Short-Term Psycho.*, *3*(2), 123–159.

15. The Interactional Dimension of Countertransference

Robert Langs

It is the basic purpose of this paper to outline, discuss, and synthesize a series of clinical postulates regarding countertransference, developed through an adaptational approach to this dimension of therapeutic and analytic relationships. These postulates are based on clinical observations and an extensive review of the psychoanalytic literature (Langs 1976a,c), and were shaped with a view toward enhancing our understanding of the treatment interaction and with some stress on their pertinence to analytic and therapeutic technique.[1] The present investigation of countertransference is somewhat different than the prior explorations I have undertaken (1974, 1976a,c), in that I shall focus here almost exclusively on the interactional aspects of countertransference and shall concentrate on recent conceptions developed largely since those earlier publications—some of which have not previously been considered at all, either by myself or by others. I shall adopt an approach that concentrates on the delineation, elaboration, and clinical illustration of these postulates and, while the ideas presented here have been contributed to significantly by earlier writers, I will not provide an historical survey since I have done so in an earlier work (1976c). Without further introduction, then, I shall turn now to the basic definitions that we will need in order to define and comprehend the interactional dimension of countertransference.

BASIC DEFINITIONS

I shall proceed in outline form, offering only the essentials (the interested reader may find the elaborating literature in Langs 1973a,b, 1974, 1975a,b,c, 1976a,c, 1978a,b).

1. *The bipersonal field* (Baranger and Baranger 1966, Langs 1976a,c) refers to the temporal-physical space within which the analytic interaction

Reprinted by permission of Jason Aronson, Inc. from *Countertransference*, L. Epstein and A. H. Feiner, eds., Northvale, 1979, pp. 71–103.

takes place. The patient is one term of the polarity; the analyst is the other. The field embodies both interactional and intrapsychic mechanisms, and every event within the field receives vectors from both participants. The field itself is defined by a framework—the ground rules of psychoanalysis—which not only delimits the field, but also, in a major way, contributes to the communicative properties of the field and to the analyst's hold of the patient and containment of his projective identification.

Communications within the field take place along an interface determined by inputs from both patient and analyst, and possessing a variety of characteristics, including, among others, psychopathology, depth, and stability. The major interactional mechanisms in the field are those of projective and introjective identification, although other interactional defenses, such as denial, splitting, the creation of bastions (split-off sectors of the field; see Baranger and Baranger 1966), and additional unconsciously shared forms of gratification and defense are also characteristic. The major intrapsychic defenses are those of repression, displacement, and the other well-known classically described mechanisms.

2. The investigation of the communicative medium provided by the frame of the field and the communicative mode of each participant is essential for an understanding of the analytic interaction and therapeutic work. The basic communications from each participant occur verbally and nonverbally, through words and actions serving a variety of meanings and functions. As a fundamental means of categorizing these communications, they can be classified as manifest content and as Type One and Type Two derivatives (Langs 1978a,b). The first term refers to the surface nature and meaning of a communication, while a Type One derivative constitutes a relatively available inference or latent theme extracted from the manifest content. In contrast, a Type Two derivative is organized around a specific *adaptive context*—the precipitant or instigator of the interactional and intrapsychic response—and entails definitive dynamic meanings and functions relevant to that context. Further, within a given bipersonal field, every communication is viewed as an interactional product, with inputs from both participants.

3. On this basis, we may identify three basic styles of communicating and three related forms of interactional field (Langs 1978a). The Type A style or field is characterized by the use of symbolic communications, and the bipersonal field itself becomes the realm of illusion and a transitional or play space. In general, the patient's associations can be organized around a series of specific adaptive contexts, yielding a series of indirect communications

that constitute Type Two derivatives. These latent contents and themes fall into the realm of unconscious fantasy, memory, and introject on the one hand, and unconscious perception on the other. For the development of a Type A field, both patient and analyst must be capable of tolerating and maintaining a secure framework; in addition, the analyst must have the ability to offer symbolic interpretations of the patient's communications.

The Type B field or style is one in which action, discharge, and the riddance of accretions of psychic disturbance is central. The primary mechanism in this field is that of projective identification and living (acting) out, and both language and behavior are utilized as means of discharge rather than as vehicles for symbolic understanding.

While the Type A and Type B fields are positively communicative, each in its own way, the essential characteristic of the Type C is the destruction of communication and meaning, and the use of falsifications and impervious barriers as the main interactional mode. Here, language is used as a defense against disturbed inner mental contents. The Type C field is static and empty, and is further characterized by the projective identification of both emptiness and nonmeaning, finding its only sense of meaning in these efforts to destroy communication, links, and meaning itself. While resistances in the Type A field are characterized by the availability of analyzable derivatives, and those in the Type B field are amenable to interpretation based on the defensive use of projective identification, defenses and resistances in the Type C field have no sense of depth and possess a persistent, amorphous, and empty quality.

4. Within the bipersonal field, the patient's relationship with the analyst has both transference and nontransference components. The former are essentially distorted and based on pathological, intrapsychic unconscious fantasies, memories, and introjects, while the latter are essentially nondistorted and based on valid unconscious perceptions and introjections of the analyst, his conscious and unconscious psychic state and communications, and his mode of interacting. Within the transference sphere, in addition to distortions based on displacements from past figures (genetic transference), there are additional distortions based on the patient's current intrapsychic state and use of interactional mechanisms (projective distortions). Further, nontransference, while valid in terms of the prevailing actualities of the therapeutic interaction, always includes important genetic components—though essentially in the form of the actual repetitions of past pathogenic interactions (for details, see Langs 1976c).

The analyst's relationship with the patient is similarly constituted in terms of countertransference and noncountertransference. The former entails all inappropriate and distorted reactions to the patient, whatever their source, and may be based on displacements from the past as well as on pathological projective and introjective mechanisms. Factors in countertransference-based responses range from the nature of a particular patient, the quality and contents of his communications, the meaning of analytic work for the analyst, and interactions with outside parties—other patients and others in the analyst's nonprofessional and professional life.

The noncountertransference sphere of the analyst's functioning entails his valid capacity to manage the framework, to understand the patient's symbolic communications and offer meaningful interpretations, and a basic ability to contain, metabolize, and interpret symbolically the patient's projective identifications. There are a wide range of additional aspects of the analyst's valid and noncountertransference-based functioning which will not be detailed here (see Langs 1976c).

THREE INTERACTIONAL POSTULATES REGARDING COUNTERTRANSFERENCE

Postulate 1: As a dimension of the bipersonal field, countertransference (as well as noncountertransference) is an interactional product with vectors from both patient and analyst.

Among the many implications of this generally accepted postulate, some of which have not been specifically identified and discussed in the literature, I will consider those most pertinent to psychoanalytic technique and to the identification and resolution of specific countertransference difficulties. In this context, it is well to be reminded that countertransference-based interventions and behaviors are often not recognized as such by the analyst, due largely to the fact that countertransference is itself rooted in unconscious fantasies, memories, introjects, and interactional mechanisms. The adaptive interactional approach to countertransference greatly facilitates their recognition and resolution.

This initial postulate implies that each countertransference-based response from the analyst has a specific and potentially identifiable adaptive context. While this stimulus may reside in the personal life of the analyst or in his work with another patient, it most often entails stimuli from the relationship with the patient at hand and is, as a rule, evoked by the communications from the patient. Any unusual feeling or fantasy within the analyst, any failure by the patient to confirm his interventions (whether interpretations or management of the framework), any unusual or persistent symptom or resistance in the patient, or any regressive episode in the course of an analysis should alert the analyst to the possible presence of countertransference factors.

Value of Interactional Approach. The interactional approach proves to be of special value in these pursuits in three important ways: (1) by establishing the finding that the patient's communications and symptoms may be significantly derived from the countertransferences of the analyst; (2) by indicating that through the process of introjective identification the patient becomes a mirror and container for the analyst, in the sense that the patient's communications will play back to the analyst the metabolized introjects derived from his countertransference-based interventions (and his valid, noncountertransference-based interventions as well); and (3) by directing the search for the form and meaning of countertransferences to the sequential interactions of each session.

If we consider these sequential clues first, we may recognize that the immediate precipitant for the countertransference-based reaction can be found in the material from the patient that precedes the erroneous intervention (inappropriate silences, incorrect verbalizations such as erroneous interpretations, and mismanagements of the framework). While there is often a broader context to the countertransference-based intervention in the ongoing relationship between the analyst and his patient, and while there may be, as I have noted, additional inputs derived from relationships outside of the immediate bipersonal field, clinical experience indicates that these immediate adaptive contexts provide extremely important organizing threads for the detection and comprehension of the underlying countertransference fantasies. When dealing with a countertransference-based positive intervention (as compared to silence, which I could consider a negative intervention), it is, of course, the last of the patient's associations that prompts the analyst's response. If this communication is viewed within the overall context of the patient's material, and understood in terms of manifest and latent content, and if all of this is addressed in interaction with the manifest and latent content of the analyst's erroneous intervention, the amalgam provides important and immediate clues as to the nature of the analyst's underlying difficulty.

The Interactional Sequence. Thus, the interactional sequence for a countertransference-based response is (1) adaptive context (especially the stimulus from the patient at hand), (2) the analyst's erroneous reaction (positive or negative intervention, whether interpretation or management of the frame), and (3) response by the patient and continued reaction by the analyst. If countertransferences are to be understood in depth, they must be organized around their specific adaptive contexts, so the analyst may understand himself in terms of Type Two derivatives, including both unconscious fantasies and perceptions. Without such an effort, he would be restricted to an awareness of the manifest content of his erroneous intervention or to readily available inferences—both fraught with possible further countertransference-based effects.

This sequence also implies that the analyst may recognize the presence of a countertransference difficulty at one of several junctures—as the patient is communicating disturbing material, while he is intervening, or after he has intervened—and that this recognition may be based either on his own subjective reactions or on subsequent communications from the patient. Much has already been written regarding subjective clues within the analyst who has a countertransference problem, while less consideration has been given to those leads available from the patient; let us now examine these latter more carefully.

The bipersonal field concept directs the analyst to the investigation of his countertransferences when any resistance, defense, symptom, or regression occurs within the patient or himself. Since the adaptational-interactional view considers all such occurrences as interactional products, it generates as a technical requisite the investigation of unconscious factors in both participants at such moments in therapy. As a rule, these disturbances, when they occur within the patient (to take that as our focus), will have unconscious communicative meaning. In the presence of a prevailing countertransference-based communication from the analyst, they will reflect the patient's introjective identification of this disturbance, his unconscious perceptions of its underlying basis, and his own realistic and fantasied metabolism of the introject. That patient's reactions to the disturbed intervention from the analyst may include exploitation, the creation of misalliances and bastions, and use of the intervention for the maintenance of his own neurosis (a term used here in its broadest sense), as well as unconscious efforts to detoxify the introject and cure the analyst.

In terms of the patient's associations and behaviors following an incorrect intervention, the interactional model directs us to the intervention itself as the adaptive context for the patient's subsequent association. In this way, the patient's material can, as a rule, be treated as Type Two derivatives in response to the particular adaptive context. I term these associations *commentaries* on the analyst's intervention, in that they contain both unconscious perceptions and unconscious fantasies.

Hierarchy of Tasks for the Analyst. It is here that we may identify a particular hierarchy of tasks for the analyst, based in part on the recognition that this discussion implies that the patient's association always take place along a *me-not-me interface* (Langs 1976c, 1978a) with continuous reference to self and analyst. Thus, valid technique calls for the monitoring of the material from the patient for conscious and unconscious communications related to the analyst before establishing those related to the patient; actually, the one cannot be identified without an understanding of the other. In addition, in both spheres—self and analyst—the analyst must determine the patient's valid perceptions, thoughts, and fantasies before identifying those that are distorted and inappropriate; here too, the identification of one relies on a comprehension of the other. Ultimately, of course, these determinations have as their most essential basis the analyst's self-knowledge, and especially his in-depth understanding of the conscious and unconscious meanings of his communications to the patient.

In the adaptive context, then, of the analyst's interventions, the patient's responsive associations are an amalgam of unconscious perceptions of the manifest and latent qualities of the intervention, on the one hand, and, on the other, their subsequent elaboration in terms of the patient's valid and distorted functioning. Thus, in addition to determining whether such associations truly validate the analyst's intervention by providing genuinely new material that reorganizes previously known clinical data (i.e., constitutes a *selected fact,* as Bion [1962] has termed it) and evidence for positive introjective identification, the analyst must also consider this material in terms of the patient's experience and introjection of his communication—valid and invalid. This introjective process takes place on the cognitive level as well as in terms of interactional mechanisms. The analyst must therefore be prepared to recognize that both cognitive-symbolic communications and projective identifications are contained in his interventions; in fact, he must be prepared to recognize his use of interventions as facades, falsifications, and barriers as well (see below).

This interactional approach enables the analyst to make full use of his patient's conscious and unconscious resources, and of the analysand as an unconscious teacher and therapist. The analytic bipersonal field is not, of course, designed primarily for such a use of the patient, but these occurrences are inevitable in every analysis, since countertransference can never be totally eliminated. In addition, in actuality, these experiences often have enormously therapeutic benefit for the patient (see Searles 1975), so long as the analyst has not deliberately misused the analysand in this regard, and is in addition capable of understanding and responding appropriately to the patient's curative efforts. In this respect, it is essential that the analyst make silent and unobtrusive use of his patient's introjection of his countertransference and of his additional therapeutic efforts on his behalf, responding without explicit acknowledgment and with implicit benefit. This latter implies the analyst's ability to follow the patient's leads and to benefit through efforts at self-analysis based on the patient's unconscious perceptions and the therapeutic endeavors; it also requires a capacity to actually rectify—correct or modify—any continued expression of the countertransference difficulty and to control most, if not all, subsequent possible expressions. In addition, it may entail the analyst's *implicit* acknowledgment of an error in technique and a full analysis of the patient's unconscious perceptions and other responses in terms that accept their validity—work that must in addition address itself eventually to the patient's subsequent distortions, and to the pathological misappropriations and responses to these countertransference-based difficulties within the analyst.

Postulate 2: The analyst's unconscious countertransference fantasies and interactional mechanisms will influence his three major functions vis-à-vis the patient: his management of the framework and capacity to hold the patient; his ability to contain and metabolize projective identifications; and his functioning as the interpreter of the patient's symbolic associations, projective identifications, and efforts to destroy meaning.

A complementary postulate would state that the analyst's countertransferences can be aroused by, and understood in terms of, not only the patient's associations and behaviors, but also in terms of the analyst's responses to the framework of the bipersonal field, and to the holding and containing capacities of the patient.

While some analysts, such as Reich (1960) and Greenson (1972), have questioned the invariable relationship between technical errors and countertransference, my own clinical observations clearly support such a thesis. However, virtually the entire classical psychoanalytic literature prior to my own writings (see especially 1975b,c, 1976a,c, 1978a) considered as the sole vehicle of countertransference expression the analyst's erroneous verbal interventions, especially his errors in interpreting. A number of Kleinian writers, especially Grinberg (1962) and Bion (1962, 1963, 1965) have also investigated countertransference influences on the analyst's management of projective identifications and on his containing functions. A full conceptualization of possible avenues of countertransference expression would include all these areas, as well as the analyst's management of the ground rules and his capacity to hold the patient.

As we have already seen in the discussion of the first postulate, the adaptational-interactional view helps to deepen and render more specific our understanding of the interplay between countertransference and the analyst's interpretive interventions. Not unexpectedly, it leads us to include missed interventions and inappropriate silences along with the expression of countertransference, and provides us extensive means for identifying, rectifying, and interpreting the patient's responses to these errors. Much of this has been discussed above, tends to be familiar territory for most analysts, and has been considered rather extensively in prior publications (see especially Langs 1976a,c); I will therefore restrict myself here to a consideration of those aspects of this postulate that have been relatively disregarded.

Management of Ground Rules. Perhaps the single most neglected arena for the expression of the analyst's countertransferences is that of his management of the ground rules—the framework of the bipersonal field. In part, because virtually every analyst has to this day been analyzed within a bipersonal field whose framework has been modified, the influence of countertransferences on the analyst's management functions has been virtually ignored by all. Nonetheless, I have garnered extensive evidence for the basic and necessary functions of a secure framework (Langs 1975c, 1976a, 1978a), demonstrating its importance in creating a therapeutic hold for the patient, in establishing the necessary boundaries between patient and analyst, and in affording the bipersonal field its essential open and symbolic communicative qualities.

However, the maintenance of a secure framework requires of the analyst a tolerance for his patient's therapeutic regression and related primitive communications, a renunciation of his pathological and countertransference-based needs for inappropriate gratification and defenses, and a capacity to tolerate his own limited regression and experiences of anxiety, which are inevitable under these conditions. Thus, because the management of the frame is so sensitively a function of the analyst's capacity to manage his own inner state, and to maintain his psychic balance, his handling of the framework is in part a direct reflection of the extent to which he has mastered his countertransferences. Further, because of the collective blind spots in this area and the sanction so implied, analysts will tend to monitor their verbal interventions for countertransference-based influences, while neglecting to do so in regard to their management of the frame. Clearly, any alternation in the framework can provide the analyst countertransference-based and inappropriate gratifications, as well as defenses and nonadaptive relief from anxiety and other symptoms; all possible deviations in the frame should therefore be explored for such factors (see Langs 1975c).

Three Types of Containing Pathology: Problems of Countertransference. Interactionally, one of the analyst's basic functions is to receive, contain, metabolize, and interpret the patient's projective identifications (interactional projections) and other interactional inputs. Due to underlying countertransferences, an analyst may be refractory to such containment and impervious to both the patient's communications and his interactional efforts. Much of this is based on what Bion (1962) has described as the container's dread of the contained, and which he has characterized as fears of denudation and destruction. An analyst may indeed dread the effects on himself of the patient's communications and projective identifications, and may respond on a countertransference basis with nonlistening, with distancing or breaking the link with the patient (Bion 1959), or by undertaking active efforts to modify the patient's disturbing communications and projections—often through the use of irrelevant questions, distinctly erroneous interpretations, and sudden alterations in the framework.

A second form of countertransference-based disturbance in the analyst's containing function may occur in regard to the processing or metabolizing of the patient's projective identifications (see Langs 1976b). Grinberg (1962) has termed this *projective counteridentification:* a situation in which the analyst receives a projective identification, remains unconscious of its contents, meaning, and effects, and inappropriately and unconsciously reprojects the pathological contents back into the patient—either directly or in some modified but detoxified form. Bion (1962) has termed this containing function the capacity for *reverie,* and has stressed the importance of the detoxification of dreaded and pathological projective identifications, leading to reprojections back into the patient that are far more benign than the original projective identifications. In my terms, this detoxification process entails the appropriate *metabolism* of a projective identification, the awareness in the analyst of its conscious and unconscious implications, and the symbolic interpretation of these contents in terms of defense-resistance functions and the revelation of pathological introjects. In this regard, countertransference-related anxieties, introjects, and disruptive fantasies may disturb the metabolizing and detoxifying process within the analyst, and may render him incapable of becoming aware of the nature of the patient's projective identifications and unable to interpret them. Under these conditions, he will, as a rule, pathologically metabolize the introject in terms of his own inner disturbance, and reproject into the patient—through verbal interventions and mismanagement of the framework—a more terrifying and pathological projective identification than that which orginated from the analysand.

A third type of containing pathology entails what I have described as a pathological need for introjective identifications—a countertransference-based need to inappropriately and excessively contain pathological introjects (Langs 1976a,b). This tends to be expressed through provocative interventions—whether interpretive or in respect to the frame—that are unconsciously designed as intrusive projective identifications into the patient, intended to evoke responsive pathological projective identifications from the analysand. These analysts have a hunger for pathological expressions from their patients, and find many means of inappropriately disturbing their patients and generating ill-timed pathological projective identifications.

The Analytic Bipersonal Field. The analytic bipersonal field is designed for the cure of the patient, and for the analytic resolution, through cognitive insight and implicit positive introjective identifications, of his psychopathology. It has proved difficult for analysts to accept that a valid and secondary function of the same bipersonal field—valid only so long as it is, indeed, secondary—is that of the analytic resolution of more restricted aspects of the analyst's psychopathology. This idea is often misunderstood to imply a belief in the use of the patient and the analytic situation as a primary vehicle for the cure of the analyst. Despite explicit disavowal of such intentions, the recognition that this will inevitably be a second-order phenomenon is viewed as exploitation of the patient, rather than as a relatively silent and actually indispensable benefit that will accrue to the well-functioning analyst. In the course of overcoming the many resistances against accepting this postulate—more precisely, a clinical observation—it has become evident that this attribute is an essential component of the bipersonal field, and that it is unlikely that the analyst could function adequately in its absence. Without it, it would be virtually impossible for him to master the inevitable anxieties and disturbances that will occur within him, as interactional products, in the course of his analytic work with each patient. Their inevitable presence has not only a potential therapeutic effect on his behalf, but also renders him a far more effective analyst for his patients.

The basic framework—the ground rules—of the psychoanalytic situation provides a hold, appropriate barriers, and the necessary communicative medium for analyst as well as patient. This hold affords him a valuable and appropriate sense of safety, a means of defining his role vis-à-vis the patient, assistance in managing his inappropriate impulses and fantasies toward the patient (his countertransferences), and insures the possibility of his use of language for symbolic interpretations (it is therefore essential to his interpretive capacities).

Just as certain aspects of the analyst's behavior and stance are essential dimensions of the framework, the patient too offers a hold to the analyst. Such factors as the regularity of his attendance at sessions, his being on time, his payment of the fee, his complying with the fundamental rule of free association, his listening to and working over the analyst's interpretations, and his own adherence to the ground rules and boundaries of the analytic relationship contribute to a holding effect experienced by the analyst. Further, the patient will inevitably serve as a container for the analyst's projective identifications—both pathological and nonpathological—a function through which, once again, the analyst may implicitly benefit.

As for the influence of countertransference in these areas, these may derive from undue or pathological (instinctualized: aggressivized or sexualized) holding needs, and an unconscious fear of, or need to repudiate, the patient's hold, a dread of the patient as container, and an excessive need to utilize the patient's containing capacities. These countertransference influences are manifested through the analyst's mismanagement of the frame, his erroneous interventions, his failures to intervene, and, overall, through conscious and unconscious deviations in the analyst's central commitment to the therapeutic needs of the patient. The analyst who inordinately requires a rigid and unmodified frame will be intolerant of his patient's alterations of that frame; these may take the form of latenesses, missed sessions, necessary requests to change the time of an hour because of changed life circumstances, unnecessary requests for such changes in schedule, and a variety of gross and subtle efforts to alter the basic ground rules of analysis—such as efforts to engage the analyst in conversation after an hour.

It is my empirically derived conclusion (Langs 1975c, 1976a,c) that it is the analyst's main responsibility to maintain, to the extent feasible, the framework intact in the face of all inappropriate efforts at deviation. I am therefore in no way advocating conscious—or unconscious—participation in inappropriate modifications of the frame. I wish to stress, however, that analysts with pathological needs for a rigid frame—in contrast to the necessary rigorous frame (Sandler, in Langs et al., in press)—will have difficulty in recognizing those rare valid indications for an alteration in the framework (e.g., a suicidal emergency), a change that is in essence a revised version of the basic framework without its destruction or defective reconstitution. In addition, such an analyst will have a great deal of difficulty in dealing with his patient's efforts to modify the framework and in recognizing such endeavors as a crucial adaptive context for the organization of the analysand's subsequent material. He also will have major problems in understanding the unconscious implications of these intended or actual alterations in the frame, and in carrying out effective, relevant analytic work. Further, he will dread those interpretations to his patient that might generate moments of hostility and rejection, and which might unconsciously prompt the patient to modify in some way his usual, implicit hold of the analyst.

The Pathological Container. Those analysts for whom the patient's inevitable hold generates a threat, whether related to fears of intimacy, instinctualization of the patient's holding capacities in terms of seductive and aggressive threats, or the dread of the necessary and therapeutic regression evoked by such a hold, unconsciously will make efforts to disturb the patient's holding capacities. It seems evident that the patient derives a degree of implicit and necessary gratification in regard to his capacity to safely hold the analyst, a satisfaction that is not unlike those derived from his unconscious curative efforts on the analyst's behalf (Searles 1965, 1975, Langs 1975b, 1976a,c). Thus, the repudiation on any level of the patient's appropriate holding capacities not only generates active countertransference-based inputs into the bipersonal field, but also denies the patient a form of growth-promoting gratification that forms an important complementary means of achieving adaptive structural change, in addition to the more generally recognized means derived from affect-laden insights and inherent positive introjective identifications. It is evident too that the analyst's need to repudiate the patient's appropriate hold will prompt him to generate interventions and mismanagements of the framework designed unconsciously to disturb that holding function, create artificial and undue distance, and erect pathological and inappropriate barriers between himself and the patient.

Every analyst at some time in the course of an analytic experience, and a number of analysts in the course of much of their work with all of their patients, will be burdened by countertransference pressures that prompt the inappropriate use of the patient as what I have termed a *pathological container* for his own disturbed inner contents (Langs 1976a). At such junctures, the analyst's interventions are not primarily designed for the meaningful insight of the patient and for the appropriate maintenance of the framework, but instead unconsciously function as efforts at projective identification as a means of placing into the patient the analyst's burdensome psychopathology and inappropriate defensive needs. And while, as I have mentioned above, the patient can indeed accrue adaptive benefit from his own unconscious capacities to function as a pathological container for the analyst's projective identification and from his curative efforts on the analyst's behalf, such gains are dangerously intermixed with the destructive aspects of such interactions. These include the overburdening of the patient with the analyst's pathology to a degree that evokes a pathological regression that not only will be difficult to manage and interpret, but also may be essentially misunderstood by the analyst who has unconsciously evoked the regressive process and who maintains his unconscious disturbed needs for the patient's containing ability. Failures by the patient to contain the analyst's pathological projective identifications, and to metabolize them, however unconsciously, toward insights for the analyst, will be unconsciously resented by the analyst, and will considerably complicate the analytic interaction. The influence on the patient of the pathological introjects generated by the analyst also may be quite destructive, and may in a major way reinforce the patient's own pathological introjects and defenses. In large measure, such an interaction may constitute the repetition of an important past pathogenic interaction which helped to generate the patient's emotional problems in his formative years.

On the other hand, the analyst may dread any even momentary and limited use of the patient as a container—not only for his pathological projective identifications, but for his valid interventions as well. Under these conditions he will experience an extreme constriction in his capacity to interpret to the patient and excessive anxiety in communicating freely to him, however consciously these interventions are founded on a wish to be appropriately helpful. Often, the dread of containing the patient's projective identifications is based on conscious and unconscious fears of being driven crazy by the patient, and related fears of psychic disintegration or loss of control; fears of similar effects on the patient may inhibit the analyst's necessary projective communications to the analysand.

Postulate 3: Countertransferences have a significant influence on the communicative properties of the bipersonal field, and on both the analyst's and the patient's style of communicating.

It is evident that the communicative style of the analyst (and of the bipersonal field of which he is a part) is a function of a wide range of factors, the most immediately obvious being inborn tendencies; acute and cumulative genetic experiences; personality and character structure; ego resources; ego dysfunctions; intrapsychic conflicts; unconscious fantasies, memories, and introjects; and the overall extent of emotional health or psychopathology. The focus here on the influence of countertransference is, then, an attempt to delineate simply one vector among many that coalesce to effect a particular communicative style and field.

Ideal Model of Communication: Type A. Initial clinical evidence suggests that the ideal analyst basically employs the Type A mode of communication, with its essential symbolic qualities, and that he has a capacity to manage the framework of the analytic situation in order to create with the patient a potential field for a Type A communicative interaction. Such an analyst would undoubtedly, from time to time, and based on many factors, momentarily shift to the Type B, action-discharge mode of communication and to the Type C, barrier-negation mode. He would, however, through his own awareness and through communications from his patient, be capable of recognizing these shifts in communicative style, of self-analyzing their underlying basis, of rectifying their influence on the patient and the therapeutic bipersonal field, and of interpreting to the patient his conscious and unconscious perceptions of this communicative shift and its unconscious meanings and functions.

Type B Mode. In contrast to the Type A therapist, the Type B therapist experiences repeated difficulty in deriving symbolic formulations of his patient's associations and in generating symbolic interpretations. While his conscious intentions may well be to offer such interventions—there is considerable lack of insight within analysts in regard to their communicative mode—his use of language will be unconsciously aimed at projective identification into the patient and internal relief-producing discharge. While at times patients may undoubtedly derive some type of symptom relief from such therapeutic interactions—based primarily on relatively benign projective identifications from the analyst and on positive self-feelings derived from unconscious curative efforts and containing responses to his pathology—such gains are not embedded in valid cognitive insights and modulating, positive introjective identifications. As a result, they are quite vulnerable to regression and are without the necessary substantial foundation characteristic of lasting adaptive structural change. In addition to their use of verbal interventions that function interactionally as pathological projective identifications, these analysts are quite prone to unneeded modifications of the framework which similarly serve their needs for pathological projective identification, action, and discharge. Elsewhere (Langs 1976a,c) I have designated as *misalliance and framework cures* the noninsightful, unstable symptom relief, in either patient or analyst, that may be derived in a Type B communicative field.

Type C Mode. The analyst who is prone to a Type C communicative style will seldom be capable of a truly symbolic interpretation. His verbal interventions make use of language not primarily as communication, but as a form of noncommunication and as an effort to destroy meaning. These analysts make extensive use of the psychoanalytic cliché and, unconsciously, their interventions and mismanagements of the framework are designed to destroy the communicative qualities of the bipersonal field and to render it frozen and static. Based on the massive defensive barriers and falsifications offered by these analysts, patients will from time to time experience symptom relief through reinforcement of their own Type C communicative style or through the development of impermeable defensive barriers that momentarily serve as a protection against disruptive underlying contents—fantasies, memories, and introjects. This type of *misalliance cure* (Langs 1975b, 1976a,c) may well account for a large percentage of symptom relief among present-day psychotherapeutic and psychoanalytic patients, and within their therapists and analysts as well.

The Type A therapist will, of course, tend to be rather comfortable with a Type A patient, and will be capable of interpreting his communications. Countertransference-based anxieties may occur because of the regressive pressures that he experiences in a Type A field and, in addition, will arise when the communications from the Type A patient touch upon areas of continued vulnerability. With a Type B patient, he will be capable of containing, metabolizing, and interpreting his patient's projective identifications, though countertransference difficulties may intrude when these projective identifications are massive or touch upon areas of excessive sensitivity. Some Type A analysts experience discomfort with the action-prone, projectively identifying Type B patient, and will experience difficulties in containing, metabolizing, and interpreting their interactional projections.

A Type C patient may be quite boring to the Type A analyst, who will consciously and unconsciously experience the envy, destruction of meaning, and attack on the analyst's ability to think and formulate that is characteristic of these patients. The Type A analyst may be vulnerable to these qualities of the negative projective identifications of these patients, and he may also have difficulty in tolerating their use of massive, impenetrable, and uninterpretable defensive barriers. Still, he is in the best position to identify the qualities of a Type C communicative style and to patiently interpret the primary defensive aspects. In addition, he is best prepared to tolerate, contain, and interpret the underlying psychotic core of these patients.

While clinical evidence indicates that it is possible to conduct a successful analysis with a Type B or Type C patient (Langs 1978a), it appears likely that the reverse is not true: Type B and Type C analysts cannot be expected to generate bipersonal fields characterized by an openness of communication, the use of symbolic language, the rendering of symbolic interpretations that lead to cognitive insight and mastery, and the interactional experience of positive projective and introjective identifications—all culminating in adaptive structural change and growth for the patient. While, as I have noted above, Type B and Type C analysts may indeed afford their patients periods of symptom relief, and while these may on occasion structuralize and lead to the disappearance of symptoms, the underlying basis for these symptomatic changes are infused with pathological mechanisms and are quite vulnerable to regressive pressures. There can be no substitute for a personal analysis and for the self-analytic efforts designed to master a given analyst's propensities for the Type B and Type C communicative modes.

In concluding this delineation of interactional postulates related to countertransference, two points implicit to this discussion deserve to be specified. First, in virtually every countertransference-based intervention there is a nucleus of constructive intention and effect. While in general, this kernel of valid effort is by no means sufficient to compensate for the hurt and damage done by a countertransference-based intervention—effects that may range from the relatively modifiable to the quite permanent—this positive nucleus often can be used as a center of constructive therapeutic work during the therapeutic interludes evoked by the consequences of an unconscious countertransference fantasy or introject. Second, it follows from this observation, and from more general clinical impressions, that considerable insightful analytic work can prevail throughout the rectification-analysis phase of such countertransference-dominated interludes. Thus, we must maintain a balanced view of the effects of the analyst's countertransferences: to some degree, they damage the patient and reinforce his neurosis (a term I again use here in its broadest sense), and thereby perpetuate or even intensify his psychopathology; in addition, however, so long as the countertransference-based effects are recognized, rectified, and fully analyzed with the patient—and of course, subjected to self-analysis by the analyst—these experiences also can provide extremely moving, insightful, positive introjective moments for both patient and analyst.

CLINICAL VIGNETTE

I will now present a single condensed vignette as a means of illustrating these postulates. Because of my commitment to total confidentiality regarding my direct work with patients, this material will be drawn from a supervisory seminar. While this approach is somewhat limiting in the area of countertransference, the interested reader will find additional data in several recent publications (Langs 1976a,b, 1978a); most important, he should have ample opportunity to clinically document these postulates in his own therapeutic endeavors.

Mr. A. was married, in his mid-thirties, depressed, and afraid of growing old and dying. Early in his analysis, during sessions in which his analyst took notes and intervened largely in terms of questions and reflections of the patient's anxiety about initiating treatment, the patient seemed concerned with a certain deadness in the analytic situation: it was, he said, like talking into a tape recorder. He spoke a great deal of tennis, of the homosexual discussions of his closest male friend, and of his fears of divorce, despite feelings that his marriage was killing him. His wife, he said, often loses control and acts crazy; she is overdependent on him. He also expressed wishes that he could invent a machine that could do psychoanalysis. He spoke of friends who fared poorly in analysis, and the analyst suggested that the patient had doubts about his own treatment. The patient disagreed, but said, however, that he wanted it to be quiet and peaceful, like smoking pot. He was not afraid of talking about homosexuals, though he felt that a physician who worked for him had many such fears.

In the next session, he reported a dream in which he found himself in bed with two women. Earlier that day, he had lingered at his tennis club after one of the members had died of a heart attack or sudden stroke. Mr. A. had fantasies of dropping dead on the tennis court, but spoke instead of feeling quite alive and interested in some medically related research in which he and a male friend were engaged.

The analyst asked the patient how he felt in the dream and inquired about other details. The twosome reminded the patient of a harem and of how he often thinks of other women during intercourse with his wife. He thought of a madam in a movie who had been destructive toward the girls who worked for her, and added that he never understood women and feared them. Further questions along these lines by the analyst led to additional allusions to discussions with friends about homosexuality and to curiosity about what was going on in the analyst's mind. When he plays tennis, the patient said, he thinks of nothing—his mind is blank. The analyst pointed out that the patient seemed frightened of his thoughts concerning homosexuality, but that having two women at one time could hardly be called "homosexual." In response, Mr. A. wondered why he comes to analysis at all. When his friends told him that homosexuals hate women, he panicked; these women were his slaves. He spoke of his hatred for his mother and of his close relationship with a research physician, and wondered what he saw in him; he was always involved with other men; it would be awful to be homosexual.

In the next hour, Mr. A. reported a dream of being late for his session. He was standing outside his analyst's office. The analyst came out to move his car and everybody started to laugh. His tire hit a rock, which then hit a taxicab and disabled it. A black woman got out of the cab and called the analyst crazy; he then pushed the cab around because it couldn't go. In associating, the patient alluded to the previous session and how analysis was a dangerous field because the wrong people can influence you. He feels constricted in what he says while on the couch. The dream followed tennis. He can't be close with anyone; he fights with his wife; everything he does brings him unhappiness.

The analyst asked a series of questions related to the manifest dream, and the patient spoke of how his friends and father think that he is crazy for coming to analysis, though in the dream people are calling the analyst crazy. His father accuses him of trying new things and dropping them. After some rumination, the patient spoke of feeling constricted in the sessions and of possible envy of the analyst; he had to arrange his life in keeping with the analyst's schedule. The analyst responded that the patient skips out in the dream, but the patient rejoined that it was the analyst who had been late— not he. He said he recognized that he is not the analyst's only patient and that the analyst's life does not center around him, as is true for himself in relation to the analyst. If he missed an appointment, he mused, would the analyst lie down? That would be reversing their roles and would make the analyst the crazy one. The analyst responded that the patient seemed afraid of being laughed at, and the patient agreed, suggesting again that the whole thing was a big reversal. The analyst emphasized again that the dream reflected the patient's fears of being laughed at, criticized, and going crazy.

The patient was late for the next session and spoke of a friend who had become a college professor; the patient felt guilty that he had not taken the right path for his own life. There were further references to being crazy, to being in analysis, and to the static qualities of his marriage. The research center at which the patient had done his postgraduate work was probably going to close because it could not get enough funds or students. Many of the staff had died, and the patient spoke of a fear of cancer that he had felt since beginning his analysis. He had had gastrointestinal symptoms; his mother was always preoccupied with gynecological problems; and at his engagement party he had suffered food poisoning. When his father had had his recent surgery, the patient had experienced an intense fear of dying. His father was seldom available when Mr. A. was a child and would never play tennis with him. Mr. A. recalled several accidents in his childhood, and spoke considerably of his father's disinterest, coldness, and lack of care; if he had been different, the patient would have realized his potential far more than he had. His mother, on the other hand, would get hysterical to the point that no one could talk to her; she was only concerned when he was hurt.

At this point, the analyst suggested that the patient write a short biography of himself for the analyst. Without responding directly, the patient continued to associate: he could always make his mother cry and yet she never hated him as did his father, who held grudges.

In the next hour the patient reported that he had not written the biography; he hadn't had time. He spoke of his research physician friend who had come to Mr. A.'s office to get some downers (sleeping pills) that the patient kept on hand. This doctor was a man worried about aging, and yet Mr. A. still idealized him. He was, however, beginning to see new things and maybe this doctor friend was becoming more human. He felt at any rate that he was more honest with himself than this other man was, and Mr. A. was thinking of leaving the area. He wondered if he should get a nursemaid for his infant daughter and spoke again of his tennis club. He wished his wife would be more aggressive and wondered how women ever develop into good mothers. If he left her, he said, she'd fall apart, and all the time he spends with his men friends interferes with his love for her. So much of this had happened since he started analysis, and it came up too because he'd been talking to his physician friend about that analytic jargon about homosexuality and castration anxiety. His friend felt that analysis is actually insignificant and that one day Mr. A. would have a gnawing pain somewhere, and they'd open him up and find something that would mean that everything would soon be over. Mr. A. would sometimes think about childhood and sex, but not about his parents in that respect. He said he felt he should have read more before he came into analysis, and here the analyst noted that the patient seemed to be looking for some kind of guidelines. The patient said that analysis is like an examination, and he spoke of his secret purchase of nudist magazines. His parents never talked about sex. He had his first sexual relations quite late in life; it was a difficult experience and he had trouble getting an erection and had considered turning on with some kind of drug.

The Patient's Unconscious Perceptions. I will focus here solely on those aspects of this material that are pertinent to this discussion. The early fragments of this material are in part an unconscious response to the analyst's note-taking and questions—nonanalytic work with manifest contents. At the time this material was presented, the supervisee indicated some sense of confusion with this patient and stated that the note-taking was an effort to get a better idea about what was going on in this analysis; it was also based on a wish to discuss this case with colleagues. The patient's unconscious perceptions and experiences of the note-taking serve us well in attempting to define its unconscious implications, especially those related to the analyst's countertransferences: the analyst is not alive, but a tape recorder and analytic machine; his wife loses control and acts crazy; craziness is connected with homosexuality; his wife is excessively dependent; and there is worry about a physician who worked for the patient.

I will take this as sufficient commentary on the note-taking, and will not attempt to trace out its implications in the additional clinical material. We can therefore pause here and suggest that the note-taking did indeed serve as a significant adaptive context for the patient's associations. It is a meaningful organizer of these communications from the patient, which may be viewed as symbolic in nature and largely in terms of Type Two derivatives: disguised unconscious perceptions of, and fantasies about, the analyst. Much of this falls into the realm of unconscious perceptiveness, and conveys possibly valid unconscious fears, motives, and needs within the analyst that have prompted him to take notes—motives of which the analyst was largely unaware, if we are to take his justifications as reflecting the extent of his insight into himself. It would be difficult here to identify and establish the patient's own unconscious homosexual anxieties and fantasies, fears of losing control and going crazy, and needs for mechanical protective devices, since he can justifiably project and conceal them within the analyst's own evidently similar anxieties, efforts at inappropriate gratification, and pathological defenses, expressed, however unconsciously, through the note-taking.

The Patient's Communicative Mode. In terms of the postulates developed here, I also would suggest that this patient is making extensive efforts at Type A communication and toward the development of a Type A bipersonal field. The analyst, for his part, both through the alteration in the framework reflected in his note-taking and through his use of noninterpretive interventions—questions directed at the surface of the patient's associations—is utilizing a Type C mode of communication and is endeavoring to create a static, surface-oriented, falsifying communicative field. While there are, in this material, occasional efforts by the analyst at projective identification which I will soon consider, many of his interactional projections are attempts to place a sense of emptiness and void into the patient, and to develop impenetrable, clichéd defenses—the negative type of projective identification characteristic of the Type C field. The main hypothesis, then, is to the effect that the note-taking and the surface-oriented interventions are unconsciously designed by this analyst to satisfy his own needs for a Type C barrier and, actually, to destroy the patient's openness to symbolic communication—to the expression of anxiety-provoking contents that are too disturbing for this analyst.

This hypothesis is supported by the patient's material, and while under other conditions these associations might well reflect the patient's own need for a Type C field, here the data suggest that this is not at all the case: the patient seems to be making repeated efforts at Type A communication, and his allusions to Type C mechanisms appear to be based on introjective identifications with the analyst.

The patient's associations, then, support the formulation that the note-taking and questioning unconsciously reflect impairments in the analyst's capacity to safely hold the patient and to contain the patient's projective identifications. The analyst's behaviors also convey his inappropriate needs to be held by the patient and for the patient to contain his anxieties—implications to which the patient is quite sensitive. On a communicative level, these interventions reflect an unconscious effort by the analyst to modify this potential Type A field into a Type C field in which he would feel better held and safer, especially in regard to disturbing communications and projective identifications from the patient.

The very act of writing down every word from the patient, with its striking containing and incorporative qualities, reflects a dread of actually containing in an affective way the patient's projected contents and a distinct incapacity to metabolize them toward interpretation. Instead, much as the patient unconsciously perceives the therapist's interventions—in respect to the frame and verbally—the note-taking is an effort to deaden the analytic situation, to make it mechanical, and to render it static. The mention of the tape recorder, and the later reference to a psychoanalytic machine, are metaphors of the analyst's containing functions rendered inanimate, probably because of inordinate fears of the patient's projective identifications—the container's fear of the contained (Bion 1962). To state this another way, in terms of the patient's unconscious perceptions and Type Two derivative communications, the therapist fears being driven crazy by his patient and his material, and attempts a Type C mode of expression and set of defenses in a massive effort to seal off this potential craziness and to prevent the contained contents from destroying him—a formulation quite in keeping with an earlier delineation of the Type C field and its function (Langs 1978a).

Among these terrifying contents and projective identifications, those related to latent homosexual themes, uncontrolled destructiveness, and annihilation seem most prominent. While, as I pointed out earlier, the patient may well have intense anxieties in each of these areas, for the moment these formulations apply very directly to the analyst. These countertransferences and their manifestations must be rectified in actuality, and the patient's responses to them analyzed, before the latter's own disturbances could surface in derivative and analyzable form in this bipersonal field. The patient himself refers to the conditions of this field, in which the communicative interface, and the elements of psychopathology it contains, has shifted toward the analyst, by referring to efforts to put himself in the analyst's shoes and the reference to role reversal. The analyst's unneeded deviations in the frame and inappropriate interventions unconsciously express his countertransferences and his wish to have the relevant contents contained by the patient and in a sense, therapeutically modified.

The Psychoanalytic Cliché. In this context, the analyst's intervention that the patient seemed to have many doubts about treatment may be seen as what I have termed a *psychoanalytic cliché*—a psychoanalytically derived generalization based on manifest content or Type One derivatives that primarily serves to destroy the true underlying meaning of the patient's communications, and to substitute a defensive falsification (Bion 1965, Langs 1978a). The patient's response to this intervention, in which he referred to feeling peaceful when he smoked pot, reflects again the unconscious obliterating qualities of the analyst's interventions—a characteristic of almost all the interventions described in this vignette—and suggest in addition that the patient's own propensities toward the Type C mode are being intensified in this therapeutic interaction. The patient rather wisely concludes this hour with a further allusion to the underlying homosexual anxieties unconsciously shared by both himself and the analyst.

In a general way, the analyst confirmed aspects of this formulation in indicating that he was having a difficult time understanding the patient's material and that he was feeling somewhat anxious about the patient's pathology and the initial course of this analysis. These conscious feelings and thoughts are related to the analyst's difficulty in holding this patient and in containing his projective identifications; they also suggest a countertransference difficulty related to the patient's hold of the analyst. In some way, this patient's material and reactions were not providing the analyst a sense of safety. But rather than tracing out the sources of the analyst's discomfort, he turned to note-taking as a means of artificially and mechanically (how well the patient senses this!) providing himself with a holding device and a containing substitute that will protect him from the postulated dreaded inner destruction—denudation and annihilation, as Bion (1962) terms it.

The Framework Cure. In addition, it may well be that the analyst's sense of dissatisfaction regarding the hold that he is experiencing in this analytic interaction has been intensified, rather than reduced, by his own alteration in the framework: his note-taking. Unconsciously, analysts tend to have anxieties in regard to their need to take notes, their anticipation of presenting such material to colleagues and exposing their vulnerabilities, and their use of what I have termed *framework cures* (Langs 1975c, 1976a,c) to resolve underlying countertransference problems. The note-taking itself is often distracting. The entire constellation, conscious and unconscious, actually disrupts the analyst's sense of security rather than enhancing it.

Impaired Holding. In evaluating the next hour, it would appear that in addition to continuous specific precipitants (the analyst's note-taking and erroneous interventions—questions and generalizations) there was a specific and related adaptive context in the patient's outside life: the death of a member of his tennis club. This day residue can be readily related not only to the patient's fears of death, but also to his unconscious perception of similar anxieties in the analyst—based on earlier material not presented here. However, in the actual session, these day residues were not integrated with the dream, which appears to have been a response to these precipitants; instead the analyst chose to focus on the manifest content of the dream and on its postulated role as a defense against homosexual fantasies and anxieties.

Keeping to ideas relevant to this presentation, it would appear that interventions of this kind, offered without a specific adaptive context and in terms of manifest content and Type One derivatives—the direct reading of a manifest dream and limited associations for latent content, rather than the use of an adaptive context to generate dynamically meaningful Type Two derivatives—characteristically serve to reinforce the Type C, falsified, and static qualities of the bipersonal field. As this session illustrates, such interventions almost always are designed to avoid a specific adaptive context which connects on some level to the patient's relationship with the analyst, and usually they are designed to cover over the patient's unconscious perceptions of the analyst's countertransference-based interventions. This approach facilitates an emphasis on the patient's pathology, and on his unconscious fantasies rather than his unconscious perceptions, and often deals with anxieties extraneous to the analytic relationship; it is a major form of defensiveness in respect to the influence of the analyst's countertransferences on the analytic interaction, the bipersonal field in which it occurs, and the analysand.

Interventions of this type are experienced by patients in terms of an impaired sense of holding, and especially as a reflection of the analyst's refractoriness in regard to his containing functions. Here, the unconscious communication from the analyst is to the effect that death, and especially sudden death, is to be denied, rendered nonexistent, and split off into a bastion of the bipersonal field (Baranger and Baranger 1966). A more general and widespread effort at obliteration may follow, creating a Type C field.

To some extent, these hypotheses are supported by the patient's response to the analyst's general interpretation of the patient's concerns about homosexuality and the dream of the two women as defensive in this regard. The patient rightly wonders why he comes to analysis at all, implying that if important meanings are to be destroyed in the analytic bipersonal field, effective analytic work will be impossible. There are also further indications of his doubts regarding the analyst's capacity to contain, manage the frame, and interpret, and, in respect to his stress on underlying homosexual anxieties, it might be asked whether these are primarily the analyst's concerns, and whether as such they serve as a deflection from more disturbing worries.

In the following hour, the patient had a dream that he immediately linked to the previous session. In terms of the patient's associations, it alludes to the analyst's craziness and his fear of doing damage—and by implication, of being damaged. The patient comments on the dangers of being an analyst, a point quite pertinent to the present discussion. He also describes his sense of constriction in the sessions, conveying both the extent to which the Type C mode is being imposed upon him and his unconscious perceptions of the analyst's own needs to constrict. It is then that the patient refers to his envy of the analyst and his security. On one level, this alludes to the analyst's envy of the patient, who feels secure enough to communicate his unconscious fantasies, introjects, memories, and anxieties—a communicative mode that is quite difficult or perhaps even impossible for this analyst.

It is also noteworthy that when the analyst attempts to suggest that the dream reflects the patient's wish to leave analysis, the patient points out that it is the analyst who had the problem in the dream—a formulation in keeping with the assessment of this material being offered here. It is in this context that the patient implies the projection into himself by the analyst of the wish that patient become therapist in this bipersonal field—the reversal of roles. The analyst's rejoinder is to emphasize the patient's paranoid feelings and anxieties, partially, it seems, to deny his own concerns and partially to projectively identify them into the patient as well.

In the next hour, the patient was late and the analyst felt concerned about the course of the analysis. Patients frequently respond to failures in the analyst's holding, containing, and interpretive capacities with disruptions in the framework that impart to the analyst a sense of being held poorly and a related sense of disturbance.

Container's Fear of the Contained. The hour itself begins with direct and indirect allusions to having made a mistake in entering analysis. The patient then returns to the theme of death and his own fear of cancer—an image that would suggest, in the context of this discussion, both the patient's dread of containing the analyst's pathological projective identifications and the analyst's comparable fear. It is a metaphor of the container's fear of the contained, and is the reprojection of the analyst's pathological projective identification in a form that is further imbued with toxicity and destructiveness. The patient's reference to food poisoning conveys similar implications.

The interactional qualities of this material are supported by the patient's reference to his own fears, as well as those of his mother, and his allusion to his father's surgery. Unconsciously, he then reprimands the therapist for his insensitivity and distance, but sees it as an alternative to utter loss of control—hysteria.

It was at this point in the session that the analyst experienced an intense sense of disquietude and concern about the patient's pathology and asked him to write a biography. Consciously, he had been concerned about the dream of the previous hour, in which he had appeared undisguised, and while he wondered whether this was an indication of some type of countertransference difficulty, most of his thoughts related to anxieties about serious underlying pathology in the patient. The request for the biography was made by the analyst as another effort to learn more about the patient in order to understand his pathology more clearly.

Once again, we will allow the patient's response to guide us in evaluating this intervention—another alteration in the frame. First, he did not write the biography, and he soon spoke of a physician friend who asked him for some sedatives. This consciously idealized physician was now being seen as human and vulnerable, and in some sense, as dishonest with himself. Here we have a metaphor for the analyst's projective identification into the patient of his own anxieties and need for noninsightful, artificial, drug-based relief. It is the patient who is to offer a healing reprojection—the pill or the biography—to relieve the analyst of his inappropriate anxieties. The danger, as the patient puts it in Type Two derivative form, is that the analyst might fall apart; the dread is of something deadly inside. Exhibitionism, voyeurism, sexual impotence, and homosexuality are all implied as related anxieties and themes.

At this point in his presentation, the analyst was able to describe some unresolved anxieties regarding death. He soon realized that the request of the patient that he write a biography was an effort to undo the anxieties by creating a permanent, indestructible record of the patient with which he— the analyst—could reassure himself. It is interesting that this patient refused to serve as a pathological container for the analyst's anxieties, at least on this level, and that he also refused to join in the sector of misalliance and in the framework cure offered by the analyst. Apparently recognizing unconsciously that the biography was an effort at artificial communication and an effort to erect a barrier to the disturbing contents that were emerging in this analysis, the patient unconsciously communicated these perceptions to the analyst and became engaged in additional unconscious efforts at cure— largely through a series of insightful unconscious interpretations related to the analyst's need to obliterate, his wish for the patient to serve him as a nursemaid and good mother, his homosexual and bodily anxieties, and his fears of death, containing, and sexuality.

While considerably more could be said in regard to this vignette, I will conclude this discussion by suggesting that only a series of self-insightful efforts directed toward resolution of the analyst's underlying countertransference difficulties, and the actual rectification of his difficulties in holding, containing, interpreting, and creating a Type A rather than a Type C communicative field—and the full interpretation of the patient's unconscious perceptions, introjections, and reactions to these inputs by the analyst—could redirect the interface of this bipersonal field to the pathology of the patient, and provide him a Type A communicative medium and an opportunity for insightful therapeutic work.

CONCLUDING COMMENTS

I will not attempt a comprehensive discussion of these postulates regarding countertransference, nor will I endeavor to delineate further the special advantages of viewing countertransference as an interactional product of the bipersonal field. I shall conclude by simply emphasizing the importance of an adequate and full listening process, of a validating clinical methodology, and of self-knowledge in applying these concepts regarding countertransference in the clinical situation, and more broadly in the expansion of psychoanalytic knowledge.

As many other analysts have noted (Langs 1976a), transference was first seen by Freud as the major enemy and obstacle to psychoanalysis, and only later recognized as its greatest ally—a quality that is by no means fully appreciated even to this day, so that the patient as the enemy and as resisting dominates the analyst's unconscious images, while the patient as ally and as curative is still far less appreciated. Similarly, with an even greater sense of dread, countertransference was first viewed as an enemy to analytic work; and while Freud never specifically acknowledged its constructive aspects, later analysts have indeed attempted to do just that. There has been a recent trend toward identifying the constructive dimensions of countertransference, and these very much deserve to be put into perspective.

However, it is well to conclude this discussion with a recognition that despite the many parallels between transference and countertransference (in their narrowest sense), there are important differences. While both are inevitable in the course of an analysis, transference manifestations are absolutely vital to the analytic work and are bound to be a major component of the patient's constructive experiences with the analyst and of his unconscious communications to him. By contrast, it is essential that countertransference expressions be kept to a reasonable minimum, that they not dominate the experiences and communications of the analyst, and that they not overfill the bipersonal field. However human such expressions are, and however meaningful the rectification and analysis with the patient may be, countertransference-based communications do traumatize the patient to some degree and these effects must be fully appreciated. It can be seen, then, that a properly balanced view of countertransference is extremely difficult to maintain. It is my hope that the present paper has enabled the reader to develop a more sensitive conception of this most difficult subject.

NOTE

1. The clinical observations and formulations to be developed in this paper are equally pertinent to psychotherapy and psychoanalysis. Since almost all the prior literature on this subject is derived from the psychoanalytic situation, I will adopt that as my model for this presentation.

REFERENCES

Baranger, M., and Baranger, W. (1966). Insight and the analytic situation. In *Psychoanalysis in the Americas,* ed. R. Litman, pp. 56–72. New York: International Universities Press.

Bion, W. (1959). Attacks on linking. *International Journal of Psycho-Analysis* 40:308–315.

———— (1962). *Learning from Experience.* New York: Basic Books. Reprinted in *Seven Servants.* New York: Jason Aronson, 1977.

———— (1963). *Elements of Psycho-Analysis.* New York: Basic Books. Reprinted in *Seven Servants.* New York: Jason Aronson, 1977.

———— (1965). *Transformations.* New York: Basic Books. Reprinted in *Seven Servants.* New York: Jason Aronson, 1977.

Greenson, R. (1972). Beyond transference and interpretation. *International Journal of Psycho-Analysis* 53:213–217.

Grinberg, L. (1962). On a specific aspect of counter-transference to the patient's projective identification. *International Journal of Psycho-Analysis* 43:436–440.

Langs, R. (1973a). The patient's view of the therapist; reality or fantasy? *International Journal of Psychoanalytic Psychotherapy* 2:431–441.

———— (1973b). *The Technique of Psychoanalytic Psychotherapy,* vol. 1. New York: Jason Aronson.

———— (1974). *The Technique of Psychoanalytic Psychotherapy,* vol 2. New York: Jason Aronson.

———— (1975a). The patient's unconscious perception of the therapist's errors. In *Tactics and Techniques in Psychoanalytic Therapy, Volume II: Countertransference,* ed. P. Giovacchini. New York: Jason Aronson.

———— (1975b). Therapeutic misalliances. *International Journal of Psychoanalytic Psychotherapy* 4:77–105.

———— (1975c). The therapeutic relationship and deviations in technique. *International Journal of Psychoanalytic Psychotherapy* 4:106–141.

———— (1976a). *The Bipersonal Field.* New York: Jason Aronson.

———— (1976b). On becoming a psychiatrist: discussion of "Empathy and intuition in becoming a psychiatrist" by Ronald J. Blank. *International Journal of Psychoanalytic Psychotherapy* 5:255–279.

———— (1976c). *The Therapeutic Interaction.* 2 vols. New York: Jason Aronson.

———— (1978a). Some communicative properties of the bipersonal field. *International Journal of Psychoanalytic Psychotherapy* 7:89–161.

———— (1978b). Validation and the framework of the therapeutic situation. *Contemporary Psychoanalysis* 14:98–124.

Langs, R. et al. (in press). *Psychoanalytic Dialogues III: Some British Views on Clinical Issues.* New York: Jason Aronson.

Reich, A. (1960). Further remarks on counter-transference. *International Journal of Psycho-Analysis* 41:389–395.

Searles, H. (1965). *Collected Papers on Schizophrenia and Related Subjects.* New York: International Universities Press.

———— (1975). The patient as therapist to his analyst. In *Tactics and Techniques in Psychoanalytic Therapy, Volume II: Countertransference,* ed. P. Giovacchini. New York: Jason Aronson.

16. The Case of "Mrs. X"

D. W. Winnicott

I now wish to include an illustration of an interview with a parent. There is no essential difference between an interview with a parent and an interview with a child except that with adults, as with older adolescents, it is unlikely that an interchange of drawings would be appropriate.

This is a case chosen from my hospital clinic. The daughter had been in our care, transferred by a colleague who is a pediatrician. In the initial interview with the child we discovered that there were features showing us that the mother's attendance with her child at the hospital indicated a need in the mother herself. The mother was unable, however, to think of what she was doing in this way, and she was constantly bringing her daughter for one doctor or another to examine her and to treat her for ailments the severity of which was not as great as the mother's anxiety would seem to indicate. It was necessary in this case for the child psychiatry team to keep in contact with the mother and daughter and to hold the case while waiting for developments. Gradually, after months, the mother lost her suspicion and revealed herself as a person very much in need of personal help.

I was told from the social-work side of the team that the moment had come for me to interview the mother, and I give a description of this interview. The result of this interview was favorable from the point of view of the clinic's efforts to give suitable help to the child since the mother, having communicated about herself, was now able to do a new thing, which was to hand over the management of her daughter to the casework organisations. As a result therefore of the interview we were able to place this girl in a suitable school which in fact carried her through the next few years. Contact between the child and the mother could be maintained because of the school's own special attitude to this matter.

A description of this interview is given not so much as evidence of the cure of the mother, which indeed would require an immense amount of work on the part of someone, as to illustrate the way in which by waiting we

Reprinted by permission of HarperCollins Publishers, Basic Books from *Therapeutic Consultations in Child Psychiatry*. New York, 1971, pp. 331–41.

arrived at the moment for a communication of a very personal kind. Incidentally, the way the mother gave her history provides a picture of a deprived child as given by that child now become an adult herself with an illegitimate daughter. It is possible to claim in addition that this mother became better able to manage her own affairs following the interview and its sequel: the proper care of the daughter.

I saw Mrs. X. alone.

I said: "Hello! You look rather thin."

She said: "As a matter of fact I am fat and I can't get my clothes on."

She was looking serious and worried.

I said: "Let's talk about Anna—it will break the ice." (Anna was 6 years old.)

Mrs. X. said: "She is really good, you know. She does not have a very nice life—I never talk to her, for instance, simply because no-one ever talked to me when I was a child. If I am upset it is then that Anna gets worse, and perhaps really naughty."

She went on to talk about the handicap she herself had experienced through not having taken the appropriate exams at school, so that she could not be a nurse or other things that she had wanted to be. At 20 she saw a woman doctor at a clinic and was shown the report which said that she was "amoral, had no background, and was permanently adolescent"; but, as she said, "It is no good having treatment to let you know what you are like when you know already." She insisted on her own badness, and in this she persisted to the very end of the consultation.

"The trouble is," she said, "if I like someone, male or female, for me that is sex. At 19 I had my first hug and kiss and this was the first time anybody was affectionate toward me, so the two came at the same time."

I said: "I can't think how you managed."

She said: "Well, I masturbated a great deal."

This was clitoric only. She never knew about deep orgasm until quite recently.

She said: "The trouble is I ruin everything by becoming possessive. I don't mean to, but I am all 'What have you done? where have you been?' as if the man or woman had done everything to hurt me. One of them said: 'I can't even go to the lavatory without your being jealous.' "

I said: "Children are often like that—probably Anna has been?"

She said: "Yes, but isn't it awful when I'm still a child!"

It was here that she started crying.

She said: "It doesn't matter at all whether it is a man or a woman—if anyone is affectionate then there is a sexual experience for me. I have had two affairs with women, which were perhaps the most satisfactory things that have happened."

They were both big, plump women—a lot of sex play and breast manipulation and so on.

I said: "Well, all that is terrible. Something good has happened to you elsewhere but it has got lost. I am sure of that because you can recognise good things in Anna."

So she went over some of the details of her story again.

She was made a ward of the ——— Corporation because her mother was cruel to her. She had her mother until she was 3 or 4 and I said: "Perhaps mother may have been all right at the beginning from your point of view?"

She said: "She could not have been if she was so cruel that I had to be taken away from her."

We talked here about her desperate loneliness, a state which she described both ways: "I get lonely by being unpopular, but I get terribly jealous of anyone who is popular, especially my girl friend."

I made a comment here, saying: "Being alone is safe."

She said: "That is what I said to my friend, Daisie, a week or two ago," and she went over again what I had said in her own language.

She went on to talk about Daisie, who is extremely pretty, vivacious, gay and theatrical, 22 years old. She has done everything, she can talk her way into everything, has two bank accounts and plenty of money.

Here and elsewhere it was obvious that she kept her normal self going in the personality of her friends, of whom (in consequence, perhaps) she is inordinately jealous.

I said to her, because of her description of Daisie: "Did you have any brothers or sisters?"

She said: "I remember an orphanage Christmas Party during which someone said: 'And this is your sister'; she was very pretty. I never saw her again."

This led on to her telling me that she was called Polly in the orphanage, but when she saw her birth certificate she found that her father was "Y." and her mother "Z." There was no mention of the name she had been called. She found she was born in ———! She often wonders whether there had been a crime in the family so that the orphanage changed her name to save her from shame. She was in the ——— Corporation Society Orphanage, starting off in a big place for 150 small children, and being in smaller homes until eventually going to ———. In one of these there was a Miss ———, a woman from abroad who was the superintendent.

I asked for permission to make enquiries about her childhood and she said she would be glad if I would, but she has always kept away from making enquiries for fear of finding that things are much worse than she thinks. The scanty details she gave me turned out to be correct. All this happened in the thirties.

She went on to describe fits of depression. She has always dealt with these by going to bed early and *daydreaming*. At these times she always pretends that she is something special and is very good at something or other. Actually she has never been either of these two things. She was a plain, thin child, she said, and for this reason went to hospital. This reminded her of something and made her cry again.[1] She had had one kind person in her life. When 8 or 9 she was in a fever hospital, in a small room, and she had no visitors during the whole of her stay there. One day a woman stopped at her cubicle, opened her bag, and said: "Choose something." She chose her mirror. The woman then went and gave it to the nurse, who eventually came to her with it. She says of this that it was "the only kind thing that ever happened to me in my childhood." She had no visitors at all during the six months that she was in the hospital. It must have been six months that she was there because she had both her birthday (summer) and Christmas there. She remembered being wheeled into the ward in black stockings and gradually being persuaded to walk. She does not know what was the illness. She then remembered being taken by a man in blue from the orphanage into the ambulance.

I spoke of the awfulness of being taken from an orphanage, which was different from being taken from one's own home, because of the uncertainty about returning. She went into an isolation ward and remembers Father Christmas, who turned out to be the doctor. I made a remark here about the ward having dealt with her body but seemed to leave out the rest of her. According to her pattern she immediately felt very guilty as she said: "I feel that people owe me things, but of course it is *me* who is wrong. But because I feel I am owed something I cannot let anything go well. If it is going well I destroy it halfway, and so I hurt myself."

I said: "It must be very difficult for you to know what to be angry with, and yet there must be violent anger in you somewhere."

She said: "Yes, but it takes an odd form—I feel a shudder going through me. It is a feeling as if *for a split second* (she found it very difficult to describe this) *I might go mad*, but I remember where I am, and it's over."

I said: "You mean you *do* go mad, only it is done so quickly that it is all over. Your fear is that you will find you have done something awful while you have been mad."

She then told me something which she said she had "never told anyone," and she was very distressed. When she was 14 or 15 she could not be placed out in a factory because it was said that she would be no good, so she was kept to work in the nursery opposite the orphanage where children came from their homes. She had to help with the children or infants and take the place of a teacher who might be absent, and so on. A child was screaming, and it got on her nerves and she nearly strangled it. (This illustrated what I had said perfectly.) She took it by the neck and shook it, but then stopped. On another occasion she would hug children hard in order to get sexual feelings. "This is horrible and dirty—do any other women ever do anything like this? Sometimes Anna gets into bed and hugs me and I feel sexy. Has *any* mother *ever* felt this? Of course in the nursery school I was given all the dirty jobs, including cleaning up the babies, but I was never allowed to do anything of the kind that would be important for a baby."

Those babies in the nursery were all going to be collected by their parents and so I suggested that this could be one reason why she nearly murdered this child, she herself having never had a home to go back to.

She then went on. At 18 she was a maid in somebody's house and she had to get her birth certificate. She repeated herself, telling me that this was very upsetting, for in her day-dreams there were always wonderful things she *might* one day discover about her parents, but when she saw that her name was not the same as the name she knew herself by and that her father was a hawker of no fixed address, she broke down in tears.

So in this house where she was a maid with a wage of 15s. a week, the young mistress had lovely clothes and a beautiful sitting-room, which she was not allowed to use, and the young mistress always carried a lot of money in her bag. Mrs. X. stole a pound to buy herself something pretty, but in spite of having so much money this woman missed the pound and Mrs. X. was sacked.

I went on talking about the anger that must be in her without her knowing where to put it.

I said: "God, for instance."

She said: "In the orphanage we were taught terrible things about God, and until I was 13 I always slept with my arms crossed in case I died so that I would not go to hell. As soon as I left the orphanage I stopped confession and have had no belief in anything since. Once I wanted to be a nun but that was only so as to look pious. I have wanted a baby terribly since I was 12. Here I am—I've made a mess of my life—how can I recover? Cyril (father of Anna) and his mother did not like me and I am sure it was because of the orphanage. I always blame everything on the orphanage and feel ashamed of it all the time. But some people like Marilyn Monroe make films and let everybody *know* they were in an orphanage, because they have the strength of character which I have not got. We had a lot of beatings. Auntie (as she was called) used the wooden spoon on your hands. I stole a lot of food in the night, biscuits, sugar and cocoa. We never had sweet things except on Sundays when we had a biscuit or a piece of cake."

She remarked that this craving for sweet things had persisted.

I asked her again about her mother and the question of research into the past, and she said she had not done any lest she got a worse shock which she could not bear.

She said: "You see, she never came near me all those years from 3 to 16. A friend said to me, though, 'you are always searching for something.' "

I interpreted here about the link between the compulsive stealing and searching for something, perhaps for a lost bit of good relationship with her mother. She said she does not steal ever now but she still has a terrible urge for sweet things. At any minute she may have a desperate need and have to rush out and buy a cake, even when giving Anna her bath.

I then asked her about dreams and she said: "Daydreams?"

I said: "No, real dreams." Her real dreams are all frightening, about a mouse or a rat. She said: "On the television there was a mouse and I could not sleep at all that night. It is a terrible thing I have about rats and mice. There is a rat in all my nightmares. Even an advertisement about rat poison gives me the shivers. This was a dream I had three times: *I was in a room with someone and an orange. A rat had been eating the orange and there was no food left so that I had the choice of starving or eating the orange which had been bitten by the rat.* I always woke in a terrible state from these dreams and I always keep a light on in any case. I tried to cure myself by going to the zoo with Anna, but the rats and mice there were pretty, and so it was no good. It has always been the same, since I was 18 at any rate."

"The most awful thing was Emergency Ward 10:[2] a girl had a disease caught from rats and they went to her room and there was a picture of all the rats in her bed. The shock was so bad that I was nearly sick and I couldn't sleep all night."

I asked what the trouble was and she said: "Oh, I think they will eat me."

I withheld using this dream.

She said: "There are dreams when you are just falling asleep and wake suddenly — *a line with a train coming and I just wake* — or *I climb a tree and never get to the top* — another, *I run and run and thousands and thousands of little people are running after me. They have little bodies and huge heads.* As a child I used to fall asleep every-where — at tea, in school, and so on — and I always had a dirty head. The lice in my head would run over the pillows and I felt compelled to touch my head, although it was all terrible. I have always wanted someone to love or cuddle me, but I was never kissed until I was 19. Auntie never kissed any of us good-night. I am all the time ashamed of the orphanage."

Here she put in an illustration that showed her sense of fun. She said:

"Once on a bus the conductor said to Auntie (who was a nun): 'Are all these your kids?' Auntie was flustered and said: 'Yes, but they have all got different fathers!'"

This was like an oasis in the desert. She quickly returned to the desert with:

"This was terrible for me."

I said: "It is as if with all these insects you are talking about your own fertility. You longed from the age of 12 to have a baby, which would have been all right, but before then fertility was all mixed up with feces and dirt and infestation and so on."

She said: "I thought having babies must be something awful, my mother would never do that! But then (it must have been Coronation time when I was 10) I read about the princesses, and I saw the queen, and in that way I got away from the horror which came from not being told anything at all about babies. My first period I had in the middle of the night. I was very frightened and woke Auntie ———. She was cross. 'Everything you do is different' was all she said. But I had seen blood and I thought I was going to die."

No one explained anything at all, but Auntie gave her some towels, saying "You must clean these yourself," and this made her feel more ashamed than ever.

I asked her about mixed classes in the orphanage. She said that there were boys, but the boys had bath nights on different nights.

She added, as if remembering something that had been forgotten:

"When I was 9 I saw a boy showing himself" (she was confused about details). "He was asking a girl to kiss him. I remember the words: 'Give it a kiss,' and the children laughed. In walked Auntie and we all got the wooden spoon."

She said that Auntie was a woman who was really not suitable for this job. She was eventually dismissed.

"As an instance, there was a boy who was liable to wet the bed, and I am upset even now seeing him being sent to sleep "all curled up" in the cot each time as a punishment. She was naturally unjust. She had a relief twice a week. Some of these were horrible. One was nice, so of course we all took advantage of her; we came home late, ate too much butter and too much jam, and did all our work wrong. You see, she was so sweet that we all went mad. Sometimes she would send the older ones out to get chips and then we would eat them all together! But what I remember about this time was work, work, work."

And she gave a vivid description of life in a rush.

"We had to do everything, scrub the floors of the school, rush home two miles, get the lunch ready, rush back to school after washing up, rush home to prepare tea, clear up the tea, and then darn socks. We watched the children play, but we had no time for anything."

Then she remembered a lot of details about brass that had to be cleaned and steps to be whitened. Auntie never talked with the children, and she never remembers having had any toys. I asked her about toys to cuddle. She said that Anna had none and nor did she. She as a child would pull her pillow down and put her head under the sheets so that she could see no light, but she always woke herself at 5 a.m. for two hours of daydreaming. This daydreaming involved having her hands between her legs, and she also demonstrated something which was in the pattern of her childhood right through: rocking backward and forward with her thumbs in her armpits. She had had a lot of smacks for this habit.

I made an *interpretation* here. It seemed to me that we had nearly had enough, each of us, and I must do some work. I must act now or not act at all.

I said: "You know, it may be that these rats and mice are *in between you and the breast* of the mother that was a good mummy. When you get back to infancy and you think of your mother's breasts the best you can do is rats and mice."
She seemed shocked, and she shuddered and said: "How can that be!"

I said dogmatically that the rats represented her own biting, and the breast turning up as a biting object indistinguishable from her own biting. I related this to the fact that her own mother had failed her during the time when she was dealing with the new problem of the urge to bite in her personal development. She accepted this and immediately started looking for something in the relationship to the mother which could be carried over. She said she never had had a nice dream. She may have had a sad one and she said that she always felt she would die unnaturally (not suicide) and that she would never last long enough. Then a significant thing happened. She said that she remembered something—being carried—it had to do with the time before the orphanage. There were two things. One thing had to do with "pobs," a cereal food in her home county, and so with the period before the orphanage; "but the other thing is an important memory because I remember going to the orphanage [that is, when she was 4] always trying to think of this rather frightening episode, *because it was the only thing I could carry over from the time before the orphanage.*"

She tried very hard to get it.

"There is a voice—feet are running—I know doors are opening—there was a man there—people are shouting and someone has a bag or case." This was the moment of being taken from home to the orphanage.

This was a memory which was extremely precious to her and which she felt sad to be losing, although it never quite got her back to the early days as the word "pobs" did.

Mrs. X. had now reached back over the gap, and to some extent had recovered the memory of her own "good" mummy.

I ended by saying that it would be quite possible for the relationship between her mother and herself to have been good at the start, although from the point of view of people observing, the mother was being cruel to her. We had to leave things in this state. She said, however, that if I really liked she would show me her birth certificate, which she never shows to anyone as she keeps it locked up. Once she could have got married to someone very nice, but at the last minute her birth certificate had to be produced so she ran away from the whole thing.

Although this was an interview with a parent there was the same playful evolution of ideas and feelings as in the interviews with the children. This mother gives quite naturally and in an unsophisticated way the relationship between stealing and both deprivation and hope.

RESULT

As described in the preamble to the case-presentation, this interview led to a new opportunity for the child to be managed by the clinic team in the way that she really needed and in the way that we had long waited for. The mother had to be given time to gain the confidence in us that was necessary before she could make use of this kind of interview in which it was she herself who was the ill person of the couple. After this interview she stopped using the daughter as ill and in need of medical care. The child went into substitute care, and the good relationship between her and her mother was maintained and enriched. Anna is now almost an adult.

NOTES

1. My hope is that by now the reader will have got the feeling that, in spite of my freedom in the use of myself, the structuring of the interview truly comes from the patient.

2. TV series.

PART IV

Patient Selection: In Sickness
and in Health

The four selections in this part share the same general philosophy of therapeutic change. They show how—despite patients who span a great spectrum
from health to sickness—the authors use much the same considerations in
patient selections. Sifneos's constituency is healthier, "analyzable" patients.
Leibovich's borderline patients need ego-building and ego-organizing maneuvers by the therapist. And Malan's patients fall somewhere between the two.
(Earlier Malan, that is. In recent years, Malan's ideas have converged almost
entirely into Davanloo's.) But in the initial evaluation, all three pay careful
attention to the history of the patient's prior relationships and the quality of
the patient's relationship with the therapist. (Leibovich's clearest account of
selection *per se* is in an earlier paper.)[1]

Why should it be that a reasonable ability to connect with the therapist is
the litmus for patient selection in very diverse dynamic treatments? Apparently, two patients at the same level of health but unequal capacities to form
a bond with the therapist would have quite different prognoses in the dynamic
therapies—the more schizoid patient being expected to do poorly. There is
no single answer why this might be the case, but there is sufficient consensus
to suggest that, indeed, positive *engagement* is a major (if not *the* major)
criterion for patient selection.

As mentioned in part III on therapist activity, what the therapist does
(especially with reference to transference interpretations) is related to patient
selection. And patient selection is related to diagnosis; healthier patients
generally get selected for interpretive work, sicker ones do not. But the
theoretical basis of the majority of therapies in this book is that transference
distortions in everyday life cause maladaptation; that transference distortions
in the therapy can be examined to reverse maladaptation; but that examination of the transference in the treatment is limited by the patient's pathology.
For sicker patients, work with transference is indirect if it occurs at all, and
"ego-building techniques" are a major therapist activity. (For a masterful

discussion of ego-building techniques, see Blanck and Blanck.)[2] For relatively direct work with the transference, patients are excluded if they are schizoid, missing an important developmental step, or unable to "get it" when the therapist makes connections between behaviors and unconscious conflicts.

Regarding patient selection, Gustafson speaks for many dynamic practitioners when he says:

I believe that the selection for brief dynamic therapy can be simplified to three fundamental questions. Has the patient been able to navigate safely through the worst periods of disturbance of his life? Has the patient been able to have a deep give-and-take with another person? Does the trial therapy bring about an actual breakthrough to deep feelings and the recurrent focal problem in the patient's life?[3]

A final word about patient selection and connectedness concerns "motivation." Usually "motivation" was mentioned as a good thing for the patient to have if short-term dynamic therapy is to succeed. The problem was, nobody seemed quite clear what it was or how to recognize it. Was "motivation" the amount of energy the patient brought to the encounter? The amount of suffering the patient had? The amount of time and money the patient would spend to get rid of it? Or perhaps motivation was just something the therapist imagined when there was a good connection.

In addition to his contribution regarding therapist activity in part III, Davanloo also has something to say about motivation and patient selection.

Until the late 1970s I believed in criteria for selection and considered motivation an important criterion; but since then my position has changed totally, based on my research. I consider motivation a criterion created by therapists who cannot treat highly resistant, complex patients. I have demonstrated that the most reliable criterion [for predicting outcome] is the unconscious therapeutic alliance mobilized after unlocking the unconscious, weakening the whole force of resistance during the initial interview; and we can do that with every psychoneurotic patient, no matter the degree of resistance. . . .

Until 1980 I considered a fragile character structure a contraindication [to my method]; but our research data, all audiovisually recorded, shows that they are the best candidates and that we can bring about major structural character changes.[4]

Davanloo believes his research population constitutes a truly representative outpatient sample. In no way to diminish the contribution of Davanloo to the field, I question whether his patient population is representative of patients either seen in the clinic generally or in private practice: All Davanloo's patients must consent to be videotaped throughout evaluation and treatment, and this says something profound about how they regard privacy. Thirty years ago when I entered therapy, I would not have agreed to being taped; twenty-five years ago, when I entered analysis, I would not have agreed to being taped. Even today, I doubt I would permit it. So it may be that I have a blind spot for understanding any individual who could so readily throw away the privacy built into the doctor-patient relationship. (How you come down on the question of the validity of Davanloo's research may mostly hinge on how you respond to the idea of having your own psychotherapy videotaped.)

REFERENCES

1. Leibovich, M. "Short-Term Psychotherapy for the Borderline Personality Disorder." *Psychother Psychosom* 35 (1981):257–64.
2. Blanck, G., and R. Blanck. *Ego Psychology II, Psychoanalytic Developmental Psychology.* New York: Columbia University Press, 1979, esp. 210–55.
3. Gustafson, J. P. "An Integration of Brief Dynamic Psychotherapy." *Am J Psychiatry* 141 (1984):935–44, esp. 942.
4. Davanloo, H. Letter to JE Groves, October 30, 1994, 1–2.

17. The Frontier of Brief Psychotherapy

David H. Malan

SELECTION

The Convergence of Statistical and Clinical Evidence

During a number of recent years I have been acting in two parallel roles
concerned with brief psychotherapy: first, as a research worker studying the
material provided by Balint's team, and second, as a clinician trying to
provide a service at the Tavistock Clinic, by running a unit in which trainees
treat patients with brief therapy under group supervision.

This dual role has had some interesting and important consequences. In
the brief therapy unit I have operated as a pure clinician, always allowing
research findings to be over-ridden by intuition if the two appeared to be at
variance. It might be thought that this is yet another example of the divorce
between research and clinical practice and the lack of impact of the one on
the other (and I have sometimes been deceived into thinking this myself) but
it is not so. What has repeatedly happened is that principles reached on
purely clinical grounds on the one hand, and those derived from research on
the other, even when appearing to differ, are found on closer examination
to coincide.

The most striking example of this comes from the relative importance of
the two selection criteria, *motivation* and *response to interpretation*, which
will be considered below.

In this chapter I shall try to present a distillation of the principles of brief
therapy as I see them at the present time after the convergence of these two
lines of evidence. The clinical examples will mostly be taken from the
Tavistock brief therapy unit, and I should at once like to thank the therapists
involved for permission to publish their work, into which they have poured
so much of their own dedication and life experience. I have often thought—
a sober judgment made entirely without false modesty—that in many cases
they have done far better work than I am any longer capable of myself.

Reprinted by permission of Plenum Publishing Co. from *The Frontier of Brief Psychotherapy*.
New York, 1976, pp. 247–57, 263–65, 349–58.

Intensive Brief Psychotherapy

Before we consider the problem of selection, we need to define the form of brief psychotherapy for which the patients are being selected. Earlier, I pointed out that there was a continuum between what Sifneos calls crisis support at one end, and what he calls brief anxiety-provoking psychotherapy at the other. The form of therapy described here obviously comes under the latter heading, but we need a term that more exactly describes its essential character. Both Sifneos's term, and Balint's term, focal therapy, describe simply a kind of technique. I want a term that gives weight to the fact that in this form of therapy the aim is really to *resolve* either the patient's central problem or at least an important aspect of his psychopathology. If this seems to involve rather a large claim, I hope I have presented enough clinical evidence to suggest that such an aim is not unrealistic. I would have preferred the word "radical" which of course I have used extensively in *SBP** and earlier in the present book in connection with the two opposing views of brief therapy; but I have been warned that, as a label, it might have somewhat unfortunate connotations in America. I cannot entirely avoid this word, but in general have fallen back on another—suggested to me by Dr. John Nemiah—namely, "intensive." I should emphasize that I am proposing it for descriptive purposes and nothing else; there are too many terms, coined by various workers in this field, and used as flags for particular schools of psychotherapy.

The Assessment of Patients for Psychotherapy

Much of what follows will differ little from what many others have practiced or have written on the subject of assessing a patient for psychotherapy. If differences are to be found, they will lie in the emphasis on forecasting and therapeutic planning, but even these features were long ago strongly emphasized by other workers, notably Finesinger (1948) and Alexander and French (1946).

The first steps in selection are—or should be—the same for all forms of psychotherapy: They must start with a *thoroughgoing psychodynamic assessment,* the successive aims of which are as follows: (1) to understand the patient's illness as deeply as possible; hence (2) to be able to make a

---

* Malan (1963).

forecast of what will happen if the patient is taken on for psychotherapy; (3) to decide from this which patients are unsuitable, and which are suitable for which forms of psychotherapy; (4) to assign the patient to the appropriate form of psychotherapy; and (5) to make a therapeutic plan for the form of therapy chosen.

The idea of *therapeutic planning* is central to our form of brief therapy; and I think that an increasing number of therapists are beginning to realize that it needs to play a major part in all forms of psychotherapy, with the exception of full-scale analysis. I hope the days in which patients are taken on "in the hope that something useful will happen," are numbered. At the Tavistock Clinic the following kind of plan for medium-term therapy is becoming increasingly heard: "This deprived patient needs something like six months in which she can learn to trust her therapist, a year in which she can make use of the relationship, and six months to work through her feelings at the loss of regular sessions, with a long relationship after that."

To repeat, the ability to plan depends on the psychodynamic assessment, and this in turn must involve certain elements, each of which is undertaken in the context of trying to forecast what will happen if the patient begins to undergo uncovering psychotherapy. The first of these is a *proper psychiatric history*.

This is something that tends to be neglected, but a few examples will serve to show its importance: For instance, you cannot plan therapy realistically if you do not know (1) that a patient complaining of difficulty in making close relationships was admitted to hospital for two years with tuberculous glands between the ages of one and three; or (2) that a similar patient has one sibling who was once in a delusional state, and another who failed a university degree and is now working as a laborer; or (3) that an apparently mildly depressed patient had a previous attack of depression that was incapacitating, or (4) made a previous suicidal attempt with a large number of tablets, in circumstances in which he was unlikely to be discovered; or (5) once got into a state in which he danced on the desk in his office and did target practice with an air pistol; or (6) that a woman complaining of overeating had an episode in her teens in which she was thirty pounds below her normal weight, missed her periods for two years, and was admitted to the hospital, where her life was in danger; or (7) that what appears to be an agoraphobic patient is in fact afraid of going out because she is afraid that people in the street are talking about her; and so on and so on.

One hardly needs to point out the kind of forecast that can be made on the basis of the above items in a patient's history: (1) that this patient's inability to make relationships is probably based on an inability to face his true feelings about the traumatic separation in his childhood, that getting him to form a therapeutic relation will be difficult, and that if this succeeds he is likely to become dependent in a primitive way; (2) that the disturbance in this patient is probably the consequence of genetic loading and/or some highly pathological family situation, which may have resulted in a much deeper disturbance in this particular patient than may appear on the surface; (3), (4) and (5) that any attempt at working through the patient's central problem will probably result in his becoming *at least as severely depressed or as severely manic as when he was at his worst in the past,* with the result that hospital admission may well become necessary; (6) that this is probably a very deep-seated and primitive condition, that it will require prolonged psychotherapy if it is to be helped at all, and may well involve periods of undereating even with possible danger to life; and finally (7) that in this patient, overenthusiastic interpretation is quite likely to precipitate an overt psychotic state.

I would not necessarily say that any of the above features are absolute contraindications to intensive brief therapy, but they come near to being so, and must make any potential therapist consider very carefully the type of intervention that he is going to make.

The second important feature of the assessment is what may be called the *full-scale psychodynamic history,* which of course overlaps with the psychiatric history in many features. The aim of this is to try to understand the events of the patient's life in emotional terms, and to see how they have contributed to the present illness, and how they give evidence of the patient's ability to cope with difficulties and to face his anxieties. There is one particular type of situation the assessor needs to try and create time and again, and which has an extreme relevance to brief therapy: that the precipitating events leading to the recent onset of symptoms can be seen to have something of emotional significance in common with events leading to the past onset of symptoms, and that these in turn can be understood in terms of the patient's original family relationships. This is the kind of situation that most frequently leads to the possibility of formulating a *focal problem,* and furnishes one side of the triangle of insight, the link between current and past relationships, which will need to be used extensively in therapy.

The psychodynamic history must include a thorough history of the patient's relationships, with particular reference to any clear-cut patterns that emerge. This can lead to an assessment of the depth of disturbance in relationships, and also to the possibility of forecasting the type of transference likely to develop. As an example, a patient may show a pattern of running away from a relationship as soon as there is any threat of involvement. If this is severe, the assessor may well conclude that the patient is unsuitable for psychotherapy; and in any case he will know that this inability to become involved is what must be dealt with in therapy, and that the patient's wish to withdraw will probably constitute the main danger to therapy in the early stages.

The quality of the patient's relationships will give one clue to his strength and potential for growth. Other clues will be given by the amount of "good experience" he has had in his early life, his ability to progress and mature in the past, his ability for achievement in the face of difficulties, his work history, his interests, and his capacity for creativeness.

The above history of the patient's relationships must, of course, include an exploration of his current relationships, and indeed of his whole current life situation. In addition to the patient's own internal strength, it is important to know how much support he will receive from the people currently in his life; and, on the other hand, what obstacles such people may put in the way of his improvement. One of our research findings has been that patients who are tied in difficult current relationships tend to have long therapies. (This work was undertaken at a time when it was not routine at least to interview a marital partner, let alone to try and involve him or her in the therapy.) It must always be borne in mind that conjoint marital therapy, rather than brief individual therapy, may be the treatment of choice in such cases. We did achieve occasional successes by treating one partner only, examples being the Maintenance Man (not included in the present book) and to a lesser extent the Pesticide Chemist; but no one can say that these results might not have been better if the partner had been treated as well. Exactly the same considerations apply to patients who are involved in difficult family situations, where it may be possible and right to involve the whole family in the treatment.

The next important feature in the psychodynamic assessment comes from the quality of the interview itself, seen in terms of the interaction between the patient and interviewer. It is important to be able to assess the patient's capacity to speak honestly about himself, to see his problem in emotional terms, to allow the interviewer some degree of emotional closeness. Above all, and *provided there is no contraindication,* it is quite essential that the interviewer should make trial interpretations, carefully thought out and no deeper than is necessary to serve the purposes for which they are intended. These purposes are as follows: first, to deepen the rapport between patient and interviewer, to reduce resistances, to obtain fresh and spontaneous material, to get more honest answers to questions; second, to assess the patient's capacity to use interpretative psychotherapy; and third, to begin to test hypotheses about the origins of the patient's illness, which will be used both in the planning of therapy, and in the therapy itself if this is undertaken. Evidence about the response to such interpretations is thus one of the most important elements in the assessment.

It is also important to note that these trial interpretations may well involve the transference. Much evidence has been accumulated at the Tavistock Clinic in recent years that transference may already be present to an intense degree in the initial interview, and that transference interpretations may have a dramatic releasing effect. The possibility of transference interpretations should therefore be always borne in mind, particularly when the patient is showing obvious signs of finding it difficult to open up. On the other hand, this can of course be overdone, and the routine relating of every interpretation to the transference is something that I regard as artificial and mistaken. It must always be remembered, however, that interpretations may set in train a chain of events that is quite undesirable. This is particularly so where there is potential psychosis, where ill-chosen interpretations may face the patient with feelings that he is not ready to cope with, may make him more disturbed, and may even precipitate a psychosis. The following story, mentioned in passing in *SBP*, may serve as a warning:

A man walked into a hospital where I was casualty officer, complaining of the fear that he might kill his wife. Questioning revealed that while he was serving abroad in the Army during the war his wife had had an affair with another man and had had a child. Being inexperienced and full of enthusiasm for the power of interpretations, I said to him, "So you have good reason to want to kill your wife." He made no clear response to this and went off. Two days later he came back in an exalted state, demanding of everybody, "Do you believe in the Lord?" He was clearly psychotic and had to be admitted as an emergency.

It must also be remembered that correct interpretations, or even just behavior that enables a patient to share his inner feelings, constitute a most potent gift that the patient may never have experienced before, and that carries with it an implied promise of more. If the patient is *not* suitable for psychotherapy, or if there is no appropriate vacancy, the resulting rejection will be all the more traumatic. I once gave a major interpretation to a woman patient, summarizing her life problem. She fell in love with me and was still writing me poems two years later, flattering for me no doubt but not so satisfactory for her husband. Another example is of a severely deprived young man who spent the first half-hour of his interview in silence, and who was eventually led to talk by a combination of sympathetic attention and interpretation deliberately kept as superficial as possible. This was enough to make him write a letter two days later in which he wanted to share his psychotic thoughts. We did have a vacancy to treat him, but if we had not we might well have been faced with an immediate emergency.

To sum up, whereas interpretations are an essential part of assessing a patient whom we accept, they can be used irresponsibly and there should be a constant interaction at interview between the desire to make contact, the severity of disturbance suspected or revealed, and the availability of vacancies for treatment.

At this point the reader may well ask why I emphasize the importance of response to interpretation, when in fact this variable showed only a small positive relation to outcome when judged by Dreyfus and Shepherd on the initial assessment material. The answer is concerned with problems of using statistics on selected samples. The patients whom we accepted in the present series were those who either responded well to interpretation in the initial interview, or else made sufficient contact with the interviewer to indicate that they had a potential for responding. In fact, as has already been mentioned earlier, our assessment of this was 100 percent accurate: In no patient was there any difficulty in obtaining a response to interpretation soon after the beginning of therapy. Thus, the only patients selected were those at the upper end of the scale of contact with the interviewer, and it was within this context that the correlation with outcome did not appear. I can only say that if some of the rejected patients listed earlier had been selected—notably, for instance, Miss L.—the correlation would almost certainly have emerged very clearly.

The fourth important factor to come out of the initial interview is the patient's motivation. My own use of motivation has never been as systematic as that of Sifneos. My position can probably be described as follows: I regard very high motivation, such as that shown at initial interview by the Indian Scientist, as being a most encouraging sign for intensive brief therapy: Equally, very poor motivation I regard as a more or less absolute contraindication: On the other hand, I do not regard *moderately* low motivation as a contraindication, *provided other signs, and particularly the ability to see a focus, are favorable.* One must always remember that the therapist has the chance to create higher motivation through interpretation of his chosen focus, the more so the more he is sure that it is correct. It seems that we always intuitively realized this, and the confirmation that it could lead to successful outcome was given clinically by such cases as the Buyer, and statistically by the clear interaction between motivation and focality presented above.

At the end of the psychiatric interview, therefore, it should be possible to make a full psychodynamic diagnosis and to see whether there seems to be some circumscribed aspect of pathology that can be made into a focus, and hence whether there appears to be a possible therapeutic plan. These are all aspects of the therapist's role, and thus represent only half of the information that has been provided. It should also be possible to answer many questions to do with the patient's role: to forecast likely events if he undergoes uncovering psychotherapy, and to assess his capacity for insight, ability to respond to interpretation, strength to face anxiety-provoking material, potential for growth, and motivation to carry him through the stresses of therapy.

I am by now convinced, however, by long and sometimes salutory experience, that a single psychiatric interview by itself is rarely enough to be able to assess the patient's suitability for brief therapy. Sometimes the information clearly appears insufficient, e.g., when the emotional meaning of precipitating events is not clear; but even when it appears to be sufficient, in my view the interview should often be followed either by another, or, more frequently, by a projection test. This latter should ideally be given in the context of definite questions asked of the psychologist:

How much is this an Oedipal problem and how much a problem in the two-person mother-child relation? How much dependence is there? How much evidence is there of good experience? What is his capacity to face his primitive impulses? Is there evidence for homosexuality? Is there any evidence for psychotic features? . . . and so on. It may also be possible, if, for instance, a male patient was interviewed by a man, to assign him to a female psychologist in order to highlight both his reactions to women and to triangular situations. With one such patient in our recent experience, the female psychologist has provided the third apex for interpretations about the Oedipal triangle; and he eventually admitted that he was convinced that the psychologist was the therapist's wife, despite the fact that she had an entirely different name.

In several recent cases the projection test has revealed entirely unexpected features and has saved us from making serious mistakes. A particular example was a young man with what appeared to be a simple Oedipal problem; who, on testing by a woman psychologist, revealed an almost psychotically paranoid attitude to women.

Of course, even the interview and projection test may sometimes not be enough, and it may save many wasted sessions if the patient is given further exploratory interviews. It is here that the statistical results on motivation and focality become relevant: The patient is regarded as suitable if his motivation increases and the therapist finds himself able to keep interpretations focal. Our recent experience suggests the following recommendations here: that with less experienced therapists these exploratory interviews should be kept as few as possible, as otherwise there is difficulty in rejecting the patient if he appears to be unsuitable; that the number should be left vague, as otherwise the patient may tend to open up falsely in what he knows to be his last session; and that this work should be undertaken by the original interviewer rather than a different potential therapist—it is then more naturally part of the assessment procedure, rather than a clear-cut situation of being on probation, and it is easier to transfer the patient if the final decision is that he is unsuitable.

Criteria for Acceptance for Intensive Brief Therapy

When the initial assessment has been completed the selection procedure may be described as a series of stages:

1. Elimination of Absolute Contraindications. Earlier I gave a list adapted from Hildebrand of severe and disabling conditions, the presence of which mean rejection without further consideration. These shade into the next heading.

2. Rejection of Patients with Whom Certain Dangers Seem Inevitable. These are patients for whom certain types of event are forecast. They have been listed above, to which the reader is referred. Examples of patients showing these features are given earlier.

3. Formulation of a Focus from the Therapist's Point of View. As always, this is some circumscribed aspect of psychopathology, formulated in terms of a basic interpretation, which it seems feasible to try and work through in a short time.

4. The Focus from the Patient's Point of View. It may be easy enough to formulate a focus, but the next essential question is whether there is evidence that it is acceptable to the patient. Ideally, the following conditions should be fulfilled:

   (a) The patient has shown a good capacity to think of his problems in emotional terms.

   (b) He apparently has the strength to face disturbing material.

   (c) Interpretations based on the focus have been given during the assessment period, and there has been a reasonably good response to them.

   (d) He appears to have the motivation to face the stresses of therapy.

The statistical results presented earlier may be incorporated into this selection procedure by considering the balance between motivation and focality. This means that a patient can be accepted either (a) with only moderate motivation but high focality—i.e., it is possible to see a focus very clearly, and the forecast is made that this will generate enough motivation to carry the patient through; or (b) with high motivation but low focality—where it is possible to forecast that the patient's high motivation will lead to the clarification of the focus within a short time. It must always be remembered, however, that in the latter case therapy tends to be longer.

Summary of Selection Procedure

Although the process of assessment is thus very complex, the process of selection can really be formulated very briefly:

A focus can be found, the patient has already responded to it positively, motivation is sufficient, and certain specific dangers do not seem inevitable.

Time Limits

In the brief therapy unit at the Tavistock Clinic we almost invariably set a time limit from the beginning, telling the patient this as soon as he is taken on. Since many of the therapists have only a limited time at the clinic, we often cannot offer the patient the possibility of irregular sessions according to need after termination, though in my view this should always be done where possible. As I wrote in *SBP,* a time limit gives therapy a definite beginning, middle, and end—like the opening, middle game, and end game in chess— and helps to concentrate both the patient's material and the therapist's work, and to prevent therapy from becoming diffuse and aimless and drifting into a long-term involvement. It enables the prospect of termination to be brought in quite naturally as the time for this approaches; and often this enables a therapy that had been in danger of becoming diffuse to become clear and focal again. To adapt Dr. Johnson, being under sentence of termination doth most marvelously concentrate the material.

With trainees under supervision, we now have a standard limit of thirty sessions. This is well above average for the nine short favorable cases in the present series (mean 20.0, median 18), but it gives opportunity to make up for mistakes that may hold up the work for several sessions. In exceptional therapies that are expected to be more complex or more difficult, we have used a time limit up to one year (roughly forty-six sessions, with holidays).

We have also come to realize that in fact it is much better to set a time limit in terms of a definite *date* rather than a number of sessions. This obviates the necessity for both therapist and patient to keep count, which is not easy; and it also removes at one stroke all sorts of complications to do with whether or not to make up sessions that the patient has missed, and having to judge whether his absences were due to reality or to acting out. If he has a long and unavoidable absence, the time can always be made up to him.

PLANNING AND TECHNIQUE

When I was writing *SBP* I was always coming up against the observation that two or more aspects of brief therapy that appeared originally to be separate were really interdependent. Thus, the possibility of using transference interpretations (an aspect of *technique*) clearly depends on the type of patient chosen (an aspect of *selection*). We meet the same phenomenon here: Not only is the ability to make a therapeutic plan an important criterion for *selection;* but a plan means an intention to conduct therapy in a particular way and hence is an implied *prediction;* and the intention to conduct therapy in a particular way immediately involves *technique*—and moreover, the more detailed the planning, the more do aspects of technique need to be described in the plan. Thus, planning, prediction, and technique are best all considered together.

This leads at once to the answer to a question that I am often asked at discussions of brief psychotherapy, How is it possible to keep interpretations focal? I have always found this a difficult question, but the reason, I think, is

that the true answer often lies not in technique at all but—before therapy
starts—in selection and planning. Put briefly, the best way of keeping
interpretations focal is to select focal patients in the first place and then to
formulate a correct therapeutic plan.

We may elaborate on this by the description of an ideal type of case, not
an idealized case, since approximations to this situation are quite frequently
met in practice. It is in cases of this kind that brief therapy can be at its
most radical.

In formulating a therapeutic plan, the ideal situation to meet at initial
assessment is one in which as many as possible of the following seven
conditions are fulfilled:

1. *The Current Conflict.* There is a precipitating factor that gives a clue to
   the current conflict.
2. *The Nuclear Conflict.* There are (a) previous precipitating events, or
   (b) early traumatic experiences, or (c) family constellations, or (d)
   repetitive patterns, which give a clue to the nuclear conflict.
3. *Congruence between Current and Nuclear Conflict.* The current conflict and the nuclear conflict can be seen to be basically the same.
4. *Response to Interpretation.* The patient responds to interpretations
   about aspects of this conflict.
5. *Motivation.* After interviews in which these interpretations have been
   given, the patient's motivation remains high or increases.
6. *Transference.* The conflict is one that is likely to manifest itself in
   the transference.
7. *Termination.* The nature of the termination issue can be foreseen, and
   this in turn can be related to the nuclear conflict.

If most of these conditions are met, it is hardly too much to say that—
with a reasonably competent therapist—(1) therapy cannot help being focal,
(2) its aims can be clearly defined, and (3) its course, though not, of course,
its outcome, can be broadly predicted.

These three statements may be taken in turn. First, therapy cannot help
being focal because the patient shows a single type of problem running
through his life. It seems probable that any material that he brings will
represent an aspect of this problem, and all the therapist will have to do is to
interpret each aspect as it arises.

Second, the aim of therapy can be clearly defined in the light of the
principles discussed earlier. This will be to clarify the three components of

the impulse–defense triad of the nuclear nuclear conflict, and then to complete the triangle of insight.

Third, provided the formulation is correct, the course can equally be predicted. The early part of therapy will be concerned with clarifying the impulse–defense triad, working toward deeper and more disturbing material; the middle part will be concerned more and more with making the T/P link; and the later part of therapy will be concerned with bringing out feelings about termination, expressing these in terms of the nuclear conflict, and making the T/P link in this area as well.

This kind of statement may well be greeted with some skepticism, or even (as I have heard in the past) with the epithet "omnipotent." Yet, even at the time of Balint's workshop, some of us tried to formulate such predictions before the beginning of therapy; and in recent years I have been doing the same in the Tavistock brief therapy unit. It is only as I write now, clarifying in my own mind principles that I have been teaching for years, that I see how almost automatic the process of prediction can sometimes be.

In fact the seven conditions listed above could easily lead to the headings of an Initial Assessment Form and a Prediction Form, as will be illustrated in some of the following cases.

We have never in fact formulated our predictions quite as exactly as described in this way, but it is clear that we understood how to do it implicitly, as some of these examples will show. Furthermore, as already discussed, prediction will involve both selection and technique; and this subject will therefore provide an opportunity to illustrate many of the principles that have crystallized from this whole work, clinical and statistical, together with some thinking about the future.

Because most of the examples are fairly recent, follow-ups are relatively short, and it is possible that some of the therapeutic results may be reversed by later events; but I feel I have justification for believing that *over the whole sample,* as in fact happened with the later follow-up of the *SBP* cases, the basic principles would still hold firm.

THE PRESENT POSITION

It remains to consider the overall position of brief psychotherapy and to put the present work into perspective.

This work was originally undertaken at a time of complete chaos in the theory and practice of brief psychotherapy, when all possible opinions could be found, from the most conservative to the most radical, on selection criteria, technique, and outcome. As now becomes clear, this illustrates most pointedly how fallacies arise from clinical impression unsupported by systematic evidence:

Anyone who practices long-term psychotherapy occasionally meets a type of patient who may be described as a "ripe plum," ready for picking, a phrase introduced by Henry Dicks in the early discussions in Balint's workshop. This is often a basically healthy patient suffering from symptoms due to an acute conflict, whose unconscious is very close to the surface, and who responds dramatically to a simple piece of insight that, to an experienced psychotherapist, is utterly obvious. Robert Knight (1937) quotes a typical example: a farmer suffering from weakness of his right arm, which was very clearly a conversion symptom designed to prevent him from being able to express his wish to hit people; and which was relieved almost immediately by what amounted to a single interpretation. In this type of situation, what the therapist sees is the dramatic relief of symptoms. He does not, of course, conduct any systematic follow-up; and if he is a well-trained analyst he assumes that since the deep anxieties have not been worked through, the therapeutic effects can go no further. He then reaches a generalization, expressed quite explicitly in this paper by Knight:

Short psychotherapy of this kind, based on analytical understanding, is valuable in relatively acute but not too severely sick cases in which quick help is needed and in which more prolonged, orthodox psychoanalysis is inexpedient. It should be understood that such treatment is more or less symptomatic and palliative, tends merely to relieve the distressing symptoms and does not alter to any great extent the underlying personality. It may be, however, that the insight gained by the patient from such psychotherapy may enable him to understand himself better and thus strengthen him against breaking down under the stress of similar situations in the future.

Thus is born the conservative generalization about *selection criteria* and *outcome;* and since this type of therapy usually involves neither the transference nor the roots of neurosis in childhood, there are also born conservative generalizations about *technique*.

This kind of generalization is strengthened by various other situations. The first occurs when a patient breaks off treatment in the early stages with apparently little achieved. Here he may later find that he cannot manage and he then returns and undergoes long-term treatment. These are the patients that we know about and who therefore lead to biased observations. We know nothing about the ones who do not return, and we do not take them into account in drawing conclusions.

Similar considerations apply to another situation, when a patient shows dramatic improvement after a short period of treatment and suggests termination. Long, and quite valid, experience has taught us that this is often (always?) a "flight into health," and it is our duty to convince the patient that he is not well at all and to bring him back into treatment. Here there are three alternatives: (1) We fail in this endeavor and he later relapses and returns; (2) we succeed, and he goes on to long-term treatment; or (3) we fail, and he is never seen again. Once more, our observation is biased because it is patients in the first two circumstances whom we know about, and both of these circumstances involve relapse. Thus is born the generalization that no patient can really get better unless he receives long-term treatment and his deep anxieties are resolved.

A third type of situation arises when the therapist is concerned with short-term therapy in a busy psychotherapeutic clinic. Here a large part of the population of patients may well be those in crisis, and the therapist aims to give the patient as much insight into the crisis as possible and to return him quickly to normal life. The observation is often made that the patient may use this as a point of growth, and thus the quite valid generalization is made that the outcome of such therapy may be permanent personality change; but the *in*valid generalization is then made that these patients in crisis are the only types for whom brief therapy is possible.

A fourth type of situation results from the observation of the use of the orthodox psychoanalytic technique in long-term therapy. Here we employ the standard techniques of interpretation of resistance and transference, and after a time we observe the development of the transference neurosis, and we go on to use this therapeutically in a process that is, of course, uniformly time-consuming. We do not observe exceptions to this, and reach the generalization that this is the inevitable consequence of techniques based on psychoanalysis, and a necessary condition to the patient's recovery.

There is in all these situations a single common type of fallacy: The circumstances of our work cause us to observe certain phenomena repeatedly, and we come to believe that these are the only phenomena to occur, without asking ourselves whether there may be hidden unobserved exceptions.

In fact, these exceptions *have* been observed from time to time ever since brief psychoanalytic therapy began; and the more often, the more systematic the investigation has been. Among the more recent authors we need to mention Pumpian-Mindlin (1953), Sifneos (1972), and Wolberg (1965); but really priority must be given to Alexander and French. Anyone who reads their case histories can see the clinical (not, of course, the statistical) evidence for the great majority of what has been written in the present work; to generalize, the use of all the basic psychoanalytic principles, especially interpretation of the transference and transference/parent link, in a radical technique of brief therapy leading to radical outcome.

Why then were their conclusions not immediately accepted? It seems to me that their unconscious must have been involved in the way they presented their findings, because they cannot have consciously intended to convey the impression that they were advocating a universal modification of psychoanalytic technique, rather than simply the flexible application of basic psychoanalytic principles to brief psychotherapy. If anyone wishes to be reminded of the effect of their book on orthodox psychoanalytic opinion, he should read the vituperative review by Ernest Jones in the *International Journal of Psychoanalysis* (1946), where, after an attempt to soften what has gone before, the "return of the repressed" occurs with shattering impact in the last paragraph:

So far this review may appear to be mainly adverse. Nevertheless we consider the book to be a valuable and useful one. To practitioners having little or no knowledge of psychoanalysis, and perhaps holding a position at a clinic attended by a large variety of patients, it should prove not only valuable but illuminating. Such penetration, skill, and tactfulness in the handling of patients as are here demonstrated will show other workers the advantages of an inspired and highly trained team. Our only criticism is that such a reader would be left in ignorance of the important fact that besides the various methods here described there is such a thing as real psychoanalysis.

The word "unconscious" is not mentioned in the index, nor have we been able to find it in the text itself. Perhaps indeed it is not germane to the content of the book.

(After quoting this passage I was relieved to find that the word "unconscious" does occur in the present book, and I will take care to ensure that it is included in the index.)

Jones's last paragraph is, of course, absurd, because the case histories deal with nothing but the patients' unconscious in an entirely psychoanalytic way.

This passage illustrates very clearly how, although a reader might have taken note of the case histories themselves, he was left with the overall impression of an attack on orthodox psychoanalytic technique. As a result the empirical evidence contained in the case histories was totally overlooked.

The trouble was, of course, that quite apart from Alexander and French's presentation, these radical observations stood in complete contradiction to general clinical experience. The effect on opinion has been—to use correctly, I think, a psychoanalytical term for a defense mechanism—a "splitting" between conservative views and radical evidence that has persisted to the present day.

It needs to be said again and again that the successful use of psychoanalytic methods in brief psychotherapy is a tribute to psychoanalysis, not an attack upon it; especially when, as here, it is shown that the more psychoanalytic the technique, the more successful the therapy. The only unpalatable fact to emerge is that patients may sometimes appear to recover without going through the deepest psychoanalytic processes; but this is an empirical observation as surprising to us as to everyone else, and it has to be faced.

In fact, we were started on the road to these discoveries by chance: We stumbled upon the fearless use of psychoanalytic technique, and the treatment of relatively disturbed patients, the first because of our training, and the second because of the relative rarity of "suitable" cases; and the combination of the two generated a momentum of its own. This in turn generated the desire to find out what really happened to patients under a variety of conditions. We have thus filled in some of the gaps left by relying on clinical impression alone, and—as always when any scientific problem is investigated—some of the results have been quite unexpected.

These results may now be summarized in the form of five major generalizations, from each of which important clinical consequences follow:

The first generalization is that *the capacity for genuine recovery in certain neurotic patients is far greater than has hitherto been believed.*

This has the following important clinical consequence:

Brief interventions of all kinds, from the most conservative to the most radical, can be therapeutically effective, and one of the tasks of the clinician is to determine how radical an intervention is needed in any given case.

The second generalization is that *there exists a type of patient who can benefit radically within the limits of brief psychotherapy from partially working through his nuclear conflict in the transference.*

It is important to note that this type of patient is very different from the "ripe plum" as described by Knight. With the type considered here, the therapist needs to do far more than just give a simple piece of insight in one or two sessions. On the contrary, he needs to use the full range of psychoanalytic technique to face the patient with his conflicts, and then a number of sessions to work them through. This is hard psychoanalytic work, involving such basic principles as the interpretation of resistance, watching for the development of the transference, and perceiving and interpreting the link to childhood.

The third generalization is that *such patients can be recognized in advance through a process of dynamic interaction, which must be allied with clinical experience of the dangers of dynamic psychotherapy.*

The principles of selection embodied in this generalization are the most difficult to convey; but it can be said that such patients are responsive, well motivated, appear to have the strength to face their disturbing feelings and to carry on their own lives independent of therapy; that a circumscribed focus can be formulated; and the many possible dangers of dynamic psychotherapy appear to be avoidable.

The fourth generalization is that, with such patients, within limits, *the more radical the technique in terms of transference, depth of interpretation, and the link to childhood, the more radical are the therapeutic effects.*

The fifth generalization is that *there exist certain more disturbed or more complex patients with whom a carefully chosen partial focus can be therapeutically effective.*

This is the area above all that needs further investigation.

Some of these generalizations are new, some are not, but even those that are not have never been generally accepted. They all amount to an extension of the limits of brief psychotherapy toward the more radical end of the spectrum. Perhaps, therefore, one of our major contributions will have been to support this extension with overwhelming evidence.

When these kinds of intensive brief therapy are added to the full range of methods—including crisis intervention, as enumerated by Sifneos; and to these are added all kinds of marital, family, behavioral, and newer techniques—perhaps brief therapeutic methods may make an important contribution, if not to the overwhelming problem of human mental health, at least to the efficiency of psychotherapeutic clinics.

Finally, at a time when psychoanalytic methods are under attack, and when much research evidence is tending toward the conclusion that therapeutic factors in many different kinds of psychotherapy are common and nonspecific, we appear to have shown on the contrary that the application of specific psychoanalytic techniques leads to radical therapeutic outcomes. This is an observation with far more than purely practical implications, which needs to be taken into account in all theories of the human personality that may be be written in years to come.

REFERENCES

Alexander, F., and French, T. M. (1946). *Psychoanalytic therapy.* New York: Ronald Press Co.

Balint, M., Ornstein, P. H., and Balint, E. (1972). *Focal psychotherapy.* London: Tavistock. Philadelphia: Lippincott.

Finesinger, J. E. (1948). Psychiatric interviewing. I. Some principles and procedures in insight therapy. *Amer. J. Psychiat.* 105, 87.

Jones, E. (1946). Review of Alexander, F., and French, T. M., *Psychoanalytic therapy. Int. J. Psychoanal.* 27, 162.

Knight, R. P. (1937). Application of psychoanalytic concepts in psychotherapy. *Bull. Menninger Clinic* 1, 99.

Malan, D. H. (1963). *A study of brief psychotherapy.* New York: Plenum Press.

Pumpian-Mindlin, E. (1953). Considerations in the selection of patients for short-term therapy. *Amer. J. Psychother.* 7, 641.

Sifneos, P. E. (1972). *Short-term psychotherapy and emotional crisis.* Cambridge, Mass.: Harvard University Press.

Wolberg, L. R., ed. (1965). *Short-term psychotherapy.* New York: Grune and Stratton.

18. Two Different Kinds of Psychotherapy of Short Duration

Peter E. Sifneos

Misunderstandings and confusion have marked the use of the terms "brief" and "short-term" psychotherapy. A variety of therapeutic techniques which have little or nothing in common with each other except the short time interval have been treated as identical with no attempt to define and describe the specialized features of each type.

This attitude may be due to the preference of most psychiatrists for long-term psychotherapy. It may be true that long-term psychotherapy is a useful psychiatric treatment and, in certain instances, the only way to help a few seriously disturbed patients, but it is not true that it is invariably the psycho-therapy of choice.

Against this trend there are a few notable exceptions (4–9, 13, 24, 25), and among these in my opinion the work of Alexander (1–3), Malan (10–12), and McGuire (14, 15) stands out.

The purpose of this chapter, which is based on nine years of experience with patients treated in the Psychiatry Clinic of the Massachusetts General Hospital, is to present a conceptual frame of reference for two different kinds of short-term psychotherapy. The criteria for selection of patients, the specialized techniques utilized, and the follow-up findings will be discussed briefly.

It must be emphasized, first of all, that shortening the period of psycho-therapy should not be an economic expedient to meet the growing demands for psychotherapeutic services in many communities, nor should it be viewed as a second-best alternative which aims at replacing long-term psychotherapy or circumventing psychoanalysis. Various kinds of short-term psychotherapy should be an addition to the psychiatrist's armamentarium and should be offered to patients suffering from a variety of mild emotional illnesses, as well as to certain patients with more severe and protracted types of psychiatric disorders (11).

Reprinted by permission of Plenum Publishing Co. from *Brief Therapies,* H. H. Barton, ed., New York, 1971, pp. 82–90.

Because they are offered to different types of patients and are technically dissimilar, psychotherapies of short-term duration may be divided into two types: (1) *anxiety-provoking* or dynamic; and (2) *anxiety-suppressive* or supportive.

ANXIETY-PROVOKING PSYCHOTHERAPY

Similar in theory to psychoanalytic or dynamic psychotherapy and offered to individuals who have some strengths of character, this kind of treatment emphasizes that a certain degree of anxiety is necessary during the interview because it motivates the reluctant patient to understand the nature of his emotional conflicts, to recognize the reactions that he utilizes to deal with them, and to enable him to have a corrective emotional experience. Anxiety generated during the interview may be used as a tool in assisting the patient to change his maladaptive behavior and to attain a state of improved emotional functioning.

Anxiety-provoking psychotherapy is goal oriented and in most cases can be: (1) *short-term therapy* (18), which I define in this chapter as lasting anywhere from two months to one year, with an average of four months; or (2) *crisis intervention* (21), defined as lasting up to two months. These time intervals are not arbitrary and are mentioned simply as guidelines. Only rarely may they be extended over longer periods of time. Psychoanalysis is, of course, anxiety-provoking psychotherapy of long-term duration.

Short-Term Anxiety-Provoking Psychotherapy

This type of psychotherapy is offered to patients selected according to the following criteria (20): (1) the patient must be of above average intelligence, as demonstrated by work or educational achievement; (2) he must have had at least one meaningful relationship with another person during his lifetime; (3) he must be flexible and able to interact with the evaluating psychiatrist by expressing some affect during the interview; (4) he must have a specific chief complaint; and (5) he must be motivated to work hard during his treatment and have fairly realistic expectations of what can be achieved.

It may appear that patients who fulfill our criteria for short-term anxiety-provoking psychotherapy are so healthy that they do not require any treatment at all. Quick value judgments about the triviality of the patient's difficulties should be avoided, however, and emphasis should be placed upon how serious the emotional disorder is and how the patient who is suffering from it can function before and after treatment (20). Before the patient is accepted for psychotherapy, his motivation for treatment must be further assessed in a final goal-setting interview (23). This is crucial prognostically.

Important as selection criteria may be, it is realized that to assess some of the points that have been outlined is not easy. Sometimes one discovers the seriousness of certain narcissistic, masochistic, dependent, or acting-out tendencies only after psychotherapy has begun.

Case 1. We saw a 35-year-old married banker who complained of anxiety when his boss talked with him about the prospects of his becoming a vice-president. He said he had been contented with his job and did not want any more responsibility. This characteristic dated back to his relationship with his father, whom he had always tried to please, and had continued subsequently with people in authority.

He liked to view himself as a "good boy," and mentioned that as an adolescent he had had syphilophobia without ever having had sexual intercourse. He remembered that his mother had reassured him about this but cautioned him not to talk to his father about it. He was fairly happy in his marriage but was always uneasy about sexual relations, which he tried to avoid whenever possible. This seemingly passive streak was considered ominous, but because he fulfilled our criteria and seemed to be functioning reasonably well, he was accepted for treatment.

In his second interview he announced that another man had been made the vice-president of the bank, and he claimed that his anxiety had disappeared. From then on he talked in his interviews only about pleasant memories, such as "basking in the sun during his vacation." His passivity had been underestimated during the evaluation and as soon as his anxiety disappeared his motivation to understand himself vanished. He developed no understanding of himself; therefore his therapy proved to be ineffective.

Requirements and Technique (18, 20, 22). The interviews are face-to-face, once a week, lasting for about 45 minutes. The therapist encourages the establishment of rapport with the patient and tries early to create a therapeutic alliance. He utilizes the patient's positive transference feelings explicitly as the main therapeutic tool. His specific goal is to concentrate on a circumscribed area of unresolved emotional conflicts underlying the patient's symptoms. He actively bypasses character traits such as masochism, excessive passivity, and dependence which give rise to therapeutic complications.

The therapist takes advantage of the fairly lengthy time lag in the appearance of the transference neurosis in relatively healthy patients in order to perform his therapeutic task. Thus he avoids its development. His emphasis is on problem solving so that such techniques as have been learned by the patient can be utilized effectively by him in the future after therapy has been terminated. The treatment ends early, when the patient starts giving hints that the goals of therapy have been achieved, or warnings that he wants to prolong therapy.

Follow-Up. This is a summary of the patients' statements about the results of treatment (18, 20). They usually point to only moderate symptomatic relief. Their original expectations of the results of psychotherapy have become more modest and realistic (16). They describe psychotherapy as "a new learning experience," "unique," "rare," or "unusual." The level of their self-esteem seems to have been raised. They show that a limited dynamic change has occurred with the substitution of a new defense mechanism for an old one. There is evidence of problem solving and acquisition of new adaptive patterns. Those who show these changes rarely return for further treatment.

Crisis Intervention (21)

An emotional crisis (17) is defined as an "intensification of a painful state which has the potential of becoming a turning-point for better or for worse." It usually follows a particularly stressful event which induces some individuals, who are otherwise emotionally healthy, to seek immediate assistance. Three factors are required to estimate properly the intensity of the emotional crisis: (1) the history of the hazardous situation which led to its development; (2) a precipitating event which produced the sudden intensification of anxiety; and (3) a series of unsuccessful attempts to cope with this anxiety. With these factors in mind, the criteria for selection of patients are similar to those used for short-term anxiety-provoking psychotherapy.

Requirements and Technique. Emotional crisis intervention focuses specifically on the resolution of the emotional crisis, using anxiety-provoking techniques. It emphasizes: (1) the quick establishment of rapport and transformation of the therapeutic work into a learning experience; (2) the utilization of the patient's positive transference, but not, however, as explicitly as in short-term anxiety-provoking psychotherapy due to the shorter time interval; (3) the active review and understanding by the patient of the steps that have led to the development of the crisis itself; (4) the challenging and minimizing by the psychiatrist of action taken on the part of the patient which the doctor considers to be antitherapeutic and which may lead to difficulties in the future; (5) the learning by the patient to anticipate situations that are likely to produce unpleasant emotions. He does this by comparing his present problems with potentially similar experiences likely to occur in the future and thus prepares himself to meet future trouble by these problem-solving rehearsals. The therapeutic intervention is terminated after a few appointments.

Follow-Up. The patients usually overcome the emotional crisis that brought them to the clinic. Some feel that they are better equipped to deal with future difficulties, having achieved a better level of emotional functioning than that which existed prior to the onset of their difficulties. They are able to anticipate. They claim to have been taught to solve problems.

The differences in technique between these two kinds of anxiety-provoking psychotherapy are a matter of degree. In short-term psychotherapy the patient's transference is utilized systematically to achieve a limited dynamic change. This is an ambitious goal. In crisis intervention the therapist encounters his patient before his emotional conflicts crystallize into a psychiatric symptom and helps the patient learn to anticipate and solve future problems. The goal here is on prevention.

In sum, anxiety-provoking psychotherapy is both a therapeutic and a learning experience for the patient.

ANXIETY-SUPPRESSIVE PSYCHOTHERAPY

This kind of psychotherapy, offered to severely disturbed patients, aims to decrease or eliminate anxiety by use of supportive techniques such as reassurance or environmental manipulation, with or without drugs. It may be: (1) *brief therapy,* lasting anywhere from two months to one year; or (2) *crisis support,* lasting up to two months. It may also be of long-term duration, such as *anaclitic therapy* (19).

Brief Anxiety-Suppressive Psychotherapy

Patients with character defects who give a history of recent and rapid decompensation from a precarious level of emotional functioning, and who complain of lifelong psychological difficulties and poor interpersonal relationships, are selected according to the following criteria: (1) ability to maintain a job; (2) a strong appeal for help; (3) recognition that these symptoms are psychological in origin; and (4) willingness to cooperate in psychotherapy.

Requirements and Technique. The therapist sees the patient in face-to-face interviews once, twice, or even three times a week lasting anywhere from a few minutes to an hour. He tries to convince the patient that he is eager to help and allows him to talk freely without interruption. He "lends himself" to the patient by taking over some of his decision-making functions. He helps him to understand the ways in which he handled his feelings when faced with hazardous situations. He predicts the patient's future behavior on the basis of his past performances and thus prepares him to avoid future difficulties. He uses appropriate medication when necessary. The following example illustrates these points.

Case 2. A 24-year-old man who had been an overt homosexual since the age of 16 entered the Psychiatry Clinic complaining of panic, inability to work, and thoughts of killing himself as a way out of his misery. These symptoms had appeared as soon as his homosexual partner, with whom he had been living, left him following an argument. He had a history of lifelong emotional difficulties and had been admitted to mental hospitals on two occasions because of suicide attempts. Both of his parents had died in an automobile accident when he was two years old, and he had been brought up by relatives.

He was an intelligent high school graduate who had a fairly steady work pattern and seemed to be eager for help. In twice-a-week psychotherapy an attempt was made to relieve the acute distress over the loss of his boyfriend. His reaction pattern to previous losses was reviewed. He was complimented for seeking help in the clinic rather than resorting to suicide. The prospect of future troubles was discussed in detail. After a while, he started to feel better and returned to work. He was able to talk about his angry feelings at having been abandoned and soon established a new homosexual relationship. In four months he was symptom free.

Follow-Up. Although we have not studied the follow-up findings of this group as extensively, there seems to be: marked symptomatic relief, some evidence of ability to avoid situations that give rise to the difficulty, a tendency to view the clinic rather than the therapist as the supportive agent, no evidence of dynamic change, and a tendency to return to the hospital at times of future difficulties.

Crisis Support

Patients similar to those selected for brief anxiety-suppressive psychotherapy and facing an acute crisis are offered crisis support. Lasting up to two months, this therapy attempts to eliminate as quickly as possible the factors

that are responsible for the patient's decompensation and to help him overcome the acutely traumatic situation in which he finds himself. The emphasis
here is also on using anxiety-suppressive techniques. Drugs are given freely.
The patient is seen frequently for short intervals, depending on his needs.
The follow-up findings are similar to those obtained in brief anxiety-suppressive psychotherapy.

DISCUSSION

It should be evident that these two different kinds of psychotherapy, anxiety-
provoking and anxiety-suppressive, should not be compared to each other
since they are neither technically similar nor offered to the same type of
patient population. On the other hand, every effort should be made to
validate separately the results of each kind by research studies.

In the last four years we have set up a research project to appraise the
results of short-term anxiety-provoking psychotherapy. More recently we
selected 40 patients according to the criteria already set forth. We designated
alternately 20 as experimental and 20 as control patients, subdivided them
into age groups of 17 to 21 and 22 to 40, and matched them according to age
and sex. Ten are males and 30 females.

All are seen by two independent evaluators and are given an MMPI. The
control patients wait for approximately the same time that it takes their
counterparts to be treated. After the end of therapy of each experimental
patient, both he and his control counterpart are again seen by the same
evaluators and given the MMPI once more. The control patients are then
taken into treatment. Every effort is being made to follow up these patients
every six months for at least two years.

Since this work is ongoing, the findings will not be presented formally at
this time. It can be stated, however, that although the difficulties of such a
research project are many, it appears that our original impressions of the
results of short-term anxiety-provoking psychotherapy are being substantiated by this more systematic approach.

SUMMARY

In this chapter two technically different kinds of short-term psychotherapy
have been presented. The *anxiety-provoking* type is similar in theory to
psychoanalytic therapy and focuses on the resolution of emotional conflicts

that underlie the patients' symptoms. It is offered to patients with well-circumscribed neurotic symptoms, selected according to specific criteria. Depending on its length of time, it is subdivided into: (1) *short-term* therapy, which emphasizes problem solving and usually achieves a limited dynamic change; and (2) *crisis intervention,* which helps the patient to overcome an emotional crisis quickly.

Anxiety-suppressive psychotherapy is offered to a selected group of seriously disturbed patients who have recently decompensated and produces symptomatic relief by use of all sorts of supportive techniques. Depending on its length of time it is also subdivided into (1) *brief* therapy; and (2) *crisis support.* In follow-up, the patients seem to benefit in different ways from these two kinds of short-term psychotherapeutic techniques.

REFERENCES

1. Alexander, F. Principles and techniques of briefer psychotherapeutic procedures. In M. S. Wortis, M. Herman, and C. Hare (Eds.), *Psychiatric treatment.* Baltimore: Williams & Wilkins, 1953.

2. Alexander, F. The dynamics of psychotherapy in the light of learning theory. *Amer. J. Psychiat.,* 1963, 120, 440–449.

3. Alexander, F., and French, T. *Psychoanalytic therapy.* New York: Ronald Press, 1946.

4. Bellak, L. *Emergency psychotherapy and brief psychotherapy.* New York: Grune & Stratton, 1965.

5. Gillman, R. D. Brief psychotherapy: A psychoanalytic view. *Amer. J. Psychiat.,* 1965, 122, 601–611.

6. Hollender, M. H. Selection of patients for definitive forms of psychotherapy. *Arch. Gen. Psychiat.,* 1964, 10, 361–370.

7. Knight, R. P. Evaluation of the results of psychoanalytic therapy. *Amer. J. Psychiat.,* 1941, 98, 434–439.

8. Knight, R. P. A critique of the present status of psychotherapies. *Bull. N.Y. Acad. Med.,* 1949, 25, 100–115.

9. Knight, R. P. *An evaluation of psychotherapeutic techniques, psychoanalytic psychiatry and psychology.* New York: International Universities Press, 1954.

10. Malan, D. H. On assessing the results of psychotherapy. *Brit. J. Med. Psychol.,* 1959, 32, 86–105.

11. Malan, D. H. *A study of brief psychotherapy.* Springfield, Ill.: Charles C. Thomas, 1963.

12. Malan, D. H.: personal communications.

13. Masserman, J. H. (Ed.), *Current psychiatric therapies.* Vols. 1–6. New York: Grune & Stratton, 1961–1965.

14. McGuire, M. T. The process of short-term insight psychotherapy. *J. Nerv. Ment. Dis.*, 1965, 141, 83–95.

15. McGuire, M. T. The process of short-term insight psychotherapy. II. Content expectations and structure. *J. Nerv. Ment. Dis.*, 1965, 141, 219–230.

16. Sifneos, P. E. Phobic patient with dyspnea: Short-term psychotherapy. *Amer. Practitioner*, 1958, 9, 947–952.

17. Sifneos, P. E. A concept of emotional crisis. *Ment. Hyg.*, 1960, 44, 169–179.

18. Sifneos, P. E. Dynamic psychotherapy in a psychiatry clinic. In J. H. Masserman (Ed.), *Current psychiatric therapies,* Vol. 1. New York: Grune & Stratton, 1961, pp. 168–175.

19. Sifneos, P. E. *Ascent from chaos: A psychosomatic case study.* Cambridge, Mass.: Harvard University Press, 1964.

20. Sifneos, P. E. Seven years' experience with short-term dynamic psychotherapy. In *Sixth International Congress of Psychotherapy, London, 1964: Selected lectures.* New York: S. Karger, 1965, pp. 127–135.

21. Sifneos, P. E. Crisis psychotherapy. In J. H. Masserman (Ed.), *Current psychiatric therapies,* Vol. 6. New York: Grune & Stratton, 1966, pp. 125–128.

22. Sifneos, P. E. Psychoanalytically oriented short-term dynamic or anxiety-provoking psychotherapy for mild obsessional neuroses. *Psychiat. Quart.,* 1966, 40, 271–282.

23. Sifneos, P. E. The motivational process: A selection and prognostic criterion for psychotherapy of short duration. Paper presented at the Fourth World Congress of Psychiatry, Madrid, Spain, September 1966.

24. Stone, L. Psychoanalysis and brief psychotherapy. *Psychoanal. Quart.,* 1951, 20, 215–236.

25. Wolberg, L. R. *Short-term psychotherapy.* New York: Grune & Stratton, 1965.

19. Short-Term Psychotherapy and Emotional Crisis

Peter E. Sifneos

THE THERAPIST AND THE PATIENT FACE TO FACE

As there is much divergence of opinion about the whole subject of psychotherapy, so there is considerable controversy about the question of technique. For example, at one extreme there are those who think that no greater sophistication than common sense is required to sit down and talk with a patient. They believe that the training of psychiatry residents under supervision is a waste of time. On the other hand, there are those who think that every movement, look, gesture, posture, and word of the therapist should be dissected and studied closely, and his entire behavior rehearsed and reenacted.

The degree of the therapist's activity is also a subject full of controversy. It is sometimes advocated that the "blank wall" or "sounding board" attitude, and silence or minimal activity on the part of the therapist are the best technical maneuvers, while others recommend giving advice or talking a great deal. Sometimes they even consider the advocacy of physical contact with the patient.

In my opinion, the therapist's attitude has to do with two most important aspects: being idiosyncratic and spontaneous. Insofar as these attitudes are concerned, one may spell out certain technical guidelines or general principles which should be kept in mind but not viewed as unconditional authoritative rules for the therapist to follow. Within the context of these dimensions the therapist and the patient come face to face. What one should remember is that the patient needs the therapist's objective and novel approach to his problems, while the therapist needs the information which only the patient can provide, thus enabling the therapist, in turn, to reach a specific psychodynamic formulation of the emotional difficulties involved and thereby to be able to help the patient solve these problems.

Reprinted by permission of Harvard University Press from *Short-Term Therapy and Emotional Crisis*. Cambridge, 1972, pp. 93–123, 393–94.

There are certain essentials for becoming a short-term anxiety-provoking psychotherapist. The knowledge of the theoretical considerations involved in the selection criteria of patients, the technical requirements, the aims and goals, the results obtained, and the experience gained by treating several patients under individual supervision is an obvious prerequisite. Above and beyond these considerations, however, there are certain personality traits which, in my opinion, every psychotherapist must possess. Imagination, flexibility, and a dissatisfaction with the mere narrow gathering of facts are excellent qualities, because they denote inquisitiveness and the curiosity to pursue and understand the patient's problems. In addition, the detached and objective ability to assess the patient's difficulties must be counterbalanced by the intuitive, sympathetic interest in another suffering human being.

The therapist should decide as soon as possible what kind of psychotherapy he plans to employ and, tempting as it may be, he must not rely on the referring source for this decision. The well-known tendency of a beginning and anxious psychotherapist to rely on the superior knowledge of the experienced older referring psychiatrist or on the opinions expressed in the psychiatry record, and the failure to decide for himself as to whether to treat the patient (who may occasionally not be a good candidate for psychotherapy), has led to many a therapeutic tragedy. If he decides to use anxiety-provoking psychotherapy, there are certain tasks which he must do as soon as possible. He must again go all over the whole evaluation process as it was described in the previous chapter. The history-taking of the patient's emotional development should be utilized for the formulation of his psychodynamic hypothesis, and, at the same time, the selection criteria should be reassessed, so that the therapist is satisfied that the patient is indeed a good candidate for this kind of treatment. The preparation of the patient for short-term anxiety-provoking psychotherapy is just as important as the therapist's conviction that he should use this technique. After this, the therapist must, first of all, spend some time in educating the patient regarding what he is to expect. This process is part of the overall structuring of the psychotherapeutic process. McGuire,[1] who has utilized Bruner's[2] original concept, emphasizes that structuring and sequencing play an important role in this kind of treatment, not only during each psychotherapeutic hour but also throughout the entire treatment process itself.

PREPARATION OF THE PATIENT

The patient meets his therapist with certain expectations which have developed as a result of the process of evaluation. Although at first he might not have been as clearly aware of the nature of his emotional problem, as a result of the evaluation interviews he has been able to select one of his various complaints which he wants to eliminate and to assign to it top priority for treatment. Consequently, he expects to be able, more or less, to understand himself and overcome this specific difficulty, which, despite his efforts in the past, he had been unable to solve alone. In other words, a shift has taken place in the patient's expectations—from a wish for symptomatic relief to a wish for a more basic change in attitudes and understanding.

REQUIREMENTS

The interviews are face-to-face, once a week, forty-five minutes long, and at a specific time. It should be explained to the patient that if he arrives late he cannot expect that the time lost will be made up at the end of the hour, because this will interfere with the timing of the interview of the next patient. If something of importance to the patient is brought up at the end of the hour it should be made clear that it cannot be discussed until the next interview.

The time set aside specifically for the patient may not be utilized by anybody else; therefore, the patient must understand that he will be charged for missed interviews unless the prospective cancellation is discussed with the therapist in advance and an agreement regarding the time is reached between them. It is possible that one may view these requirements as too rigid or artificial. I think that this clear-cut elucidation of the position of the therapist is part and parcel of the education of the patient concerning the psychotherapeutic rules. It shows the patient that the therapist takes his role seriously. An example follows.

A thirty-two-year-old male patient who had difficulties with his girl friends and was worried about the situation following the first two interviews, arrived fifteen minutes late for his third appointment. This was discussed during the interview. He missed the fourth appointment but called up to say that he would be unable to keep it. He did not appear for the fifth appointment and did not telephone.

At this point the therapist wrote him a letter, stating that he was planning to terminate the therapy unless he heard from the patient within a week. The patient called up to say that he was going to keep his next appointment. He arrived early, apologized for the previous cancellations, and started to give some details about how he had forgotten the hour. The therapist interrupted him, stating that it was not a matter of an apology but was something else which, to him, was of much greater importance. He went on as follows: "I take psychotherapy seriously and I assume that my patient also has the same attitude. The kinds of difficulty which you have with women and which we decided to look into and try to disentangle seem to indicate a serious problem which interferes with your whole life, as you yourself have acknowledged. The problem cannot be eliminated unless you are here, for us to understand it and to try to solve it together. Your absence demonstrated to me that your initial interest in this task is dwindling."

The patient was taken aback by this straightforward presentation.

Patient: I did not realize that you are so keenly interested in helping me with my problems. Maybe I was trying to test you?

Doctor: Maybe you were, and this is of importance; but I wonder what you think of all the angry feelings that you expressed at your mother, which took you by surprise after we talked about in the interview. You may remember that you were fifteen minutes late the next time, and after we discussed this delay, I again asked you about your relation to your mother—particularly after your father divorced her. You changed the subject repeatedly from then on, and I brought you back to it over and over. Do you remember?

Patient: Well, yes. I do.

Doctor: How much does your tendency to avoid talking about the subject of your relation with your mother have to do with your missing the subsequent two hours?

The patient was noncommittal. The next hour he recounted a dream about his mother and himself which had bothered him. He said that he had not expected psychotherapy to be so disturbing. He had dealt with his anxiety by evading it—a familiar pattern which he had used in the past.

In reviewing this case in retrospect, it became clear that the therapist's confrontation about the missed appointments seemed to have played a crucial role in stimulating the patient's motivation to continue his treatment, which proceeded fairly uneventfully from then on.

The patient is free to use his hour in any way he sees fit. He may smoke if he so desires. The therapist usually takes notes, although there is some difference of opinion on this point. I, personally, take notes, and I find that it does not interfere with the spontaneity of the communication with the patient. Notes become invaluable to the therapist whenever he wishes to review the trend of a psychotherapeutic process. For example, they help him remember the details and associations of a specific event, or special fantasies which were brought up in relation to a certain dream. Nothing can be more impressive to a patient than to repeat to him his own words, to confront him with his own resistance, to clarify the way he handles his own emotional conflict, and to demonstrate to him a specific pattern of his own behavior. Finally, if an interview is to be tape recorded or videotaped, written permission must always be obtained from the patient. These mechanical devices are invaluable for teaching purposes. At this point I shall summarize the main technical factors of short-term anxiety-provoking psychotherapy which will be discussed in greater detail later on in this chapter.[3]

THE ROLE OF THE THERAPIST

The therapist encourages the establishment of rapport and tries to create early a therapeutic alliance. He must set up a tentative psychodynamic hypothesis in order to arrive at a formulation of the patient's emotional conflicts, based on the evidence which he has collected during the history-taking, which will guide him throughout the psychotherapeutic process. The therapist tries to investigate and arrive at an agreement with the patient as to what symptoms or interpersonal difficulties, or both, are considered to be of top priority and must be resolved. Furthermore, he must establish how these characteristics are associated with underlying emotional conflicts. This task is referred to as the definition of the patient's emotional problem which must be solved by both the therapist and the patient during the course of the psychotherapy. It is possible that this problem may differ from that which was decided upon during the evaluation. It should be remembered, however, that since the therapist is the one who will treat the patient, his assessment of the problem and his agreement with the patient become the basis for this mutual work.

He may try to convince the patient to modify the problem which is to be solved and to focus upon a new area of emotional conflict, if this becomes necessary as a result of new material which is brought up during the psychotherapy. His specific goal is to concentrate on a circumscribed area of the unresolved emotional conflicts which may be underlying the patient's problem and to teach the patient to become aware of them and to gain objectivity concerning them. He utilizes the patient's positive transference feelings explicitly and early, as the main psychotherapeutic tool. He uses confrontation and clarification in an effort to stimulate the patient to work through the material. In the example of the patient who started to come late and missed his two subsequent appointments, confrontation was used to stimulate the patient's motivation to pursue his treatment. Confrontation is also used to help the patient experience his transference feelings during the interview. The best way to achieve this is by utilizing anxiety-provoking questions.

Clarification is less painful. The therapist, having gathered all the important available facts about a given pattern of the patient's behavior, proceeds systematically to analyze and to assemble all its aspects in detail—as if putting together the pieces of a jigsaw puzzle—until it appears that the patient has seen the overall picture, understood its purpose, and has experienced the emotions associated with it. From then on, this type of analytic-synthetic method becomes a pattern to be utilized in other situations. The therapist can refer back to this first experience and use it as an example in future sessions. He bypasses character traits consistently, such as masochism, excessive passivity, and dependence, which give rise to therapeutic complications. He prepares the patient to rehearse his reactions and utilize whatever problem-solving techniques he has learned during psychotherapy, so that he may use them effectively to avoid difficulties in the future, after therapy has terminated.

He expects to help the patient achieve a basic change, so far as his interpersonal relationships are involved, as a result of his learning to solve new problems rather than to be satisfied with only symptomatic relief. Finally, he ends the treatment early. These technical points will now be discussed in greater detail under the following headings, which represent the five major phases of short-term anxiety-provoking psychotherapy: (1) The Patient-Therapist Encounter, (2) The Early Treatment, (3) The Height of the Treatment, (4) Evidence of Change, and (5) The Process of Termination.

THE PATIENT-THERAPIST ENCOUNTER

It has long been argued that it is difficult to differentiate clearly between psychiatric evaluation and therapy. Although psychotherapy starts immediately at the first encounter between the patient and his therapist, the therapist must complete the evaluation of the patient's problem as soon as possible. He must do this in order to prepare for the smooth development of the second phase of the treatment, by taking into consideration the patient's expectations about results of the therapy. Thus, he must establish rapport by utilizing the patient's positive feelings, which are usually present at this time. This enables him to set up a therapeutic alliance between the patient and the therapist and to create an atmosphere where learning can take place.

There is a second technical point which has to do with what has already been discussed—namely, the need to have a tentative psychodynamic hypothesis in order to set up a formulation of the patient's emotional problem. The importance of having such a hypothesis cannot be overemphasized, because it is a prerequisite for obtaining a complete history of the patient's emotional development, with special emphasis placed on the interpersonal relations, which give a clear picture of how the patient deals with the realities of the outside world. All this information helps the therapist obtain the evidence necessary for setting up a psychodynamic formulation of the patient's psychopathology, which will act as a guide to him throughout the course of psychotherapy. This is a difficult task. Details of information obtained as a result of persistent questioning are gathered in the therapist's mind and become the pieces of a three-dimensional puzzle which slowly fall in place at different time levels. A picture starts to emerge on one plane which is connected sooner or later by another picture on a different level. The complicated three-dimensional patterns start to merge and help build the skeleton of the psychodynamic edifice which helps in understanding the patient's emotional problem. What is left to be done during the psychotherapy for both the patient and the therapist is to clarify certain areas and consolidate others until the final structure which emerges is firmly established.

The Patient's Expectations

Although certain attempts have been made during the extensive evaluation to assess the patient's expectation of what he hopes to achieve during the psychotherapy, it is important that this be done once more. What are the patient's goals? What does he anticipate will happen during his treatment? What does he expect will be the role of the therapist? What does he want to achieve as a result of therapy? What does he view as his own role during this experience? Some of these questions must be clarified. The first encounter gives the therapist an idea as to what to expect and, in any case, it sets the tone for things to come.

The patient's feelings of enthusiastic anticipation about his treatment, or his disappointment after he has met the therapist, may be significant. Initial transference feelings may be associated and aroused in the patient which could color and influence the rest of the therapy. Thus, the patient's opening remarks and his choice of subject may give a significant clue as to what is to follow. They usually are representative of the patient's style. They are his opening gambit.

A twenty-seven-year-old student who had difficulties with his employer at work started his first interview by giving an elaborate account of his sexual life. When, finally, the therapist asked him why he was going into so many details, the patient looked surprised, and said, "Isn't sex what you psychiatrists are interested in?" The need to please the therapist was an example of his automatic response to people in authority—the very characteristic he resented. When the therapist mentioned that the psychotherapy was not set up for his own interest but was aimed at understanding and solving the patient's emotional problems, he seemed pleased, and said, "Well, maybe, after all, this treatment is going to do me some good!"

Evaluation and History-Taking

It is usually preferable to let the patient open the first interview and talk freely about whatever he wishes; yet, at the same time, tempting as it may be pursue in greater detail these opening remarks of the patient, this should not alter the therapist's determination to complete the patient's evaluation by obtaining a detailed history. Having emphasized during the first interview that psychotherapy should become a joint venture in which the patient participates actively and not as a passive onlooker, at some appropriate point the therapist should proceed with the history-taking, even if a complete past history has already been obtained during the evaluation interview. It may seem obvious that everyone knows how to take a history, since this is one of the first techniques that every medical student learns. It is very unfortunate, however, that this is not the case; and, because it has been taken for granted, many a psychiatry resident completes his training and still does not know how to take an adequate psychiatric history.

There are two schools of thought about history-taking. The famous "brown" or "red" history-taking guide book, on which every second-year medical student relies for information concerning what questions to ask during the "system review" or what points not to overlook as he attempts to get the social history, is viewed by him as an instrument which will help him solve the riddle of the patient's diagnosis. He tends to depend heavily upon it in an understandable effort to hide his inexperience. Although it is meant to be only a flexible guideline for the student to use judiciously, most often it is followed rigidly, with the result that the history becomes complete, but artificial.

Employing a set of instructions, which offer the patient a list of forced-choice questions which he must answer by a "yes" or "no," is not the best way to take a history. It does not follow, however, that an open-ended question approach is necessarily much better. Although the student may obtain some meaningful information in one area, letting the patient ramble on and on in a guideless way, as often happens, will result in much time being wasted and perhaps some vital clue or bit of information being lost.

It is important, then, that a judicious confrontation by open-ended and forced-choice types of questions, used in such a way as to obtain a clear and continuous picture of the patient's overall emotional development, is the most appropriate way to proceed. Special attention should be focused on the developmental history as well as on interpersonal relationships, particularly with parents, that prevailed during the first few years of life, on the early family atmosphere, on the school history, and on problems that arose during puberty and adolescence. Such information will probably give some clue as to the patient's ability to deal with difficult situations during his adult life in such important areas as his relations with others, his work, and his marriage. The manner in which the patient handles his anxiety should also be surveyed from his earliest years up to the present.

Slowly the areas of conflict and the maladaptive reactions employed to handle them will appear, and the repetitive difficulties in coping with certain hazardous situations will soon start to emerge. At such a point the therapist must ask specific questions; and, from the patient's replies, he must obtain the evidence, to his own satisfaction, as to whether his suspicions about a specific area of emotional difficulty can be confirmed. Sooner or later this will lead, in most cases, to a fairly clear picture of the patient's psychodynamics. A hypothesis, then, based on definite evidence emanating from the patient and not on idle speculation is formulated in the therapist's mind. Up to this time the therapist has used the patient as a source of information; now he needs to obtain from him a systematic statement about what he considers to be the problem he wants to solve during his treatment.

If both the therapist and the patient see eye to eye on this issue, no problem is anticipated. Most of the time, however, this is not the situation; and the patient, as has already been mentioned, must be asked to assign top priority to the area of the emotional problem he wants to solve. The therapist, if he disagrees, must present to the patient what, in his opinion, appears to be a more serious problem. Usually these two positions are not as opposed to each other as they may appear at first glance. What is needed is the establishment of a connection between the underlying conflicts and the superficial complaints. This is the task of the therapist. He must try to demonstrate to the patient convincingly and, as completely as it is possible to do, why he disagrees with him. Usually a compromise can be reached, as the following example shows.

A young man who complained of pain in his chest was referred from the medical clinic after having had extensive diagnostic studies, which were negative. He said he was afraid his trouble might be due to some serious disease; he felt sorry for himself. He mentioned, also, that he had difficulty in getting along with men, but he felt equally ill at ease with women. The therapist disagreed with the recommendation of the evaluation team, which had suggested focusing during the treatment on his relations to men. He was of the impression instead that the fear of illness was used as a way of getting sympathy and attention, and also as way to evade his anger for women, which he feared but was unable to express well. From the history-taking it became clear that the patient as a little boy had obtained sympathy from his "cold" doctor-father only when he was sick. To the therapist his reaction to his mother's rejection seemed to be a bigger problem, and he suggested to the patient that he think about it and be prepared to discuss it during the next hour.

The patient returned after one week, saying that he had given the matter much thought and added that, although the pains in his chest still continued and worried him, he realized that his angry feelings toward women bothered him and he was willing to explore them also. He went on as follows: "My girl friend is very unsympathetic about my pain. She claims that it is all in my mind. This attitude of hers irritates me, as it has always done. At such times I feel sorry for myself and go and talk to the guys in the office. You know, once you talk about illness, such as the flu or something like that, everybody gets interested and has something to say. 'Take aspirin.' 'Don't.' 'Excedrin is better.' 'No. I find a hot bath and a drink works best.' Well, you know all this, but such talk makes me feel better. Mind you, they are not interested in *you,* they are interested in your headache or your cough or in the chest pain. I am not saying that the pain is in my head. It is not. I feel it right here." He pointed to his chest.

The therapist said that he did not doubt in the slightest that the patient had a pain; but what he emphasized was that he could help the patient understand his reactions to this pain which seemed to create problems for him; and he added that, since the x-rays and other findings were negative, this indicated that there was no serious disease present. "After all, muscle spasm can cause pain," he said. "What seems to be the basic problem, in my opinion, is your anger at your mother or at your girl friend. Your fear that the pain is caused by something serious and also your efforts to use this fear in such a way as to get attention when you feel you need it seems to be a secondary reaction." The patient was hesitant but agreed to look into his particular difficulties with women. He went on. "There is something inside me that says, 'Don't do it,' he said, "so I figure that it must be important and that I resist it. I am willing to give it a trial."

Thus, by the end of the first few interviews, the patient's emotional difficulty would have been defined and it was agreed upon that it was the basic emotional problem to be solved during the psychotherapy. Following is another example.

A nineteen-year-old high school senior came to the clinic complaining of being bored and depressed after the death of his mother two years before and of his having difficulty in deciding whether to go to college or join the army. It was thought during the evaluation that an unresolved grief reaction seemed to be the main problem, but the therapist was not exactly sure that this was the only difficulty. In the second interview he was impressed by the fact that this young man had serious difficulties with his father and other male friends, and he pointed this out to the patient. "It seems that your angry outbursts at your friends when they try to advise you about what to do are like your angry outbursts at your father when he inquires about your future career." The patient admitted that he was angry with his father and saw joining the army as a way out of his dilemma. "In Vietnam I could get away from it all." The therapist then asked, "Now, what in your opinion is a bigger problem for you—your feelings of sadness for the loss of your mother or the problem with your father, your friends, and this need to run away." The patient was silent for a while. Finally, he said, "In a way, I know I miss my Mom. She was nice to me and my sadness has a lot to do with the way I feel. But at the present time my big problem is my indecision about the army and college. This is what I want to figure out."

Finally, the therapist must set up certain criteria as to the barest minimum necessary to be achieved during the treatment and make predictions for himself as to whether they can be accomplished.[4] These minimum conditions should be stated in writing, if possible, so that they could be used eventually by those who might be interested in evaluating the results of psychotherapy. Both patient and therapist, as a result of their initial encounter and their different points of view, have a common task, i.e., the solution of the patient's specific emotional problem which must be attempted during the ensuing psychotherapy.

EARLY TREATMENT

The Patient

During the early part of the therapy the patient's positive feelings for the therapist are at their height. After having tried repeatedly but unsuccessfully to solve his own difficulties, the patient has reached the point where he sees the possibility of success becoming a reality, and he looks upon the therapist as someone with whose assistance he would be able to finally succeed. Expectations of the therapist's magical ability to produce a cure, if they have persisted until now, are beginning to recede rapidly. The elaborate efforts made by the evaluators and by the therapist should dispel and dissipate any unrealistic expectations still remaining. The patient has been treated as an adult. His role as a participant—as someone who has the capabilities of working hard and of solving his own problems, which have been emphasized—gives him a sense of well-being. He is grateful to his therapist. Furthermore, he feels excited as a result of the work on the definition of the emotional problem. A wider horizon is opened to him. Not only may his symptoms improve but he may now have the opportunity to learn more about himself and to effect a change. He is imbued with eager anticipation.

This is how one patient expressed himself: "I never expected that psychotherapy could be like this. Although I knew that there were not going to be any miracles and that it was not like going to see your family doctor, and although everybody made it quite clear that it was up to me to work and solve my problems, I somehow, deep inside, couldn't believe it. The first two sessions made all the difference. It is hard to explain how. I know, realistically, that we decided on what we had to do. This, I am sure, helped a lot. It clarified things. But—what was even more important—I felt convinced that it was really up to me. I felt that you trusted me and had confidence in my being able to do the work. This was very satisfying. After each of the sessions I went to my room and did a lot of thinking. The amazing thing was that I started to think in a different way. This was very exhilarating. The possibility that I might discover a new way of looking at myself made a great difference. I just want to mention this today because it is very important to me." These words give a vivid picture of the early phase of the treatment.

The Therapist

The therapist not only must not ignore such positive attitudes but must take advantage of them and utilize them explicitly and vigorously. Here is the golden opportunity to bring the old family conflicts into the atmosphere of the newly developing doctor-patient relationship. The therapist must then confront the patient with his transference feelings and use them as the main psychotherapeutic tool.

The term "transference" must be defined. It is an emotional interaction between two people, having both conscious and unconscious aspects.[5] Freud's[6] discovery of transference became the basis of psychoanalysis, as well as of all kinds of psychodynamic psychotherapy. Freud himself thought, however, that transference occurred not only during but also outside of psychoanalysis, and Glover[7] considered it as "a normal affective phenomenon governed by unconscious mechanisms of displacement and promoting social adaptation." In this way transference is considered as applying not only to neurotic patients but to everyone, including the therapist. In addition to Freud and Glover, several psychoanalysts have been interested in transference phenomena and have written extensively about it. Recently, Greenson[8] emphasized that repetition and inappropriateness are outstanding characteristics of transference, and Alexander and French[9] stressed that a distinction should be made between transference reactions adequate to realistic present situations and significant repetitive reactions to a person from the past.

An example of an instantaneous development of transference that relates to past experiences is found in a patient of mine in her third year of psychoanalysis who admitted with some embarrassment that she was surprised to find out that my nose was "perfectly normal." When I asked her to elaborate, she admitted that ever since her first evaluation interview she had felt sorry for me because of my "crooked nose." This conviction of hers was associated with her wish to make men turn into women, which had been worked through very slowly during her psychoanalytic treatment, before her final willingness to give up this neurotic idea. It was at this point that she was willing to acknowledge to herself that her analyst's nose (which was supposed to have been "flattened out and eaten by disease") was "perfectly normal."

The emphasis up to now has been on the patient's positive feelings. This, of course, does not mean that ambivalent feelings do not exist. It simply means that the positive ones predominate. This obvious distinction should also be kept in mind because feelings from the past should be differentiated from those of the present. Thus, the patient's anger at the therapist may be perfectly legitimate, justifiable, appropriate, and realistic, and may have nothing to do with past situations.

A further distinction is also necessary at this point: one should differentiate clearly between transference and transference neurosis. Transference neurosis is the transfer of all conscious and unconscious fantasies, emotions, and attitudes for all people in the past on to the therapist during the height of the psychoanalysis of neurotic patients. Glover states: "Everything that takes place during the analytic session, every thought, action, gesture, with reference to the external thought and action, every inhibition or thought or action relates to the transference situation between the patient and his analyst." Although the line of demarcation between these two terms may not be clear cut, it is helpful to keep them apart. For practical purposes, it is in degree that they differ.

In any case, the therapist must take advantage of the long time lag in the appearance of the transference neurosis in fairly healthy patients. The longer this time lag, the healthier the patient. The analyst, by use of free association, has access to the patient's fantasies and unconscious conflicts and is therefore able to analyze the transference neurosis successfully before psychoanalysis ends. The transference neurosis is, of course, an intense experience. In one form or another, however, and after some time has passed, the transference neurosis will appear during the course of psychotherapy. If the therapist lets this happen, invariably complications are likely to develop which may prove to be insoluble, because the therapist is limited by the once-a-week, face-to-face interactions and has at his disposal only limited access to the patient's unconscious conflicts. He is, therefore, unable to analyze successfully the transference neurosis, and the therapy ends in an impasse. This is one of the main reasons why the therapy must be conducted with relative speed and must end quickly.

From all this it should be clear that the therapist should be on the alert to pick up the early manifestations or delays in the appearance of the patient's transference feelings for him. Thus, as soon as the patient makes reference to him, even in a casual way, the therapist must express interest and be willing to discuss it, even if this happens in the first or second interview. The therapist does not have to wait until transference appears as a resistance. This principle, which has been recommended by Freud and several analysts, involves the unrealistic and unconscious aspects of the transference feelings which should not be gratified or manipulated. On the contrary, what is emphasized in short-term anxiety-provoking psychotherapy is that confrontation of the positive transference does not need to be postponed. The patient is capable of examining every aspect of his behavior, tracing the origins of his emotional problem in the past, and seeing for himself the ways in which his conflicting desires give rise to symptoms that have produced his difficulties. To do all this, he must first understand his reactions toward his therapist. The therapist, in turn, must use his wisdom in reference to this which, in my opinion, is what Felix Deutsch [10] calls "the correct use of the doctor-patient relationship." In a different dimension, this is an ingredient in the education of the patient concerning psychotherapy, because it involves the teaching of the rules—an integral part of the preparation for the work to be done during the height of the treatment.

THE HEIGHT OF THE TREATMENT

The following case is an example of a patient at the height of therapy.

A thirty-two-year-old man, while on his honeymoon, suddenly developed acute obsessive-compulsive symptoms consisting of a need to pick up papers or pieces of metal from the floor or from the street. He had the urge to make sure he had picked up everything and to know that everything was clean. He was also tormented by the preoccupying thought that he might have been in some way responsible for his father's death, although he realized the absurdity of such thoughts. He was intelligent, he related very well, and had a good work history and fairly good relations with other people. He responded well during the evaluation interview and was eager for help because his symptoms interfered with his marriage and his work.

His father had died six months before the treatment was started. He said that although he cried during his father's funeral, he had noticed on other similar occasions an inappropriate tendency to laugh. Soon after his father's death he met a young woman, fell in love with her, and, after a courtship of four months which involved satisfactory sexual relations, they decided to be married. While on their honeymoon, his wife received a wedding present. She hurriedly opened the package, and, in her delight at its contents, she forgot to gather up the wrappings that were strewn all over the floor of the hotel room. When the patient saw them he meticulously started to pick them up and experienced a feeling of intense anger as he did so.

He always came early for his interviews, related well to his therapist, and made a genuine effort to understand himself. At the fourth interview, he arrived ten minutes late and was silent when the therapist pointed this out. After a moment, he turned to him angrily and said, "You're blaming me for being late." The therapist emphasized that this was not his intention, at which the patient apologized, was silent for a while, and then said that an entirely irrelevant episode from his childhood had crossed his mind. He was encouraged to talk about it, and, as he reminisced, he said that when he was twelve years old he liked to go fishing with his father. On one occasion he dropped his fishing rod accidentally, and, as he tried to retrieve it he almost overturned the boat. His father was very angry at him, and said, "You are always so careful. How can you be so careless now? I could have drowned!" He said he remembered being angry at that time and that this irrelevant thought had entered his mind: "How can my dad be so sloppy and leave his desk in such a mess!" He again became silent. When asked what he was thinking, he said he had noticed several sheets of paper lying on the psychiatrist's desk. Upon being asked what this reminded him of, he answered, "Dad did not give up. He called me to his study and kept on lecturing to me about safety. I didn't care. The only thing I could think about was the sheets of paper strewn all over his desk," and then, with a smile, he added, "You have a cute secretary."

At the next interview the patient was fifteen minutes late. He said that his compulsive symptom had been very bothersome for the whole week. He then announced that he had an irrelevant urge to take the wastepaper basket and strew its contents all over the doctor's desk. At this point he became visibly anxious, his hands started to shake, and he said that this thought was in some way connected with the fear that he was somehow responsible for his father's death. As the therapist drew a parallel between his attitude toward him and his attitude toward his father, the patient admitted having the fantasy that he wished the therapist would drop dead suddenly. "Then I can sleep with your secretary," he added. The patient was on time for the next appointment and told about the following dream: He had gone hunting with a girl friend when, suddenly, a huge ostrich appeared and started to chase him. Although he wanted to kill the bird to impress his girl friend, he was unable to do so because his gun "would not fire." He woke up feeling somewhat relieved. When asked about his association to the dream, he remembered that when he was six years old he tried to peek at his older sister while she was taking a shower and felt vaguely that this was a wrong thing to do. Later on during the interview he remembered his father returning from fishing. He had caught several fish, and they were all lying on the kitchen table. What had impressed him most was a rainbow trout that appeared to have been decapitated accidentally. He shuddered at the idea and was visibly shaken. In the next few interviews he talked a great deal about the relations he had had with women. He had loved to give parties, and women were very much attracted to him, but he had had a tendency to disregard his own date and flirt with his best friend's girl. He said that his mother always liked to give dinner parties when his father was on fishing trips. His father disapproved of this. For those dinner parties, he remembered, his sister always dressed seductively. He remembered having dreams of being married to his sister but always woke up feeling very anxious because a dark figure would invariably threaten him. He also noted that his wife looked very much like his sister.

The psychodynamics of this case are obvious. The therapist brought together repeatedly the attitude of the patient toward his father and toward the therapist. His anger at the therapist and his wish that he would drop dead were associated with the fishing episode, the decapitated rainbow trout, and his father's death. His attitude toward his sister, his marriage after his father's death, and his wishes for the psychiatrist's secretary were also linked together. As a result of the interviews the patient reexperienced his past emotional conflicts with his father which were underlying his obsessive symptoms and thus he was able to solve his emotional problem. His symptoms improved dramatically and soon disappeared. Therapy was discontinued after the sixteenth interview. Three years later he was asymptomatic.

The Therapist

The height of the treatment is characterized by the repeated efforts of the therapist to concentrate in the areas of unresolved conflicts which underlie the patient's emotional problem and to avoid the difficulties involving character traits which are considered to be more primitive. To accomplish this, the therapist utilizes confrontation and anxiety-provoking questions in order to bring into the open the patient's emotions to help them become "alive," so to speak, during the interview in order to help him look into the areas of difficulty he tends to avoid. These techniques stimulate the patient to reexamine past conflicts and instruct him repeatedly how to analyze, scrutinize, and understand his reactions and his emotional behavior. Confrontation is an invaluable technical tool of short-term anxiety-provoking psychotherapy. It is a forceful approach which the therapist chooses to use in order to achieve his therapeutic goals because he is convinced that it will produce better results than a gentler, more persuasive technique. Confrontation creates pain, but the therapist is convinced as a result of the detailed assessment of the patient's strengths of character that he deals with someone who can withstand a considerable degree of strain. Finally, he encourages the patient to employ new ways to deal with his conflicts and to solve his problem. Let us now consider these points in greater detail.

Concentration on Areas of Unresolved Emotional Conflicts. The therapist is aided in this task by his psychodynamic hypothesis of the patient's difficulties. He then proceeds to get more information from the patient about past experiences and to assess his evidence. Sooner or later the transference may appear as a resistance, and at this point the therapist switches from getting information about conflicting situations with people in the past to confronting the patient with his resistant feelings toward the therapist in the present. As soon as this has been accomplished the therapist may resume getting information about past events.

One could conceptualize the work of the therapist as a walk on two parallel tracks. He steps at first on one and then, after a while, he shifts to the other. One track deals with the transference relationship; the other is concerned with the patient's past. As long as the patient is able to stay on the subject which is being worked through currently in the treatment, there is no need for the therapist to bring the transference into the open. Sooner or later, however, resistances start to appear. The whole tone of the interviews start to change. Instead of the smooth narrative and eager attempts of the patient to understand what happened, silences interrupted by efforts to avoid and to change the subject start to appear. The patient may even hint at the transference by shifting and talking in oblique ways about the therapist. The whole interview seems fragmented. At such time the therapist should shift his attention to difficulties arising within the transference relationship, which must be clarified before the therapy can proceed smoothly again.

In addition to confrontation, clarification is also an important technical tool. Whenever he has a clarification to make, the therapist uses (as already mentioned) clear-cut examples which have come up within the context of the transference relationship, and, at such times, he may quote verbatim the patient's statements from past interviews. This usually makes a very marked impression on the patient, who may be startled, surprised, or even shocked to hear his own words spoken back to him. It is like hearing one's own voice on a tape recorder. There is usually a sense of slight embarrassment on the part of many of us on such occasions. "Do I really sound like that?" we ask. This is due, possibly, to our inability to see or hear ourselves from the outside or to conceptualize the way we really look or sound to other people. In this sense, note-taking comes in handy for the therapist, because if he does decide later to quote the patient he must do so correctly.

Slowly the conflicts start to emerge, as well as the emotions and the reactions utilized to handle them. Following is an example.

A twenty-year-old student, who was treated for a depression, had talked repeatedly about his tendency to look down on himself, not to care about his appearance, and generally to let himself drift. He had said in several interviews that when he was young he got a lot of attention from both of his parents (who were obsessed about cleanliness) when he dirtied his clothes while playing. He had, in passing, during the first interview, admitted that he, as a child, purposely smeared mud on his shirt. He also had mentioned having begged for money once from an old woman while playing in the park. She, seeing that he was well-dressed but covered with mud, felt sorry for him, gave him a quarter, and washed off his coat for him herself.

In his interview the patient told how he had spent all of his money and had gone out of his way to ask several of his friends for loans. He also complained of feeling weak, incapable of doing anything well, and of being "deflated" and sad. After hearing all this for a while, the doctor exclaimed, "You emphasize how sad you are, but we know you enjoy the attention you get from being broke, from begging, and from being helpless." "Good point," the patient said, and was silent for a while. He then added, "I understand, but you don't seem to care how I feel"; and then much more emphatically he went on, "You are so disinterested you don't give a damn. You don't give me a thing in the way of help."

Doctor: Like what, for example?

Patient: Food for thought, anything, any old crumb.

Doctor: So. Although you profess to understand, you are, right this minute, still begging, asking me to give, begging for crumbs.

Patient (pause): Damn you!

Doctor: I can see you are angry when your manipulations fail. The question is whether begging for money and for bread crumbs or "smearing your clothes with mud" is to your best interest. Yet we do know that you are capable at other times of getting along without all this self pity.

Patient: I know what you mean. I am surprised, however, that you do know all this.

Doctor: At this time you may interpret what I told you as having given you those bread crumbs. Actually I gave you back what *you told me* in our first interview.

Patient: I had completely forgotten! (He looked thoroughly surprised.)

This type of clarification of the patient's behavior was used several times during the psychotherapy, until the patient seemed to refer to "his sad sack ways" with amusement.

Active Avoidance of Characterological Complications. Knight[11] emphasizes the importance of "the optimal level of positive feeling in the patient which is conducive for effective psychotherapeutic work," and Alexander stresses that if the transference neurosis is "allowed to reach great intensity" it can "impair the therapy." These technical points, discussed already, are best achieved, in my opinion, only if the therapist actively avoids dealing with deep-seated characterological traits in the patient, such as excessive passivity, narcissistic gratification, or dependence. When the patient introduces such material, it is best for the therapist to intervene and change the subject, despite the fact that this may tend to make the patient angry.

A thirty-two-year-old single obese male teacher had a quarrel with a colleague. The episode reminded him of a similar experience when he was in college and his roommate had succeeded in taking his girlfriend away from him. He said that at that time he was so angry he felt hungry and had gone to the most high-priced restaurant and "spent a fortune" eating the most expensive foods. From then on, he continued to talk about his enormous enjoyment of eating and of food, as he had done in previous interviews. This was his favorite reaction to competitive and frustrating situations. The therapist cut short these ruminations by asking for details about the recent encounter with the other teacher.

Use of Anxiety-Provoking Questions. The fact that the patient must become aware of his feelings "alive," so to speak, during the interview, has been emphasized already. This can best be done by bringing to the patient's attention the negative feelings he experiences toward his therapist because of the use of anxiety-provoking questions. This initiates the final stage of this phase of short-term psychotherapy, when the patient must be confronted with his anger, fear, anxiety, and sadness, which result from the examination of the areas of emotional conflict that underlie his problem. It is understandable, of course, that the patient has evaded, more or less, such painful feelings. Now it is time that they should be brought into the open more systematically and understood more clearly. The patient, by expressing these unpleasant emotions toward his therapist without being judged, experiences what Alexander calls "a corrective emotional experience" with all its therapeutic value.

The therapist, as a result of his previous work on the patient's positive transference, has established himself as an ally, a trustworthy teacher, and a reliable friend. Thus, he is now able to increase the patient's desire to understand his conflicts, even at the expense of some pain.

Keeping the patient's energy within the problem area, as emphasized by Semrad,[12] is a crucial technical procedure in short-term psychotherapy, but this is no easy task.

In another interview, a patient I have already mentioned, who complained of chest pain and talked at length about feeling sorry for himself and about his need to be taken care of, was recounting with much emotion how he managed to get his friends to reassure him. He went on, "They know I'm miserable, that

I don't have much stamina, that I am so strong—I mean, so weak." The therapist thought it was appropriate to utilize this slip of the tongue, to show the patient how he used weakness to cover up his strength. "Are you strong?" the therapist asked. The patient blushed. Looking annoyed, he denied it vehemently and emphasized that he did not "believe in all this Freud stuff." But the therapist persisted. He went back relentlessly to the conflict, despite the patient's annoyance, and gave him specific examples. The patient finally retorted, "You keep on needling me and it hurts, but you may be right. I shall think about it."

The therapist's counter-transference feelings also play an important role. He must be aware of this so that he does not use anxiety-provoking questions to punish the patient, to see the patient suffer, or to enjoy a position of superiority. It is clear that such attitudes will create difficulties, and it is because of this that the therapist should have had psychotherapy or a personal analysis as a part of his education, so as to be at least partially aware of any of his sadistic tendencies.

This type of persistent work and anxiety-provoking questioning is difficult for residents to learn to employ, and it is particularly important that the supervisor help them to become aware of their own feelings and reactions. One of our residents was repeatedly unable to deal with his counter-transference feelings for a seductive female patient who was in the process of expressing (in a roundabout way at first, but progressively more openly) her positive transference feelings for him. For example, when she talked about her sexual involvement with men who had the physical characteristics of her therapist, he ignored her remarks and changed the subject repeatedly. She soon became angry and started to criticize him at an increasing rate. The case was being presented to a group of residents as a teaching exercise, and this made the task more difficult for the therapist. Tension was rising, and it was obvious that, unless the issue was dealt with directly, the therapy would be unsuccessful. At this point, the resident was encouraged to tackle the transference issue head on. After three agonizing interviews, the therapist, urged and supported by the group, was able (to his own amazement) to deal with the transference, counter-transference issues. The ensuing relief on the part of the patient was just as great as the general enthusiasm which his interpretation produced on both his colleagues and his supervisor.

The therapist demonstrates repeatedly the pattern the patient has employed in order to deal with his conflicts. Again and again he uses, and quotes from, the patient's interview material and from the transference relationship notes.

He urges the patient to look at the pattern of his behavior and helps him to learn how his present-day interpersonal relationships are associated with his past neurotic difficulties, and how, for example, his regressive behavior or his tendency to act in a certain way in order to avoid his unpleasant feelings have created unnecessary complications in his life and caused him much discomfort. By concentrating and focusing on the understanding of the means he has used to avoid anxiety, the therapist helps the patient to examine, and repeatedly reexamine, past problems in the light of the present situations, and to experiment with new ways to solve his emotional problem. His role, thus, is clearly one of an unemotionally involved teacher.

The Patient

The patient, as we have seen, is becoming aware of his feelings, positive and negative, during the interview. He soon starts to raise questions on his own and tries to find the answers to them without needing to rely exclusively on his therapist's probing. As a result of his own self-questioning and the persistent and relentless anxiety-provoking work of the therapist, the patient slowly allows himself to experience painful reactions, and his motivation to come to grips with and solve his emotional problem becomes intensified. When he starts, during his treatment, to ask the kinds of questions about himself which might have been raised by the therapist, this is a sign that the psychotherapy is proceeding well.

One evidence that the patient is learning to solve emotional problems is his ability to bring into his interviews spontaneous associations which reenforce or add to the understanding of the emotional difficulties discussed during the previous interview, as if there had been no interruption of one week. The patient gradually becomes convinced that he must face up to his painful affects and interpersonal difficulties.

At some point, the patient usually identifies with the therapist.[13] The distinction should be made here between imitation and identification. The former involves paying lip service to, or agreeing with, the therapist's words without understanding what they mean. Identification, on the other hand, is a dimension of the learning process which involves motivation and selectivity and which encourages independence. It gives the patient an opportunity to make free choices. Interference with identification may become a hindrance to learning and may develop into the crucial point of failure in the psychotherapeutic process.

As the patient's curiosity rises, his motivation increases. Instead of avoiding and evading his painful feelings, he now knows that he must bring them into the open and examine the underlying conflicts that give rise to them. When the emotional problem is finally solved, the patient experiences a profound sense of satisfaction. On the cognitive level, this feeling is similar to what one experiences when he masters a difficult situation or solves a complicated mathematical problem. Furthermore, the realization that he was able to master his tangled interpersonal difficulties with their all-powerful emotions—something he has been unable to do before—gives him a feeling of liberation and his self-esteem is augmented. Relaxation of the probing on the part of the therapist reenforces the patient's reward and not only contributes to a decrease in tension but also gives rise to a sense of well-being.

EVIDENCE OF CHANGE

The Therapist

When the therapist is able to demonstrate repeatedly, and to the patient's satisfaction, that the emotional conflicts, as seen in the transference relationship, are a repetition of the patient's interpersonal relationships with people in the past and to show how such difficulties have been handled in the past, how they have created his current entanglements, and how the patient has learned new ways to deal with them and is able to solve them, a great deal has been accomplished. But he must not rest upon his laurels. He must first look for evidence that this has really happened. Hints that it is occurring may emerge as a result of a certain reduction of tension which he notices is taking place during the psychotherapeutic interviews. Tangible demonstration of progress in the patient's behavior must now be shown to occur outside the interview periods.

Sooner or later the patient gives signs that improvement in interpersonal relationships, in areas where difficulties previously occurred, is taking place. Such tangible evidence of progress should alert the therapist to the realization that termination should be considered. The possibility that a flight into health may be taking place must be considered by the therapist. One can easily distinguish, however, between this kind of solid demonstration of improvement, both inside and outside the psychotherapy, and some action taken by the patient to run away from his problem. When the therapist is also able to encourage the patient to utilize finally these newly developed problem-solving capabilities in other areas of emotional conflict in order to use them effectively in the future, he has succeeded in his task.

The Patient

The patient's abilities to give examples to prove that he is utilizing what he has learned during the therapeutic situation are the best evidence that such new learning has taken place as a result of the treatment. This is, I assume, what Alexander means by "interpretative learning," and Freud by "the process of reeducation." The reader should be cautioned here about the use of the word "learning," which usually implies only an intellectual acquisition of information to be used subsequently. The learning that takes place as a result of short-term anxiety-provoking psychotherapy has an emotional component, also, but this should come as no surprise. It should be remembered however that what Strupp [14] calls "therapeutic learning" depends to a large extent on the emotional tie between the patient and his therapist, and is therefore "predominantly experiential." As has already been mentioned, it has been shown that the learning of autonomic responses can take place in animals. Is it possible, then, that emotional learning can take place in humans?

THE PROCESS OF TERMINATION

The Therapist

Satisfied that meaningful progress has taken place, but realizing that all difficulties have not yet been overcome, the therapist must avoid the temptation of prolonging the treatment. He not only must be modest enough to realize that he is not indispensable to the patient but he must also remember that there are certain behavior patterns which cannot be altered by psychotherapy. The therapist's attitude toward early termination plays a very crucial role at this juncture. His counter-transference may be prejudiced against termination; his narcissism and his own intellectual curiosity may not only interfere with, but also prolong, the treatment unnecessarily. Young residents are sometimes fascinated both by the "material" and also by the desire to become "amateur psychoanalysts." They are inclined, then, to prolong psychotherapy, hoping to turn it into quasi-psychoanalysis. This tendency is also caused by the attitude of those residents' supervisors who, as analysts, have abandoned psychotherapy long ago and have tended to think of it as a second-best alternative compared with psychoanalysis. In their capacity as supervisors of psychiatry residents, they tend to encourage the prolongation of the treatment. There should be a choice not as to what is the "best" treatment but as to what is the "best" treatment for *whom* and for *what*.

At times, a patient who may show early improvement is treated for several years without any further evidence of progress. Actually, he may be worse off for having become dependent upon the therapist. This, in part, may be due to the false impression that improvement can result only after long treatment and that any other kind of success is only short-lived. Glover gives an example of an obsessive patient who improved after being treated for only a few months. In a casual, accidental follow-up thirty years later, the improvement had been maintained with no evidence of any returning symptoms. Fenichel [15] also emphasizes that some patients with obsessive-compulsive symptoms of short duration can improve rapidly. Thus, at times, these early improvements are long-lasting.

The therapist must watch for hints about termination emanating from the patient; or, if they are not forthcoming, he must initiate the talk about termination himself and emphasize that he trusts the patient to carry on his work alone. At this point the therapist concentrates on working through the patient's ambivalent feelings, which usually predominate at times when termination is contemplated. Separation and loss are invariably painful. The therapist must help the patient to recognize that positive and negative emotions may coexist at such times and may be unusually strong. It should be remembered that such emotions are, in reality, aimed at the therapist, although they may have existed at times of separations in the past. Keeping the discussion, then, focused on the present relationship and the prospect of its ending helps to overcome this phase fairly quickly. Otherwise, prolonged discussion of previous separations tends to lengthen the treatment.

After talking about the prospect of termination, a young woman discussed a dream during her next session: She was walking alone on a narrow street when she noticed that her therapist was driving a huge convertible car full of beautiful blondes. She waved at the therapist as he passed by, but he paid no attention to her. Instead, he seemed to laugh at a joke made by one of the girls. Then she realized suddenly, to her horror, that the car was on a dead-end street and that it was going to crash. She called out, without being heard. She screamed just before the car hit a brick wall. She rushed to the scene of the crash and by performing mouth-to-mouth resuscitation, she was able to save the therapist's life. By the time she came for her appointment she had analyzed her jealousy, had recognized that the blondes represented other patients who were going to take her place after the end of her treatment. She was disturbed, however, by the thought that she had wished the accident to occur. The therapist explained to her that such emotions were to be expected at a time of separation and that, because they exist, it does not mean that her good responses toward him in the past have disappeared. "After all," he said, "you did save my life with a kiss!"

Part of this work involves making an effort to predict the patient's future course on the basis of what was learned during the treatment and to help to prepare him for his life after psychotherapy has ended. The therapist should encourage the patient to talk about his expectations of what could happen after psychotherapy is concluded. Again, here the role of the therapist has to do with the education of the patient concerning his future. The emphasis should be on encouraging him to take over the role of the therapist as it was formulated during psychotherapy and to make it a part of himself after the treatment is terminated. Thus, the patient should be expected to continue to raise questions about himself which he must try to answer and to anticipate hazardous situations which are likely to produce crises and cause him to become anxious. He should be warned that during such times he *may* revert back to some of his old ways, but he must persist in trying to solve the emotional conflict which is responsible for the crisis in the same way that he has done during his treatment. Teaching the patient to anticipate is a crucial dimension of the termination phase. If this process of reeducation, with its emphasis on preparing the patient for the future, is successful, it carries with it the promise of victory far greater than what was achieved during psychotherapy. Learning a new way of looking at and questioning himself offers the patient the key to overcoming his future emotional difficulties. It is like a vaccine which immunizes him from future ills.

Formal agreement about termination should be reached as soon as possible, but this should be done in a flexible way. We have been unwilling to set up artificial time limits, such as a fixed number of interviews. Every patient should be given time enough to solve his emotional problems, provided he does not take advantage of this to unnecessarily prolong his psychotherapy.

The Patient

When the patient starts to experiment successfully on his own, outside the treatment period, as a result of his solid problem-solving accomplishments during the psychotherapy, he begins to wonder whether termination should be considered. At such times he feels confident that he can face the future with the new weapons he has acquired, and, as already mentioned, he gives hints to the therapist in the form of such questions and comments as: "Where do we go from here"? or "It seems that we have accomplished what we set out to do." He anxiously and eagerly expects his therapist's agreement, even though, at the same time, he feels sad at the prospect of losing the therapist who has been an ally and a friend, and of ending psychotherapy, which has been, on the whole, a meaningful experience for him. Ultimately, the wish to be independent, to trust himself, and to experiment with his new freedom are stronger and healthier desires than the wish to perpetuate the relationship with his therapist.

REFERENCES

1. M. T. McGuire, *American Journal of Psychotherapy*, 22 (April 1968) 218–232. M. T. McGuire and P. E. Sifneos, "Problem-Solving in Psychotherapy," *Psychiatric Quarterly*, 44 (October 1970), 667–674.
2. J. S. Bruner, *On Knowing: Essays for the Left Hand* (Cambridge, Mass., Harvard University Press, 1962); Toward a Theory of Instruction (Cambridge, Mass., Harvard University Press, 1966).
3. P. E. Sifneos, "Short-Term Anxiety-Provoking Psychotherapy," *Seminars in Psychiatry*, 1 (November 1969), 389–399.
4. D. H. Malan, *A Study in Brief Psychotherapy* (Springfield, Ill., Charles C. Thomas, 1963) and *The British Journal of Medical Psychology*, 32 (1959), 86–105.
5. P. E. Sifneos, "Dynamic Psychotherapy in a Psychiatric Clinic," in *Current Psychiatric Therapies*, ed. J. Masserman (New York, Grune and Stratton, 1961), pp. 168–174.
6. S. Freud, "The Dynamics of Transference. On Transference Love on Beginning Treatment," in *The Complete Psychological Works of Sigmund Freud*, vol. XII (London, Hogarth Press, 1958).
7. E. Glover, *The Technique of Psychoanalysis* (New York, International Universities Press, 1955).
8. R. Greenson, *The Technique and Practice of Psychoanalysis* (New York, International Universities Press, 1967).
9. F. Alexander and T. French, *Psychoanalytic Psychotherapy* (New York, Norton, 1945).
10. F. Deutsch and W. Murphy, *The Clinical Interview*, vol. I (New York, International Universities Press, 1954).
11. R. Knight and C. Fredman, *Psychoanalytic Psychiatry and Psychology* (New York, International Universities Press, 1954).
12. E. V. Semrad et al., "Brief Psychotherapy," *American Journal of Psychotherapy*, 20 (October 1966), 576–599.

13. P. E. Sifneos, "Learning to Solve Emotional Problems: A Controlled Study of Short-Term Anxiety-Provoking Psychotherapy," in *The Role of Learning in Psychotherapy,* ed. Ruth Porter (London, J. and A. Churchill, 1968), pp. 87–97.

14. H. Strupp,"Teaching and Learning in Psychotherapy," *Archives of General Psychiatry,* 21 (August 1969), 203–212.

15. O. Fenichel, *Psychoanalytic Theory of Neurosis* (New York, Norton, 1945).

20. Why Short-Term Psychotherapy for Borderlines?

Miguel A. Leibovich

The effectiveness and appropriateness of prescribing brief psychotherapy for borderline individuals is generally disclaimed. Assertions about its feasibility and usefulness are commonly met with skepticism.

In this paper I will delineate some of the reasons underlying my contention that short-term integrative psychotherapy (STIP) should definitely be considered as a therapeutic modality during the clinical evaluation of a patient presenting a borderline personality disorder.

It should be kept in mind, however, that short-term treatment is not indicated for all borderlines and that careful criteria for the selection of patients should be followed before the recommendation is made.

In arriving at an understanding of why STIP is effective in the treatment of borderlines, consideration is given to: (1) the technical strategies specific to the briefer procedures and (2) the particular symptomatic and characterological manifestations of this patient population.

Among the reasons that pertain to the technical aspects of the short-term therapies are: (1) time, (2) acceptability, (3) expectations, (4) therapist's activity, (5) therapist as a real person, (6) focused approach, (7) emphasis on patient's determination, (8) withdrawal and regression.

Among the reasons that relate to some of the particular characteristics and symptoms of borderline patients are: (1) autonomy, (2) relationships, (3) structure and controls (4) choice, (5) engulfment drives, (6) fantasied universe, (7) reality, (8) ego functions.

REASONS THAT PERTAIN TO THE TECHNICAL ASPECTS OF THE SHORT-TERM APPROACHES

Time

In STIP, from the very beginning, the fact that the therapeutic encounter will be short is emphasized. Circumscribing the therapy to a definite time period

Reprinted by permission of S. Karger A. G. from *Psychother. Psychosom.* (1983) 39:1–9.

is a most important element. It has to be discussed thoroughly during the therapeutic agreement. From the start, it places a central emphasis on the eventual separation. Borderlines' recognition of boundaries, as we well know, is fragile. The incipient commitment to this short-term relationship stresses the reality of other inevitable limits and frustrations experienced in their daily living. It is also an acceptance of the separateness, distinctiveness and aloneness of the self, of separations and losses that need to be faced and deprivations that must be felt and endured. Borderlines are exquisitely sensitive to imagined or real rejections. Knowing early about the psychotherapy's end gradually accustoms these patients to the fact of that planned "abandonment," making it less devastating.

Shortening the treatment time establishes an understandable, observable and manageable segment of reality during which many of these human dilemmas must be acknowledged, owned and wrestled with. It also evokes feelings of frustration, disappointment and resentment as a result of patients' realization that their wishes for a "merged" relationship with the therapist will not materialize. The setting of a schedule creates a different attitude from that of long-term therapy, especially if the patient is told or made to assume that the length of treatment is open-ended.

The concept of briefness poses a challenge, encouraging patients to accomplish more in a shorter period. It also implicitly reflects the therapist's confidence on the patient's ego resources. The commitment to a treatment period with a time constraint, with a beginning and an end in sight, gives a transitory sense of purpose. This is significant since these patients do not usually set and maintain purposeful plans and activities. One patient expressed it this way: "At least, for now, I have this period of purpose."

Borderlines have the tendency to minimize or reject their own accomplishments. The completion of the short period of treatment usually implies an accomplishment. Even if a positive outcome is rejected by the patient, the reality of having persisted with the therapeutic task is in itself an achievement.

STIP provides a time period that patients can tolerate and finish. They are usually left with a positive experience of a relationship that opened, continued and closed, hopefully on a good note. It is an ego-integrating experience in finishing something.

Acceptability

Borderlines exhibit externalization, concreteness, poor introspective capacity, reduced phantasy formation, proneness to action, low frustration tolerance and subsequent demandingness for immediate gratifications and solutions.

In clearly defining the therapeutic work and its focus STIP is more easily understood and accepted by these patients. Not unusually, they do resist longer psychotherapies that stress personality change, envisioning them as less immediately rewarding. Monetary matters also add weight to these patients' preference for short-term interventions.

The effectiveness of STIP is more tangibly assessable. If the outcome of the treatment is positive, this brief experience becomes the preamble for the future acceptance of further therapeutic work. Therefore, acceptability by this patient population is another valid reason for considering STIP as an alternative in the clinician's armamentarium.

Expectations

Borderlines may show distrust and marked skepticism for psychotherapy and have low expectations for its results.

Behavior is not entirely affected by the past. It is also influenced by expectations of future consequences. There is evidence that the outcome of therapy can be influenced significantly by what the patients are led to expect. During the therapeutic contract and agreement it is explained, tentatively, what can be expected from the treatment, both in terms of process and results. The patient is told that therapy will be only temporary, from 9 to 12 months or less, that an understanding of the precipitating events that led the patient to seek treatment will be attempted, that probably the symptoms and difficulties will decrease, that an improvement of the patient's self-esteem may occur and that a resumption of his previous level of functioning (if this is impaired) will be aimed at. In general, any intervention which heightens the expectation of help and relief will lead to some of those changes.

Briefness creates, per se, an anticipation that a shift will occur within the time allocated. This expectation in itself contributes to actual beneficial changes. Patient's optimism surges. The therapist also conveys the belief that therapy is a task that can be ordered and the problems solved. Ordering is of importance for borderlines as it assists in the organizing capacity of the ego.

Therapist's Activity

The therapist's active verbal role is basic for conducting STIP. It brings a strengthening of the patient's self-definition, differentness and separateness by demarcating and accentuating the boundaries between the two individuals. Unresponsiveness and silence may become intolerable and threatening. They elevate feelings of anxiety and uncertainty favoring decompensation, especially at first when the relationship is still tenuous.

Through this active, empathetic therapeutic stance the therapist reflects, absorbs, transforms and feeds back the patient's material, clarifying and gently confronting, while persistently maintaining contact, showing concern and understanding, setting limits when necessary via integrating comments and ego-supportive assertions.

The Therapist As a "Real Person"

In treating borderlines the therapist must present himself/herself as a "real person." This enhances the patient's deficient internalization and identification processes. It serves as a model for the establishment of other real object relationships. The encouragement obtained through the relationship with the therapist who acts as a responsive, real person involved in a respectful empathetic dialogue with the patient soon creates the impetus for trying new interactions on the outside, previously perceived as too threatening. In taking a natural and genuine stance the therapist need not cross the line of professionalism.

Focused Approach

For STIP's focused, problem-solving and structuring approach, patients must recognize and isolate the existence of a focal, troublesome issue, symptom or characteristic. There should be congruence between patient and therapist about the validity and relevance (in terms of the patient's life situation and priorities) of the focus selected for therapeutic work. For example, the chosen conflicts could be: low tolerance for frustration and consequent explosive destructive behavior, weakened ability to delay immediate gratifications, tendency to develop entangled interactions and relationships, vague self-other differentiation, tendency to externalization, diminished capacity for bearing anxiety, depression or other unpleasant affects, high degree of "personalization" in human contacts, exaggerated manipulative traits, overdependency which stunts the utilization of the patient's ego resources, etc. The agreed-upon focal issue is explored thoroughly and always kept in the foreground during the sessions. Excursions into unplanned areas are avoided.

This tactic creates an active participating therapeutic alliance which quickly enhances the patient's realistic internalization of aspects or functions of the therapist. The ego-building process that results from this interactional experience tends to neutralize the rage so typical of the borderline and avoid the primitive transference reactions so frequently the cause of therapeutic cessations or impasses.

Emphasis on Patient's Determination

An omnipresent sense of unworthiness causes the patients to be enveloped by doubts and uncertainties about how much they can do for themselves, how well they can understand their troubles and how much control they can exert over their maladaptive patterns.

The therapist conveys his faith in the patient's undeveloped ego capability to change his/her behavior and life predicament. There is an explicit emphasis on the importance of digging out, tilling and cultivating their unutilized determination. This enhances their budding motivation for using their capabilities for active work. For some patients, whose powerful oral strivings veer them toward passivity and symbiosis, this emphasis can be too threatening, requiring a more balanced approach.

Withdrawal and Regressions

Not uncommonly, psychotherapies of long duration, nebulous in their goals, and not conceived on meeting the concrete and immediate needs of borderline people, are abruptly abandoned.

We all know of the proneness of borderlines for premature withdrawals from several therapeutic attempts. STIP's active, time-circumscribed, agenda-focused methodology engenders a higher degree of interest, stimulation and optimism in the course of therapy which energizes patients into continuing with their introspective work. The therapeutic process and the patient's movement during that period are intermittently reality-tested and supported, thereby helping to avoid intense overreactions and decompensating manifestations.

REASONS THAT RELATE TO SOME OF THE PARTICULAR CHARACTERISTICS OF BORDERLINES

Autonomy

Psychological autonomy is greatly impaired in these people. Short-term therapy aims principally at continuing the development of patient's synthetic capacities and toward the coordination and integration of the fragmented ego functions. The major thrust is to obtain a better functioning of the organizing sector of the ego. Small achievements during the therapeutic process in the areas of competence, self-assertion, separateness and individuation are realizations of ego autonomy which eventually produce a greater solidity of the self.

Relationships

Borderline's relationships are chaotic, tainted by feelings of distrust, fury, envy and jealousy, uncertainties and fears, intense fusing and distancing reactions, entitlement, demandingness, etc.

During STIP's encapsulated time period, the patient may examine an ongoing external interaction as well as that with the therapist and thereby zoom in and learn about his/her sensitivities and responses to other people.

Early on, they begin to observe their abilities for experiencing and tolerating intense emotions more effectively. Their fears about being overwhelmed and completely at the mercy of hurtful and unpleasant overreactions decrease. This brings encouragement for handling feared strong feelings in the context of interactions with others, in contrast to retreating into withdrawal or destructive activities.

Structures and Controls

Borderline's ego suffers from poorly developed inner control mechanisms. This approach provides a containing environment via a "structured life experience with another individual, the therapist," and a consistent limited period of self-exploration occurring within the framework of a "controlled reality." This brings about, rather soon, an understanding and better management of the patient's impaired impulse-control functions.

Choice As an Exercise for Ego Functions

Borderlines present considerable uncertainties about their right to choose and doubt their abilities for doing so. By selecting an "issue" for therapeutic work the patient exercises a choice. Through this process the problems have to be acknowledged and delineated, alternatives and consequences come into consideration, limits have to be perceived, emotions experienced and accepted, and responsible actions become actual possibilities. The ego functions of perception, thinking and execution (usually not adequately de-veloped) are activated and strengthened. Learning to make choices is also ego-organizing. It results in patients experiencing more keenly a sense of self as distinct from others. This recognition propels their self-acceptance, and firms up their sense of responsibility. It is an experience of ego awareness usually not previously perceived by them.

Engulfment Drives

As much as they crave it, borderlines intensely dread "closeness and en-gulfment." *Modell* [1968] has said: "These people experience the harrowing dilemma of extreme dependence coupled with an intense fear of closeness. They believe that 'closeness' to the 'other person' will be mutually destruc-tive. The true danger arises not so much from their aggression as from the more tragic fact that their love is destructive. They feel that to give love is to impoverish oneself and to love the other person is to drain him." The limited nature of this short-term therapeutic relationship and the explicit demarcation of the roles of therapist and patients evanesce the stormy clouds of fusion and engulfment. Patients are less threatened by these drives. They know realistically that the therapy and the relationship will be interrupted soon.

Fantasied Universe

Many borderlines have a loose concept of what "measured periods" are. They seem to exist suspended in a "timelessness and fantasied environment." For them, the customary moments or hours for something to happen, begin or end appear unimportant. They operate within the realm of a fantasied universe. STIP as an ego- and reality-oriented approach interferes with and alters this state. It mobilizes dormant ego resources which aimlessly meander within that timeless self. It formulates and initiates clearer directions for constructive pursuits.

Reality

The sense of reality and reality testing are partially defective in borderlines. STIP centers around the utilization of the ongoing therapeutic encounter, as an experience of reality, rather than transference. The emphasis is on the here and now, on the therapist-patient relationship and on the patient's current conflictual situations. It attempts to correct the distortions and misperceptions. The more nebulous framework of some of the long-term therapies often impairs the patient's grip on their own reality, engendering panic, insecurities, confusions and disorganization.

Ego Functions

Inherent in the definition, borderlines are people with solid resources as well as frightening vulnerabilities. It is most important to identify and explicitly emphasize the intact and stable ego functions. These patients actually need to hear about their assets.

This interweaves with the exploration and repair of some of their maldeveloped ego capabilities.

CONCLUSIONS

In this paper, I have sketched some of the basic concepts of short-term integrative psychotherapy for borderlines and only a few of the reasons underlying my contention about its benefits.

I propose here that when a clinician assesses a borderline individual, short-term treatment should be strongly considered and attempted. It is an oversimplification to conceptualize borderlines as exhibiting only one kind of clinical picture. As we know, there is a great variety of syndromes within this diagnostic category.

Of major importance is the accurate diagnosis, based on the discernment of their symptoms, primitive defense mechanisms, ego configurations, psychodynamics and relationships. Borderlines can be arrested at any of the developmental subphases of the "separation-individuation phase," be it the "differentiation," "practicing," "rapprochement" or "separation-individuation proper" subphases.

STIP, based on a structured, stable, consistent, empathetic and focus-oriented therapist-patient relationship, can be quite beneficial for these individuals arrested at different levels of development and presenting a mixture of strong and weak ego functions. The therapeutic goals, technical strategies and expected results will vary for each group of borderlines. The criteria for patient selection, contraindications for its application, and methodology (described in previous papers) have to be carefully thought out.

REFERENCES

Bellak, L.; Small, L.: Emergency psychotherapy and brief psychotherapy; 2nd ed. (Grune & Stratton, New York 1977).

Leibovich, M.; Short-term adaptive psychotherapy. Proc. VIIth Int. Congr. Psychother. Psychother. Psychosom. *15:*1–38 (1967).

Leibovich, M.: Short-term psychotherapy for hysterical personalities: stages of the therapeutic processes. Psychother. Psychosom. *24:*67–78 (1974).

Leibovich, M.: An aspect of the psychotherapy of borderline personalities; in: What is psychotherapy? Proc. IXth Int. Congr. Psychother. Psychother. Psychosom. *25:*53–57 (1975).

Leibovich, M.: Short-term psychotherapy for the borderline personality disorder. Psychother. Psychosom. *35:*257–264 (1981).

Leibovich, M.; McGuire, M. T.: The use of intact ego functions in short-term psychotherapy, Proc. VIIth Int. Congr. Psychother. Psychother. Psychosom. *15:*1–46 (1967).

Mahler, M. S.: A study of the separation-individuation process and its possible application to borderline phenomena in the psychoanalytic situation. Psychoanal. Study Child *26:*403–425 (1971).

Modell, A. H.: Object love and reality (International Universities Press, New York 1968).

Oberman, E.: The use of time-limited relationship therapy with borderline patients. Smith College Studies in Social Work, February 1967.

Sifneos, P.: Short-term psychotherapy and emotional crisis (Harvard University Press: Cambridge 1972).

PART V

Brevity Revisited: When Less Means More

Frances and Clarkin's prescription of no treatment in chapter 21 is of course the briefest "treatment," but not to treat at all may occasionally be best if the first aim is to do no harm. Evaluation is also treatment, as Malan and colleagues' follow-up of "untreated" controls in chapter 22 suggests.

Freud's brief treatment of Katharina is included as chapter 23 because it is brief, focused, and active. And it shows his willingness to adapt the therapeutic frame to the temporal situation of the "patient." (It is equally remarkable for the artistic tension and narrative force that survive translation and partly explain Freud's being nominated in the late 1920s for the Nobel Prize—not in medicine but in literature.)

This selection of essential readings ends with the last paper Donald Winnicott submitted before his death in 1971. Winnicott's relevance to brief therapy is shown in his handling of cases in which he strategically helped the patient remove blocks to normal development and displayed a genius for lightning-quick flashes of shared insight. Gustafson[1] speaks for many when he says that nobody but Freud had as much impact on the quotidian practice of the average clinician. Winnicott's thinking is fiercely original, and his writing style reflects his idiosyncratic thought processes—to the puzzlement of those accustomed to a linear reading of clinical papers. To get the most from Winnicott, read him the way you read poetry—with the heart—rather than the way you read a medical journal.

The more one lives with Winnicott's cases, even the longer therapies, the more it appears that he did not view treatment hours as, say, beads on a string, stretching back into the past and forward into the future—he approached each session as a single unit, a whole, a treatment *in itself*. Especially as he grew older and knew his time was running out, he brought to each session a special type of activity that made every hour count, working as if each session would be his last.

REFERENCE

1. Gustafson, J. P. *The Complex Secret of Brief Psychotherapy.* New York: W. W. Norton, 1986.

21. No Treatment As the Prescription of Choice

Allen Frances and John F. Clarkin

We have previously outlined indications for several types of psychiatric treatment and have presented a decision-tree approach to differential therapeutics.[1,2] This article continues the exploration of treatment choices by specifying tentative criteria for an important but too often neglected clinical option, the prescription of no treatment. The findings of outcome research demonstrate psychotherapy to be, on the average, more effective than no treatment. Nonetheless, some patients have a negative response or nonresponse and others would have experienced spontaneous improvement. Although it is sometimes harmful or unnecessary, psychiatric treatment is in practice rarely withheld. In our own clinic, a recent survey of 500 consecutive evaluations revealed only four occasions when no treatment was recommended. It is not surprising that patients were more inclined to this alternative than were consultants; 52 patients refused continued evaluation or treatment. This article outlines a set of tentative guidelines for recommending no treatment and suggests the need for further systematic research to support or refute them. A clarification of this question will ultimately benefit both the inappropriate patient and the mental health system by keeping them apart.

Therapeutic enthusiasts emphasize that the patients likely to qualify for no treatment often are the most unfortunate of people, those with no other prospect of relief, and are precisely the persons most in need of help. Although therapeutic zeal has a place, it ignores two problems. (1) Treatment has a risk-benefit ratio; the potential harm it can inflict on some people (by inducing new symptoms, recurrences, or an addiction to therapy) may outweigh its possible benefits. (2) Treatment has a cost-benefit ratio; the resources of the mental health system expended on this person are not available for someone else perhaps more likely to benefit. In formulating relative indications for no treatment, we do not advocate austerity or pessimism, but rather we hope to define realistic limits and boundaries. Psychotherapy is potent, can work both for good and ill, and must be prescribed with the same

Reprinted by permission of the American Medical Association from *Archives of General Psychiatry* 38 (1981) 542–45.

care and specificity necessary in dispensing medication. In our experience, the psychotherapies, like drugs, can produce addiction, side effects, complications, and overdosage if prescribed in an unselective fashion.

REVIEW OF THE LITERATURE

This section briefly summarizes the findings and methodological problems encountered in outcome research to define patients likely to experience a negative response or nonresponse to psychiatric treatment or a spontaneous remission. These three patient outcomes indicate that treatment may have been harmful or unnecessary. After this review, we conclude that there is no convenient or simple research design able to predict the group of patients for whom no treatment would be the prescription of choice. Nonetheless, a more precise investigation of this question is clearly an important goal of all future outcome research.

Negative Response

Until fairly recently, insufficient attention to negative outcomes obscured the potency of psychotherapy because differences between treated and control groups were lessened by averaging good and bad effects.[3] Bergin and Lambert[4] reviewed 40 studies of negative effect. In the nine best studies, the reported rates were from 3% to 28%, but the value of these findings was compromised by various design limitations (not involving psychotherapy at all or confounding it with other interventions,[5,6] not distinguishing negative response and nonresponse,[7] or assuming negative response only on the basis of differential variance).[8,9]

There is still very little information on the specific patient attributes that predict negative response. Poorly controlled studies suggest that the conditions of severely disturbed patients may deteriorate in some psychoanalytic and group therapies,[6,10–13] but these same patients might have benefited from other forms of treatment and do not, on the face of it, constitute a no-treatment group. An active clinical literature describing negative responses to psychotherapy originated with Freud[14] and was recently expanded by Strupp and associates.[15] His survey of experienced therapists revealed their consensus that negative responses do occur and may be related to, among other things, patient personality factors (borderline and masochistic, low ego strength, and low motivation).

Nonresponse

The nonresponders (or no-change group) can be divided into the following three distinct and very different categories: (1) patients who would have gotten worse except for the beneficial effects of treatment and are really veiled positive responders; (2) those who would have gotten better but for the noxious effect of treatment and are veiled negative responders; and (3) those who are untouched by treatment and continue to follow the natural course of their disorder. Since the rate of positive response to psychotherapy in various kinds of treatment tends to cluster at roughly 65% to 70%,[4] nonresponse and negative response may occur roughly in 30% to 35% of cases. The current data do not allow a more accurate or specific apportionment. It must also be remembered that the size of the no-change group may be overstated because of the relative narrowness of most outcome measures; the patient may have changed and benefited in ways that have not been tapped.

Spontaneous Improvement

The third group of no-treatment candidates comprises those patients with a positive outcome who might have done just as well independent of therapy. It is methodologically impossible to measure spontaneous improvement occurring within treatment. In control no-treatment groups, spontaneous improvement is reported to vary with diagnosis, ranging from 9% of borderline persons and schizophrenics to 52% of all others.[16] A summary of 17 well-controlled studies[4] yielded a median spontaneous remission rate of 43%. The interpretation of these data is complicated because initial evaluations, waiting lists, or research procedures may themselves constitute a form of treatment.[17] The rate of spontaneous remissions may also be overstated since it usually refers only to symptom improvement and ignores other types of positive outcome (e.g., character change) that may occur but are more difficult to measure. The patients with the best prognosis for treatment (those with good premorbid functioning, an environmental crisis, and/or a remitting disorder) probably also have the best prognosis without treatment.

To more clearly define the characteristics of negative responders and nonresponders and spontaneous remitters, outcome research must increasingly identify the differential effects of particular treatments on particular patients. It is unfortunate that even as these data accumulate, they will be of only limited application in providing criteria for no treatment. The results of each study are restricted to the effects of only the one or the few treatments under investigation. To discriminate those patients who would fail in all possible treatments, and who therefore should receive none, one must isolate the shared characteristics of the poor responders in each and every treatment modality. An alternate strategy might involve the investigation of response patterns in high-risk patients as they experience a sequence of treatments. Neither approach is very practical.

Since decisions about no treatment must be made now and since research findings will be long in coming, it is timely to offer preliminary and very tentative clinical guidelines for no treatment. These relative criteria have not been tested, require much further discussion and validation, and cannot be applied literally or rigidly. What we are suggesting is a judicious weighing of research hints on negative effects and no effects and spontaneous improvement to supplement the clinical assessment of the patient's current status, prognostic indicators, and prior response to psychotherapy. A major national effort to study psychotherapy outcome is likely to be launched in the near future. Certainly an attention to and measurement of its possible negative effects should be included in research designs.

RELATIVE INDICATIONS FOR NO TREATMENT

Patients at Risk for Negative Response

Those borderline patients [10-12] who have, in previous treatments, displayed poor tolerance for the ambiguities, temptations, and frustrations of the transference situation are at risk for a negative response. These patients actualize transference fantasies rather than investigate them; they often do this in the most self-destructive and provocative way imaginable, and perhaps, at times, with a delusional intensity. Repeated treatment may contribute to, rather than sort out, the chaos in such a patient's life. This result can sometimes be predicted in patients who have never been in therapy by studying their initial response to an extended consultation or brief trial of treatment. More often, the inadvisability of treatment is based on the patient's unsuccessful previous experiences. The exceptions are as follows: those (1) borderline patients who have an isolated, focused problem amenable to brief, circumscribed treatment; (2) those borderline patients who have had good treatment, life experiences, and/or prognostic indications that suggest treatment suitability; (3) those borderline patients whose lives are so endangered and/or intolerable that the risks of treatment are worth taking; and (4) cases in which a therapist who is expert in treating borderline patients is available.

Patients Prone to Severe Negative Therapeutic Reactions. Such reactions occur most commonly in masochistic, narcissistic, and/or oppositional personality disorders.[14-18] In response to appropriate technical interventions, when therapy seems most likely to be beneficial, the patient's condition paradoxically becomes worse. In masochistic patients, this may represent a need to be punished either to assuage an abiding sense of guilt or to maintain a relationship with an ambivalently perceived, punishing love object. In narcissistic or oppositional patients, it may represent a need to remain autonomous, distant, and superior to the therapist. Negative therapeutic reactions constitute no more than workable resistance in some patients, but in others they lead to intractable stalemates and, in severe cases they can be life-threatening. Those patients who have had repeated life-threatening or treatment-destroying negative therapeutic reactions should probably be offered another therapy only if the need is very great. If treatment is unavoidable, it should probably be brief and unambitious; this kind of patient is compelled to defeat therapeutic optimism. The exceptions are as follows: (1) patients with mild and workable negative therapeutic reactions and (2) patients whose lives are so endangered and/or intolerable that the risk of treatment is worth taking.

Patients Who Enter Treatment Primarily to Justify a Claim for Compensation or Disability or to Support a Lawsuit. The possible psychiatric and material benefits to be derived from treatment must be balanced against the danger that secondary gains of illness will lead to chronic invalidism. The exceptions are as follows: (1) the patient has a treatable psychiatric disorder, and it is worth the risk of increasing secondary gain; and (2) the patient is already disabled by secondary gain.

CASE 1: A Negative Responder. The patient is an attractive, 30-year-old, single woman who has difficulty in her relationships with men. She works as a secretary, has a close woman friend, and does well except when she falls in love. She then becomes temperamental, possessive, devaluing, and infuriating, and she finally precipitates a stormy breakup. This pattern has been repeated many times and has not responded to a variety of treatments. In two separate exploratory psychotherapies, one with a woman and another with a man, powerful transference feelings quickly developed, she occasionally became briefly delusional about the therapist, and she finally required two short hospitalizations. She has also had adequate trials of phenothiazines, tricyclic antidepressants, and monoamine oxidase inhibitors, and she was briefly taking lithium carbonate. The consulting psychiatrist indicated to the patient that treatment seemed more to complicate her life than to help her and that she would be wise to make do on her own. She agreed. On a follow-up six months later she was functioning at her usual level and was still out of treatment.

Patients at Risk for No Response

The Chronically Dependent, Treatment-Addicted Patient. This type of patient has already had extensive and seemingly endless therapies, often of many different kinds, without sustained improvement. Treatment has become a way of life rather than a means to an end. The possibility of this outcome is occasionally clear even in a person who has never had therapy, but more typically one predicts the risk after evaluating the patient's repeated poor response, but persistent clinging, to previous treatments. Often this patient might well survive, and should attempt, at least a temporary break from the routine of treatment. In current practice, such weaning is recommended too infrequently. The exceptions are as follows: (1) the patient does require continuous, perhaps lifetime, maintenance therapy as indicated by a history of serious suicide attempts, decompensation, or deterioration when out of treatment, or a need for a long-term medication regimen; and (2) the patient requires a brief and limited crisis intervention, perhaps to promote a weaning from treatment.

Antisocial or Criminal Behavior. Because psychiatrists attend to unconscious process and psychic determinism, they often regard antisocial behavior as the culmination of forces outside the person's willed control. This may account for the continued tendency of mental health systems to accept responsibility for treating and changing criminal offenders despite a long history of small success in this endeavor.[19] The clinician should evaluate to what extent an offender has a treatable psychiatric disorder (psychosis, organic brain disease, etc). If this is not the case, the most appropriate disposition is generally a legal or correctional one. Quite often the legal system, the individual offender, or both together are insistent that a legal charge be converted into a psychiatric problem. Psychiatrists should limit their participation to those situations within their competence and be especially cautious if the person will evade legal responsibility by becoming a patient. The exceptions are as follows: (1) the patient has a treatable psychiatric disorder (this usually does not include antisocial personality); and (2) psychiatric treatment does not offer secondary gain (e.g., it is provided within, not as an alternative to, the legal system).

Patients with Factitious Illness. Such patients feign physical or psychological symptoms to acquire psychiatric treatment. With such patients psychiatric interventions tend to be futile and enormously wasteful of professional time.

Patients Who Are Poorly Motivated and without Incapacitating Symptoms. Motivation for treatment is always ambivalent; the most motivated have resistances, the least motivated may covertly beg for help. It is not our purpose to discuss ways of predicting motivation or promoting its growth. In general, however, treatment should not be sold to or imposed on people who do not want it, except under the following conditions: (1) treatment is necessary to avoid considerable short- or long-term disability; (2) an effective treatment does exist; and (3) because of his disorder, the patient is unable to make the most prudent decision without help.

CASE 2: A Nonresponder. The patient is an attractive, 40-year-old, divorced, childless woman who handed the interviewer a typewritten list detailing her obsessive ruminations and rituals. She had "been through" 18 almost-consecutive years of treatment, including "a traditional, a lay, and a Jungian analyst, a behavior therapist, two groups, one brief hospitalization, and every available psychotropic medication." Her therapy repeatedly bogged down in intellectualization, actualization, mutual recrimination, and disappointment. She would leave in a huff, move on with great expectations, but again feel disappointed and humiliated. The patient described her life and therapy as unrelieved suffering and waste, and she saw herself as a victim. Fortunately, in spite of severe symptoms, she managed to support herself and dated occasionally. The patient told her story without affect. "I've done it 30 times before," and she insisted on another behavior therapy. She had terminated treatment with her last therapist after a battle about her "self-destructiveness," and she disliked his "insight orientation" because "my symptoms weren't being addressed." She also resented behavior therapy because it focuses on symptoms and ignores self-destructiveness.

This patient is chronically dependent and has made treatment an established way of life, with little prospect of change but with immense secondary gain. The consultant was unimpressed by her need for lifetime support or her suicide potential, thought it remotely possible that she could accept no treatment, and estimated that the only risk was her going elsewhere.

Patients Likely to Have Spontaneous Improvement

Patients in the Midst of a Grief Reaction or Crisis. Such patients have sufficient psychological and social-network resources to manage without psychiatric assistance. Although the short-term effectiveness of crisis intervention is well documented, not all persons require treatment to negotiate each life crisis.[4,16] The exceptions are as follows: (1) the patient already has pathologic symptoms or mourning patterns or these had developed in response to similar stresses in the past; (2) the patient displays an inability to mourn or to face the crisis; and (3) nontechnical help (family, clergy, doctor, etc.) is unavailable or has not worked.

Patients Who Are Generally Healthy. Therapy is not warranted for patients who may have some problems but who are generally too healthy to make treatment necessary. An exception in this case is therapy for training purposes.

CASE 3: A Spontaneous Remission. The patient is a 22-year-old male college senior who was upset by his parents' refusal to attend his forthcoming wedding. He was generally a well-integrated, likable young man, and he would have made a fine treatment case either alone or with his family. On the other hand, he had no enduring psychiatric symptoms, had handled similar family crises on his own in the past, had managed an appropriate separation from his family, and was able to use the consultation to clarify his feelings and options. No further treatment was required. He called back three months later to inform the therapist that he was now married and had been successful in persuading his parents to attend the wedding.

Miscellaneous Technical Indications

A No-Treatment Recommendation As a Specific Therapeutic Intervention. An example is a patient who can function on a higher level but who wants treatment to justify regression. Refusing treatment provides a message to the patient that he is healthier than he thinks. The no-treatment recommendation can also be used as a paradoxical injunction to oppositional patients with poor motivation but a need for treatment.

The Proper Timing of Treatment Requires at Least a Temporary Delay. It is generally unwise for a patient to embark on a new therapy just after ending a previous one. Participation in a linked chain of therapies does not allow the patient to fully experience his separation from any one therapist or to integrate the impact of the treatment he has left. Exceptions include the patient who requires maintenance support or if one therapy has been intended as an induction to another.

Very often, a particular therapy or therapist of choice is unavailable at the moment. In this case, no treatment now may be indicated if something is worth the wait.

CASE 4: No Treatment as a Treatment Technique. The patient is a 28-year-old oppositional man who had been hospitalized six times for depressions and/or suicidal gestures and was obviously proud of his untreatability. Somewhat unexpectedly, he now responded well to a confronting therapist who refused to be optimistic about his treatment but who stayed closely involved. The patient's victory over his therapist required that he begin work for the first time, saying, "You never thought I'd make it this far, huh Doc?"

Several months later, he terminated treatment but would call occasionally to report progress and difficulties. Several times, when he felt like quitting work,. he was seen for one session. After two years, the patient suddenly quit his job, demanded an immediate interview, and declared that he had tried his best but was not meant for work. The therapist explored the patient's anger with a new supervisor, his sense of entitlement, and his desire to be cared for. The patient seemed to be working hard in the session, but declared toward the end, "All this is true but I need a rest. I need therapy for a while before going back to work." The therapist told the patient that whatever could be gained by resuming treatment would be purchased at too high a price of continued dependency and inadequacy. He offered the patient a return visit in three weeks, but he stated that he would not consider resuming treatment unless the patient was regularly employed. The patient resented this, remarked that life might not be worth living, and implied that the therapist was driving him to desperate measures. The therapist did not think that suicide was as big a risk to the patient's overall adaptation as was the renewal of treatment, and he told the patient this. Later, the patient called to cancel the scheduled appointment and was back at work.

COMMENT

Many of our criteria assume that the nonsuccess of previous efforts is the best predictor that yet another treatment may not be indicated. All too frequently patients are routinely offered a long series of treatments regardless of impressive evidence that repeated trials have been harmful or have ended in a stalemate. Nonetheless, there are occasions when the clinician is correct to forge ahead in spite of a dire treatment history. Several variables other than patient characteristics may have determined previous treatment failure (i.e., the therapist's lack of skill, a poor therapist-patient match, the choice of the wrong treatment, environmental conditions, and so on). A patient who has done poorly in one form of therapy (e.g., dynamic psychotherapy) may of course be quite suitable for other forms of therapy (e.g., behavior therapy or the use of psychotropic drugs) that address different target symptoms with different techniques and require different patient enabling factors. Patients also change over time in their motivation, circumstances, and ability to use treatment; such changes must be balanced against the previous record. It is common for patients to retrospectively distort their previous therapy experiences and report them in the least favorable light. One must carefully question both the patient and previous therapists to determine the actual nature of the previous results.

The decision to offer no treatment, particularly in response to what is often a desperate or chaotic situation, requires courage and the conviction that this constitutes the best possible course of action. It makes sense to have more than one consultant evaluate the patient's condition and share the responsibility for making and presenting the decision. This reduces the possibility that the recommendation arises from any one therapist's countertransference feelings and also conveys to the patient that the decision is a careful one, one made with his welfare in mind, and not a brush-off. In many instances there is no need to render an all-or-none verdict, and we have deliberately avoided any clear definition of "no treatment." Treatment can always be instituted at some future time after a reevaluation of the patient's condition, and often it is wise to provide a small amount rather than no treatment at all. This may take the form of a follow-up visit or a brief therapy, or it may be part of the therapeutic consultation itself.

Even in the most unlikely circumstances, psychiatric treatment may be indicated because its possible benefits, although remote, outweigh the risks and costs, and nothing better is available. This decision must result from a conscious and thoughtful consideration that weighs the risks of no treatment (suicide, homicide, unnecessary suffering, decompensation) against the risks of treatment and compares the potential benefits of both.

The benefits of no treatment deserve more consideration than they generally receive. No treatment may serve to (1) protect the patient from iatrogenic harm (particularly to interrupt a sequence of destructive treatments); (2)

protect the patient (and clinician) from wasting time, effort, and money; (3) delay therapy until a more propitious time; (4) protect and consolidate gains from a previous treatment; (5) provide the patient an opportunity to discover that he can do without treatment; and (6) avoid a semblance of treatment when no effective treatment exists. The decision to embark on a psychiatric treatment is too important to be made lightly. It is especially crucial to identify and protect those patients likely to be harmed by treatment. Our first obligation is to follow the injunction *primum non nocere;* second is the identification of patients we neither help nor hurt; third, and sometimes most difficult, is to allow patients on their way to spontaneous improvement to recover without us.

A possible criticism of our approach comes from studies that find that the prediction of psychiatric treatment outcome is not very accurate.[20] Moreover, the consensus of many studies is that treated groups of patients tend to fare better than untreated groups.[21,22] One could combine these two results to form the opinion that treatment should be offered to everyone on the assumption that it is generally useful and that we are not good at guessing who will do poorly in it. We are not content with this conclusion because it does not attend to the specifics of the given patient and instead plays the odds derived from group means. Largely on clinical grounds, we have described subsets of patients for whom no treatment, or no treatment now, should be considered. These very tentative indications are meant to stimulate clinical discussion and demonstrate the need for further systematic investigation of this question.

REFERENCES

1. Clarkin JF, Frances A, Moodie J: Selection criteria for family therapy. *Fam Process* 18:391–403, 1979.
2. Frances A, Clarkin JF, Marachi J: Selection criteria for outpatient group psychotherapy. *Hosp Community Psychiatry* 31:245–250, 1980.
3. Bergin AE: The evaluation of therapeutic outcomes, in Bergin AE, Garfield S (eds): *Handbook of Psychotherapy and Behavior Change: An Empirical Analysis.* New York, John Wiley & Sons Inc, 1971, chap 7.
4. Bergin AE, Lambert MJ: The evaluation of therapeutic outcomes, in Garfield, S, Bergin AE (eds): *Handbook of Psychotherapy and Behavior Change: An Empirical Analysis,* ed 2. New York, John Wiley & Sons Inc, 1978, chap 5.
5. Powers E, Witmer H: *An Experiment in the Prevention of Delinquency.* New York, Columbia University Press, 1951, chap 4.

6. Fairweather G, Simon R, Gebhard ME, et al.: Relative effectiveness of psycho-therapeutic programs: A multicriteria comparison of four programs for three different patient groups. *Psychol Monogr* 74(whole No. 492):1–26, 1960.

7. Cartwright RD, Vogel JL: A comparison of changes in psychoneurotic patients during matched periods of therapy and no therapy. *J Consult Psychol* 24:121–127, 1960.

8. Carkhuff RR, Truax CB: Lay mental health counseling: The effects of lay group counseling. *J Consult Psychol* 29:426–431, 1965.

9. Mink OG, Isaksen HL: A comparison of effectiveness of nondirective therapy and clinical counseling in the junior high school. *School Counsel* 6:12–14, 1959.

10. Kernberg OF, Burstein ED, Coyne L, et al.: Psychotherapy and psychoanaly-sis: Final report of the Menninger Foundation's Psychotherapy Research Project. *Bull Menninger Clin* 36:1–267, 1972.

11. Aronson H, Weintraub W: Patient changes during classical psychoanalysis as a function of initial status and duration of treatment. *Psychiatry* 31:369–379, 1968.

12. Weber JJ, Elinson J, Moss LM: The application of ego-strength scales to psychoanalytic-clinic records, in Goldman GS, Shapiro D (eds): *Developments in Psychoanalysis at Columbia University: Proceedings of the 20th Anniversary Confer-ence.* New York, Columbia Psychology Clinic for Training and Research, 1965, pp. 215–273.

13. Yalom ID, Leiberman MA: A study of encounter group casualties. *Arch Gen Psychiatry* 25:16–30, 1971.

14. Freud S: *The Ego and the Id,* standard ed. London, Hogarth Press Ltd, vol 19, 1961, pp. 49–52.

15. Strupp HH, Hadley SW, Gomes-Schwartz R: *Psychotherapy for Better or Worse: An Analysis of the Problem of Negative Effects.* New York, Jason Aronson Inc, 1977, chap 1.

16. Endicott NA, Endicott J: 'Improvement' in untreated psychiatric patients. *Arch Gen Psychiatry* 9:575–585, 1963.

17. Malan DH, Heath ES, Bacal HA, et al: Psychodynamic changes in untreated neurotic patients: Apparently genuine improvements. *Arch Gen Psychiatry* 32:110–126, 1975.

18. Sandler J, Holder A, Dare C: *The Patient and the Analyst.* New York, International Universities Press, 1973, chap 8.

19. Liss R, Frances A: Court-mandated treatment: Dilemmas for hospital psychia-try. *Am J Psychiatry* 132:924–927, 1975.

20. Luborsky L, Mintz J, Auerbach A, et al.: Predicting the outcome of psycho-therapy: Findings of the Penn Psychotherapy Project. *Arch Gen Psychiatry* 37:471–481, 1980.

21. Luborsky L, Singer B, Luborsky L: Comparative studies of psychotherapies: Is it true that 'Everyone has won and all must have prizes'? *Arch Gen Psychiatry* 32:995–1008, 1975.

22. Smith ML, Glass G V: Meta-analysis of psychotherapy-outcome studies, *Am Psychol* 32:752–760, 1977.

22. Psychodynamic Changes in Untreated Neurotic Patients: Apparently Genuine Improvements

David H. Malan, E. Sheldon Heath, Howard A. Bacal, and Frederick H. G. Balfour

The work reported here was performed at a time of great confusion in psychotherapy research, when most known controlled studies had given null results, and evidence seemed to suggest that about two-thirds of neurotic patients improve "spontaneously" without treatment. This latter statement of course originated with Eysenck,[1-3] and has been reexamined by Bergin, who concluded that the median rate was nearer 30%.[4] Nevertheless, Bergin's evidence is not free from objection, and the true figure remains unknown. In Bergin's collaboration with Strupp,[5] he also acknowledges a qualitative gap in our knowledge that badly needs to be filled: by what mechanisms do these so-called spontaneous improvements occur? To this, we may add a second equally important question: what is the quality of these improvements in psychodynamic terms? It is time, therefore, that a series of untreated patients should be studied by methods sensitive to the subtleties and complexities of psychodynamic change, and that the detailed evidence should be published in such a way that the reader can judge it for himself. This report describes part of a study by four psychoanalysts that attempts to meet these criteria.

PREVIOUS WORK

A classified bibliography through 1966, together with a full discussion, was given in a previous report in which part of this work was published:[6] Later reviews are given by Bergin[4] and Rachman.[7] Meltzoff and Kornreich[8] have also carried out the most comprehensive review of all time of studies of psychotherapy in which there was a control group, which of necessity gives evidence about spontaneous remission. No one can hope to compete with the thoroughness of these authors, and the reader is referred to them for further

Reprinted by permission of the American Medical Association from *Archives of General Psychiatry* 32 (1975):110–26.

information. Comprehensive as this work has been, however, none of the studies quoted answers the questions that we have posed.

HISTORY AND DESCRIPTION OF THE PRESENT STUDY

Our work was carried out between the years 1962 and 1966, starting as a pilot study, and continuing with support from the David Matthew Fund of the London Institute of Psychoanalysis and the Mental Health Research Fund. It is a two- through eight-year follow-up of 45 adult neurotic patients who were seen for consultation at the Tavistock Clinic, London, but who—for any reason—did not have treatment. We made it an essential criterion that by the time each patient was asked to come for follow-up, he *should not have been interviewed by a psychiatrist more than twice in his whole life.* In fact, it so happens that the majority of the patients with whom this report is concerned had only been interviewed *once* by a psychiatrist in their lives—which, we believed, was as near to having the patients genuinely untreated as it is possible to get.

Our study was specifically designed to provide evidence both on two qualitative questions and a quantitative prediction. The qualitative questions were: What kinds of change can take place in neurotic patients without treatment? Can these changes be in any way comparable with those that we aim to attain in dynamic psychotherapy? The quantitative prediction was as follows: that, although we may expect to find quite a high proportion of these patients symptomatically improved, clear evidence can be obtained that many of these improvements are questionable on dynamic criteria.

This latter prediction was in fact confirmed. If we now incorporate one altered judgment and one later follow-up, then of the 45 patients, 23 (51%) were judged to be at least "improved" symptomatically, but only 11 (24%) were judged to be improved dynamically. Moreover, whereas ten (22%) were "recovered" symptomatically, only two (4%) were recovered dynamically. The detailed evidence on the 13 symptomatically improved but dynamically questionable patients was presented in our previous report.[6] The present report is concerned with those 11 patients whose improvements, even if only partial, appear to be genuine.

NATURE OF THE SAMPLE

The reader is referred to our previous report for a more complete exposition of this.[6]

During the period covered (dates of first consultation were between August 1957 and February 1964), there were 164 patients thought to be eligible whose last known address was within reasonable range of London. Attempts were made to interview all these patients. We were successful with 45 (27%). This represented 1.6% of the 2,847 patients recorded in the books of the Adult Department between these two dates. The minimum follow-up period for all patients was chosen as two years, the maximum being over nine years.

As far as the *reason for not receiving treatment* was concerned, this varied widely: practical difficulties, various forms of mutual rejection, outright rejection by either the clinic or the patient, or mutually agreed policies of "wait and see." Thus, no generalization can be made. It is true, however, that only a small proportion (seven of the 45) were regarded by the interviewing psychiatrist as basically unsuitable for dynamic psychotherapy. This includes two of the patients described here (Nos. 14 and 15).

Thus, although the patients do not *manifestly* differ noticeably from a sample given psychotherapy, the very fact of not receiving treatment means that they must, in fact, differ in important respects. The quality that all the 11 patients had in common was, ultimately, the feeling that they could manage their lives without treatment.

PRINCIPLES OF ASSESSING PSYCHODYNAMIC CHANGE

A thorough discussion of this, and of methods used by other authors, is given both in our previous paper,[6] and in earlier publications by one of us (D.H.M.).[9,10] The essential point that we try to make in these publications is that most previous methods of assessing "improvement," however apparently thorough (e.g., the Minnesota Multiphasic Personality Inventory) or apparently objective (e.g., the self-ideal correlation), are liable to serious error, because they are based essentially on the numerical addition—or other purely arithmetical treatment—of a number of changes, without any possibility of weighting these by taking into account what they mean in terms of the underlying disorder. This is true even of some of the scales devised by psychoanalysts surveying various areas in a patient's life, including personal relations, such as that of Knight.[11] We believe firmly that, to be valid, any method must employ a psychodynamic appraisal of the patient and his situation *as a whole*. Of all methods known to us and used in other studies, we believe that only the three methods used in the Menninger Psychotherapy Research Project, i.e., the Health-Sickness Rating Scale, the Absolute Global

Change Scale, and the Global Change Scale based on the method of paired comparisons, fulfill these criteria.[12–14]

The discrepancy between assessments based on arithmetical manipulation on the one hand, and those based on an overall dynamic view on the other, was illustrated in detail with an example in our previous report. Since all but one of the patients described here were judged to be at least "improved" on symptomatic as well as on dynamic criteria, this discrepancy is of much less importance for these particular patients, and will receive little emphasis. Instead, we shall illustrate the principles of psychodynamic assessment with one of the most striking examples taken from the 11 patients to be described in the present report.

The patient. "The Polish Refugee" (case 14), was a single woman of 33 years of age who was referred to us complaining of depression and the feeling that she was unable to carry on. Her history was one of very severe trauma. She was an only child, and much spoiled. In her teens, the Germans invaded Poland and both her parents were sent to concentration camps. Her father died there, and, though her mother survived, she returned in a state of chronic ill health. After the Russian invasion of Poland, the patient became promiscuous, and had a series of unsatisfactory relations with unsatisfactory men. She left school at age 18 years and drifted from one job to another, coping inadequately with all of them.

When she was 27 years old her mother died, and the patient had a breakdown in which she neglected her flat, sold everything that was valuable, largely refused to work, and lived mainly on money sent to her by her relatives in England. Two years before being seen, she managed to get out of Poland and came to Britain. Here she carried on as before, working on and off, drifting from one job to another, always feeling weak and exhausted and full of other physical symptoms, having one unsatisfactory affair after another, and being supported by her relatives. After one of these unhappy love affairs, she became afraid of everything, cried all day, and felt like committing suicide. It was this that brought her to the clinic.

The first step in psychodynamic assessment is to make a list of the patient's "disturbances" together with all relevant evidence from the patient's history. In this particular case, the two are inseparable, and the above historical account is probably the best way in which the material can be summarized. The list of disturbances is analogous to a list of symptoms and signs in medicine. The next step in medicine is to make a "diagnosis," i.e., an explanatory hypothesis by means of which the symptoms, signs, and history may be linked in terms of known pathological processes. In a neurotic patient, the conventional diagnosis—as in the above patient, "depressive reaction in a passive-dependent, hysterical personality"—is often purely descriptive, and may add very little to our knowledge. On the other hand, the introduction of even a small amount of additional thinking—in this case it is not even "psychodynamic"—may make a very large difference to our understanding. With this particular patient, we can summarize her whole history by saying that she has never learned to deal adaptively with stress of any kind; and that, on the contrary, she has developed a pattern of following the whims of the moment, and collapsing into illness when things go wrong, with the hope that others will take the responsibility for her life. Her reaction is nonetheless pathological for the fact that the traumas that she has suffered have been very severe indeed.

We are thus able to make a formulation in terms of a *maladaptive reaction* to a *specific type of stress,* the latter probably being *frustration* of any kind, and also *loss.*

Now in medicine, in any condition of clearly understood pathology, it is possible to say exactly what is meant by true recovery in terms of the underlying disorder of structure or function. In a neurotic illness no such formulation is possible. Nevertheless, if a diagnosis has been made in terms of a pathological reaction to a specific stress, then it is perfectly possible to formulate empirical or operational criteria of recovery, as follows: (1) that the patient should have been exposed to the specific stress or stresses; and (2) should now have shown a different and adaptive response to them.

Let us suppose, however, that her life had been such that these stresses had not recurred. There are then two possibilities: either we have to say that her recovery is "not proven"; or else we may search in her history for evidence of what we may call a *specific predisposition,* which may be defined as some detectable evidence that, if she had been exposed to the specific stress, she would have shown the same maladaptive pattern. The specific predisposition thus becomes a pathological characteristic that can be detected *in the absence of the specific stress.* In this particular case, the general predisposition is what may be called *emotional immaturity,* and, for instance, might be detected if the patient were found to be unable to make use of long-term planning, or clearly always managed to be cared for by someone who took responsibility for her life.

These principles can be made clearer by taking the medical analogy further. The example that we use is of a patient suffering from a congenital heart lesion, who becomes breathless on slight exertion. The predisposition is then the heart lesion itself and the specific stress is exertion. If, after surgery, the patient is to be regarded as recovered, it is essential that he or she should have been exposed to reasonable exertion and be shown to be able to cope with this without undue breathlessness. The predisposition may also be detectable without exposing the patient to exertion, e.g., by listening to the heart sounds and hearing a murmur.

This medical analogy should make clear that, for a true recovery, it is the change in the predisposition that matters, and that only one of the ways of detecting this—though the most important—is by exposure to the specific stress.

Now our ideas about these concepts have only developed gradually, and, at the time we carried out this work, we did not use these terms specifically. Nevertheless, they were clearly implied in our criteria of recovery; and, for clarity, we have introduced them where appropriate.

Another useful though less fundamental concept that this particular patient illustrates is as follows: her inability to react adaptively to stress means that she cannot take active steps to alter the stress, and thus she inevitably sets up a *vicious circle* between herself and her environment. This is shown, for instance, in her reaction to men: since she cannot actively choose a suitable man and work through the stresses in her relationship with him, she can never win a man who can give her real satisfaction, which in turn might alleviate her unhappiness and her symptoms. A criterion of recovery is thus that a patient who is subject to such a vicious circle should, if possible, have broken it by her own efforts. This concept is particularly important in patient No. 15 (see below).

In other cases it may not be possible to make a clear formulation in any of these terms. Even then, however, it is still possible to lay down criteria that go further than a simple statement that the various disturbances must disappear. Here we state that any disturbances must not merely disappear but must be *replaced by something positive;* or, put in another way, that any "inappropriate" reaction—in terms of feeling or behavior—must be replaced by the corresponding appropriate reaction. An example is given by case 19, a man suffering from transvestist and fetishistic impulses. This condition cannot be formulated in terms of a reaction to any specific stress; but it is possible to say simply that these impulses must be replaced by "normal" heterosexual impulses, which should ultimately lead to a mutually satisfactory relation with a woman. Finally, another important empirical concept constantly used is that of "constructive aggression" or "constructive self-assertion." This may be defined, in general, as a type of aggression that benefits both the patient and his environment—as an example, the submissive, resentful employee, who, after standing up to his boss, finds the relation between the two of them on a much more open and friendly basis. Wherever we find a disturbance of aggressiveness, whether inhibited or excessive aggressiveness, an automatic criterion of recovery is that this should be replaced by constructive self-assertion.

To return to this particular patient, she had a single interview with a psychiatrist at the Tavistock Clinic, and no other contact with psychiatry during her life whatsoever. She was not offered treatment because the psychiatrist did not think she had the motivation to help herself.

Our procedure, in this case as in all the others, was first to contact the patient and make sure she was willing to come for follow-up; and then to use the information in the case notes, *before seeing the patient for follow-up,* to make first an *explanatory hypothesis* of the patient's disturbances, and then to lay down criteria that must be met if the patient is to be regarded as dynamically "recovered." Here we wrote as follows:

Hypothesis

As a spoiled only child, she has never learned mature behavior. On the contrary, she has always followed her immediate impulses, has been unwilling to make efforts on her own behalf, and, under stress, has retreated into depression, exhaustion, and helplessness, hoping that others will take responsibility for her. Here we may now add that her specific predisposition was emotional immaturity, and that specific stresses for her were frustration and loss.

Criteria

General. The essential criterion is that she should have changed over into mature behavior, resulting in the ability to take responsibility for her own life, to behave realistically and with a long-term aim in view, to cope actively with difficulties herself, and not to demand that others cope for her. She should have held jobs with reasonable stability. Symptoms should not have returned, except perhaps transitorily under stress.

Relation to Men. We had the information that she was now married. Ideally, therefore, we would like to see that the above behavior manifested itself before she knew that she would have a lasting relation with a man. This is in order to exclude the possibility that she can only function with a man's protection.

Her relation with her husband should be one of reasonable equality and give-and-take. She should not be unduly dependent, and should not expect him to take excessive responsibility for her. She and her husband should have a good degree of companionship, and the sexual relation should be mutually satisfactory. The patient was then asked to come for a follow-up interview.

Follow-Up
(Seven Years and Five Months Since Her Original Interview)

The history that she reported since her original interview was as follows:

Symptoms. She began to improve soon after her diagnostic interview. Her symptoms improved considerably though not completely.

Work. She got a new job as a secretary soon after her interview, and held it for five years. She was eventually dismissed because she took too much time off from work, which was partly due to recurrent gastrointestinal symptoms. She immediately got another job, also as a secretary, which she held until her marriage, i.e., for about two years.

Relations with Men. After a brief relation with one man, she met her future husband and has been with him ever since. He was already married. She accepted his statement that he did not intend to marry her, and she described their relationship as a good one both sexually and as far as companionship was concerned. Nevertheless, she described attacks of gastric trouble in a way that made clear that they were a substitute for anger. Finally, about two years ago, she began to say openly that she wanted to marry him. They had a stormy time, involving several partings and reconciliations, and finally she told him that either he married her or she was going to leave him. They parted for three weeks, and then he phoned her. She said she would not speak to him and was going to bang down the receiver. He said, "Don't do that, for I am going to start divorce proceedings." They got married seven months ago.

She described her husband and her marriage in most glowing terms. He is considerate, tender, and loves her very much. She said with considerable insight that she had been *spoiled* but she had never been *loved* before. She added that it was not just the sexual relationship, which appeared to be entirely satisfactory, but everything else as well. When asked about disagreements, she said they never disagreed. She gave evidence, however, of being able to understand why he was sometimes irritable, and to be able to handle it in an apparently mature way.

She said that she did not like films with blood and fighting in them, which still made her feel uncomfortable. Her symptoms had to some extent persisted up to her marriage, but since then they have entirely disappeared.

COMMENT

As will be seen, practically all the criteria are met. Possible reservations are as follows:

1. She is still at the honeymoon stage of her marriage and the relation with her husband seems somewhat idealized.
2. Since she did not become symptom-free until she had finally got what she wanted, *the tendency to react to stress with symptoms* may still to some extent be present.
3. She may still have problems over aggression.

Nevertheless, she has replaced a vicious circle by a benign circle by means of her own efforts. In spite of the reservations, we believed that she ought tentatively to be judged as psychodynamically "apparently recovered."

DISCUSSION OF DYNAMIC HYPOTHESES AND CRITERIA OF RECOVERY

There are two main possible types of objection to our procedure, which come from opposite ends of the theoretical spectrum. The first, from the more strictly scientific and less dynamic approach, may suggest that the hypotheses are too subjective and contain too much unvalidated theory, and that the criteria are based on a series of value judgments that are not made explicit and can only be a matter of opinion. The second, from a more psychoanalytic approach, may suggest that the hypotheses are too superficial, often say nothing about certain causal factors, may ignore over-determination, and may leave the inner mechanisms of some manifestations of the illness quite unexplained.

We have thought very deeply about these problems over many years and have discussed them in detail elsewhere.[6,9,10] Both objections are best answered by a description of how our procedure developed.

When we started, we tried to make our hypotheses "deeper" and more psychoanalytic in an attempt to answer the second type of criticism. The result was absolutely clear, fully justifying the first type of criticism: the independent judges imposed their own theoretical bias on the material, often producing hypotheses that had little in common with one another. The policy that we then needed to adopt in reaching a consensus became equally clear: the amount of theory had to be reduced to the point at which agreement could be reached. In fact, this process coincided with the purely scientific principle of keeping the hypotheses as close as possible to the available evidence. In the example just given, for instance, a psychoanalytic approach might well result in a hypothesis attributing the depression to guilt-laden anger against the parents. This would be based on a psychoanalytic generalization stating that all depression must involve unexpressed aggression turned against the self. It must be said at once that we do not allow ourselves to accept such generalizations, and that we only use them if there is direct evidence for them in the particular case—which here there was not. It would have been quite a different matter, for instance, if the patient had suffered from the depressive feeling that she had been responsible for her father's death. Thus, we would immediately have realized that such a hypothesis was scientifically unacceptable, and we would have sought the *highest common factor* on which we could all agree, and which we believed would be reasonably acceptable to an open-minded observer who at least believed in a certain amount of psychodynamic theory. In this patient, there surely is no room for disagreement over the *value judgment* that her behavior is unsatisfactory and maladaptive—no one is happy as a result of it, neither she nor her relatives. To take the next step and label her behavior as the expression of *emotional immaturity* is then both absolutely logical, makes use of the evidence in her history of her being a spoiled only child, and is much more than being purely descriptive—it brings in a vast body of knowledge about the behavior of children and neurotic adults, it suggests other maladaptive patterns that the patient might show and should be looked for at follow-up, and it immediately points forward to criteria of recovery.

With regard to the criteria themselves, we also accept unashamedly that they contain value judgments, which we believe cannot be avoided. This has been discussed at some length elsewhere.[10] Here we can only say: (1) that our values are clearly implied by the criteria used in the following pages; (2) that the fact that these criteria have often been exactly fulfilled confirms their relevance; and (3) that since the evidence is published in some detail, the reader is free to make his own hypotheses and criteria and to reach his own conclusions about the extent to which these patients are to be regarded as improved.

JUDGMENTS OF IMPROVEMENT

Two of us (D.H.M. and H.A.B.) have made these judgments by consensus on the usual scale of recovered, much improved, improved, slightly improved, and essentially unchanged. The patients described here are those of the 45 who were judged to be at least "improved" on dynamic criteria.

We should add here that by now we have very extensive experience of rating dynamic improvement on a numerical scale of zero to 4, rising in $\frac{1}{2}$ points, and have achieved what we believe to be a very high reliability indeed. This is shown particularly when independent judges are divided into those contaminated and those blind to events of therapy, and the mean of one is correlated with the mean of the other (usually two judges in each case). In a series of 30 patients given brief psychotherapy, this gave a reliability of $r = +.83$,[15,16] and in a series of 39 patients given group therapy, a reliability of $r = +.90$. We deliberately did not use this scale in this work because we did not want to imply any spurious comparisons with treated series selected by entirely different processes.

Presentation of the Clinical Material

For reasons of space we cannot present all the other ten cases in detail, but have chosen five patients who are either most striking or else feature most significantly in the discussion. The most important of these are cases 18 and 19—the latter probably being more striking than case 14, already presented. All 11 cases are summarized in the Table 22.1.

Psychiatric Diagnoses

These are well recognized to be somewhat arbitrary and unreliable, but, for completeness, diagnoses along both British and American principles have been included. The British diagnoses have been given by D.H.M., the American by Alan Morgenstern, M.D.

Table 22.1. Summary of Changes

Case no.	Sex	Pseudonym	Age, yr	Marital status	Specific stress	Main pathological reactions to specific stress	Length of follow-up, yr mo	Situation at follow-up	Dynamic criteria
14	F	Polish refugee	33	Single	Frustration & loss	Depression, inadequacy, promiscuity, physical symptoms	7 5	Constructive self-assertion in face of difficulties, married, symptom free	Recovered
15	F	Mrs. T.	33	Married	Frustration Sex	Uncontrollable hysterical outbursts; refusal of intercourse.	7 1	Realistic moves, including self-assertion & acceptance of intercourse; has broken vicious circle with her husband	Improved
16	M	Printer's assistant	26	Single	Competition with other men Challenge to his masculinity	Symptoms: anxiety in social situations & at work; difficulties with women; problems over aggression	2 0	Improved at price of peptic ulcer; much more responsible job; married; improved	Improved
17	F	Economics student	21	Single	Competition with other women	Depression; examination anxiety; social withdrawal	2 5	Passed exams without anxiety; resolved depressive attack by self-analysis; social & heterosexual involvement	Improved
18	M	Geologist	26	Single	Conflict over his mother's severe depression	Vacillates between neglect & unrealistic self-sacrifice; social withdrawal	3 0	Has dealt realistically with problem over his mother; married a girl "good at people," which has helped him with his social withdrawal; still has difficulty asserting himself	Much improved

No.	Sex	Description	Age	Marital status	Precipitating stress	Symptoms			Follow-up	Assessment
19	M	Research chemist	31	Single	Prospect of a mature relation with a woman	Impotence, transvestism, fetishism; feeling inferior as a man	2	6	He has fallen in love with a girl and has a pleasurable relation with her short of intercourse; his "perverse" feelings have disappeared: he is more able to be self-assertive; relation with girl is only 7 weeks old	Improvements too recent for final assessment
							9	11	He has now been married for 6 yr; marriage contains deep satisfactions & ordinary relation is passionate, there is no problem over potency & "perverse" impulses have largely disappeared; he no longer feels inadequate as a man	Recovered
20	F	Convent girl	23	Single	Deprivation; bad mother figures	Depressive attacks; inability to enjoy herself; never had a boyfriend	4	2	No recurrence of depressions; able to handle stress; able to enjoy herself; relation to men basically unchanged	Improved
21	F	Evacuee	27	Single	Loss of person or environment on which she is dependent	Depressive attacks	11	6	Married	
							2	1	Reacted to subsequent loss without depression; now engaged; still very dependent	Improved?

Table 22.1. *Summary of Changes (continued)*

Case no.	Sex	Pseudonym	Age, yr	Marital status	Specific stress	Main pathological reactions to specific stress	Length of follow-up, yr mo	Situation at follow-up	Dynamic criteria
22	M	Junior lecturer	26	Single	Competition with other men; male authority	Anxiety, passivity, submissiveness; unwilling to get involved with women	2 1	Complete confidence in work & relation to men; allows involvement with women but now preoccupied with jealousy	Improved
23	F	Miss V.	21	Single	Ambivalence toward men	Frigidity; involved with sadistic man; works far below her capacity	2 7	Sex much more enjoyable, but no orgasm; still involved with same man but copes very well; work now makes use of her intelligence	Improved
24	F	Lesbian teacher	23	Single	Intense ambivalence toward men	Overt homosexuality; no heterosexual feelings; "masculine protest"	2 1	No homosexual feelings; involved with two men between whom companionship & sexual feelings (short of intercourse) seem to be split; no evidence of masculine protest	Improved

REPORT OF CASES

CASE 15. A 33-year-old woman who was married and worked as a typist showed severe hysterical reactions. She complained of constant tension and restlessness. Also, she had the following additional symptoms: attacks of feeling ill; recurrent minor physical complaints; attacks of hysterical crying; and outburst against her husband and daughter.

Background

Her mother was tense and emotional and suffered from a number of neurotic symptoms. There was constant bickering between the patient and her mother. The father was a chronic invalid. The patient adored him and felt he could do no wrong. He died ten years ago.

Previous Personality. She has always been extremely nervous. When she was 5 years old her school physician said she really ought to be sent away from home, as she was suffering from all her mother's neurotic symptoms. All her life she has suffered from frequent uncontrollable outbursts of crying and screaming in which she shakes all over.

Long History of Hysterical Behavior and Sexual Inadequacy (the latter with a possible physical basis). Her first menstrual period was at 18 years of age. From the beginning she suffered from severe dysmenorrhea. She was found to be suffering from an infantile uterus and vagina. After the use of dilators, her vagina was considered to be normal but she was told she could never have a child. At 19 years of age she married a man for whom she now admits she felt no physical attraction. She has always felt a severe repugnance against intercourse and the marriage is unconsummated. Eight years ago she adopted a little girl.

Six years ago, after a quarrel with her husband's family, she started to suffer from violent attacks of screaming, went to bed, and refused to get up for several months. She was eventually shocked out of this by her physician, who threatened her with admission to a mental hospital. She "screamed and screamed at him," but after this was able to get up again.

Four years ago her husband said he could tolerate the situation no longer and applied for an annulment. She made a histrionic gesture, trying to hang herself while her husband was in the house. She decided to contest the annulment and her husband dropped the idea.

During this time she knew that her husband was being unfaithful. At interview, she complained of his censorious preaching attitude, and his refusal to be sociable with her friends.

She then admitted that on one occasion she had had intercourse with another man, really to prove that she was normal. To her surprise, her sexual feelings were aroused, and she experienced no pain or difficulty. Nevertheless, she is convinced that intercourse with her husband will always be impossible. She cannot bring herself to show any affection toward her husband, even to kiss him. She knows her feeling of tension is due to the sexual situation.

A British psychiatric diagnosis of her condition would be severely hysterical personality; American, hysterical personality (histrionic personality disorder). Her only contact with psychiatry was one diagnostic interview with a psychiatrist at the Tavistock Clinic. The reason for her not having treatment was that the psychiatrist wrote that her attitude to sex has become a fixed pattern that she has no wish to change, and that any attempt to get her to face her emotional problems might precipitate severe hysterical reactions.

Hypothesis. We could say no more than that she suffers from extreme emotional immaturity, and sexual inhibition that may partly—but clearly only partly—have a physical basis. Her specific predisposition is extreme emotional immaturity, and specific stresses for her are frustration of any kind and sex.

Criteria. The essential criterion is that she should be able to handle situations of stress by active and realistic intervention rather than histrionic behavior and the development of symptoms.

She should at least make active attempts at bringing about a reconciliation with her husband. Ideally, she should be able to obtain at least as much sexual pleasure with him as in her extramarital relation. Also ideally, she should be able to have a mutually satisfactory relation with him, and should be able to order her life in such a way that her family does not suffer.

Follow-Up (Seven Years One Month). Events before the original interview as recounted at follow-up:

Up to a few months before her original interview, she and her husband had lived close to his family, which had resulted in her quarrelling with them. Finally, in order to get away from them, she had firmly told her husband that she was moving to the nearest town (Liverpool) and he could follow her if he wanted. She went, and he did in fact follow her. They later both moved to London, and it was about three months after this move that she was first seen at the clinic. She said that her main motive in staying with her husband was that this was important for her daughter's sake.

Subsequent Events. About three months after her original interview, she said she didn't know how it happened, but when her husband indicated his usual wish for intercourse, she accepted him; and since then they have been having intercourse regularly two or three times a week. It turns out, however, that she gets no enjoyment from this whatsoever. It is also true that she still gets mildly interested and sexually aroused outside marriage, but she has not had another extramarital encounter. She said that the crucial factor in driving her to allow the sexual relation was her fear about the emotional welfare of her daughter.

She said that she felt there was a deep feeling of affection and love between her and her husband, although this did not include sexual or romantic love. She said that their relation was now warmer in every other sense of the word. She can now allow him to be affectionate with her, which she couldn't before, because she was always terrified that affection might develop into sex, which she couldn't handle.

Symptoms. Although she still gets tense at times, she made clear that this was much improved. She said she was no longer restless. However, she has been taking tranquillizers for the last six months. She still suffers from minor physical complaints, but said these no longer worry her, and she rarely goes to the doctor about them.

Self-Assertion in General. It seemed that she was better able to assert herself at work but not really at home. The key phrase that she used was that she had learned to accept things as they were.

Summary

The crucial change has been her ability to accept the sexual relation with her husband, even though she does not enjoy it. Without question, this was an active and realistic move on her part, and thus the essential criterion is partly fulfilled. It also seems certain that this action on her part has broken the vicious circle between her and her husband, has led to a great improvement in their relation and in the tension at home, and to some reduction in her symptoms. On symptomatic criteria she was judged to be "much improved," and on dynamic criteria she was judged to be "improved."

CASE 16. A 26-year-old single man who worked as a printer's assistant was suffering from anxiety in relation to competition with men. He has had long-standing complaints of depression and social anxieties.

Disturbances

For many years he has had the following symptoms: (1) difficulty in getting to sleep; (2) lack of concentration: when studying, his mind wanders; (3) indecision; (4) he always feels to blame if things go wrong at work, and often takes the blame when it is not his fault; (5) at times he feels extremely sorry for himself and feels that he is much worse off than other people.

Social Anxieties. He is very anxious in company and has very little social life. He becomes detached and silent, especially when he is the center of attention; and if he feels he has to speak, what he says is often nonsense. He cannot speak spontaneously and his mind goes blank. He feels inferior and is much preoccupied with the feeling that other men are waiting to make him appear ridiculous in front of women. In these circumstances he becomes full of anger inside and his voice fails, only to become deep and masculine again when he gets out of the situation.

Difficulties with Women. The above social anxieties become very much worse if there are women present, particularly if they are attractive. He has had some casual sexual relations, usually after he has drunk a lot, and on these occasions he describes his voice as disappearing completely.

Difficulties over Aggression. His state alternates between withdrawal, passivity, and inability to stand up for himself, particularly with bosses; and getting suspicious of people, feeling that they want to humiliate him, and then becoming argumentative and obnoxious.

Background

His father was away from home a great deal. His mother both nagged and spoiled him. She did things for him when he was old enough to do them himself. He made her send his younger brother to boarding school in order to get him out of her clutches.

A British psychiatric diagnosis of his condition would be character disorder with depression and anxiety; American, depressive neurosis in a man with a schizoid personality. His only contact with psychiatry was a history taken by a psychiatric social worker, followed immediately by one diagnostic interview with a psychiatrist, both at the Tavistock Clinic. The reason for his not having treatment was that he was put on the waiting list for group treatment, was offered a vacancy at a time that he could not manage, and was not offered anything further.

Hypothesis. He appears to be very insecure in his masculinity (specific predisposition) and very sensitive to possible humiliation. Specific stresses for him are competition and challenges to his masculinity.

Criteria. The essential criterion is that he should develop confidence in himself as a worthwhile man and be aware of his real assets and limitations. This should lead to the following: (1) disappearance of symptoms; (2) ability to make comfortable relations with others, and to behave spontaneously and appropriately in social situations; (3) ability to form a good relation with a girl who attracts him, and ultimately a stable and satisfying one, including the sexual relation; and (4) ability to achieve a balance over the expression of aggression—not to be unnecessarily aggressive, but to be able to be active and assertive in an appropriate way.

Follow-Up (Two Years Eight Months). As far as his previous symptoms were concerned, the position was now as follows: (1) insomnia; whereas previously it took him one to two hours to get to sleep, it now takes him one half to three fourths of an hour; (2) lack of concentration; since he has now been able to pass exams, this can no longer seriously affect him; (3) indecision: he is now able to make many decisions a day, quickly; (4) anxiety about doing things right: he was not asked about this; (5) depression: these feelings have disappeared; and (6) it is important to note, however, that he has now developed a peptic ulcer, which began one month after he had been given a more responsible job.

With regard to social anxieties in general and work, the evidence suggests that he is not improved very much. He says he is less shy, but he still feels very awkward and goes silent among a group of strangers. What he does say often still comes out jumbled. He still has very little social life.

In work, up to a point, there has been considerable improvement. He has got a much more responsible job and is now able to make decisions quite easily.

He has undertaken a new course of study and has passed his preliminary exams. He feels confident that he could do a similar job in a much larger company. However, all this seems to have been bought at the price of a peptic ulcer.

Relations with Women. He said he was now not afraid to ask a girl to dance, was better at small talk, and no longer felt inferior to attractive girls. He is now married. However, he completely blocked on being asked about his relation with his wife, and the interviewer could get no real information about this at all. He claimed that the sexual relation was satisfactory, but he said it in such a way that it was impossible to tell what this meant.

Problems over Aggression. He said that he was less sensitive to feeling humiliated; and that although he still tended to jump on people aggressively, this now occurred only at the office and only when he felt it was fully justified. He described one occasion on which he was able to stand up to a boss effectively, but he said he still had a problem in this area.

Summary

There is an improvement in the original symptoms, and very great improvement at work, together with the development of a substitute symptom in the form of a peptic ulcer. He has succeeded in getting married, but the evidence suggests that he is unable to have a deep relation with his wife. It is probably giving him the benefit of the doubt to judge him as "improved." On symptomatic criteria he was judged to be "slightly improved," and on dynamic criteria "improved." This is the only patient of our 45 who was judged as more improved on dynamic than on symptomatic criteria.

CASE 17. A 21-year-old single female economics student was suffering from anxiety about competition with other women. She also had complaints of depression and examination anxiety.

Disturbances

Depression. She has felt especially lonely during the past six months. This brings on attacks of feeling miserable, worthless, a fraud, and that people wouldn't have anything to do with her if they knew her real self. In these attacks she tends to overeat. Her sleep is not affected. She finally went to the doctor after an uncontrollable fit of weeping brought on by an intense feeling of loneliness.

Anxiety. As her second-year exams approached she was told she would be likely to get a first in her finals. She began to get increasingly anxious about the exams and to suffer from nightmares. She was seen at the Tavistock Clinic after her exams were already over.

Social Relations. She has difficulty in making relationships. Though she joins in the activities at college, she always feels lonely and out of it. She also has difficulties with men. She wants boyfriends but is frightened of them. She feels that all they want is physical success, whereas she wants to be loved for herself. At interview, although she was pleasant to talk to, she gave the impression of physical unattractiveness.

Background

She was extremely close to her father, who behaved to her something like an elder brother rather than a father. Her family was extremely enlightened and she was treated as an adult from an early age—all family discussions and decisions being carried out in her presence.

Her father's work was in connection with the Foreign Office, and her schooling was much disrupted by changes. At school she missed the close relation with her parents, which she did not have with her teachers.

A British psychiatric diagnosis of her condition would be anxiety state and reactive depression; American, mixed neurosis with anxiety and depression. Her only contact with psychiatry was one brief interview with a doctor at the student health service, who made no attempt to go deeply into her problems, and one diagnostic interview with a psychiatrist at the Tavistock Clinic. The reason for her not having treatment was that since her second year exams were already over, it was left that she could come back after her summer holiday. She wrote saying that she was feeling better and did not need to come.

Hypothesis. Although it was easy to speculate on psychoanalytic lines about the origin of these disturbances, we did not believe there was firm evidence. We saw the crucial disturbances as a feeling of worthlessness, and anxiety in competitive situations (specific stress) brought on by the exams. There was no certain evidence which of these was primary or more important.

Criteria. The essential criteria are that she should feel of value as a person and as a woman, be able to use her assets, and be able to compete without anxiety or compulsiveness. This should lead to the following:

(1) loss of depression, with the attainment of self-confidence and the ability to enjoy life; (2) no undue anxiety about further exams; (3) ability to make mutually satisfying relationships in general, and to enjoy social life; and (4) she should at least lose her fear of men and look forward to physical as well as intellectual relationships with them.

Follow-Up (Two Years Five Months). Her history is best presented in chronological order, starting with the precipitating factor for her original breakdown, as recounted at follow-up.

She said that she had been alone in her room at college, had heard all the other girls playing radios, and had suddenly become intensely aware that they all had boyfriends and she hadn't. It was this that had precipitated her uncontrollable fit of weeping.

She said that since her breakdown her life had been punctuated by important events, which she referred to as "coincidences," after each of which she had been able to make an important emotional advance.

The first of these had occurred on her holiday shortly after her interview. She had met a young man with whom she had talked deeply, although he was engaged to a girl in England. She had never been as close to a boy as this before, and she felt it made a great difference to her.

On her return, she found that she had got the equivalent of a first in her second-year exams. During her third year at college she felt much freer socially. She described one of the changes as a new-found ability to realize that friends were concerned about her.

As her final exams approached, she again had nightmares, but these now were different—trying to push herself through a crowd of people all going the other way. Apart from this, she suffered little examination anxiety. In the end she got an upper second, which she said was what she expected—she had never expected to get a first.

She had then had a sexual experience with another postgraduate student. She had broken this off because he was very tied to his parents. She said this had not upset her very much. She had been considerably sexually aroused, but had not had orgasm. Shortly after this she had a fleeting sexual encounter with a young man in which the element of a triangular relation was very prominent.

Some time later, she had again been on holiday with a young man, with whom she had a platonic relation, and another girl. The boy began to talk more to the other girl than to her, and she began to have a depressive attack, accompanied by a feeling of self-loathing, and she described herself as "descending into a pit." She had then begun to realize that the cause of her depression was her intense jealousy. One evening she had again had an outburst of crying and the other two had heard her and had come in. She was then able to talk about her feelings. This had a considerable therapeutic effect, for not only had her depression disappeared, but she felt from then on that she was able to participate in group situations in a new way—no longer as an outside observer, but as a member of the group.

Dynamics of the Follow-Up Interview. The interviewer was in conflict between science and humanity—whether to leave this girl as an untreated patient or to make use of all this material about jealousy and triangular situations in a therapeutic interpretation. He decided on the latter course, relating the jealousy to the original triangle between herself, her father, and her mother. Her response to this was to tell how her mother and her father had different views about her appearance. Her mother wanted her to dress in such a way that she looked smart but somehow not particularly attractive to men; whereas the way in which her father wanted her to dress made her look much more beautiful. In fact she tried to dress in a way that resembled neither of these, but if it resembled either, it was the way her mother advocated. She also said that she still suffered from acne, and she could not stop herself from picking the spots and making them worse. The interviewer interpreted that perhaps she didn't quite dare to be attractive in the way her father wanted, because of guilt about wanting to take her father away from her mother.

It is important to note that at the follow-up interview (in contrast to the original interview) she gave the impression of being a very attractive girl.

In answer to a question as to her present feelings about herself, she said that she felt much more confident in herself as a *person*, but that her feelings about herself as a *woman* were lagging behind. She currently had no boyfriend, and did not want to get involved because she was going to spend a year in the United States. She also mentioned that she still sometimes needs to comfort herself by overeating.

Criteria at Follow-Up. In general, she certainly feels of value as a person; and she has made considerable progress in her feelings of value as a woman, though there is still some way to go. She is able to use her assets in work. She has made remarkable progress in her loss of depression, attainment of self-confidence, and ability to enjoy life. She had one depressive attack, but was able to resolve it by self-analysis.

With regard to examination anxiety, this criterion is largely fulfilled, though it is possible that an upper second was below her potential. Her enjoyment of social life also seems to be greatly improved. As far as her relations with men are concerned, this criterion was deliberately made rather unambitious because of the psychiatrist's description of her as essentially unattractive. As the criterion stands, she has exceeded it. If the criterion is made more ambitious, then it is clear that she had made very great progress, but there are important reservations: she has not been able to have orgasm; there has still been, at least until recently, a preoccupation with triangular relationships, which have carried both fascination and anxiety and guilt; and she may be employing a rationalization to prevent further development of her relations with men. On symptomatic criteria she was judged to be "recovered," and on dynamic criteria "improved."

CASE 18. A 24-year-old single male geologist was suffering from a conflict between resentment and guilt in relation to his mother. He sought advice at the clinic for a specific problem.

Disturbances

Conflict over His Mother. Since his father's death three years ago, his mother has suffered from recurrent severe depression. She has been in hospital on and off for two years and has been treated with electric convulsive therapy, but there has been no permanent improvement and she is unable to care for herself. The patient vacillates between feeling that he ought to give up his career and go and live near her; feeling that he ought to get her transferred to a hospital near where he works, but doing nothing about it; and he has ended up by comparatively neglecting her and feeling guilty about it—e.g., he went on a geological expedition to Iceland for six months, and he may not visit her for as much as two months at a time.

Social Difficulties: Immaturity. The interviewing psychiatrist made the judgment that the patient was solitary and that he had directed his interests toward *things* rather than *people* because the latter were too much for him to cope with. The patient remarked that he could not imagine himself as the father of children. The psychiatrist wrote, "I have the very strong feeling that he has considerable neurotic problems."

Background

Both parents were described as quiet. The mother devoted her life to looking after the father, who was often ill. No aggression seemed to be expressed in the family. The patient felt close to neither of his parents.

A British psychiatric diagnosis of his condition would be anxiety in an immature personality; American, anxiety neurosis in an immature personality. His only contact with psychiatry was one diagnostic interview with a psychiatrist at the Tavistock Clinic. The reason for his not having treatment was that it was left that the patient could get in touch again if he felt the need. He did not do so.

Hypothesis. We believe that the original source of trouble was that both his parents were distant from him. This probably resulted in his being angry; this had to be suppressed because anger was not expressed in his home; and the buried anger in turn gave rise to guilt. The present situation with his mother, in which he is required to make sacrifices for her, has reactivated both the anger and the guilt. Probably because of conflicts connected with those mentioned above, he has withdrawn from people in general.

Criteria. The problem with his mother would be regarded as solved if he could reach a reasonable compromise between her needs and his, neither neglecting her nor sacrificing himself excessively.

With regard to relations in general, there should be a substantial increase in his ability to become personally involved and to form satisfactory relations with people of all kinds. He should be able to make reasonable compromises between their needs and his.

Follow-Up (Three Years). His mother is still in the same hospital and has consistently refused to be transferred, in spite of his efforts to get her to do so. Moreover, she has at times refused to eat, and the hospital seems to have neglected this. One day he complained, but he was told there was nothing to worry about. A few days later she was transferred to a medical ward and found to be suffering from protein deficiency. She is now in a chronic ward, and he is not happy about it, but there seems little he can do.

As far as visiting her is concerned, he seems to have reached a reasonable compromise. He goes about once in three weeks, and is able to combine this with other things that he can enjoy.

In relations with people, he said that he was well aware of the difficulties that he had in making contact with people. Nevertheless, looking back on it, he clearly did not feel that he had been as withdrawn as the original psychiatrist thought. He had close relations with people who had the same kinds of interest as he had, but he did have difficulty in breaking away from this group. At this time he also had a rather unsatisfactory relation with a girl whom he did not feel competent to cope with.

Some time after his original interview, he succeeded in breaking out of his narrow circle of friends. He first made friends with another man who helped him to develop much wider interests. He then met a girl who was involved in a quite different type of work from his and who seems to be very sociable and good at relations with people. He fell in love with her, and they have now been married for over a year. All the indications at follow-up were that this was a good marriage between two people who loved each other. She has a wide circle of friends, and this has greatly enriched his social life. Their sexual life was described as satisfactory.

Two reservations emerged: (1) during the interview, he was extremely nervous and unsure of himself; and (2) he gave some evidence of difficulty in asserting himself in situations that he encountered in everyday life, saying that he tended to put on a show of anger rather than actually being angry.

Summary

As far as the problem over his mother was concerned, we had no means of knowing whether or not any more effort on his part would have produced a more satisfactory solution. With this reservation, our criteria seem to have been fulfilled. He certainly seems to have reached a reasonable compromise within the limits of the present situation.

It is also very striking how he realized that his problem was concerned with breaking out of his narrow circle of friends, and how he enlisted the help of other people in doing this. His marriage to this particular girl must be considered as an extremely healthy move. Perhaps the interviewing psychiatrist overestimated his degree of withdrawal.

Of course some difficulties remain, as shown for instance by his behavior at interview. But on symptomatic criteria he was judged to be "recovered," and on dynamic criteria "much improved."

CASE 19. A 31-year-old single research chemist was suffering from transvestist and fetishistic impulses. His complaint was impotency. He came to the clinic because he thought that he might shortly become engaged.

Disturbances

All his known disturbances are connected with sexuality. He had no interest in women up to the age of 18 years, but then had some mild love affairs without allowing himself intercourse. He first attempted intercourse at 22 years. He had no difficulty in lovemaking, felt a great desire for the woman, and got an erection, but this collapsed the moment he attempted penetration. Exactly the same has happened on several occasions since.

At the age of 5 years he began to think how exciting it would be to be a woman. He began to get a strange feeling of excitement and pleasure from imagining himself in his mother's clothes. Only on a few occasions in his adolescence did he actually put on his mother's clothes, but he has never been able to get rid of the preoccupation with being dressed as a woman, feeling like one, and being taken for one.

Accompanying the transvestist feelings is an intense preoccupation with women's shoes. He feels compelled to stare at and study a woman's shoes to the point of intense sexual excitement, with erection and ejaculation, followed by intense anxiety, shame and self-reproach. At times he is compelled to handle a woman's shoes as if there were something mysterious in them, and shoes with a soft smooth texture have a special attraction for him. Next to touching and stroking a woman's body, the handling and stroking of such a shoe produces the greatest sexual excitement. When he is dictating letters to his secretary he may become preoccupied with her shoes, and lose the thread of what he is saying. He is afraid that this may one day betray him.

Although socially and academically he has done very well, he has an intense feeling of inferiority as a man. "My whole life has given me nothing but a sense of shame, ignorance, and ineptitude in everything connected with sex. I am beginning to feel a fraud. I am not a man with men, and with women I feel like an embarrassed boy."

Background

He is an only child. His father, a solicitor, was shy and awkward, and felt ill at ease with his wife and child. Everything was left to the mother, who absolutely doted on her son, and enjoyed keeping him as a little child to cuddle and fuss over. The patient felt that his mother was father and mother to him. "She seems to radiate strength and confidence, and I could never imagine her yielding or deferring to a man in anything."

There was no further information in the notes about his prospective engagement mentioned above.

A British psychiatric diagnosis of his condition would be impotence with transvestist and fetishistic impulses: American, psychophysiologic genitourinary disorder, namely, impotence, and sexual deviation, namely, fetishism and transvestism.

In the original diagnostic interview with the psychiatrist at the Tavistock Clinic, he was advised to have psychoanalysis. Two years later he wrote saying that he had rejected this advice, terrified of the amount of money and time he would have to sacrifice. Since then, his engagement had been broken off, "not by me and not as a result of the disorders mentioned." His condition had not changed and he asked to be put in touch with an analyst again. He was seen by the original psychiatrist for a second interview, but this time the psychiatrist felt much less sure that he needed treatment and left him to decide.

Hypothesis. Although there are many pointers in the history allowing speculation along psychoanalytic lines, we did not want to get involved in problems to do with the cause of sexual disorders of this kind.

We would only say that he was treated as a baby by his mother, and had no masculine father on whom to model himself; and therefore, it is understandable that he has grown up with a feeling of immaturity and uncertainty about his sexual identity. A *specific stress* seems to be the prospect of a mature relation with a woman.

Criteria. The essential change is that he should have a clear sense of identity as a man, and be able to express and enjoy his masculinity with both women and men. This should lead to the following: (1) successful and pleasurable emotional and sexual relation with a woman; (2) loss of "perverse" tendencies; (3) the ability to be constructively aggressive with both men and women, if this was not present before; and (4) the above changes should be accomplished without loss of effectiveness in the areas where he has been successful before.

First Follow-Up (Two Years Six Months Since the First Psychiatric Interview). He now made it clear that his transvestist and fetishistic impulses had not been constantly present throughout his life. Each time they went away he would hope that they had gone for good, and he would destroy the women's clothes that he had used.

The crucial recent event was that eight weeks ago he started going out with a girl for whom he seemed to have deeper feelings than he had ever experienced before, and this has resulted in the complete disappearance of his "perverse" tendencies during this period. He has intense sexual feelings with her and strong erections, but he has not yet put his potency to the test.

As far as self-assertiveness was concerned, he described incidents in which he was able to stand up to a man on behalf of someone else, but there did seem to be considerable residual difficulty in this area. In his work there was certainly no loss of effectiveness.

Second Follow-Up (Nine Years Eleven Months Since the First Interview). There had been no contact with psychiatry since the first follow-up interview.

The relation with the girl mentioned in the previous follow-up came to an end, and between then and his marriage about six years ago he formed relations with about four different girls. The pattern tended to be that he became deeply involved, proposed marriage, was refused, and then became very demanding of affection, with the result that the girl got put off and left him. Finally he met his wife and married her within three months. They now have two sons, aged 3 years and a few months, respectively.

The relation with his wife appears to be essentially satisfactory, with shared interests, companionship, shared friends, and intense shared love for the children. It also contains ordinary difficulties, such as those concerning in-laws and his working too much at home.

Subsequent Sexual History. He told an amazing story of sexual ignorance and sexual discovery. The degree of sexual ignorance in which he had been brought up was such that until past the age of 30 years he did not realize that sexual intercourse needed to involve pelvic thrusting—he said with considerable humor that having read Hemingway, he thought "some sort of cosmic vibration would be provided from the center of the earth." As a result, in his attempts at intercourse he had simply inserted his penis, had waited for something to happen, and had ejaculated because he was so tense, without giving the girl any satisfaction. He had first realized that something more was needed from hearing some of his friends' ribald discussion of the sexual act as described in a novel. The next time he had the chance of a sexual relation, he acted on his discovery, and it really seems as if this was the turning point in the overcoming of his impotence. In subsequent relations he has, in general, had no difficulty with his potency. His sexual needs have been strong, and the relation with one girl broke up because he wanted intercourse more than twice a night and she didn't, which resulted in quarrels between them and premature ejaculation on his part.

With his wife, he described a passionate sexual relation, in the early stages of their marriage, with no difficulty over potency.

Transvestism and Fetishism. He made clear that the situation reported at the previous follow-up had not lasted, and that these impulses, although fluctuating, had later returned in full force. In the early relation with his wife he had sometimes put on items of her clothing as part of their foreplay, and had found himself intensely excited by this. His wife had noticed the quality of his excitement and had questioned him about it, and he had told her about his impulses. Her attitude was not to be shocked, but not to encourage him, and to question whether it was wise to go on in case it became a habit. It seems that from this time his impulses have receded, and he said he had not acted on them for perhaps six months. Occasionally the idea comes to him, but in the end he feels it's not worth the bother.

In a letter written after the interview, the interviewer asked him whether or not this meant that some quality of excitement was missing in his sex life. On the whole he did not think this was so, writing that "there are even now times occasionally when I want something I haven't got and these moments are associated with the stirring of some of the old perverted desires." On the other hand, "the thought of the rituals themselves now seems boring and silly. I think I really may have outgrown them. But the thought of the consummation they seemed to promise lingers and there is *something* I occasionally feel I still want, though I have not the least idea what that something is or would be. . . . These thoughts occur to me only occasionally and then only in a very mild form. They certainly don't torment me. Perhaps I shall realize one day that what I wanted was what I have now."

Feeling of Identity as a Man.—Difficulties in this area had persisted up to the time of his marriage, e.g., he felt inferior at being no good at doing maintenance jobs on the car or in the house. He now does these jobs, but feels his wife is better at some of them. When asked directly about his previous intense feeling of inadequacy, he did not really seem to remember it and said that he no longer had such a feeling and never thought about it. He went on to talk about self-assertion, and spoke of being able to tell off a colleague at a committee meeting in such a way that the colleague had apologized and been very pleasant about it afterwards. This had happened quite spontaneously, and he said how much better it was than thinking afterwards what one ought to have said.

The following is a further quotation from the letter mentioned above: "You asked me what was the happiest time of my life. The answer I gave on the spur of the moment was the period just after I married. On reflection, I would now say that the present seems to me the happiest time, though it may sound a little spurious or effusive to put it that way. Since our second child was born, we have been exhausted and compelled to be wholly committed to the business of bringing the two of them up. But we have both found the life deeply satisfying. Our eldest boy gives us enormous pleasure, especially as he seems to be not in the least jealous, as we were afraid he might be, of his brother but on the contrary very affectionate and proud. I find the satisfactions and pleasures of being married and having a family—something incidentally I have wanted all my life—far deeper than the ghastly cerebral excitement of perversion."

Summary

The above material speaks for itself. It seems to us that, unless one is going to be obsessionally perfectionistic about the *absolute* disappearance of the transvestist and fetishistic impulses, which in any case would be suspect if it happened, there is no reason to judge him as anything other than "recovered."

Comment

A comparison can be made between the observed changes and those that might have resulted from psychotherapy. Although in all cases but two the improvements are only partial, they appear to us to be real, and we, therefore, see no way of distinguishing between these partial improvements and those that might have resulted from long-term psychotherapy. Consequently, we believe that it would be possible to devise convincing imaginary reports by fictitious therapists, which might read as below:

CASE 14: the Polish refugee: "After many sessions the patient at last began to realize that her previous patterns of behavior are unsatisfactory, and that if she wants to receive any satisfaction she must first take responsibility for her own life. This has resulted in a noticeable diminution of symptoms and an improvement both in her frustration tolerance and in her relations with everyone around her. It led ultimately to her making a satisfactory marriage."

CASE 18: the geologist: "It was finally possible to bring home to him his intense conflict between resenting his mother's demands on him and his guilt about not doing enough for her. This resulted first in the ability to handle the situation over his mother in a far more realistic way. This cleared the way for an increased ability to relate to other people. This in turn culminated in his marriage to a girl whose interpersonal relations appear to be very healthy, who has thus been in a sense able to take over his therapy. Although he still has some anxieties about aggressiveness, it was believed that this was a very satisfactory therapeutic result, and therapy was terminated by mutual agreement."

CASE 16: the printer's assistant: "After repeated interpretation of his oedipal problems in the transference, he began to realize his intense competitiveness and his irrational view of all men as waiting to pounce on him. This has resulted in a substantial reduction in his anxieties at work, an increased ability to relate to women, and ultimately to marriage. Nevertheless, the anxiety at work appears to have resulted in a peptic ulcer, and his intellectual defenses remain strong. Therapy continues."

We believed that if these patients had been given long-term therapy, such accounts would be natural, and clinicians would accept without question that therapy was responsible for the improvements. Since the patients did not receive therapy, we concluded that we had uncovered the existence of "spontaneous remission" of a depth and extent that none of us had believed possible. This seemed to illustrate most pointedly how easy it is to find some event in therapy that accounts for improvements observed, when in fact the improvements might have occurred in the absence of any therapy whatsoever; and consequently, it also emphasized the vital need for a control series in any study of psychotherapy involving outcome.

Additional Evidence. This was the stage of discussion at which we began to write the present report. We may now introduce our surprise. The reader has been cheated, because part of the evidence has been suppressed. The more we wrote, the more cogent this evidence appeared to be, to the point at which it became overwhelming.

The evidence is concerned with what happened in the single diagnostic interview that each of these patients was given, and what some of them said about this at follow-up. It is set out below for the three patients whose fictitious reports were given above.

CASE 14: the Polish refugee: The interviewing psychiatrist wrote to this patient's general practitioner, who had referred her, as follows:

"She is asking now for treatment as a further attempt at securing somebody else to take full responsibility for her. I do not think that under these circumstances any treatment will help her unless she is capable of making some serious and sustained effort on her own. I put this situation firmly and squarely to her in the hope that it might make some impression on her. Although she seemed to be impressed, I am very doubtful if this will prove lasting."

Parts of the account by the psychiatrist who carried out the follow-up interview read as follows: "She said that she was in a very bad way when she came here the first time. She spontaneously said that the interview with the other psychiatrist had helped her a great deal." In fact, the firm handling by the interviewing psychiatrist had been continued both by her relations and by a family friend who was a physician, who had told her that there was nothing wrong with her.

CASE 18: the geologist: The interviewing psychiatrist wrote as follows about the original interview: "It was very easy for me to show him that in fact the real problem he was dealing with was his own feelings of *having* to take the responsibility, and of *having* to pay the price, one way or the other, about dealing with his mother. I dealt with this directly in terms of his guilty and aggressive feelings towards the demands being made on him by his parents, and his desire to serve his own needs, getting tangled up in making any decision. This was obviously an enormous relief to him. We ended the session by his saying that he realized now that he did not want to pay any price at all, but that he had better pay a price which was reasonable, rather than throwing up his career, which would leave him with so much resentment that he would not be helping his mother at all. I said that if he wanted to talk over this again, he could always make another appointment, to which he replied that he did not think he would, but held my hand quite firmly for quite a long time, telling me how grateful he was for the interview."

The follow-up interview with this particular patient was tape-recorded, and the following is an extract from the transcript (the patient is speaking): "The main point of the interview was that it made me realize much more clearly that I was having feelings of anger towards my mother for being ill; that this sort of thing could be expected to happen and must be taken into consideration; and that if, for her sake, I'd given up the work I'd set my heart on, these aggressive feelings would have come up and I would have needed to be quite sure I could combat them." In other words, he seems to have remembered almost word for word the basic interpretation given to him three years before.

CASE 16: the printer's assistant: This patient was originally interviewed by a psychiatrist whose practice is to make transference interpretations routinely in all his interviews. The following is a quotation from his account of the interview with this patient: "For a long time silences were prevalent in spite of my attempts to confront him with various things he said. Links between peculiarities of his voice and his potency played a great part in the exchanges between him and me. His constant waiting for the battle to develop with other men also appeared clearly in the here-and-now, and at one point following such a here-and-now interpretation he started to tell me *with a radiant face* [our italics] how true this was, and how he always felt an audience at the back looking on what happened, and at the battle that was developing between us now."

It is quite clear from this account, and from the words in italics in particular, that the patient must have been profoundly affected by the interview at the time. At follow-up, however, he would not admit that the original interview had had any effect; but when pressed, he grudgingly admitted that a number of improvements had followed not long afterwards.

The point that we wish to make is that, with the sole exception of the references implying long-term treatment, *the fictitious accounts of therapy that we gave above may possibly be in all essentials entirely accurate.* In fact, it suddenly appears that the extreme care that we took to exclude all patients who had had more than two interviews with a psychiatrist in their whole lives was a wasted effort, because powerful therapeutic effects may follow from a single interview. In other words, we seem to have met the reverse of a problem frequently encountered in psychotherapy research—not a study of psychotherapy contaminated to an unknown degree by spontaneous remission, but a study of spontaneous remission contaminated by psychotherapy.

We choose to give three additional cases as examples because of the ease with which fictitious accounts of therapy could be devised. If these were the only examples, they would together make an interesting observation, but, in fact, the evidence is far more extensive and far more striking than this, as the following accounts will show.

CASE 23: Miss V. illustrates the impact of the psychiatric interview in a more striking way than any other of these patients, as is shown by the following extract from the verbatim transcript of her follow-up interview:

"My first interview here was like having to do a very complex algebraic problem, and somebody sits down with you and tells you how to work it out and get the answer. *I didn't realize that my feelings were quite so strong and that my father was there behind things. Since that time I have been able to see it. This has helped.* I don't remember a great deal about the interview except that it made a tremendous impression on me. The word association test before it upset me terribly for some unknown reason. The interview upset me, not because someone told me something I didn't want to know, but I felt as if I had been *run over.* You know, if you have a small accident, you feel sort of shaky afterwards."

CASE 17: the economics student illustrates both the impact of the interview, and the acquisition of a capacity for self-analysis leading quite clearly to therapeutic effects.

At follow-up she described a series of events, or "coincidences," each of which had enabled her to make some advance in her life. The first of these had in fact been her diagnostic interview. When I asked her what she remembered about her interview with the psychiatrist, she told me that the thing that she remembered above all was that he started by asking about her parents. She had felt this had been one of the coincidences. She was impressed with this, wondering if it was just chance, or how he could have known.

CASE 20: the convent girl resembles the printer's assistant in three respects: (1) a highly interpretative interview, (2) evidence for some response to the interpretations, (3) a coincidence between the theme of the interpretations and the areas of improvement, but finally (4) a denial by the patient that the interview had any importance.

> One of the problems that she presented was an inability to go out and enjoy herself. The interviewing psychiatrist repeatedly pointed out to this deprived girl the pattern of denying her own needs in favor of those of others, and the probable feelings behind this of guilt and anger. After much resistance, the patient eventually got as far as saying that once she started to go out she felt it would be "difficult to keep her indoors." When asked at follow-up about the original interview, she said she could hardly remember even coming at all, let alone anything that happened in it. Yet one of the main areas of improvement lay in her ability to enjoy herself, and the pattern of serving others' needs seemed also to have largely disappeared.

CASES 15 and 22 resemble the Polish refugee, in that the therapeutic mechanism appears to be the realization that they must take responsibility for their own lives. Below are quotations from the account of the follow-up interviews.

> Mrs. T's (case 15) original complaint was refusal of sexual intercourse. Her original interview with Dr. F. represented to her something like the last thing that could be done to help her. Added to this, he threw the whole thing back at her, making her feel it was up to her to change herself. She doesn't know how it happened, or what made her able to do it, but about three months after her interview, when her husband as usual indicated his wish for intercourse, she accepted him, and since then they have been having regular intercourse about two or three times a week.

> The junior lecturer (case 22) was complaining of a quite severe anxiety state, with a fear of authority and of responsibility, which had been precipitated by his arrival in England from his country of origin. "When he had seen the psychiatrist, he had been much preoccupied with the idea of going back to his home country. The psychiatrist had refused to advise him about this and had left him to make his own decision. The result of this had been that he had decided to stay in England, and the fact that he had taken the decision himself had greatly increased his confidence." At follow-up all his anxieties concerned with his direct relation with men had apparently disappeared, though those concerned with a triangular relation between himself and another man and a woman were still clearly present.

Finally we may add some interesting evidence on case 19, the research chemist. The following is a quotation from the account of the first follow-up interview:

After the first consultation with the psychiatrist, he had felt considerably disturbed by receiving the impression that there was something seriously wrong with him. On the other hand, after the second consultation two years later, he was much relieved when the psychiatrist didn't think he needed treatment, and *this had caused his fetishistic impulses to disappear completely for a few weeks.*

In addition, this patient apparently found the first *follow-up* interview helpful, as is illustrated by the following quotation from the account of the second follow-up interview:

He expressed some gratitude for my previous interview with him, in which I had given him the impression that he may well not need treatment. He said that this had been a great reassurance to him and that it had been "important."

Discussion of the Qualitative Evidence

An examination of this material thus suggests strongly that these single diagnostic interviews had some powerful therapeutic effects. This conclusion is reinforced by the fact that three of these patients wrote to their interviewing psychiatrist not long after their interview, stating that they felt better and clearly implying that this had happened through the acquisition of insight.

The geologist (case 18), four weeks later wrote, "I soon found it easy to talk to the psychiatrist and feel that the discussion did get somewhere in clarifying the situation and the different possible courses of action."

Miss V. (case 23) four weeks later wrote, "Several hints from the psychiatrist have helped me and already the situation has improved."

The economics student (case 17), three months later wrote, "I found my talk with you at the end of last term most helpful and *productive of self-examination* [our italics]. This, plus a most enjoyable holiday, seem to have driven away my depression."

It was considerations such as these that finally forced us into the realization that, at least in many of these cases, we had not been studying spontaneous remission at all, but one-session psychotherapy.

Quantitative Evidence

Before drawing any final conclusion, however, we need to consider the following question: granted that we have found evidence for therapeutic factors in a high proportion of the dynamically improved patients, is it possible to find similar factors in a high proportion of the dynamically unimproved patients as well? If this were possible, then the evidence that improvements were due to these therapeutic factors would be weakened.

With this in mind, we have searched the material on our whole sample for the following: (1) evidence of interpretations at diagnostic interview, to which there was some response; (2) letters written to the psychiatrist after the diagnostic interview, with any implication that the interview had been help-ful; or (3) statements at follow-up with any implication as in (2). If any one of these is found, that case is judged as "therapeutic factors present."

We have made an exhaustive statistical analysis of the evidence. Our conclusion can be stated quite simply: without question these therapeutic factors are present in a significantly higher proportion of dynamically im-proved patients, in contrast to those who are unimproved or are improved on symptomatic criteria only.

This may be illustrated most simply below (N = 45).

Therapeutic factors	Unimproved	Improved	Total
Present	11	9	20
Absent	23	2	25
Total	34	11	

For this distribution, $X^2 = 6.35$, df $= 1$, which is significant at the .01 level (one-tailed test).

The corresponding distribution for symptomatic criteria is as below (N = 45).

Therapeutic factors	Unimproved	Improved	Total
Present	7	13	20
Absent	15	10	25
Total	22	23	

This gives $X^2 = 1.87$, for which P lies between .05 and .1.

Now there is a possible fallacy in drawing any conclusion from this: that those patients who are unimproved, symptomatically or dynamically, have no reason to say that the interview was helpful; and thus, causation may be operating the wrong way round—not that the absence of therapeutic factors causes lack of improvement, but that lack of improvement causes absence of therapeutic factors. This fallacy may be at least partly eliminated by omitting all patients who were unimproved on both symptomatic and dynamic criteria, and plotting those patients judged to be improved on symptomatic criteria only against those improved on dynamic criteria, as below (N = 24).

	Symptomatic		
Therapeutic factors	Only	Dynamic	Total
Present	5	9	14
Absent	8	2	10
Total	13	11	

This distribution is significant at the 5% level by the Fisher Exact Probability Test (one-tailed).

Moreover, we are also quite sure that if the quality or intensity of these therapeutic factors is taken into account, so that they are judged on a scale containing more than two points, the positive correlation with outcome is increased. Thus there was no patient among those who were not dynamically improved who directly attributed his improvement to insight, as three of these patients did; or who remembered an interpretation with such clarity as did the geologist; or who described the impact of the interview in such dramatic terms as did Miss V.

Thus the statistical evidence strongly reinforces the clinical evidence already presented, confirming the likelihood of powerful therapeutic effects from these single interviews.

THERAPEUTIC MECHANISMS

We are now in a dilemma. Having started out to study "spontaneous remission" and its mechanisms, we have ended with considerable evidence about one-session psychotherapy, and apparently little evidence about spontaneous remission at all.

In fact, the latter difficulty can be overcome, but, even if it could not, this would be no great tragedy. One of the almost insuperable difficulties about the study of long-term psychotherapy is that, because there is time for so much to happen, it is almost impossible to draw any conclusions about factors responsible for therapeutic effects. Here, in those patients who began to improve soon after their diagnostic interview, we have an unrivaled opportunity to study evidence about the effects of single interventions. Moreover there are various ways in which, notwithstanding these therapeutic effects, the clinical material can be used to provide evidence about spontaneous remission as well.

First of all, a study of what these patients said about their interviews discloses unequivocally the presence of two therapeutic factors that are entirely distinct. The first is *insight,* and the second is being brought face-to-face with the *necessity for taking responsibility for their own lives.*

Insight

As far as this is concerned, the most striking example is clearly the geologist (case 18). He illustrates a neurotic mechanism that may be called the "all-or-nothing" phenomenon, in which a patient who is suffering from two incompatible and partly unconscious internal forces, can only alternate between one and the other extreme and can never integrate the two. In his case, the simple expedient of bringing out his hidden resentment against his mother, and his guilt about it, apparently transformed the situation into one in which he could make a realistic and reasonable compromise between his mother's needs and his own. The evidence that this change was the direct consequence of the therapist's interpretation seems to us to be overwhelming. The quotation given above from the follow-up interview with Miss V. similarly shows the effects of acquiring insight, though in a less clear and less well-documented way; but we have her letter four weeks later clearly bearing witness to therapeutic effects.

Thus, both these patients give evidence of therapeutic effects arising from insight acquired during the diagnostic interview. The economics student illustrates the same, but she illustrates also the possibility of *acquiring insight quite independently of therapy.* The first evidence of this comes from events before she was seen; as her exams approached, she began to suffer from a series of nightmares. These in fact were not dreams of examination anxiety but thinly disguised sexual dreams about her father, which, in the latest of them—the night before her breakdown—she had finally been able to admit. This experience clearly prepared her for receiving further insight from her interview, which, apparently simply through the psychiatrist's questioning, and not through interpretation, crystallized for her that her relation with her parents was an important factor in her difficulties.

But we now meet something that seems to go well beyond what happened in the interview. In the later part of the follow-up period, she had been faced with a kind of triangular situation that seemed to lie at the heart of her difficulties; and this threatened to precipitate an attack of depression similar to that which had brought her to the clinic originally. On this occasion, however, two things happened that were quite different from events of the previous crisis. First, she began to realize that her depressive feelings were due to jealousy; and second, she succeeded in talking out these feelings and expressing them to the other two people involved, in such a way that the crisis was completely resolved.

This patient, therefore, illustrates the acquisition of a capacity that is one of the major aims of dynamic psychotherapy, namely the ability to resolve a situation first by self-analysis and then by taking appropriate constructive action on the insight achieved. This constitutes the discovery of a *new way of handling emotional difficulties,* the teaching of which is one of the explicit aims of "anxiety-provoking brief psychotherapy" as described by Sifneos.[17] Now, of course, no one can determine the extent to which this new capacity was the result of the diagnostic interview, but one can be quite sure that it was not taught directly to the patient during this interview. In any case, a moment's thought will show that the sudden realization of what one's feelings really are, followed by the ability to talk these over and express them, can hardly be regarded as the exclusive prerogative of people who have undergone psychotherapy.

Ways in Which Evidence Can Be Obtained for Spontaneous Remission

This latter consideration represents one of the general ways in which these single-interview patients can be used to indicate some of the mechanisms of spontaneous remission, namely, what one may call "extrapolation to zero therapy." This patient apparently acquired the capacity for self-analysis after the very minimum of therapeutic intervention. Presumably, she might well have achieved the same without any therapeutic intervention at all. In this connection it is worth noting that the atmosphere in which she grew up was one of very considerable psychological sophistication.

Another way in which these patients may illustrate possible mechanisms of spontaneous remission is when the therapeutic effects go well beyond what might be expected from the content of the psychiatrist's original interpretation. Here we may return to the geologist. The insight that he received at interview was concerned purely with the conflict over his mother. The improvements found at follow-up included not only the problem concerning his mother, but his whole social life; and this led ultimately to his making what appeared to be a highly satisfactory marriage. It is, of course, possible that the type of problem that he had with his mother made a major contribution to his problem with people in general, but this explanation does not seem entirely convincing. It seems quite possible that his improvement in relations with people had little to do with the other problem, and would have occurred anyway. At first sight there would appear to be no way of reaching any conclusion about this.

However, we may introduce here a piece of evidence put forward by the patient himself at follow-up, namely that his movement toward people started to occur *before* he came for his diagnostic interview. Although this trend may have been facilitated by the therapeutic effects of his original interview, there seems no reason to suppose that it would not have continued if there had been no such interview; and every reason to suppose that such factors occur with other people who never come to see a psychiatrist. Once more, extrapolation to zero therapy has furnished an example of a type of emotional maturation that may well constitute a factor in spontaneous remission.

The statement that improvements had already begun before the original interview was also made by the lesbian teacher, who said that she thought that the homosexual phase of her life was coming to an end before she came to the clinic. Similarly Mrs. T's new-found ability to use constructive self-assertion also started before she came to the clinic, when she moved to Liverpool and told her husband he could follow her if he wished.

To summarize, three patients said that their improvement had already started before their diagnostic interview, and they thus provide direct evidence for the beginnings of spontaneous remission free from the effects of psychiatric intervention.

Therapeutic Relationships in Everyday Life

The geologist also provides two separate examples of another possible factor in spontaneous remission, namely, what may be called a *therapeutic relationship* that enables a patient to grow. The less important example of this is with the friend who helped him to broaden his interests and therefore his social contacts; the more important is, of course, with his wife.

During the course of long experience both of psychotherapy and of follow-up work, we have been repeatedly struck with two contrasting phenomena: the first is what Freud called the "compulsion to repeat"—patients who repeat incessantly a neurotic type of relationship, and who actually seek out from their environment a particular type of partner with whom this repetition is inevitable. Clinicians may be less aware of the opposite phenomenon, namely the ability to seek out a kind of relationship through which a neurotic pattern may be broken.

The geologist illustrates this particularly clearly. One of his problems was a difficulty in getting on with people; and he specifically said that the girl whom he chose to marry was someone who was especially gifted in this direction. We have found many similar examples during our follow-up of treated patients, in a number of whom the evidence strongly suggests that the ability to find such a partner was in no way the consequence of therapy.

Patients' Ability to Take Responsibility for Their Own Lives

As psychoanalysts we are trained to have little faith in the therapeutic effects of saying to a patient that he must "pull himself together," or "snap out of it," or that "he can manage if he tries," and other seemingly platitudinous exhortations. Nevertheless, our present material provides one direct, and two indirect, examples of powerful therapeutic effects when this is the message that the patient receives.

The most striking example is of course the Polish refugee (case 14), whose pattern of collapsing into illness and sponging on her relatives was both chronic and apparently ingrained and immutable. Here we may quote the interviewing psychiatrist's description of his own intervention: "I was rather downright with her, and told her that no one could help her if she was not willing to help herself." At follow-up, she made clear that not only had this interview in itself been helpful, but that her own family and a friend who was a physician had continued the good work, telling her that there was nothing wrong with her and that she could manage perfectly well. This continuation of informal therapeutic work, of a kind that might have been given by a formal therapist, of course means that this particular patient was probably the least "untreated" of the whole series—though there is no reason to suppose that the therapy involved any attempt to give her insight into the origins of her illness. Nevertheless, the seven-year follow-up bears witness to the extraordinary therapeutic effectiveness of these interventions. This is one of two examples in our work of Bergin's speculation that many of the improvements that are loosely called "spontaneous remission" are really the results of informal therapy by professional helpers such as general practitioners and clergymen.[18] The other example is provided by Mrs. T. (case 15) (see the account of her previous history).

The other two examples of the ability to take responsibility only fail to be spectacular by comparison with the Polish refugee, and in fact provide equally instructive lessons. Patient No. 15 described very clearly how she had hoped for some magical cure in her contact with the clinic, and how the psychiatrist "threw the whole thing back at her, making her feel that it was up to her to change herself." It seems that the message was not directly given but was only implied. Here it is worth noting that the tone of the psychiatrist's report was the most pessimistic in the whole series: "The pattern of complete repudiation of sexual response to her husband is rigidly fixed. She is convinced that she can never change."

In the junior lecturer (case 22), the effect was even more indirect and apparently arose simply from the fact that he pressed the psychiatrist for advice about whether or not he should return to his home country, and the latter refused to give it. The result of this was that the patient decided to stay in England, "and the fact that he had taken the decision himself had greatly increased his confidence."

Therapeutic Mechanisms in the Research Chemist

This intensely interesting and complex story merits a special section. First of all, some psychodynamic thinking needs to be introduced. It seems clear that the basic disturbance in this man (case 19) was one of sexual identity, and that he had, as a result, a profound sense of inferiority as a man. Few psychoanalysts would believe that such a condition could respond to anything short of intensive long-term psychotherapy. In fact, it seems that what the patient needed was a series of events that helped to break the vicious circle between a sense of inadequacy on the one hand and failure in a man's role on the other—or, in terms of learning theory, the vicious circle in which his sense of inadequacy was constantly being "reinforced" by failure. One category of such events, but only one, was his contact with the clinic: from both the second consultation and the first follow-up interview he had received the reassurance that he was not so irreparably damaged as he had always feared, and, therefore, the confirmation of his potential as a man. Thus *genuine* reassurance, like the exhortation to take responsibility for one's own life, is a type of intervention that we may sometimes unjustifiably despise.

The second category of event is a pure learning experience, namely, his chance discovery of an elementary piece of knowledge about the technique of sexual intercourse. It is quite clear that this discovery led to the complete disappearance of the complaint that had originally brought him to see a psychiatrist, which was not transvestism but impotence. This result raises the question, given great point by the work of Masters and Johnson, of the extent to which simple instruction in the art of lovemaking may relieve apparently severe sexual disabilities.

From this discovery and the resulting improvement in potency, there clearly followed the possibility of learning that he was in fact a perfectly adequate man, and this in turn paved the way for the possibility of choosing an adequate partner and coping with the stresses of a close relationship.

The final act in the drama was the confession of his transvestist impulses to his wife, and her sympathetic but discouraging reaction to them. Here psychoanalysts would probably say that these impulses were merely re-pressed, which of course is a possibility; but another possibility is that—as we know happens in psychotherapy—they were already weakened and were only awaiting some decisive event to be in some way "extinguished." If the mechanism had been merely repression, we should expect the result to be a definite loss of sexual excitement. Here we can only say that the patient's honest and carefully thought out description of his feelings does not suggest that this was so.

There is however something even more striking and unexpected in this history than any of the features so far mentioned, which may be introduced as follows: in psychotherapy, we are familiar with the occurrence of radical alterations in a patient's view of the people in his past life. This patient demonstrates the same phenomenon to a remarkable degree. At his original consultation, he conveyed a clear impression of his mother's dominance, his father's subordinate position, and his own lack of contact with either of them. By the time of the second follow-up interview, it had become clear that this picture emphasized only one aspect of the truth, or that it empha-sized only one period of his life. After this earlier interview, the material to be published was submitted to the patient, who replied by letter as follows:

I am amazed if I ever said that my mother had been both "mother and father" to me. Perhaps I did, but my relations with my father have been close and strong, especially when I was a child and during the last ten years or so of his life. When I was a child we were constant companions. We were estranged, somewhat, during my adoles-cence. In my late teens I was not allowed to accompany my father to the pub. Finally I took the law into my own hands and announced that I was joining him—a dramatic moment in our lives. He enjoyed the political arguments we had and after a short while he would ask me to join him. . . .

Here again we meet a striking moment of maturation long before the patient ever thought of seeing a psychiatrist.

If this patient had had psychotherapy, we would very probably be saying that the resolution of his oedipal rivalry had allowed him to see the positive side of his relation with his father. In actual fact, much the same may be true, the factor being the patient's realization of his own manhood.

Thus yet another phenomenon has been shown, perhaps against all expectation, not to be the exclusive prerogative of patients who have undergone in-depth psychotherapy.

The Relative Therapeutic Importance of the Psychiatric Interview and Life Experience

It needs to be emphasized that the relative therapeutic importance of the psychiatric interview and life experience apparently varies over a wide range in the patients presented here.

At one end of the spectrum, e.g., in the research chemist, the interviews were probably only a minor facilitating factor in the patient's recovery. At the other end, e.g., in the Polish refugee and Mrs. T., the single psychiatric interview seems to have represented a turning point in the patient's life.

Therapeutic Mechanisms: Conclusion

The mechanisms that these patients illustrate may now be summarized as follows: (1) insight; (2) the capacity for self-analysis; (3) working through feelings with the people involved; (4) normal maturation and growth; (5) therapeutic relationships, especially the therapeutic marriage; (6) the patient's taking responsibility for his own life; (7) the breaking of a vicious circle between the patient and his environment; (8) genuine reassurance; and (9) direct learning.

The first eight mechanisms appear to have been facilitated in one or more of these patients by the single diagnostic interview; but all the evidence suggests that every one of the eight could perfectly well appear in its own right, in the absence of any therapeutic intervention. Thus this extraordinarily rich clinical material provides us with important information both about mechanisms in psychotherapy and about spontaneous remission, suggesting strongly that the two types of mechanism are basically the same.

There is a final quantitative question: are patients who can be helped by a single interview really as common as is implied by the present study, where they apparently make up nine out of 45, or 20%? It seems to us that this cannot possibly be so, and that the mechanism of self-selection inherent in the way the study was conducted must have concentrated these patients in our sample. Presumably patients who were satisfied with their contact with the clinic were more willing to return for follow-up.

Clinical Implications

An important question is whether or not patients who will improve after a single interview can be recognized in advance. Our material does not provide evidence on this question. As might be expected, several of the patients described here were young people of apparently good personality, e.g., the geologist, the economics student, the junior lecturer, and Miss V.; but on the other hand, there were two grossly hysterical and apparently inadequate personalities (the Polish refugee and Mrs. T.); two suffering from sexual deviations (the research chemist and the lesbian teacher); and two with very deprived backgrounds (the convent girl and the evacuee). We really have no answer to this question, but it does raise a crucial problem for further research. Even without an answer, however, the existence of such patients has important implications in the operation of psychotherapeutic clinics. Clearly, psychiatrists who undertake consultations should not automatically assign patients to long-term psychotherapy or even to brief psychotherapy, but should be aware of the possibility that a single dynamic interview may be all that is needed. On the other hand, it can also be said that some of the patients described here might well have benefited considerably more from deeper work spread over a few therapeutic sessions. Such sessions might well be at long intervals spread over a period of months or even years. The highly interpretative follow-up interview on the economics student gives an example of this kind of therapy. Finally, dynamically oriented psychiatrists should also be aware of the powerful potential therapeutic effects both of telling a patient that he must take responsibility for his own life, and of reassuring him that he can manage without therapeutic help.

CONCLUSION

We should like to reiterate that our conclusions about the therapeutic effect of single interviews are not the result of biased examination of the evidence by authors anxious to prove the value of psychotherapy. We started to write this report as a warning to psychotherapists to take spontaneous remission seriously. Some three months, 40 crossed out pages, and 40 correlation coefficients later, we concluded that the evidence for therapeutic effects was stronger than that for spontaneous remission. Nevertheless, the evidence for spontaneous remission is there, and does need to be taken seriously; and one of us (D.H.M), at any rate, is convinced of its presence in two series of treated patients, one given brief psychotherapy and the other group treatment, which have been under intensive study. It is a delightful paradox that two studies of psychotherapy should have provided so much evidence about spontaneous remission, and the present study of spontaneous remission about psychotherapy.

REFERENCES

1. Eysenck HJ: The effects of psychotherapy: An evaluation. *J Consult Psychol* 16:319–324, 1952.

2. Eysenck HJ (ed): *Handbook of Abnormal Psychology.* London, Pitman, 1960.

3. Eysenck HJ: The effects of psychotherapy. *Int J Psychiatry* 1:99–144, 1965.

4. Bergin AE: The evaluation of therapeutic outcomes, in Bergin AE, Garfield SL, (eds): *Handbook of Psychotherapy and Behavior Change.* New York, John Wiley & Sons Inc, 1971.

5. Strupp HH, Bergin AE: Some empirical and conceptual bases for coordinated research in psychotherapy. *Int J Psychiatry* 7:18–90, 1969.

6. Malan DH, Bacal HA, Heath ES, et al.: A study of psychodynamic changes in untreated neurotic patients: I. *Br J Psychiatry* 114:525–551, 1968.

7. Rachman S: *The Effects of Psychotherapy.* Oxford, England, Pergamon Press, 1971.

8. Meltzoff J, Kornreich M: *Research in Psychotherapy.* New York, Atherton, 1970.

9. Malan DH: On assessing the results of psychotherapy. *Br J Med Psychol* 32:86–105, 1959.

10. Malan DH: *A Study of Brief Psychotherapy.* London, Tavistock, 1963, 49–50.

11. Knight RP: Evaluation of the results of psychoanalytic therapy. *Am J Psychiatry* 98:434–446, 1941.

12. Wallerstein RS, Robbins LL, Sargent HD, et al.: The psychotherapy research project of the Menninger Foundation: Rationale, method, and sample use. *Bull Menninger Clin* 20:221–278, 1956.

13. Luborsky L: Clinicians' judgments of mental health: A proposed scale. *Arch Gen Psychiatry* 7:407–417, 1962.

14. Kernberg OF, Burstein ED, Coyne L, et al.: Psychotherapy and psychoanaly-

sis: Final report of the Menninger Foundation's psychotherapy research project. *Bull Menninger Clin* 36:3–275, 1972.

15. Malan DH, Rayner EH, Bacal HA, et al.: Psychodynamic assessment of the outcome of psychotherapy, in Porter R (ed): *The Role of Learning in Psychotherapy*. London, J & A Churchill. 1968, 61–67.

16. Malan DH, Therapeutic factors in analytically-oriented brief psychotherapy, in Gosling RH (ed): *Support, Innovation and Autonomy*. London, Tavistock, 1973.

17. Sifneos PE: *Short-Term Psychotherapy and Emotional Crisis*. Cambridge, Mass, Harvard University Press, 1972.

18. Bergin AE: Some implications of psychotherapy research for therapeutic practice. *J Abnorm Psychol* 71:235–246, 1966.

23. Katharina

Sigmund Freud

In the summer vacation of the year 189– I made an excursion into the Hohe Tauern* so that for a while I might forget medicine and more particularly the neuroses. I had almost succeeded in this when one day I turned aside from the main road to climb a mountain which lay somewhat apart and which was renowned for its views and for its well-run refuge hut. I reached the top after a strenuous climb and, feeling refreshed and rested, was sitting deep in contemplation of the charm of the distant prospect. I was so lost in thought that at first I did not connect it with myself when these words reached my ears: "Are you a doctor, sir?" But the question was addressed to me, and by the rather sulky-looking girl of perhaps eighteen who had served my meal and had been spoken to by the landlady as "Katharina." To judge by her dress and bearing, she could not be a servant, but must no doubt be a daughter or relative of the landlady's.

Coming to myself I replied: "Yes, I'm a doctor: but how did you know that?"

'You wrote your name in the Visitors' Book, sir. And I thought if you had a few moments to spare . . . The truth is, sir, my nerves are bad. I went to see a doctor in L—— about them and he gave me something for them; but I'm not well yet.'

So there I was with the neuroses once again—for nothing else could very well be the matter with this strong, well-built girl with her unhappy look. I was interested to find that neuroses could flourish in this way at a height of over 6,000 feet; I questioned her further therefore. I report the conversation that followed between us just as it is impressed on my memory and I have not altered the patient's dialect.

"Well, what is it you suffer from?"

* [One of the highest ranges in the Eastern Alps.]

Sigmund Freud. Studies on Hysteria (1893–95). *Standard Edition*, vol. 2 London: Hogarth Press, 1955, pp 125–34. Reprinted by permission of HarperCollins Publishers (U.S.) and Random House U.K. Ltd.

"I get so out of breath. Not always. But sometimes it catches me so that I think I shall suffocate."

This did not, at first sight, sound like a nervous symptom. But soon it occurred to me that probably it was only a description that stood for an anxiety attack: she was choosing shortness of breath out of the complex of sensations arising from anxiety and laying undue stress on that single factor.

"Sit down here. What is it like when you get 'out of breath'?"

"It comes over me all at once. First of all it's like something pressing on my eyes. My head gets so heavy, there's a dreadful buzzing, and I feel so giddy that I almost fall over. Then there's something crushing my chest so that I can't get my breath."

"And you don't notice anything in your throat?"

"My throat's squeezed together as though I were going to choke."

"Does anything else happen in your head?"

"Yes, there's a hammering, enough to burst it."

"And don't you feel at all frightened while this is going on?"

"I always think I'm going to die. I'm brave as a rule and go about everywhere by myself—into the cellar and all over the mountain. But on a day when that happens I don't dare to go anywhere; I think all the time someone's standing behind me and going to catch hold of me all at once."

So it was in fact an anxiety attack, and introduced by the signs of a hysterical "aura"*—or, more correctly, it was a hysterical attack the content of which was anxiety. Might there not probably be some other content as well?

"When you have an attack do you think of something? and always the same thing? or do you see something in front of you?"

"Yes. I always see an awful face that looks at me in a dreadful way, so that I'm frightened."

Perhaps this might offer a quick means of getting to the heart of the matter.

"Do you recognize the face? I mean, is it a face that you've really seen some time?"

"No."

"Do you know what your attacks come from?"

"No."

"When did you first have them?"

"Two years ago, while I was still living on the other mountain with my

---

* [The premonitory sensations preceding an epileptic or hysterical attack.]

aunt. (She used to run a refuge hut there, and we moved here eighteen months ago.) But they keep on happening."

Was I to make an attempt at an analysis? I could not venture to transplant hypnosis to these altitudes, but perhaps I might succeed with a simple talk. I should have to try a lucky guess. I had found often enough that in girls anxiety was a consequence of the horror by which a virginal mind is overcome when it is faced for the first time with the world of sexuality.*

So I said: "If you don't know, I'll tell you how *I* think you got your attacks. At that time, two years ago, you must have seen or heard something that very much embarrassed you, and that you'd much rather not have seen."

"Heavens, yes!" she replied, "that was when I caught my uncle with the girl, with Franziska, my cousin."

"What's this story about a girl? Won't you tell me all about it?"

"You can say *anything* to a doctor, I suppose. Well, at that time, you know, my uncle—the husband of the aunt you've seen here—kept the inn on the ———kogel.† Now they're divorced, and it's my fault they were divorced, because it was through me that it came out that he was carrying on with Franziska."

"And how did you discover it?"

"This way. One day two years ago some gentlemen had climbed the mountain and asked for something to eat. My aunt wasn't at home, and Franziska, who always did the cooking, was nowhere to be found. And my uncle was not to be found either. We looked everywhere, and at last Alois, the little boy, my cousin, said: 'Why, Franziska must be in Father's room!' And we both laughed; but we weren't thinking anything bad. Then we went to my uncle's room but found it locked. That seemed strange to me. Then Alois said: 'There's a window in the passage where you can look into the room.' We went into the passage; but Alois wouldn't go to the window and said he was afraid. So I said: 'You silly boy! I'll go. I'm not a bit afraid.'

---

* I will quote here the case in which I first recognized this causal connection. I was treating a young married woman who was suffering from a complicated neurosis and, once again, was unwilling to admit that her illness arose from her married life. She objected that while she was still a girl she had had attacks of anxiety, ending in fainting fits. I remained firm. When we had come to know each other better she suddenly said to me one day: "I'll tell you now how I came by my attacks of anxiety when I was a girl. At that time I used to sleep in a room next to my parents'; the door was left open and a night-light used to burn on the table. So more than once I saw my father get into bed with my mother and heard sounds that greatly excited me. It was then that my attacks came on."

† [The name of the "other" mountain.]

And I had nothing bad in my mind. I looked in. The room was rather dark, but I saw my uncle and Franziska; he was lying on her."

"Well?"

"I came away from the window at once, and leant up against the wall and couldn't get my breath—just what happens to me since. Everything went blank, my eyelids were forced together and there was a hammering and buzzing in my head."

"Did you tell your aunt that very same day?"

"Oh no, I said nothing."

"Then why were you so frightened when you found them together? Did you understand it? Did you know what was going on?"

"Oh no. I didn't understand anything at that time. I was only sixteen. I don't know what I was frightened about."

"Fräulein Katharina, if you could remember now what was happening in you at that time, when you had your first attack, what you thought about it— it would help you."

"Yes, if I could. But I was so frightened that I've forgotten everything."

(Translated into the terminology of our "Preliminary Communication" this means: "The affect itself created a hypnoid state, whose products were then cut off from associative connection with the ego-consciousness.")

"Tell me, Fräulein. Can it be that the head that you always see when you lose your breath is Franziska's head, as you saw it then?"

"Oh no, she didn't look so awful. Besides, it's a man's head."

"Or perhaps your uncle's?"

"I didn't see his face as clearly as that. It was too dark in the room. And why should he have been making such a dreadful face just then?"

"You're quite right."

(The road suddenly seemed blocked. Perhaps something might turn up in the rest of her story.)

"And what happened then?"

"Well, those two must have heard a noise, because they came out soon afterwards. I felt very bad the whole time. I always kept thinking about it. Then two days later it was a Sunday and there was a great deal to do and I worked all day long. And on the Monday morning I felt giddy again and was sick, and I stopped in bed and was sick without stopping for three days."

We [Breuer and I] had often compared the symptomatology of hysteria with a pictographic script which has become intelligible after the discovery of a few bilingual inscriptions. In that alphabet being sick means disgust. So I said: "If you were sick three days later, I believe that means that when you looked into the room you felt disgusted."

"Yes, I'm sure I felt disgusted," she said reflectively, "but disgusted at what?"

"Perhaps you saw something naked? What sort of state were they in?"

"It was too dark to see anything; besides they both of them had their clothes on. Oh, if only I knew what it was I felt disgusted at!"

I had no idea either. But I told her to go on and tell me whatever occurred to her, in the confident expectation that she would think of precisely what I needed to explain the case.

Well, she went on to describe how at last she reported her discovery to her aunt, who found that she was changed and suspected her of concealing some secret. There followed some very disagreeable scenes between her uncle and aunt, in the course of which the children came to hear a number of things which opened their eyes in many ways and which it would have been better for them not to have heard. At last her aunt decided to move with her children and niece and take over the present inn, leaving her uncle alone with Franziska, who had meanwhile become pregnant. After this, however, to my astonishment she dropped these threads and began to tell me two sets of older stories, which went back two or three years earlier than the traumatic moment. The first set related to occasions on which the same uncle had made sexual advances to her herself, when she was only fourteen years old. She described how she had once gone with him on an expedition down into the valley in the winter and had spent the night in the inn there. He sat in the bar drinking and playing cards, but she felt sleepy and went up to bed early in the room they were to share on the upper floor. She was not quite asleep when he came up; then she fell asleep again and woke up suddenly "feeling his body" in the bed. She jumped up and remonstrated with him: "What are you up to, Uncle? Why don't you stay in your own bed?" He tried to pacify her: "Go on, you silly girl, keep still. You don't know how nice it is."—"I don't like your 'nice' things; you don't even let one sleep in peace." She remained standing by the door, ready to take refuge outside in the passage, till at last he gave up and went to sleep himself. Then she went back to her own bed and slept till morning. From the way in which she reported having defended herself it seems to follow that she did not clearly recognize the attack as a sexual one. When I asked her if she knew what he was trying to do to her, she replied: "Not at the time." It had become clear to her much later on, she said; she had resisted because it was unpleasant to be disturbed in one's sleep and "because it wasn't nice."

I have been obliged to relate this in detail, because of its great importance for understanding everything that followed.—She went on to tell me of yet other experiences of somewhat later date: how she had once again had to defend herself against him in an inn when he was completely drunk, and similar stories. In answer to a question as to whether on these occasions she had felt anything resembling her later loss of breath, she answered with decision that she had every time felt the pressure on her eyes and chest, but with nothing like the strength that had characterized the scene of discovery.

Immediately she had finished this set of memories she began to tell me a second set, which dealt with occasions on which she had noticed something between her uncle and Franziska. Once the whole family had spent the night in their clothes in a hay loft and she was woken up suddenly by a noise; she thought she noticed that her uncle, who had been lying between her and Franziska, was turning away, and that Franziska was just lying down. Another time they were stopping the night at an inn at the village of N———; she and her uncle were in one room and Franziska in an adjoining one. She woke up suddenly in the night and saw a tall white figure by the door, on the point of turning the handle: "Goodness, is that you, Uncle? What are you doing at the door?"—"Keep quiet. I was only looking for something."—"But the way out's by the *other* door."—"I'd just made a mistake" . . . and so on.

I asked her if she had been suspicious at that time. "No, I didn't think anything about it; I only just noticed it and thought no more about it." When I enquired whether she had been frightened on these occasions too, she replied that she thought so, but she was not so sure of it this time.

At the end of these two sets of memories she came to a stop. She was like someone transformed. The sulky, unhappy face had grown lively, her eyes were bright, she was lightened and exalted. Meanwhile the understanding of her case had become clear to me. The later part of what she had told me, in an apparently aimless fashion, provided an admirable explanation of her behavior at the scene of the discovery. At that time she had carried about with her two sets of experiences which she remembered but did not understand, and from which she drew no inferences. When she caught sight of the couple in intercourse, she at once established a connection between the new impression and these two sets of recollections, she began to understand them and at the same time to fend them off. There then followed a short period of working-out, of "incubation," after which the symptoms of conversion set in, the vomiting as a substitute for moral and physical disgust. This solved the riddle. She had not been disgusted by the sight of the two people but by the memory which that sight had stirred up in her. And, taking everything into account, this could only be the memory of the attempt on her at night when she had "felt her uncle's body."

So when she had finished her confession I said to her: "I know now what it was you thought when you looked into the room. You thought: 'Now he's doing with her what he wanted to do with me that night and those other times.' That was what you were disgusted at, because you remembered the feeling when you woke up in the night and felt his body."

"It may well be," she replied, "that that was what I was disgusted at and that that was what I thought."

"Tell me just one thing more. You're a grown-up girl now and know all sorts of things . . ."

"Yes, now I am."

"Tell me just one thing. What part of his body was it that you felt that night?"

But she gave me no more definite answer. She smiled in an embarrassed way, as though she had been found out, like someone who is obliged to admit that a fundamental position has been reached where there is not much more to be said. I could imagine what the tactile sensation was which she had later learnt to interpret. Her facial expression seemed to me to be saying that she supposed that I was right in my conjecture. But I could not penetrate further, and in any case I owed her a debt of gratitude for having made it so much easier for me to talk to her than to the prudish ladies of my city practice, who regard whatever is natural as shameful.

Thus the case was cleared up.—But stop a moment! What about the recurrent hallucination of the head, which appeared during her attacks and struck terror into her? Where did it come from? I proceeded to ask her about it, and, as though *her* knowledge, too, had been extended by our conversation, she promptly replied: "Yes, I know now. The head is my uncle's head—I recognize it now—but not from *that* time. Later, when all the disputes had broken out, my uncle gave way to a senseless rage against me. He kept saying that it was all my fault: if I hadn't chattered, it would never have come to a divorce. He kept threatening he would do something to me; and if he caught sight of me at a distance his face would get distorted with rage and he would make for me with his hand raised. I always ran away from him, and always felt terrified that he would catch me some time unawares. The face I always see now is his face when he was in a rage."

This information reminded me that her first hysterical symptom, the vomiting, had passed away; the anxiety attack remained and acquired a fresh content. Accordingly, what we were dealing with was a hysteria which had to a considerable extent been abreacted. And in fact she had reported her discovery to her aunt soon after it happened.

"Did you tell your aunt the other stories—about his making advances to you?"

"Yes. Not at once, but later on, when there was already talk of a divorce. My aunt said: 'We'll keep that in reserve. If he causes trouble in the Court, we'll say that too.' "

I can well understand that it should have been precisely this last period— when there were more and more agitating scenes in the house and when her own state ceased to interest her aunt, who was entirely occupied with the dispute—that it should have been this period of accumulation and retention that left her the legacy of the mnemic symbol [of the hallucinated face].

I hope this girl, whose sexual sensibility had been injured at such an early age, derived some benefit from our conversation. I have not seen her since.

DISCUSSION

If someone were to assert that the present case history is not so much an analyzed case of hysteria as a case solved by guessing, I should have nothing to say against him. It is true that the patient agreed that what I interpolated into her story was probably true; but she was not in a position to recognize it as something she had experienced. I believe it would have required hypnosis to bring that about. Assuming that my guesses were correct, I will now attempt to fit the case into the schematic picture of an "acquired" hysteria on the lines suggested by a previous case. It seems plausible, then, to compare the two sets of erotic experiences with "traumatic" moments and the scene of discovering the couple with an "auxiliary" moment. The similarity lies in the fact that in the former experiences an element of consciousness was created which was excluded from the thought-activity of the ego and remained, as it were, in storage, while in the latter scene a new impression forcibly brought about an associative connection between this separated group and the ego. On the other hand there are dissimilarities which cannot be overlooked. The cause of the isolation was not an act of will on the part of the ego but *ignorance* on the part of the ego, which was not yet capable of coping with sexual experiences. In this respect the case of Katharina is typical. In every analysis of a case of hysteria based on sexual traumas we find that impressions from the pre-sexual period which produced no effect on the child attain traumatic power at a later date as memories, when the girl or married woman has acquired an understanding of sexual life. The splitting-off of psychical groups may be said to be a normal process in adolescent development; and it is easy to see that their later reception into the ego affords frequent opportunities for psychical disturbances. Moreover, I should like at this point to express a doubt as to whether a splitting of consciousness due to ignorance is really different from one due to conscious rejection, and whether even adolescents do not possess sexual knowledge far oftener than is supposed or than they themselves believe.

A further distinction in the psychical mechanism of this case lies in the fact that the scene of discovery, which we have described as "auxiliary," deserves equally to be called "traumatic." It was operative on account of its own content and not merely as something that revived previous traumatic experiences. It combined the characteristics of an "auxiliary" and a "traumatic" moment. There seems no reason, however, why this coincidence should lead us to abandon a conceptual separation which in other cases corresponds also to a separation in time. Another peculiarity of Katharina's case, which, incidentally, has long been familiar to us, is seen in the circumstance that the conversion, the production of the hysterical phenomena, did not occur immediately after the trauma but after an interval of incubation. Charcot liked to describe this interval as the "period of psychical working-out" [*élaboration*].

The anxiety from which Katharina suffered in her attacks was a hysterical one; that is, it was a reproduction of the anxiety which had appeared in connection with each of the sexual traumas. I shall not here comment on the fact which I have found regularly present in a very large number of cases — namely that a mere suspicion of sexual relations calls up the affect of anxiety in virginal individuals.*

---

* (*Footnote added* 1924:) I venture after the lapse of so many years to lift the veil of discretion and reveal the fact that Katharina was not the niece but the daughter of the landlady. The girl fell ill, therefore, as a result of sexual attempts on the part of her own father. Distortions like the one which I introduced in the present instance should be altogether avoided in reporting a case history. From the point of view of understanding the case, a distortion of this kind is not, of course, a matter of such indifference as would be shifting the scene from one mountain to another.

24. Basis for Self in Body

D. W. Winnicott

My intention in writing this article is to explore clinical material that throws light on the inter-relationship between the growing child and his or her body. The subject is obviously a very wide one, and a specialization in one area leads automatically to neglect in other areas. Nevertheless, it is possible for me to take the word *personalization,* which I have used in another context, and to see how it becomes illustrated in detailed clinical work in child psychiatry and psychoanalysis. I adopted the term *personalization* as a kind of positive form of *depersonalization,* a term that has been used and discussed fairly fully. Various meanings are given to the word *depersonalization,* but on the whole they involve the child's or the patient's loss of contact with the body and body functioning, and this implies the existence of some other aspect of the personality. The term *personalization* was intended to draw attention to the fact that the in-dwelling of this other part of the personality in the body, and its firm link with whatever is there which we call psyche, in developmental terms represents an achievement in health. This is an achievement which becomes gradually established; and it is not unhealthy, but indeed a sign of health, that the child can use relationships in which there is maximal trust, and in such relationships at times disintegrate, depersonalize, and even for a moment abandon the almost fundamental urge to exist and to feel existent. The two things go together, therefore, in healthy development: the sense of security in a relationship maintaining opportunity for restful undoing of integrative processes, while at the same time facilitating the general inherited tendency that the child has toward integration and, as I am stressing in this paper, the in-dwelling or the inhabitation of the body and the body functioning.

Forward development is very much associated with in-dwelling as with other aspects of integration, but forward development is in all respects frightening to the individual concerned, if there is not left open the way back to total dependence. And this is particularly true in the clinical field, from the years two to five, after which in terms of clinical experience the return

Reprinted by permission of *International Journal of Child Psychotherapy* 1 (1972):7–16.

to dependence becomes obscured in a whole series of sophistications. At adolescence there is a new period in which, because of the vast implications of the new and rapid advances in meeting and coping with the world, there recurs a need to keep open a way back to dependence. Clinically, this phase is liable to be manifested at the prepuberty phase, when the adolescent is twelve to fourteen years old. After this phase the dependence may very easily become absorbed in a natural dependence, which is free from regressive elements relative to the parents, which already looks toward the adult status, and which is called "being in love," and in the experiences of every possible kind that surround such a state.

The term *personalization*, which I have used for my own benefit, may not be acceptable in a general way, but it has enabled me to gather together the examples in my clinical work that are relevant to this aspect of achievement in human development. An important case from my point of view is one that I do not propose to treat fully in this context, as I have published it in detail elsewhere (Winnicott, 1971). Here, I wish to refer to the case in my own language.

I refer to a significant interview with a boy, Iiro, nine years nine months. I have often described this interview as an illustration of communication with a child because there was no common language between the boy and myself. We exchanged drawings on the basis of the squiggle game* and we had an interpreter. In spite of these handicaps, the boy communicated to me his special need which belonged both to his own development and to a complication in his mother's attitude towards his disability. Iiro was under almost constant orthopedic treatment because of a condition of syndactyly, in which the fingers and toes are joined together. In Iiro's case there was no clear indication for the orthopedic surgeon where to create fingers and toes out of the chaotic state that existed. This is an hereditary disease, and Iiro, in the middle of a fairly large family, was the only child who had inherited the disorder. The surgeon said that this boy cooperated almost too well, and wondered why. The boy had had innumerable operations on his hands and feet. Some of the urgency in the use of the orthopedic surgeon's skill came from the fact that the mother had the same condition, and she could only

* For the reader who is not familiar with Winnicott's "squiggles," the game begins with the therapist pencilling his nonspecific scribble on a blank piece of paper. The child then makes it into a recognizable form by adding lines in accordance with what he "sees" in it. On a second sheet of paper the child then draws *his* squiggle, and the therapist similarly transforms it into a distinguishable object. Each drawing serves as a point of departure for a variety of therapeutic interchanges.

accept this boy on the basis of doing everything possible to cure him of a deformity for which she felt responsible. On the basis of having everything possible done for him, she had found herself more fond of this boy than of any of her other children. Here was a clear situation, therefore, of a boy—a happy, likeable, and intelligent boy—who nevertheless, along with his mother, was constantly in search of further orthopedic help, asking indeed for better plastic surgery than the surgeon was capable of putting into practice.

The interest of the case lies in the fact that at a deeper level this boy communicated something other than his need to be made normal. Although it made sense to him to have everything possible done by surgery (he did not know, of course, of his mother's tremendous sense of guilt), he indicated that he needed one thing: he must be certain that, first of all, he was loved as he was when he was born, or at some theoretical start to his existence. If accepted as deformed, which implied that it would be normal to be born with feet and hands like his, then he could go forward with any amount of cooperation with his mother and the surgeon. He communicated this, without conscious motivation, in terms of his great love of ducks, and the first squiggle he saw as the webbed foot of a duck. Further on in the interview he was able to use an eel as symbolic of his early state—that is to say, before the question of arms and legs or of fingers and toes became relevant.

Several points of theoretical interest follow an examination of this case. Obviously a child does not know about a disparity like this at the beginning. Gradually, in the course of time, the child has to recognize the fact of the deformity. It is possible that Iiro never recognized this fact until the interview with me, when he was nine years and nine months old. What the boy must be able to adjust to is the attitude of his mother and of other people towards his deformity, and eventually it becomes necessary for him to see himself as abnormal. At the start, however, normality for the child must be his own somatic shape and function. As he starts, so he must be accepted. So he must be loved. It is a matter of being loved without sanctions.

It is very easy to carry this observation over to an examination of the needs of children who are not deformed. Being loved at the beginning means being accepted, and it is a distortion from the child's point of view when the mother figure has the attitude: "I love you if you are good, if you are clean, if you smile, if you drink it all up." These sanctions can come later, but at the beginning the child has a blueprint for normality, which is largely a matter of the shape and functioning of his or her own body. It may be thought that surely these matters belong to a later age, when the child has become a relatively sophisticated person. The observation cannot be neglected, however, that these are matters of the very earliest days of the child's life. It is truly at the beginning that the child needs to be accepted as such, and benefits from such acceptance. A corollary would be that almost every child has been accepted in the last stages before birth—that is to say, when there is a readiness for birth—but love is shown in terms of the physical care which is usually, but not always, adequate when it is a matter of the fetus in the womb. In these terms, the basis for what I call personalization, or an absence of a special liability to depersonalization, starts even before the child's birth. It is certainly very much a matter of significance once the child has to be held by people whose emotional involvement, as well as physiological responses, need to be taken into account. The beginning of that part of the baby's development, which I am calling personalization (and which can be described as an in-dwelling of the psyche in the soma), is to be found in the mother or mother figure's ability to join up her emotional involvement, which originally is physical and physiological. In the development of this theme one could take many diverse paths. My method will be to use another clinical example, chosen because of its availability in my mind.

I am reminded of a consultation that a girl, Jill, aged seventeen, had with me in 1968. She used this consultation in a positive way, and in fact it enabled her to go forward with her development, which had become held up. From her mother's letter, which I received before the consultation, I learned this:

Jill has been feeling a bit lost. It might seem as though her problems were mainly social or educational. Her overt and articulate complaints are chiefly about herself "vis-à-vis the world." She does not make friends readily. She feels stupid and lacks a sense of purpose. I feel that these complaints of hers may be masking a deeper resentment against her family, or lack of one, or against me, for various reasons she cannot express. It is "they" surely who have somehow failed to equip her with self-confidence, so that instead of joining in with her contemporaries' battle for freedom, she is, as it were, stuck in the doorway, possibly still hoping to make up on what she has missed before she can move on.

And the mother added a biographical note:

She was born in 1950: breast-fed for nine months, and though small, a satisfactory greedy infant. When she was three her father (who was of *my* father's generation) died. I do not think the impact of his death was blurred or blunted for her. For a long time afterwards she spoke of it and of its effect on both of us. She would make drawings representing the two different situations: hers and mine. She had, and still has, a grandfather and several uncles, but in her day-to-day life there has not been any consistently available or really important male figure.

She gave the impression of being an ordinarily happy, often rather gay, small child. She had good resources in the way of imaginative play. When she was twelve, I had a breakdown (severe depression) and went to a mental hospital for ten months. She has never talked much about this time. Once, when asked, she said: "I knew you would come back, of course."

The following is my description of the interview, dictated from notes within hours after the interview.

Jill, aged seventeen years. Consultation: 2 July 1968. First and only child. The father died when she was three. Addition to the family: Tommy (adopted), whom I once saw in consultation. He was then six and she was eight. The father was thirty years older than the mother.

Jill came alone. She was a very slight person, dressed in a gray corduroy frock. She might have been thirteen. One of the first things that she said was that she was nearly eighteen. Evidently she was rather self-conscious about seeming to be so slight.

At first there was a rather sticky period in which it was not certain how we could use each other. I went through the ordinary preliminaries about her coming. Did she come because she was sent or because she wanted help? She said that it was only at school that she had trouble, and her work there worried her. She had a mental block when she wrote essays, and this made her very depressed. In greater detail she described the way in which she collected material for an essay, then started to put it together, and soon reached a place from which she could not proceed. She thought she would like to go to a university, but felt bound to fail in her application. She was not sure she wanted to go to college, which might be simply a continuation of everything that had happened at school. In other words, she feared she would be held up again by the block in her mental functioning.

Jill did not have many friends in high school. She seemed to feel that her subjects were not really worthwhile studying. One of them was art, and she was obsessed with the question, "What sort of art is any good?"

I talked a little bit about Jill and her setting. I told her I knew that she was living with her mother with no father, that her mother had told me about her own (the mother's) depressions, and that Jill's life at age twelve was disturbed by the mother's breakdown (ten months in the hospital).

Jill tried to explain to me that she had always thought things in her life were really all right until some incident, probably an accident, occurred, since which she had felt a lack of confidence that her ultimate outcome could be satisfactory. In describing this, she said that she had previously believed that she could curl up her body for a successful defense, but since the accident she no longer felt that this protection could be relied upon. As we talked about this, it seemed clear that she felt that some part of herself, sticking out, was in danger from the environment, but, when curled up, this part was not in danger. Naturally, I thought of the idea of a penis with castration anxiety, but this seemed to be too crude a language to describe what was happening in this girl's mind. I could explore around this area without harm, and I was left with the idea that this was not a good enough way of describing her anxiety.

At some point we transferred over to the squiggle game. I felt that Jill would be more at ease with something that we were doing together, and certainly it seemed to work out that way. So we went ahead as if we were children together, and it all seemed quite natural.

1. My first squiggle she turned into a sort of swan.
2. Her first squiggle I transformed into a girl's head, with a length of hair like Jill's.
3. My next squiggle she changed very imaginatively into a dog, seen at a curious angle from behind.
4. Her next squiggle I turned into what she called a colt.
5. My next she could do nothing with. She said, "There is too much in it already." This corresponded with something she had already said about life—how complex it can be at any one moment, with all sorts of possibilities crowding in.
6. Her next I turned into a vase. She agreed that it was a recognizable shape for a glass vase and seemed relieved that we had got to something more simple and circumscribed.
7. Of my next she simply said, "That's a modern chair."
8. I made her next into some kind of little dog. This led to the fact that Jill's family has a border terrier for a pet.
9. She changed my next into architecture—a concert hall of a very modern variety. She had worked in an architect's office for a few months doing menial jobs, but she evidently liked the idea of architecture as a job.
10. Her next I turned into a pair of glasses like mine.

While all this was going on, we were talking together. Jill said that her dreams were not nice—something like falling in the street or downstairs, with her legs giving way. She told me that her left leg was actually a centimeter shorter than her right one—a fact which was not apparent, although she was wearing a very short miniskirt, but evidently it had great meaning for her. She mentioned that in a dream she felt as if she were missing a limb. Then we returned to the subject of her inability to concentrate. I pointed out that Jill felt that if she gathered together all the bits of herself and had a look, in order to see how she could put them all together, there would be something missing, just as when she gathered material for an essay. I related this to the fact that she had had to live her life without a father. She appeared to have no feeling at all about the death of her father, except that she was irritated when people who knew him talked about him so that she felt very much left out. It was something they knew about and she did not.

Then Jill told me about the way that her defense (curling up) had broken down following a street accident. She had another accident in which she broke her front teeth, causing her to lisp, and she was very self-conscious about this. She described how stupid the accident was. She was emptying a wheelbarrow, with a dog on the lead. The dog was scared and Jill turned round, angry with the dog, but the handle of the wheelbarrow jumped up and broke her teeth. She said, "It's ironical. I was being angry with the dog, and I was the one to get hurt." The accident gave her considerable shock and undoubtedly upset her mother, too, because it altered Jill's appearance. In this I recognized the existence of a truly external factor, like the death of her father when she was three. She talked about her father being very old anyway.

For the time being we discussed Jill's feelings about being a girl. She very much wanted to be a boy from the time Tommy came, when she was seven or eight, right up till she was ten; now she probably preferred being a girl. I fished around for envy of Tommy's penis, but she simply said that she knew all about the differences between boys and girls before Tommy came. It should be remarked that Tommy was always a very difficult boy. I asked Jill if she had dreams in which she was a boy, and her answer was that she definitely did not. She had some friends, perhaps three girls.

Now came the significant part of the consultation. Jill drew a picture of the aforementioned dream of the broken-off limb, the missing part that she always felt about herself. She talked about the color of it. It was like the stump of a leg. Its flesh was pale and mauve, like the flesh of a dogfish (biology dissection). It was a dead color. In talking about it, she said that she thought of it more as a limb bitten off by a wild animal than as something hurt in an accident. This reminded me of the dog in the accident, in which "ironically" it was Jill's own teeth that got knocked out.

Eventually I made an interpretation, saying that I thought that this was the nearest Jill could get to her reaction to her father's death. She did not remember him as a person, and she did not mourn his loss. Nevertheless, when he died, a bit of her life died with him, so that there was something missing. At the same time, it could be said that she bit off something of him, because we had to remember the importance of her teeth which she had discussed in connection with the accident with the wheelbarrow. I talked about the way in which little children of three play with and bite around their father's fingers, watch chain, or some other belonging, and it could be fairly certainly assumed that Jill played in this way with her father. His death and removal then would feel to her as if she had really bitten instead of playing at biting, this resulting in a fantasy of severance of the finger or whatever. Jill was able to accept this for consideration. In the end, she expressed a certain amount of astonishment at her drawing of the limb, which had brought this central theme so much into the foreground—that is, her feeling that in any examination of herself something would be found to be missing. It turned out that the limb that was torn off in her dream was the left one, which was her short one.

We made some sort of resumé at the end and discussed the possible value of such an interview and also the possibility that she might be disturbed by it. Finally, she was quite positive. She quite simply said, "I am glad I came. Good-bye." My comment to her was that the appropriate word was *sad*, not *glad*. If she could get away from the anxiety about there being something missing, then she might find that the appropriate statement would be that it is very sad for a three-year-old girl when her father dies. Then Jill left in a state of friendliness.

Jill's case illustrates the way in which a small child, although unaware that one of her limbs is shorter than the other, can eventually be forced— because of the attitude of parents, doctors, and particularly her mother, with hypochondriacal anxieties occasionally consolidating into a depressive illness—to accept that there is something wrong somewhere. In this case the deformity was so slight that it could have been ignored completely. Nevertheless, when Jill came to arrange herself and her personality around the fact of not having a father and the detail of having lost him at the age of three (when, according to the family saga, she was very fond of him), she elaborated this insignificant fact into the dream of a leg bitten off by a wild animal. The same mechanism was at work in her mental life, and until the consultation she was unable to go forward in her emotional or intellectual growth. It happened that she was able to resume her development following the consultation, and the follow-up has shown that effectual psychotherapy was in fact achieved.

Integration in the developing human being takes a wide variety of forms, one of which is the development of a satisfactory working arrangement between the psyche and the soma. This starts prior to the time when it is necessary to add the concepts of intellect and verbalization.

The basis of a self forms on the fact of the body which, being alive, not only has shape but also functions. Observations relevant to this (which I have called personalization [Winnicott, 1945, 1949] in order to link up with the disorder called depersonalization) are made primarily in direct study of infants and their mothers interacting naturally. As a useful adjunct to such observations, I draw attention to the help that can be derived from a study of children with physical abnormalities. In this paper there was room only for two examples, but these may suffice to illustrate the way in which clinical details may throw light on such complex phenomena. Many physical abnormalities are not of such a nature that a baby could be aware of them as abnormalities. In fact, the baby tends to assume that what is there is normal. Normal is what is there. It is often a fact that the baby or child becomes aware of deformity or abnormality through perception of unexplained facts, as in the attitude of those, or of some of those, in the immediate environment. A very complex example is mental defect, when the apparatus for dealing with complex perceptions is itself crippled by the same deformity that is causing the environmental distortion. I have not discussed such a case here.

It will be possible, I think, to extract one principle from these cases that has almost universal application, and I can use the message given me by Iiro, chosen for my first case. In effect, what he said in discussing his congenital syndactyly was, "I will cooperate with anyone who can help to mend my abnormality, provided I am first of all accepted and loved as I am." Being accepted and loved "as I am" meant to Iiro "as I knew myself through knowing my own body before I found people saw me as abnormal; and they were right because, as I gradually came to see and understand, I am deformed."

In this way, a deformed baby can grow up into a healthy child with a self that is not deformed and a sense of self that is based on the experience of living as an accepted person. Distortions of the ego may come from distortions of the attitude of those who care for the child. A mother with a baby is constantly introducing and reintroducing the baby's body and psyche to each other, and it can readily be seen that this easy but important task becomes difficult when the baby has an abnormality that makes the mother feel ashamed, guilty, frightened, excited, or hopeless. Under such circumstances she can do her best, and no more.

A corollary is that the psychotherapist need not say that a child cannot be helped because of a physical abnormality. The child's self, his sense of self, and his ego organization may all be intact because of their being based on a body that was normal for the child in the formative period.

The key word in this article is *self*. I wondered if I could write something down about this word, but, of course, as soon as I came to do it, I found that there is much uncertainty even in my own mind about my own meaning. I found I had written the following:

For me the *self,* which is not the *ego,* is the person who is me, who is only me, who has a totality based on the operation of the maturational process. At the same time the self has parts and, in fact, is constituted of these parts. These parts agglutinate from a direction interior-exterior in the course of the operation of the maturational process, aided as it must be (maximally at the beginning) by the human environment, which holds and handles and, in a live way, facilitates. The self finds itself naturally placed in the body, but may in certain circumstances become dissociated from the body or the body from it. The self essentially recognizes itself in the eyes and facial expression of the mother and in the mirror which can come to represent the mother's face. Eventually the self arrives at a significant relationship between the child and the sum of the identifications which (after enough incorporation and introjection of mental representations) become organized in the shape of an internal psychic living reality. The relationship between the boy or girl with his or her own internal psychic organization becomes modified according to the expectations that are displayed by the father and mother and those who have become significant in the external life of the individual. It is the self and the life of the self alone that makes sense of action or of living from the point of view of the individual, who has grown so far (and who is continuing to grow) from dependence and immaturity towards independence and the capacity to identify with mature love objects without loss of individual identity.

REFERENCES

1. Winnicott, D. W. (1945), Primitive Emotional Development. In *Collected Papers*. London: Tavistock Publications, 1958.

2. ———(1949), Mind and its relation to the psyche-soma. In *Collected Papers*. London: Tavistock Publications, 1958.

3. ———(1971), *Therapeutic Consultations*. London: Hogarth Press and the Institute of Psycho-Analysis.

Index

"ABC Method" of Ellis, 232, 233
ABRAHAM, K., 119
Abreaction: encouraged in denial/numbing stage, table 5.2; facilitating, 29, 30, 34; in Freud's trauma theory, 103; vs. information processing, 109; in treatment with hysterical style, table 5.3. *See also* Catharsis
Abstract/concrete: information processing, 125
Abuse, drug and alcohol, 17, 47, 55, fig 3.4
Accident: as precipitant, 44, 101–5; shaping life course, 52, 53; as stimulus to therapeutic work, 34
Acting out: character, 35, 402; defense, 337; resistance, 391
Action, human. *See* Narrative, narratology
Action language, good to think with, 177. *See also* SCHAFER, R. R.
Active-passive/role reversal, as defense, 114–15, 123
Activity: therapist's, table 1.1, 75, 97, 99; as brief therapy "essence," xi, 1–5, 249–51; therapist's, with borderlines, 437. *See also* Interpretation
Acts of others, toward self, 183
Acts of self: and TLDP focus, 182–84; toward self, 183
Adaptation, table 1.1, 50–51; adaptive viewpoint (psychoanalysis, cf. genetic), 66, 79–82, 89; of construct system, 226; failure of, 275, 277, 465; and stress response syndromes, 105, 106, 109
Adaptational approach, to countertransference, 335, 336
Addiction to therapy, 449, 454
ADLER, A., 231
Adolescence, table 1.1, 8, 9, 517; time and, 68, 82
Adult. *See* Ego states, in TA
Advice, 40; useless, 276
Affect, affective, table 1.1; and "associative anamnesis," 81; contagion, 367; inhibition

in depression, 137; mediated by cognition, 230, 235; redundant theme, 191. *See also* Anxiety; Anger; Rage; etc.
"After-education," 278
Aggression, table 1.1; aggressor, self as, table 5.1; disturbed capacity for, 267, 269; pathologic manifestation of, 21
Agreement, treatment, 73, 84. *See also* Contract; Frame, framework; Therapeutic alliance
Alcoholism, 106, 115; in TA, 163, fig. 7.1, 170 n. 5. *See also* Abuse, drug and alcohol
ALEXANDER, F., 4, 5, 27–42, 55, 56, 75, 266, 382, 396, 397, 400, 421, 428, 432. *See also* "corrective emotional experience"; "Flexibility" principle; Frame, framework; FRENCH, T. M.
Alliance. *See* Agreement, treatment; Contract; Frame, framework; Therapeutic alliance
"All-or-nothing" thinking, 236
Alternative explanations, role in cognitive therapy, 240
Ambiguity, therapist tolerance for, 188
Ambivalence: and separation, 89; about time, 70
Anaclitic therapy, 404
Anal-sadistic phase, 119
Analysand. *See* Patient
Anamnesis, 84. *See also* Initial interview; Evaluation, initial
Anger: chronic, 234; and counterprojection, 288; Davanloo's approach, 300–334; guilt-laden, 470; in hysterical style, 112; in obsessional style, 123; resistance to, table 1.1, 6, 7; somatized, 313, 477; during stress response syndrome, table 5.1, 108; symptomatic, 419; as therapist changes subject, 427; during termination, 91–93; and TLDP narrative, 178. *See also* DAVANLOO, H.
Anniversary reactions, 18, 19

Homosexuality: in evaluation and formulation, 388, table 22.1; fear of, by analyst, 352–62; as phase, 499

Honeymoon, as precipitant, 423

"Honeymoon." *See* Disillusionment

Hope, pathologic, 292, 294

HOROWITZ, M. J., x, table 1.1, 16–19, 97, 99, 101–33. *See also* Stress response syndromes

Hospitalization, 40, 165, 453, 454, 520; fallback for failure of interpretation, 297, 384, 386

"Hour" as "sessions," "interviews," or "meetings" if not sixty minutes, 78

Humor, 128, 129, 169

Hunger, analyst's, for pathology, 345

Hyperactivity syndrome, 233

Hypnoid state, 115, 510

Hypnosis, 1, 514; mesmerian, psychoanalysis's *bête noire*, 26; and narcohypnosis, table 5.2

Hypochondria by proxy, 374

Hypothesis. *See* Formulation

Hysteria, 507–15; conversion in, 513; hallucinations in, 513; hypnosis and, 514; splitting of psyche in, 514, 515; symptom as pictographic script, 510

Hysterical style, 107, 108, table 22.1, 475; defects of, table 5.3; in response to stress, 111–18; victim-aggressor, child-parent, rescue/rape themes, 113

Iatrogenic, 458, 459

Id, contains no negation, 68

"IDE" focus (interpersonal developmental, existential), 18–19, 27, 28, 43–49, fig. 3.1. *See also* BUDMAN, S. H.

Ideal, idealize, idealization. *See* Defense, narcissism

Identification, identifications, table 5.2; with an introject, 298 n. 1; with therapist, 430; trial, position in therapy, 298 n. 6; promoting trust, 273. *See also* Projective identification

Identity, 50, 97, 525; and self-characterization, 211

Illegitimacy, 367–74

Images, table 5.2

Impasse, 37, 86, 422

Imperative statements, 286

Implosion, 130, 131

Impotence. *See* Sexual dysfunction

Improvement: criteria of, 466, 495; symptomatic vs. dynamic, 462, 464

Impulse, 109, 311, 314, 325; breakthrough of, 303, 333; "Impulse/feeling," 301, 316; impulsive personality, 130

Inadequacy, feelings of, sexual, 488

Inappropriate behavior: barrier, by analyst, 348; gratification, 343, 344; silence, 339, 343; smile, 321, 330

Incest, 111, 507–15

"Incubation" period, before symptoms appear, 513, 515

Information: completion of, 109, 110; in microanalytic studies, 186; overload, 103; processing, 102–33, table 5.2; and TLDP, 171, 172

Inhibition, 42, 114; ideational, 117

Initial interview, 82, 378. *See also* Evaluation, initial; Formulation; History, historical

Insight, 5, 34, 35, 38, 39, 267; capacity for, and patient selection, 388; in Davanloo's method, 315; in moment of *Erlebnis*, 275; as therapeutic factor, 498, 503; not sought in Fixed Role Therapy, 227; independent of therapy, 497; triangle, 384, 385

Insomnia, 46. *See also* Sleep disturbance, insomnia

Instinctual drive, 103

Intake evaluation, in Mann's method, 77. *See also* Formulation; History, historical; Initial interview

Integrative fields, 104

Integrity, protection of character, 219, 220

Intellectualization, 120

Intelligence, selection criterion, 401, 405, 423

Intentionality: autonomy, 87, 282; choice, 443; ego functions, 20, 31, 39, table 5.2, 437–45, 282; personal responsibility, 277

Interminability, of treatment, 62, 90

Internalization, in termination, 60, 91, 92. *See also* Guilt

Interpersonal: conflict, 45, fig. 3.1; contrasted with genetic, biochemical, developmental, and personality factors, 134; deficits as